Windows Vista™:
The Complete Reference

John R. Levine
Margaret Levine Young

New York Chicago San Francisco
Lisbon London Madrid Mexico City
Milan New Delhi San Juan
Seoul Singapore Sydney Toronto

The *McGraw·Hill* Companies

Cataloging-in-Publication Data is on file with the Library of Congress

McGraw-Hill books are available at special quantity discounts to use as premiums and sales promotions, or for use in corporate training programs. For more information, please write to the Director of Special Sales, Professional Publishing, McGraw-Hill, Two Penn Plaza, New York, NY 10121-2298. Or contact your local bookstore.

Windows Vista™: The Complete Reference

1234567890 DOC DOC 01987

ISBN-13: 978-0-07-226376-3
ISBN-10:   0-07-226376-8

Sponsoring Editor	**Copy Editor**	**Composition**
Megg Morin	Bill McManus	International Typesetting and Composition
Editorial Supervisor	**Proofreader**	**Illustration**
Janet Walden	Tulika Mukherjee	International Typesetting and Composition
Project Manager	**Indexer**	
Vasundhara Sawhney	Kevin Broccoli	**Art Director, Cover**
Acquisitions Coordinator	**Production Supervisor**	Jeff Weeks
Carly Stapleton	Jean Bodeaux	
Technical Editor		
Diane Poremsky		

Rob Tidrow
dedicates this book
to his family.

About the Authors

John R. Levine is the author of two dozen books, ranging from *Linkers and Loaders* to *The Internet For Dummies*. He also runs online newsgroups and mailing lists, hosts a hundred web sites, and consults on programming language and Internet topics. He lives in the tiny village of Trumansburg, New York, where in his spare time he's the mayor (really). John is also active in the anti-spam movement, is a board member of CAUCE (Coalition Against Unsolicited Commercial E-mail), and runs the abuse.net web site.

Margaret Levine Young is the co-author of over two dozen books with various co-authors, including *The Internet For Dummies*; *Internet: The Complete Reference, Millennium Edition*; and *UNIX For Dummies*. She holds a B.A. in Computer Science from Yale University, writes software for the Unitarian Universalist Association of Congregations at www.uua.org, lives near Middlebury, Vermont, and experiments in e-commerce at her family's Great Tapes for Kids web site at www.greattapes.com.

Will Kelly is a freelance technical writer and consultant in the Washington, DC area. He has also worked as a courseware developer, project manager, trainer, and analyst. Much of Will's career has focused on helping commercial and Federal government IT organizations develop, deploy, and support desktop, mobile, and web technology products and services.

Will was the technical editor of over 30 computer books between 1994 and 2004. His articles about mobile computing and Small to Medium Enterprise topics regularly appear in *Processor Magazine* and *PC Today Magazine*. And he never misses spinning class or the gym (even on deadline nights).

Rob Tidrow is Publications Senior Specialist for Affiliated Computer Services (ACS, Inc.). He has also been a freelance technical writer and consultant for several years, specializing in Windows technologies and networking. Rob has a wife (Tammy) and two sons (Adam and Wesley). He lives in Centerville, Indiana, on a 34-acre "micro-farm," enjoys playing golf (even in the cold temperatures), and never seems to get enough seat-time on his tractor.

Contents at a Glance

Contents

Part V   **Windows Vista on the Internet**

Acknowledgments

The authors would like to thank the following people for valuable assistance in writing this book: Rob Tidrow and Will Kelly, for doing the heavy lifting to get all the details about Windows Vista correct; Megg Morin, for making the book happen and for putting up with the foibles of the authors; Tonia Saxon, Jordan Young, and everyone on the Microsoft Beta Support Team, for answering lots of questions. We also thank our friends and (most of all) our families for putting up with us during the seemingly endless process of updating such a long book.

From Will:

- Megg Morin, for gently shepherding me through this book project.
- Diane Poremsky, technical editor, for keeping me honest.
- My friends, clients, and colleagues, who challenge me to be a better person, writer, and professional.
- Spinning class at Washington Sports Club, for providing an outlet for the stress and frustration I felt after yet another crash or reinstall of the Windows Vista beta or Release Candidate.

From Rob:

- Megg Morin, for keeping after me throughout the book project.
- Diane Poremsky, for reviewing all the technical aspects of the book and even pointing out my typos.
- Carly Stapleton, for organizing material and renaming a bunch of my screenshots.
- Carole McClendon, my agent, who is quite simply the best in the business.
- My family, for allowing me to work on this book for many weeks without much interaction with them.

Introduction

Microsoft has been working on Windows Vista for over five years. It provides several enhancements over its direct predecessor, Windows XP, Service Pack 2. As soon as you start up your computer and log into Windows, you will notice a difference. A new Start menu, new desktop backgrounds, and even the new Sidebar that docks on the right side of your screen will tell you that you are experiencing something new. Then go ahead and click the new Start menu button (it no longer says "Start") and navigate the menus to launch a program. No longer does your screen fill with multiple layers of menus that reach to the edge of your screen and back. Instead, each time you drill down in a menu, it overlays the previous menu to make it easier to find the program you want and not lose track of where you are.

Other new features include new programs (such as Windows Calendar, Windows Photo Gallery, Windows Media Center, and Windows Fax and Scan), handy networking tools (the Network and Sharing Center, for example), a redesigned Control Panel, and many more advancements. You even get a few new games to help pass the time of day.

Who Is This Book For?

This book is primarily intended for general users of Windows Vista Ultimate, the full edition of Windows Vista. If you have another version, such as Windows Vista Basic or Windows Vista Business, this book is for you too. Some of the features that are available in Windows Vista Ultimate are not available in those other versions, but Windows Vista Ultimate includes all features of those editions so you can find information about those features in this book. You might have a lot of experience with other computer systems, or Windows Vista may be your first exposure to computing.

Your computer might be the only one in your home or office, or it may be one of many on a local area network. You probably have a modem or network card, although Windows works perfectly well without either. Chances are, your computer is connected to the Internet, or will be soon.

If your computer is connected to a large network, we don't expect you to be the network administrator, but if you're in a small office with two or three computers, we tell you how to set up a small, usable Windows network. If you have a modem, we discuss in detail what's involved in getting connected to the Internet, because Windows Vista includes all the software you need to use the Internet.

What's in This Book?

This book is organized around the kinds of things that you want to do with Windows, rather than around a listing of its features. Each part of the book concentrates on a type of work you might want to do with Windows.

Part I: Working in Windows Vista

Part I covers the basics of using Windows. Even if you have used Windows forever, at least skim through this section to learn about XP's entirely new interface environment. If you are new to Windows, you'll want to read it carefully.

Chapter 1 starts with the basics of working in Windows: using the mouse and managing your windows. Chapters 2 and 3 explain how to run and install programs beyond those included with Windows—including using the enhanced compatibility mode options that can run even the oldest DOS and Windows Me/9x/XP programs. Chapter 4 covers the newly revamped Help And Support tool, including how to get assistance from friends, coworkers, and Microsoft over the Internet. Chapter 5 looks at the many ways to move and share information between and among programs. User accounts, which have been vastly improved in Windows XP, are described in Chapter 6. Finally, Chapter 7 introduces you to the new scheduling program, Windows Calendar.

Part II: Managing Your Disk

All the information in your computer is stored in disk files and folders, and Part II helps you keep them organized and safe. Chapters 8 and 9 cover day-to-day file and folder operations, including how to use Windows Explorer (also known as Computer) to manage your files. Chapter 10 describes the backup program that comes with Windows, and how to set up a regular backup regime.

Part III: Configuring Windows for Your Computer

Windows is extremely (some would say excessively) configurable. Part III tells you what items you can configure and makes suggestions for the most effective way to set up your computer.

Chapter 11 covers the redesigned Start menu, the gateway to the features of Windows and your installed programs. Chapter 12 details the desktop, the icons, and other items that reside on your screen, such as the new Sidebar and Gadgets feature. Chapter 13 explains your keyboard and mouse (yes, lots of options exist just for the mouse), and Chapter 14 tells you how to add and set up additional hardware on your computer. Chapter 15 covers printing, including setting up printers and installing fonts, and using the new Fax and Scan features. Chapter 16 highlights the special features that are useful to laptop computer users, including the new Windows Mobility Center to help laptop users manage mobile devices. Chapter 17 covers the Ease of Access features that make Windows more usable for people who may have difficulty using conventional keyboards and mice, seeing the screen, or hearing sounds.

Part IV: Working with Text, Pictures, Sound, and Video

Chapter 18 discusses Windows' simple but useful text and word processing programs and calculator feature. In Chapter 19, you read about new features for viewing, editing, printing, e-mailing, and burning DVDs of your pictures using the Windows Photo Gallery program. Chapters 20 and 21 examine Windows' extensive sound and video multimedia facilities, including the powerful new Windows Media Player 11. Finally, Chapter 22 introduces you to Windows Media Center, an application that makes your computer the hub of your entertainment world.

Part V: Windows Vista on the Internet

Windows offers a complete set of Internet access features, from making network connections to e-mail and the World Wide Web.

Chapter 23 explains the intricacies of setting up a modem to work with Windows, whether you use a dial-up account or a high-speed cable, ISDN, or DSL connection. Chapter 24 tells you how to use that modem to create and set up an account with an Internet service provider or online service. Chapter 25 describes Windows Mail (the upgrade to the ubiquitous Microsoft Outlook Express), the Windows accessory program that handles your e-mail. Chapter 26 covers the new Internet Explorer 7.0, Microsoft's updated web browser. Chapter 27 examines online conferencing with Windows Live Messenger, and Chapter 28 discusses the other Internet applications that come with Windows.

Part VI: Networking with Windows Vista

Because it is based on Windows 2000, which itself was derived from a network server operating system, Windows Vista has extensive built-in networking features. You can set up your Windows machine as a workstation in a large network, as a server in a small network, or as both.

Chapter 29 introduces local area networks, including key concepts such as client-server and peer-to-peer networking. Chapter 30 walks you through the process of creating a small network of Windows systems. Chapter 31 tells you how to share printers and disk drives among your networked computers. Chapter 32 explains how to share one Internet account and modem among all the computers on a LAN. Chapter 33 covers the network security features that Windows Vista provides, including the Windows Firewall.

Part VII: Windows Housekeeping

Windows is sufficiently complex that it needs some regular maintenance and adjustment, and Part VII tells you how. Chapter 34 discusses disk setup, including removable disks and new hard disks that you may add to your computer. Chapter 35 tells you how to keep your disk working well and how to use the facilities that Windows provides to check and repair disk problems, including defragmenting and taking out the garbage. Chapter 36 explains how to tune your computer for maximum performance, and Chapter 37 reviews the process of troubleshooting hardware and software problems. Chapter 38 describes the other Windows resources available on the Internet and elsewhere, including automatic updates, which can automatically identify and install updated or corrected Windows components.

Part VIII: Behind the Scenes: Windows Vista Internals

Part VIII covers a few advanced Windows topics. Chapter 39 describes the configuration files that Windows uses, and Chapter 40 describes the Registry, the central database of program information that is key to Windows' operation.

Appendix

The appendix describes how to install Windows Vista as an upgrade to a Windows system, or from scratch on a blank hard disk.

Conventions Used in This Book

This book uses several icons to highlight special advice:

TIP *A handy way to make Windows work better for you.*

NOTE *An observation that gives insight into the way that Windows and other programs work.*

CAUTION *Something to watch out for, so you don't have to learn the hard way.*

When we refer you to related material, we tell you the name of the section that contains the information we think you'll want to read. If the section is in the same chapter you are reading, we don't mention a chapter number.

When you see instructions to choose commands from a menu, we separate the part of the command by vertical bars (|). For example, "choose File | Open" means to choose File from the menu bar and then choose Open from the File menu that appears. If the command begins "Start |," then click the Start button on the taskbar as the first step. See "Giving Commands" in Chapter 2 for the details of how to give commands.

New and Improved Features in Windows Vista

Windows Vista is a major upgrade from previous Windows system. The Aero interface is a fantastic change to the older, Luna interface available with Windows XP. Not only are there surface-level changes, but a whole lot more. Here is a list of a few of the new (or greatly improved) features:

- **Remote Assistance** enables you to ask a friend, coworker, or a support professional to take over your computer via the Internet and fix a software problem (see Chapter 4).
- **User accounts** make it convenient to create and use a separate user account for each person who uses a single computer (see Chapter 6).
- **Windows Calendar** is a new scheduling program provided with Windows Vista (see Chapter 7).
- **Windows Aero** interface provides a brand new look and feel to Windows (see Chapter 12).
- **Sidebar and Gadgets** adds small applications (called gadgets) to your desktop for quick access and viewing (see Chapter 12).
- **Windows Photo Gallery** enables you to view and perform some edits on your digital photographs (see Chapter 19).

- **Backup** is still here, but vastly improved! The Backup Status and Configuration tool lets you set up automatic backups of the important data on your computer. You also can run CompletePC Backup to create a backup copy of your entire computer—including programs and system files (see Chapter 10).

- **Internet Explorer (IE)** version 7.0 is an upgrade to Microsoft's powerful web browser (see Chapter 24).

- **Windows Mail** is the newest version of Microsoft's e-mail and newsgroup program (see Chapter 25).

- **Windows Media Player 11** provides a new interface to viewing videos, playing music, and managing your media. Windows Media Player 11 makes it easy to burn audio discs and DVDs, synchronize music playlists with your digital music players, and download media from the Internet (see Chapter 20).

- **Windows Media Center** allows you to make your computer the hub of your entertainment system, including viewing and recording television shows through your computer (see Chapter 22).

Windows Vista also removed a few programs that came with some earlier Windows versions. For example, Windows Vista no longer includes the Windows Messenger Chat program. You can, however, use the supplied link to download a replacement program called Windows Live Messenger (see Chapter 27).

Differences Between Windows Vista Editions

Windows XP comes in various versions:

- **Windows Vista Starter** is available in 119 emerging markets and includes features that help new users use their computer. Microsoft does not plan to sell this version in the United States, Canada, the European Union, Australia, New Zealand, and other world markets that have high income levels.

- **Windows Vista Home Basic** includes basic features, such as features allowing you to easily set up Internet connections, features to set up parental controls, and ways to create documents. Many of the advanced Windows Vista features, however, are not included with Home Basic.

- **Windows Vista Home Premium** provides your computer with Media Center so you can turn your computer into a media hub. Home Premium includes the new Vista Aero design.

- **Windows Vista Business** is primarily suited for the business user. It includes security tools and Microsoft Backup. However, it does not include the media tools, such as Windows Photo Gallery.

- **Windows Vista Ultimate** includes everything, including business tools, multimedia features, and Aero. Vista Ultimate is a hybrid of Vista Business and Home Premium. It lets you use your computer as a media center, but has the enhanced business features, too.

- **Windows Vista Enterprise** boasts drive encryption and other high-end features, such as compatibility mode.

Talk to Us

We love to hear from our readers. Drop us an e-mail note at winxptcr@gurus.com to tell us how you liked the book or just to test your e-mail skills. Our mail robot will answer right away, and the authors will read your message when time permits (usually within a week or two).

Also visit our web site at http://net.gurus.com/ for updates and corrections to this book.

PART

I

Working in Windows Vista

The Basics of Windows Vista

Windows is the most widely run computer program in the world, and Windows Vista is the latest version of Windows. Most of the software written for personal computers—indeed, most of the software written for any computer—is written for computers running Windows.

This chapter explains what Windows Vista is and explains the objects you see on the Windows screen—the desktop, icons, the taskbar, the Start menu, and windows. It also explains the Control Panel, a collection of programs that enables you to control how Windows and your computer work. Many Control Panel programs run *wizards*, special programs that step you through the process of creating or configuring an object on your computer. *Properties* are another way of choosing settings for the objects in your computer. This chapter also describes how to start Windows, shut it down, and suspend Windows operation when you're not using your computer.

TIP *If you've used Windows 95, 98, Me, 2000, or XP you can probably skip this chapter since you already understand windows, icons, and the desktop. Just skim through to see what's changed!*

What Is Windows Vista?

Windows Vista is the latest desktop version of Microsoft's Windows series of programs. It's the upgrade to the consumer versions of Windows (95, 98, Me, and XP) as well as to the business, server, and power-user versions (Windows NT, 2000, and 2003). Windows is an *operating system*, a program that manages your entire computer system, including its screen, keyboard, disk drives, memory, and central processor. Windows also provides a *graphical user interface*, or *GUI*, which enables you to control your computer by using a mouse, windows, and icons. You can also use the keyboard to give commands; this book describes both methods.

You can upgrade to Windows Vista from Windows XP, or you can do a "clean install" to replace any previous version of Windows on your computer. You can also buy a computer with Windows Vista preinstalled. Once Windows Vista is installed, you can run Windows-compatible *application programs* (programs for getting real-world work done).

Versions of Windows Vista and Windows 2003

For years, Microsoft has produced two editions of Windows, one for desktops (that is, for individual users, including for use on laptops) and one for servers (computers that provide services over networks). The desktop versions were Windows 3.1, 95, 98, Me, and XP and were intended for workstation use—that is, on computers that people used directly. The server versions were Windows NT 4, 2000, and 2003, and were intended for use on servers (computers that provide services to other computers on a network) as well as by high-end users.

Windows Vista is designed to work for individuals and power users, and comes initially in five versions:

- **Windows Vista Business**   For businesses and organizations
- **Windows Vista Enterprise**   For large corporations that have complex information technology infrastructures
- **Windows Vista Home Premium**   For home users who use computers for entertainment, Internet and e-mail tasks, and homework
- **Windows Vista Home Basic**   For home users who need a computer to do just the basics
- **Windows Vista Ultimate**   Includes all the best business, mobile, and entertainment features of the other versions of Windows Vista

This book describes Windows Vista Ultimate. The Microsoft web site contains details about Windows Vista at www.microsoft.com/windowsvista/getready/editions/default.mspx.

Windows Vista comes bundled with many programs, most of which aren't actually part of the operating system, including Internet connection software (dial-up connections), an e-mail program (Windows Mail), a web browser (Internet Explorer), a simple word processing program (WordPad), a calendar program (Windows Calendar), local area network (LAN) support, utilities that help with hard-disk housekeeping, and dozens of other programs.

What Appears on the Screen?

Like previous versions of Windows, Windows Vista uses windows to display information on your screen, icons to provide pictorial buttons for you to click, and a taskbar, which is a "mission control" center for your computer. All of these objects appear on your Windows desktop—your screen. Microsoft made a major effort to clean up the screen in Windows Vista: you'll see many fewer icons and menu commands. Of course, you can always create icons and add commands for the programs and files you use frequently—in fact, Windows does this for you.

What Hardware Do You Need?

Windows Vista requires the following computer hardware:

- A CPU running at a speed of at least 800 MHz.
- At least 512MB of RAM memory (although Microsoft recommends at least 1GB).
- A hard disk with at least 20GB total space with at least 15GB free.
- A DVD drive from which to install Windows.
- A monitor, keyboard, and mouse or other pointing device.
- If you plan to listen to sounds played by Windows and other programs, you need a sound board and speakers attached to your computer (See "Configuring Windows to Work with Sound" in Chapter 20). To participate in voice or video chats, you need a microphone or digital video camera, too.
- If you plan to use your computer to connect to the Internet, you need a dial-up modem and a regular phone line, an ISDN modem and an ISDN line, a DSL modem and a DSL line, a cable modem and cable connection, or a LAN connection (see Chapter 27).

Windows shows the following items:

- **Desktop**   Windows uses your screen as a *desktop*, a work area on which you see your programs. The desktop, shown in Figure 1-1, can contain windows, icons, and the taskbar.
- **Taskbar**   The taskbar is a row of buttons and icons that usually appears along the bottom of the screen, as shown in Figure 1-1. You can configure Windows to display the taskbar along the top or side of your screen. You can also tell Windows to hide the taskbar when you aren't using it. The taskbar has several parts, including the Start button, task buttons, toolbars, and notification area.
- **Start menu**   When you click the Start button on the taskbar, the Start menu appears, as shown in Figure 1-2. You can also display the Start menu by pressing the WINDOWS key (if your keyboard has one) or by pressing CTRL-ESC. The Start menu lists commands and additional menus that list most of the programs that you can run on your computer. Vista has a new way to access additional folders on the Start menu. Instead of program menus displaying to the right side of the Start menu, each subsequent menu you select, such as the Accessories menu, displays on top of the previous folder.

Welcome to Windows Vista!

When you start Windows Vista, the Vista Welcome Center appears onscreen. The Welcome Center includes icons and links to help you get started with some of the basic Windows tasks, including setting up hardware, adding a printer, and using a mouse.

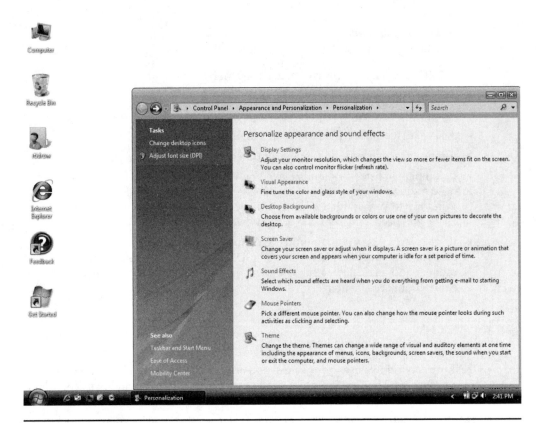

<small>**FIGURE 1-1**   The Windows Vista desktop</small>

TIP *In this book, we indicate commands on the Start menu and its submenus like this: Start | Help
And Support. This means you should click the Start button and choose Help And Support from the
Start menu. We also capitalize the first letter of each word in menu selections and dialog box
options (such as Help And Support) so that you can easily identify them from the surrounding text.*

- **Task buttons**   Task buttons are the buttons on the taskbar that represent each
  program that is running. If a program displays more than one window, more than
  one task button may appear. Each task button displays the icon for the program and
  as much of the program name as can fit. Click a window's task button to select that
  window—that is, to make that window active. You can also right-click a button to
  see the system menu, a menu of commands that you can give regarding that
  window, including opening and closing the window. If the taskbar gets too full to fit
  task buttons for all the open windows, Windows groups the buttons together, with
  one button for each application.

FIGURE 1-2   The Windows Vista Start menu

- **Notification area**   The notification area appears at the right end of the taskbar and contains the system clock along with a group of tiny icons. When you move the mouse pointer to the clock, after a moment the current date also appears. The icons in the notification area represent programs that need your attention. Windows Vista displays fewer icons here than previous versions of Windows did, displaying them only when you need to do something.

TIP   *If there are too many icons to fit in the notification area, you see a left-pointing (<) button that you can click to see the rest of the icons. This button allows Windows to hide the icons that don't fit, so they don't clutter up your taskbar.*

How Do You Configure Windows and Other Programs?

To use Windows effectively, you need to configure it to work with your computer's hardware and with your other programs. When configuring Windows, you encounter these concepts:

- **Properties**   Settings for many different objects in your computer's hardware and software

- **Control Panel**   Enables you to see and change many Windows settings

- **Wizards**   Programs that help automate the processes of installing hardware, installing software, and configuring software

FIGURE 1-3   A Properties dialog box displays the properties of an object and may enable you to edit them.

What Are Properties?

Every object in Windows—the hardware components of your computer, software programs, files, and icons—has *properties*, the settings that affect how that object works. For example, a file might have properties such as a filename, size, and the date the file was last modified.

To display the properties of almost anything you see on the screen in Windows, right-click the item and choose Properties from the menu that appears. You see a dialog box with a title that usually includes the word "Properties." Figure 1-3 shows the properties of an icon on the desktop.

If the object has too many properties to fit in a dialog box, tabs may run along the top of the dialog box. Click a tab to see the settings on that tab. Windows may let you change some of the settings, depending on the type of object. For example, to see the properties of the Windows desktop, right-click the desktop in a place where it is not covered by icons or windows. You see the Display Properties dialog box (see "What Are Display Properties?" in Chapter 12) When you have finished looking at the properties shown and possibly changing some of the properties that can be changed, click OK to save your changes (or click Cancel to cancel them) and exit the Properties dialog box.

What Is the Control Panel?

The *Control Panel*, shown in Figure 1-4, is a window that displays icons for a number of programs that enable you to control your computer, Windows, and the software you have installed. These programs help you see and change the properties of many parts of Windows.

Figure 1-4   The Control Panel window

To see the Control Panel, choose Start | Control Panel. Windows Vista displays a newly redesigned window with categories of tasks—Windows calls this *Category View*. Clicking a category in the Control Panel displays a list of tasks in that category. Windows Vista also includes links to each category in the category pane on the left side of the Control Panel window. To see this pane, click a category, such as the Network and Internet category. Vista now displays each option available for the Network and Internet category, but also shows links to the other Control Panel categories in the left pane.

If you are used to the "Classic" Windows 95, 98, or Me Control Panel icons, click the Classic View option. You see most of the same Control Panel icons that appeared in earlier versions of Windows; double-click them to run them. These icons also appear in Category View, below the tasks.

The details of what you can change in each category and what each Control Panel icon does are discussed throughout this book, in the related chapters.

What Is a Wizard?

Windows, like many other Microsoft programs, includes many *wizards*, programs that step you through the process of creating or configuring something. For example, the New Connection Wizard leads you through the many steps required to set up a dial-up connection to the Internet (see Chapter 22).

Wizards include instructions for each step, telling you what information you must provide and making suggestions regarding your choices. Most wizards display window after window of information and questions, with Back, Next, and Cancel buttons at the bottom of each window. Fill out the information requested by the wizard and click the Next button to continue. If you need to return to a previous wizard window, click the Back button. To exit the wizard, click the Cancel button. The wizard's last screen usually displays a Finish button because there's no next screen to see.

Starting Up Windows

On most systems, Windows starts automatically when you turn on the computer. You see whatever messages your computer displays on startup, followed by the Windows *splash screen* (logo). If your computer is on a LAN or is set up for multiple users, you also see a welcome screen, showing the user accounts defined on the system. Click your user account name; if the account requires a password, type your password and press ENTER.

If your computer system has been put into sleep or hibernate mode, Windows hasn't been shut down; instead, it is "sleeping." To start up where you left off, just resume operation of your computer, which usually is accomplished by moving the mouse, pressing a key (such as the SHIFT key), or (if you use a laptop) opening the cover.

Another possibility is that someone locked the computer screen by pressing WINDOWS-L (that is, holding down the WINDOWS key, which not all keyboards have, and typing L). If so, you see the same welcome screen you saw when Windows started: click your user account name to continue.

TIP *If your computer's hard disk contains more than one bootable partition (that is, another section of your hard disk that contains an operating system), you may see the message "Please select the operating system to start," with a list of bootable partitions. Use the arrow keys to select the operating system you want and press ENTER. For information about partitions, see Chapter 34.*

Choosing Lock Button Modes

Windows Vista includes Lock buttons. Lock buttons display on the Start menu and provide options for putting Windows or your computer in a different operating mode. For example, when you are ready to shut down your computer, you can use the Shut Down mode. The following list describes each mode Vista provides:

- **Switch User**   Allows you to change from the current user to another user without shutting down the computer.
- **Log Off**   Allows you to log off from Windows and any network connections you have established.
- **Lock**   Allows you to lock your computer so users cannot access it, but it allows your programs to continue running. This is handy if you are downloading a large file and you need to walk away from your computer while it continues to download.
- **Restart**   Shuts down Windows, and then reloads it (useful if your computer starts acting funny).

> **When Can You Turn Off the Computer?**
>
> We recommend you *do not* turn off the computer when you have finished using it. Windows likes to perform housekeeping tasks when you aren't using the computer, so leaving it on, even when you're not working, is a good idea. You can schedule programs to run at specified times (see "Running Programs on a Schedule Using Task Scheduler" in Chapter 2)—for example, you can schedule Windows to collect your e-mail at 7:00 every morning.
>
> Many computers power down the monitor, hard disk, and fan after a set time of inactivity. The computer itself, however, is still running. If your screen doesn't power off automatically, you should turn off your monitor when you aren't using the computer. Many computer monitors (except for LCD monitors) use the lion's share of the electricity consumed by a computer (see "Managing Your Computer's Power" in Chapter 15).

- **Sleep**   Puts the computer into a sleep mode, which shuts down the hard drive and turns off the monitor to conserve power consumption. Programs remain open and your documents are automatically saved. When you awaken your computer, these devices turn back on.

- **Hibernate**   Puts your computer into a power-saving mode that is similar to the Sleep mode. Hibernate is available only if you use the advanced power settings in Windows.

- **Away**   Makes it appear that your computer is shut down, but some tasks like burning CDs and recording television programs still run. If you move the mouse or type on the keyboard, nothing happens.

- **Shut Down**   Shuts down Windows. Windows displays a message when you can safely turn off the computer. Don't turn off the computer until you see this message. Computers with advanced power management shut off automatically.

Setting Windows to Shut Down by Itself

Windows includes *OnNow*, technology that powers down the computer when nothing is happening and powers it back up when the computer is needed again. To use OnNow, choose Start | Control Panel, click System And Maintenance, and then run the Power Options program (see "Managing Your Computer's Power" in Chapter 16).

Choosing Between Single-Click and Double-Click

You can choose how icons on the Windows desktop and in Explorer windows behave (as you could in Windows Me, 98 Second Edition, and XP). Your choices are

- **Single-click**   (Web style) To select the icon without running or opening it, move your mouse pointer to the icon without clicking, and wait a second. To run or open the icon, click it once. Icon labels appear underlined (like web page links).

- **Double-click**   (Classic Windows style) To select the icon, click it once. To run or open the icon, click it twice. Icon labels are not underlined.

Follow these steps to choose between single-click and double-click:

1. Choose Start | Control Panel. Click the Appearance And Personalization category.

2. Click the Folder Options icon. You see the Folder Options dialog box, shown in Figure 1-5. If the General tab isn't selected, click it.

TIP   *Whether you use single-click or double-click, you can right-click icons to see a shortcut menu of commands you can perform on the icon (see "Choosing Commands from Shortcut Menus" in Chapter 2).*

3. In the Click Items As Follows area, click either the Single-click or Double-click radio button. If you choose Single-click, choose whether you want icon titles to be underlined all the time (Consistent With My Browser) or only when your mouse pointer is on the icon (Only When I Point At Them).

4. Click OK.

FIGURE 1-5   The General tab of the Folder Options dialog box, where you can specify how Windows icons work.

Running Programs

Running Windows Vista itself doesn't get you very far. The point of Windows is to let you run programs that help you get work done. To take advantage of Windows' capability to multitask (do several things at the same time), this chapter explains how to run several programs at the same time and how to switch among them. Because programs display information in windows, you also learn how the windows you see on your screen work.

You can control the size and location of the windows in which programs display information. Once a program is running, you can give it commands using the mouse and keyboard. This chapter also explains how to configure Windows to launch automatically the programs you always use so that you're ready to work as soon as you start Windows, how to schedule programs to run at preset times, and how to define shortcut keys for quick-starting programs you use frequently. Windows Vista's new compatibility mode enables many older programs to run without problems.

> **TIP** *If you've used previous versions of Windows, you probably know everything in this chapter— just flip through to familiarize yourself with the terms you'll see throughout the rest of the book.*

What Are Programs and Windows?

A *program* is a sequence of computer instructions that performs a task. Programs are stored in *program files*, which have the filename extension .exe or .com. When you run a program, your computer executes the instructions in the program file.

Programs can do several things at once; for example, a word processing program may be able to print one document while you edit another. One program can run several *tasks* or *processes* at the same time. Windows itself runs many tasks at the same time, including tasks that monitor the hard disk, screen, and keyboard; update the onscreen clock; and run programs on a schedule, for example. The heart of Windows is its capability to *multitask*—that is, to run many processes at the same time.

An *application* is a program that does real-world–oriented work. Word processors, spreadsheets, and databases are widely used types of applications. A *systems program* does computer-oriented work—an operating system like Windows itself is the most important systems program you use. Printer drivers (which control the actions of a printer) or disk scanners (which check disks for errors) are other examples of system programs. A *utility* is

a small, simple, useful program (either a small application or a small systems program).
Windows comes with many utilities, like Calculator and Notepad.

TIP *If you have user accounts on your system, you can run a program as if you logged in as another user, assuming that you know the user account's password (see "Running a Program as Another User" in Chapter 6).*

Each program displays information in one or more *windows*—rectangular areas on the screen that display information from a running program (see the next section, "What Do the Parts of Windows Do?"). Some windows are divided into sections, called *panes*. To run more than one program at the same time, go ahead and run one program, then another, then another. The first program you run continues to run when the second program starts. Each program's window(s) can be minimized, maximized, or restored (see "Controlling the Size and Shape of Your Windows" later in the chapter). A button appears on the taskbar for each program.

One window is always *on top*, which means it is the *active window*. The title bar of the active window is a different color than the color of the title bars of all the other windows on your screen; in the default Windows desktop color scheme, the title bar of the active window is blue, while the other title bars are gray. Where the active window overlaps with another window, the active window obscures the other window.

Whatever you type on the keyboard is directed to the program in the active window. The programs in the other windows continue to run, but they don't receive input from your keyboard. To type information into a program, you switch the active window to a window displayed by that program.

What Do the Parts of Windows Do?

Figure 2-1 shows a program (this example shows WordPad, a simple word processor that comes with Windows) running in a window. Although what's inside the window frame changes from program to program, most windows you see in Windows include the following components:

- **System Menu button**   Displays a menu of commands you can use to move and resize your window (see "What Is the System Menu").

- **Title bar**   Displays the title of the window and provides a way to move the window around within the screen.

- **Minimize button**   Shrinks the window to an icon on the taskbar (see "Controlling the Size and Shape of Your Windows").

- **Maximize or Restore button**   When you click the Maximize button, the window expands to cover the whole screen (see "Controlling the Size and Shape of Your Windows"). Once a window has been maximized, the Maximize button disappears and is replaced by the Restore button. When you click the Restore button (with two overlapping rectangles), the window shrinks to its previous size and the Maximize button reappears.

- **Close button**   Closes the window and exits the program (see "Controlling the Size and Shape of Your Windows").

- **Menu bar**   Provides a row of menus you can use to choose commands (see "Giving Commands").

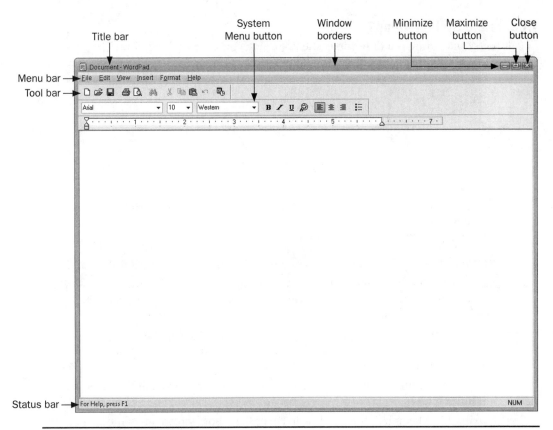

FIGURE 2-1   The parts of a window

- **Toolbar**   Provides a row of buttons you can click to give commands (see "Giving Commands").

- **Status bar**   Displays information about the program. Some programs enable you to give commands by clicking parts of the status bar.

- **Scroll bar**   Provides a way to "pan" your window up and down, or left and right, to show information that doesn't fit in the window. Scroll bars may be horizontal (running along the bottom edge of a window) or vertical (running down the right edge of a window). All scroll bars have arrow buttons at each end and a sliding gray box somewhere in the scroll bar; some programs display scroll bars with additional buttons (for example, to scroll one page of a document at a time). The length or width of a scroll bar represents the entire length or width of the document you are viewing, and the sliding box represents the part of the document you can currently see. To change which part of the document you can see, click the arrow button at one end of the scroll bar, or click-and-drag the sliding gray box along the scroll bar.

- **Window borders**   Provide a way to drag around the edges of the window to change the size and shape of the window (see "Controlling the Size and Shape of Your Windows").

What Is the System Menu?

The *System Menu* button is a tiny icon in the upper-left corner of each window. The icon shows which program you are running. When you click the icon, you see the *System* menu:

You can also display the System menu by pressing ALT-SPACEBAR or by right-clicking the title bar of the window.

The commands on the System menu do the following:

- **Restore**   Resizes the window to its previous size, the same as the Restore button.
- **Move**   Enables you to move the window around on your screen by using the cursor (arrow) keys. This command does the same thing as dragging the window's title bar with the mouse. Press ENTER to finish moving the window.
- **Size**   Enables you to change the size of the window by using the cursor keys. This command does the same thing as dragging the window borders with the mouse (see "Controlling the Size and Shape of You Windows").
- **Minimize**   Minimizes the window, shrinking it to a small icon, the same as the Minimize button.
- **Maximize**   Maximizes the window to cover the whole screen, the same as the Maximize button.
- **Close**   Closes the window, the same as the Close button.

Some applications also add their own commands to the System menu.

Starting Programs

Windows gives you many ways to start a program, including clicking its icon on your Windows desktop, choosing it from a menu, clicking a document you want to edit or view by using the program, clicking the program filename, and typing the program name into a Run or DOS window. The following sections describe these methods.

Starting Programs from the Desktop

If an icon for the program appears on your Windows desktop, click the icon either once or twice to run the program. If the labels under the icons on your desktop are underlined, click once. If the labels are not underlined, double-click. You can control whether you need to single-click or double-click icons to run programs by setting your Folder options (see "Choosing Between Single-Click and Double-Click" in Chapter 1).

Starting Programs from the Start Menu

Chapter 1 describes the Start menu, including the all-important Start button. To launch a program from the Start menu, click the Start button. You see the Start menu, as shown here:

The Windows Vista Start menu has two sides. At the top of the left side are Internet and E-mail, which run your default web browser and e-mail program. You can add other programs, too (see "Reorganizing the Start Menu" in Chapter 11). Below that are icons for programs you've run frequently and recently: Windows chooses these programs according to your usage. Toward the bottom of the left side is the All Programs button, which displays menus that usually include the rest of the programs that are installed on your computer. At the bottom of the left side is the new Start Search field. In this field you can type search criteria (such as the name of a file) that you want Windows to locate.

The right side of the Start menu lists the folders that Microsoft suggests you use for your files (Documents, Pictures, and Music) and Computer (to run Windows Explorer). If your computer is on a network, Network appears. The other choices are usually Control Panel (for computer administration), Connect To (if your computer is on a LAN or the Internet), and Help And Support. At the bottom of the right side is the new Lock Button area. This is where you shut down, restart, and lock your computer (see "Choosing Lock Button Modes" in Chapter 1).

If you can't find the program you want, and you think it's been installed on your computer, click the All Programs button on the Start menu (that is, choose Start | All Programs). You see the Programs menu, which now looks different than the Programs menu in previous versions of Windows:

With Windows Vista, the Programs menu displays on top of the All Programs menu. When your mouse pointer is on a menu name, a submenu appears (on top of the current menu). Point to menus until you see the name of the program you want to run, then click the program name. Most programs appear on the Programs menu or on its submenus (because most installation programs add commands for the programs that they install). You might need to try several menus to find the one that contains the program you want. You can always press ESC to cancel the menu you are looking at (moving your mouse pointer off the menu and clicking usually cancels the menu, too). For example, WordPad appears on the Accessories submenu of the Programs menu. To run WordPad, choose Start | All Programs | Accessories | WordPad.

NOTE *In this book, we tell you to run programs from the Start or Start | All Programs menus where the programs appear in a standard Windows Vista installation. If you've customized your Start menu, commands may not be where we say they are. Also, if you've run a program recently, it may appear on the left side of the Start menu—if so, ignore our instructions for finding the program and click the command you see.*

You can rearrange the programs on your Start and Programs menus so that the programs you most frequently run appear on the Programs menu or the Start menu rather than on a submenu. You can also create desktop icons for any programs on these menus (see "Reorganizing the Start Menu" in Chapter 11).

CAUTION *You can change the order of the items on the Start and Programs menus by dragging them up and down on the menus. You can also drag an item from one menu to another, or "pin" a program to the top-left side of the Start menu by right-clicking it and choosing Pin To Start Menu. If you don't intend to reorganize your menus, don't click-and-drag the commands on them.*

Starting Programs Using the Windows Key

You can run a program without using your mouse. If your keyboard has a WINDOWS key, press it to display the Start menu; if not, pressing CTRL-ESC does the same thing. Press the LEFT-ARROW, RIGHT-ARROW, UP-ARROW, and DOWN-ARROW keys to highlight a command from the Start menu and press ENTER to choose the command. The same method works for choosing commands from submenus. The RIGHT-ARROW key moves from a command to its submenu (which is usually to the right on the screen). The LEFT-ARROW and ESC keys cancel a submenu and return to the previous menu.

Starting Programs by Clicking Program Filenames

Programs are stored in files, usually with the filename extension .exe (short for "executable") or .com (for "command"). Windows displays the names of program files in Explorer windows. To run the program, single-click or double-click the filename of the program you want to run.

For example, if you double-click the filename Mspaint.exe, Windows runs the Microsoft Paint program. You can usually guess the program name from the filename, though some filenames can be cryptic.

Starting Programs by Clicking Document Filenames or File Icons

Windows knows which programs you use to open which types of files. For example, it knows that files with the .doc extension are opened using Microsoft Word. When you install a program, the installation program adds a file association to Windows, so Windows knows what kinds of files it can open.

To run the program that can open a particular file, you can click or double-click the filename in an Explorer window. If the filenames are underlined, you single-click the filename to open it. If the filenames are not underlined, you double-click the filename. Windows runs the appropriate program to handle that file (if the program isn't already running) and opens the file in that program. If an icon for a file appears on your desktop, clicking or double-clicking the icon tells Windows to do the same thing.

For example, if your desktop icon labels aren't underlined and you double-click a file with the extension .mdb (a Microsoft Access database file), Windows runs Microsoft Access and opens the database file. Windows may be configured not to display extensions (the default setting is for extensions to be hidden); you can identify many types of files by their icons. To tell Windows to display full filenames, including the extensions, see "What Are Extensions and File Types?" in Chapter 8.

If you try to open a file for which Windows doesn't know which program to run, you see a window asking what you want to do. Your options are

- **Use The Web Service To Find The Appropriate Program**   Windows runs your web browser to display information about the type of file that you want to open, and helps you find a program that can open it.

- **Select The Program From A List**   Windows displays the Open With dialog box, shown in Figure 2-2. Choose the program that can open the type of file you clicked; if the program doesn't appear on the list, click the Browse button to find the filename of the program. If you always want to run this program when you click this type of file, leave the check mark in the Always Use The Selected Program To Open This Type Of File check box. Optionally, you can type a description of the type of file: this description appears when you select a filename and choose Views | Details. Then click OK.

You can control which program runs for each type of file (see "Associating a Program with a File Extension" in Chapter 3).

TIP   *If you want to open a file using a different program from the one Windows automatically runs, right-click the filename and choose Open With from the menu that appears. Windows displays the Open With dialog box shown in Figure 2-2, and you can choose the program you want to run.*

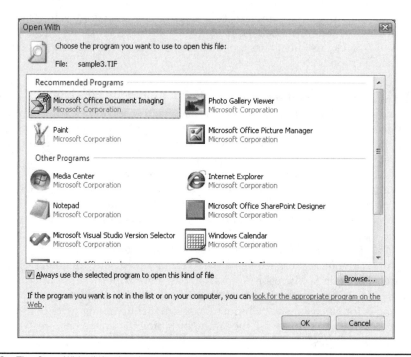

FIGURE 2-2   The Open With dialog box lets you tell Windows which program can open the file you clicked.

Starting Programs Using Shortcut Keys

If a shortcut (see "What Is a Shortcut?" in Chapter 9)—an icon with a tiny arrow in its lower-left corner—exists for a program, you can define shortcut keys to run the program. *Shortcut keys* for programs are always a combination of the CTRL key, the ALT key, and one other key, which must be a letter, number, or symbol key.

To define shortcut keys for a program:

1. Right-click the shortcut icon that launches the program and choose Properties from the menu that appears. You see the Properties dialog box for the shortcut.

2. Click the Shortcut tab.

3. Click in the Shortcut Key box (which usually says "None") and press the key you want to use in combination with the CTRL and ALT keys. For example, press *M* to specify CTRL-ALT-M as the shortcut key combination. To specify no shortcut keys, press SPACEBAR.

4. Click OK.

Once you define shortcut keys for a program, you can press the keys to run the program.

NOTE *If another program uses the same combination of keys, that combination of keys no longer performs its function in the program; instead, the key combination runs the program to which you assigned the shortcut keys. However, few programs use CTRL-ALT key combinations.*

Starting Programs from the Run Dialog Box

Before Windows, there was DOS, which required you to type the filename of a program and press ENTER to run the program. If you prefer this method, it still works in Windows—sometimes it's easier than finding the program in the maze of Start menu options. Choose Start | All Programs | Accessories | Run, and you see the Run dialog box, shown in Figure 2-3.

To run a program, type in the Open box its executable name (such as Notepad) or its full path and filename (that is, the exact filename, including the folder that contains the file), or click Browse to locate the filename. Then press ENTER or click OK. Windows runs the program.

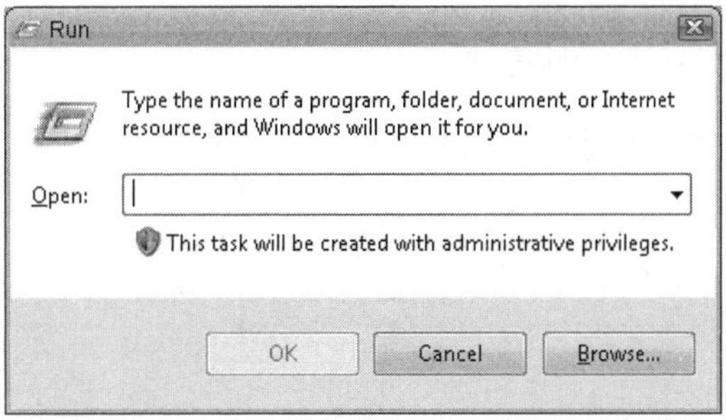

FIGURE 2-3   Use the Run dialog box to launch programs using a command-line entry.

Depending on the program, you may need to type additional information after the filename. For example, to run the Ftp program (an Internet file transfer program that comes with Windows), type **ftp**, followed by a space and the name of a computer on the Internet (like **ftp.microsoft.com**). When you press ENTER, Windows runs the Ftp program by using the additional information you typed.

TIP *If you've typed the filename in the Open box recently, click the downward-pointing button at the right end of the Open box and choose the filename from the list that appears.*

Starting Programs when Windows Starts

When Windows starts up, it looks in the Startup folder of your Start menu for shortcuts to programs (see "What Is a Shortcut?" in Chapter 9). This folder is usually stored in C:\Users*username*\App Data\Roaming\Microsoft\Windows\Start Menu\Programs (assuming that C: is the partition where Windows is installed). If any programs or shortcuts to programs are stored in this folder, Windows runs them automatically when it has finished starting up.

For example, you can use this Startup folder to run your word processor and e-mail programs automatically each time you start Windows. Just create shortcuts in your Startup folder (see "Making Shortcuts" in Chapter 9).

NOTE *The Windows Registry, which stores information about Windows and your applications, can also tell Windows to run programs automatically on startup (see "Running Programs on Startup" in Chapter 40).*

Controlling the Size and Shape of Your Windows

Windows enables you to control the size and position of most windows, so you can arrange your open windows to see the information you want to view. A window can be in one of three states:

- **Maximized**   The window takes up the entire screen, with no window borders.
- **Minimized**   All that appears is the window's button on the taskbar.
- **Restored (or in a window)**   The window is displayed with window borders (see Figure 2-1). You can change the height and width of restored windows. Most windows on your screen are restored windows.

Table 2-1 describes how you can manipulate windows.

TIP *Minimize windows when you want to unclutter your desktop without exiting programs.*

Giving Commands

Almost every Windows program enables you to issue commands to control what the program does. For example, the WordPad program includes commands to create a new document, save the document you are working on, print the document, and exit the program (among its

Action	Description
Move a window	To move a window, click anywhere in the title bar of the window, except for the System Menu button or the buttons at the right end of the title bar. Next, drag-and-drop the window to the place you want it to appear.
Minimize a window	To minimize a window—make a window disappear, leaving nothing but its taskbar button—click the window's Minimize button, the leftmost of the three buttons on the right end of the title bar, or click the window's System Menu button and choose Minimize from the menu.
Minimize all windows	To minimize all the open windows on your screen, right-click a blank area on the taskbar and choose Show The Desktop from the shortcut menu. If the Shows Desktop icon appears on your taskbar (it's on the Quick Launch toolbar, usually right next to the Start button), you can also click this icon to minimize all your windows. (See "What Can Appear on the Taskbar?" in Chapter 11 for a description of the Quick Launch toolbar.) To reverse this command, right-click a blank area on the taskbar and choose Show Open Windows.
Maximize a window	To maximize a window—expand it to cover the whole screen—click the window's Maximize button, the middle button on the right end of the title bar, or click the window's System Menu button and choose Maximize from the menu. When a window is maximized, its Maximize button is replaced by the Restore button, which returns the window to the size it was before you maximized it. Double-clicking a window's title bar switches between maximized and restored. If the window is currently minimized and you want to maximize it, right-click the button on the taskbar for the window and choose Maximize from the menu.
Restore window to previous size	After you maximize a window, you can restore it—return it to its previous size. Click the window's Restore button to restore the window, or click the window's System Menu button and choose Restore from the menu. The Restore button appears (as the middle button on the right end of the title bar) only when the window is maximized. If the window is currently minimized and you want to restore it, click the taskbar button for the window.
Arrange all windows	To see all the windows on your desktop at the same time, you can ask Windows to arrange them tastefully for you. Right-click a blank area of the taskbar and choose one of the following commands from the menu: • **Cascade Windows** Opens all the windows so they overlap, with their upper-left corners cascading from the upper-left corner of the screen, down and to the right • **Show Windows Stacked** Opens all the windows with no overlap, with each window extending the full width of the screen and one window below another • **Show Windows Side by Side** Opens all the windows with no overlap, with each window extending the full height of the screen and one window next to another

TABLE 2-1   Controlling Windows

Action	Description
Change a window's size and shape	To change a window's height or width, click the border around the window and drag it to the place where you want it. If you click along a top, side, or bottom border, you move one window border. If you click the corner of the window border, you move the borders that intersect at that corner. When your mouse pointer is over a border, it changes to a double-pointed arrow, making it easy to tell when you can start dragging. If a window is minimized or maximized, you can't change its size or shape.
Close a window	Click the Close button (red X) to close a window. This is the same as choosing File|Close from the window's menu. If the program appears in only one window (the usual situation), closing the window exits from the program, the equivalent of choosing the File|Exit command.

TABLE 2-1   Controlling Windows *(continued)*

many other commands). Most programs provide several ways to issue commands, including choosing commands from menus and clicking icons on the toolbar.

Choosing Commands from the Menu Bar

The *menu bar* is a row of one-word commands that appears along the top of a window, just below the title bar. To choose a command from the menu bar or to choose a command from any drop-down menu, click it. For example, to choose the File | Open command, click the word "File" on the menu bar and click the word "Open" on the File drop-down menu.

When you choose a command on the menu bar, a *drop-down menu* usually appears. Each drop-down menu is named after the command that displays it. For example, most programs include a File command as the first command on the toolbar. Choosing the File command displays the File drop-down menu, shown here, with a list of commands that have something to do with files, such as opening, closing, or saving files.

When a drop-down menu is displayed, you can see a different drop-down menu by clicking a different command on the menu bar. To cancel a drop-down menu (that is, to remove it from the screen), click somewhere outside the menu.

If your screen doesn't have room for the entire drop-down menu to appear, you see a downward-pointing triangle at the bottom of the submenu; click the arrow to see the rest of the menu. Many programs use a Windows feature that displays only the most frequently used commands or the commands you've chosen recently. At the bottom of the menu is a double-*V* character (a double downward-pointing arrow) that you can click to see the rest of the available commands.

TIP   *When displaying a menu, many programs display more information about each command as you point to the commands with your mouse. The additional information usually appears in the status bar, the gray bar along the bottom edge of the window.*

Symbols on Menus

Other information may appear next to commands on menus:

- Commands that have a rightward-pointing triangle to their right display another menu.

- Commands that have an ellipsis (three dots) after them display a dialog box.

- Some commands represent an option that can be turned on or off. A command of this type has a check mark to its left when the option is on (selected) and no check mark when the option is off (not selected). For example, a View menu might have a Status Bar command that is checked or unchecked, controlling whether the status bar is displayed. To turn an option on or off, choose the command; the check mark appears or disappears.

- Some menus contain several options, only one of which may be selected. A large dot appears to the left of the selected option. To select an option, choose the command; the dot appears to its left.

- For some commands, a button on the toolbar performs the command. On the drop-down menu that contains the command, the toolbar button appears to its left, just as a reminder.

- Some commands have a keyboard shortcut. For example, many programs provide the key combination CTRL-S as a shortcut for choosing File|Save. Keyboard shortcuts appear to the right of commands on drop-down menus.

Commands on a menu may appear in gray, indicating that the command is not currently available.

Choosing Menu Commands with the Keyboard

In most programs, one letter of each command in each menu is underlined. Previous versions of Windows displayed these underlines all the time, but with some programs, Windows Vista displays them only if you press the ALT key. For example, most programs underline the *F* in File on the menu bar. To choose a command from the menu bar by using the keyboard, hold down the ALT key while you type the underlined letter of the command you want. Or, press and release the ALT key. The first command on the menu bar is selected and appears enclosed in a box. Press the underlined letter of the command you want. To choose a command from a drop-down menu, press the underlined letter for that command. For example, to choose the File|Open command, press ALT-F, and then o.

TIP *You can mix using the mouse and the keyboard to choose commands. For example, you can use the mouse to click a command on the menu bar, and then press a letter to choose a command from the drop-down menu that appears.*

To cancel all the drop-down menus that appear on the screen, press the ALT key again. To back up one step, press the ESC or LEFT-ARROW key.

Clicking Buttons on the Toolbar

Most (but not all) Windows programs display a *toolbar*, a row of small buttons with icons on them, just below the menu bar; for example:

Clicking a toolbar button issues a command, usually a command that you also could have issued from the menu bar.

To find out what a toolbar button does, rest the mouse pointer on the button, but don't click. After a second, a small label appears near the button, naming or explaining the button (this label is sometimes called a *tool tip*). Some programs display toolbar buttons that contain text along with icons, for people who like words with their pictures.

Some programs let you move the toolbar to other locations, including into a separate floating window. Try clicking a blank part of the toolbar and dragging it to another location in the program window. And some programs that come with Windows Vista enable you to lock the toolbar, to prevent anyone from changing or moving it. Right-click a blank place in the toolbar to see if a command like Lock The Toolbars appears.

Choosing Commands from Shortcut Menus

Windows and most Windows-compatible programs display special menus, called *shortcut menus* (or *context menus*), when you click with the right mouse button. The shortcut menu displays commands appropriate to the object you clicked. For example, if you right-click a blank space on the Windows taskbar, the shortcut menu that appears contains commands you can perform on the taskbar or desktop, as shown here.

Commands on shortcut menus contain the same symbols (ellipses, triangles, and toolbar buttons) that appear on drop-down menus (see "Choosing Commands from the Menu Bar" earlier in the chapter). Commands that appear in gray are currently unavailable.

After you have displayed a shortcut menu, you can choose a command from the menu by clicking the command (with the left mouse button) or pressing the underlined letter in the command. If no letters are underlined in the commands on the menu, pressing a letter usually selects the first command that starts with that letter. To cancel a shortcut menu, click outside the menu or press the ESC key.

TIP *You can't always guess where shortcut menus will appear or what will be on them. To use shortcut menus, right-click the item you want to work with and see what appears!*

You can display a shortcut menu by using only the keyboard; select the item you want to right-click and press SHIFT-F10 to display the shortcut menu. Newer keyboards include an "application key" that has a small picture of a menu on it.

The application key has the same effect as right-clicking at the mouse pointer location. Use the UP-ARROW and DOWN-ARROW keys to select the command you want, and then press ENTER to select it, or press ESC to dismiss the menu.

Choosing Settings on Dialog Boxes

A *dialog box* is a special kind of window that enables you to change settings or give commands in a program. For example, in most programs, when you give a command to open a file, you see an Open File dialog box that enables you to specify which file you want to open. You must exit the dialog box before continuing to use the program. Most dialog boxes include buttons to exit, with names like OK, Close, and Cancel.

As programs have gotten more complicated, with more and more settings, dialog boxes (like the one shown in Figure 2-4) have also gotten fancier. They may also include a menu bar, a toolbar, tabs (like the ones on manila folders), graphics, and buttons that display other dialog boxes.

When a dialog box is displayed, choose the settings you want. When you have finished, click the OK or Close button to dismiss the dialog box. You can also click the Close button in the upper-right corner of the window. If you don't want to keep the changes you have made, click the Cancel button or press the ESC key. While a program is displaying a dialog box, the program usually won't accept any other input until you've closed the dialog box.

***

TIP *If a window has a question-mark button in its upper-right corner, click it and then click the setting about which you want help. If the window doesn't have a question-mark button, click the Help button, if there is one, or press F1. Another way to obtain help is to right-click the setting you need information about and choose the What's This? command from the shortcut menu, if it appears.*

***

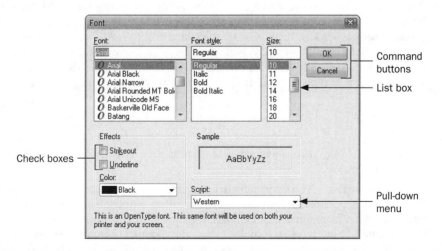

FIGURE 2-4   Dialog boxes may contain many types of settings.

Settings in Dialog Boxes

Dialog boxes contain various types of settings, and different software companies use different types of settings. The following are the most common types of settings in dialog boxes:

- **Text box**   A box you can type in. To change the text in a text box, click in the box and edit the text. To replace the text with new text, select the entire contents of the box and type the new text. Some text boxes accept only numbers and have tiny up- and down-arrow buttons that you can click to increase or decrease the number in the box.

- **List box**   A box that contains a list of options, one of which is selected. If the list is too long to fit in the box, a scroll bar appears along the right side of the box. To select an option from the list, click it. When a list box is selected, you can use the UP-ARROW or DOWN-ARROW keys to select an option. In many list boxes, typing a letter jumps down to the first item on the list that begins with that letter—a useful maneuver for long lists. Some list boxes include a text box just above them so you can type an entry in the text box or click an entry from the list box—your choice.

- **Check box**   A box that can either be blank or contain a check mark (or *X*). If the check box is blank, the setting is not selected. To select or deselect a check box, click it. When a check box is selected, you can press SPACEBAR to select or deselect it.

- **Radio button**   A round button that can either be blank or contain a dot. If the button contains a dot, it is selected. Only one of the radio buttons in a group or related radio buttons can be selected at a time. To select one button in a group of radio buttons, click it. When a button in a group of radio buttons is selected, you can press cursor-motion (ARROW) keys on the keyboard to select the button you want.

- **Pull-down menu**   A box with a downward-pointing triangle button at its right end (also called a drop-down menu). The box displays the currently selected setting. To choose a setting, click in the box or on the triangle button to display a menu and click an option from the menu. When you select a pull-down menu, pressing the DOWN-ARROW key usually displays the menu of options; if it does display the menu, press DOWN-ARROW repeatedly until the option you want is highlighted and press ENTER.

- **Menu bar**   A row of commands, such as the menu bar at the top of a program window.

- **Toolbar**   A row of buttons that give commands, similar to the toolbar at the top of a program window.

- **Command button**   A box you can click to perform a command. Most dialog boxes include an OK or Close button and a Cancel button. If the label on the command button ends with an ellipsis (three dots), the button displays another dialog box. One command button on each dialog box is the default command button and has a darker border. Pressing ENTER has the same effect as clicking this button. When a command button is selected, you can press SPACEBAR to perform its command.

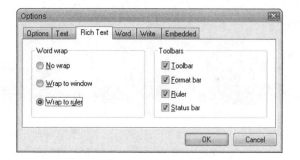

FIGURE 2-5   A dialog box with tabs is like a dialog box with multiple pages.

Except for command buttons, most settings have labels (explanatory text) to the left or right (or occasionally above) the setting.

Some dialog boxes have too many settings to fit in the window, so they contain several pages, or *tabs*, of settings. Figure 2-5 shows a dialog box with tabs running along the top of the dialog box. When you click a tab, the rest of the dialog box changes to show the settings associated with that tab.

Moving Around Within a Dialog Box

One setting in the dialog box is selected, which means it's currently active. The selected setting is affected if you press a key on the keyboard. The selected setting is highlighted or outlined, depending on the type of setting.

Here are ways to select a setting in a dialog box:

- Click the setting you want to select.

- Press the TAB key to select another setting, usually below or to the right of the current setting. Press SHIFT-TAB to select the previous setting.

- If the setting you want to select has an underlined letter in its label, hold down the ALT key while you type that letter. For example, to select a setting labeled Save In, press ALT-I.

- If the dialog box has tabs along the top, you can see the settings associated with another tab by clicking that tab or pressing CTRL-TAB or CTRL-SHIFT-TAB. To select a tab along the top of the dialog box, click the tab or press the ALT key and type the underlined letter in the label on the tab. Once you select a tab, you can use the LEFT-ARROW and RIGHT-ARROW keys to display the settings for each tab. The UP-ARROW and DOWN-ARROW keys move from setting to setting, too—though their action varies from dialog box to dialog box.

Open, Save As, and Browse Dialog Boxes

The Open, Save As, and Browse dialog boxes in most programs have some special settings. All three dialog boxes provide you with a way of specifying a disk drive, a folder, and a file to work with. Windows Vista introduces new standard versions of these dialog boxes, such as the one shown in Figure 2-6.

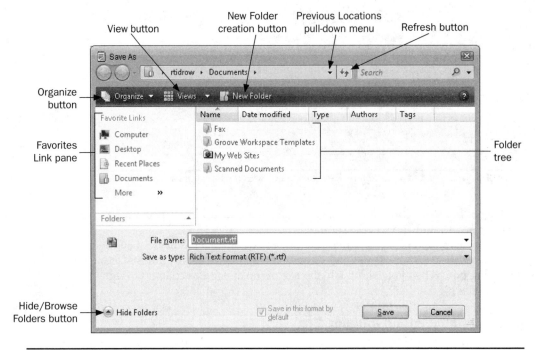

View button | New Folder creation button | Previous Locations pull-down menu | Refresh button

Organize button

Favorites Link pane

Folder tree

Hide/Browse Folders button

Figure 2-6   The WordPad Save As dialog box

Most Open, Save As, and Browse dialog boxes have the following items:

- **Favorites Link pane**   Vertical pane down the left side of the dialog box with icons that usually include Documents (for files you've used recently, regardless of their location), Computer (for a list of your computer drives), Desktop (for the top-level view of the items in your computer), Recent Places (for a list of recently saved to places), and More (for a list of additional folders in which to save files). Click one of these buttons to change the view in the folder tree to the right.

- **Previous Locations pull-down menu**   The Save, Open, and Browse dialog boxes contain a Previous Locations pull-down menu that enables you to specify a recently used folder that contains the file you want to open or the folder to which you want to save a folder.

- **Folder tree**   This large list box displays the current contents of the folder you have selected (see "What Is the Folder Tree?" in Chapter 8). Press F5 to update the display if you think that the folder contents have changed.

- **Organize**   Clicking this button lets you view options for managing the contents of the selected folder.

- **Views**   Clicking this button displays a list of the views you can choose: Large Icons, Small Icons, List, Details, and Thumbnails.

- **New Folder**   Clicking this button creates a new folder within the current folder (see "Creating Files and Folders" in Chapter 8).
- **Files Of Type box**   Clicking in this box displays the types of files currently displayed in the folder tree. For example, in Microsoft Word, the Files Of Type box is usually set to display only Word documents, but you can choose to see all filenames.

Switching, Exiting, and Canceling Programs

Windows enables you to run many programs at the same time, each in its own window. You can exit from one program while leaving other programs running, and you can choose which program window is the active window—the window you are currently using.

Switching Programs

To *switch programs*—choose another window as the active window—you can

- Click in the window for the program.
- Click the button for the window on the taskbar. If the window was minimized, clicking its button returns the window to its size before it was minimized.
- Press ALT-TAB until the window you want is active, or press ALT-SHIFT-TAB to cycle through the open windows in the reverse order.
- Press ALT-TAB and don't release the ALT key. A window appears with an icon for each program that is running, with the program in the active windows highlighted, as shown here:

The name of the highlighted window appears at the bottom of the window. To switch to a different program, keep holding down the ALT key, press TAB to move the highlight to the icon for the window you want, and then release the ALT key.

NOTE   *Perhaps the least convenient way to switch to a program is by using the Switch To button on Windows Task Manager. Press CTRL-ALT-DELETE to display Windows Task Manager, select the program you want, and click Switch To.*

Windows Flip and Windows Flip 3D

Windows Vista has two new features for switching between open windows. These are called Windows Flip and Flip 3D. With Windows Flip, you can switch through open windows by using ALT-TAB, but Windows displays a thumbnail picture of the open window instead of a generic-looking icon. The thumbnail picture gives you a better idea of the windows' contents so you can quickly switch to the one you want.

Windows Flip 3D lets you switch between open windows using the mouse scroll wheel. The open windows display as a 3D stack of windows that you can scroll through to get to the one you want to view.

NOTE   *To use the Windows Flip and Flip 3D features, your computer's graphic's card must support the Windows Display Driver Model (WDDM) graphics standard. You can learn more about WDDM at www.microsoft.com/whdc/device/display/graphics-reqs.mspx.*

Turning On Windows Flip

If your graphics card supports the new Windows Aero feature (an advanced graphics technology available in Windows Vista), you will be able to switch between open windows using the Windows Flip feature. Windows Flip allows you to see a small thumbnail view of your open windows as you press the ALT-TAB keyboard combination to switch between windows.

To see how this works, open two or more windows, preferably each from a different application (just to let you see how different windows look with Windows Flip). Next, press and hold down the ALT key, and then press the TAB key once (keep the ALT key held down). The Windows Flip window appears, like the one shown in Figure 2-7. Of course, the appearance of your window will be different from the one shown here, depending on which windows you have open. To move the highlighter to another window, press TAB. Continue pressing TAB until the highlighter rests on top of the window you want to make active. Release both the ALT and TAB keys to display that window.

Turning On Windows Flip 3D

Another feature of Windows Vista Aero is the Windows Flip 3D feature. It does the same thing as the Windows Flip feature (ALT-TAB) in that it allows you to switch to another open window. The difference between Windows Flip and Windows Flip 3D is that the latter shows a much larger image of the open windows and displays the windows in a three-dimensional, angled stack, as shown in Figure 2-8.

FIGURE 2-7   Press ALT-TAB to use Windows Flip.

Figure 2-8   Use Windows Flip 3D to scroll through a stack of open Windows.

To use this feature, do one of the following:

- Press and hold down the WINDOWS key on your keyboard and press TAB repeatedly to flip through each of the open windows. When you see the window you want, release both keys. You also can use the scroll button on your mouse after you display the Windows Flip 3D stack.

- Press CTRL-WINDOWS-TAB to keep the stack open. Roll the scroll button on your mouse to flip through the windows. Click a window in the stack to display it as the active window. Or, press ENTER to display the front window.

- Click the Switch Between Windows button on the Quick Launch toolbar on the taskbar. This displays the Windows Flip 3D stack. Roll the scroll button on your mouse to flip through the windows. Click a window in the stack to display it as the active window. Or, press ENTER to display the front window.

NOTE   *If you do not have the Quick Launch toolbar open, right-click the taskbar and choose Toolbars | Quick Launch.*

Exiting Programs

Most programs provide several ways to exit, including some or all of these:

- Choose File | Exit from the menu bar.
- Click the Close button in the upper-right corner of the program window. If a program displays multiple windows, close them all.
- Press ALT-F4.
- Click the System Menu button in the upper-left corner of the program window and choose Close from the menu that appears.
- Right-click the program button on the taskbar and choose Close from the menu that appears.

If you have trouble exiting a program, you can use Windows Task Manager, described in the next section.

Canceling Programs

When you are running several programs at the same time, you can exit a program as described in the previous section. For example, click the Close button for all the windows the program displays or choose File | Exit or File | Close.

Another way to exit a program when multiple programs are running is to press CTRL-ALT-DELETE and click Start Task Manager to display Windows Task Manager (shown in Figure 2-9, and described in more detail in Chapter 36). The Applications tab lists all the programs currently running.

FIGURE 2-9   Windows Task Manager

To cancel a program, click the program name in Windows Task Manager and then click the End Task button. If you were using the program to edit a file, you may lose some work.

> **NOTE** *The End Task button is designed for canceling programs that have "hung"—stopped responding to the keyboard or mouse. To avoid losing unsaved work, always try exiting a program by clicking its Close button, pressing ALT-F4, or choosing File | Exit before resorting to Windows Task Manager.*

Running Programs in Compatibility Mode

Some older programs, especially games, do not run correctly under Windows Vista, XP, or 2003. Windows XP introduced a new feature called *compatibility mode* that emulates previous versions of Windows—Windows 2000, NT 4.0, Me, 98, and 95. Windows Vista includes the Program Compatibility Wizard to simulate earlier Windows environments.

Compatibility mode can also set the display to the lower resolutions that were standard several years ago. If you have a program that used to run well but balks at Windows Vista, compatibility mode may fix the problem.

> **CAUTION** *You should not use compatibility mode with programs that are designed specifically for earlier versions of Windows. For example, a virus checker that is designed for use with Windows 95 should not be run with Windows Vista.*

Start the Program Compatibility Wizard by choosing Start | All Programs | Accessories | Program Compatibility Wizard. The wizard guides you through selecting and picking

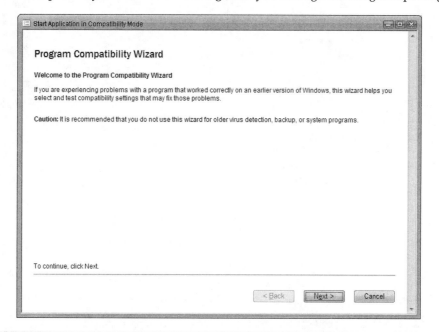

FIGURE 2-10 Use the Program Compatibility Wizard to help run older Windows programs.

settings for the program you want to run. Click Next and then select how you want the program set up. Figure 2-10 shows the first screen of the Program Compatibility Wizard. Click Next between the wizard pages to complete the Program Compatibility Wizard.

After you select the program to run, select the operating system recommended for this program. The Program Compatibility Wizard provides the following operating system modes:

- Windows 95
- Windows NT 4.0 with Service Pack 5
- Windows 98
- Windows Me
- Windows 2000
- Windows XP with Service Pack 2

The next Program Compatibility Wizard screen lets you select display settings for the program, including the number of colors, screen resolution, visual themes, and so forth. Figure 2-11 shows this screen.

You are then asked if the program requires administrator privileges. If so, select Run This Program As An Administrator and be prepared to enter an administrator password to run the program. To finish, click Next to test how well the program runs in compatibility mode.

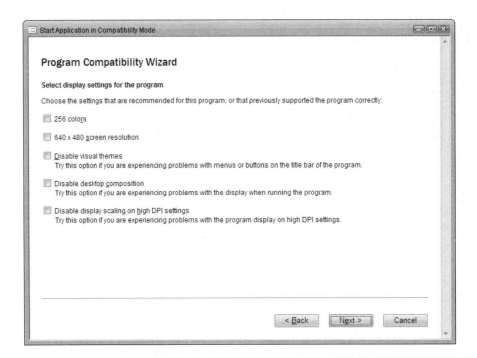

FIGURE 2-11 Select display settings for the program you want to run in compatibility mode.

Installing Programs

Windows Vista comes with a number of useful programs, and many new computers come with lots more software preinstalled, but you'll want to install some programs yourself sooner or later. For example, you might want to install some of the programs included on the Windows Vista CD-ROM that may not have been installed on your system.

Or, you may want to do just the reverse—uninstall programs that you no longer use or that are outdated. You can free up some disk space by uninstalling Windows components that you never use. Windows comes with a built-in system for installing and uninstalling programs.

When you install a program, Windows keeps track of what types of files the program can create and edit. You can change which program Windows uses to open each file type.

What Happens During Program Installation and Uninstallation?

Before you can install a program, you have to get it—you have to buy or download the program. You may receive a program on a CD-ROM, as a stack of floppy disks or as a file downloaded from the Internet. Once you have a program, you install it, usually by running an installation program to copy the program to your hard disk and configure it to run on your system.

If you download a program, it usually arrives in the form of an *installation file* (also called a *distribution file*), which is a compressed file containing all the files required for a program to run, along with an installation program. For example, the installation file may contain the installation program, the program itself, the help file for the program, and a few other files that the program needs. You can download (copy) installation files from the Internet or other sources. If your computer is connected to a local area network (LAN), the installation file may be stored on a network disk (see Chapter 31). The files that make up the program are usually compressed to take up less space and so that they can be packaged together as one file.

NOTE *When installing programs, you must be logged on with a user account that is a member of the Administrator group (see Chapter 6). Standard and Guest user accounts can't install programs. If you haven't set up user accounts, you are probably logged on automatically as Administrator.*

What Happens During Program Installation?

Most programs come with an installation program named Setup.exe or Install.exe. When you install a program, the installation program usually does the following:

- Looks for a previous version of the program on your hard disk. If it finds a previous version, the program may ask whether you want to replace the previous version.

- Creates a folder in which to store the program files. Most installation programs ask where you'd like this folder. Some installation programs also create additional folders within this folder. Windows creates a folder named Program Files, usually in C: (if Windows is stored in a partition or drive other than C:, the Program Files folder is usually in the same partition). We recommend that you install all your programs in folders within the Program Files folder.

NOTE *Some software vendors have the bad habit of installing application programs in locations other than your Program Files folder. You can't do much about this; the additional folders may clutter up your root folder, but they don't do any harm.*

- Copies the files onto your hard disk. If the program files are compressed, the installation program uncompresses them. Usually, the installation program copies most of the files into the program's folder, but it may also put some files into your C:\Windows, C:\Windows\System, or other folders.

- Checks your system for the files and hardware it needs to run. For example, an Internet connection program might check for a modem.

- Adds entries to the Windows Registry to tell Windows which types of files the program works with, which files the program is stored in, and other information about the program (see Chapter 40).

- Adds a command for the program to your Start | All Programs menu (some programs add submenus to the Start | All Programs menu to contain several commands). The installation program may also add a shortcut to your Windows desktop to make running the program easy for you, or to a taskbar toolbar. You can change the position on the Start menu of the command for the program, get rid of the command, or create a command if the installation program doesn't make one. You can also create a shortcut icon on the desktop, if the installation program hasn't done so, or move or delete the program's shortcut (see "Making Shortcuts" in Chapter 9).

- Asks you a series of questions to configure the program for your system. The program may ask you to type additional information, like Internet addresses, passwords, or software license numbers. It may also ask which users should be able to run the program.

Every installation program is different, because it comes with the application program, not with Windows. If your computer is connected to a LAN or to the Internet, the installation program may configure your program to connect to other computers on the network.

What Happens During Program Uninstallation?

The perfect uninstallation program exactly undoes all the actions of the installation program, removing all the files and folders the installation program created, and putting back everything else to where it was originally. Unfortunately, we've never seen a perfect uninstallation program, but most uninstallation programs do an acceptable job of removing most traces of a program from your system.

Installing Programs

Windows Vista includes a Control Panel applet called Programs that helps you find, modify, and remove programs installed on your computer. Unlike previous versions of Windows, Vista does not have the Add Or Remove Programs applet that you can use to install programs. Instead Vista relies on individual programs to provide their own automatic setup routine when you insert the program's CD-ROM or DVD disc.

If you are installing a program from a CD or DVD disc, insert the disc into its drive. The program's installation routine automatically launches and guides you through installing the program. If you are installing a program from a file on your hard disk or on a network drive, locate the file called Setup.exe or Install.exe and double-click it. The installation program runs. Follow the instructions on the screen to install the program.

Once you install a program, the program name usually appears in the Installed Programs window. This window is available by opening the Control Panel, selecting Programs, and then clicking the Installed Programs link. Figure 3-1 shows the Installed Programs window.

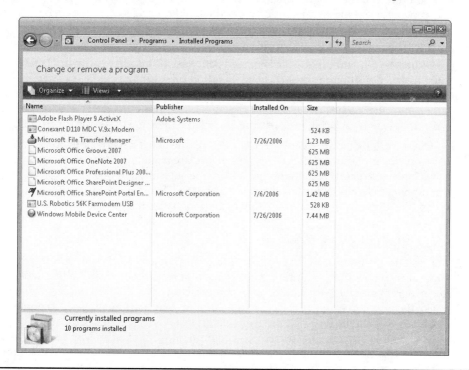

FIGURE 3-1 The Installed Programs window

Running an Install or Setup Program

If you know the pathname of the installation file for the program you want to install, you can run the installation program directly (see "Starting Programs" in Chapter 2)—double-click its filename in Windows Explorer or use the Start | All Programs | Accessories | Run command. Follow the instructions on the screen to install the program.

Installing Programs Without Installation Programs

Older programs, such as those designed to run with Windows 3.1 or DOS, don't have installation programs. Instead, the programs are delivered as a set of files. Some older programs arrive as a *ZIP* file, a file that contains compressed versions of one or more files (see "Working with Compressed Folders" in Chapter 9). ZIP files have the extension .zip (if you can't see filename extensions in Windows, see "What Are Extensions and File Types?" in Chapter 8 to display them).

To install a program from a ZIP file, you can use the Windows compressed folders feature, which treats ZIP files like folders (see "Working with Compressed Folders" in Chapter 9). Alternatively, you can install an unzipping program such as WinZip (www.winzip.com), which comes with its own commands for unzipping (uncompressing) and installing programs from ZIP files.

To install a program that you receive as a set of files or as a ZIP file, using the Windows compressed files feature, follow these steps:

1. If you received the program as a ZIP file, open the ZIP file. In an Explorer window, it appears as a folder with a little zipper on it. Otherwise, look at the set of files in an Explorer window.

2. Look at the list of files to find files with the .exe or .com extension; these are executable programs. If one file is named Setup.exe or Install.exe, run it. Then follow the instructions on the screen. The installation program may ask you a series of questions to configure the program for your system. If one file is named Readme.txt (or some other name that suggests it contains instructions), read the contents of the file. If its extension is .txt, click or double-click the filename to see the file in Notepad.

3. Otherwise, look for an executable file with a name like the name of the program; this may be the program itself. For example, if you are installing a program called Spam Be Gone version 4.3, you might find a filename such as Spambg43.exe. To run the program, click or double-click the program name. The first time you run the program, it may ask you for information with which to configure the program for your system.

Finishing Installation of a Program

After you install a program, you may still need to configure it to work with your system. Many programs come with configuration programs that run automatically, either when you install the program or when you run the program for the first time.

To make the program easier to run, you can add it to your Start menu (see "Reorganizing the Start Menu" in Chapter 11). If the program has an installation program, the installation program may do this for you. The installation program may even put an icon on the Quick Launch toolbar (the small icons on the taskbar you can click to run a program). If not, you can add an icon yourself (see Chapter 11).

You can also add a shortcut for the program to your Windows desktop (see "Making Shortcuts" in Chapter 9). The installation program may have created a shortcut already. You can create shortcuts right on the desktop or in a folder.

Finally, you can add a shortcut to a taskbar toolbar by dragging and copying a shortcut to the toolbar.

Installing and Uninstalling Programs that Come with Windows

Windows Vista comes with several preinstalled components. For example, Windows includes Windows Calendar, Windows Contacts, Windows Defender, and Windows Mail. Other features can be installed after you set up Windows for the first time.

If you want to install some of the programs that come on the Windows Vista CD-ROM, follow these steps:

1. Choose Start | Control Panel. You see the Control Panel window.

2. Run Programs. You see the Programs window.

3. Click Turn Windows features on or off. You see the Windows Features window, as shown in Figure 3-2. The check box to the left of each type of program is blank (meaning none of the programs of that type are selected), gray with a check mark (meaning some, but not all, of the programs of that type are selected), or white with a check mark (meaning all the programs of that type are selected). The selections show which Windows programs have already been installed.

4. To install additional programs, click the check mark next to each of the types of programs that you want to install (scroll down the list to see the rest of the program types). Most of the items on the list include a number of programs.

5. To select all the programs of that type, click plus next to each subfolder to expand the list. Then click each check box next to the programs you want to install.

FIGURE 3-2   You can install additional programs from the Windows Vista CD-ROM.

6. You can uninstall previously installed programs at the same time you install new programs. To uninstall a program, deselect it; that is, clear the check in its check box by clicking the box. Don't clear a program's check box unless you want to uninstall it.

7. After you select all the programs you want installed and deselect all the programs you don't want installed, click OK to install and uninstall the programs. Windows determines which programs you are installing and which you are uninstalling, and copies or deletes program files appropriately. The wizard may ask you to insert the Windows Vista disc.

8. Depending on which programs you install, you may need to restart Windows when the installation is complete, and you may be directed to run wizards or other configuration programs to set up the new programs.

Using Windows Easy Transfer

Windows Vista provides an updated tool for transferring files from one computer to another, called Windows Easy Transfer. Although Windows Easy Transfer was available for computers running Windows XP, users had to download it from the Microsoft web site. Now Easy Transfer is part of Windows Vista.

What Is Windows Easy Transfer?

Windows Easy Transfer enables you to transfer the following items from one computer to another:

- User accounts
- Folders
- Files
- Program settings
- Internet settings
- Internet favorites (bookmarks)
- E-mail settings
- E-mail contacts
- E-mail messages

Because of licensing restrictions, actual programs are not transferred from one computer to another. If this were possible, users would be able install a program on one computer and then share it with any other computer, regardless of the number of end-user licenses purchased. Windows Easy Transfer does, however, enable you to transfer program settings (such as custom configurations you have set up for a program) from one computer to another.

Transferring Files and Settings to a New Computer

To transfer files and settings from one computer to another, you need some way of transferring the files. Easy Transfer provides the following ways:

- Removable media, such as a flash drive or ZIP disk
- CD-ROM or DVD

- Network share
- USB PC-to-PC cable

The Easy Transfer program is a two-part process. First you run Easy Transfer (which is a wizard that guides you through the process) to save files from your old computer. Then, you run Easy Transfer on your new computer to transfer the files from the old computer to the new one.

Before running Easy Transfer, there are some easy maintenance tasks you may want to perform on your old computer. For example, you may want to run the Disk Cleanup utility to remove temporary files and Internet Explorer cached files. This reduces the number of unneeded files to be transferred, especially if you decide to transfer Internet Explorer settings.

To run Easy Transfer, follow these steps:

1. Close all open programs.
2. Choose Start | All Programs | Accessories | System Tools | Window Easy Transfer to open the Windows Easy Transfer window, shown in Figure 3-3.

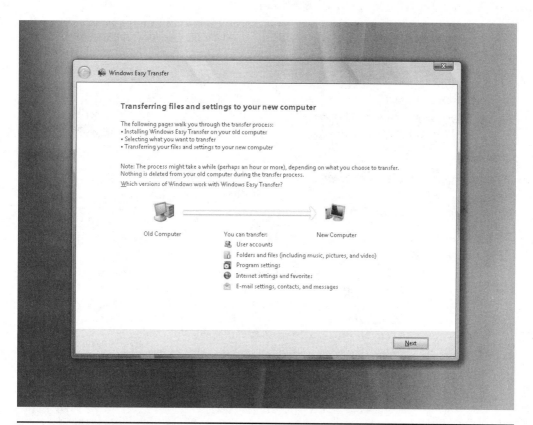

FIGURE 3-3   The Windows Easy Transfer program helps you transfer files from one computer to another.

3. Click Next and select the option that suits your situation. For example, if you are using Easy Transfer for the first time, you are probably using your old computer now so as to transfer files from that computer to your new one. If so, select This Is My Old Computer.

4. Work through the next few wizard screens to select the transfer method and files to transfer.

5. After you finish saving the files to transfer, run Easy Transfer on your new computer and select the This Is My New Computer option when prompted. You then select the location where your transfer files are stored and finish the transfer process.

NOTE *Resist the temptation to transfer all your files from your old computer to the new one. By transferring all your files over, you may cause some device driver or DLL problems if Windows Vista confuses your old files for new, updated files. Instead, focus on transferring files that you know you will need to get your work done or need for family situations. For example, consider transferring all your music and picture files over to the new computer.*

Associating a Program with a File Extension

Many programs create, edit, or display files of a specific type. For example, the Notepad program (a text editor that comes with Windows) works with text files that usually have the filename extension .txt. When you open a file with the extension .txt, Windows knows to run Notepad.

The Windows Registry stores *file associations*, information about which program you use to edit each type of file. Installation programs usually store this information in the Registry, but you can change the default file associations in the Registry. Chapter 40 describes how to view and edit the Registry with the Registry Editor program, but you can use other tools to change your file associations.

Associating Files with Programs when Opening a File

In an Explorer window, you can tell Windows which program to use when opening files with a particular extension. Follow these steps:

1. In an Explorer window, find a file with the extension that you want to associate with a program.

2. Right-click the filename and choose Open With from the menu that appears. (If Open With doesn't appear on the menu, you have to use another method of associating the file type with the program; see the next section.) You see the Open With dialog box shown in Figure 3-4. (If a small submenu of programs appears, select Choose Default Program to display the Open With dialog box.)

3. Select the program to run, or click Browse to find the program file.

4. Click the Always Use The Selected Program To Open This Kind Of File check box and click OK.

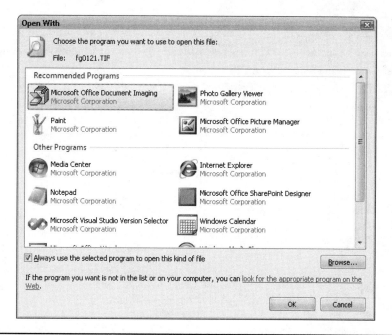

FIGURE 3-4   Which program do you want to run to open this file (and files like it)?

Windows Explorer permanently saves the association of the filename extension with the program, and it opens the file you selected with the program you specified.

Associating Files with Programs by Using the Default Programs Option

Another way to associate a file type (file extension) with a program (or change which program is associated with a file type) is to use the Default Programs feature in Windows Vista. This feature enables you to view the program that runs a file type. It also lets you change the default program that is associated with a file type.

To create or edit a file association, follow these steps:

1. Choose Start | Default Programs | Associate A File Type Or Protocol With A Program. The Set Associations window appears, shown in Figure 3-5.

2. Click a file type.

3. Click the Change Program button. The Open With window opens.

4. Select the program to run, or click Browse to find the program file.

5. Click OK.

Windows Explorer permanently saves the association of the filename extension with the program, and it opens the file you selected with the program you specified.

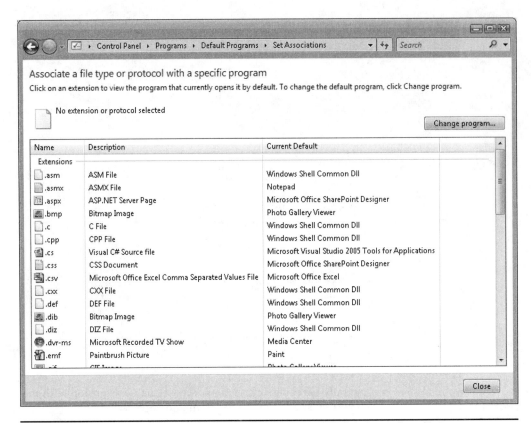

FIGURE 3-5 The Set Associations window lets you change the default program for a file type.

Uninstalling Programs

If you have a program on your computer that you don't use, you can uninstall it to free up space on your hard disk (unless it's one of the many components of Windows that cannot be uninstalled). You can also uninstall older versions of programs before installing new versions. The best way to uninstall a program is by using the Installed Programs window. If the program doesn't appear on the Windows list of installed programs, run the program's uninstall program; if the program doesn't have one, you'll have to delete files manually.

Uninstalling Programs Using the Programs Window

When you want to uninstall a program, first try using the Installed Programs window. Follow these steps:

1. Choose Start | Control Panel and click Programs. You see the Programs window.
2. Click the Uninstall A Program link. You see the Installed Programs windows, as shown in Figure 3-6.

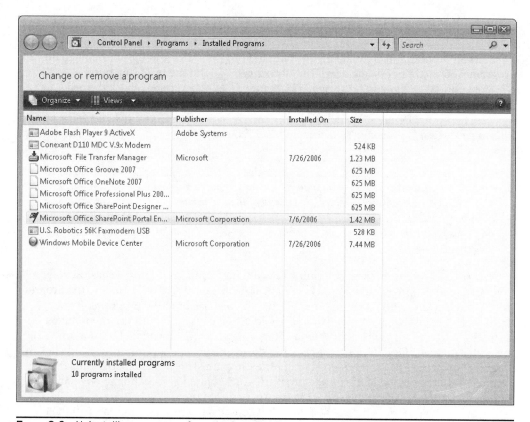

FIGURE 3-6   Uninstalling a program from the Installed Programs window

3. In the list of installed programs, click the program you want to uninstall. Windows tells you how much disk space the program occupies, the publisher of the software, and when you installed the program.

4. Click the Remove button. Windows uninstalls the program, during which it displays messages to let you know what's happening.

If the program doesn't appear in the Installed Programs window, you have to uninstall the program another way, as described next.

NOTE   *Sometimes Windows can't uninstall a program, usually because it can't find the files it needs to perform the uninstallation.*

Running an Uninstall Program

Many programs come with uninstall programs, usually named Uninstall.exe. Look for an uninstall program in the same folder where the program is stored. Run the uninstall program, and then follow the directions on the screen. The uninstall program may also be on the Start | All Programs menu on the same submenu as the program.

Uninstalling Programs Manually

What if a program doesn't appear in the Installed Programs window and doesn't come with an uninstall program? You can delete by hand the program files and the shortcuts to the program. You might not delete every last file connected with the program, but the remaining files usually won't do any harm. Before deleting anything, check the program's documentation for instructions. Be sure to back up your hard disk or create a System Restore checkpoint before uninstalling a program by hand, in case you delete a file your system needs (see "Returning Your System to a Predefined State with System Restore" in Chapter 37).

TIP *Before you delete a program, you might first want to rename the folder containing the program files, adding something like "deleted" to the end of the folder name. Then, wait a few days. If other programs are using those files, you'll see error messages when those programs run. If no programs report errors within a week, then you know it's safe to delete the folder containing the program files.*

To delete the program files, determine which folder contains them. The easiest way to find out where the program is stored is to look at the properties of a shortcut to the program (see "What Is a Shortcut?" in Chapter 9). Right-click a shortcut to the program on your desktop, on the taskbar, in a folder, or in the folder that contains your Start menu items (usually C:\Users\All Users\Start Menu\Programs). Choose Open File Location from the menu that appears. Or you can right-click the shortcut icon, choose Properties, and click the Shortcut tab on the Properties dialog box for the program. The Target box contains the full pathname of the executable file for the program. Click Open File Location to open an Explorer window for the folder that contains the program file.

To delete the program, delete the folder that contains the program files and all the files in it (see "Deleting Files and Folders" in Chapter 8). After uninstalling a program, you might see shortcuts to the program lying around on your desktop, in folders, on the taskbar, or in your Start menu. Delete these shortcuts by right-clicking the shortcut and choosing Delete from the menu that appears, or by dragging the shortcut into the Recycle Bin on the desktop.

TIP *If at all possible, use a program's uninstaller instead of just deleting all the files, because the uninstaller is safer and more comprehensive. Uninstallers remove files in C:\Windows, C:\Windows\System, C:\Windows\System32, and other locations in which the program might have installed them. Uninstallers also delete the Registry entries for the program (see Chapter 40).*

Getting Help

Windows has always come with *online help*—helpful information stored on your computer that you can look at using a Help command. Windows Vista comes with online help, too, but this help is "online" in two senses: the help system includes help files stored on your computer's hard disk, as well as a connection to online help information via the Internet. You look at the online help stored on your own computer by using the Help And Support tool. When you are using a program, you can use its "question mark" Help button to find out what the items on the screen mean.

Windows Vista includes Remote Assistance, which enables you to allow a friend or coworker to take control of your computer over the Internet or a LAN to fix software problems you may have. Microsoft also offers online newsgroups, discussion groups about all aspects of Windows.

> **NOTE** *The Help And Support tool contains information about Windows Vista and some of the programs and accessories that come with it. Other programs that come with Windows, and most third-party applications, have separate help systems. Most programs have two ways of displaying Help screens. Choose Help from the menu bar, or press the F1 key.*

What Is the Help And Support Center?

The Help And Support tool is a set of web pages about Windows and the programs and accessories that come with it. The pages are stored on your hard disk and are displayed by a special Internet Explorer window. Other programs you install may also come with their own online help.

Displaying Help Screens

To see the Help And Support tool window (shown in Figure 4-1), choose Start | Help And Support. The toolbar shows some commonly used tools, including Back, Forward, Home, and Print. You also see Browse Help, Ask someone or expand search, and Options.

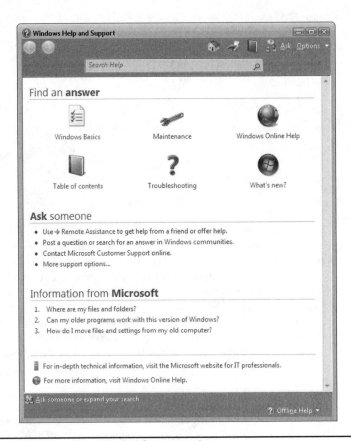

FIGURE 4-1 The home page of the Help And Support tool

When the Help And Support tool window first appears, you see that the main window has four main areas: Search Help, Find An Answer, Ask Someone, and Information From Microsoft (click Home on the toolbar to return to it).

The Find An Answer area includes the following links that provide links to additional areas of help:

- **Windows Basics**   Provides a list of topics that discuss fundamentals about Windows, running programs, the Internet, and other topics

- **Maintenance**   Provides a list of topics to help you maintain the health of your computer

- **Windows Line Help**   Links you to help located on the Internet

- **Table of Contents**   Links you to a complete list of help topics you can read

- **Troubleshooting**   Provides a list of topics to help you fix problems you may be having with your computer and Windows

- **What's New?**   Provides a list of topics showing you what's new in your version of Windows Vista

Another feature to notice on the Help And Support home page are the navigation buttons at the top-left corner. Use these buttons when you need to move forward and backward between help topics you have displayed.

Finding Topics

When you need to find a help topic, usually the quickest way is to use the Search Help field at the top of the Help And Support window. Type a word or phrase in the field and press ENTER. Windows displays a list of help topics that have the word or phrase you typed, as shown in Figure 4-2.

Scroll through the list of help topics for what you need. If the list of help items is over 30 items, Windows displays only the first 30 items. To see additional ones, scroll to the bottom of the screen and click the More Results For link.

When you find a topic of interest, click its link. Windows displays the help item in the Help And Support window. The help item will probably have additional help items you can click to read more about related topics.

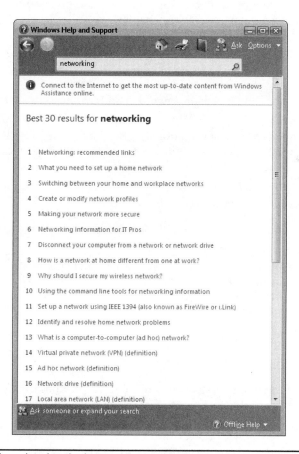

FIGURE 4-2   Help topics related to the keyword "networking"

Copying Help Information to Other Programs

You can use cut-and-paste to copy information from the Help And Support window to other programs (see "Cutting, Copying, and Pasting" in Chapter 5). Select the part of the text in the window that you want to copy. If you want to copy the entire help topic, right-click in the window and choose Select All from the menu that appears. Then right-click in the page and choose Copy from the menu that appears (or press CTRL-C). Windows copies the text to the Windows Clipboard. Now you can paste the text into a document by using the Edit | Paste command (or pressing CTRL-V) in the program you use to edit the document.

Getting Help from Microsoft or from a Friend

You can get helpful information over the Internet about Windows. Click the Help And Support Home button on the toolbar to return to the Help And Support tool home page. You will find the following items to help you get help from Microsoft or from a friend:

- **Ask Someone**   Using Remote Assistance, you can ask a knowledgeable friend to take control of your computer via an Internet connection (see "Allowing a Friend to Control Your Computer" later in the chapter).

- **Information From Microsoft**   If your PC is online, you can sign up for a Microsoft .NET Passport, which identifies you to Microsoft, and get information from the Microsoft web site. Once you sign in with your .NET Passport name and password, you can contact a Microsoft support technician for help, check on the status of problems you've submitted, or download and install software that enables Microsoft to upload files from your computer to resolve a software issue.

- **Microsoft Website For IT Professionals**   Read information written for information technology workers to gain an in-depth knowledge of how Windows Vista works and how to troubleshoot problems with Vista.

- **Windows Online Help**   Visit the Windows Vista Help And Support web site for additional help topics associated with Vista.

You must be connected to the Internet to use these Internet-based resources.

TIP *If you are asking for help from Microsoft, you may be asked for information about your computer system. You can right-click the Computer icon on your desktop and click Properties to see information about your computer, including processor name and speed, memory amount, and computer name.*

Other Help Options

Here are other things you can do in the Help And Support Center window:

- Click the Back button on the toolbar to move to the previous topic you displayed, or click the Forward button to return to the next topic you displayed before clicking Back.

- To print a help topic, click the Print button or right-click the help topic and choose Print from the menu that appears.

Finding Out What an Onscreen Object Is

Many dialog boxes in both Windows and application programs have a small question-mark button in the upper-right corner, next to the Close button. This Help button enables you to find out what an object is. Click this question-mark Help button and then click an item in the dialog box—an icon, button, label, or box. A small window appears with a description of the object you clicked. To dismiss the window, click anywhere in the dialog box.

Another way to display information about an item on the screen is to hover the mouse pointer over the item. A help box appears with a brief description of the item. Click anywhere onscreen to close the help box.

Allowing a Friend to Control Your Computer

Programs have been available for years that allow someone to control another computer over the phone or the Internet. Carbon Copy and pcAnywhere are popular programs because they allow support technicians to look at and fix a computer without having to visit the office where the computer sits. In another example of bundling programs with Windows, Windows Vista comes with Remote Desktop, which provides this same functionality (see "Accessing Other Computers with Remote Desktop Connection" in Chapter 16). Remote Assistance is a special version of Remote Desktop Connection that enables you to invite someone to control your PC to help you solve a software problem.

With Remote Assistance, you invite a specific person to take control of your computer. You can contact the person via an instant messenger program (such as MSN Messenger, available at http://get.live.com/messenger/overview) or by e-mail. If the person agrees, then the helper can control the mouse pointer and type as if he or she were at your computer. You can also chat by typing or talking (if you have microphones and speakers), and send files.

Inviting a Friend to Help

To invite someone to take control of your PC:

1. Open the Help And Support tool window by choosing Start | Help And Support.

2. Click Windows Remote Assistance in the Ask Someone section. You see the Windows Remote Assistance window, shown in Figure 4-3. Click Invite Someone You Trust To Help You in the window that appears.

3. If this is the first time you have used Remote Assistance, you may need to set up your computer to use Remote Assistance. Click the link called Click Here To Open System Properties. You see the System Properties dialog box with the Remote tab open. Click Remote Assistance Invitations Can Be Sent From This Computer. Also click the option User On This Computer Can Be Offered Remote Assistance From Instant Messaging Contacts. Click OK.

4. Click Invite Someone You Trust To Help You again.

5. Choose whether to contact your helper by using e-mail or saving the invitation as a file. Here we choose to use e-mail.

6. Type and retype a password that you can provide to a person you invite to your computer. Do not use your normal login password for this password.

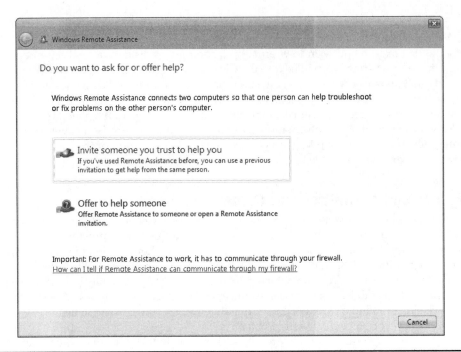

FIGURE 4-3 Send an invitation for someone to help you fix your Windows problem.

7. Click Next and identify the person in the To: field of the e-mail address line. A generic message is provided to ask for help. You can add your own personal comments at the bottom of the message. Click Send.

8. Wait for your helper to get the invitation and to respond. When your helper receives the invitation and types in the password in response to your invitation, respond that you want to proceed.

Once Windows makes the Remote Assistance connection, you can do the following:

- **Share control of your computer**   When the helper clicks Take Control, you see a dialog box asking whether you want to let the helper share control of your computer. Click Yes to do so. While the helper is using your computer, keep your hands off the mouse and keyboard—it's terribly confusing when two people try to control the mouse pointer or type at the same time! Press ESC (or any key combination with ESC) to end sharing control, or click Stop Control.

- **Send a file**   Click Send A File and specify the filename.

- **Voice chat**   Click Start Talking if you and your helper have speakers and microphones on your computers, to start a voice chat. Click Settings to set the audio quality. If the helper clicks Start Talking first, you see a message asking whether you'd like to start a voice chat.

Click Disconnect when you are done being helped, unless the helper disconnects first.

Responding to an Invitation for Remote Assistance

If you receive an invitation to help someone by using Remote Assistance, you get an e-mail or Windows Messenger message that says something like this:

```
Fred H would like your assistance. A personal message may be included
below. You can easily provide assistance from your computer by following
the instructions at:
http://windows.microsoft.com/RemoteAssistance/RA.asp
Caution:
* Accept invitations only from people you know and trust.
* E-mail messages can contain viruses or other harmful attachments.
* Before opening the attachment, review the security precautions and
information at the above address.
Personal message:
Help. I need assistance.
```

The message includes an attached file named rcBuddy.MsRcIncident. (The first part of the filename may be different.) Click the link in the message to read a web page about how Remote Assistance works. (This web page works only in Internet Explorer.)

Follow these steps when you receive an invitation from someone you know (who has contacted you with the password to use) and you want to help:

1. Make sure that you are either connected to the Internet or (if both computers are on the same LAN) to the LAN.

NOTE   *If you can't make a connection, one of the computers may be behind a firewall, and you may need to ask the network administrator to enable the port used by Remote Assistance (port 3389).*

2. Open the attached file. You may see a warning that attached files may contain viruses. Go ahead and open the file. You see the Windows Remote Assistance dialog box:

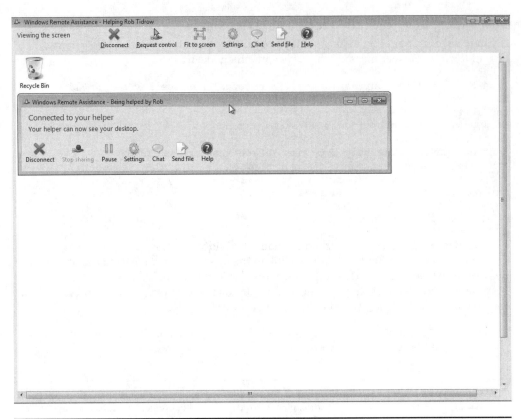

FIGURE 4-4 Hosting a Remote Assistance session on your computer

3. Type the password and click OK to connect. Remote Assistance makes the connection over the LAN or the Internet. You see a Remote Assistance window similar to Figure 4-3. The user on the other end must allow you to connect to his or her computer before you see this screen.

4. Start a chat session with the remote users by clicking the Chat button (see Figure 4-4). In the area in the lower-left part of the Remote Assistance window, type a message and click Send to send the message to the other computer.

Once Windows makes the Remote Assistance connection, you can do the following:

- **Control the other person's computer** Click Request Control and wait for the other person to give permission for you to proceed. When you see a message indicating that you are sharing control, click in the right side of the Remote Assistance window, where the image of the other person's computer screen appears. While your mouse pointer is in that part of the window, its movements also move the mouse pointer on the other computer. However, the other person can also use the mouse and keyboard, and it gets confusing if you both try to do so at the same time. You can click Fit To

Screen if the image of the other computer screen doesn't fit in the Remote Assistance window, but it usually becomes unreadable: click Actual Size to display the other computer screen at actual size. Press ESC (or any key combination with ESC) to end sharing control, or click Release Control.

- **Send a file**   Click Send A File and specify the filename.

- **Voice chat**   Click Start Talking to start a voice chat. If the other person clicks Start Talking first, you see a message asking whether you'd like to start a voice chat. Both computers need microphones and speakers.

Click Disconnect when you are done helping, unless the other person disconnects first.

TIP *If someone sends you an invitation to help from a computer that has a higher screen resolution than your computer, you won't be able to see much of the other person's screen in your Remote Assistance window (if you click Scale To Window, it will be unreadable). Set your screen resolution as high as you can.*

Copying, Moving, and Sharing Information Between Programs

Windows Vista provides two methods of sharing data between different application programs (although each method has variations): You can cut or copy and then paste using the Windows Clipboard, or you can use Object Linking and Embedding (OLE). In general, cutting-and-pasting (or its variant, dragging-and-dropping) works well for the simpler tasks—moving text from one application to another, for instance. OLE is useful when you want all the features of one type of program to work with an object in another program. For example, if you want to display an Excel spreadsheet in a Word document, and you want to be able to update a complicated formula and display the correct answer in the Word document, then you need to use OLE.

Sharing Data Through the Windows Clipboard

Copying or moving information from one location to another within a program is easy using the Cut and Paste commands that almost all Windows programs support. Cutting-and-pasting uses the Clipboard to store information temporarily. Moving or copying information between programs is also easy using the Clipboard. Some programs also let you use your mouse to drag information from one location to another.

You can use the Clipboard to move or copy text, a range of spreadsheet cells, a picture, a sound, or almost any other piece of information you can create with a Windows application. The Windows Clipboard can hold only one chunk of information at a time, so you either have to paste it somewhere else right away or not cut or copy anything else until you've pasted the information where you want it. If you cut or copy another chunk of information, it replaces the information already on the Clipboard. To use the Clipboard to move or copy information within or between files, or to share information between programs, you cut or copy the information from one window and paste it in another.

Cutting, Copying, and Pasting

Cut-and-paste is a feature of Windows that enables you to select information from one file and move or copy it to another file (or to another location in the same file). Cut-and-paste works by storing information temporarily on the Clipboard. The following cut-and-paste techniques enable you to copy or move information within or between almost any Windows application:

- **Cut**   Removes selected information from its current location and stores it (temporarily) on the Clipboard
- **Copy**   Copies selected information and makes a (temporary) duplicate of it on the Clipboard
- **Paste**   Copies information from the Clipboard to the location of the cursor in the active application

To move information, you select it, cut it to the Clipboard, and then paste it in the new location. To copy information, you select it, copy it to the Clipboard, and then paste it in the new location.

You can cut, copy, and paste information by using the following methods (some methods might not work in some applications):

- **Menu**   Choose the Edit menu's Cut, Copy, and Paste commands.
- **Keystrokes**   Press CTRL-X to cut, CTRL-C to copy, and CTRL-V to paste.
- **Buttons**   Many applications have toolbars with Cut, Copy, and Paste buttons.
- **Mousing**   Many applications provide shortcut menus that include the Cut, Copy, and Paste commands. Right-click an object to see a shortcut menu.

TIP *The Cut and Copy buttons may be disabled if you haven't selected information in the window, and the Paste button may be disabled if no information is on the Clipboard.*

The following steps explain how to copy or move text from one location to another:

1. Select the information you want to copy or move.

   - You can select information by highlighting it with the mouse or by holding down the SHIFT key as you use the arrow buttons. The help system of the application you're using will contain more information regarding how to select in that application.
   - Be careful when you have information selected. Depending on the application, you can inadvertently replace the whole selection by typing a character or space or by pressing the DELETE or BACKSPACE keys. Usually, a simple click deselects the information, ending the danger.

TIP *If you're afraid you deleted something by mistake, press CTRL-Z to undo the change in most programs.*

2. If you want to copy the information, press CTRL-C, click the Copy button, or choose Edit | Copy. If you want to move the information, press CTRL-X, click the Cut button, or choose Edit | Cut.

3. If you are copying, you don't see any change on the screen when you give the Copy command. If you are cutting, however (which is useful if you want to move information), the selected information disappears from the screen—it is now stored on the Clipboard.

4. Move the cursor to the place you want the information to appear. This may mean changing applications by clicking a button on the taskbar, or even opening a new application. As long as you don't cut or copy anything else or turn off the computer, the information will be available to be pasted to a new location.

5. Paste the text by pressing CTRL-V, by clicking the Paste button, or by choosing Edit | Paste. The information you cut or copy appears at the location of the cursor.

Once you cut or copy information onto the Clipboard, you can make multiple copies of it by pasting it as many times as you want.

TIP *Information on the Clipboard takes up RAM, limiting the resources your computer has available to do other things. Therefore, if you cut or copy a lot of information to the Clipboard, paste it quickly. Then, cut or copy something small—one letter or word, for instance—which replaces the large chunk of information on the Clipboard and makes most of the RAM available again. Some programs clear the Clipboard.*

If you use Microsoft Office 2000 or later, you may see the small Office Clipboard window (in Office 2000) or the task pane (in Office XP and Office 2007). The Office Clipboard stores up to 12 (for Office 2000) or 24 (for Office XP or Office 2007) "clips" from Office applications. Rest the pointer on a clip to see its contents. You can paste any clip by clicking its icon on the Office Clipboard. The Office Clipboard opens automatically after you cut more than one selection for Office applications.

NOTE *Some programs have problems with cut-and-paste. If you have trouble pasting into a program, first paste the information into Notepad. Then copy it from Notepad and try pasting into the program where you actually want the information to appear.*

What Is Drag-and-Drop?

Drag-and-drop is another method of moving or copying information from one file to another, or to another location in the same file. To move information from one location to another, select it with your mouse and drag it to its new location.

Not all programs support drag-and-drop. Some programs copy the information you drag, rather than move it. Some programs enable you to choose whether to move or copy the information (for example, a program may enable you to copy the information by holding down the CTRL key while dragging).

Capturing Screens Using the Clipboard

Many products can take a *screenshot*, a picture of whatever is on the screen. This book is littered with screenshots that are used as figures. If you need to create a screenshot, you can use the Clipboard to create one. Use the PRINT SCREEN key that appears on your keyboard—it

> **What Is DDE?**
>
> Dynamic Data Exchange is another way for programs to exchange information. With DDE, the programs send messages among themselves. For example, say you are running Microsoft Word and you open a DOC file (a file with the extension .doc) in Windows Explorer. Windows uses DDE to send a message to Microsoft Word so that the DOC file opens in the current Word window, rather than starting up a second copy of Word. You can control what DDE messages your programs send, but programming is required, using macros in programs like Microsoft Office Word 2007 or Excel 2007, or using a programming language such as Microsoft Visual Basic 2005.

often is above the cursor control keys with the SCROLL LOCK and PAUSE keys. You can take two different kinds of screenshots:

- A picture of the whole screen by pressing PRINT SCREEN
- A picture of the active window by pressing ALT-PRINT SCREEN

NOTE *Windows Vista includes the Snipping Tool, which enables you to drag the cursor over an area onscreen and take a picture of that area. See Chapter 19 "Using the Windows Snipping Tool," for more information about the Snipping Tool.*

Once the picture is on the Clipboard, you can paste it somewhere else. You may want to paste the picture into a graphics program, such as Paint (which comes with Windows), so you can save it in a graphics file format and use it later (see "Drawing Pictures with Microsoft Paint" in Chapter 19). Or, you might want to paste it into a file, such as a word processing document containing an explanation of that screen or window.

Sharing Information Using OLE

Object Linking and Embedding is far more flexible and can be far more complicated than cut-and-paste or drag-and-drop. OLE enables you to use all your software applications to create an integrated document. For instance, you might want to create an annual report that includes these components:

- Text you create and format by using a word processor, such as Microsoft Word or Corel WordPerfect
- A company logo stored in a graphics file created by Adobe Photoshop, Paint, or some other graphics application
- Data and calculations on operating costs stored in a Microsoft Excel spreadsheet
- Graphs and charts, which may come from your spreadsheet package or another graphics package

These components may not reflect exactly what *you* want to do, but the point is the same—if you want to combine the output of different applications, OLE offers many advantages over the Clipboard. Why? Because, when you use OLE, the original program retains ownership of the object, and you can use the program to edit the object. For instance, if you use OLE to embed a portion of a spreadsheet in a word processing document, you can always use the spreadsheet application to edit the object and the spreadsheet in the word processing document will reflect those changes. If, instead, you use the Clipboard to copy the numbers from the spreadsheet and then you paste the numbers to the word processor, they would just sit in the word processor, oblivious to their origins—you could use only the tools available in the word processor to edit the numbers. This means that if you later change the original spreadsheet, the numbers pasted in the word processing document won't change.

In OLE, an *object* refers to a piece of information from one application that is placed in a *container file* created by another application. For example, a spreadsheet or graphic is an object when it is included in a word processing document. OLE actually is two similar methods of sharing information between applications—embedding and linking. Sticking with the previous example, *embedding* means putting the spreadsheet object in the word processing document (container file) and asking the word processor to take care of storing the object. So, although the word processor enables you to edit the spreadsheet object by using the spreadsheet application, the spreadsheet object is stored with the word processing document. *Linking*, on the other hand, allows the object to retain a close relationship with its origins—so close, in fact, if the numbers in the original spreadsheet file change, the linked spreadsheet object in the word processing document changes to match. This occurs because the word processing document doesn't really contain the object it displays—it only contains a reference to the file where the information is stored.

You may also choose to insert a *package* into another file. A package is a small file that uses OLE, but instead of displaying content owned by another application, it displays an icon, which, when clicked, opens the owner application and displays the object. Packages can be either linked or embedded. Whether you choose to embed or link objects, the process is similar: you create an object in one application, and then link or embed the object into another application.

Although using OLE to link files can be wonderfully convenient and can save you hours of revisions, it should be used judiciously. If you plan ever to move the file containing linked objects or to send it to someone, you must make sure one of the following occurs:

- The linked files also get moved or sent.
- The linked objects don't get updated. This means the host application won't go looking for the information in the linked file. To break the link, delete the object and paste in a nonlinked version instead.
- You edit the links so the host file knows where to find the source files for the linked objects.

Otherwise, your beautifully organized and time-saving document can become a complete mess. If you are going to move a document with linked objects in it, you need to know how to maintain links, a topic covered later in this chapter.

If you don't need the automatic updating you get with linked objects (for instance, if the source file isn't going to change, or if you don't want the object to reflect changes) or if you know you are going to move or send files, then stick with embedded objects—they're easier to maintain. However, embedding a large object may take more disk space than linking.

NOTE *Some applications enable you to link one file to another in a different way—by using a hyperlink (see "What Is the World Wide Web?" in Chapter 26). A hyperlink actually takes you from one file to another, opening the application for the second file, if necessary.*

Creating Linked or Embedded Objects

The way you link or embed an object depends on the application programs you're using—the program into which you want to embed or link the object. Most programs have a menu command to create an object by using OLE, but you may have to use the online help system to find the command. In Microsoft Word, for instance, you can use Home | Paste | Paste Special to create an object by using OLE. When using Home | Paste | Paste Special in Microsoft Word or its equivalent in another program (usually Edit | Paste Special), you may see the Display As Icon option. This option allows you to create a package, an icon that, when clicked, opens the object in its native application. The following two techniques may also work to link or embed an object: dragging-and-dropping and using Home | Paste | Paste Special. Neither technique is supported by all applications.

Embedding an Object by Dragging-and-Dropping

The easiest way to embed an object is to drag the information from one program and drop it in the other program. For this method to work, both applications must support drag-and-drop embedding. Check the documentation for the program that contains the information you want to embed. When dragging the information you want to embed, use the same technique you use to copy selected information *within* the application (some applications require you to hold down the CTRL key while dragging the information). For instance, in Excel, you have to click-and-drag the border of the selected area to move or copy it.

Follow these steps to use drag-and-drop embedding:

1. Select the information you want to embed.

2. Use drag-and-drop to drag the selected information to the other application; use the same drag-and-drop technique you use to copy information within an application. If the second application isn't visible on the screen, you can drag the information to the application's taskbar button—hold the mouse pointer there for a second, and the application window opens.

3. Drop the information where you want it; if the application supports OLE, you automatically create an embedded object.

TIP *You may be able to specify that the information be linked rather than embedded (the usual default when OLE drag-and-drop is supported) by holding down the SHIFT key—try it to see whether the application you are using supports this feature.*

Linking or Embedding an Object Using Paste Special

You may want a little more control over the object than you have when you drag-and-drop it. To achieve more control over the object, use the Home | Paste | Paste Special command found in many applications. The procedure is much like using the Clipboard to cut-and-paste, except you paste by using OLE instead, as follows:

1. Select the information you want to link or embed.

2. Press CTRL-C or CTRL-X to copy or cut the information (or use another method to copy or cut).

3. Move the cursor where you want the object to appear.

4. Choose Home | Paste | Paste Special. You see a dialog box similar to the one shown in Figure 5-1. Choose the correct application from the choices displayed. Make sure to choose the application you want to use to edit the object—in the figure, that is Microsoft Office Excel. If you choose another option, you won't be using OLE—instead, you will be using the Clipboard to do a simple paste of information from one application to another.

5. Choose the correct setting either to embed the object in the new file or to link the two files together. To embed the object, choose the Paste option; to link the object, choose the Paste Link option. Figure 5-1 shows the settings to embed a Microsoft Excel object into a Word document.

6. Change the Display As Icon check box setting, if necessary. If you choose to display the object as an icon, you don't see the information itself. Instead, you create a *packaged object* that shows the information it contains only when you open its icon.

7. Click OK to link or embed the object. You see the object in the container file, as in Figure 5-2.

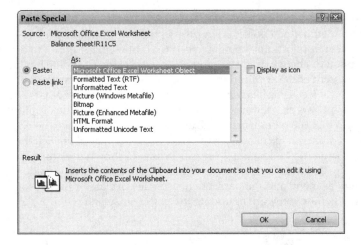

FIGURE 5-1   Use this dialog box (or one like it) to embed an Excel document into another file.

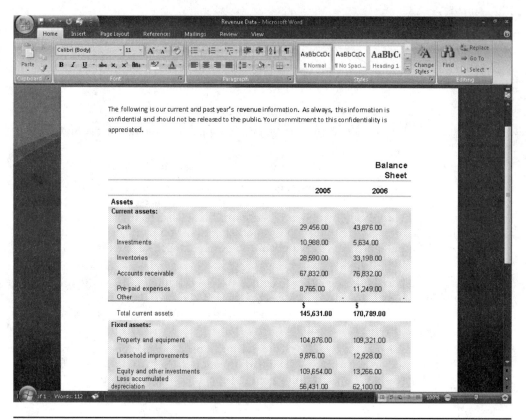

FIGURE 5-2   Part of an Excel worksheet embedded in a Word document

Editing a Linked or Embedded Object

Editing a linked or embedded object is simple—in most applications, you just double-click the object. For other applications, you may need to right-click the object to display a menu with an Edit option or change modes so you are in Edit mode (if you're having trouble, check the help system of the application containing the object). Once you figure out how to edit the object, the object's application opens. Next, the menu and toolbars of the window in which the object appears are replaced by the menu and toolbars of the application assigned by the Registry to that file type (usually the application used to create the object). In other words, if you're editing an Excel object in a Word document, double-click the object to display Excel's menu and toolbars in Word's window, as shown in Figure 5-3. You can edit the object by using that application's tools. When you're done, click outside the object to reinstate the regular menu and toolbars, or choose File | Update or Exit in some applications. If you're asked whether you want to update the object, answer Yes.

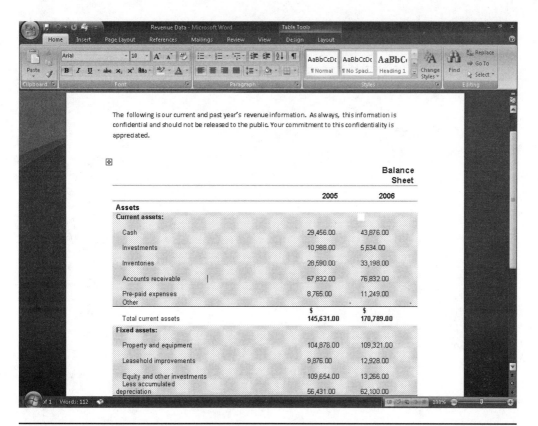

FIGURE 5-3   Edit an Excel object in a Word document by using the Excel menu and toolbars that appear when you double-click the object.

If the object is linked rather than embedded, you can also edit the object by editing the source file itself. If the file containing the object is also open, you may have to update it manually to see the new information in the object. Closing and opening the file containing the object may be the easiest way to update the object.

To delete an object, click it to select it—you'll probably see a box around it—and then press the DELETE or BACKSPACE key.

Sharing Your Computer with Multiple Users

Because Windows Vista is based on Windows XP (which was based on Windows 2000), it has a bevy of security-oriented features that were never present in Windows Me/9x. Windows Me/9x (like the original DOS operating system on which they were based) had almost no built-in security, with no way to prevent one user from reading another user's files. For example, if you create multiple user profiles on a computer running Windows 98 Second Edition, you see a password dialog box when you start Windows. This suggests that the computer is secure, but you can simply click Cancel and get complete access. Windows Vista can require a username and password, and if someone makes too many unsuccessful attempts to gain entry, Windows Vista can deny further attempts for a period of time.

Windows Vista includes Fast User Switching, so that multiple people can be logged on and running programs at the same time. Once you have created separate user accounts for the people who will use the computer, you can set file and folder permissions to control who can open, run, modify, or delete files and folders. Windows Vista also provides Simple File Sharing, which makes it easy to share access to files and folders with other people who use your computer. This chapter examines how to set up Windows for multiple users, including creating user accounts, assigning passwords, logging on, and switching users. It also describes how to log on and off, and how to check who's logged on.

Chapter 31 describes how to share files, folders, and printers with other people on a local area network (LAN) rather than on a single computer. For network security topics, such as how to send secure e-mail, control what information Internet Explorer stores on your disk, and protect your computer from viruses, see Chapter 33.

If your computer is part of a LAN that includes a Windows 2003 Server (or similar server operating system), it is probably part of a *domain*—a workgroup that is controlled by a server computer. If your computer is part of a domain, don't set up or modify user accounts on your computer without consulting your network administrator, because user accounts are probably managed on the server using Windows authentication services. The instructions in this chapter apply to workgroup-based, not domain-based, LANs.

CAUTION   Windows Vista Home Basic Edition doesn't contain all the features described in this chapter. Microsoft decided that home users were unlikely to be connected to large, domain-based networks.

What Password Protection Does Windows Offer?

Windows has many different resources that can be password protected. The major passwords are the following:

- **User password**   The password for your user account. You type it when you start up Windows or switch from one user to another, if your computer has user accounts for which passwords have been created. You can change your password at any time. Windows also stores a *password hint*—a word or phrase that would remind you of your password if you forget it, but that wouldn't give the password away to anyone else. If you are truly concerned about forgetting your password (we always are!), you can also create a *password reset disk*, a floppy disk or a USB flash drive that you can use to log on to your user account even if you forget your password. If your computer does not have a floppy disk drive, or you do not have a USB flash drive, you cannot make a password reset disk.

NOTE   You have the option to not have a password. Simply choose not to enter one when prompted by the Windows Vista Setup Wizard, or remove the password later (see the Appendix). Regardless of your choice, if you plan on being the only user of your computer, you can opt to automatically log into your machine. Just make sure you aren't offering free access to sensitive data to unauthorized individuals.

- **Domain password**   The password used to validate your username to host computers on a LAN that is controlled by Windows 2003 Server, Windows .NET Server, Windows .NET Advanced Server, Windows 2000 Server, Windows NT, or compatible LAN servers. If your domain password is missing or invalid, you can't gain access to disks or printers on the LAN.

- **Encrypted ZIP compressed folders**   You can assign a password to a ZIP compressed folder (see "What Are Compressed Folders?" in Chapter 9).

- **NTFS encryption password for a file or folder**   In Windows Vista Ultimate, Business, and Enterprise editions, you can assign a password to files and folders stored in NTFS partitions (see "What Are Attributes?" in Chapter 9). Encryption isn't available on FAT32 partitions.

This chapter describes how to create user passwords to secure your computer and your Documents folder. See Chapter 33 for additional information if your computer is on a LAN.

What Is a User Account?

When two or more users share a computer, they don't have to argue about what color the background should be, what programs should be on the Start menu, or whether to use single-click or double-click style. Instead, each user can have a *user account* (called a *user profile* in versions of Windows prior to Windows XP). User accounts can be stored in one of two places:

- **Local user accounts**   Information about a local user account is stored r in the C:\ Users folder that contains files that describe each user's preferences. Each time a user logs on, Windows finds the appropriate user account and makes the appropriate changes. If you change any of your preferences (for example, choose a new wallpaper), that information is stored in your user account, so that the change will still be there the next time you log on, but not the next time someone else logs on. Whenever your computer acquires a new user, you should establish a new user account (see "Setting Up a Computer for Multiple Users" later in the chapter). User accounts enable several people to share one computer, or to share folders and other resources on a LAN.

- **Domain accounts**   Information about domain accounts is stored by the Active Directory (AD) program running on Windows NT, 2000, .NET Server, or Windows 2003 Server. When you log in using a domain, your computer gets information from Active Directory about what your settings are and what you have permission to do. Domain accounts are used on larger networks where maintaining accounts stored in each individual computer would be impractical. Domain accounts can use *roaming user profiles*, which allow people to use their own user account from any computer on a LAN, or *mandatory user profiles*, in which only administrators can make changes.

Windows Vista enables you to password-protect the files in your Documents folder, so that other people using the same computer later won't be able to read them (see "Keeping Your Files Private"). Each user's Documents folder can be protected from view from the other users.

Another feature protects your computer if you don't assign passwords to your user accounts. If your user account doesn't have a password, you can log on to your account only at your own computer; you can't use Run As (described in "Running a Program as Another User" later in this chapter) or Remote Desktop Connection to use the computer with your user account (see "Accessing Other Computers with Remote Desktop Connection" in Chapter 16).

If your computer is on a small LAN, you can set up local user accounts on all the computers on the LAN so that people can use any computer and see their own files and desktop. See Chapter 31 for details.

TIP   If you are wondering which user account you are logged on as, click the Start button. The user account name appears at the top right of the menu.

User Account Control when Starting Programs

User Account Control (UAC) is a new technology provided in Windows Vista. It enables users and organizations to better secure desktop environments against potential security breaches and malicious threats. UAC also provides a better way to manage desktops in an enterprise environment. UAC enables you to allow a nonadministrator to log in as an administrator with limited rights and access. When a user logs into Vista using an administrator account, the account is "split" into two accounts—administrator and standard user. As the user is performing nonadministrator tasks, such as running applications, using items on the desktop, and so forth, a user token is created. When an administrator task is performed, such as installing a program, Vista creates a second token, an administrator token, so the user can perform those tasks. The user is required to click a Continue button to allow the action to happen. This reduces the amount of security problems that previous versions of Windows had when a user could log in as an administrator and perform any task without restrictions.

When a standard user logs into Vista, only one type of token is created—a standard user token. This restricts the user from performing system-wide changes to the computer. A standard user trying to perform an administrator-level task is required to sign on with a username and password for a valid administrator account.

Vista segregates tasks into administrator and standard user tasks. For example, the following are tasks that are administrator level:

- Installing programs
- Changing system times
- Changing firewall settings
- Configuring security policies
- Accessing some Control Panel applets

On the other hand, the following tasks are standard user–level tasks:

- Changing desktop wallpaper
- Adding a printer
- Changing time zones

Vista displays the Windows Shield icon on user interface items, such as a button on a dialog box, to indicate UAC items.

Vista automatically turns on User Account Control when you install Vista. You can, however, turn it off if you determine you do not need the level of security it provides. For example, a home user that is using Vista in a nonnetworked or nonshared environment would probably not require UAC turned on. However, to turn off UAC, you do need administrator privileges, so a user in a corporate environment would probably not have the rights to shut off UAC.

To quickly turn off UAC for an account, do the following:

1. Choose Start | Control Panel.
2. Click User Accounts And Family Safety.
3. Click User Accounts.

FIGURE 6-1   The User Account Control window

4. Click Change Security Settings. The User Account Control message window appears, as shown in Figure 6-1.

5. Click Continue.

6. Click to deselect the Use User Account Control (UAC) To Help Protect Your Computer option.

7. Click OK.

8. Click Restart to shut down and restart Windows. When Windows restarts, the UAC feature is turned off.

To enable UAC, use the preceding steps, except click to select the option in Step 6. You will need to shut down and restart the system to activate the UAC feature.

UAC is an advanced technology that can be configured in a number of different ways. The way just described is one way, albeit simple and per user—the changes you make are only for the currently logged-in user. For computer-wide changes to UAC, you must use the Security Policy tool, available from the Administrative Tools section of the Control Panel. However, using the Security Policy tool is something most end users will not have to bother with.

NOTE   The Security Policy tool is a powerful tool. Do not use it if you are not comfortable making system-wide changes to Windows Vista. Incorrect settings you make can render Vista or your computer unusable without reinstalling Windows Vista.

What Types of Users Can You Create?

Windows Vista enables you to set up local user accounts. If you are logged into a Windows 2003 Server, Windows .NET, 2000, or NT server with administrative privileges, you can create and maintain domain accounts on a domain-based LAN, but you should talk to your LAN administrator before doing so.

Table 6-1 lists and briefly explains the types of users Vista can have.

You can create as many administrator or standard accounts as you want. You can't create guest accounts.

Account Type	Description
Administrator	Enables access to all accounts. Each computer needs at least one administrator account at all times. You can have more than one, if you like. When using an administrator account, you can give commands to create, edit, and delete all user accounts, and you can install software. Windows Vista comes with one administrator account named Administrator. Microsoft recommends that you use it only for installing programs and managing the system.
Standard	Enables access to your own account. When using a standard account, you cannot perform tasks that affect other users' accounts on the computer, such as install software, open files in other people's Documents folders, change system settings, or change other people's user accounts. You can run programs that are already installed, and you can modify your own user account (except that you can't change it into an administrator account). You should log on with a standard account for day-to-day work, to avoid viruses and other programs that might try to install themselves when you aren't looking.
Guest	Enables access only to programs that are installed on the computer. Each computer running Windows Vista has one guest account (named Guest). When using the guest account, you cannot change any user accounts, open files in other people's Documents folders, or install software.

TABLE 6-1   Windows Vista User Account Types

Table 6-2 lists some of the files and folders that are stored separately for each local user account. These items are stored in the user account's *user profile*—the folder that contains all the settings for the user. A user profile is usually in the C:\Users*username* folder, where *username* is replaced by the name of the user account. (If Windows is installed on a partition other than C:, so is this folder.) You need to configure Windows Explorer to display hidden files and folders to see them (see "What Are Hidden Files and Folders?" in Chapter 9).

Fast User Switching allows you to switch from one user account to another without the first user logging off. For example, suppose that a user named Jordan is running Windows Mail and Microsoft Office Access 2007. Another user, named Meg, needs to check her mail and asks Jordan if she can use his computer to do so. Fast User Switching lets Jordan step aside and Meg switch the computer to her user account. Jordan's programs are on hold until Meg is done using the computer. When Jordan switches back to his account, his programs are just where he left them.

Fast User Switching is enabled by default if your Windows system has at least 64MB of RAM. With less RAM, the system doesn't have enough space to store one user's environment, including its running programs and open files, while another user is active.

NOTE   *You can't use Fast User Switching if your computer is part of a domain (that is, connected to a domain-based LAN). You also can't use it if you use the Classic logon screen instead of the Welcome screen for logging on.*

Item	Contents
Ntuser.dat, Ntuser.dat.log, and Ntuser.ini files	This user's configuration settings and other information.
Application Data folder	This user's application program configuration settings.
Cookies folder	The cookies stored by Internet Explorer while run by this user (see "What Are Cookies?" in Chapter 26).
Desktop folder	The items that appear on this user's desktop.
Favorites folder	Items this user has added to the Favorites folder.
Local Settings\History folder	Shortcuts to web sites this user has viewed recently.
Local Settings\Temporary Internet Files folder	Recently viewed web pages.
Documents folder	The files and folders that appear in this user's Documents folder when the user is logged on. You can tell Windows to look in a different location for your Documents folder; see "Modifying User Accounts" later in this chapter.
NetHood folder	This user's network shortcuts, which appear in the Network folder when the user is logged on.
PrintHood folder	This user's shared printers.
Recent Items folder	Shortcuts to files this user has opened recently.
Send To folder	Shortcuts to folders and devices that appear on the Send To menu when the user right-clicks a file or folder.
Start Menu folder	The shortcuts and folders that Windows uses to display the Start and More Programs menus for this user.
Templates folder	Template files for word processors and other programs, used when this user creates a new document.

TABLE 6-2   Information Stored in Local User Account Profiles

Setting Up a Computer for Multiple Users

When several people share a computer, local user accounts allow each person to personalize the user interface without inconveniencing the other users. The user accounts can have passwords, to prevent people from logging on as each other, or you can dispense with passwords, if security isn't a concern.

TIP   *We recommend creating a password for each user account, even if it's an obvious one. Passwords prevent toddlers or bored passersby from using your computer, even if the password is simply "xxx" or the same as the username.*

When you start using Windows Vista, you are automatically logged on with an administrator user account named Administrator unless you tell the Windows Vista Setup

Wizard the names of the people who will use the computer (which causes the Setup Wizard to create administrator accounts for each of them). Using this administrator account, you can create user accounts for the people who will use the computer, giving each person the appropriate type of account (administrator or standard) based on the person's level of use.

Creating, Modifying, and Deleting User Accounts

If your user account is an administrator account and you run Windows Vista, you have full control over local user accounts.

Creating New User Accounts

Follow these steps to create a local user account in the User Accounts window:

1. Choose Start | Control Panel, and click User Accounts And Family Safety | Add Or Remove User Accounts to display the Manage Accounts window (see Figure 6-2).

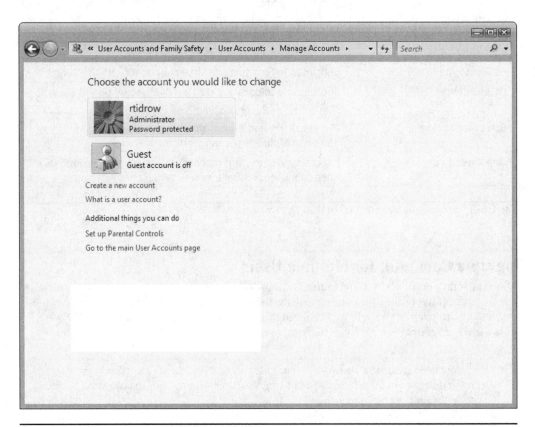

FIGURE 6-2   Add a new account with this window.

2. Click Create A New Account. Windows prompts you for the account name and the type of account. You have only two options: standard user or administrator.

3. Click Create Account. Windows creates the account.

New accounts start with the Windows default settings, as well as settings that have been stored for all users. For example, when programs are installed, they usually create desktop icons and Start menu commands in the C:\Users\All Users folder, so that all users, including new user accounts, can run the program.

If you have Windows Vista Ultimate, you can also create new accounts in the Computer Management window, which lets you set many more configuration options for the account. Follow these steps:

1. Choose Start, right-click Computer, and choose Manage from the menu that appears. You see the Computer Management window shown in Figure 6-3.

2. Open the Local Users And Groups folder and then the Users folder.

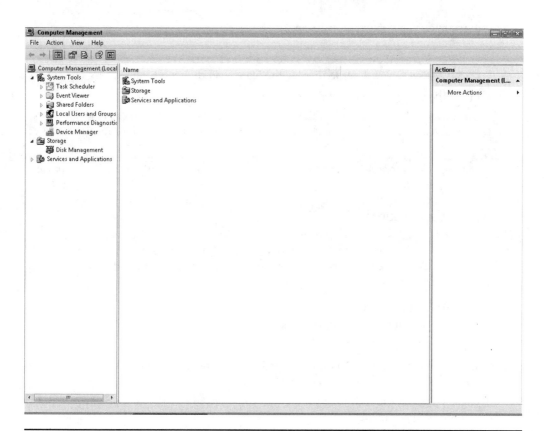

FIGURE 6-3   The Computer Management window

FIGURE 6-4   Adding a new user

3. Chose Action | New User to display the New User dialog box (shown in Figure 6-4).

4. Fill in the information about the user account.

5. Click Create. Windows creates the user account and adds it to the Users group. The first time that the user logs on, Windows creates a Documents folder for the account.

TIP *Unless you don't care about security, be sure to modify the new account to have a password, as described in the next section.*

Modifying User Accounts

You can change a few user account settings from the User Accounts window and (if you have Windows Vista Ultimate) change most of the rest of the settings from the Computer Management window. A few options, such as the locations of the Documents and Favorites folders, are set in other ways.

Modifying Basic User Account Settings

If you want to modify the name, picture, or account type for a user account by using the User Accounts window, follow these steps:

1. Choose Start | Control Panel, and click User Accounts And Family Safety | User Accounts to display the User Accounts window.

2. Click a link corresponding to the change you want to make. The following are the changes you can make:

   • Change your password

   • Remove your password

- Change your picture
- Change your name
- Change your account type

3. Click a setting and enter the new value.

4. To return to the list of user accounts, click the Back button on the toolbar.

Tip *We recommend that you rename the Administrator account to use another name. Breaking into your system is harder if the hacker doesn't know the name of an existing user account, especially an administrator account.*

Modifying Advanced User Account Settings

To modify other user account settings, you need to use the Local Users And Groups program in the Computer Management window. Follow these steps:

1. Choose Start, right-click Computer, and choose Manage from the menu that appears. You see the Computer Management window, as previously shown in Figure 6-3.

2. Open the Local Users And Groups folder and the Users folder.

3. Click a user account and click the Properties button on the toolbar. Or, right-click a user account and choose Properties from the menu that appears. You see the Properties dialog box for the user. The General tab contains information about the user password and the status of the account (disabled or locked out). The Member Of tab is for adding this user account to groups. The Profile tab is shown in Figure 6-5.

4. Make your changes and click OK.

FIGURE 6-5   The Profile tab of the Properties dialog box for a user account

---

TIP *When you specify a pathname that includes the user account name (such as the pathname of the user's Documents folder), you can type **%username%** instead of the user account name. This trick enables you to enter the same path for different users' settings.*

Changing the Location of the Documents Folder

The Documents folder for a user is normally in C:\Users*username*\Documents (assuming that Windows is installed on C:). You can tell Windows Vista to use a different folder instead, by following these steps:

1. Click Start, right-click Documents, and choose Properties from the menu that appears. You see the Documents Properties dialog box, with the General tab selected. Click the Location tab (see Figure 6-6). The text box contains the current location of your Documents folder.

2. To tell Windows that you want to store your files in another folder, click the Move button and browse to the folder in which you plan to store (or already store) your files. You can click the New Folder button if the folder doesn't exist yet. Click the Network link if you want to choose a folder on another computer on your network. Click Select Folder when you have selected the folder.

FIGURE 6-6   Specifying the location of your Documents folder

3. To switch back to the original (default) location of the Documents folder (in C:\ Users*username*), click the Restore Default button.

4. Click OK. Windows asks if you want to move the files that are in your old Documents folder to your new Documents folder.

5. Click Yes or No.

TIP *Keeping your Documents folder on a separate disk drive or partition makes it easy to back up or move your files separately from your programs. Wherever it is, be sure to back up your Documents folder regularly.*

Changing the Start Menu for All Users

Each user can customize her own Start menu, but an administrator user can customize everyone's Start menus with one command. For example, you might want to add a command to display a program that everyone in your workgroup will use, or a shortcut to a shared folder. Here's how:

1. Right-click the Start button and choose Open All Users from the menu that appears. You see the Start Menu window, which is an Explorer window displaying the files that make up the default Start menu for all user accounts. These files are usually stored in C:\Users\All Users\Start Menu (if Windows is installed on C:).

2. If you want the command to appear in everyone's All Programs menu, open the Programs folder. Otherwise, stay in the Start Menu folder to create a command that appears on everyone's Start menu.

3. Right-click and choose New | Shortcut to run the Create Shortcut Wizard.

4. Following the wizard's prompts, create a shortcut to the program, folder, or file that you want on everyone's Start menu.

The shortcut you create appears on each user's Start or All Programs menu the next time each person logs on. You can use the Start Menu window to move or delete shortcuts for all users, too.

Adding or Removing Passwords

If you don't want other people to be able to log on as you, assign your account a password. When you create a password for your own account, Windows also offers you the option of a private Documents folder—one that other people can't open. If an administrator creates a password for you, your Documents folder is already private.

Follow these steps to add a password to your own user account in the User Accounts window (administrators can use the same steps to add a password to another user's account):

1. Choose Start | Control Panel, and click User Accounts And Family Safety | User Accounts to display the User Accounts window.

2. Click Create A Password. You see the Create A Password For Your Account window, as shown in Figure 6-7.

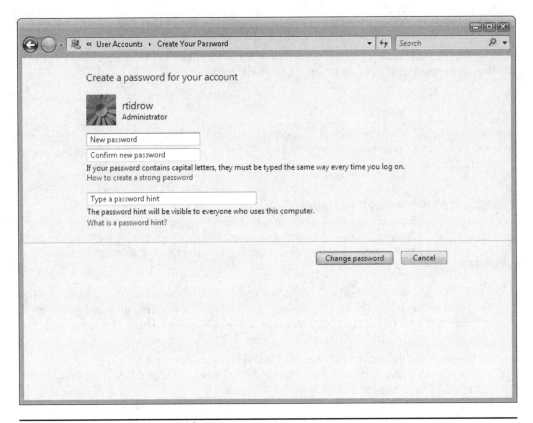

Figure 6-7 Changing the password for a user account

3. Type the password into each of the first two boxes (you see only dots, in case someone evil is looking over your shoulder). You can also type a password hint (that is, a word or phrase that will remind you of your password, without giving it away to anyone else) in the third box.

4. Click Change Password when you have typed the password and password hint.

5. If you are setting a password for your own user account, Windows asks, "Do you want to make your files and folders private?" Click Yes Make Private to create a private folder for your files, or click No not to. If you choose Yes Make Private, your Documents folder can be opened only by you and by administrators.

6. To create a password reset disk for use in case you forget your password, click Prepare For A Forgotten Password on the task pane. You see the Forgotten Password Wizard.

7. The wizard steps you through creating a password reset disk. You need a blank, formatted floppy disk, and you need to know your current password.

If you have an administrator or power user account and you use Windows Vista Ultimate, you can create or remove passwords from a user account by using the Computer Management window. Follow these steps:

1. Choose Start, right-click Computer, and choose Manage from the menu that appears. Click the Local Users And Groups item. You see the Computer Management window, as shown earlier in Figure 6-3.

2. Right-click the user account and choose Set Password from the menu that appears. You see a dire warning about lost files, but this warning appears to refer to files that the user has encrypted with a password (see "What Are Attributes?" in Chapter 9). We're not actually sure that *any* information will be lost, but we can't guarantee it. If you choose to go ahead, click Proceed and you see the Set Password dialog box.

3. Type the new password in each of the two boxes and click OK.

4. Let the user know his new password, and suggest that he change it as soon as possible to a password he can remember.

You can remove the password from your own account (or, if you have an administrator account, from other users' accounts). If you don't want the user account to have a password any more (so that anyone can log on by clicking the username on the Welcome screen), open the User Accounts window, click Remove The Password (or Remove My Password, if it's your account), and then click the Remove Password button to confirm.

If you change your password later (and we recommend that you change it from time to time), you don't need to re-create the password reset disk.

TIP *We recommend that you create passwords for all your user accounts. If you're not worried about security, make all the passwords the same, but don't omit them altogether, unless your computer isn't connected to the Internet. We don't know of specific holes in Windows Vista user account security, but why take a chance?*

Enabling and Disabling the Guest Account

If you set up passwords for your accounts, you may also want to make sure that the Guest account is disabled (Windows disables it by default). If the Guest account is enabled, anyone can use your computer without a password.

To disable the Guest account, choose Start | Control Panel, and click User Accounts And Family Safety | User Accounts to display the User Accounts window. Click Manage Another Account to display the Manage Accounts window. Click the Guest account and click Turn Off The Guest Account. You can turn it back on again by clicking the Guest account from the User Accounts window and clicking the Turn On button.

Deleting User Accounts

If someone with a user account on your computer will never, ever use the computer again, you can delete the user account. When you delete the account, Windows deletes the user's internal security ID (SID), and even if you create a new account with the same name, it will have a new SID and a new profile and settings. So don't delete a user account if the person will be away temporarily—disable it instead.

To delete a user account, an administrative or power user can use either the User Accounts window or the Computer Management's Local Users And Groups utility (for Windows Vista Ultimate users)—we recommend the User Accounts window, because it cleans up the user's account folders when it deletes the account. (You can't delete the account you are currently using.) In the User Accounts window, select the account name and click Delete The Account. Windows asks what you want to do with the files on the user's desktop and in the user's Documents folder. Click Keep Files to move the files to a folder on the desktop, or click Delete Files to delete them. Either way, the user's folder in C:\Users is deleted.

You also can use the Local Users And Groups program in the Computer Management window to delete a user. However, if you use the Action | Delete command in the Computer Management window to delete a user account, the user's folder remains in the C:\Users folder, which strikes us as untidy.

To temporarily disable an account in Windows Vista, open the Computer Management window (click Start, right-click Computer, and choose Manage from the menu that appears), click Local Users And Groups, click the Users folder, right-click the user account, choose Properties from the menu that appears, and click the Account Is Disabled check box. While a user account is disabled, it doesn't appear on the Welcome screen, and you can't log onto it from the Classic logon screen, either.

Using a Shared Computer

Unlike Windows Me/9x, with Windows Vista you are always logged on with a user account (either a local user account or a domain account). If you haven't yet set up user accounts, you are logged on automatically as Administrator. Once you set up additional user accounts, you can log on as any user (as long as you know the appropriate password), logging out when you are done. Using the new Fast User Switching feature, you can also switch from one user account to another in the middle of your work.

TIP *Don't use Administrator or any administrator account for your day-to-day computer work. You can do less accidental damage from a standard account.*

Logging On

Once you have created user accounts, whenever your computer powers up or a user logs off, you see a logon screen. If you are not on a LAN, or you are connected to a peer-to-peer workgroup-based LAN, you normally see the Welcome screen, as shown in Figure 6-8. Click your username and type your password, if your account has a password (which we recommend). Windows loads your user account, and you can see the desktop.

Resuming Work after Locking Windows

If your computer is configured to use the Welcome screen for logging on, pressing WINDOWS-L (that is, holding down the WINDOWS key and pressing L) to lock the computer also displays the Welcome screen. Log back in to continue working. Windows Vista has Fast User Switching turned on by default.

FIGURE 6-8   The Welcome screen greets you when you start up Windows, log out, or press WINDOWS-L to switch users.

Logging Off

If you are done working but don't want to shut down the computer, you can log off. Choose Start and Log Off from the Switch User menu. Windows exits all your programs, logs you off, and displays the Welcome screen.

Switching Users

When Windows starts up, you choose which user to log on as by clicking or typing the username in the Welcome screen. If Windows is already running, you can switch users by logging off and letting the other user log on.

Fast User Switching provides a faster way to switch users: press WINDOWS-L. Alternatively, you can choose Start | Log Off, and then click the Switch User button on the Welcome screen. Click Switch User again and then log on as another user. The currently logged-on user has Logged On displayed underneath their username. When you switch users with this method, Windows doesn't exit the programs you were running; instead, they continue running in the background until you switch back to the first user account.

Setting the Screen Saver to Require You to Log Back On

If you are worried about someone using your computer when you step away from it, you can set the screen saver to require you to log back in using your user account name and password. Follow these steps:

1. Right-click a blank place on the desktop and choose Personalize to display the Personalization area of the Control Panel.

2. Click Screen Saver and set the Screen Saver box to an option other than None.

3. Select the On Resume Display Welcome Screen check box.

4. Click OK.

Now when you return to your computer and click a key or move the mouse to wake Windows up, it displays the Welcome screen.

Changing Your Password

You can change your own password any time. Follow these steps:

1. Choose Start | Control Panel, and click User Accounts And Family Safety to display the User Accounts window.

2. Click Change Your Windows Password to display the Make Changes To Your User Account window.

3. Click Change Your Password to display the Change Your Password window.

4. Type the existing password and your new password (twice). Also type a password hint, to remind you of your password if you forget it.

If you created a password reset disk for your user account, you don't have to create or modify the disk when you change your password.

TIP *Be sure to create a password reset disk for yourself—it saves lots of headaches if (when) you forget your password. Choose Start | Control Panel, click User Accounts And Family Safety, and choose Prepare For A Forgotten Password from the task pane.*

Keeping Your Files Private

If file sharing is disabled on your computer, your folders are stored on a drive or partition formatted with NTFS, and you use Windows Vista, you can see and set who has permission to open your folders or files.

To see the permissions for a file or folder, right-click it in an Explorer window and choose Properties from the shortcut menu that appears. You see the Properties dialog box for the file or folder. Click the Security tab, which only appears for files and folders on NTFS drives when Simple File Sharing is disabled (see Figure 6-9).

The Security tab shows who has permission to do what with the file or folder. Table 6-3 lists what these permissions allow.

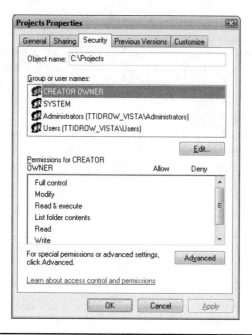

Figure 6-9   The Security tab of the Properties dialog box for a file

Permission	Allows for Folders	Allows for Files
Full Control	All operations	All operations
Modify	Traverse and list folder Read and write attributes Create files and folders Read permissions Delete	Execute file Read, write, and append data Read and write attributes Read permissions Delete
Read & Execute	Traverse and list folder Read attributes and permissions	Execute file Read data Read attributes and permissions
List Folder Contents	Traverse and list folder Read attributes Read permissions	(Not applicable)
Read	List folder Read attributes and permissions	Read data Read attributes and permissions
Write	Create files and folders Write attributes Read permissions	Write and append data Write attributes Read permissions
Special Permissions	Advanced permissions	Combination of permissions

Table 6-3   File Permission Settings

Select an entry in the Group Or User Names list, and the permissions for that group or user account appear in the Permissions list in the lower part of the dialog box. For any permission that is allowed, you can click the Deny check box to revoke that permission for that user or group. For permissions that are denied, you can click the Allow check box. If you don't have permission to change the permission, the check box appears dimmed.

Sharing Files with Other Users

To store your files so that other users of your computer can read, edit, or delete them, store the documents in the Shared Documents folder that appears under Computer in the folder tree. (This folder is actually called C:\Users\All Users\Shared Documents, assuming that Windows is installed on C:.) All users, including the Guest account, can open the files in the Shared Documents folder. To see the Shared Documents folder, choose Start | Computer and click Shared Documents in the task pane.

CAUTION   *If you haven't disabled the Guest account, then files in the Shared Documents folder can be opened by anyone who uses the computer (see "Enabling and Disabling the Guest Account," earlier in the chapter).*

If you want only some people to be able to read or modify material you store in the Shared Documents folder, see the preceding section for how to set the permissions for a file or folder.

Running a Program as an Administrator

If you know the password for an administrator account, you can run a program as if you were logged on as that user. Some older programs can't run unless the user account has full rights on the system (for example, it insists on making system configuration changes that would ordinarily be forbidden for your user account). The Run As Administrator dialog box enables you to run a program and specify what user account to run it as.

To see the Run As Administrator dialog box, hold down the SHIFT key while you right-click an icon for the program (either on the desktop or in an Explorer window). Choose Run As Administrator from the menu that appears. Select a user (that has administrator privileges), enter the user's password, and click OK.

Managing Appointments and Schedules with Windows Calendar

It seems as if our days are getting shorter or the number of appointments, meetings, and tasks is growing. To help manage schedules, many people use electronic calendar and scheduling software. Windows Vista includes a new scheduling program called Windows Calendar. It enables you to create appointments, make a task list, share calendars with other people, and create multiple calendars. This chapter discusses how to use Windows Calendar to perform those tasks.

What Is Windows Calendar?

Windows Calendar provides an easy-to-use digital calendar to help you keep track of your daily activities. Some people jot down meetings and to-do lists on Post-It notes, backs of envelopes, or a wall calendar. If that's the system you use and it works, great. If it doesn't work or you don't have a system yet, try the Windows Calendar to help you manage your daily appointments and tasks.

Windows Calendar also enables you to create multiple calendars to keep track of different parts of your life. For example, you may want to create a separate calendar that shows your children's extracurricular activities on it. You can do this. Another example is having multiple calendars for work; create one for each project you are working on, for instance. As you create calendars, the original calendar becomes the master calendar that shows all the dates from all your custom calendars. Each calendar can be color-coded to help you distinguish which calendar is which. You also can send e-mail invitations to other people so that they can stay abreast of new appointments you set up.

Finally, Windows Calendar provides a way to share your calendar with other people and to subscribe to other users' calendars. This is handy if you work on a team project in which sharing meeting times is important (and your company does not use a messaging and scheduling program like Microsoft Outlook and Exchange). Another way sharing calendars comes in handy is for after-work activities that you are involved with. Perhaps you need to set up an annual calendar of events for a local charity and then share that calendar with other volunteers. With Windows Calendar it's very easy to set up a calendar and publish it so others can import it into their Windows Calendar program.

Using Windows Calendar

To start Windows Calendar, choose Start | All Programs | Windows Calendar. This displays a blank calendar window, like the one shown in Figure 7-1. The Windows Calendar interface is divided into three main areas. On the far left is the Navigation Pane. It includes the following items:

- **Date**   This is a small calendar that shows an entire month. By default, Windows Calendar shows the current month with the current day highlighted. Click the left and right arrow buttons next to the name of the month to navigate backward and forward to see different months.

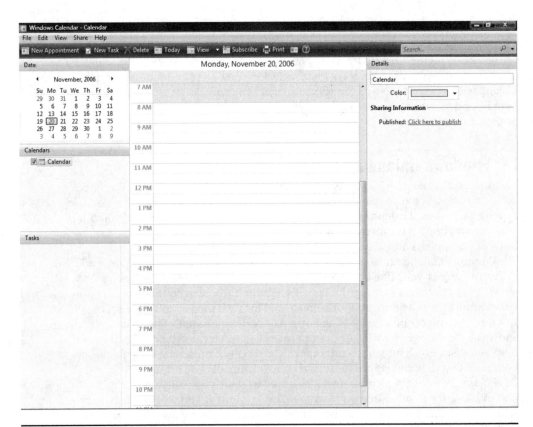

FIGURE 7-1   Use Windows Calendar to set up appointments, create tasks, invite others to a meeting, and more.

- **Calendars**   In this area you can see a list of your calendars. By default, one calendar shows. After you import calendars and create new ones, those calendars appear as well.

- **Tasks**   This area shows your to-do list. You can view task names here and "check off" tasks as you finish them. To see details of a task, simply click it and the details are shown in the Details pane.

In the middle of the Windows Calendar window is the appointment pane. It shows the current calendar in different views, including the following:

- Day
- Work Week
- Week
- Month

The right side of the Windows Calendar window is the Details pane. Here you can view details for a selected appointment, calendar, or task. For example, when you select an appointment in your calendar, you can see when the appointment starts and ends, find out if the appointment is a recurring one, and see the individuals invited to join you in the appointment (if you have invited them).

You can turn off the Navigation Pane or Details pane by clicking the View menu. At the bottom of the menu are choices for showing or hiding the Navigation Pane and Details pane. When you hide these panes, the view of the calendar enlarges.

Configuring Windows Calendar

Windows Calendar enables you to modify some of the settings of the calendar window and calendar features. For example, you can change the starting work day of the week to match your work week. If you generally have Sundays and Mondays off, for instance, start your work week on Tuesday and ending on Saturday. The default, of course, has the work week running from Monday to Friday.

Another modification you may want to make is the work hours you want displayed. By default Windows Calendar shows the work day starting at 8:00 A.M. and finishing at 5:00 P.M. For many users, this setting is fine. But if you work a different schedule (such as 3–11), change the Windows Calendar Day Start and Day End settings to match your work times.

To set Windows Calendar options, choose File | Options. The Options dialog box appears (see Figure 7-2).

The Options dialog box is divided into three main areas: Calendar, Appointments, and Tasks.

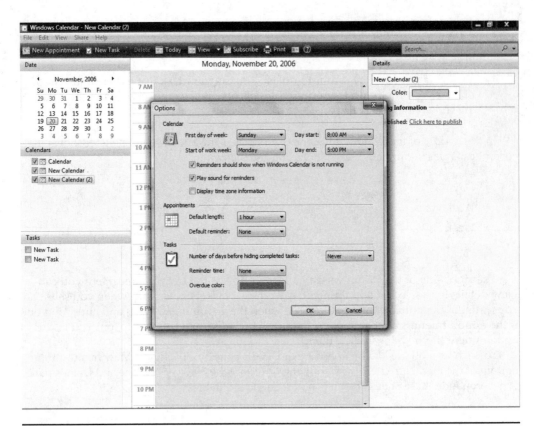

FIGURE 7-2   Set Windows Calendar options using the Options dialog box.

Configuring Calendar Options

In the Calendar Options area, you can set how Windows Calendar should display days of the week, work days, and other options. The following are the settings you can modify:

- **First Day Of Week**   Click the drop-down list of days to choose when you want the calendar week to begin. What you choose here will determine which day of the week appears first (to the far left of days) in the small calendar in the Navigation Pane. By default Sunday is the first day of the week in the United States.

- **Start Of Work Week**   Click the drop-down list of days to choose when you want the work week to begin. This determines how the Work Week view option displays work days when you are viewing your calendar. By default Monday is the first work day of the week in the United States.

- **Day Start**   Click the drop-down list of times to choose when your work day begins. By default the time is set to 8:00 A.M.

- **Day End**   Click the drop-down list of times to choose when your work day ends. By default the time is set to 5:00 A.M.

- **Reminders Should Show When Windows Calendar Is Not Running**   Provides a way for Windows Calendar reminders to display and notify you even if you do not keep Windows Calendar running. When a reminder displays, and Windows Calendar is not running, you can click to view details of the reminder, which then launches Windows Calendar.

- **Play Sound For Reminders**   Instructs Windows Vista to play a sound to alert you when a reminder displays.

- **Display Time Zone Information**   Displays the time zone information in the Details pane when you view information about an appointment. This is handy if you share calendars or receive meeting invitations with workers who work in different time zones and countries.

Configuring Appointments Options

Windows Calendar includes two appointment options:

- **Default Length**   Determines the default length of time for new appointments. This is set to 1 hour when you initially launch Windows Calendar.

- **Default Reminder**   Determines the length of time in advance of an appointment that the reminder should activate. For example, if you set it to 30 minutes, a reminder pops up at 1:30 P.M. for a 2:00 P.M. appointment.

Configuring Tasks Options

Tasks are your individual "to-do" items, such as "Pick up milk and bread." You can set the following options for tasks:

- **Number Of Days Before Hiding Completed Tasks**   Enables you to specify when Windows Calendar should hide tasks that you have completed. If you choose None, all completed tasks remain visible on the Tasks pane.

- **Reminder Time**   Enables you to set a time when reminders are displayed for your tasks. By default, Windows Calendar does not remind of tasks that need to be completed. However, if you like a little tickler message prior to the end of the day, set the time to 4:30 P.M. (or half an hour before your end of day). This helps you remember to get short tasks completed before the end of the day, and reminds you to pick up that milk as you head home!

- **Overdue Color**   Enables you to set a color that the task changes to when the task become overdue. The default overdue color is red.

Understanding Appointments in Windows Calendar

Probably the Windows Calendar task you will perform the most is creating new appointments. Appointments appear in the Calendar view. They are called appointments, but they can also be meetings, tasks that have specific deadlines and that may involve other people, or blocks of time you want to designate as Busy Time so you can limit disruptions and get important work done or make phone calls.

Creating Appointments

To create a new appointment, double-click the time on the calendar at which you want the appointment to begin. You also can click a time and choose the New Appointment button on the Windows Calendar menu. Or, choose File | Appointment when you have a time selected.

The block of time for the appointment (by default 1 hour) changes color to your calendar color (such as light green) and displays the words New Appointment. Type a name for the appointment, such as District Manager Review Meeting, and press ENTER. Windows Calendar displays the new appointment, with its details displayed in the Details pane.

You can move an appointment by dragging-and-dropping it to a different time. If you need to increase or decrease the time of an appointment, simply click-and-drag the top or bottom edge of the appointment to resize the appointment box. Appointments can be shown in half-hour increments on the calendar. You can get more granular on an appointment's time by defining it in the Details pane.

Showing Details in Windows Calendar

To add details to an appointment, such as the location of the meeting, insert them in the Details pane. Here's a look at the settings there:

- **Name**   Displays the name of the appointment. You can add several lines of information here for your appointments.

- **Location**   Enables you to specify a location of the appointment.

- **Calendar**   Enables you to choose which calendar the appointment belongs to if you have multiple calendars. For example, if you have three calendars, one of which is the master calendar, you can use it to set up all your appointments. Then specify on the Calendar drop-down list in the Details pane which calendar the appointment belongs to (such as work, home, and so on).

- **URL**   Enables you to enter a web site address if the appointment involves additional information that you can obtain from a site.

- **Appointment Information**   Provides an area to modify the time of the appointment and if the appointment is recurring. Recurring appointments are those that occur at the same time each day, week, month, or year. You also can set up recurring meetings that occur at specific intervals, such as every first Monday of the month.

- **Reminder**   Enables you to specify how long in advance of the meeting start time that Windows Calendar should alert you. This setting overrides the default setting you set in the Options dialog box.

- **Participants**   Enables you to invite other people to your meeting using the Windows Contacts list of contacts. When you click Attendees, the Windows Calendar contacts list appears (see Figure 7-3). Double-click the people you want to invite and click OK. The names of the invitees appear in the Invite box on the Details pane. Click the Invite button to launch your e-mail program's (Windows Mail for instance) new message window (like the one shown in Figure 7-4). In the To field are the attendees' e-mail addresses, and the appointment information is contained in an attached file that the

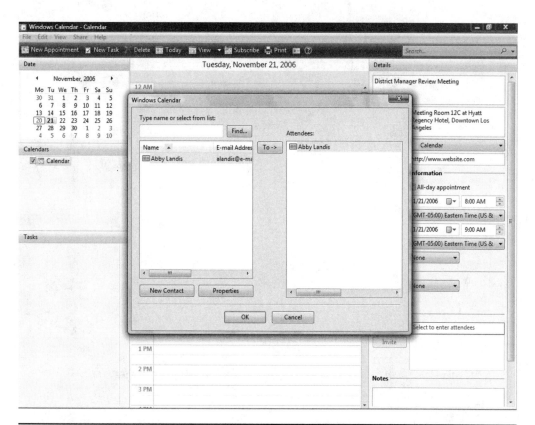

FIGURE 7-3   You can select attendees to attend your appointment.

recipients can download to their copy of Windows Calendar or to a calendar program that supports invitations. Enter some message text and click Send to deliver your appointment invitation.

- **Notes**   Provides an area in which you can enter other information about the meeting, such as a list of topics you want to cover or filenames of supporting documents you plan to present.

Figure 7-5 shows an appointment with several details shown. One thing to notice about the appointment is that after you add attendees, make the appointment a recurring one, add notes, and specify a reminder time, icons appear on the appointment in the calendar to show that these details are included.

NOTE   *Windows Calendar uses the Internet Calendar file format for sharing calendars and for inviting others to an appointment. The file format is ICS (.ics file extension) and is a standard for many calendaring and scheduling programs that work under Windows, Apple Macintosh, and Linux. For example, Microsoft Office Outlook 2007 enables you to import multi-event ICS files.*

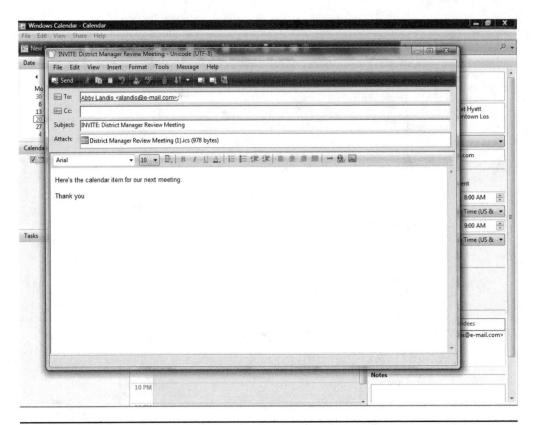

Figure 7-4   You can send calendar invitations to attendees by using e-mail.

You can click outside the appointment to hide the appointment's details.

To remove an appointment, simply click it and press DELETE. When you do this, Windows Calendar does *not* ask if you are sure you want to remove the appointment. It simply deletes it, and you cannot undo the deletion.

Creating a Task in Windows Calendar

Tasks are helpful reminders for to-do items you have to complete, but are not appointments that you set up in your calendar. Examples of tasks include the following:

- Design new process workflow
- Buy milk on the way home
- Call Tracy in Marketing re: Sales Flyers
- Pick up kids at wrestling practice

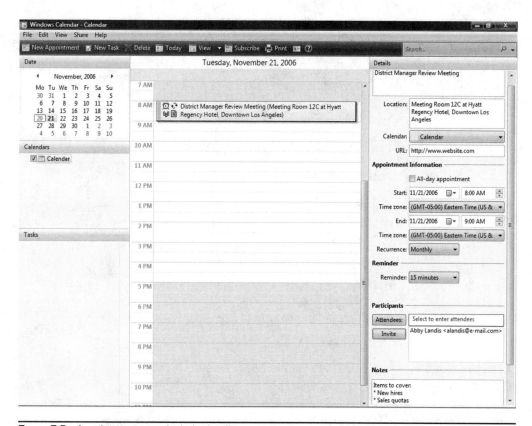

FIGURE 7-5   Appointments can include details.

To create a new task, right-click inside the Tasks area in the Navigation Pane. A submenu appears. Click New Task. A New Task item appears. Type the task item and press ENTER. The new task item appears in the Tasks area, as shown in Figure 7-6. In the Details pane, you can add more information about the task, including the following:

- **Description**   Enables you to add a lengthy description of the task. Only part of this description can be seen in the Tasks area, but you can add several lines of text here.
- **Calendar**   Enables you to choose which calendar the task belongs to if you have multiple calendars.
- **URL**   Enables you to enter a web site address if the task involves additional information that you can obtain from a site.
- **Completed**   Shows if a task is completed.
- **Priority**   Enables you to select the importance of a task. You can choose Low, Medium, High, or None.

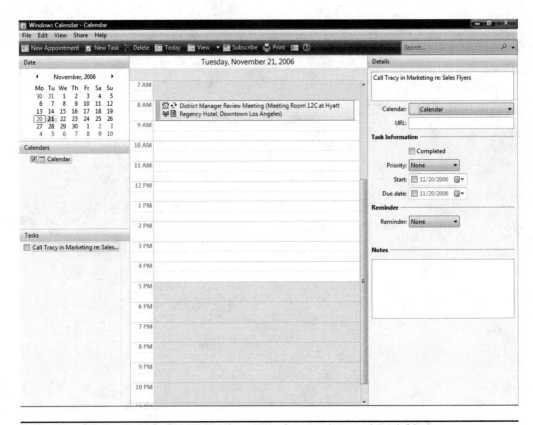

Figure 7-6   Create new tasks to help you keep track of your projects and "to-do" items.

- **Start**   Enables you to specify the starting date of your task. This is handy if you have a task that must be measured in terms of days to complete or a similar matrix.

- **Due Date**   Enables you to specify when a task is due to be completed. If you have reminders set up for tasks, the reminder will display based on the Due Date you specify.

- **Reminder**   Enables you to set Windows Calendar to alert you when a task is due. You can set either None or On Date.

- **Notes**   Provides an area to type additional information about the task. This is a good place to add supporting documentation, helpful tips on completing the task, phone numbers, and so on.

To specify that a task is completed, click inside the task's check box. Also, if you need to delete a task, click it and press DELETE. Again, Windows Calendar does not ask if you are sure you want to delete a task. It just deletes it and you cannot undelete it.

Printing a Calendar

An electronic calendar is very handy when you have access to your computer. But even if you are going to be away from your computer, you can print a copy of your calendar and carry it with you. When you print a calendar, you have a few choices in the layout of it. You can choose from the following layouts:

- Day
- Work Week
- Week
- Month

Choose File | Print to open the Print dialog box (see Figure 7-7). Select which of the preceding layouts you want to use from the Print Style area. In the Print Range area, select the range of dates you want to print. For example, if you select Day as the Print Style, Windows Calendar defaults so only one day—the current day—prints. To change this to multiple days, change the End date parameter to the last day you want to print. Windows Calendar prints all the days' calendar information that falls between the Start and End Print Range dates.

When you are ready, click OK. Windows Calendar prints your calendar.

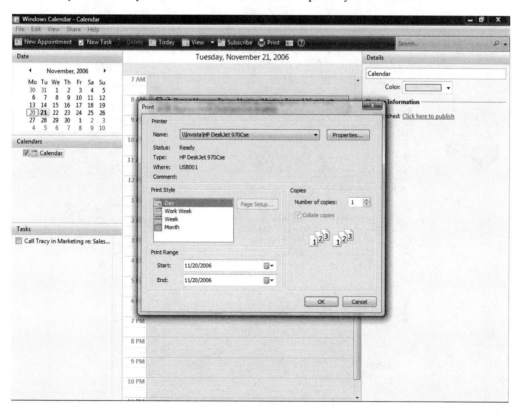

FIGURE 7-7   Printing a hard copy of your calendar is handy for those times you're away from the computer.

Sharing Calendars in Windows Calendar

Windows Calendar enables you to share calendars with other people by publishing your calendar to an Internet site or shared network site. Once you publish the calendar, Windows Calendar can keep your calendar information updated as you change the calendar. Furthermore, other users can subscribe to your calendar, download it to their computer, and import it into their Windows Calendar program. In fact, other calendar programs that use the Internet Calendar format (ICS) can also import your calendar. You also can subscribe to other users' calendars, download them, and import them as additional calendars within Windows Calendar.

Publishing a Calendar

To publish a calendar, you must have a site to publish to. For example, some web sites allow users to post their calendars and share with others. In a company setting, your network administrator may have set up a shared folder in which calendars can be stored for sharing. In either case, you need to know the full path name for the shared site so you can fill out the Publish Calendar window.

To publish a calendar, follow these steps:

1. Choose Share | Publish. The Publish Calendar dialog box appears (see Figure 7-8).

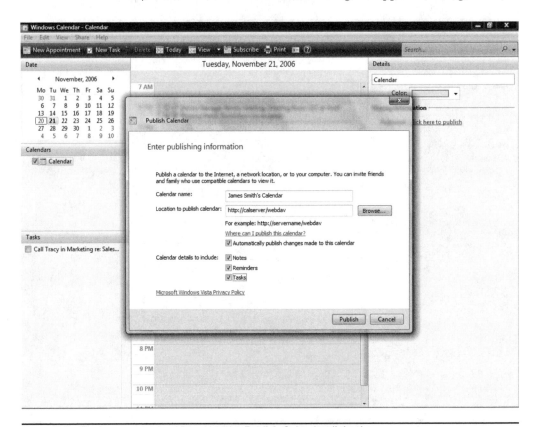

FIGURE 7-8   To share your calendar, set up the Publish Calendar dialog box.

2. Type a name in the Calendar Name box. This helps identify your calendar when others import it into their calendar program.

3. Enter the path to the location where you will publish the calendar. If the location is on a local area network (LAN), you can click the Browse button to find it. Otherwise, you must enter the full path to a web address that supports published calendars.

4. Specify if you want Windows Calendar to publish changes to the calendar. If you do this, then those who subscribe to your calendar will be able to stay current with your calendar as you modify it.

5. Select the details of your calendar that you want published. You can include Notes, Reminders, and Tasks.

6. Click Publish. Windows Calendar publishes your calendar and displays the window shown in Figure 7-9.

7. If you want to send an e-mail out to announce that your calendar is published, click Announce. (If you do not want to send out an announcement, click Finish.) That launches a new mail message with the address of the calendar showing in the message body area. You can address the message to recipients and click Send. Click Finish.

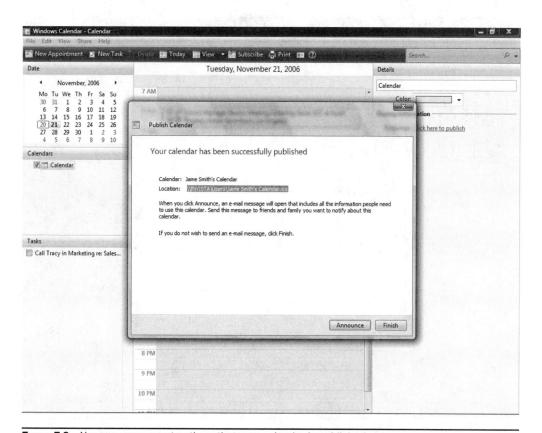

FIGURE 7-9   You can announce to others that your calendar is published.

If you want to stop publishing your calendar and remove your previously published one on the calendar-sharing server, you must unpublish your calendar. To do this, choose Share | Stop Publishing. A message appears asking if you are sure you want to stop publishing your calendar. To remove the calendar that you have published to the server, make sure the Delete Calendar On Server option is selected. Click Unpublish.

Subscribing to Calendars

To import another user's calendar, you must subscribe to it. Choose Share | Subscribe from the Windows Calendar menu bar. This opens the Subscribe To A Calendar dialog box, as shown in Figure 7-10. Type the full path to the calendar, including the name of the calendar followed by **.ics**. An example is http://sharedcalendars/calendar.ics. If the shared calendar is on a LAN drive, you would use the format //networkdrive/calendar.ics.

Click Next. The Calendar Subscription Settings dialog box appears. You can set update intervals, such as Every 15 Minutes, Every Hour, Every Day, or Every Week. Select if you want to include reminders and tasks, and then click Finish. Windows Calendar imports the calendar and displays it as an additional calendar in the Calendars list in the Navigation

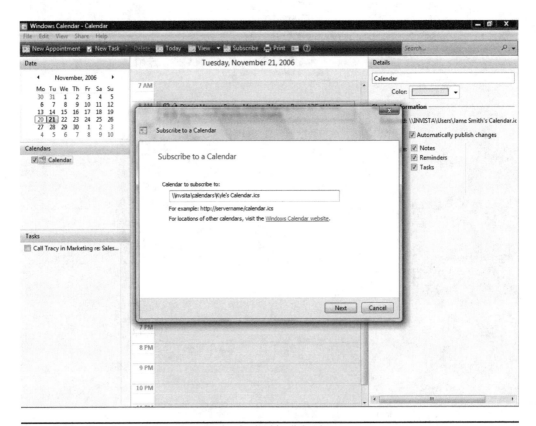

FIGURE 7-10   Type the path to a shared calendar in this dialog box.

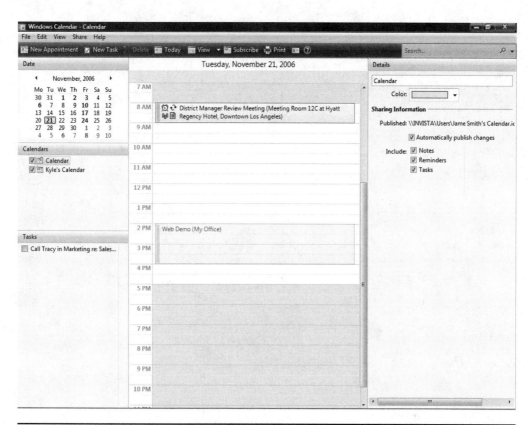

FIGURE 7-11   A subscribed-to calendar appears in your Calendars list in the Navigation Pane.

Pane (see Figure 7-11). Appointments from calendars you import will show up as a lighter shade (and different color if that user specified a different calendar color) on your calendar.

NOTE   *If you receive an e-mail from another user announcing a calendar that is being published, click the link in the e-mail message to subscribe to that calendar.*

Click the subscribed-to calendar in the Navigation Pane to view appointments from that calendar in a darker shade. You can also use the Color drop-down list in the Details pane to change the color of that calendar. Now you can easily discern which appointment is from your master calendar and which is from a different calendar.

Managing Your Disk

Using Files and Folders

Computers are tools for working with information—creating it, accessing it, and rearranging it. Windows stores information in files and organizes those files into folders. Everything you do with your computer involves files and folders.

This chapter describes the basic file-and-folder skills you need to operate your computer. The next chapter discusses the longer-term issues involved in managing your files efficiently. This chapter explains the anatomy of the Explorer windows in which you manipulate files and folders, and their toolbars. It tells how to use Windows Explorer to create, select, name, open, move, copy, and delete files and folders. You also learn the easiest ways to undo or recover from common mistakes, as well as how to burn your own CDs.

This chapter assumes you are working with the default settings of Windows Explorer— the way Windows Explorer works before you change anything. The next chapter covers how to adjust Windows Explorer to suit your tastes and habits.

What Are Files and Folders?

Files and folders are two of the most fundamental concepts of the Windows operating system. No matter what you use your computer for, you create and organize files and folders as soon as you decide to save your work. If you have worked with any other operating system, you are probably already acquainted with the concept of a file. You probably are familiar with folders as well, though you may know them as *directories*. If you aren't already familiar with files and folders, spending a small amount of time learning their properties will serve you well.

What Is a File?

A *file* is any collection of related information that is given a name and stored so it can be retrieved when needed. A file may contain any kind of information: a program or application (Movie Maker, for example, is in a file called MovieMk.exe); a document; a part of a document, such as a table or an illustration; a sound or piece of music; a segment of video; or any number of other things.

Many files are part of the Windows system itself. Windows uses files to store the information it needs to function, such as information regarding the appearance of your desktop, the kind of monitor or printer you use, the various dialog boxes and error messages, or how to display different fonts. Similarly, the applications on your computer typically have a number of auxiliary files in addition to the file containing the main program. Some of these files, for example, contain the choices you make about the program's optional settings. When you change these settings, you are not altering the program itself; you are editing some of its auxiliary files.

What Is a Folder?

Because of all the files associated with Windows and the various applications on your computer, your hard drive contains thousands of files before you begin creating files of your own. If your computer is part of a network, you may have access to millions of files. The Internet has billions of files. You would have no hope of keeping track of all those files if they weren't organized in some efficient way. In Windows (as in most other major operating systems), the fundamental device for organizing files is the folder.

Technically, a *folder* is just a special kind of file—one that contains a list of other files. The files on the list are said to be *in* the folder, and each file is allowed to be in only one folder. A folder can be either open or closed. When a folder is closed, all you see is its name and the folder icon, as shown here:

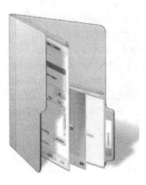

Windows comes with several folders that Microsoft suggests that you use for your files—Contacts, Documents, Music, Videos, Pictures, to name a few. Another icon, Computer, looks like a folder, and contains all the disks accessible from your computer. These customized folders have unique icons:

Contacts   Desktop   Documents   Downloads   Favorites   Links   Music   Pictures   Saved Games   Searches   Videos

When a folder is open in Windows Explorer, it has its own window, and the files contained in the folder are displayed in the window (see "What Is Windows Explorer?" later in the chapter).

The terms "file" and "folder" were chosen to remind you of a more familiar information retrieval system—the filing cabinet. Like the folders in a filing cabinet, the Windows folders are named objects that contain other objects. For example, a Windows folder named Budget might contain four spreadsheet files for First quarter, Second quarter, Third quarter, and Fourth quarter.

What Is the Folder Tree?

The organizational power of the folder system comes from the fact that it is *hierarchical*, which means folders can contain other folders. This feature enables you to organize and keep track of a great many folders, without straining your memory or attention.

If Folder A is inside Folder B, Folder A is a *subfolder* of B. Any folder can contain as many subfolders as you want to put there, but each folder (like each file) is contained in only one folder. In the same way, a mother may have many daughters, but each daughter has only one mother. And so, a diagram showing which folders are contained in which other folders looks something like a family tree. This diagram is called the *folder tree*, or sometimes the *folder hierarchy*. Windows Help calls it the *folder list*.

Figure 8-1 shows the top levels of the folder tree as they appear in the Folders Explorer bar. At the top of the folder tree (the founder of the Folder family, so to speak) is Desktop. Immediately under Desktop are Computer, Recycle Bin, Control Panel, Network, and whatever files and folders you might have copied to the desktop. The manufacturer of your computer may also have put some files or folders on your desktop.

NOTE *The Computer icon may not appear on your desktop. But Computer still shows up directly under Desktop in the folder tree.*

Underneath Computer are icons representing all of your system's storage media: hard drives, floppy drive, DVD drive, CD-RW drive, and so on. (Your system configuration may differ somewhat from that pictured in Figure 8-1.) Also under Computer is Control Panel, the window you use for configuring your computer.

What Are Filenames?

To store a file and retrieve it later, Windows has to give it a *filename*. Often you are asked to invent a name for a file. Good filenames are evocative without being too cumbersome. They also have to conform to some rules. Fortunately, the file-naming rules were liberalized when Windows 95 came out, and Windows Vista retains these liberalized rules. You can change a filename using Windows Explorer, as well as in the Open and Save As dialog boxes of many applications.

FIGURE 8-1   The upper levels of the folder tree.

What Filenames Are Legal?

In DOS and Windows systems prior to Windows 95, filenames could be only eight characters long, followed by a three-character extension that told the file's type—Filename.txt, for example. Inventing coherent, easily remembered filenames was an art similar to composing good vanity license plates. Even so, one frequently had to stare at files like Jnsdecr.doc for some time before remembering it was John's December report.

Fortunately, Windows 95 changed all that by introducing long filenames, and Windows Vista retains that advance. File and folder names can be up to 215 characters long, and can include spaces. So Jnsdecr.doc can become John's December Report.doc.

Folders, likewise, can have names up to 215 characters long. These names are automatically of type "folder" and have no extension.

In addition to periods and spaces, some characters that were illegal for file and folder names prior to Windows 95 are now legal, including

    + , ; = [ ]

Still, there are some characters you can't use in filenames, including

    \ / : * ? " < > |

and any character you make by using the CTRL key.

What Are Extensions and File Types?

Filenames are still followed by a period and an *extension*, which is usually three letters long. The extension denotes the *file type* and, among other things, tells Windows which program to use to open the file and which icon to use to represent the file. Windows handles most file-type issues invisibly. Files you create with a particular program are typically given a type associated with that program (unless you specify otherwise), and the appropriate extension is added to the name automatically. For example, web pages usually have the extension .htm or .html, and text files usually have the extension .txt.

You can do many things in Windows without paying any attention to file types; therefore, Windows doesn't even show you the extensions unless you ask to see them. We recommend you configure Windows to display extensions for two reasons: to help you know the complete names of your files and to help you determine the types of files you receive from others. To see the extensions:

1. Choose Start | Control Panel. You see the Control Panel window.

2. Select the Appearance And Personalization category, and then click the Folder Options icon. The Folder Options dialog box appears.

3. Click the View tab. The Advanced Settings box contains a long list of options.

4. Click the check box next to Hide Extensions For Known File Types. If the box is checked, the extensions are hidden; if it's not checked, the extensions are shown.

5. Click OK to make the Folder Options dialog box go away, and close the Control Panel.

When you install a program, the installation program usually tells Windows the file types the program handles (see "What Happens During Program Installation?" in Chapter 3).

What Are Addresses?

An *address* is information that tells you (and Windows) how to find something. The four kinds of addresses are:

- **File addresses**   Tell you how to find files on your computer. A typical file address looks something like C:\Windows\Explorer.exe.

- **UNC (Universal Naming Convention) addresses**   Used when referring to files on some local area networks (LANs). UNC addresses are in the format *computername*\ *drive**pathname*, where *computername* is the computer's name on the LAN, *drive* is the disk drive on that computer, and *pathname* is the file address on that drive. For example, if you needed to open a file called Budget03.xls in the C:\ Documents folder on a computer named DebB, you'd open \\DebB\C\ Documents\Budget03.xls.

- **Internet addresses**   More properly called *URLs*, specify how to find things on the Web (see "What Is a URL?" in Chapter 26). The URL of Microsoft's home page, for example, is www.microsoft.com.

- **E-mail addresses**   Tell you how to find the e-mail boxes of the people to whom you want to write.

The Address box in Windows Explorer handles every kind of address except e-mail addresses. Typing a file address into the Address box opens the corresponding file or folder on your computer, typing a UNC address opens the corresponding file or folder on your LAN (if your computer and the computer that has the file or folder are logged into the LAN and you have permission to open it), and typing a URL opens the corresponding web page on the Internet (if your computer is online).

NOTE *E-mail addresses are still handled differently from the other kinds of addresses. You can send e-mail by typing **mailto:** followed (with no space) by an e-mail address into the Address box (see Chapter 25).*

File addresses, also called *paths* or *pathnames*, work in the following way. Files and folders are stored on disks. Each disk drive has a drive letter that is its address (see "What Are Drive Letters?" in Chapter 34). Drives A: and B: typically are reserved for floppy drives, and C: denotes your computer's main hard drive. Subsequent letters are used for other hard drives, DVD drives, CD-RW drives, CD-ROM drives, flash drives, removable drives, drives on other computers on your LAN (if any), and other devices. In file addresses, drive letters are always followed by a colon (:).

Each file or folder address begins with the letter of the drive on which the file or folder is stored. The *root folder*—the main or top-level folder on the disk—is designated by a backslash immediately after the drive letter and colon. (So C:\ is the root folder of drive C:.) The rest of the address consists of the names of the folders on the folder tree between the given file or folder and the drive that contains it. The folder names are separated by backslashes (\).

For example, the address C:\Windows\Temp refers to a folder named Temp, inside the folder named Windows, which is stored on the C: drive. If the file Junk.doc is contained in Temp, Junk.doc's address is C:\Windows\Temp\Junk.doc.

> **NOTE** *Both file address and UNC addresses use backslashes (\) to separate the pieces of the address. But URLs (for historical reasons) use slashes (/) for the same purpose.*

What Is Windows Explorer?

Windows Explorer is a versatile tool for viewing and manipulating files and folders. It appears whenever you open Computer or any other folder on your desktop, and you can also run it by choosing Start | All Programs | Accessories | Windows Explorer. The program has many features that you can display or hide, and several different views of the features it displays.

Windows Explorer is a twin of Internet Explorer, which is the Windows built-in web browser (see "What Is Internet Explorer?" in Chapter 26). Running either program opens an *Explorer window.* The Explorer window is extremely versatile and has many parts, which you may or may not decide to display. When all parts of the Explorer window are made visible, it looks like Figure 8-2.

The major parts of the Explorer window are described in Table 8-1.

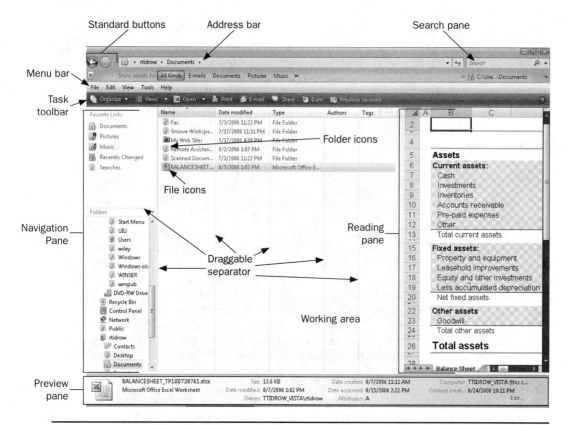

FIGURE 8-2   Anatomy of Windows Explorer window. You can choose to display as many or as few of these components as you like.

Item	Description
Standard buttons	The two leftmost toolbar buttons are navigation buttons: Back and Forward. They behave like the corresponding web browser buttons. The Back button takes the window back to the previous folder it displayed, and the Forward button undoes Back. The Forward button has an arrow attached to it; clicking the arrow produces a drop-down list of locations to which you can directly go. To the right of the Address bar is the Refresh button. Click it to refresh the view of the open folder.
Address bar	The Address bar displays the name of the open folder. When you click the arrow at the right end of the Address box, a diagram appears. It displays the top levels of the folder tree, and allows "long-range navigation" by clicking any top-level item you want to open.
Search pane	The search pane helps you find files or folders on your computer system, web pages on the Internet, or people in a directory (see "Searching for Files and Folders" in Chapter 9).
Menu bar	You issue commands to Windows Explorer by clicking toolbar buttons. By default, Vista does not show the menu bar. To turn it on for your current session, press ALT. To keep it on, choose Organize I Layout I Classic Menus.
Task toolbar	This toolbar displays common tasks you can perform on the selected drive, folder, or file, and changes depending on the type of tasks you can perform on the item you have selected. For instance, when you select a file, an icon for the associated program appears, enabling you to click the icon to open the file.
Draggable separator	The various separators provide separation between panes, columns of data, and other Explorer items. To resize a pane, you can grab a separator with the mouse and move it.
Navigation Pane	Displays a hierarchical view of the desktop, computer, drives, and other items. To view the contents of these items, double-click them. Subfolders and files appear in the working area.
Working area	This area displays icons corresponding to all the drives, files, and folders contained in the open folder. In this area, you can open folders, subfolders, and specific files.
File icons	File icons represent individual files on your computer or network device.
Folder icons	Folder icons represent individual folders and subfolders on your computer or network device.
Reading pane	The Reading pane displays a view of the currently selected document or graphic file. This gives you an idea of the file's content without opening its associated program. You can navigate the document (such as move around in an Excel worksheet), but you cannot edit the file here.
Preview pane	The Preview pane displays file information about the objects you select. When a file is selected, for example, the Preview pane shows the file's type and size. When a drive is selected, it displays the file system type (such as NTFS), free space, and capacity of the drive. When a folder is open and no object is selected, it tells you the number of objects in the folder and how many of them are hidden.

TABLE 8-1   Main Features of the Windows Explorer Window

PART II

Working with Windows Explorer

When you open the Computer icon on the desktop, Windows Explorer opens an Explorer window, as shown in Figure 8-2. Any folder you open from the desktop creates a new Explorer window. You can also run Windows Explorer by choosing Start | All Programs | Accessories | Windows Explorer. Alternatively, you can put a shortcut to Windows Explorer somewhere more convenient, such as on the desktop, on the Quick Launch toolbar, or at the top of the Start menu.

Every aspect of the Explorer window has numerous optional configurations, which are covered in the next chapter. This chapter describes how to do basic file and folder operations under the default configuration. If your computer works differently, someone has probably changed Windows Explorer's settings. If you want, you can change them back as follows:

1. Start Windows Explorer either by opening a folder on the desktop or by selecting Start | All Programs | Accessories | Windows Explorer. An Explorer window opens.

2. If the menu bar is showing, select Tools | Folder Options. Otherwise, press ALT first and then choose Tools | Folder Options. The Folder Options dialog box appears with the General tab displayed.

3. Click the Restore Defaults button in the Folder Options dialog box.

4. Click OK.

Navigating the Folder Tree

Windows Explorer enables you to view the contents of any folder on your system. The process of changing your view from one folder to another is referred to as *navigating*. The Explorer window provides you with navigation tools you can use to go up or down in the folder tree and back or forth along the path you have taken. In addition, you can jump to any folder near the top of the folder tree by clicking its icon on the list that drops down from the Address box on the toolbar. Or you can click an item in the Address box to jump back to that folder or drive.

If you like to use the keyboard, you can use UP ARROW and DOWN ARROW to move up and down a column of folders, or use LEFT ARROW and RIGHT ARROW to move back and forth in a row. You can select a folder by typing the first letter of its name.

Viewing the Folder Tree with the Navigation Pane

The Navigation Pane, shown in Figure 8-3, is a map of the folder tree. You can expand or contract this map to whatever level of detail you find most convenient. (Naturally, your folder tree will not have exactly the same folders as shown in Figure 8-3.)

The folder tree is displayed outline-style in the Navigation Pane. At the top of the tree, displayed flush with the left edge of the window, is the Desktop icon. Below Desktop, and indented slightly to the right, are the folders contained in the desktop: Computer, Recycle Bin, Control Panel, Network, Public, and the user folder (named rtidrow in this example).

A folder that contains other folders has a small arrow next to it. A clear arrow pointing to the right indicates that the folder has subfolders, but that they are not shown. A black arrow pointing down and to the right indicates that the folder's subfolders are listed below and slightly to the right of the folder. In Figure 8-3, the user folder contains several subfolders, such as Contacts, Desktop, Documents, and so forth. These folders include subfolders that are not shown.

FIGURE 8-3   The folder-tree map, as shown in the Navigation Pane.

If the subfolders of a folder are not shown, you can display them (in other words, expand or open the folder) by clicking the arrow next to the folder's name. Clicking the black arrow next to a folder's name removes its subfolders from the list (contracts or closes it, in other words). Any portion of the folder tree can be expanded as much or as little as you like.

The arrows enable you to look at the overall structure of your files without losing sight of the folder whose contents are displayed in the working area. Opening a new folder in the working area automatically expands the folder tree in the Navigation Pane to show you the new folder. If you use the arrows in the Navigation Pane to contract a folder that contains the currently open folder, that folder is closed and the working area changes to display the contents of the folder you just contracted.

Navigating by Using the Address Box
The Address box displays the name of the folder whose contents appear in the working area. An abbreviated folder-tree diagram drops down from the Address box. It shows only the top layers of the folder tree, together with the folders between the open folder and the drive that contains it. You can use this area to jump to a new location in the folder tree by clicking any of the location icons shown. New in Vista are drop-down menus that display when you click the arrow next to an Address box item. This shows subfolders within the selected folder, such as those shown in Figure 8-4.

Going Up and Down the Folder Tree
Under the default settings, the Up button on the toolbar (or the equivalent View | Go To | Up One Level command on the menu bar) "moves" the window up one level of indentation in the folder tree. The window then shows the contents of the folder containing the previously viewed folder. For example, if a window displays the contents of the C:\Windows folder and you then click the Up button, a window displays the contents of the C: drive. Click Up again,

FIGURE 8-4   Vista's new Address bar includes context menus to help you choose where you want to navigate.

and you see the contents of Computer. Wherever you begin, if you click Up enough times, you reach the desktop.

To move the window one step down the folder tree, open a subfolder of the currently open folder.

Going Back and Forth on the Folder Tree

Under the default settings, the Forward and Back buttons on the toolbar (or the equivalent commands View | Go To | Forward and View | Go To | Back) move the window back and forth among the previously displayed folders. The Back button returns to the previously open folder. Clicking the Back button again returns to the folder before that, and so on. The Forward button undoes the Back button: clicking Back and then clicking Forward leaves you where you started. Until you have clicked Back, there is no place to go forward to, so the Forward button is gray, indicating that nothing will happen if you click it. Similarly, once you have returned to the first folder you opened, the Back button turns gray.

Lists of folders to which you can go back or forward drop down when you click the arrow next to the Back or Forward button, respectively. Jump to any folder on the list by clicking its name.

Jumping to Somewhere Else Entirely

The arrow at the right end of the Address box pulls down a list of recently visited or viewed folders, web pages, drives, and other items. You can jump to one of these items by clicking it on this drop-down list.

Another way to quickly navigate to a common location within Explorer is to type the location name in the Address bar and then press ENTER. You can type the following locations in:

- Recycle Bin
- Games
- Documents
- Computer
- Contacts
- Pictures
- Music
- Videos
- Control Panel
- Favorites

> **Where Is the Desktop Really?**
>
> The Windows interface makes the desktop look as if it contains all hard disks, floppies, DVDs, CD-ROMs, and other storage devices. But the desktop is only a virtual object, not a piece of hardware; so where is the Desktop folder stored?
>
> Each user has his or her own Desktop folder. The shortcuts, files, and folders you move to the desktop are actually stored in the folder C:\Users*your user name*\Desktop (assuming that Windows Vista is installed on C:).

What Is the Recycle Bin?

Files and folders deleted from your hard drives don't go away completely, at least not right away—they remain inside the *Recycle Bin*. From there, they can either be restored to the folder they were in before you deleted them or moved from the Recycle Bin to any other folder via cut-and-paste or drag-and-drop.

The Recycle Bin icon lives on the desktop and looks like a wastebasket. When you open the icon, Windows Explorer shows you the files and folders that were deleted since the Recycle Bin was last emptied.

Recycle Bin

The Recycle Bin is a hybrid object that behaves like a folder in some ways, but not in others. Like a folder, it contains objects, and you can move objects into and out of the Recycle Bin, just as you do with any other folder. Unlike a folder, even an unusual folder like the Desktop folder, the Recycle Bin is not contained on a single drive. Instead, each of your computer's hard drives (or partitions of hard drives, if your drive is partitioned) maintains its own Recycle Bin.

Folders that have been sent to the Recycle Bin aren't considered part of the folder tree: they don't appear in the Navigation Pane, and they can't be opened. If you want to examine the contents of a folder in the Recycle Bin, you first must move the folder out of the Recycle Bin to a different location. Likewise, files in the Recycle Bin cannot be opened, edited, or worked on otherwise.

The intention of the designers is clear: the Recycle Bin is not to be used as a workspace. Instead, it is a last-chance repository. You can put things in the Recycle Bin or take things out—that's all.

Working with the Recycle Bin under the default settings is covered in "Retrieving Files and Folders from the Recycle Bin" later in this chapter. Reconfiguring the Recycle Bin settings is covered in the next chapter (see "Managing the Recycle Bin" in Chapter 9).

Making and Working with Files and Folders

The basic file and folder operations—creating, selecting, naming, and opening—are relatively unchanged from earlier versions of Windows.

Creating Files and Folders

New folders and files of certain types can be created on the desktop or in Windows Explorer. On the desktop, right-click any empty area and choose New on the shortcut menu. In Windows Explorer, click the folder in which you want to create the new object and then choose File | New (or right-click any empty spot in the working area and choose New on the shortcut menu). All of these actions produce a submenu that lists the new objects you can create: folders, shortcuts, and a variety of types of files. Select an element of this list, and Windows creates the appropriate object. You can also create shortcuts by using this method (see Chapter 9).

You can create files of types other than the types listed from within application programs.

Selecting Files and Folders

Files and folders are represented on the desktop and in Windows Explorer by icons, with the name of the file or folder printed underneath or beside its icon. A *file icon* is a rectangle that looks like a piece of paper. The rectangle bears the design of the default program that opens the file. An Excel file icon, for example, looks like this:

BALANCESHEET_T
P100738761.xlsx

A *folder icon* looks like a manila folder. A compressed folder icon looks like a folder icon with a zipper on it.

Under the default settings, you select a file or folder by clicking its icon, and you open it by double-clicking. If you don't like all this clicking (or you're afraid of getting repetitive stress syndrome), you can adjust Windows Explorer so that resting the cursor on an icon selects the corresponding object, and single-clicking opens the object (see "Replacing Double-Clicks with Single-Clicks" in Chapter 9).

To select more than one object, select the first object and then press CTRL while you select others. (If you don't press CTRL, selecting one object deselects all the others.)

If the objects you want to select are close together, move the cursor to an empty spot nearby, hold down the left mouse button, and drag the cursor. A rectangle forms, and any object inside the rectangle is selected. When you release the mouse button, the rectangle disappears, but the objects it contained continue to be selected. You can get the same effect by using SHIFT instead of dragging the mouse: Select an object, and then hold down SHIFT and select another object. All objects in an imaginary rectangle containing the two selected objects are also selected.

More complicated patterns of objects can be selected by combining the two methods:

1. Drag out a rectangle that contains most of the objects you want to select (and perhaps some others). That is, click in one corner of an imaginary rectangle, hold down the mouse button, and drag the mouse pointer to the opposite corner of the rectangle.

2. Release the mouse button and press CTRL.

3. While pressing CTRL, deselect unwanted objects (if any) by clicking them.

4. Keep pressing CTRL, and select any additional objects you want by clicking them.

To select all the items in a folder, open the folder and choose Edit | Select All from the Explorer window's menu bar or press CTRL-A. To select all but a few objects in a folder, choose Select All and then hold down CTRL while you deselect those few objects.

You can also use the keyboard to select multiple files. To select consecutive files in a single list or column, select the first file and then hold down SHIFT while pressing the DOWN ARROW key until you reach the last file. To select all the files in a rectangular grid, select the file in one corner of the rectangle and then hold down SHIFT while pressing the UP or DOWN ARROW key until you reach the opposite corner.

To select files that aren't listed together, select one file, hold down CTRL, press the UP or DOWN ARROW key to move to the next file you want to select, and press SPACEBAR to select it. Continue holding down CTRL, moving, and pressing SPACEBAR until you select all the files you want.

TIP *If you want to select most of the files in a folder, select all the items you* don't *want to include. Then choose Edit | Invert Selection to deselect the selected items and to select the deselected ones.*

Naming and Renaming Files and Folders

Newly created folders and files are given default names, such as New Folder and New Microsoft Word Document. To rename a file or folder, click its icon and choose File | Rename from the menu bar (press ALT if the menu bar is not displayed), right-click the icon and choose Rename from the shortcut menu, or press F2. A box appears around the current name, and the entire name is selected. Type the new name in the box and press ENTER.

You can also rename by selecting an object and then clicking the name next to the icon. Again, a box appears around the current name and you proceed as before. Be sure to pause slightly between selecting the object and selecting its name—otherwise, you open the object.

If the new name is only a minor change from the old one, edit the old name instead of typing the new one. Click inside the name box at the place where you want to begin typing or deleting.

Changing a File's Extension

Changing a file's extension changes its file type. Don't do this unless you know what you're doing. If you assign the file a type that Windows doesn't recognize, it won't know how to open the file. If you assign the file a type Windows does recognize, whenever you open the file, Windows uses the application associated with that file type. Unless you prepare the file in such a way that is appropriate for that application, the opening fails. (Consider, for example, the Paint program trying to open an audio file—it doesn't work.)

Before you rename a file, check whether Windows Explorer is displaying the file extensions (see "What Are Extensions and File Types?" earlier in the chapter). Just look at some files and see whether their names end with a period and three or four letters. If file extensions are hidden, you can't change them when you rename a file. If they are displayed, you can change them. When you rename a file whose extension is displayed, you must include the extension in your renaming or else the file type is lost. Conversely, if you type in a file extension when the extension is hidden, you wind up with a double extension, like Report.doc.doc. (It's perfectly legal to name a file Report.doc.doc, but you could confuse yourself.)

NOTE *Windows* always *displays file extensions that it doesn't recognize. You can tell that Windows doesn't recognize a file's extension if the file has a generic icon like this:*

file.abc

If you change a file's extension (and thus its file type), Windows gives you a warning that the file may become unusable and asks you to confirm your decision. This feature, although annoying, may save you from making an occasional mistake.

Opening Files and Folders

You can open a folder by double-clicking its icon. The folder contents are displayed in an Explorer window.

Double-clicking a file icon opens the file using the default application for that file type. You can open a file in some other compatible application by right-clicking the file icon and selecting an application from the Open With menu, by dragging-and-dropping the icon onto an application's icon, or by using the File | Open command from the application's menu.

You can change the settings of Windows Explorer so that only a single-click is required to open a file or folder (see "Replacing Double-Clicks with Single-Clicks" in Chapter 9).

Opening a File with the Default Application

If a file has a file type that Windows recognizes, double-clicking the file icon in an Explorer window opens the file with the application associated with that file type.

If you open a file in an Explorer window and Windows doesn't recognize its file type, or if that file type has no associated application, a message box appears letting you know Windows cannot open the file. You can use the web service to let Windows automatically locate a program to open the file type or you can manually select a program to use.

Some file types may have more than one application associated with them (see "Associating a Program with a File Extension" in Chapter 3). To check, right-click the file icon and see if a command like Edit appears under Open in the shortcut menu. For example, in the default configuration, image files open with Image Preview but are edited with Paint.

With Vista, you also can choose the down arrow of the Open button on the Explorer window. Then select Choose Default Program, which displays the Open With dialog box. Figure 8-5 shows the Open button's Choose Default Program command.

FIGURE 8-5   Use Vista's new Open button to display options for selecting the application to launch a file.

Opening a File from the Open With Menu

At times, you might want to open a file with an application other than the one associated with its file type. For example, Windows by default associates HTML files (with extension .htm or .html) with Internet Explorer; but, if you want to open an HTML file with Mozilla Firefox instead, you can right-click the file's icon in an Explorer window (or on the desktop) and select an application from the Open With menu. The Open With menu lists the applications that Windows knows can open the selected type of file. Initially, these are probably only Microsoft applications like WordPad or Paint. But if you don't see the application you want, select Browse to see an Open With dialog box and a larger list of applications.

When you have found and selected the application you want to use to open the file, click the Open button in the Browse window. You return to the Open With dialog box, and the application you found is now listed and selected. If you want this application to become the new default application for this file type, check the Always Use The Selected Program To Open This Kind Of File check box. Whether you have checked this box or not, click OK to make the Open With dialog box disappear and open the file.

This may seem like an arduous process just to open a file, but fortunately you only have to do it once. Now that you have used the Open With menu to open a file of this type with this application, the application should appear on the Open With menu for any file of this type. In addition, the application appears in the Open With dialog box for files of any type.

Opening a File by Dragging-and-Dropping

If both the file icon and the application icon (or shortcuts to either) are visible on your screen, drag-and-drop the file icon onto the application icon. If you do this frequently with a particular application, create a shortcut to the application on the desktop (see "Making Shortcuts" in Chapter 9).

Opening a File from Within an Application

If an application is open, choose File | Open from its menu bar. The Open window appears and enables you to indicate which file to open.

Rearranging Files and Folders

The quest for the perfect system of file organization is endless—you frequently need to move or copy files and folders to somewhere other than where they were originally created. You can rearrange your files and folders by using the following:

- Options on the Organize menu
- Commands from the menus
- Drag-and-drop techniques

Moving and Copying with Two Explorer Windows

If both the source and target folders are already open in their own Explorer windows, you can move and copy files and folders easily. You can drag-and-drop objects from the source window to the target window, or you can do the following:

1. Select the objects to be moved (or copied) from the source folder's window.

2. Select Edit | Cut (or Edit | Copy). Ghostly images of the objects remain in their original places until the objects are pasted elsewhere. (An alternative method is to right-click the selection and choose Cut or Copy from the shortcut menu.)

3. Click the spot in the target folder's window where you want to place the objects.

4. Select Edit | Paste, or right-click an empty spot in the Explorer window and choose Paste from the shortcut menu.

Dragging and Dropping Files and Folders

Drag-and-drop is often the simplest way to move or copy objects from one drive or folder to another or between a folder and the desktop (see "What Is Drag-and-Drop?" in Chapter 5). You can also delete objects by dragging and dropping them onto the Recycle Bin icon. To drag-and-drop files or folders:

1. Set up window(s) so you can see both the source and the target folders (remember, the desktop itself is a kind of "window"). Our preference is to have the source folder open in the working area of an Explorer window, and the target folder visible in the Folders Explorer bar, but you can also have the source and target folders open in two separate Explorer windows.

2. Select the icons of the objects you want to move or copy.

3. While holding down the left mouse button, drag the icons to the target. (You can also drag with the right mouse button. This is discussed in the following Tip.) If the target is an open window, drag the icons to an open space in the window. If the target is a folder icon in an open window, drag until the cursor rests over the icon. The target icon changes color when you have the cursor in the right place.

4. Drop by releasing the mouse button.

Drag-and-drop has one unfortunate aspect. If you experiment, you soon notice it doesn't do the same thing in all circumstances—sometimes it moves an object, sometimes it copies it, and sometimes it makes a shortcut. The reason for this behavior is that the programmers at Microsoft have gone a bit overboard in trying to be helpful. Windows does what it guesses you intend to do, based on the file type of the objects being dragged, the locations of the source and target folders, and a few other things we haven't figured out.

Here's what happens when you drag-and-drop:

- **Objects to the same disk** If you drag objects (other than programs) from one folder and drop them in another folder on the same disk, the objects are moved. They disappear from the source folder and appear in the target folder. The rationale is that you are probably just rearranging your files. (Remember, the desktop is a folder on the C: drive. Anything else on the C: drive is considered to be on the same disk as the desktop.)

- **Objects to a different disk** If you drag objects (other than programs) from one folder and drop them in another folder on a different disk, the objects are copied. Separate copies exist in both the source and target folders. The rationale is that you are probably making a backup copy on another disk or making a copy to give to someone else.

- **Programs** If you drag a program, it may behave like any other object, but for some programs, Windows makes a shortcut in the target folder and leaves the program file where it was in the source folder. We haven't come up with a firm rule describing this, although, in general, the more complex the program, the more likely it is that dragging-and-dropping it will create a shortcut. So, for example, you'll get a shortcut if you drag-and-drop Windows Media Player, but not Calculator (you can move Calculator only if you have sufficient User Access Control rights, such as administrator rights).

Windows Vista provides information on what it's going to do with the objects you drop. When the object icons are in a droppable position, a transparent icon appears with the message Move to *Folder name*:

TIP *If you want to use drag-and-drop, but you neither want to memorize how it works nor trust Windows to guess your intentions, drag with the right mouse button rather than the left mouse button. When you drop in the target folder, select the action you intended from the shortcut menu.*

You can also control drag-and-drop behavior by using the keyboard: If you left-drag with SHIFT pressed, the objects are moved when you drop them. Left-dragging with CTRL pressed copies the objects when you drop them. You can easily remember the distinction between using SHIFT and using CTRL when left-dragging by noting that copy and CTRL both begin with C, and that when you move an object, you are "shifting" the object from one location to another.

Using the Send To Menu

Send To is a menu found on the File menu of Explorer windows and on the shortcut menu when you right-click a file or folder. The Send To menu enables you to copy files to preselected locations quickly and easily. To use Send To for this purpose:

1. Open a folder that contains files you want to copy.

2. Select the file(s) and folder(s) to copy (see "Selecting Files and Folders" earlier in the chapter).

3. Choose File | Send To from the menu bar, or right-click the item(s) you selected and choose Send To from the shortcut menu. Either way, a menu of possible destinations appears. The Windows installation program creates a default Send To menu that varies according to the resources available to your computer. Here is a sample Send To menu:

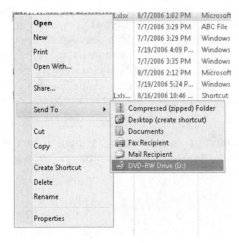

4. Choose a destination from the Send To menu. The files are copied to the destination.

Deleting Files and Folders

To delete a file, folder, or collection of files and folders in a single Explorer window:

1. Select the objects to be deleted.

2. Do any of the following actions: choose File | Delete from the menu bar, right-click the object and select Delete from the shortcut menu, or press DELETE. A dialog box appears that asks whether you really want to send the objects to the Recycle Bin (if they are deleted from your computer's hard drive) or delete the objects (if they are on a removable disk).

3. Click Yes in the dialog box.

Under the default settings, objects deleted from your computer's hard drives go to the Recycle Bin, from which they can be recovered. You can reset your preferences so that objects are deleted immediately and don't go to the Recycle Bin (see "Streamlining the Deletion Process" in Chapter 9). Objects deleted from floppy drives or other removable disks don't go to the Recycle Bin, although they may be recoverable by other means. For this reason, be especially cautious when deleting objects from floppies or other removable disks.

TIP *You can delete files or folders directly, without sending them to the Recycle Bin, if you are certain you won't change your mind. To delete a file or folder irrevocably, select it, press SHIFT-DELETE, and then click Yes when the confirmation box appears.*

Making Your Own CDs

All CD drives on computers can read CDs, but many can write CDs as well. Windows Vista includes software for burning CDs.

NOTE *To learn how to burn files to a DVD, see Chapter 21.*

What Are CD-R and CD-RW?

You can create two different kinds of CDs:

- **CD-R (compact disc-recordable) discs**   Can be written on once (they are *WORM*, or write once, read many). They can't be changed after they are written (though you can write on them many times until they are filled up). You can read CD-R discs in normal computer CD-ROM drives, as well as in audio CD players, so CD-R is the type of CD to use when creating music CDs or CDs to distribute to lots of people. Blank CD-Rs are relatively cheap (we've seen them for as little as 10 cents apiece in the United States).

- **CD-RW (compact disc-rewritable) discs**   Can be written and rewritten many times, like a floppy disk. CD-RW discs can be rewritten about 1000 times. You can use them as removable storage for sets of files that you want to update regularly (as a backup media). However, they are only readable in other CD-RW drives, and sometimes only by the same model of drive. So, for example, you might put all your documents on a CD-RW and conveniently carry them to the other side of the world, where you could read and update them on another computer with a compatible CD-RW drive.

Both types of writable CDs hold approximately the same amount of data: about 650MB for 74-minute discs and about 700MB for 80-minute discs. CD-R drives can write only CD-R discs, not CD-RW discs. CD-RW drives can write both types of discs.

CD-burning Basics

To create (or *burn*) a CD-R or CD-RW, you collect a group of files that you want to save on the CD, and then write them in one *session*. You can write multiple sessions to both CD-R and CD-RW discs, but not all CD-ROM drives will be able to read them: audio CD players usually see only the first session on a CD-R disc, and data CD-ROM drives usually see only the last session.

Previous versions of Windows required third-party software to save files on CD-Rs and CD-RWs. If you do a lot of work with CD-Rs and CD-RWs, you may still find it convenient to get software like Easy Media Creator Suite (www.roxio.com) or Nero Burning (http://ww2 .nero.com/enu/index.html). However, Windows Vista integrates CD into Windows Explorer. When you put a CD-R or CD-RW disc into your CD-R or CD-RW drive, Explorer recognizes what kind of disc it is and integrates it into the folder tree.

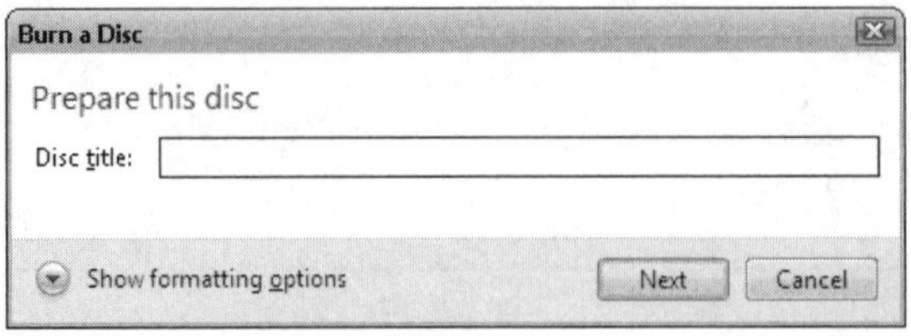

FIGURE 8-6   Give the new disc a title.

Burning CDs from Windows Explorer

Once you know what you want to store on a CD, and whether you have a CD-R or CD-RW drive, follow these steps to create a CD-R or CD-RW disc:

1. Buy some blank discs from your local computer store or mail-order or online catalog. Be sure to check whether you are getting CD-R or CD-RW discs.

2. Place the disc in the CD-R or CD-RW drive and close the drawer. Windows Vista indicates that it has detected a CD by displaying the AutoPlay window, asking you which task you want to perform: Burn A CD With Windows Media Player or Burn Files To Disc Using Windows.

3. Click Burn Files To Disc to display the Burn A Disc window (see Figure 8-6).

4. Type a title for the disc, such as a brief description of the contents.

5. Click Next to display a new blank window.

6. Drag or copy all items that you wish to store on the disc into the new disc window. Your data automatically burns to the CD.

7. Try out the CD in the type of drive in which you want it to work (audio CD player, computer CD drive, CD-R drive, or CD-RW drive).

Another way to add items to a CD is to open Windows Explorer, click the file or folder to burn, and click the Burn button on the Task toolbar. This burns the file or folder to the CD.

Fixing Your Mistakes

Even the most experienced computer user occasionally clicks the mouse and then stares at the screen in horror, asking, "What did I just do?" Fortunately, the horror needn't be lasting—Windows provides tools for recovering from many common errors.

Fixing Big Mistakes

Computers have been known to start misbehaving after you install new software, add a hardware device, or otherwise change delicate settings. Understanding exactly what has gone wrong and fixing it can be a laborious and unrewarding process, and sometimes you just don't care. You just want to put things back the way they were and forget this ever happened.

Windows Vista contains a powerful tool for addressing these situations, System Restore (see "Returning Your System to a Predefined State with System Restore" in Chapter 37). Using System Restore, you can return your computer's hardware/software configuration to the way it was on some previous date—when it presumably worked better than it does now.

Reversing Your Last Action Using the Undo Command

Windows Explorer has an Undo command that allows you to recover quickly from simple mistakes like deleting or moving the wrong file. Just press CTRL-Z or select Edit | Undo. Repeat either of these commands to step back through your recent actions.

Retrieving Files and Folders from the Recycle Bin

If you change your mind about deleting a file or folder and it's too late to use the Undo command described in the previous section, you can still retrieve it from the Recycle Bin—if it was deleted from a hard drive and you haven't emptied the Recycle Bin in the meantime.

 Emptying and configuring the Recycle Bin is discussed in the next chapter (see "Managing the Recycle Bin" in Chapter 9).

Opening the Recycle Bin

The easiest place to find the Recycle Bin is on the desktop, where its icon looks like a wastebasket. You can also find the Recycle Bin on the folder tree directly under the desktop, below your computer's disk drive and other devices.

Searching the Recycle Bin

If you know exactly what file or folder you are looking for, any view will do. But if the Recycle Bin is crowded and you need to do some real detective work to determine which objects you want to retrieve, the Details view (shown in Figure 8-7) is best. Choose View | Details. The working area becomes a list with columns showing the following:

- The name and icon of the file or folder
- The address of the folder from which the object was deleted
- The date and time the object was deleted
- The user who deleted the file or folder
- The size
- The file type
- The date and time the object was last modified

 Clicking the column header sorts the list according to that column's attribute. For example, if you know the date when you deleted the file, click the Date Deleted header to put the objects in the order in which they were deleted. All objects deleted on the same date you deleted the file appear together. If you remember the name of the file, but know you deleted several versions of it, clicking the Name header arranges the list alphabetically by name. All the versions appear next to each other, and you can easily see which is the most recent version.

Recovering Objects from the Recycle Bin

The simplest way to recover an object from the Recycle Bin is to follow these steps:

1. Open the Recycle Bin.
2. Select the object (or collection of objects) you want to recover.
3. Choose Restore This Item from the Explorer toolbar.

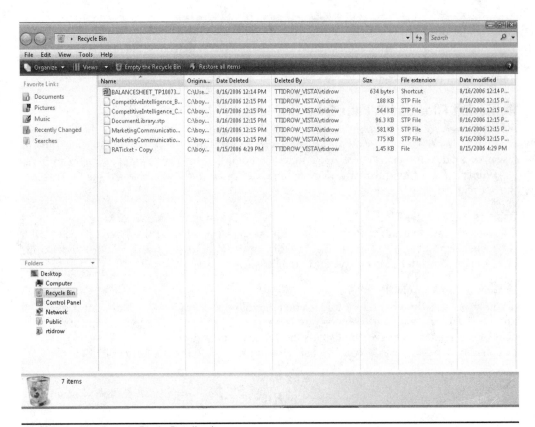

FIGURE 8-7   The Recycle Bin in Details view

You can also right-click the item you want to recover and choose Restore from the shortcut menu.

The object returns to the folder it was deleted from—the address given in the Original Location column of the Details view. If the object is a folder, all its contents return with it. You can use Restore even if the object was deleted from a folder that no longer exists. A folder of the appropriate name is then created to contain the restored object. You can restore everything in the Recycle Bin to its original location by clicking the Restore All Items option on the task pane.

To recover an object but put it in a new place, you can either cut-and-paste from the Recycle Bin to the new location or do the following:

1. Open the Recycle Bin.

2. Expand the folder tree in the Navigation Pane so the target folder icon is visible.

3. In the working area, select the object(s) you want to recover.

4. Drag-and-drop to the target folder on the Navigation Pane.

Managing Files and Folders

The previous chapter explained what you need to know to start working with files and folders: creating and deleting them, opening them, seeing what's in them, naming them, and moving them from one place to another. This chapter discusses issues that may not come up immediately as you work with files and folders, but that you should know about if you are going to have a long-term relationship with your computer.

To a beginner, having a lot of choices is more of a burden than a convenience, but as users become more familiar with their computers, they develop their own ideas about how things should work. For this reason, Windows has default settings that cause the system to work automatically in the way the designers believe is simplest for beginners. A large number of Windows' behaviors are reconfigurable, however, so more advanced users can make their own choices.

The longer you work with your computer, the more files you create. At some point, putting them all in the Documents folder, or splitting them into two folders called Work and Home, is no longer adequate. You need to come up with a system that organizes your files into smaller, coherently related piles. Discussing organizational systems goes beyond the scope of this book, but you should know about one valuable organizational tool: the shortcut. Shortcuts enable you to access the same file or application from many different points in the folder tree, without the disadvantages that come with having several copies of the same file.

You should also know about compressed folders, which save the same files in a smaller amount of disk space, at the cost of some functionality.

Even the best-organized people occasionally forget where they put something, so you need to know how to use the Search bar. You can also speed up your searches with Indexing Service.

Being able to retrieve deleted files from the Recycle Bin (described in the previous chapter) is a convenience; but, in time, the bin becomes crowded with long-forgotten files that take up disk space for no purpose. You need to know how to manage the Recycle Bin so that it continues to be useful without unduly burdening your hard drive.

Finally, files and folders have properties (see "What Are Properties?" in Chapter 1). The Properties dialog box for a file or folder contains much useful information and lets you make certain choices regarding the object's properties and attributes.

What Is a Shortcut?

Technically, a *shortcut* is a file with an .lnk extension. Less technically, a shortcut is a placeholder in your filing system. A shortcut has a definite position on the folder tree, but it points to a file or folder that is somewhere else on the folder tree.

The purpose of a shortcut is to allow an object to be, for most purposes, in two places at once. For example, you usually should leave a program file inside the folder where it was installed, so you don't mess up any of the relationships between it and its associated files. At the same time, you might want the program to be on the desktop, so that you can conveniently open files by dragging them to the program's icon. Solution: leave the program file where it is, but make a shortcut pointing to it, and place the shortcut on the desktop. When you drag a file to the shortcut icon, Windows opens the file with the corresponding program.

Maintaining multiple copies of documents on your system is both wasteful of disk space and potentially confusing—when one copy gets updated, you could easily forget to update the others. And yet, files often belong in many different places in a filing system. If, for example, Paul writes the office's fourth-quarter report, the document may belong simultaneously in the Paul's Memos folder and in the Quarterly Reports folder. Putting the document itself in Quarterly Reports and a shortcut to it in Paul's Memos solves the problem, without creating multiple copies of the document. Clicking the shortcut icon opens the associated document, just as if you had clicked the icon of the document itself.

You can recognize a shortcut icon by the curving arrow that appears in its lower-left corner. A shortcut icon otherwise looks just like the icon of the object it points to: a document, folder, or application. A shortcut can be on your desktop or in a folder. A shortcut to the Word document Revenue Data.doc looks like this:

You can create, delete, move, copy, and rename shortcuts from Explorer windows, just as you would any other kind of file (see "Working with Shortcuts" later in the chapter).

NOTE *Windows also has things called "shortcut keys" and "shortcut menus," which have nothing to do with shortcuts (see Chapter 2). Network shortcuts are shortcuts to files and folders on a LAN, and appear in the Network folder.*

What Are Properties of Files and Folders?

Like almost everything else in Windows, files and folders have *properties*—information about a file or folder you can access and, perhaps, change without opening the file or folder.

To view this information and make changes, select the file or folder in Windows Explorer, and then choose File | Properties (or right-click the file or folder and select Properties from the shortcut menu). The Properties dialog box appears, with the General tab selected (see Figure 9-1).

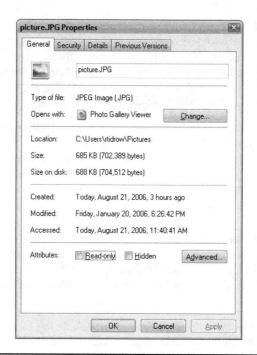

FIGURE 9-1 The properties of a file

The General tab of a file's Properties dialog box displays the following details about the file:

- Name and icon
- File type (see "What Are Extensions and File Types?" in Chapter 8)
- The default application that opens files of this type (see "Associating a Program with a File Extension" in Chapter 3)
- Location in the folder tree (see "What Is the Folder Tree?" in Chapter 8)
- Size (including both the actual size of the file and the slightly larger amount of disk space allocated to the file)
- Date and time of creation, most recent modification, and most recent access
- Attributes (see the next section)

Depending on a file's type, it may have additional tabs of properties that you can access by clicking them individually. The properties of most image files, for example, include a Summary tab where you can enter the kind of information people write on the backs of photographs: who took the picture, who the people in the picture are, and so on.

Because a folder is technically a special kind of file, the General tab of its properties contains much of the same information: icon, name, type (File Folder), location, size (the number of bytes taken up by the folder and all its contents, including the contents of subfolders), date created, and attributes. The General tab of a folder's properties has one additional item, Contains, which reports the number of files and folders contained in the folder and all its subfolders.

For some folders (such as folders that people or programs create, rather than folders that come with Windows), the Properties dialog box includes a Customize tab, which enables you to control what the folder looks like, both when it appears as an icon and when you open the folder. The Customize tab includes these settings:

- **Use This Folder Type As A Template**   This is a drop-down list of predefined folder templates (see "What Is a Folder Template?" later in the chapter). The default template is Documents. If the folder will contain pictures or music, choose one of the other options so that Windows can include Picture Tasks or Music Tasks in the task pane when you open the folder. You can click the Also Apply This Template To All Subfolders check box if the folder contains subfolders with the same types of files.

- **Folder Pictures and Folder Icons**   These two tab sections enable you to control how the folder's icon looks. If you have a picture that you would like to appear as part of the folder icon in Thumbnails view, click Choose Picture and select it. To control how the folder icon looks in other views, click the Change Icon button and choose another icon.

Some files, such as the one shown in Figure 9-1, include the Details tab. This tab includes sections of information about the file, such as Description, Origin, and detail sections. The detail sections for a photograph, for instance, list the image size, resolution, name of camera used, and other specifics.

If your computer is on a local area network, folders also have a Sharing tab, with information about whether the folder (and the files and folders it contains) are shared on the network (see "Sharing Disk Drives and Folders on a LAN" in Chapter 31).

TIP   *To find the total size of a group of files and folders, select them all, right-click anywhere in the selected filenames, and choose Properties from the shortcut menu. Windows displays the total number of files and folders, as well as their combined size. Note that you can't select multiple folders in the Folder Explorer bar—display the list of files and folders in the working area of the Explorer window.*

What Are Attributes?

The attributes of a file or folder appear at the bottom of the General tab of the Properties dialog box. For files and folders stored on NTFS partitions, click the Advanced button to see additional attributes.

The *attributes* of a file or folder include these settings, which can be selected or deselected for each file or folder:

- **Read-only**   You can read and even edit this file or folder, but when you try to save your changes, Windows reminds you that this is a read-only file and asks you to save your new version as a different file. If you try to delete a read-only file or folder, Windows reminds you that it's read-only, but deletes it if you insist.

- **Hidden**   A file or folder with this attribute doesn't usually appear in Explorer windows, but can be made visible if you want to see it (see "What Are Hidden Files and Folders?" later in the chapter).

- **Archive**   This setting may mean the file or folder has been changed since the last time it was backed up, depending on which backup program you use. Windows Vista comes with Microsoft Backup (see Chapter 10). To see this attribute on an NTFS (NT File System) partition, click the Advanced button to see the Advanced Attributes dialog box, where it appears as the File Is Ready For Archiving attribute (see "What Is a File System?" in Chapter 34).

- **Indexed**   This setting determines whether the file will be included in the Windows Indexing Service index, which is used when searching for files. You can set this attribute on for files stored in an NTFS partition.

- **Compressed**   A file or folder with this attribute is compressed to save space. Compression is available only for files or folders stored on NTFS partitions. Compressed files and folders cannot be encrypted. This type of compression is different from the compressed folders described in the next section.

- **Encrypted**   A file or folder with this attribute is encrypted (encoded) so that only the user who created the file or folder can open it later (see "Can Windows Vista Keep Files Private?" in Chapter 6). The encryption attribute is only visible (and settable) for files and folders on NTFS partitions.

What Are Compressed Folders?

Compressed folders are folders whose contents are stored in such a way as to conserve disk space. The amount of disk space you can save by storing a file in a compressed folder varies depending on the kind of file it is; a Word document of 100K, for example, might only take up 40K in a compressed folder, while an Acrobat document of 100K might still take up 80K in a compressed folder.

Windows Vista actually has two types of compressed folders: *NTFS compressed folders* and *ZIP compressed folders*. NTFS compression, which is available for both files and folders, works only on NTFS partitions, and is completely invisible in operation. You compress or uncompress an NTFS compressed folder (or file) by changing its Compress Contents To Save Disk Space attribute on the Advanced Attributes dialog box (right-click the folder or file, choose Properties from the menu that appears, click the General tab, and click the Advanced button to see this attribute). A ZIP compressed folder, unlike an ordinary folder, is actually a file—in this case, a ZIP file (with the extension .zip). All the files in this type of compressed folder are actually stored in the ZIP file. ZIP compressed folders are "virtual folders"—files that masquerade as folders in Windows Explorer. Most other programs see ZIP compressed folders as single files, though, and can't read or write the files contained in compressed folders.

The icon representing a ZIP compressed folder is a folder with a zipper on it, as shown here.

BALANCESHEET_TP100738761.xlsx - Shortcut.zip

You pay a price for compression: files in ZIP compressed folders are harder to work with. They take longer to open than an identical uncompressed file, and most applications can't open them directly. If you open a document by single- or double-clicking its filename in an Explorer window, Windows makes an uncompressed copy of the file and runs the program associated with that type of file, but the copy is opened as a read-only file. Most applications can't save files in ZIP compressed folders at all. If you want to edit the document and save your changes, you must give the file a new name and save it in an ordinary folder. You can move the file into the ZIP compressed folder later, using Windows Explorer.

Given their virtues and vices, ZIP compressed folders are best for archiving information that you don't access or change often. ZIP compressed folders are also useful for sharing information with other people; being smaller than normal folders, they take less time to transmit and occupy less disk space. (For example, large files that you download from the Internet are frequently in ZIP format.) The recipients can read the files, though, only if they have Windows Vista, Windows XP, Windows Me, or a third-party utility like WinZip. If you want ZIP files to look like folders in Explorer windows, including opening and saving directly from ZIP files (compressed folders), get ZipMagic (www.allume.com/win/zipmagic/), which combines the power of WinZip and the convenience of Windows compressed folders.

A more detailed description of the techniques for working with ZIP compressed folders is given later in this chapter (see "Working with Compressed Folders"). Windows Vista refers to both NTFS and ZIP compressed folders as compressed folders, and in the rest of this chapter, when we talk about compressed folders, we mean ZIP compressed folders.

Compressed folders can also be encrypted. You can attach a password to the folder so that no one else can open any of the files in the folder without knowing the password.

What Are Hidden Files and Folders?

Windows contains a number of files that a beginner might find confusing, and that you don't want to delete or change accidentally. As a safety feature, these files are *hidden*, which means, by default, they don't show up in Windows Explorer and can't be opened, deleted, or moved in Windows Explorer unless you choose to make them visible. For example, the folder C:\Windows\Spool keeps track of technical information regarding your printers— stuff you mostly don't want to mess with. But if you open Computer, the C: drive, and then the Windows folder, you won't find the Spool folder. If you want to see C:\Windows\System 32\Spool (and all the other hidden files and folders), follow these steps:

1. Choose Tools | Folder Options from the menu bar of any Explorer window (press ALT to display the menu bar). The Folder Options dialog box appears.

2. Click the View tab. The Hidden Files section contains two radio buttons: Do Not Show Hidden Files And Folders and Show Hidden Files And Folders.

3. Click the Show Hidden Files And Folders radio button.

4. Click OK.

When hidden files and folders are shown, their icons appear as ghostly images, like the folder shown here on the left. The folder on the right is the normal folder (unhidden).

To hide files and folders again, repeat the preceding procedure, but select the Do Not Show Hidden Files And Folders radio button in Step 3.

Hidden files and folders usually don't play a significant role in the everyday life of the average computer user. For that reason, we recommend you leave them hidden whenever you are not working with one. This policy minimizes the chances you will alter or delete something important by accident.

Nonhidden files and folders contained in a hidden folder have an in-between status: they retain their original attributes and show up in Explorer windows if you move them to a nonhidden folder, but they are hidden in practice as long as they stay inside the hidden folder, because the path that connects them to the top of the folder tree includes a hidden link.

CAUTION   *A hidden file or folder shouldn't be considered secure. The Search command not only finds hidden files and folders, but anyone who finds your file by using this command can open it directly from the Search window (see "Searching for Files and Folders" later in the chapter). Also, you can see from the preceding discussion that viewing hidden files is not difficult. If other people use your computer and you don't want them to find particular files, you should encrypt those files, store them in your Documents folder (assuming that your Windows user account has a password), or move them to a removable media device, such as a jump drive, USB key, or similar device, and keep it hidden in a more conventional way. See Chapter 6 for how to set up a password-protected user account with a private Documents folder, and Chapter 33 for a description of Windows' other security features.*

You can hide a file or folder by following this procedure:

1. Select the file or folder.
2. Click the Properties button on the toolbar, or right-click the file or folder and choose Properties from the shortcut menu. The Properties dialog box appears.
3. If it is not already selected, click the General tab. Near the bottom of the General tab is a list of attributes, one of which is Hidden.
4. Select the check box next to Hidden.
5. Click OK to make the Properties dialog box disappear.

To unhide the file, repeat the same steps, but deselect the Hidden check box.

What Is a Folder Template?

Some folders look and behave differently from others. A folder of pictures or music, for example, can be set up to have special links in the task pane or special display properties so that it is easy for you to find the file you want and do what you want with it. A *folder template* is a predefined set of properties that you can choose to apply to a folder. Windows Vista comes with five folder templates: All Items, Documents, Pictures and Videos, Music Details, and Music Icons.

The default folder template is All Items. You can choose a different template from the Customize tab of a folder's Properties dialog box.

Configuring Windows Explorer

You can configure many facets of Explorer windows to your own taste. Some of the basic choices were described in the previous chapter. At the simplest level, you can resize and move the windows themselves just like any other windows. You can also make more complex changes in Windows Explorer's behavior, the information it displays, and how that information is presented.

In addition to changing the look and behavior of Windows Explorer in general, you also can add features to individual folders. You can choose a special icon for a folder or select a picture that appears when you look at the folder in Thumbnails view.

Changing the Behavior of Explorer Windows

The Explorer windows of Windows Vista are descended from two parents: the folder windows of Windows 95 and the browser windows of Internet Explorer. The default settings of the Explorer windows borrow a little from each parent. If you don't like this compromise, you can change your settings from the Folder Options dialog box, shown in Figure 9-2. To open this dialog box, choose Tools | Folder Options from the menu of Windows Explorer, or open the Control Panel and choose Folder Options from the Appearances and Themes category.

If, after experimenting with new settings, you decide the designers of Windows Vista had it right after all, you can return to the Folder Options dialog box and click the Restore Defaults button.

Opening a New Window for Each Folder

The default setting of Windows Explorer is for a window to "navigate" up and down the folder tree, like a web browser: when you open a subfolder of the currently displayed folder, the contents of the currently displayed folder vanish from the working area and are replaced by the contents of the subfolder. However, you still have the option of choosing the original Windows 95 behavior: the new folder can open in a new window, leaving the old window unchanged. If you do, the Windows Explorer's Forward and Back buttons stop working.

The new behaviors only apply to windows you create by opening folders on the desktop, however, or opening folders displayed in windows that already have this behavior. If you start Windows Explorer by choosing it from the All Programs menu, for example, it behaves in the default (that is, the web browser) way.

FIGURE 9-2   The General tab of the Folder Options dialog box, with the default settings

Replacing Double-Clicks with Single-Clicks

Under the default settings, a single mouse click selects a file or folder, and a double-click opens it. If all that clicking seems like too much work, you can change the settings so a file or folder is selected when the mouse pointer hovers over it and is opened by a single-click, as in web browsers.

To make the change, choose Tools | Folder Options to open the Folder Options dialog box, shown in Figure 9-2. Then click the Single-Click To Open An Item radio button. To change back, click the Double-Click To Open An Item radio button in the Folder Options dialog box.

Changing Views

Windows Explorer can display file and folder icons in the working area in six different views: Extra Large Icons, Large Icons, Medium Icons, Small Icons, Details, and Tiles. However, you can specify exactly how large you want the icons to display between the Small Icons and Extra Large Icons using a slider control to set the size of the icons. You can find all these options on the View menu. Folders that have been assigned special folder templates may have additional view options.

Tiles and Icons are graphical views that enable you to arrange the icons in any two-dimensional pattern you like. Details and List views both put the objects into a list. Details view includes more information in its list and enables you to reorder the list according to various criteria.

Tiles and Icons Views

Tiles view and Icons view are both graphical ways of presenting the contents of a folder—you can drag-and-drop the files and folders in the window in any way that makes sense to you, just as you might arrange objects on a desktop, piling up some and spreading out others.

Icons is the more visual view, Tiles the more informative. In Icons view the icons can be shown in different sizes to give you different views of the file's content. Extra Large Icons, Large Icons, and Medium Icons provide a thumbnail view of the file. The Small Icons view is also a thumbnail, but on most displays the view is really too small to see anything. Tiles view shows text labels to the right of the icons, and the types and sizes of files are given in the text labels.

Details View

Details view puts the contents of a folder into a list. Details, as the name implies, gives a more detailed list that includes columns of information, such as Name, Date Modified, Type, Date Taken (created), Tags, Size, Total Size, and Rating (see Figure 9-3 for an example of a folder shown in Details view).

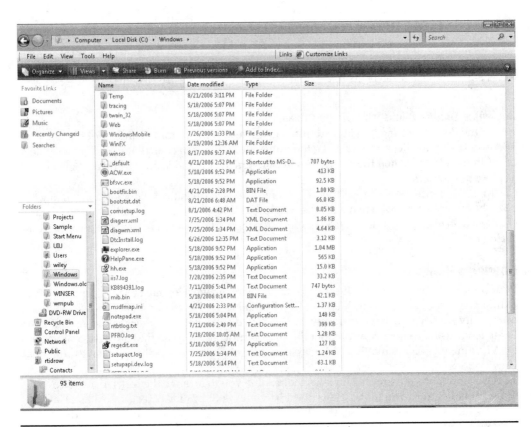

FIGURE 9-3   In Details view, you can sort by clicking any column head.

If you think Details view would be more informative if it had a different set of columns, right-click the bar that displays the column headings. The shortcut menu displays a list of possible column headings, with the currently displayed ones checked. Check or uncheck any you like. (Many of the headings are only appropriate for special types of files or folders; for other files or folders, the corresponding column is empty.) The changes you make apply to the current folder only, but will be remembered the next time you open that folder. You can also change Details view for all folders (see the next section, "Changing How the View Settings Work").

Details view also enables you to sort the list of files and subfolders according to any column by clicking its column head. For example, clicking Name sorts the contents in alphabetical order, such as shown in Figure 9-3. Clicking a column head twice sorts the contents in reverse order. For example, clicking the Size column head once sorts from the smallest file to the largest, and clicking Size twice re-sorts from the largest file to the smallest.

You can adjust the width of the columns in a Details view by dragging-and-dropping the lines between the adjacent column heads. You can switch the order of the columns by dragging-and-dropping the column heads.

Changing How the View Settings Work

By default, each folder has its own view settings. If you choose a new view from the View menu, you change the view for the currently displayed folder only. Windows remembers the new view the next time you open that folder, but all other folders are unchanged. But another method enables you to change the view for all folders in one fell swoop.

Defining One View for All Folders

If you decide you like Details or Large Icons (or some other) view and want to use it for all your folders, you can. Here's how:

1. Configure a folder the way you want all the folders to appear.

2. With that folder open, select Tools | Folder Options. The Folder Options dialog box appears (shown earlier in Figure 9-2).

3. Click the View tab. In the Folder Views area at the top, click the Apply To Folders button.

4. A confirmation box appears, asking whether you really mean to change the default view settings. Click Yes.

5. Click OK to close the Folder Options dialog box.

If you want to reset all folders back to the default settings, follow the previous instructions, except in Step 4, click the Reset Folders button.

NOTE *Changes that you make to the layout of columns in Details view can't be extended to all folders by this technique.*

Defining a View That Stays with a Window

You may also decide you want the view settings to belong to the window, not to the folder. In other words, when you switch to, say, Large Icons view, you want every folder you open from that window to come up in Icons view until you change to something else. To change window settings:

1. Select Tools | Folder Options in Windows Explorer. The Folder Options dialog box appears (shown earlier in Figure 9-2).

2. Click the View tab.

3. In the Advanced Settings box, uncheck the Remember Each Folder's View Settings check box.

4. Click OK.

To restore the default behavior, repeat the process, but check the box in Step 3.

One thing you can't do is have Windows Explorer behave in different ways for different folders, such as open with a single-click in one folder and open with a double-click in another. Whatever decisions you make on the General tab of the Folder Options dialog box are applied automatically to all Explorer windows.

Changing View Settings

The stray odds and ends of how Explorer windows look and behave are controlled from the View tab of the Folder Options dialog box. From this tab, you can tell Windows whether to display the following:

- Hidden files and folders
- File extensions (see "What Are Extensions and File Types?" in Chapter 8 for directions on how to display them)

You can make your experience of Windows Explorer a little more comfortable by setting its options the way you like them. To open the View tab of the Folder Options dialog box, choose Tools | Folder Options from the Windows Explorer menu bar, and then click the View tab. The View tab contains the Advanced Settings box, which is a long list of check boxes, most of which are self-explanatory. For example, checking the Show Pop-Up Description For Folder And Desktop Items check box enables Windows to display a pop-up help window for folder and desktop items.

If you decide that whatever you changed on the View tab was a bad idea, but you can't remember exactly what you changed, go to the View tab and click the Restore Defaults button.

Sorting and Arranging the Contents of a Folder

Windows Explorer can sort the icons in an Explorer window automatically according to any column that appears in Details view. For most folders this means the icons can be sorted by name (alphabetically), by file type, by size (from smallest to largest), or by date (earliest to most recent). Even if you aren't in Details view, you can access the same choices via a shortcut menu or on the View | Sort By menu. Adding a column to Details view adds the same choice to the View | Sort By menu.

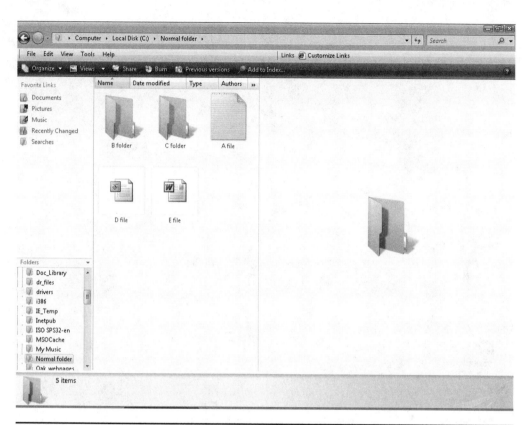

FIGURE 9-4   A folder's contents sorted by name

In any of these sortings, folders are listed before files. Thus, in Figure 9-4, the B Folder and the C Folder come before the A File. In Tiles and Icons views, the contents of the folder are sorted in rows (if the window is wide enough for more than one column). The first element in the order is located in the window's upper-left corner, the second is to its right, and so on. In Details view, the contents are sorted in a list, starting at the top of the window.

In Details view, sorting is particularly easy: click the column header to sort according to that column. Click it again to sort in reverse order (in which folders automatically go to the end of the list). The column by which the list is sorted displays a small arrowhead, which points up for a sort in ascending order and down for a sort in descending order.

In Tiles and Icons views, you can also arrange icons manually, by dragging them. Figure 9-5 shows a folder whose contents have been arranged manually—notice the irregular spacing and the overlapping icons. Metaphorically, manual arrangement is more like sorting stacks of paper on a table than sorting items in a filing cabinet. The effect can be similar to having subfolders: you can put work files on the right half of the window and home files on the left, instead of having Work and Home subfolders. If you decide you want tidy rows and columns again, select something off the View | Auto Arrange menu.

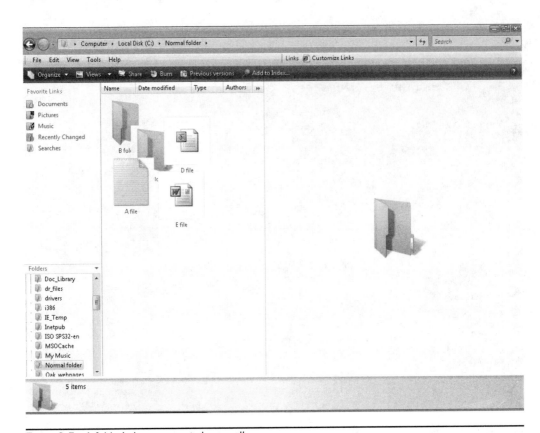

FIGURE 9-5   A folder's icons arranged manually

CAUTION   *If you overlap an icon too closely with a folder icon, Windows will think you want to put the corresponding object inside the folder.*

You can also group files and folders automatically according to name, size, type, or date modified. Choose View | Group By, then choose Name, Date Modified, Type, Authors, or Tags.

Working with Shortcuts

Sometimes you want a file to be in two places at once: the place where it really belongs and on the desktop where you can easily get to it. Sometimes your filing system has two logical places to put the same file. Shortcuts enable you to deal with these situations, without the disadvantages that come from having two independent copies of the same file (see "What Is a Shortcut?" earlier in the chapter).

Making Shortcuts

Shortcuts are created when you do any of the following:

- Drag-and-drop certain applications to a new folder or to the desktop.
- Hold down the right mouse button while you drag any object to a new location, and then select Create Shortcut(s) Here from the menu that appears when you drop the object.
- Invoke the Create Shortcut Wizard either by selecting File | New | Shortcut in an Explorer window or by right-clicking an open space on the desktop or in an Explorer window and selecting New | Shortcut from the shortcut menu.

In the first two cases, the original file or folder stays in its old location, and a shortcut to that file or folder is created in the drop location. In the third case, the shortcut is created in the folder from which the Create Shortcut Wizard was invoked.

Windows makes shortcuts automatically in certain circumstances. When you add a web page to your list of Favorites, for example, a shortcut is created and put in the folder C:\Users*your username*\Favorites.

We find that drag-and-drop techniques are the easiest way to create shortcuts. But if you prefer, you can use the Create Shortcut Wizard as follows:

1. Open the destination folder, the one in which you want to create the shortcut. If you want the shortcut to be on the desktop, make sure part of the desktop is visible on your screen.

2. Choose File | New | Shortcut in the destination folder's window. Or, if the desktop is the destination, right-click an empty place and select New | Shortcut. Either of these techniques launches the Create Shortcut Wizard.

3. If you know the address of the file or folder to which you want to create a shortcut (the target), you can type it into the Type The Location Of The Item box on the wizard's first page. If you have the address written in another file, you can cut-and-paste it into the Type The Location Of The Item box by using CTRL-V to paste. If you use the Type The Location Of The Item box, skip to Step 7.

4. Click the Browse button. A Browse For Files Or Folders dialog box appears.

5. Use the Browse For Files Or Folders dialog box to find the target file.

6. Select the target file or folder, and then click OK. The Browse For Files Or Folders dialog box disappears. The first page of the Create Shortcut Wizard now contains the target's address.

7. Click Next. The second page of the Create Shortcut Wizard appears. If you don't like the suggested name for the shortcut (usually the same as the original object), type a new one in the Type A Name For This Shortcut line.

8. Click Finish.

Shortcuts can also point to web pages on the Internet. These shortcuts have filenames that end with the extension *.url*, and you can also make them with the Create Shortcut Wizard. The procedure is the same, except in Step 3 you type the page's Internet address or URL (see "What Are Addresses?" in Chapter 8).

Using Shortcuts

For almost all purposes, a shortcut to a file or folder behaves just like the target file or folder. Opening the shortcut, dragging-and-dropping the shortcut, or dragging-and-dropping something onto the shortcut produces the same result as performing the same action with the target file or folder.

The most convenient place to put shortcuts is on the desktop. Documents you are currently working on can reside in the appropriate place in your filing system, yet a shortcut on the desktop can make them instantly available. Programs you use frequently can remain in the folders they were installed into, yet be accessible with a single click. For programs you use frequently, you can add an icon to the Quick Launch toolbar on the taskbar (see "Editing the Quick Launch Toolbar" in Chapter 11).

Working with Compressed Folders

Everyone who has packed a suitcase knows the basic idea of a compressed folder—it's a trick for getting the same quantity of information to fit in a smaller space on a disk (see "What Are Compressed Folders?" earlier in the chapter). Windows 98 and earlier versions of Windows required that you have a third-party application such as WinZip or ZipMagic to work with compressed folders. In many ways, these applications are still more useful and convenient than the Compressed Folders utility in Windows Explorer. If you are going to work with ZIP files every day, you probably want to acquire ZipMagic or some similar program; for occasional use, the Compressed Folders utility in Windows Explorer works just fine.

Creating a Compressed Folder

To create a compressed folder on the desktop, right-click an empty space and choose New | Compressed (Zipped) Folder from the shortcut menu. To create a compressed folder inside another folder, open or select the folder and choose File | New | Compressed (Zipped) Folder.

Either of these techniques creates a compressed folder called New Compressed (Zipped) Folder.zip (you won't see the extension if you have Explorer set to hide file extensions). You may rename it as you would any other folder, though (as usual) you probably don't want to change the file extension.

To create a compressed folder with a specific file or files already inside it, select the files you want to include, right-click one of the selected files, and then choose Send To | Compressed (Zipped) Folder from the shortcut menu. The selected files remain unchanged, and a copy of them is created inside the compressed folder. The name and location of the folder is the same as the file you right-clicked. The name of the new compressed folder is the same as the name as the last of the selected files.

Working with Files in a Compressed Folder

To add a file to a compressed folder, drag the file onto the folder's icon or into its open window, and then drop it. The file remains in its original location and a copy is created inside the compressed folder. To move the file without leaving the original behind, drag-and-drop it with the right mouse button, and then choose Move Here from the shortcut menu.

To many applications, a compressed folder appears to be simply a file of a type that the application doesn't know how to open properly. You can't, for example, use the File | Open command in Word to open a Word file that lives inside a compressed folder.

You can open a file in a compressed folder by double-clicking it, but the file usually lacks its full functionality. Windows uncompresses the file into a temporary location, and then runs the program that handles the file. A Word file in a compressed folder, for example, opens in read-only mode. To regain functionality, you need to *extract* the file. The extracting process creates an uncompressed copy of the file outside the compressed folder.

To extract a file from a compressed folder, drag it from the compressed folder and drop it onto the desktop or into an uncompressed folder. One copy of the file is left behind in the compressed folder and a new, uncompressed copy appears in the new location. To extract the file without leaving a copy in the compressed folder, drag-and-drop with the right mouse button and choose Move Here from the shortcut menu.

To extract all the files in a compressed folder at once, select File | Extract All from the menu if the file is open, or right-click the folder's icon and choose Extract All from the shortcut menu. The Extract Compressed (Zipped) Folders Wizard guides you in selecting a destination folder for the extracted files.

In many respects, the compressed folder and its files behave just as other folders and files. You can arrange and view the files within the folder in the usual ways, for example. However, Microsoft didn't completely integrate compressed folders into its filing system. Here is a short list of things Microsoft might want to fix:

- Compressed folders don't appear on the Folder Explorer bar.

- Compressed folders don't show up in Browse windows. So, for example, you can't save a Word document into a compressed folder by choosing File | Save As from the Word menu bar. Most programs can't open a file that's stored in a compressed folder.

- You can't customize a compressed folder.

- The columns in Details view are different for a compressed folder because there is more to know about a compressed file: the size of the compressed file, the size of the extracted file, the ratio between the sizes, whether the file is encrypted, and the method of compression.

- You can't drag-and-drop or cut-and-paste a file from one compressed folder to another unless one of the folders contains the other.

Encrypting and Decrypting Compressed Folders

You can attach a password to a compressed folder so that Windows will ask for the password before opening or extracting any of the files in the folder. This technique encrypts the entire folder. If you want to encrypt some of the files in a compressed folder, but not other files, create a new compressed folder, move the files you want to encrypt to the new folder, and encrypt that folder. The password scheme used in compressed folders can be broken by a determined attacker and isn't a substitute for a serious encryption program, but it's adequate to deter casual snooping.

To encrypt a compressed folder, right-click its icon and select Properties, click the General tab, and then click Advanced. Select Encrypt Contents To Secure Data in the Advanced Attributes dialog box. Click OK. Click OK again in the compressed folder's Properties dialog box. An Encryption Warning dialog box appears. Select to encrypt the file and its parent folder or to encrypt only the selected file. If you encrypt only the file, the folder in which the file is stored will still be accessible (that is, there will be no encryption on it). Click OK.

Opening and extracting files from encrypted compressed folders works exactly the same as opening and extracting files from ordinary compressed folders, except you have the file's encryption key and certificate set up under the currently logged-on user.

To decrypt an encrypted folder so that a certificate and key are no longer needed to access its files, right-click the folder's icon and select Properties from the shortcut menu, click the General tab, and then click Advanced. In the Advanced Attributes dialog box, deselect Encrypt Contents To Secure Data. Click OK twice.

After you encrypt a file or folder, take the time to back up the encryption key and certificate. This ensures that if the key and certificate are lost or damaged on your computer, you will have another copy of them to allow you to open the encrypted file. A message appears on the task tray asking if you want to back up the encryption certificate and key. Click the message and then do the following:

1. Click Back Up Now (Recommended). The Certificate Export Wizard appears.

2. Click Next.

3. Select the file format for the backup file.

4. Click Next.

5. To protect the encryption certificate and key, enter a password and confirm it. This will protect the backup file so only authorized users can load it.

6. Click Next.

7. Specify a filename for the export file. You can click the Browse button to specify a different folder other than the Documents folder in which to store the export file. You may, for example, want to store the backup file on removable media, such as a flash disc or CD-R. Click Save if you do this.

8. Click Next.

9. Click Finish.

10. Click OK when the export finishes.

Searching for Files and Folders

Even with a well-organized file system, you can occasionally forget where you put a file or even what the file's exact name is. Fortunately, Windows Vista provides an advanced Search tool to help you. By using Search, you can find a file:

- By name or part of a name
- By date created, modified, or last accessed
- By file type
- By size
- By a string of text contained in the file
- By some combination of all the previous points

Windows Vista includes a search index (see "Using Indexing Service" later in the chapter) that enables Windows to dynamically keep track of your files on your system. The index keeps track of filenames, modification dates, author name, tags, and ratings. All these are searching criteria you can use to locate files using the Search bar. When you search, Windows saves the found files in a Saved Searches folder. You can access the Saved Searches folder to manage or open files.

Along with the Search tool, Windows Explorer includes a new toolbar, called the Search pane. It includes buttons to help you filter the type of files to display in the Saved Searches folder. Some of the buttons you can use to filter by include the following:

- All Kinds
- E-mails
- Documents
- Pictures
- Music
- Attachment
- Picture
- Web History

To start a search, click the Search box on the Windows Explorer toolbar or click Start and Start Search. To display the Search pane on the Windows Explorer window, choose Organize | Layout | Search Pane. Figure 9-6 shows the Search pane with all the filter choices displayed.

Starting a Search

The most basic way to search for a file is to enter the filename and extension in the Search box and press ENTER.

TIP *You can use as many different criteria as you want to narrow your search.*

When the search is done, the Search Folder area displays the files or folders that meet your criteria. From this window you can

- Open any of the files or folders listed.
- Copy, cut, move, or drag-and-drop any of the files or folders to the desktop or some other window.
- Sort the files or folders. If you have set the view to Details (the default, if you opened Search from the Start menu), you can sort by name, address, size, or file type by clicking the corresponding column header.

Searching by Name

The simplest kind of search is when you know the name of the file (or most of its name), but can't remember where it is located.

FIGURE 9-6 Search pane and search filtering choices

If you know only part of the name of a file, type that part into Search. As soon as you enter a part of the name (or the complete name if you type quickly), Windows displays any found files matching your criteria. The viewing area displays all the files and folders whose names include that text string. (Even if you type in the full name, Search treats it as a substring, and returns all the files and folders whose names contain that text string.) For example, searching for "June" might yield the files june07.doc, Next June.txt, and 07 june quarterly report.wks, plus the folders June's Recipes and Juneau Alaska.

NOTE *You must press* ENTER *for Windows to start searching for files that are not indexed. This can include files that are on network drives, new ones that have not been indexed yet, or Internet resources.*

If you don't remember much about the name of the file ("It had an *A* in it somewhere"), the resulting list of files and folders is likely to be daunting. You can make your search more specific by combining keywords with other criteria, or by using case sensitivity and wildcards in the search (as described in the next section).

Wildcards

The asterisk (*) and question mark (?) characters play a special role in filename searches. Neither is allowed to be part of a filename, so when you include them in a filename search, Windows knows you intend for it to do something special with them. The asterisk and question mark are called *wildcards* because (like wildcards in poker) they can stand for any other character.

The question mark stands for any single character, so you can use it when you either don't know or don't want to specify a character in a filename. If, for example, you can't remember whether a file is named Letter to Tim or Letter to Tom, search for Letter to T?m—either Tim or Tom will match T?m. Similarly, you can find both Annual Report 2006 and Annual Report 2007 by using Annual Report 200? in your search.

An asterisk stands for any string of characters. Searching for Letter to T*m would find not only Letter to Tim and Letter to Tom, but also Letter to Travel Management Team.

Using Indexing Service

If you have ever searched through a book looking for a particular passage, you know what a difference it makes to have someone do the upfront work of making an index or concordance. That, in a nutshell, is what Indexing Service does. It is a utility that creates and maintains catalog files that keep track of the contents of the files on your computer. Having Indexing Service enabled makes searches (especially text searches) much faster, at the cost of a certain amount of overhead: Indexing Service requires some time to construct an initial catalog, which it must update from time to time as you create new files and change old ones.

By default, Windows Vista turns on Indexing Service. To modify Indexing Service options, choose Start | Control Panel | System And Maintenance | Indexing Options. The Indexing Options dialog box appears, as shown in Figure 9-7. You can change the locations that Indexing Service indexes (choose Modify and deselect the locations to ignore).

Looking in the Right Place

If you know where the desired files or folders are located in the folder tree, search only that portion of the folder tree. That search doesn't take so long and yields fewer false "finds." Select the folder or drive in which to look for the file using the Navigation Pane in Windows Explorer. Only that folder and its subfolders are searched. Another way to tell Windows where to search is by right-clicking the folder you want to search and choosing Search from the menu that appears.

By default, the Look In box is set to the folder that was open when you started the search or (if you opened Search from the Start menu) your local hard drives.

Searching by Author

If you remember who created the file, use the Search tool's Author criteria. Type the name of the author into the Search box and press ENTER. The Search Folder returns all the files that match the author name.

Searching by File Type

Another way to search for files is by file type. This can be by specifying a wildcard, such as *, and then the file extension of the file you are searching. For example, if you are looking

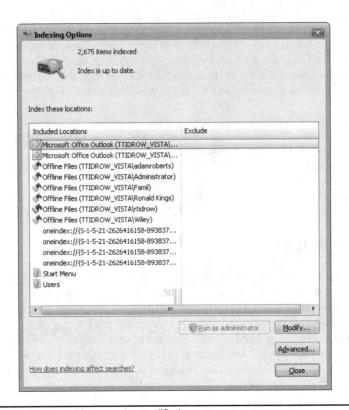

Figure 9-7 Indexing Service options can be modified.

for a Microsoft Office 2007 PowerPoint presentation file, you would need to search for a PPT file. To locate all these types of files on your system, click in the Search box, type ***.PPT**, and press ENTER. The Search Folder shows all the files that match these search criteria.

Searching by Tags

Tags are words or phrases that you add to your files on the Details tab of the file's Properties dialog box. To find files based on tags, type the tag in the Search Box and press ENTER. Windows returns files that contain the tag word or phrase.

Saving and Retrieving a Search

After performing a search, you can save the search parameters by clicking the Save Search button on the Windows Explorer toolbar. The Save As dialog box appears. Enter a name for the search and click Save. Saved search files use the extension .search, which is automatically applied to the filename you save.

After you save a search file, you can recall it by opening Windows Explorer and opening the Searches folder, as shown in Figure 9-8. To open the search, click it to see the files located in that search folder.

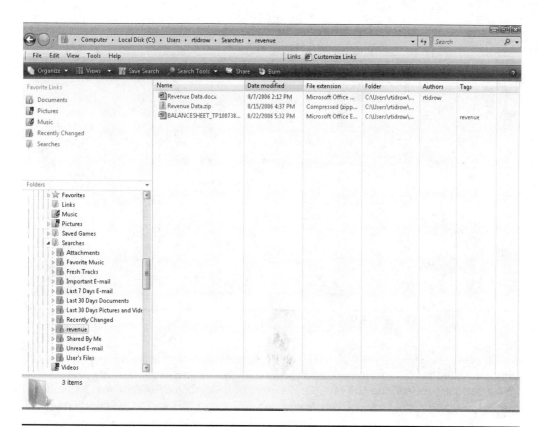

FIGURE 9-8   Saved searches are located in the Searches folder.

Managing the Recycle Bin

Files and folders sent to the Recycle Bin may disappear from the folder tree, but Windows still stores them on your hard drive and keeps track of them. Eventually, one of four things happens:

- You eliminate things in the Recycle Bin, either by emptying it or by deleting some of the files and folders there.

- You retrieve files from the Recycle Bin and put them in some other folder (see "Recovering Objects from the Recycle Bin" in Chapter 8).

- The Recycle Bin gets full, and starts permanently deleting its oldest files to make space for new ones.

- You turn off the Recycle Bin so deleted files aren't put there anymore.

This section covers all these possibilities except the second one, which was covered in the previous chapter. In addition, this section tells you how to streamline the deleting process, if you want to do so.

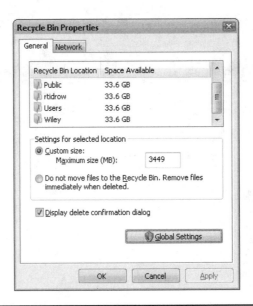

FIGURE 9-9 The Properties dialog box of the Recycle Bin

Like most other things in Windows, the Recycle Bin has properties. To display them, right-click the Recycle Bin icon on the desktop and choose Properties from the shortcut menu. The Properties dialog box for the Recycle Bin is displayed, as shown in Figure 9-9. The Properties dialog box contains a General tab, a Network tab, and a button called Global Settings for configuring Recycle Bins shared by other users on your computer.

Emptying the Recycle Bin

Deleting old files serves two purposes: it clears useless files away so you don't confuse them with useful files, and it reclaims the disk space they occupy. The first purpose is served by deleting a file—once it's in the Recycle Bin, you aren't going to open it or work on it by mistake. But a file in the Recycle Bin still takes up disk space: the space isn't reclaimed until the Recycle Bin is emptied.

To empty the Recycle Bin:

1. Right-click the Recycle Bin icon on the desktop.
2. Choose Empty Recycle Bin from the shortcut menu. A dialog box asks you to confirm your choice.
3. Click Yes.

To purge selected files or folders from the Recycle Bin without completely emptying it, open the Recycle Bin folder and delete the files in the usual way (see "Deleting Files and Folders" in Chapter 8). Objects deleted from an ordinary folder on a hard drive are sent to the Recycle Bin, but objects deleted from the Recycle Bin are really deleted.

To purge only those objects that have been in the Recycle Bin a long time:

1. Open the Recycle Bin.
2. If the window is not already in Details view, choose View | Details.
3. Click the Date Deleted header to put the objects in order of date.
4. Use the enclosing-rectangle method to select all the objects deleted prior to a certain date (see "Selecting Files and Folders" in Chapter 8).
5. Press the DELETE key on the keyboard.
6. When the dialog box appears, asking whether you really want to delete these objects, click Yes.

Resizing the Recycle Bin

By default, the maximum size of the Recycle Bin on any hard drive is 10 percent of the size of the drive itself. For example, a 100GB hard drive has a maximum Recycle Bin size of 10GB—a lot of space to use up for files you've decided to delete. If you delete an object that would cause the Recycle Bin to exceed that size, Windows warns you with an error message.

Having a maximum size for the Recycle Bin forces you not to clutter your hard drive with useless, deleted files, and 10 percent is as good a maximum size as any. But you may decide either to raise this limit (because you don't want to lose any of the files currently in the Recycle Bin) or lower it (because disk space is getting tight), either of which you can do by following this procedure:

1. Right-click the Recycle Bin icon on the desktop and choose Properties from the shortcut menu. You see the Properties dialog box of the Recycle Bin (see Figure 9-9).
2. Select a location that you want to modify.
3. Set the Custom Size field to a new Maximum Size (MB) setting.
4. Click OK.

Streamlining the Deletion Process

Many times, we've been thankful that Windows makes it so hard to eliminate a file on a hard drive. Four different actions are usually necessary: deleting the file in the first place, confirming the deletion in a dialog box, emptying the Recycle Bin (or deleting the file from the Recycle Bin), and then confirming *that* decision in a dialog box. (If you let the Recycle Bin get full, however, the oldest recycled files will be lost when new ones are recycled.) But even though this process can occasionally be a life-saver, it can also be tedious (particularly if you are trying to get rid of sensitive files that you don't want hanging around in the Recycle Bin).

CAUTION *Even deleting a file from the Recycle Bin doesn't destroy the information right away. Windows makes the file's disk space available for reassignment, but doesn't immediately write over that disk space. People with the proper tools could still read the file.*

Deleting Selected Files or Folders

If you want certain files and folders gone *right now*, with no shilly-shallying about confirmation dialog boxes, Recycle Bins, or Undo buttons, hold down the SHIFT key while you drag the files and folders onto the Recycle Bin icon. (Of course, you should be *very sure* you want the files and folders gone, and that you haven't dragged along any extra objects by accident.) Holding down the SHIFT key while you click the Delete button (or press the DELETE key) is almost as quick: you have to click Yes in a confirmation dialog box, but the objects are deleted for real, not just sent to the Recycle Bin.

Eliminating Confirmation Dialog Boxes

To eliminate the confirmation dialog box when you send something to the Recycle Bin:

1. Right-click the Recycle Bin icon on the desktop and choose Properties from the menu.

2. From the General tab of the Properties dialog box, uncheck the box labeled Display Delete Confirmation Dialog.

3. Click OK.

Even after carrying out these steps, deleting something from the Recycle Bin (that is, getting rid of it for good) still requires a confirmation. If you decide later that you've made the deletion process too easy, you can reinstitute Display Delete Confirmation Dialog; repeat the preceding steps, but check the check box in Step 2.

Turning Off the Recycle Bin

If you want to stop sending deleted files to the Recycle Bin:

1. Right-click the Recycle Bin icon on the desktop and choose Properties from the shortcut menu. You see the Properties dialog box of the Recycle Bin (see Figure 9-9).

2. On the General tab, check the box labeled Do Not Move Files To The Recycle Bin. Remove Files Immediately When Deleted.

3. Click OK.

After you complete this procedure, files you delete from your hard drive are gone, just as are files deleted from floppy drives. Files that were already in the Recycle Bin, however, remain there until you empty the Recycle Bin, delete them, restore them, or move them to another folder.

You can turn the Recycle Bin back on by following the same procedure, by unchecking the check box in Step 2.

CAUTION *If you turn off the Recycle Bin, don't forget you did. The Recycle Bin remains off until you turn it on again. A more prudent choice might be to make your Recycle Bin smaller, but to leave it on.*

Backing Up Your Files with the Backup Utility

The most important thing to say about backing up your files is this: Back up your files. You can back up your files onto floppies, tapes, flash drives, network servers, extra hard drives, DVDs, writable CDs (CD-Rs or CD-RWs), tape drives, or whatever you happen to have. The new Windows Backup Status and Configuration tool, however, does limit the devices you can back up to when making a partial or complete backup. For instance, if you use Backup Status and Configuration, you can back up to a hard drive, CD-R, DVD-R, or network drive. How you back up your files is much less important than that you do it. If you have only a few files or folders to back up, you can use Windows Explorer to make the copies to floppy disks, USB flash drives, or other portable devices.

Windows Vista includes the Backup and Restore Center, which provides access to four main backup and restore features:

- **Back Up FilesWizard**   Guides you through backing up types of files
- **Complete PC Backup**   Creates an image of your hard disk
- **Restore FilesWizard**   Enables you to restore files and folders from a backup
- **Complete PC Restore**   Enables you to restore your computer from a backup image

Windows Vista Backup also includes a technology called Shadow Copy Backup that controls backups of open files and shared documents on Windows servers.

To fix problems on your system, Windows Vista still includes the System Restore utility that was introduced with Windows XP.

What Is Backing Up?

Backing up means making copies of your files so that you can get the information back should anything happen to the originals.

Many unfortunate things can happen to files:

- A physical disaster like fire, flood, or cat hair could destroy your computer.

- A hardware failure could make your disk unreadable.

- A software problem could erase some of your files. For example, installing an upgrade to an application program might accidentally write over the folders in which you stored the previous documents that were created with that application.

- On a business computer system, a disgruntled employee might steal, erase, or corrupt important files.

- A well-meaning roommate, spouse, child, or coworker might delete or alter files without realizing it.

- You might get confused and get rid of files you meant to keep.

Any one of these possibilities might seem remote to you. (We used to think so, until we learned better.) But when you put them all together, it's amazing how often having a recent backup copy of your files turns out to be handy.

What Should You Back Up?

Ideally, you should back up everything; but (depending on the speed of your machine, the size of your hard drive, and the type of backup medium you use) a complete backup can take a considerable length of time. Once you have a complete backup to work from, updating that backup takes considerably less time.

A backup of only files that are new or have changed is called an *incremental backup*. A complete backup of all files and folders is called a *full backup* or *baseline backup*.

Backing up files is a little like flossing teeth: we all know it's good for us, but few of us do it as often as we know we should. If it takes you a month or two to get around to doing a complete backup, you should consider backing up the following parts of your system more often:

- **Documents you are working on**   Many applications put new documents in your Documents folder or its subfolders. You may choose to put your documents anywhere you like, but for backup purposes, it is convenient to have them organized in subfolders of one easy-to-find folder.

- **Databases to which you regularly add data**   For example, if you use Quicken to balance your checkbook once a month, back up the file in which Quicken stores your checkbook data.

- **Correspondence, especially your e-mail files**   Letters and memos that you write are probably already in your Documents folder(s). E-mail files, however, are usually stored in whatever folder you set up when you installed your e-mail program. Many Microsoft programs put your data in the C:\Users*username* folder (replace *username* with your Windows user account name, described in Chapter 6).

If you back up these files frequently, a hard drive disaster is much less of an ordeal. Still, nothing beats the security of knowing that you have backups of *everything*.

Programs are not on the list of important items to back up because you (or the person who maintains your machine) should still have the CDs or DVDs that you used to install the programs in the first place. Make sure you know where the discs are, that they're in a safe place, and that each program's installation key (sometimes referred to as its "CD key") is with the disc. If you have downloaded programs, you might want to reserve one backup media (such as a DVD-R or external hard drive) for the downloaded installation files. If you lose your hard disk, reinstalling all of your software is a nuisance, but not a disaster. You would, however, lose all the special settings that you have made to personalize the software for yourself. If reselecting all of those settings would be an ordeal, then you need to either back up the entire program folder or find out which specific files contain those settings.

If you like, however, you can back up all the files on your entire system, including your programs and Windows itself. If you do this, be sure to include the Windows Registry as part of the backup (see Chapter 40).

How Often Should You Back Up?

Different sources will tell you to back up your files daily, weekly, or monthly, but the real answer is that you should back up your files as soon as you have created or changed something that you don't want to lose. You need to balance the regular nuisance of backing up your files against the possible ordeal of regenerating your creative work.

If you work on a document daily, a single day's work can be a lot to lose. System files change when you reconfigure the settings of your system or when you install new hardware or software. Only you know how frequently your databases change or how much e-mail you are willing to lose in an accident. Backing up these frequently updated files need not be as involved as a full system backup (see the preceding section, "What Should You Back Up?").

If your machine is part of a larger network, such as an office-wide local area network, check with the network administrator to see whether your hard drive is backed up automatically and, if so, how often. If it isn't, you might consider nagging an appropriate person about it. Programs exist that allow a network administrator to back up all the hard drives on the network automatically. Many offices do this every night, relieving individuals of the need to worry about backups at all.

What Should You Do with Your Backup Disks, Discs, or Tapes?

Put your backup disks, discs, or tapes in a safe place, preferably as far from your computer as practical. Backups that sit right next to your computer may be handy in a hardware or software crash—but they don't protect you at all in the event of fire, theft, or sabotage. If your backups are magnetically stored (tapes, removable disks, or hard drives—anything but DVDs, CD-ROMs, and flash drives), keep them away from strong magnets. You may want to store an extra backup disk or tape offsite (in a different building).

What Is Windows Backup Status and Configuration?

Windows Backup Status and Configuration is an updated version of the Windows Backup program that originally shipped with Microsoft Windows 2000. It is installed as part of Windows Vista (Windows Vista Home does not come with the Complete PC utility of Windows Backup Status and Configuration). Its purpose is to allow you to back up and recover files quickly and efficiently using file compression techniques to use as little disk space as possible in storing your backups. It can also spread your backup files across many floppy disks or other removable media without confusing itself.

Windows Backup Status and Configuration can make backups from all types of Windows-compatible partitions: NTFS, FAT32, and FAT (see Chapter 34). It makes a *volume shadow copy* of all the files you specify, including files that are open (many backup programs skip open files). You can continue to use your computer during a backup, even storing and editing files that are part of the backup.

NOTE *To run the Windows Backup Status and Configuration, you need to be logged into Windows as an administrative user (see Chapter 6)—Owner, Administrator, or another user account with administrative privileges. If you are logged in as a non-administrative user, you can still run the program, but you can back up only your own files, and you can store the backup only on backup media that you have permission to use.*

Backing Up a Few Files or Folders

Even if you can't get around to a complete backup, you can protect yourself against the worst without too much effort by backing up your most valuable files and folders each day that you work on them.

Copying Files onto a USB Drive

Even on a slow system, it usually takes only a minute or two at the end of each day to connect a USB drive to your computer and copy the files you worked on that day. It's a good habit to develop.

If you typically work on only a few files each day, follow these steps:

1. Connect your USB drive to your computer.
2. Run Windows Explorer (choose Start | All Programs | Accessories).
3. Find the files you want to back up.
4. Drag-and-drop the files onto the USB drive in the folder tree (see "Dragging and Dropping Files and Folders" in Chapter 8). Or, select the files, choose File | Send To (or right-click the file and choose Send To from the menu that appears), and choose your USB drive from the list of Send To destinations that appears.

If you work on a larger number of files, search for recently changed files to make sure that you don't miss any. Choose Start | Search to search for all files modified within the last day. You can drag-and-drop files directly out of the Search Results window onto a USB drive icon in Windows Explorer. Or you can right-click any file in the Search Results window and choose Send To from the menu.

TIP *If you use Search to list the files you've worked on today, construct your search in such a way as to avoid finding all the temporary files that Windows creates in the course of a day. (If you do a lot of web browsing, there can be hundreds of them.) These temporary files are contained in subfolders of the C:\Windows folder (or whatever folder Windows is installed in).*

Copying Files onto Larger Drives

Anything you can copy onto a USB drive you can also copy onto a writable DVD or CD, a ZIP drive or other removable disk, a second hard drive, or another machine on your LAN. You can drag-and-drop the files to these media in the same way you copy files to USB drives.

A larger backup drive makes it less important to be selective about what you copy. You probably can copy, without too much time or trouble, your entire Documents folder (whether it is C:\Users*username*\Documents or some other folder that you have chosen) at the end of each day. You probably can copy your entire e-mail folder as well (see "What Should You Back Up?" earlier in the chapter).

Running Windows Backup Status and Configuration

Windows Backup Status and Configuration has several advantages over a more informal system of copying key files onto floppies or other storage media:

- It can copy files in a compressed form, so that they take up less disk space.

- It can backup files to a network location, secondary hard drive (you cannot back up to the local hard drive), CD-R discs, and DVD-R discs. For CD-R and DVD-R discs, Windows Backup Status and Configuration can spread a single backup job over several discs. This feature makes it possible to back up larger jobs.

- When you define a backup job, you decide the types of files you want to back up. You don't have to go through the decision process every time you do a backup.

- It is automated. Once the job starts, all you need to do is feed it a new disc if it asks for one. If you are backing up onto an external hard drive or some other medium with sufficient size, you don't need to do anything at all.

- It can back up files that are open. Windows Backup takes a volume shadow copy—that is, what the files contain at the moment that the backup occurs.

In Windows Vista, you can start Windows Backup in one of these ways:

- Selecting Start | All Programs | Accessories | System Tools | Backup Status and Configuration.

- Right-click a disk drive in an Explorer window, choose Properties to display the drive's Properties dialog box, click the Tools tab, and click the Backup Now button.

- Open Control Panel | Back Up Your Computer (it's in the System and Maintenance category).

When you start Backup using the first two methods, the Backup Status and Configuration window appears, as shown in Figure 10-1. However, when you use the Control Panel method, the Backup And Restore Center window appears, as shown in Figure 10-2. When you click the Back Up Files button or the Restore Files button from the Backup And Restore Center window, you see the Backup Status and Configuration window.

Remember that you must be logged on as an administrative user (or with a user account that is a member of the Backup Operators group) to be able to back up or restore files (see Chapter 7).

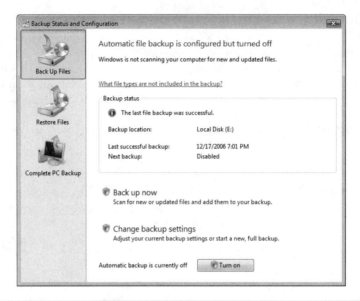

FIGURE 10-1 Backup Status and Configuration window.

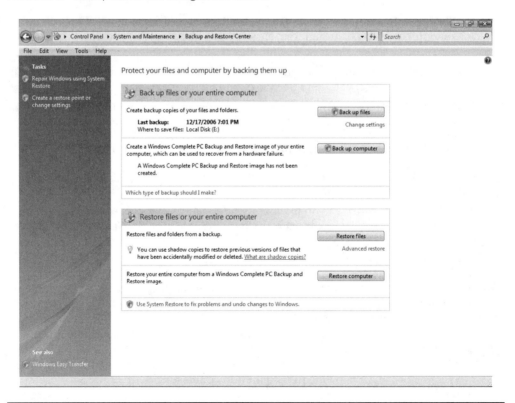

FIGURE 10-2 Backup And Restore Center window.

Each time you run Backup Status and Configuration, it checks your system for devices onto which you can copy files (backup devices). Then it displays the Backup Status and Configuration window, which includes buttons to Back Up Files, Restore Files, or run the Complete PC Backup tool.

Backing Up Files with Windows Backup Status and Configuration

Backing up files is something you should do regularly, so it's worth taking some time to configure your backup settings so that files that are the most important to you will be backed up on a regular basis, such as daily or weekly.

If you want to back up just some files or folders, set up Windows Backup Status and Configuration's Back Up Files utility. To do this, perform the following:

1. Choose Start | All Programs | Accessories | System Tools | Backup Status and Configuration. Or open Control Panel, click Back Up Your Computer, and click the Set Up Backup button (and go to Step 3). If a backup has already been set up, click Back Up Files and go to Step 2.

2. Click Change Backup Settings.

3. Specify the location where you want to store the backup files, as shown in Figure 10-3.

4. Click Next.

5. Specify the types of files you want to back up, as shown in Figure 10-4. Based on the types of files you specify, Windows Backup Status and Configuration searches for the types selected and backs them up regardless of the owner of the file (that is, which username created the file originally).

6. Click Next.

FIGURE 10-3   Specify where Windows Backup Status and Configuration stores the backup files.

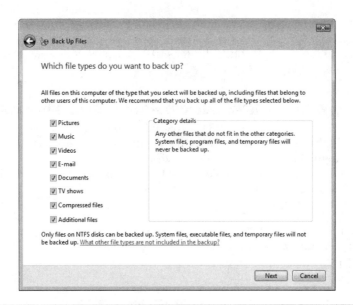

FIGURE 10-4   Specify the types of files to back up.

7. Specify how often, which day, and what time the backup is to run, as shown in Figure 10-5. Windows Backup Status and Configuration starts at the time you specify and backs up your files automatically (in the background), even while you are working.

8. Click Save Settings and Exit.

FIGURE 10-5   Determine how often and what time your backup will run.

The backup process begins and will back up the files you selected in Step 5. Depending on the speed of your computer, how many files to back up, and the speed of the backup device, this backup may take several minutes or hours. After the backup completes, Windows displays a pop-up window showing that the backup is complete.

Restoring Files with Windows Backup Status and Configuration

To restore files that you have backed up with Windows Backup Status and Configuration, you can use the Restore Files feature. You can restore files from the latest backup set, from an older backup set, or from a backup created on a different computer.

NOTE *Windows Backup Status and Configuration stores backed-up files in a special format, and you need to use Windows Backup Status and Configuration to restore them. You can't just copy the files from an Explorer window back to where you want to use them. Windows Backup Status and Configuration can't restore backups made by other backup programs, either, including those made by the Windows Me/9x backup utilities.*

To restore files from a backup, follow these steps:

1. Start Windows Backup Status and Configuration. If you open the Backup And Restore Center window, click Restore Files and go to Step 3. If you open the Backup And Restore Configuration window, click Restore Files and go to Step 2.

2. From the Restore Files page of the Backup Status and Configuration window (see Figure 10-6), click Restore Files.

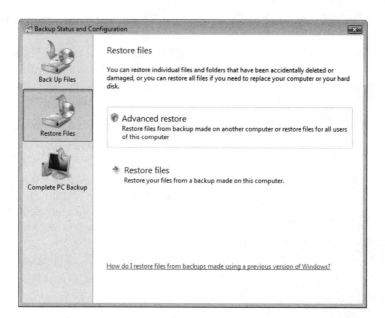

FIGURE 10-6   Start restoring files from the Backup Status and Configuration window.

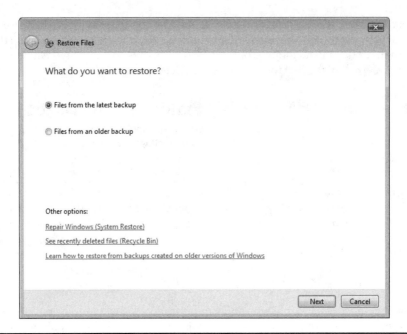

FIGURE 10-7   Choose what backup job you want to restore.

3. From the What Do You Want To Restore wizard page (see Figure 10-7), click Files From The Latest Backup.

4. Click Next. The Select the Files and Folders To Restore wizard page appears (see Figure 10-8).

5. Click the Add files button to select individual files to restore. Or, click the Add Folders button to select individual folders to restore. The Search button enables you to conduct a search of files or folders you want to restore (see Figure 10-9).

6. Click Next when you have selected the files and folders to restore.

7. Specify where you want the files to be restored. You have the following choices:

   - **In The Original Location**   Restores the files back to where they were when the backup ran.

   - **In The Following Location**   Restores files to a location different from the one when the backup ran. This is handy when you want to restore a file but not copy over files that are currently in the original location on your computer. Once restored to a different location, you can compare the files to see which one you want to keep.

8. Click Start Restore. The Restore Progress window appears while Windows Backup Status and Configuration restores your files.

9. After the restore completes, the Successfully Restored Files window appears. Click Finish.

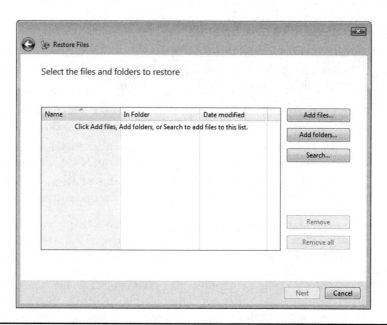

FIGURE 10-8   You can restore everything from the backup or choose individual files and folders to restore.

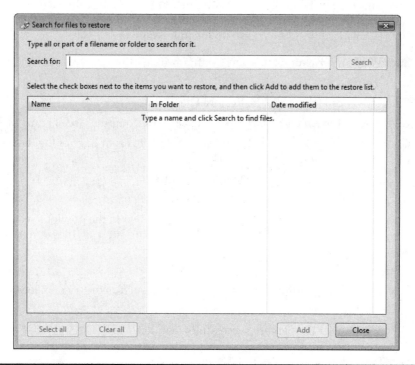

FIGURE 10-9   Search for files or folders to restore.

Restoring Files Using Windows Backup
Status and Configuration Advanced Restore

The Advanced Restore option in the Restore Files window enables you to choose other backup jobs to restore. You can choose the following options:

- **Files From the Latest Backup Made On This Computer**   Restores from the latest backup (the same as using Restore Files from the previous window)

- **Files From An Older Backup Made On This Computer**   Enables you to restore files from a backup made on this computer prior to your latest backup

- **Files From A Backup Made On A Different Computer**   Enables you to restore files from a backup made on a computer other than the one you are using

The reason you may want to restore from an older backup is that it may contain files that have been deleted prior to your latest backup. Or, the files on the latest backup may contain errors, so you need to go use a backup that has the same files on them before they became corrupted.

The last option, restoring from a computer other than yours, is handy for companies or organizations in which files need to be restored but the original computer is not currently available. For example, suppose that a company backs up its main employee database every night. One night a fire breaks out and destroys the computer on which this database resides. To restore the backed-up files from the database (say from a backup made the night before the fire), the company obviously needs to use a computer other than the original one. Windows Backup Status and Configuration makes this possible.

To use the Advanced Restore Wizard, do the following:

1. Start Windows Backup Status and Configuration.

2. Click Restore Files.

3. Click Advanced Restore in the Restore Files window (see Figure 10-6).

4. Click Files From An Older Backup Made On This Computer (see Figure 10-10).

5. Click Next to display the Select the Date To Restore From page of the Restore Files (Advanced) wizard (see Figure 10-11).

6. Select the backup set from which to restore files.

7. Click Next.

8. Select which files and folders to restore. As discussed in the previous section, "Restoring Files Using Windows Backup," you can restore all files or manually select files or folders to restore.

9. Click Next.

10. Select where you want the files to be restored to, such as the original location.

11. Click Start Restore.

12. Click Finish after the files are successfully restored.

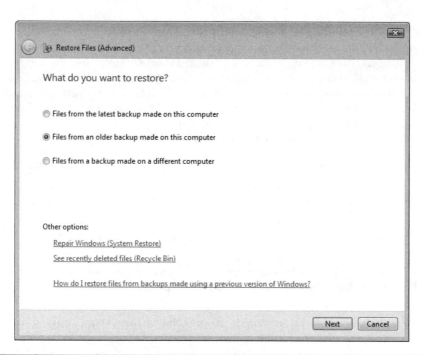

FIGURE 10-10   Choose to restore files from a previous backup.

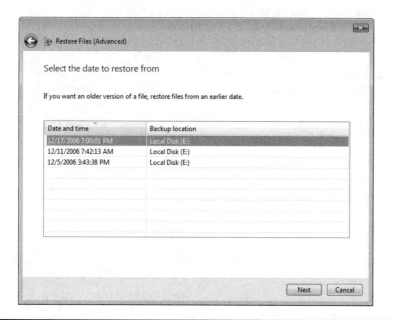

FIGURE 10-11   Specify the backup job date from which to restore.

Backing Up Your Computer Using Complete PC Backup

To back up all the files on your computer, such as if you want to have a mirror image (called a *system image backup*) of the computer's hard disk, use the Complete PC Backup tool. In the event that you need to re-create your entire hard disk, Complete PC Backup enables you to do so using the Windows Recovery Environment. The Windows Recovery Environment is not available in Windows. Instead, you activate it by booting your computer, pressing F8, and then choosing Windows Recovery Environment.

When you create a system image backup, be aware of the following:

- You can use only CDs, DVDs, or secondary hard disks to create the image backup.
- If you are using a secondary hard drive for the image backup, the hard drive must be formatted the same as the hard drive you are backing up. In most cases, the hard drive must be formatted NTFS.
- If you are using CD or DVD discs to create the image backup, be ready to use a lot of them.
- Complete PC Backup does not enable you to pick and choose the files or folders to back up. Instead, the entire computer is backed up.
- During the restore, you cannot choose files or folders to restore. Instead, the Windows Recovery Environment restores the entire system, copying over the current environment.
- Plan to run the Complete PC Backup tool when you are not currently busy. The backup process can take several hours for large hard drives.

Create a System Image Backup with Complete PC Backup

To create a system image backup, do the following:

1. Start Windows Backup Status and Configuration.
2. Click Complete PC Backup. If you are using the Backup and Restore Center, click Back Up Computer and skip to Step 4. The Create A Complete PC Backup page appears (see Figure 10-12).
3. Click Create a Backup Now. The Where Do You Want To Save The Backup? screen appears (see Figure 10-13).
4. Select the device on which to create the system image backup.
5. Click Next. The Confirm Your Backup Settings window appears.
6. Click Start Backup.
7. After the system image backup is created, click Finish.

TIP *During the Complete PC Backup process, you can click the Stop The Backup button to cancel the backup. Click Exit to return to the Backup And Restore Configuration window.*

Keep the system image backup disk or discs in a safe place in case you need them to recover from a Windows boot failure.

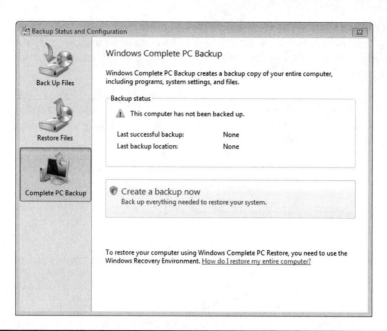

FIGURE 10-12   Create a system image backup using Complete PC Backup.

FIGURE 10-13   Specify where you to save the system image backup.

Restore Your System Using Windows Automated Recovery

If your computer fails or you have a hard disk failure, you can use the system image backup to restore your computer. To restore your system using the system image backup disk or discs, do the following:

CAUTION *Before using the Windows Automated Recovery utility, understand that your entire system will be replaced with the contents on the system image backup disk or discs. You cannot recover only select files or folders from this backup set.*

1. Make sure the first DVD or CD disc of the system image backup is inserted into the disc drive, or connect the external disk to your computer.

2. Start your computer and press F8 when the computer boots. This displays the Windows Recovery Environment.

3. Click Windows System Image Backup.

4. Follow the instructions on the screen to walk through the restoration process.

What Is the Removable Storage Service?

Windows Vista, as with Windows 2000, includes the Removable Storage Service, a service that can keep track of your tapes or other large-scale removable storage (but we refer to all storage media as tapes in this section, for brevity). Removable Storage doesn't manage backup discs, despite the name; however, it can label your discs and keep track of which one you need to insert and when. It also works with Windows Backup Status and Configuration and other backup or storage programs that use removable media.

Removable Storage refers to a backup device (such as an external hard disk) and its backup media (such as the DVD-R discs that work with a DVD-R drive) as a *library*. A library can be robotic (with an automated media changer, like the 50-CD changer you can get for your music CDs) or stand-alone (manually operated). Only Windows servers usually have robotic backup devices. Removable Storage organizes them in a library into these *media pools*:

- **Import media pool** Media that has not yet been catalogued and labeled by Removable Storage. Before you can use them for backup, Removable Storage can import them into the free media pool.

- **Free media pool** Unused, available media. When an application (like Backup Status and Configuration) is done with a tape, it can return it to the free media pool.

- **Backup media pool** Media that has been reserved for use by Windows BackupStatus and Configuration. When you use Windows Backup Status and Configuration to back up onto a new tape, Removable Storage moves the tape into the backup media pool.

Before you can back up information onto tapes, Removable Storage catalogues your unused tapes and moves them to the backup media pool. You can tell Removable Storage to do this automatically when you back up onto a new tape.

III
PART

Configuring Windows for Your Computer

Setting Up Your Start Menu and Taskbar

The Start menu is nothing new—it's been around since Windows 95. But the Windows Vista Start menu has been completely redesigned so that the programs you run most often are most easily accessible. Windows Vista has Start menu features that move frequently used commands to the "front page" of the Start menu, and hide less-often used commands. Because of the Windows Vista emphasis on keeping the desktop uncluttered, you'll probably use the Start menu more and desktop icons less.

The new Vista Start menu has been changed so that submenus and commands are easier to find than in past versions of the Start menu. Also, Windows Vista includes the Start Search box at the bottom of the new Start menu to make searching for documents, files, folders, web pages, and other items quicker. To make the Start menu easier to use, you might want to reorganize it, putting frequently used programs on the initial Start menu and demoting other programs to submenus.

The taskbar shows you which programs you're already running. Windows Vista uses the same taskbar as Windows XP, such as combining the taskbar buttons for multiple windows displayed by the same program, and shrinking the notification area (located on the right end, which used to be called the system tray). The taskbar normally appears at the bottom of the screen, but you can move it, expand it, shrink it, or even make it disappear. You can also include toolbars on the taskbar—you can display any number or none at all of the predefined toolbars, display toolbars on the desktop, and even define your own toolbars.

What Is the Start Menu?

The Start menu, shown in Figure 11-1, appears when you click the Start button on the taskbar. In Windows Vista, the Start menu appears in two columns—the left column contains links to programs and Search, and the right column contains links to folders, the Control Panel, online help, and shutdown and login links. If you prefer the classic style of the Start menu, you can switch back to it by using the Customize Start Menu dialog box (see "Customizing the Windows Vista-Style Start Menu," later in the chapter). If your Start menu looks nothing like

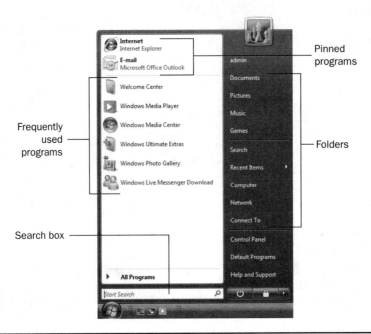

FIGURE 11-1 The Windows Vista Start menu.

the one shown in Figure 11-1, you probably have the Classic Start menu configured (the old Windows Me/98 Start menu).

The following items are usually on the Start menu (since the Start menu is customizable, your Start menu may look a little different):

- **All Programs**   Displays the *Programs menu*, a menu of programs you can run. This is the Start menu option that you are likely to use the most because you can use it to find and start programs. This menu is defined by the contents of the C:\Users\ *username*\Start Menu\Programs folder. You can change the contents of the Programs menu by changing the contents of that folder (see "Reorganizing the Start Menu," later in the chapter).

- **Start Search box**   Enables you to enter a search keyword or phrase to locate files, folders, Internet content, or other objects on your computer or a network (see Chapter 9).

- **Frequently used programs**   Lists six programs that you have used recently. Windows selects these programs based on how frequently and how recently you have run them. Click a program to run it.

- **Pinned programs**   Lists programs that are *pinned* to the Start menu—they alwa ys appear in this position so that they are easy to run. You can remove pinned programs and add new ones so that you see the programs that you use regularly.

- **Folders (Documents, Pictures, Music, Games, Search, Recent Items, Computer, Network, Connect To)**   Lists these special folders. If your Start menu hasn't been customized, you can click a folder to open an Explorer window (see "What Is Windows Explorer?" in Chapter 8). If Start menu options have been changed, you may see a submenu displaying the contents of the folder.

- **Control Panel**   Displays the Control Panel, which helps you install software and change your Windows settings (see "What Is the Control Panel?" in Chapter 1).

- **Default Programs**   Enables you to choose programs that Windows executes when you double-click a file or when a program initiates a file (see Chapter 3).

- **Help and Support**   Displays online help (see Chapter 4).

- **Power buttons**   Displays the Turn Off Computer options: Stand By (or Hibernate or Suspend), Turn Off, and Restart. Choose Turn Off if you are ready to turn off your computer. Choose Restart to restart your computer. Choose Stand By, Hibernate, or Suspend to put Windows in a power-conserving Standby or Hibernate mode. The power-conservation options available to you depend on whether you have turned them on and whether your computer supports them (see Chapter 6).

What Is the Programs Menu?

The Programs menu (also called the All Programs menu), which you display by choosing Start | All Programs, is a list of the programs you can run. This is the most commonly used part of the Start menu, and it's also the part you can customize the most. The Programs menu is hierarchical—that is, it has menus and submenus, all of which you can customize.

Figure 11-2 shows the Start menu with the All Programs option selected. With Windows Vista, instead of submenus displaying to the right of the main All Programs menu, each

FIGURE 11-2   The Start menu with the Accessories menus displayed.

subsequent menu you select—such as the Accessories menu—lays on top of the previous menu. This keeps the options on the right side of the menu, such as Control Panel, visible as you navigate to your program folders. In addition, this new look keeps all the menus in one area, so menus do not fall off the bottom or far right of the screen.

In this book, to open a game (say, Solitaire), we tell you to choose Start | All Programs | Accessories | Games | Solitaire—that is, click the Start button to display the Start menu, on the Start menu click All Programs, on the Programs menu click Accessories, on the Accessories menu click Games, and on the Games menu click Solitaire.

TIP   *Starting with Windows XP and continuing now with Windows Vista, Microsoft has abandoned the feature that shrinks the Programs menu to only those items you have used recently. However, if you miss that feature, you can have it back by using the Classic Start menu.*

When you install a new program, the installation program is likely to add a folder or other item to the Start menu or (more likely) to the All Programs menu. You may prefer to put such items in a submenu of the All Programs menu or perhaps remove them from the Start menu completely.

What Can Appear on the Taskbar?

The *taskbar* is a row of buttons and icons that usually appears at the bottom of the Windows desktop. As explained in Chapter 1, the taskbar has four parts: the Start button, the toolbar(s), the task buttons (one for each running application), and the notification area (with small icons for items that need your attention). You can customize your taskbar by moving it, changing its size, and changing what appears on it. You may also see arrows on the taskbar—click them to see buttons or other information that Windows has hidden to keep the taskbar uncluttered.

Five taskbar toolbars come with Windows:

- **Address toolbar**   Contains a text box where you can type a URL to open a web page or type a file pathname to open a file. A drop-down list enables you to choose recently used URLs and pathnames. The Address toolbar looks like this:

- **Windows Media Player toolbar**   Displays the Windows Media Player and controls as a taskbar toolbar when you have Media Player running and you minimize it. The toolbar includes buttons for playing, fast forwarding, rewinding, pausing, and controlling volume levels of items playing in Media Player:

- **Links toolbar**   Displays a button for each of the web pages Microsoft would like you to visit (you can remove Microsoft web pages and add your own favorite sites). This toolbar also appears in Internet Explorer. Click a button to open the web page. Here is an example:

- **Desktop toolbar**   Displays a button for each icon on the desktop. If a double arrow appears, click it to display the options that don't fit on the taskbar, like this:

- **Quick Launch toolbar**   Usually contains five buttons: Show Desktop, Switch Between Windows, Launch Internet Explorer Browser, Windows Live Messenger, and Microsoft Office Outlook (if you have Microsoft Office 2007 installed) You can change which buttons appear on this toolbar (see "Editing the Quick Launch Toolbar" toward the end of the chapter). Here are the standard four buttons:

- **Language bar**   Displays buttons for all installed languages and keyboard or input options that you have added using the Text Services And Input Languages dialog box, available from the Control Panel (see "Changing Language Properties" in Chapter 13). This toolbar doesn't appear as an option unless you have installed support for additional languages and keyboard layouts.

Older versions of Windows usually displayed the Quick Launch toolbar on the taskbar immediately to the right of the Start button. Windows Vista doesn't by default, but you can add it to the taskbar or move it onto the desktop (see "Adding and Removing Toolbars from the Taskbar" later in the chapter). You can also display other toolbars on the taskbar or on the desktop.

Searching the Start Menu

If you can't find the program you want in the Start menu, you can search the menu by using the Search feature. Follow these steps:

1. Right-click the Start button and choose Search from the shortcut menu that appears.
2. Type the name of the program you're looking for in the Start Search box.
3. Press ENTER.

The files that match the text you typed are displayed in the Explorer window. Windows displays the full pathname so that you can find the item in the Start menu, or you can click or double-click the item in the results list to open it. If you can't see the full path, increase the width of the Name column by clicking and dragging its right border to the right.

Customizing the Start Menu

With Windows Vista, most of the Start menu and its submenus are customizable. You can, for example, show or hide the Control Panel, remove the Documents item, or add items to the top of the Start menu. You also have total control over the Programs menu and submenus.

PART III

TIP *If your Programs menu has lots of submenus, getting to the item you want may take longer than you would like. If you find that the Start menu is cumbersome, explore the other methods of starting programs, which are covered in Chapter 2.*

Reorganizing the Start Menu

You can organize those parts of the Start menu that you are allowed to edit in three ways— you can drag-and-drop items, cut-and-paste items, or use an Explorer window to edit the Start Menu folders in the C:\Users*username*\Start Menu folder. These folders and their subfolders contain shortcuts to the programs that appear on your Start menu, and the arrangements of these shortcuts and folders define what command appears on what menu.

Here's a summary of changes you can make:

- **Add an item to the top of the left side of the Start menu**   Right-click a shortcut on the desktop or in the menu, or right-click an EXE file. Choose Pin To Start Menu from the menu that appears.

- **Add a program to the Programs menu**   Drag a desktop shortcut or the program's EXE file to the Start button. Hold it there while the Start menu opens, drag and hold it over the All Programs button until the Programs menu opens, and then drag-and-drop it where you want it to appear. (Hold it over submenus to open them.)

- **Remove an item from the menu**   To remove a program from the left side of the Start menu, right-click it and choose Remove From This List from the menu that appears. To remove a program from the All Programs menu (or its submenus), right-click the menu item and choose Delete. You can't remove items from the right side of the Start menu.

- **Rename a menu item**   Right-click the menu item and choose Rename. Type the new name and press ENTER.

If these bullet points don't cover what you need to do, or don't provide enough detail, keep reading!

Dragging-and-Dropping Programs to the Start Menu

You can create a Start menu entry for a program by dragging its program file (or a shortcut to the program) to the Start button. To add an item to the Start menu, drag the file, folder, program EXE file, or a shortcut to the program from an Explorer window or the Desktop and drop it on the Start button. Windows creates a new shortcut, and the new command appears in the top part of the Start menu.

To put the item further into the Start menu hierarchy, drag it to the Start button and hold it there until the Start menu appears. Then drag the item to exactly where you want it to appear (hold it on a submenu option to open the submenu). You may prefer to move the item in two steps, first dropping it on the Start button, and then dragging it within the Start menu, as described in the next section.

Dragging-and-Dropping Items Within the Start Menu

The easiest way to reorganize items already in the menus is to drag-and-drop the commands where you want them.

Reorganize items already in the Start menu by dragging them, like this:

1. Display the Start menu by clicking the Start button.

2. Display the menu containing the item you want to move (for instance, you might need to click All Programs to see the Microsoft Office Word 2007 option, which you might want to move to a submenu called Microsoft Office).

3. Click the item you want to move and hold the mouse button down.

4. While holding the mouse button down, move the pointer in the menu. The black bar shows you where the item you are moving will appear. You can open a submenu by highlighting it and waiting for it to open.

5. When the black bar appears in the position where you want the item to be, release the mouse button to drop the item in its new position.

Cutting-and-Pasting Start Menu Items

When you can see a Start menu command, you can right-click it and choose from the shortcut menu that appears. Two of the shortcut menu options are Cut and Copy—use them to move or copy a Start menu item.

To move (or copy) a command from one menu to another, right-click it and choose Cut (or Copy). Then give the command that displays the submenu into which you'd like to move the command, right-click, and choose Paste. For example, if you want to copy the Mozilla Firefox command from the Start | All Programs | Mozilla menu into the Programs menu, choose Start | All Programs | Mozilla to display the command, right-click it, and choose Copy. Then click Start, right-click the All Programs command, and choose Paste.

Moving Commands and Submenus by Editing the Start Menu Folders

Another way to customize the Programs menu and its submenus is to use an Explorer window to add, remove, move, and rename shortcuts. (Explorer windows are discussed in Chapters 8 and 9.) You can also rename submenus and menu items and create new submenus by using this method.

The Programs menu displays the shortcuts stored in two separate folders—one contains the Programs menu shortcuts that all users see, and the other contains the shortcuts that are visible for your personal user profile. Windows combines the two sets of shortcuts and displays a single Programs menu. The C:\Users\All Users\Start Menu folder contains common shortcuts (if Windows isn't installed on C:, substitute the correct drive letter); the other shortcuts are in the folder for your profile, C:\Users*username*\Start Menu (for example, C:\Users\Alison\Start Menu).

When you install a program that adds commands to your Programs menu, Windows asks whether you want the new menu entries to appear only in your Programs menu or on the Programs menus of all users of the computer. Adding, removing, and reorganizing the Programs menu is as simple as adding, deleting, and moving shortcuts within the two Start Menu folders. Menu items can be renamed by renaming the shortcuts.

The Start Menu folders (C:\Users*username*\Start Menu and C:\Users\All Users\Start Menu) contain the commands that appear at the top of the Programs menu. The Programs folders in the two Start Menu folders contain the rest of the commands that appear on the Programs menu. Each subfolder of the Programs folders corresponds to a submenu of the

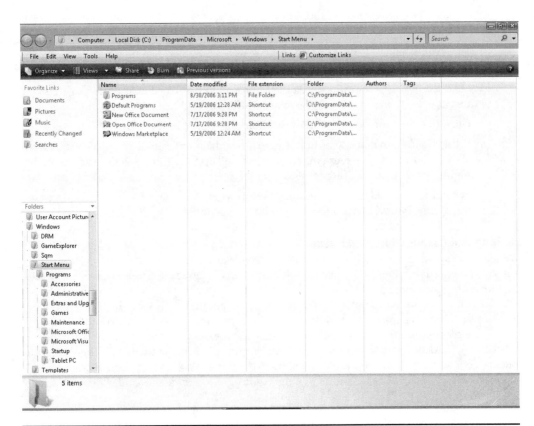

FIGURE 11-3   Using Windows Explorer to edit the Start menu.

Programs menu. For example, the shortcuts in the C:\All Users\Start Menu\Programs\ Games folder appear in the Start | All Programs | Games menu.

You can display the Start Menu folder for your user account in Windows Explorer by right-clicking the Start button and choosing Open or Explore from the menu. To display the Start Menu folder for all users, right-click the Start button and choose Explore All Users. Figure 11-3 shows the C:\Users\All Users\Start Menu folder in Windows Explorer. To see a list of installed programs on your computer, double-click the Programs folder.

To display the contents of the Programs menu, open the Programs folder in the Start Menu folders—look both in the folder for all users and the folder for your user account. You can explore the Start Menu folders by using the same methods you use to explore all folders on your computer.

TIP   *To edit any submenu of the Start menu, you can right-click it and choose Explore. Want to make changes to the Accessories submenu? Choose Start | All Programs, right-click Accessories, and choose Explore (for your user account settings) or Explore All Users. You see the C:\Users\ username\Start Menu\Programs\Accessories or C:\Users\All Users\Start Menu\Programs\ Accessories folder in Windows Explorer.*

Because the Start menu is stored as shortcuts within folders, it can be edited in the same way you edit folders and files:

- You can move an item from one menu group to another by dragging-and-dropping or cutting-and-pasting the shortcut to another folder.

- You can create a new menu group by creating a new folder. Select the folder in which the new submenu will be stored and choose File | New | Folder from the menu bar (press ALT if the menu bar in Explorer is not visible.)

- You can rename a shortcut by selecting it and pressing F2 (or right-clicking the name and choosing Rename from the shortcut menu that appears). Windows highlights the name and shows a box around it. Type a new name, or use the cursor to edit the name. Press ENTER when you finish (or press ESC if you change your mind).

NOTE *Although you can edit the Start menu by changing the contents of the Start Menu folders and their subfolders, the Start Menu and Programs folders are more than just regular folders. For instance, you can move the Programs folder out of its usual location, and you still see the Programs option on the Start menu (this can lead to complications that are hard to fix, though, so don't try it).*

Changing Start Menu Properties

In addition to changing the programs that appear on the Start menu and the order in which they appear, you can customize the Start menu in other ways. Right-click the Start button and choose Properties to display the Taskbar And Start Menu Properties dialog box, shown in Figure 11-4.

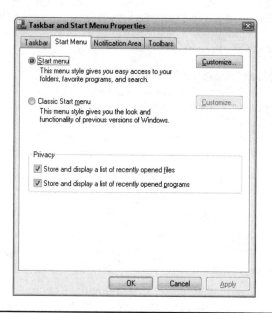

FIGURE 11-4   Choosing the style of your Start menu.

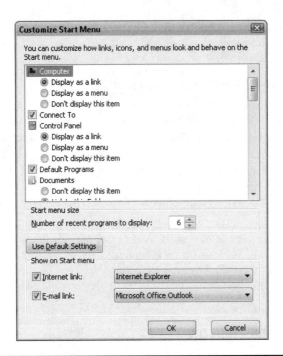

FIGURE 11-5   Changing the properties of the Start menu.

The Start Menu tab on this dialog box enables you to choose between the Start menu (the new Windows Vista design) and the Classic Start menu (the old Windows Me Start menu). Except for the section on the Classic Start menu, this chapter assumes that you are using the Windows Vista Start menu.

Customizing the Windows Vista-Style Start Menu

To customize the standard Start menu, on the Start Menu tab (see Figure 11-4), click the Start Menu radio button and then click the Customize button. The Customize Start Menu dialog box opens, shown in Figure 11-5.

This dialog box has been greatly enhanced for Windows Vista and includes several new customization options divided into categories. The following list explains these options:

- **Computer**   Includes settings for displaying the Computer icon on the Start menu. You can display it as a link or menu, or turn it off completely.

- **Connect To**   Enables you to turn on or off the Connect To item.

- **Control Panel**   Includes settings for displaying the Control Panel icon on the Start menu. You can display it as a link or menu, or turn it off completely.

- **Default Programs**   Enables you to turn on or off the Default Programs item.

- **Documents**   Includes settings for displaying the Documents folder. You can display it as a link or menu, or turn it off completely.

- **Enable Dragging And Dropping**   Enables you to turn on or off the capability to drag and drop items to the Start menu.
- **Favorites Menu**   Enables you to turn on or off the Favorites item.
- **Games**   Includes settings for displaying the Games folder. You can display it as a link or menu, or turn it off completely.
- **Help**   Enables you to turn on or off the Help and Support item.
- **Highlight Newly Installed Programs**   Enables you to select whether Windows highlights recently installed programs.
- **Local User Storage**   Includes settings for displaying the username on the Start menu, which links you to the local user's storage area. You can display the item as a link or menu, or turn it off completely.
- **Music**   Includes settings for displaying the Music folder. You can display it as a link or menu, or turn it off completely.
- **Network**   Enables you to turn on or off the Network item.
- **Open Submenus When I Pause On Them With The Mouse Pointer**   Enables you to turn on or off the capability for Windows to display submenus on the Start menu when you hover over the submenu name.
- **Pictures**   Includes settings for displaying the Pictures folder. You can display it as a link or menu, or turn it off completely.
- **Printers**   Enables you to turn on or off the Printers icon.
- **Run Command**   Enables you to turn on or off the Run icon.
- **Search**   Enables you to turn on or off the Search item.
- **Search Box**   Enables you to turn on or off the Search box, which displays directly above the Start button.
- **Search Communications**   Enables you to turn on or off the capability for Windows to search communication files.
- **Search Favorites And History**   Enables you to turn on or off the capability for Windows to search your Favorites and History folders when you conduct a search.
- **System Administration Tools**   Includes options for displaying the System Administration Tools folder on the All Programs menu or on the All Programs menu and Start menu. You also have the option of not showing the System Administration Tools folder.
- **Use Large Icons**   Enables you to set the Start menu to use large icons.
- **Start Menu Size**   Enables you to specify the number of recently used programs, from 0 to 30.
- **Use Default Settings**   Enables you to return the Start menu to its original configuration.
- **Show On Start Menu**   Enables you to specify which program you use to browse the Internet and send and receive e-mail.

Customizing the Classic Start Menu

If you choose to use the Classic Start menu, you can change many of the same customization options. To display the Customize Classic Start Menu dialog box, follow these steps:

1. Right-click the Start button and choose Properties to display the Start Menu tab of the Taskbar And Start Menu Properties dialog box.

2. Select the Classic Start Menu radio button (if it isn't already selected).

3. Click the Customize button to display the Customize Classic Start Menu (see Figure 11-6).

In the top half of the dialog box are five buttons. Use them to edit the programs on the Start menu. The Advanced button displays the Start Menu folder for your user account. Remember that most Start menu shortcuts are also stored in the C:\Users\All Users\Start Menu folder. The Sort button sorts the Programs menu alphabetically when you click it.

Most of the check boxes in the bottom half of the Customize Classic Start Menu dialog box are optional menu items—use the check boxes to select which items appear on your Classic Start menu. Use the Expand Control Panel, Expand Documents, Expand Pictures, Expand Network Connections, and Expand Printers check boxes to display the listed item as a menu rather than as a shortcut. Microsoft also included a few options that affect how the Start menu works:

- **Enable Dragging And Dropping**   The Start menu can be edited by dragging-and-dropping menu commands (see "Dragging-and-Dropping Items Within the Start Menu," earlier in the chapter).

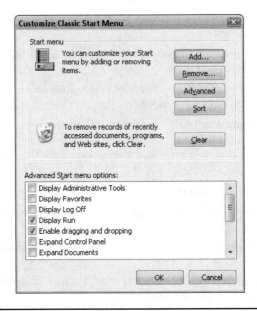

FIGURE 11-6   Changing the properties of the Classic Start menu.

- **Scroll Programs**   Scrolls the contents of the Programs menu up and down when the list is too big to fit on the screen; otherwise, the Programs menu expands to more than one column.

- **Show Small Icons In Start Menu**   By default, large icons are displayed in the Start menu. Turn on the Small Icons option to make the first level of the Start menu take up less room on the screen.

- **Use Personalized Menus**   Displays only those commands you have used recently. Turn off this option if you want to see all commands all the time.

Customizing the Taskbar

Although most Windows users find no reason to customize the taskbar, a few do. You can move the taskbar around the desktop, control its size, and choose whether it is visible all the time. The taskbar is shown in Figure 11-7.

Enabling Taskbar Changes

You can disable and enable changes to the taskbar. Some people find that they drag-and-drop items from the taskbar by accident, and they would rather have Windows prevent these changes. In fact, Windows locks the taskbar (disables changes) by default. To disable or enable editing the taskbar, right-click an unoccupied portion of the taskbar (try clicking next to the clock if you're having trouble finding an unoccupied part) and choose Lock The Taskbar. To enable changes, repeat the same steps. When the taskbar is locked, you can't edit it, move it to another edge of the screen, or change its size. You can still change the toolbars that the taskbar displays, though. (You can also lock and unlock the taskbar from the Taskbar And Start Menu Properties dialog box, which you display by right-clicking the taskbar and choosing Properties.)

Moving the Taskbar

Move the taskbar to any edge of the desktop by clicking-and-dragging it to the desired position. You have to click an unoccupied area of the taskbar—not the Start button, or a program button—to drag it. An unoccupied area of the taskbar is always available next to the clock.

When the taskbar appears on the left or right side of the desktop, it looks a little different than it does on the bottom, but it still has the same parts in the same order (the Start button is at the top). The taskbar doesn't cover icons on the desktop when it is moved—the icons shift to slightly new positions. The exception to this "icon shifting" rule is when the Auto-hide option is turned on (see "Hiding the Taskbar," later in the chapter). Then the icons don't move, but the taskbar disappears so that you can see them.

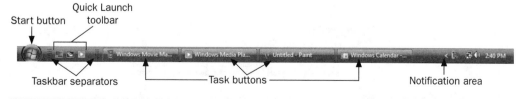

Figure 11-7   The parts of the taskbar.

Changing the Size of the Taskbar

You can change the size of the taskbar by clicking-and-dragging its inside edge—that is, the edge that borders the desktop. (Be sure that the taskbar is unlocked before you try this.) If the taskbar appears at the bottom of the screen, then change its size by clicking-and-dragging its top edge. The following illustration shows a taskbar made taller to display two rows of buttons:

A larger taskbar displays more information on each button; however, it also claims more area of the screen that could be used to display other information.

You can size the taskbar back down by clicking-and-dragging the inside edge back toward the edge of the screen—make sure to release the mouse button when the taskbar is the desired size. You can even decrease your taskbar to a thin stripe along one edge of the screen by clicking-and-dragging the edge of the taskbar to the edge of the screen. If you can't find your taskbar, try moving the mouse pointer to each edge of the screen. When the mouse pointer turns into a double-headed arrow, click-and-drag to increase the size of the taskbar.

Changing Taskbar Properties

You can change some taskbar options by right-clicking an empty part of the taskbar and choosing Properties. You see the Taskbar tab of the Taskbar And Start Menu Properties dialog box, shown in Figure 11-8.

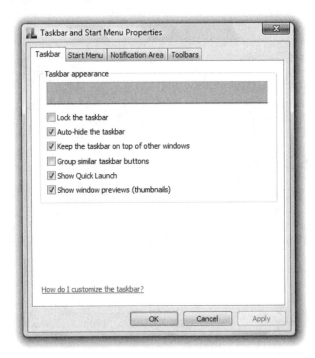

FIGURE 11-8 Changing the properties of the taskbar.

Hiding the Taskbar

You can hide the taskbar in two different ways: by decreasing its size and by using the Auto-hide option. Changing the size of the taskbar is covered in the previous section—click-and-drag the inside edge of the taskbar to the screen's closest edge. The taskbar becomes a thin blue line on one edge of the screen. The other option is to use the Auto-hide feature to hide the taskbar. Auto-hide tries to determine when you need the taskbar and displays the taskbar only when you need it.

To turn on Auto-hide, display the Taskbar tab of the Taskbar And Start Menu Properties dialog box and select the Auto-hide The Taskbar check box. When Auto-hide is on, the taskbar disappears when it isn't being used. To display it, point to the edge of the screen where it last appeared. Or, you can press CTRL-ESC or the WINDOWS key (a key with the Windows symbol that displays the Start menu) to display the taskbar and open the Start menu at the same time.

TIP   *If you can't find your taskbar, move the mouse pointer to each edge of the screen. If Auto-hide is on, the taskbar appears. If the taskbar is shrunk, the mouse pointer turns into a double-headed arrow—click-and-drag to increase the taskbar's size.*

Allowing the Taskbar to Be Covered by a Window

You can choose whether you want the taskbar to be covered by other windows by selecting the Keep The Taskbar On Top Of Other Windows check box on the Taskbar tab of the Taskbar And Start Menu Properties dialog box. When this check box is selected, the taskbar always appears over other windows. When the option is off, windows may cover the taskbar. To use the taskbar when the Keep The Taskbar On Top Of Other Windows option is turned off, move or minimize windows until the taskbar is visible, or press CTRL-ESC or the WINDOWS key to both display the taskbar and open the Start menu (press ESC once if you want to use only the taskbar). We recommend that you leave this check box selected.

Grouping Taskbar Buttons

You can group similar task buttons on the taskbar. This option, which is on by default, puts task buttons for files opened in the same program together on the taskbar. If the taskbar becomes crowded, the buttons are collapsed into a single button.

A button for grouped windows has a downward arrow on its right side. Click the button to see the individual windows, and click the window you want. You can turn this option off by deselecting the Group Similar Taskbar Buttons check box on the Taskbar tab of the Taskbar And Start Menu Properties dialog box.

NOTE   *Some people don't like grouped task buttons, because it takes an extra click to switch from, say, one Word document window to another.*

Hiding the Clock on the Taskbar

You can choose to display or hide the *system clock* that usually appears in the notification area of the taskbar. Display the Notification Area tab of the Taskbar And Start Menu Properties dialog box, and then select or deselect the Clock check box in the System Icons area.

Hiding Notification Area Icons

The notification area where the clock appears also holds icons for programs and processes that are running in the background (that is, running without you realizing that they are running). In versions of Windows prior to Windows XP, this area filled up with icons. By default, Windows Vista hides inactive icons (icons that don't require your immediate attention). You can change this setting so that icons are visible all the time by deselecting the Hide Inactive Icons check box in the Notification Area tab of the Taskbar And Start Menu Properties dialog box. You can also customize the setting by clicking Customize to see the Customize Icons dialog box, which displays a list of the icons that are currently in the notification area (whether hidden or not). Select an item and then pick from the drop-down list. For each item, you can select Hide When Inactive (the default), Hide, or Show. For your settings to take effect, be sure the Hide Inactive Icons check box on the Taskbar And Start Menu Properties dialog box is selected.

Adding Toolbars to the Taskbar

You can configure the taskbar to include toolbars, or you can display toolbars elsewhere on your desktop. Taskbar toolbars give you easy access to frequently used icons: you no longer have to minimize all open programs to display a desktop icon to open a program. Instead you can use a toolbar button. Or, you can use the toolbar button Show Desktop to minimize all open programs with one click. You can even edit the buttons that appear on a toolbar or create a completely new toolbar.

Adding and Removing Toolbars from the Taskbar

Use the Taskbar shortcut menu, shown here, to add and remove toolbars from the taskbar:

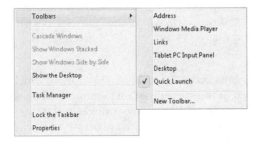

You can display the Taskbar shortcut menu by right-clicking an unoccupied part of the taskbar (even on a full taskbar, an unoccupied part is on either side of the clock).

The Toolbars command on the Taskbar shortcut menu displays a menu with the available toolbars. Toolbars that are already displayed on the taskbar appear with check marks. To display a toolbar, click its name. To remove a displayed toolbar, follow the same procedure to remove the check mark.

Microsoft provides a second way to choose whether to display the Quick Launch toolbar or not. Right-click the taskbar and choose Properties to display the Taskbar tab of the Taskbar And Start Menus Properties dialog box, which includes the Show Quick Launch check box. Checking this check box does the same thing as right-clicking the taskbar and choosing Toolbars | Quick Launch.

Controlling the Look of a Toolbar

You can control the way a toolbar works by using the Toolbar shortcut menu, shown here:

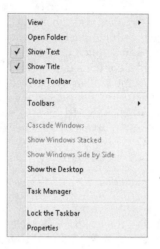

Display the Toolbar shortcut menu by right-clicking an unoccupied part of the toolbar (if you have trouble finding an unoccupied part of the toolbar, right-click the toolbar handle).

The following choices on the Toolbar shortcut menu control your toolbar (the rest of the choices that appear affect the whole taskbar):

- **View**   Allows you to display either large or small icons. The default setting is Small.

- **Open Folder**   Opens the folder where the toolbar shortcuts are stored, so that you can edit the toolbar. Once the folder is open, you can add and delete shortcuts to change the contents of the toolbar.

- **Show Text**   Displays text on each button. Choose this option again to display icons with no text. Turning off this option makes a toolbar take up less space.

- **Show Title**   Turns off or on the display of the name of the toolbar.

- **Close Toolbar**   Removes the toolbar from the screen.

- **Toolbars**   Allows you to display a new toolbar, hide a displayed toolbar, or create a new toolbar. This option is the same as the Toolbars option on the Taskbar shortcut menu.

Editing the Quick Launch Toolbar

You can easily add and remove buttons from the Quick Launch toolbar. To remove a button, right-click the button and choose Delete. To add a button, drag a shortcut or an EXE file to the toolbar. If you want to make a copy of a shortcut from the desktop in the Quick Launch toolbar, hold down the CTRL key while you drag the shortcut from the desktop to the toolbar.

Creating a New Toolbar

In addition to the existing toolbars, you can create your own toolbar to display the contents of a drive, folder, or Internet address. Depending on the options you choose for your new toolbar, it may look something like this one, which shows the contents of a folder called Consult:

In this example, the Consult folder contains four other folders and numerous files. On the toolbar, you can see the four folders—you can display the entire contents of the Consult folder by clicking the arrow at the right end of the toolbar. Notice that the subfolders are displayed as menus, so you can open a file directly from the toolbar. Clicking a folder button opens an Explorer window for that folder; clicking a file button opens the file.

CAUTION *If you create a new toolbar and then close it, it's gone. To redisplay it, you need to re-create the toolbar.*

To create a new toolbar, right-click the taskbar or a toolbar and choose Toolbars | New Toolbar from the shortcut menu that appears. You see the New Toolbar dialog box, shown in Figure 11-9, which enables you to browse available drives and folders. Click the arrow next to a folder name to expand that branch of the folder tree. You can open any folder or drive available to you in Windows Explorer—these may include drives and folders on the Internet. Click New Folder to create a new subfolder in the highlighted folder. Select the folder you want to use to create a toolbar and click OK in the New Toolbar dialog box.

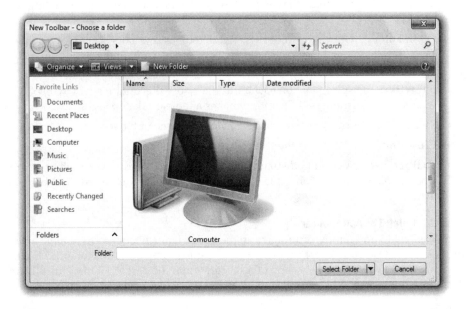

FIGURE 11-9   Select a drive or folder to create a toolbar with a button for each folder and file in the drive or folder.

Setting Up Your Desktop

When your desktop is set up in a way that is right for you, everything flows more smoothly. Files and programs are where you expect them to be. The screen is attractive and doesn't hurt your eyes. Your desktop's background and screen saver are different from everyone else's, giving your computer a familiar, homey feel. Of course, if you choose to use (and your system has the required hardware to run) Windows Vista's new Aero desktop theme, it may not feel quite so familiar at first.

This chapter describes how to configure your desktop to suit your own preferences, including choosing a desktop theme, the Vista Sidebar and gadgets, RSS feeds, background, screen saver, color scheme (using the Color dialog box), icons, other visual effects, and sound effects. Windows comes with the new Aero interface, but you can switch to a non-Aero Windows design if you prefer. This chapter also describes how to set your screen resolution and how to use multiple displays at the same time, if you have the right hardware.

What Are Display Properties?

You configure your desktop and monitor by changing Windows' display properties. For example, if you want to dress up your desktop, you can change the background color or image and change the size, color, or font of the individual elements that make up the desktop. You can add the new Sidebar and Gadgets feature to your desktop to provide quick access to mini-applications (called *gadgets*). When you step away from your computer, you can tell it to display a screen saver until you get back.

The command center for most anything having to do with your monitor or desktop is the Personalization Control Panel window, shown in Figure 12-1. You can access it from the main window of the Control Panel or by right-clicking any unoccupied spot on the desktop and choosing Personalize from the shortcut menu.

The Personalization tool has the following seven tools:

- **Window Color And Appearance** Controls the color, size, and font of every standard type of object Windows uses
- **Desktop Background** Lets you choose icons and background pictures
- **Screen Saver** Offers screen savers and automatic settings for turning off your monitor

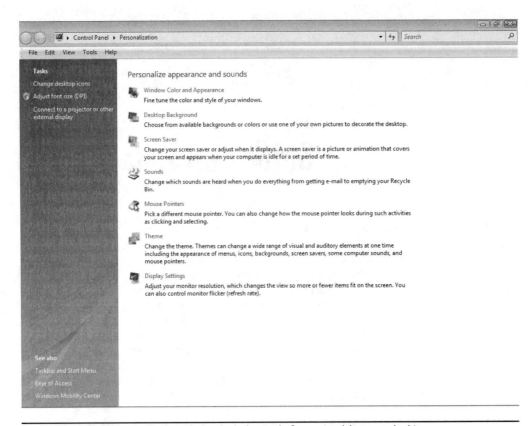

FIGURE 12-1   The Personalization window includes tools for customizing your desktop.

- **Sounds**   Provides options for modifying the sounds that play for different Windows actions and behaviors
- **Mouse Pointers**   Enables you to choose different types of mouse pointers and cursors
- **Theme**   Controls desktop themes
- **Display Settings**   Lets you set the size of the desktop (in pixels), number of colors displayed, and monitor performance

You can use these tools to change the way Windows looks. As you make changes to your display and desktop settings, the new settings are not applied until you click Apply or OK. Clicking Apply makes the change and leaves the dialog box for that Personalization tool open. Clicking OK makes the change and also closes the dialog box.

Choosing a Desktop Theme

You can change the appearance of practically anything on your desktop. However, getting a collection of colors, icons, pictures, fonts, mouse pointers, screen savers, and so on that look good together takes more time and artistic talent than most of us have. A *desktop theme* is a complete "look" for your desktop. By changing themes, you can alter everything about the appearance of your desktop in one fell swoop.

NOTE   *Windows 98 and Me had both "desktop schemes" and desktop themes. Desktop themes were separate Windows components that you could install from your Windows Me/98 CD-ROM, while desktop schemes were selected from the Display Properties dialog box. Windows XP and now Windows Vista combine most of the elements of both into desktop themes.*

A desktop theme provides not only a system of colors and fonts, but also sounds, icons, mouse pointers, a desktop background, and a screen saver. Windows Vista ships with three themes: Windows Vista, Windows Aero, and Windows Classic (which looks like earlier versions of Windows). If your system does not meet the Aero requirements, you will not see the Windows Aero option. Microsoft will also probably provide specialized themes you can download from its web site. Also, we have confidence that themes for Windows Vista will appear on third-party web sites like CNET's web site (at http://download.com), which already has countless themes for earlier versions of Windows.

Changing Themes

To change your desktop theme, follow these steps:

1. Right-click any empty spot on the desktop and choose Personalize from the shortcut menu. The Personalization window appears, as shown in Figure 12-1.

2. Double-click Theme. The Theme Settings dialog box appears, as shown in Figure 12-2.

FIGURE 12-2   Choosing a desktop theme from the Theme Settings dialog box.

3. Select the name of a theme from the Theme drop-down list. A preview of the theme appears in the Sample box below the Theme list.

4. Click OK. The Theme Settings dialog box disappears, and Windows applies the theme to your desktop.

Creating and Saving Your Own Desktop Theme

After you choose a theme, you can modify it by changing individual elements:

- The background image or color (see "Changing the Background")
- The screen saver (see "Setting Up a Screen Saver")
- The color scheme (see "Choosing a New Color Scheme")
- The windows and buttons (see "Changing Windows, Buttons, and Fonts")
- The font or size of text used in title bars, message boxes, menus, and elsewhere (see "Changing Fonts")
- The size or shape of icons (see "Choosing New Desktop Icons")
- Visual effects, like whether a menu fades or scrolls up after you're finished using it (see "Changing the Desktop's Visual Effects")
- Sound effects (see "Changing the Desktop's Sound Effects")

After you have modified a theme, it is listed as "modified" on the Theme drop-down list of the Themes tab of the Theme Settings dialog box. To save your changes as a new desktop theme, do the following:

1. Open the Personalization window by right-clicking any empty space on the desktop and selecting Personalize from the shortcut menu.

2. Double-click Theme to open the Theme Settings dialog box.

3. Click the Save As button in the Theme Settings dialog box. A Save As dialog box appears.

4. Use the Save As dialog box to find the folder where you want to store the file containing the new theme.

5. Type a name for the theme into the File Name box in the Save As dialog box.

6. Click the Save button.

7. Click OK to close the Theme Settings dialog box.

Your new theme now appears on the Theme list in the Theme Settings dialog box. To remove it (or any other theme) from the list, select it and click the Delete button.

Changing the Vista Welcome Center

Another feature you will see when you first start Windows Vista is the Windows Vista Welcome Center, as shown in Figure 12-3. The Welcome Center window comprises three main areas: a top area, a Get Started With Windows area, and an Offers From Microsoft area.

FIGURE 12-3 Vista's Welcome Center provides tools and information to help you get started using Vista.

When you click links in the Get Started area, the top area changes to reflect the choice you made. You then click the link on the right side of the area to start using the selected option. For example, the View Computer Details item shows by default. It displays a snapshot of details about your computer, including the following:

- Windows Vista version, such as Windows Vista Ultimate

- CPU name and size, such as Mobile Intel Pentium 4, 2.00 GHz

- Amount of system memory (RAM), such as 512 MB

- Computer model, such as Dell 8200

- Computer name, such as INVISTA

If this is not enough information for you, such as if you are doing system maintenance and need more data about your computer, click the Show More Details link. Windows displays the System folder, which has your computer information, computer name and domain data, activation information, and links to other computer tasks you can perform (such as viewing the Device Manager for further hardware details).

In the Get Started With Windows area of the Welcome Center, Vista displays several common tasks to help you get started using Windows and some of its new features and tools.

FIGURE 12-4   Use Welcome Center tasks to start using Windows Vista.

Also available are links to help topics and demos that provide assistance to you when you are learning how to use Vista. By default, 6 tasks show, but you can see all 14 of them by clicking the Show All 14 Items link. Figure 12-4 shows all of these tasks.

The following tasks are shown by default in the Get Started With Windows area when you initially install Vista:

- View computer details
- Connect to the Internet
- Personalize Windows
- Windows Basics
- Windows Vista Demos
- Transfer files and settings
- Windows Ultimate Extras (only if you have Window Vista Ultimate installed)
- Register Windows online
- Ease of Access Center
- Control Panel

Figure 12-5   Microsoft special offers are shown on the Welcome Center screen.

- Add new users
- What's new in Windows Vista
- Windows Media Center
- Back Up and Restore Center

All of these items are available in other areas of Windows, such as from the Start menu or Control Panel, but the Welcome Center helps you get to them quicker.

The Welcome Center also shows current special offers you can download from Microsoft's web site. As shown in Figure 12-5, seven offers are available for download at the time of this writing, including information about Windows Marketplace, technical support, and more. As offers change, you will see different ones show up here. You must be connected to the Internet to see the most current offers and to access them from Microsoft.com.

Running Welcome Center at Startup

By default, Welcome Center appears when you start Vista for the first time. It remains on your screen until you click the Close button. If you do not want to see the Welcome Center at startup, click to clear the Run At Startup check box at the bottom of the Welcome Center screen. Click the Close button. Then, when you start Windows the next time, the Welcome Center does not display.

To redisplay the Welcome Center, choose Start | Control Panel and double-click Welcome Center. Finally, check the Run At Startup check box. The next time you start Windows, the Welcome Center will display.

Showing All Welcome Center Items

When the Welcome Center window opens, it is not a maximized window. For this reason, all the items available do not show in this initial view. Instead, only a subset of all the items shows. The number of total items displays in the title for each area. For example, Get Started With Windows (14) indicates that there are 14 items in this area, and Offers From Microsoft (7) indicates there are 7 items in this area.

You can display all the Welcome Center items by clicking the Show All 14 Items link. The Welcome Center window expands and shows all the items that you can click. In the Offers From Microsoft area, you can click the Show All 7 Items link (or however many items are available), and the Offers From Microsoft area expands to show all the items.

Changing the Background

The *background* is the pattern, picture, or color that lies behind all the windows, icons, and menus on your desktop. The background used to be called *wallpaper* before people noticed that wallpapering your desktop is a mixed metaphor. With Windows XP and Windows Server 2003, the term "wallpaper" was not used as much. Windows Vista, however, includes an option for choosing Windows Wallpaper and includes a few sample black and white photos to use.

Your desktop background can be any color or image. Windows comes with several attractive photographs, as well as a number of abstract patterns, that you can use as a background. You can also use image files that you download from the Internet, copy from a friend, or get from your scanner or digital camera.

Selecting an Image or Pattern from the Background List

To select a background image or pattern for your desktop, first click the Desktop Background link on the Personalization window (shown earlier in Figure 12-1). The Desktop Background window (see Figure 12-6) lists all the background image options that Windows knows about. Click a type from the Picture Location drop-down list to see thumbnail views of the available backgrounds.

A background image is a file in an HTML or image format (with the extension .bmp, .jpg, .gif, or .tif). That image has a size, which may or may not match the dimensions of your display. If the image is smaller than the display, the position options at the bottom of the Desktop Background window give you three choices:

- **Stretch**   Stretches the image to fill the display. Photographs end up looking like funhouse mirrors, but many abstract patterns stretch well.

- **Tile**   Repeats the image to fill the display with the image. This works particularly well with colors or images designed for tiling.

- **Center**   Puts the image in the center of the display, letting the background color of the desktop form a frame around the image. This is your best choice for photographs that are slightly smaller than the display.

FIGURE 12-6 Use the Desktop Background window to select your background.

If the image you choose is larger than your display, the center and tile options both give you a single copy of the image, with the edges of the image off the screen. If this isn't satisfactory, you can use Microsoft Paint to crop the image, or you can redefine the dimensions of your display (see "Changing the Screen Resolution" later in the chapter).

When the preview in the Desktop Background window looks the way you want, click OK (which closes the window).

Making Your Own Background Images

You aren't limited to the backgrounds that come with Windows. You can use any image file—like a digital or scanned picture of your kids—as a background. Any image file that you move to your Pictures folder automatically appears in the Pictures list of the Desktop Background window. If the file is somewhere else on your system, you can click the Browse button and find the file in the Browse dialog box that appears.

Selecting a Background Color

Any background image you select automatically covers the background color of your desktop. This means that you see the background color of your desktop only if you do not choose a background (or Windows Wallpaper) image or if the image is centered with the background visible around the edges.

To select a new background color, follow these steps:

1. Right-click any empty area on the desktop and select Personalize from the shortcut menu. The Personalization window appears.

2. Click the Desktop Background link to open the Desktop Background window (shown earlier in Figure 12-6).

3. Click the Picture Location drop-down list. A list of options appears.

4. Click Solid Colors.

5. If one of the colors on the palette is what you want, click it. A small square below the selections displays the color.

6. If you don't like any of the colors on the palette, click More, and follow the directions in the section "Finding the Perfect Color" later in this chapter.

7. Click OK to change the desktop color.

Setting Up a Screen Saver

If you walk away from your computer and leave the monitor on, the same image might be on your screen for hours at a time. Years ago, this would tend to "burn in" the image permanently on the screen. To prevent such screen damage, developers created *screen savers*, which are programs that kick in when the display hasn't changed in a while. A good screen saver contains some kind of moving image, so no section of the screen is consistently bright or dark.

Monitor technology eventually improved to the point that burn-in is not a serious concern. In addition, many monitors now have an energy-saving feature that allows a monitor to turn off automatically if its display hasn't changed for some period of time (see "Managing Your Computer's Power" in Chapter 16).

But even though screen savers are no longer needed for their original purpose, many people continue to use them because they are pleasant to look at. They also discourage random passersby from reading the document you're working on when you step out for coffee. If your computer is set up with user accounts, the screen saver can require you to log back in when you return, so others can't use your computer (without your password). Built-in Windows screen savers like Aurora or Mystify make attractive geometric patterns that can be soothing to watch; others like 3D Test create a more active mood.

In offices with multiple networked computers, the screen saver can display the computer's name, suitably colorized and animated. You can also download screen savers from the Internet, enabling you to display images from the latest movie or hottest sports team when you're not working. Or you can use the Photos screen saver to cycle through pictures of your grandchildren or your vacation in Bali.

Selecting a Screen Saver

To select and activate a screen saver, follow these steps:

1. Open the Personalization window by right-clicking any empty spot on the desktop and selecting Personalize from the shortcut menu.

FIGURE 12-7   Choosing and configuring a screen saver.

2. Click Screen Saver to display the Screen Saver Settings dialog box, shown in Figure 12-7.

3. Select a screen saver from the Screen Saver drop-down list. The preview box shows a miniaturized version of what the screen saver displays. To see a full-size preview, click the Preview button. Move the mouse or click a key to stop the full-size preview.

4. When you find a screen saver you like, click either the Apply or OK button.

TIP *Windows comes with a choice of several screen savers, but that's just the beginning. Additional screen savers are available on the Internet, and most of them are free. You can begin your search at CNET's web site at www.download.com, which lists screen savers in the Utilities & Drivers department. You can also try looking on the web site of your favorite book, TV show, or movie to see whether there is a promotional screen saver. To avoid downloading spyware, viruses, and other potentially harmful program files, try to download only from reputable sources.*

Configuring Your Screen Saver

From the Screen Saver tab, you can make a number of choices about how your screen saver functions:

- **Change the settings** Click the Settings button. Each screen saver has its own list of settings; some let you change a handful of parameters; others offer an entire screen full of choices. In general, the settings of your screen saver control how fast the screen saver cycles, the colors it uses, the thickness of the lines it draws, and so forth.

- **Change the wait time** Enter a new number of minutes into the Wait box. The *wait time* is the length of time your system must be inactive before the screen saver starts up. Windows waits this long for keyboard or mouse input before starting the screen saver.

- **Require a password** Check the On Resume, Display Logon Screen check box. When the screen saver is displayed and you press a key, you will see the Locked window, asking for your user account name and password (see Chapter 6).

Choosing a New Color Scheme

A *color scheme* is a coordinated set of colors for all the basic desktop objects. With a color scheme, you can change the color of everything at once and wind up with colors that look good together and provide reasonable visibility. (You don't want to wind up with black text on black title bars, for example.) To change color schemes, follow these steps:

1. Right-click an empty space on the desktop and choose Personalize from the shortcut menu. The Personalization window opens.

2. Click the Window Color And Appearance link to display the Appearance Settings dialog box, shown in Figure 12-8.

3. Make a selection from the Color Scheme list.

4. Click OK.

NOTE *The color schemes that are available to you depend in part on your choice of window and button styles. If you choose Windows Classic windows and buttons, all the Windows Me color schemes are available.*

Finding the Perfect Color

When you choose to change the color of the desktop, the title bars, or any of the other basic objects, Windows offers a simple palette of 20 colors. If you want more choices, click Other on the color palette to display the Color dialog box, shown in woefully inadequate black and white in Figure 12-9.

The number of basic colors has now expanded to 48, shown in the Basic Colors palette on the left side of the Color dialog box. If the color you want is on this palette, click it and click OK. If even the 48 colors aren't enough for you, you can use the settings on the right side of the Color dialog box to get any color you want.

FIGURE 12-8   The Appearance Settings dialog box.

The currently selected color is shown in the Color | Solid box. To the right of the Color | Solid box are two different numerical systems of describing the current color: its hue, saturation, and luminescence (known as *HSV coordinates*); and its red, green, and blue components (known as *RGB coordinates*). Above the Color | Solid box and the coordinates is a graphical representation of the current color's HSV coordinates. The horizontal position of the cross-hairs in the large square represents the hue, and the vertical position of the cross-hairs represents the saturation. The position of the vertical slider next to the square represents the luminescence. Thus, the same

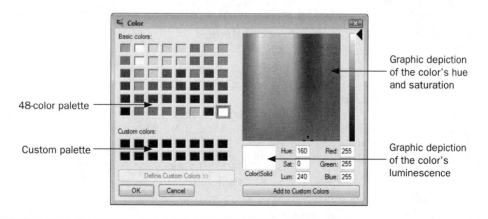

FIGURE 12-9   The Color dialog box.

color is represented three ways: as RGB, as HSV, and as a position of the cross-hairs and slider. You can select a new color by manipulating any of the three descriptions:

- Move the cross-hairs and slider with the mouse
- Type new numbers (from 0 to 240) into the HSV coordinate boxes
- Type new numbers (from 0 to 255) into the RGB coordinate boxes

When you use one of these methods to specify the color, the other two descriptions (and the Color|Solid box) change automatically to match.

If you think you might want to use this color again in the future, click Add To Custom Colors. The new color appears in one of the boxes in the Custom Colors palette on the bottom-left side of the Color dialog box. If you like, you can define several custom colors, one at a time. Like basic colors, custom colors can be selected by clicking them.

When you have created all the colors you want, select the one you want to use, and click OK. The color is applied and the Color dialog box vanishes.

Changing Windows, Buttons, and Fonts

The Windows Vista desktop theme doesn't allow many color changes—you have seven color scheme choices, and you can set the background color of the desktop. However, with the Windows Classic desktop theme, you can configure the color, size, and font of almost anything—title bars, active windows, inactive windows, message boxes, and more. These choices are made all at once (along with changes in screen savers, background images, and many other items) when you choose a desktop theme (see "Choosing a Desktop Theme" earlier in the chapter). But you may want to change the windows, buttons, or fonts while leaving the rest of your desktop alone. Or you may want to change just one or two things, like the color of title bars or the font size of tool tips.

The place to make changes to the windows, buttons, and fonts in Windows is the Appearance Settings dialog box (shown earlier in Figure 12-8). To get to this dialog box, right-click any open space on the desktop, choose Personalize from the shortcut menu, and then click the Window Color And Appearance link to display the Appearance Settings dialog box.

Changing the Appearance of Individual Items

You can edit the appearance of title bars, message boxes, and many other individual items from the Advanced Appearance dialog box, shown in Figure 12-10, which you open by clicking the Advanced button in the Appearance Settings dialog box.

To change the appearance of an item, first find it on the Item drop-down list of the Advanced Appearance dialog box (in Figure 12-10, Desktop is chosen). After you choose an item, the text boxes and buttons relevant to that item become active.

NOTE   *Not all of the text boxes and buttons of the Advanced Appearance dialog box are relevant to all items. For example, a scroll bar has no text, so the second line of buttons and text boxes becomes inactive when Scrollbar is the selected item.*

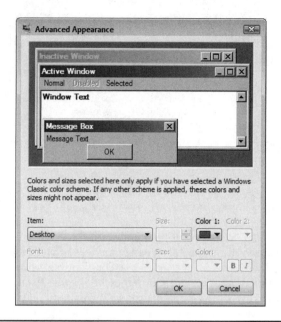

FIGURE 12-10   The Advanced Appearance dialog box gives you finer control over the look of Windows.

The first row of text boxes and buttons (Size, Color1, and Color2) refers to the item itself. So, for example, for the Active Title Bar item, the Size text box refers to the height of the title bar. Color1 is the color on the left side of the title bar, and Color2 is the color on the right side. The second row of text boxes and buttons (Font, Size, Color, Bold, and Italic) refers to the text (if any) displayed on the item.

As you enter the new information into the Advanced Appearance dialog box, the items in the dialog box's preview box change accordingly. When you are satisfied with your changes, click OK and then click OK again to close the Appearance Settings dialog box.

TIP   *It's possible to make some dreadful choices in the Advanced Appearance dialog box. You can always go back to square one by choosing one of the built-in desktop themes (see "Choosing a Desktop Theme" earlier in the chapter).*

Changing Fonts

You can fairly easily make an overall change in the size of the text that appears in menus, title bars, file labels, and other system contexts. With a little more effort, you can change not just the size, but the font as well. You also can make changes to the text used in specific contexts, rather than an overall text change.

Changing the Size of Fonts

If the default fonts that Windows uses are not large enough for you, you can easily make them bigger. Open the Personalization window (right-click the desktop and choose Personalize). Click the Adjust Font Size (DPI) link on the left side of the window. The DPI Scaling dialog box appears. Click Larger Scale (120 DPI). Click OK to save your settings.

FIGURE 12-11 Choosing special desktop effects.

TIP *Another way to increase the size of text on your screen (as well as everything else) is to use the Magnifier tool, found in the Ease of Access Center. See Chapter 17 for more information.*

The Advanced Appearance dialog box, shown earlier in Figure 12-10, gives you much finer control over Windows' fonts. You can change the font as well as the size of text, and you can change some items while leaving others alone. For example, you could choose one font for the text in menus and another for the text in message boxes. To change the font, size, or color of the text that Windows uses for a particular type of item, refer to the previous section, "Changing the Appearance of Individual Items."

Smoothing the Edges of Fonts

Fonts have a tendency to look ragged when displayed on a monitor. Windows offers a choice of two methods for combating this tendency: Standard and ClearType. The Standard method is the default. ClearType is a relatively new technique that Microsoft invented for use in e-books. We recommend taking a look at ClearType if you think that the fonts you're seeing look ragged, especially on LCD screens.

To change from one method to the other, follow these steps:

1. Open the Personalization window by right-clicking any empty space on the desktop and selecting Personalize from the shortcut menu. Click Window Color And Appearance to open the Appearance Settings dialog box (shown earlier in Figure 12-8).

2. Click the Effects button on the Appearance tab. The Effects dialog box appears, as shown in Figure 12-11.

3. Make sure that the Use The Following Method To Smooth Edges Of Screen Fonts check box is checked.

4. Choose Standard or ClearType from the drop-down list, and then click OK in both the Effects dialog box and the Appearance Settings dialog box.

Changing Icons

You can change the size or arrangement of the icons on your desktop. You can even define new icons for the various types of desktop objects.

Changing Icon Size

If your icons seem too small, you can switch from regular icons (32 points) to large icons (48 points), as follows:

1. Right-click the desktop.
2. Click View from the submenu that appears.
3. Click Large Icons.

You can make finer adjustments in icon size from the Advanced Appearance dialog box (shown earlier in Figure 12-10). Choose Icon from the Item drop-down list in the Advanced Appearance dialog box, and then choose a number between 6 and 72 in the Size box. This represents the size of icons in points. The default size is 9 points. The second row of text boxes and buttons in the dialog box controls the font and size of the labels underneath your icons.

CAUTION Making your icons too large may cause them to look ragged. Icons in Explorer windows become more visible when you switch to Extra Large Icons view (see "Changing Views" in Chapter 9).

Arranging Icons on the Desktop

You can arrange your desktop icons manually by dragging-and-dropping them. If your system is set up for single-click opening, however, you may open the corresponding objects by mistake when you try to drag-and-drop icons. If you're having this problem, use right-click drag-and-drop. Select Move Here from the shortcut menu that appears when you drop the icon.

Arranging Icons Automatically

To arrange your desktop icons automatically, right-click any open spot on the desktop, choose Sort, and then choose Arrange Icons from the shortcut menu. Windows arranges the icons in columns, starting on the left side of the desktop. The Arrange Icons menu gives you the option of arranging by name, size, type, or date modified.

CAUTION Make sure that you really want the icons arranged in columns before you use an Arrange Icons option. There is no "undo" selection on the Arrange Icons menu.

Use the Auto Arrange feature to have Windows automatically arrange icons as you move icons around or add one to the desktop. To enable Auto Arrange, right-click the desktop, choose View, and then choose Auto Arrange.

Adjusting Icon Spacing

The spacing between icons is another of the many details controlled by the Advanced Appearance dialog box (see "Changing the Appearance of Individual Items" earlier in the chapter). To change the spacing, open the Advanced Appearance dialog box and choose Icon Spacing (Horizontal) or Icon Spacing (Vertical) from the Item drop-down list. Type a number (of points) in the Size box. Larger numbers create bigger spaces.

FIGURE 12-12 The Desktop Icon Settings dialog box.

NOTE *Changing the icon spacing affects the icon arrangement of Explorer windows, as well as the icons on the desktop.*

Choosing New Desktop Icons

You can choose new icons for any of the standard desktop objects. Make these changes from the Desktop Icon Settings dialog box, shown in Figure 12-12.

To choose a new icon for Computer, Network, or the Recycle Bin, follow these steps:

1. Open the Personalization window by clicking any empty space on the desktop and selecting Personalize from the shortcut menu. Click Change Desktop Icons on the left side of the window to open the Desktop Icon Settings dialog box.

2. Select the icon that you want to change from the box of icons.

3. Click the Change Icon button. The Change Icon dialog box appears, showing you the icons available for this item. If you don't see an icon you want and know that there are other icons elsewhere on your system, you can click the Browse button and look for another file of icons.

4. When you find the icon you want, select it in the Change Icon dialog box and click OK.

5. Click OK to close the Desktop Icon Settings dialog box.

Deleting and Recovering Desktop Icons

You can remove desktop icons in the same way that you delete files and folders: select them and press the DELETE key. The only icon for which this technique fails is the Recycle Bin.

The Computer, Network, and Recycle Bin icons represent capabilities of your system that you cannot delete; you can only stop displaying them on the desktop. The objects they represent continue to appear in Explorer windows, on the Start menu, and as links on the task pane. To remove any of these icons from your desktop, open the Desktop Icon Settings dialog box (see Figure 12-12 in the previous section) and uncheck its check box in the Desktop Icons section. (This is the only way we know of to remove the Recycle Bin icon from the desktop without manually modifying the Windows registry.)

If you decide that you want these icons back on the desktop, you can restore them from the Desktop Icon Settings dialog box. Select the check boxes of the items whose icons you want to have on the desktop. Then click OK to close the Desktop Icon Settings dialog box.

Changing the Desktop's Visual Effects

Windows has a number of cute but inconsequential visual effects that create the illusion of motion or three-dimensionality on the desktop, like the thin shadow that surrounds the Start menu. You can control these effects from the Effects dialog box (shown earlier in Figure 12-11). To open this dialog box, first open the Personalization window by right-clicking any open space on the desktop and selecting Personalize from the shortcut menu. Click Window Color And Appearance to open the Appearance Settings dialog box (shown earlier in Figure 12-8). Then click the Effects button on the Appearance tab.

The check boxes in the Effects dialog box are self-explanatory. The effects themselves are harmless, so don't be afraid to experiment with them.

Changing the Desktop's Sound Effects

Most actions on the desktop (closing a window, for example) are accompanied by a sound effect. You can change these sounds all at once (or turn them off entirely) by choosing a new sound scheme, or you can change only a few sounds and leave the rest alone. A *sound scheme* is a coordinated set of sounds for all the desktop actions.

Make these choices from the Sounds tab of the Sound dialog box, shown in Figure 12-13. Open this dialog box by clicking the Sounds link in the Personalization Control Panel window, and then click the Sounds tab. Choose a sound scheme from the Sound Scheme drop-down list (Windows Vista comes with only two sound schemes: No Sounds and Windows Default).

You can also change sounds for individual events. To choose a new sound for a type of event, select the event from the Program list on the Sounds tab and then select a sound from the Sounds drop-down list. For more information about associating sounds with Windows events, see "Choosing What Sounds Windows Makes" in Chapter 20.

FIGURE 12-13 Control sound effects from the Sounds tab of the Sound dialog box.

Changing Display Settings

Windows gives you control over the dimensions of your desktop, the color resolution of your display, and many other properties. Most of this power resides in the Display Settings dialog box, shown in Figure 12-14. Open this dialog box by right-clicking any empty space on the desktop, selecting Personalize from the shortcut menu, and then clicking the Display Settings link.

Changing the Screen Resolution

The Resolution slider on the Display Settings dialog box controls the dimensions of your desktop in *pixels*, which are the colored dots on the screen. The current dimensions are stated under the slider. Increase the dimensions by moving the slider to the right; decrease them by moving the slider to the left.

Naturally, the size of your monitor doesn't change (the number of inches on your monitor is fixed), so when you increase the number of pixels on your desktop, each pixel gets correspondingly smaller, increasing the resolution. Icons and fonts shrink as well. As you increase the desktop area, you may want to increase font and icon size to compensate. (See the "Changing Fonts" and "Changing Icon Size" sections earlier in this chapter.)

The range of resolutions depends on what type of monitor you use. For a 14-inch monitor, your choices may range only from 800 × 600 to 1024 × 768. For a 17-inch monitor, you can increase the resolution up to 1600 × 1200. Larger monitors support even higher resolutions. If you have a monitor larger than 14 inches, consider increasing your screen resolution settings so that you'll be able to see more information on your screen. Here are our recommendations

FIGURE 12-14   The Monitor tab of the Display Settings dialog box.

for screen resolution based on monitor size (that is, the size of the CRT tube that can display an image, measured diagonally):

Screen Size	Maximum Usable Resolution
14 inches	640×480
15 inches	800×600
17 inches	1024×768
19 to 21 inches	1280×1024 or 1600×1200

TIP   *Windows doesn't normally support resolutions of less than 800 × 600. However, if you really want a lower resolution, open the Display Settings dialog box, click the Advanced Settings button, click the Adapter tab, click the List All Modes button, and choose a display mode of 640 × 480.*

Changing the Color Quality

The Display Settings dialog box also controls the number of colors you display. The Colors drop-down list gives you choices that depend on the quality of your monitor. Your options may include 16 colors, 256 colors, high color (16-bit, or 65,536 colors), 24-bit true color (16 million colors), and 32-bit true color (even more colors). Below the list is a color bar showing the spectrum of the selected color palette.

The choice to be made is a speed versus beauty trade-off. Displaying fewer colors or pixels is less work for your computer and may help it run faster. On the other hand, displaying more colors and pixels provides a richer viewing experience, particularly if you are looking at photographs. Using 16-bit color or higher produces much-improved image quality.

NOTE   *Colors and pixels also trade off against each other, because increasing either one uses more of the portion of RAM your system devotes to the display. Windows accounts for this automatically. If you increase the desktop area beyond the capabilities of your RAM, Windows decreases the color palette to compensate. Likewise, if you increase the color palette beyond what your RAM can handle, Windows decreases the desktop size.*

A few programs don't work properly with the new color palette until you restart your computer. In general, we recommend restarting your computer to be completely safe; but, if you change the color palette frequently, this can get to be a nuisance. You may want to experiment to see whether the software you use has any problems when you don't restart after a color change. You can set up Windows to restart automatically when you change the color palette, ask you whether to restart, or not restart (see the "Adjusting Other Monitor Settings" section later in this chapter).

Changing Color Profiles

Subtle differences occur in the ways that different monitor and printer drivers represent a color palette. These representation schemes are called *color profiles*. For most purposes, the difference between color profiles doesn't matter. However, if you must be sure the colors you see on your monitor are exactly the colors you will get when you print, you can set the color profiles of your monitor and printer to reflect the exact way your monitor and printer render colors. Matching colors is especially important if you plan to edit and print photos.

Windows comes with profiles for many popular monitors. Its default profile, called the sRGB Color Space Profile, matches most monitors reasonably well. Unless you are a graphic artist, you probably won't notice the difference between the default profile and a perfectly tuned one. Most users do not need to change their color profiles.

To change the color profile of your monitor, open the Display Settings dialog box and click the Advanced Settings button. In the new properties dialog box that opens, click the Color Management tab. Click the Color Management button to display the Color Management dialog box, and click the All Profiles tab (shown in Figure 12-15). Any profiles you have previously used are listed in the large window. To add a profile to the list, click the Add button and select from the color profiles listed. To remove a profile from the list, select it and click the Remove button.

Setting Up the Windows Sidebar and Gadgets

Windows Vista includes a new feature call Windows Sidebar. It sits on your desktop and provides an area to organize and place small, specialized applications. These applications are called *gadgets*. Windows includes a handful of gadgets that you can display on the Sidebar, but the real power of the Sidebar and Gadget feature will be realized when you download gadgets from the Web. Other users can distribute their own custom gadgets on the Web for Vista users to download and use.

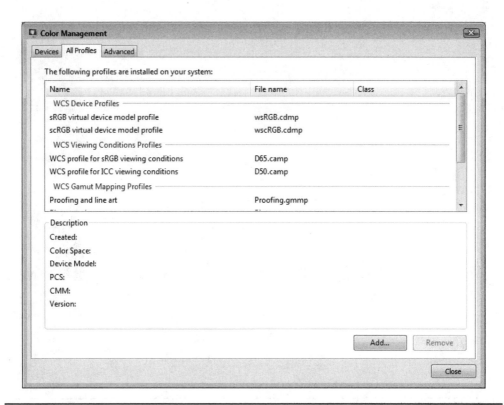

FIGURE 12-15   Setting the color profile of your monitor.

At the time of this writing, Microsoft has a web site (http://microsoftgadgets.com/) from which you can download gadgets to your computer and display them on the Sidebar. The following list describes some of the available gadgets with Vista and from the Gadgets web site:

- **Calendar**   Displays a small monthly calendar you can use to find today's date and scroll through past and upcoming months
- **Clock**   Shows the current time
- **Notes**   Provides a "sticky note" area to add brief notes and to-do lists
- **Stocks**   Displays up-to-date stock data (must be connected to the Internet to keep stock data updated)
- **CPU Meter**   Shows the percentage of CPU cycles being used and the percentage of total RAM being used by your computer

Turning on the Windows Sidebar

To turn on the Windows Sidebar and display gadgets on it, choose Start | All Programs | Accessories | Windows Sidebar. If any gadgets have been set up on the Sidebar initially,

Figure 12-16   Windows Vista includes the Sidebar, which can display gadgets.

you see them displayed on the Sidebar. Figure 12-16 shows an example of the Sidebar and a few gadgets set up.

The Sidebar really doesn't do much by itself. You usually load it up with gadgets to help you work more efficiently, to add productivity applications to your desktop, or just to have fun (there are some game and puzzle gadgets). You can move the Sidebar to the left side of the desktop from its default position on the right side. Other customization options allow you to have Sidebar open when you start Windows and change the monitor (when working with dual monitors) on which the Sidebar display. The following steps show how to modify the Sidebar:

1. Right-click the Sidebar and choose Properties to open the Windows Sidebar Properties dialog box (as shown in Figure 12-17).

2. Choose Start Sidebar When Windows Starts to have the Sidebar automatically start when Windows starts.

3. Choose Sidebar Is Always On Top Of Other Windows to keep the Sidebar visible even when you have other applications and windows open.

4. Choose the side (Right or Left) you want the Sidebar to display on.

FIGURE 12-17   Customize the Sidebar with the Windows Sidebar Properties dialog box.

5. Choose the monitor (1 or 2) to have the Sidebar switch to a different monitor when you are using the dual-monitor feature of Vista.

6. Click View List Of Running Gadgets to display the View Gadgets window. Here you can see a list of gadgets on the Sidebar. Click a gadget from the View Gadgets window and click Remove to remove the gadget from the Sidebar. Click Close to return to the Windows Sidebar Properties dialog box.

7. If you have uninstalled gadgets from your system and want to reinstall them, click the Restore Gadgets Installed With Windows button. This option is grayed out if you have not uninstalled them.

8. Click OK to close the Windows Sidebar Properties dialog box.

Adding a Gadget to the Sidebar

To add a gadget to the Sidebar, click the plus sign at the top of the Sidebar or right-click the Sidebar and choose Add Gadgets. Either way, a window showing all the installed gadgets on your system appears (as shown in Figure 12-18). This window is called the Gadget Gallery.

To add a gadget to the Sidebar, do one of the following:

1. Double-click the gadget in the Gadget Gallery. This adds the gadget to the top of the Sidebar. You can move the gadget to another location on the Sidebar by dragging-and-dropping the gadget from one location to another.

2. Drag-and-drop the gadget from the Gadget Gallery window to a position on the Sidebar.

Figure 12-18 Gadgets can be added to the Sidebar using this window, the Gadget Gallery.

Although the few gadgets provided with Windows Vista are handy, you may want to see what's available on the Internet. To do this, follow these steps:

1. Click the Get More Gadgets Online link in the Gadget Gallery window. This opens your web browser to the Windows Vista Gadget Gallery, shown in Figure 12-19.

2. Choose a category on the left side of the web page to see the gadgets that are available for download.

3. Click the Download button under the gadget you want to download.

4. Choose OK to confirm that you agree with the terms of downloading the item.

5. Click the Open button in the File Download dialog box.

6. Click Install when prompted if you want to install the gadget. Vista installs the gadget, adds it to the Sidebar, and includes it in your Gadget Gallery.

Once a gadget is on the Sidebar, you can change its properties if it includes them. Some gadgets may not have customization options (called properties sometimes). For example, the CPU Meter gadget does not include options for changing how it looks or behaves. On the other hand, the Clock gadget includes options for changing the look of the clock, setting a name for the clock (handy if you have multiple clocks showing), setting the time zone, and displaying the second hand on the clock.

To change a property, right-click the gadget and click Options. If the Options item is not there, look for something similar, such as Properties. In the resulting dialog box, choose the options you want to set. Click OK when finished. You also can display the options by clicking the gadget to display the gadget's small toolbar that appears to its right. This toolbar includes

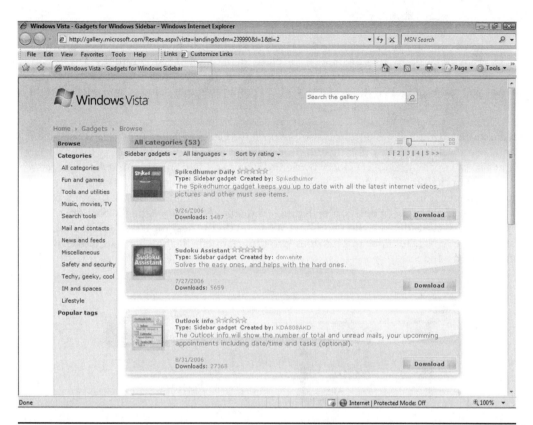

FIGURE 12-19   Microsoft has gadgets online that you can download and install.

controls for closing the gadget (an X), a properties icon (the shape of a small wrench), and a gripper icon (for moving the gadget). Click the wrench icon to open the options for that gadget.

One type of customization you can set on all gadgets is the Opacity setting. This tells Vista how opaque to display a gadget. A lower opacity setting provides less opacity; that is, the gadget is more transparent, allowing you to see better what's behind it. For instance, gadgets set at 100% opacity are fully visible. A setting of 20%, however, makes the gadget hardly visible, so that you can see what's onscreen behind it. To set the opacity, right-click a gadget, choose Opacity, and choose a setting: 20%, 40%, 60%, 80%, or 100%. By default, gadgets display at 100% opacity.

To remove a gadget from the Sidebar, do one of the following:

- Click the gadget on the Sidebar to display its toolbar. Click the close button (X).

- Right-click the gadget and choose Close Gadget.

- Right-click the Sidebar (make sure it's not on a gadget) and choose Properties. The Windows Sidebar Properties dialog box appears. Click View List Of Running Gadgets to display the View Gadgets dialog box. Click a gadget and choose Remove. Click Close.

Placing a Gadget on the Desktop

Gadgets do not have to be placed on the Windows Sidebar to display them. You can move gadgets to the desktop from the Sidebar or place them on the desktop initially. This is handy if you want to have a gadget running but do not want the Windows Sidebar to show. Also, when you put a gadget on the desktop, you are not limited to placing it on the left or right side. You can move the gadget to any location.

To add a gadget to the desktop with the Windows Sidebar open, drag-and-drop a gadget from the Sidebar to the desktop. You also can open the Gadget Gallery (right-click the Sidebar and choose Add Gadgets) and drag-and-drop a gadget from the Gadget Gallery to the desktop. You also can open the Gadget Gallery by right-clicking a gadget and choosing Add Gadgets.

You can close the Sidebar if all your gadgets are now placed on the desktop or if you just no longer want to see the Sidebar. Right-click the Sidebar and choose Close Sidebar.

Figure 12-20 shows a desktop with gadgets displayed without the Sidebar open. To quickly open the Sidebar (when you have a gadget on the desktop), right-click the gadget and choose Attach To Sidebar. This does two things: opens the Sidebar and moves the gadget to the Sidebar.

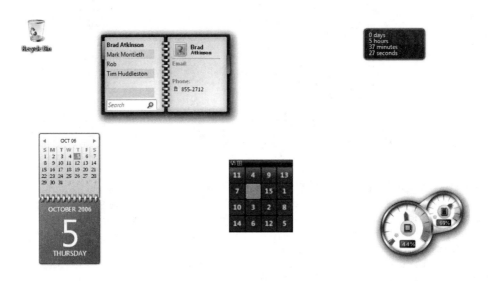

Windows Vista (TM) RC 1
Evaluation copy. Build 5600

FIGURE 12-20 Gadgets can be moved to the desktop.

NOTE *Gadgets are pretty cool, but remember that each one consumes memory and other system resources (CPU cycles, graphics memory, Internet time, etc.). Unless your computer has large amounts of memory and a fast CPU (2.0 GHz or higher), you may want to limit the number of gadgets you add to the Sidebar or the desktop.*

Getting Along with Your Monitor(s)

Windows can detect and install a driver for a Plug and Play monitor with little effort on your part (see "How Do You Add Hardware to a Windows Computer?" in Chapter 14). In addition, many newer monitors comply with the Energy Star power-saving standards, enabling you to choose to have Windows turn off the monitor if you have not used it for a certain period of time. If you have two or more monitors hooked up to your computer, your desktop can stretch across all of them, and each can have its own settings.

Using Multiple Displays

Windows can handle four screens on a single system, displaying a single desktop that spans all the screens. A pair of 17-inch monitors have considerably more screen area than a single 19-inch monitor and can be a cost-effective alternative to a single larger screen. (On the other hand, you may not have much desk space left after setting up two monitors.)

Configuring a second, third, or fourth screen is straightforward once you install the new hardware (you need a display adapter for each screen, unless you use a special adapter). Open the Display Settings dialog box, which looks like Figure 12-21 if two display adapters are installed (see "Configuring Windows for New Hardware" in Chapter 14).

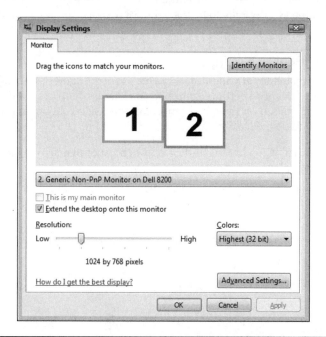

FIGURE 12-21   The Monitor tab of the Display Settings dialog box with two monitors.

To configure an additional display, follow these steps:

1. Click the picture of the new monitor to highlight it.

2. Check the Extend The Desktop Onto This Monitor check box.

3. Click Apply.

4. Click Yes if asked if you want to keep these settings.

5. Drag the monitor icons so that they correspond to the physical arrangement of your screens. For instance, if monitor 2 is on the left side of monitor 1, drag its icon to that position. This is really handy if you have three or more monitors attached and need to perform administrative tasks on them from the Display Settings dialog box.

6. Configure the new display. If possible, configure all the displays to have the same number of colors and the same screen area, to avoid confusion when you move a window from one screen to another.

7. Click OK. Windows configures the new display.

Once configured, the additional display becomes part of the Windows desktop, and you can drag windows back and forth between the displays. You can even have a single window that spans multiple screens, which can be convenient for looking at spreadsheets with wide rows. If you want to change the color depth or resolution of one of the monitors, click the monitor's icon on the Display Settings dialog box and then change the settings.

Windows considers one of your monitors to be the *primary display*, which is the monitor on which error messages and alerts appear. Some high-end DirectX graphics applications display correctly only on the primary monitor. If you have one AGP graphics card and one PCI graphics card, the PCI defaults to be the primary display, and the AGP is the secondary display.

Adjusting Other Monitor Settings

Depending on the capabilities of your monitor, some other configuration settings are available. When you click the Advanced Settings button in the Display Settings dialog box, you see a dialog box with a title based on the type of monitor you use, as shown in Figure 12-22. Tabs and settings may include the following:

- **List All Modes**   Clicking this button shows a list of display resolutions and refresh rates your monitor can support.

- **Troubleshoot**   This tab shows the Display Adapter Troubleshooter to help you fix monitor problems. For example, the Hardware Acceleration option enables you to specify how fast Windows updates your screen.

- **Color Management**   This tab specifies the color profiles you have defined.

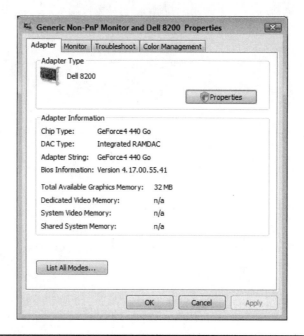

FIGURE 12-22 The advanced settings for a monitor depend on the monitor's device driver.

Configuring Your Keyboard, Mouse, Game Controller, and Regional Settings

Windows Vista, like all operating systems, sits between the programs you run and the computer you run them on. Whenever a program accepts input from the keyboard, mouse, or a game controller or sends output to the screen or printer, Windows gets involved. As a result, when you configure Windows to work with your keyboard, mouse, or game controller, the settings you choose affect all the programs you run. You can choose the keyboard layout you want to use and set the sensitivity of the mouse. If you have installed a game controller or joystick, you can also check or change its settings.

Different countries use different currencies and have different formats for writing numbers, monetary amounts, dates, and times. Windows has regional settings for most countries in the world (at least most of the countries where people are likely to use computers) to address such differences. By telling Windows which country you live in, you can cause Windows and most programs to use the date, time, monetary amounts, and numeric formats with which you are comfortable.

Windows has a built-in calendar (not to be confused with the Windows Calendar scheduling program available in Windows Vista) that all programs can use. It knows the current date and time (usually displayed at the right end of the taskbar) and understands time zones, daylight saving time, and leap years. You can set the date, time, and the time zone in which you are located so that the Windows calendar will be accurate.

You can change most of these settings in the Control Panel (see "What Is the Control Panel?" in Chapter 1). The Date And Time dialog box and the Regional And Language Options dialog box are accessible from the Clock, Language, And Region category of the Control Panel, while the Keyboard Properties, Mouse Properties, and Game Controllers dialog boxes are accessible from the Hardware And Sound category.

Configuring Your Keyboard

Configuring your keyboard can mean two subtly different things:

- Changing the way that your keyboard produces symbols (for example, how long you have to press a key before it repeats). Microsoft considers these to be keyboard properties, and you control them from the Keyboard Properties dialog box.

- Changing the way that symbols are mapped to keys (for example, choosing a different alphabet or a different keyboard layout). Microsoft considers these to be language properties, and you control them from the Text Services And Input Languages dialog box.

Changing Keyboard Properties

Opening the Keyboard icon from the Hardware And Sound category of the Control Panel produces the Keyboard Properties dialog box, shown in Figure 13-1. From here, you can control the settings listed and described in the following table.

Setting	Description
Repeat delay	Delay between starting to hold down a key and when the key begins repeating
Repeat rate	How fast the key repeats once it starts repeating
Cursor blink rate	How fast the cursor blinks

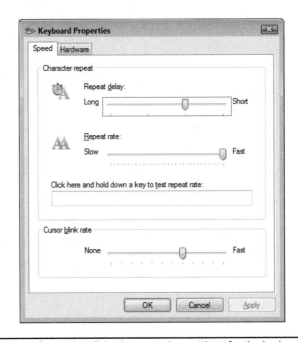

FIGURE 13-1 The Keyboard Properties dialog box contains settings for the keyboard and the cursor.

Tip   *Additional keyboard settings are available if you have trouble using the keyboard (see "Making the Keyboard More Accessible" in Chapter 17).*

Move the sliders on the Speed tab of the Keyboard Properties dialog box to set the repeat delay, repeat rate, or cursor blink rate. You can test how your keys repeat by clicking in the text box and holding down a key.

Changing Language Properties

You can also control which language layout the keyboard uses. Different languages use different letters and assign the letters to different locations on the keyboard. If you use more than one language, you can choose a key combination that switches between two keyboard layouts.

For some languages, Windows offers a selection of *keyboard layouts,* which define the physical organization of the keys on the keyboard. For example, if you choose U.S. English as your language, you can choose among layouts that include the standard 101-key layout, the Dvorak keyboard, and even the left-handed Dvorak keyboard.

These choices are controlled from the Text Services And Input Languages dialog box, shown in Figure 13-2.

Open this box as follows:

1. Open the Control Panel by selecting Start | Control Panel.

2. Click the Clock, Language, And Region icon.

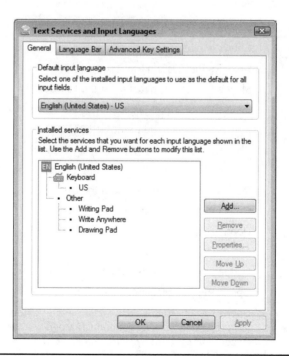

Figure 13-2   You can switch among several languages and keyboard layouts.

3. Click Change Keyboard Or Other Input Methods. The Regional And Language Options dialog box appears.

4. Click the Change Keyboards button on the Keyboards And Languages tab. The Text Services And Input Languages dialog box appears.

Configuring Your Keyboard for Another Language or Keyboard Layout

The languages and keyboard layouts that are installed on your computer are shown in the Installed Services box on the General tab of the Text Services And Input Languages dialog box. If the Installed Services box doesn't show the language or keyboard layout you want, click the Add button. When the Add Input Language dialog box appears, click the plus sign next to the language you want to install. Two subcategories appear: Keyboard and Other. Click the plus sign next to the Keyboard item to expand it to show different keyboard language options for the language you choose. Or, click the plus sign next to Other to expand it for a list of other input choices, such as Drawing Pad. Click a service from the Input Language list and then click OK. The new service is added to the Installed Services box in the Text Services And Input Languages dialog box.

NOTE *Most computer keyboards include a* WINDOWS *key, with the flying Windows logo on it. It's usually among the keys to the left of the Spacebar. The most convenient use of the Windows key is to display the Start menu, but you can use the Windows key like a Shift key in combination with other keys. Here are the Windows key combinations that work in Windows Vista.*

Key Combination	Action
WINDOWS	Opens or closes the Start menu
WINDOWS-BREAK	Displays the System Properties window
WINDOWS-TAB	Makes the next application in the taskbar into the active window
WINDOWS-SHIFT-TAB	Makes the previous application in the taskbar into the active window
WINDOWS-B	Makes the notification area active
WINDOWS-D	Shows the desktop (minimizes all windows)
WINDOWS-E	Opens Windows Explorer showing Computer (like Start ∣ Computer)
WINDOWS-F	Opens Windows Explorer with the Search pane
WINDOWS-CTRL-F	Opens the Find Computers dialog box
WINDOWS-F1	Opens Help
WINDOWS-M	Minimizes all windows
WINDOWS-SHIFT-M	Undoes minimize all windows
WINDOWS-R	Opens the Run dialog box (like Start ∣ Run)
WINDOWS-U	Opens the Ease Of Access Control Panel window for accessibility features (see "Turning On and Off Magnifier, Narrator, and the Onscreen Keyboard by Using the Ease of Access Tool")
WINDOWS-L	Locks the computer, with the option to switch to another user (see Chapter 6)

To delete a language or layout you no longer plan to use, select that language or layout from the Installed Services box in the Text Services And Input Languages dialog box and click the Remove button.

Switching Languages and Keyboard Layouts

If you install more than one language or keyboard layout on your computer, you can switch from one to another in several ways. If you switch very rarely, make the switch by choosing the language you want from the Default Input Language drop-down list in the Text Services And Input Languages dialog box. Click OK and restart your computer.

Using the Language Bar   A quick way to change languages or keyboard layouts is to use the Language bar. You can display the Language bar on your desktop or a language icon on the taskbar as follows:

1. Open the Text Services And Input Languages dialog box (shown in Figure 13-2) and click the Language Bar tab.

2. Check Docked In The Taskbar.

3. Click OK and then click OK again.

The Language bar is a small toolbar that sits just above the taskbar or can be dragged (by its left edge) anywhere on the desktop. (The Language bar that comes with Microsoft Office 2003 works similarly to the one in Windows Vista.) The Language bar has two buttons: one shows the keyboard's current language and the other is a drop-down arrow for getting help, accessing settings options, and restoring defaults. To change to a different language, click the current language [for example, EN English (United States)] and select a different language from the drop-down list [such as Arabic (Algeria)]. The keyboard changes instantly; you do not need to restart the computer.

At the far-right end of the Language bar is a small button to minimize the Language bar. If you click it, the bar disappears and is replaced by a small language icon on the taskbar next to the clock. Click the icon to change languages or restore the Language bar.

Keyboard Shortcuts for Switching Languages   You can also set a key combination for switching among languages and keyboard layouts. Your options are LEFT ALT-SHIFT (that is, the left ALT key plus the SHIFT key), CTRL-SHIFT, or none. To set up such a key combination click the Advanced Key Settings tab on the Text Services And Input Languages dialog box (shown in Figure 13-2). Find the switching action on the Action list and select it. Then click the Change Key Sequence button. Use the Change Key Sequence dialog box that appears to set up the desired key sequence.

Configuring Your Mouse

You can control what the mouse buttons do, how fast the mouse pointer (the screen object that moves when you move the mouse) moves, and what the mouse pointer looks like. You can define the shape of the mouse pointer, but not the cursor (the blinking element that shows where what you type will be inserted).

PART III

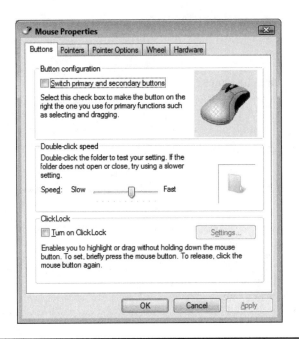

Figure 13-3   The Mouse Properties dialog box.

You can also choose the shape the mouse pointer assumes when used for pointing, when Windows is busy (the hourglass), when you are typing, when selecting text, when clicking a web link, when dragging window borders, and when performing other functions. If you choose shapes other than the Windows default shapes, you can save the set of shapes you like to use as a *pointer scheme*. Windows comes with more than a dozen predefined pointer schemes from which you can choose.

These mouse settings are controlled from the Mouse Properties dialog box, shown in Figure 13-3. Open this dialog box by opening the Mouse icon from the Hardware And Sound category of the Control Panel.

TIP   *Additional mouse settings are available if you have trouble using your mouse (see "Setting Mouse Key Ease of Access Features" in Chapter 17). You might also consider installing a trackball or other pointing device.*

Defining the Mouse Buttons

Normally, you click or double-click the left mouse button to select, open, or run items on the screen. You click the right mouse button to display the shortcut menu of commands about the item you selected (see "Choosing Commands from Shortcut Menus" in Chapter 2). Some programs use the right mouse button for other purposes.

If you are left-handed, you may find it convenient to reverse the meanings of the two buttons. In the Mouse Properties dialog box, click the Buttons tab and check the Switch

Primary And Secondary Buttons check box. To return to the default (right-handed) button configuration, uncheck the check box. Click OK to close the Mouse Properties dialog box and implement your changes.

Defining Your Double-Click Speed

Windows defines a double-click as two clicks within a specified time period, with no mouse motion during that period. That time period is called the *double-click speed*, and you can adjust it using the Double-Click Speed slider on the Buttons tab of the Mouse Properties dialog box. If you have trouble clicking fast enough for Windows to realize you want to double-click, move the slider in the Slow direction. On the other hand, if you find two single clicks often get interpreted as a double-click, move the slider in the Fast direction. To test the setting, double-click the folder icon in the Double-Click Speed box. If you can make the folder open and close, Windows is recognizing your double-clicks.

Configuring the Appearance of the Mouse Pointer

The mouse pointer changes shape depending on the context. For example, it appears as an arrow when you are selecting items, or as an *I* when you are editing text. You can choose the shape your mouse pointer assumes. In the Mouse Properties dialog box, click the Pointers tab to display a list of the current pointer shapes. To choose a different set of pointer shapes (mouse pointer scheme), choose a pointer scheme from the drop-down list. The pointers in the scheme are then shown in the Customize box.

You can mix-and-match to assemble your own pointer scheme. Click an item in the Customize box and click the Browse button. A browse window appears, showing you the pointers in the folder C:\Windows\Cursors. This folder contains two types of pointers: static cursors (with the extension .cur) and animated cursors (with the extension .ani). Find the pointer you want and click the Open button.

If you want to go back to the default pointer for an item, click the item in the Customize box, and then click the Use Default button. When you have things the way you want them, click the Save As button and give your new pointer scheme a name.

TIP *Installing a desktop theme is another way to change all your pointers (see "Choosing a Desktop Theme" in Chapter 12).*

Improving Pointer Visibility

If you have trouble following the mouse pointer when it moves, you can give the pointer a *trail*. Trails are useful on laptops and other displays that redraw the screen slowly. To turn the pointer trail on or off and to set the length of the trail, click the Pointer Options tab of the Mouse Properties dialog box. Check the Display Pointer Trails check box to turn the trail on (uncheck it to turn the trail off), and drag the Pointer Trail slider to the length you want. Click OK to implement your changes.

If you have trouble finding the pointer, check the Show Location Of The Pointer When I Press The CTRL Key check box on the Pointer Options tab and click Apply or OK. When this box is checked, pressing the CTRL key causes Windows to draw a big circle around the pointer and then zero in on it with ever smaller circles.

PART III

Setting the Mouse Speed

You can adjust how far the mouse pointer moves when you move the mouse. For example, if you move the mouse in a small area of your desk, you can adjust Windows to make the mouse very sensitive, so moving the mouse one inch (2.5 cm) moves the pointer halfway across the screen. If you have shaky hands, you can make the mouse less sensitive, so small motions of the mouse result in small motions of the pointer.

In the Mouse Properties dialog box, click the Pointer Options tab and drag the Select A Pointer Speed slider to adjust the mouse speed. To try out the new setting, click the Apply button.

TIP *If your mouse or trackball is unresponsive, it may require a low-tech solution like cleaning. Pop the ball out and look for accumulations of dust on the contacts or the ball itself.*

Setting ClickLock

ClickLock is a feature that allows you to drag objects without holding down the mouse button. To enable ClickLock, check the Turn On ClickLock check box on the Buttons tab of the Mouse Properties dialog box. After ClickLock is enabled, when you hold the mouse button down for a short time, it "locks" and you can drag the selected object without continuing to hold the mouse button down.

You can adjust the length of time that you must hold the mouse button down before it locks. To make this adjustment, click the Settings button on the Buttons tab of the Mouse Properties dialog box. When the Settings For ClickLock dialog box appears, adjust the lock time by moving the slider. Click OK to implement your changes.

Configuring Your Game Controller

Game controllers and *joysticks*—devices that enable you to play arcade-style games on your computer—come in many sizes and shapes. Windows includes drivers for many game controllers (see "What Are Drivers?" in Chapter 14).

To install a game controller, follow the instructions that come with it. Usually, you just shut down Windows, turn off the computer, plug the game controller or joystick into the game port on your computer, and turn on your computer again. Windows should recognize the new device and install it. Have the CD or DVD that came with the game controller handy, and insert it when Windows is looking for the driver. If you've downloaded a driver, tell Windows where the driver file is stored.

To find out whether Windows has recognized your game controller or to change the settings for a game controller, look at the Game Controllers dialog box, shown in Figure 13-4. To see this dialog box, open the Game Controllers icon from the Hardware And Sound category of the Control Panel.

Displaying and Changing Game Controller Settings

To see the settings for your game controller, select it from the list in the Game Controllers dialog box and click Properties. You see the game controller's Properties dialog box.

FIGURE 13-4   The Game Controllers dialog box.

One computer can have several game controllers attached. Each controller has an ID number, starting with 1. You can see and change the controller ID numbers by clicking the Advanced button in the Games Controllers dialog box.

Testing Your Game Controller

To test your game controller, select it from the list in the Game Controllers dialog box, click Properties, and click the Test tab in the game controller's Properties dialog box. Move the joystick or yoke and see whether the cross hairs in the Axes box move. Click the buttons on the game controller and see whether the button indicators light up. If not, calibrate the game controller by clicking the Settings tab, clicking the Calibrate button, and following the instructions.

Windows Regional Settings

Windows comes with predefined regional settings for most of the countries in the world. *Regional settings* affect the format of numbers, currency, dates, and times. For example, if you choose the regional settings for Germany, Windows knows to display numbers with dots between the thousands and a comma as the decimal point, to use Deutsch marks as the currency, and to display dates with the day preceding the month.

NOTE   *To reset your keyboard for other languages, see "Changing Language Properties" earlier in this chapter.*

To see or change your regional settings, look in the Regional And Language Options dialog box, shown in Figure 13-5. To display this box, open the Regional And Language Options icon from the Clock, Language, And Region category of the Control Panel.

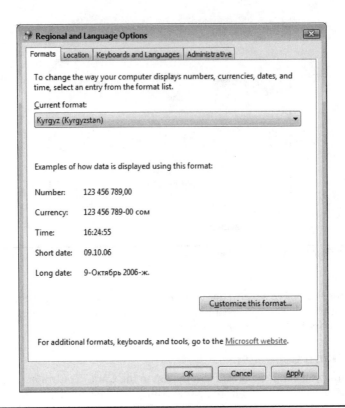

FIGURE 13-5   The Regional And Language Options dialog box displaying the regional settings for Kyrgyzstan.

Telling Windows Where You Live

Windows has predefined sets of regional settings, so you needn't select numeric, currency, date, and time formats separately. Choose the language you speak and the country where you live from the drop-down list in the Current Format list on the Formats tab of the Regional And Language Options dialog box. The list is arranged alphabetically by language, with the country in parentheses. There are, for example, 16 English entries, including English (Belize) and English (South Africa).

Setting Number, Currency, Time, and Date Formats

After you tell Windows which language you speak and where you live, it displays sample numbers, currency symbols, times, and dates on the Formats tab of the Regional And Language Options dialog box. You will probably be happy with the way these samples are formatted. If not, you can change any of these items individually by clicking the Customize This Format button. When the Customize Regional Options dialog box appears (see Figure 13-6), click the Numbers, Currency, Time, or Date tab to see the corresponding settings. You can customize settings that appear in white. Those that are in gray have set formats from which you can choose. To change any of these settings, make another selection from the corresponding drop-down list and click the Apply or OK button.

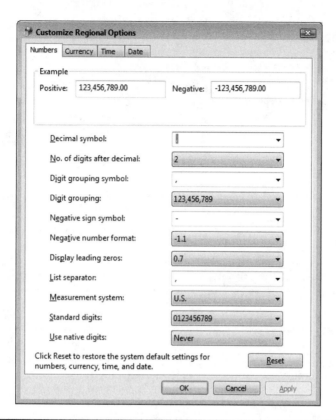

FIGURE 13-6   The Customize Regional Options dialog box.

Numbers

The following table shows the settings on the Numbers tab of the Customize Regional Options dialog box that tell Windows how you write numbers.

Setting	Description
Decimal symbol	Which character appears as the decimal point, separating the whole from the fractional portion of numbers. (In the U.S., this is a period.)
No. of digits after decimal	How many digits usually appear to the right of the decimal symbol. (The default U.S. option is two.)
Digit grouping symbol	Which character appears to group digits into groups in large numbers. (In the U.S., this is a comma.)
Digit grouping	The pattern for grouping digits in large numbers. (In the U.S., digits are grouped in threes.)
Negative sign symbol	Which character indicates negative numbers. (In the U.S., this is the minus sign, –.)

(continued)

Setting	Description
Negative number format	Where the negative sign symbol appears. (In the U.S., it appears to the left of the number.)
Display leading zeroes	For numbers between –1 and 1, whether to display a zero before the decimal symbol. (In the U.S., a zero is displayed; for example, 0.4.)
List separator	Which character to use to separate items in lists, for entering lists in Windows text boxes. (The Windows default for the U.S. is a comma.)
Measurement system	Whether you use the U.S. or metric system of measurements.
Standard digits	Shows the numbers you use.
Use native digits	Lets you choose whether native digits are used for the language you chose.

Currency

The following settings on the Currency tab of the Customize Regional Options dialog box control how Windows displays currency (money).

Setting	Description
Currency symbol	Symbol that indicates which currency is in use for amounts of money. (In the U.S., this is $.)
Positive currency format	How Windows formats positive amounts of money. (In the U.S., the currency symbol appears to the left of the amount with no space between the $ and the leftmost digit.)
Negative currency format	How Windows formats negative amounts of money. (In the U.S., negative amounts of money are enclosed in parentheses.)
Decimal symbol	Which character appears as the decimal point in amounts of money, separating the whole from the fractional portion of numbers. (In the U.S., this is a period.)
No. of digits after decimal	How many digits appear to the right of the decimal symbol in amounts of money. (In the U.S., this is two, so dollars and cents are displayed.)
Digit grouping symbol	Which character appears to group digits into groups in large amounts of money. (In the U.S., this is a comma.)
Digit grouping	The pattern for grouping digits in large sums of money. (In the U.S., digits are grouped in threes.)

Time Formats

This table shows your options for displaying the time (the settings are on the Time tab of the Customize Regional Options dialog box).

Setting	Description
Time format	Format for displaying times. In the sample, *h* represents the hour, *hh* the hour with leading zeros, *H* the hour using the 24-hour clock, *HH* the hour using the 24-hour clock and leading zeros, *mm* the minutes, *ss* the seconds, and *tt* the AM/PM symbol. (In the U.S., the format is *h:mm:ss tt*, for example, 2:45:03 PM)
A.M. symbol	Which characters or symbols indicate times before noon. (In the U.S., the default is AM.)
P.M. symbol	Which characters or symbols indicate times after noon. (In the U.S., the default is PM.)

Date Formats

The following table shows your options for displaying the date (the settings are on the Date tab of the Customize Regional Options dialog box).

Short date format	Short format for displaying dates. In the sample, *M* represents the month number with no leading zeros, *MM* the month number with leading zeros displayed, *MMM* the three-letter abbreviation for the month name, *d* the day with no leading zeros, *dd* the day with leading zeros displayed, *yy* the two-digit year, and *yyyy* the four-digit year. (In the U.S., this is *M/d/yyyy*, for example, 12/25/2000.)
Long date format	Long format for displaying dates. In the sample, *dddd* represents the name of the day of the week, *MMMM* the name of the month, *dd* the day number, and *yyyy* the four-digit year.
When a two digit year is entered, interpret as a year between *xxxx* and *xxxx*	How two-digit years are converted to four-digit years (usually 1930 to 2029). Changing the end year also changes the beginning year.

Setting the Current Date and Time

Windows is good at keeping its clock and calendar correct. It knows about U.S. daylight saving time and leap years, but depending on where you live and the accuracy of your computer's internal clock, you might occasionally need to reset Windows' clock or calendar.

To display the Date And Time dialog box, shown in Figure 13-7, right-click the time on the taskbar (usually displayed at the right end of the taskbar) and choose Adjust Date/Time, or you can open the Date And Time icon from the Clock, Language, And Region category of the Control Panel.

FIGURE 13-7   The Date And Time dialog box.

To set the date or time, click the Change Date And Time button. The Date And Time Settings dialog box appears. You can set the following items:

- **Year**   Click the year to display a list of years (such as from 1999 to 2010) and click the current year.

- **Month**   Click the left or right arrows on the calendar to move the month to the correct setting.

- **Day**   Click the day number on the calendar.

- **Hour, minute, or second**   Click the hour, minute, or second section of the clock and type a new value or click the up or down arrows.

- **A.M. or P.M.**   Click the AM or PM at the right end of the time and click the up or down arrow to the right of the time.

Click OK to save your settings.

To set the time zone, click the Change Time Zone button on the Date And Time dialog box. Click the Time Zone drop-down list and choose a new time zone. If you want Windows to adjust the clock an hour for daylight saving time in the spring and fall, check the Automatically Adjust Clock For Daylight Saving Changes check box.

Vista enables you to display two additional clocks to help you track time in other parts of the country or world. To display additional clocks, you can use the Additional Clocks tab to set them up. Click this tab and select Show This Clock. Select a time zone from the Select Time Zone drop-down list. Type a name for the clock, such as Greenland if you are tracking

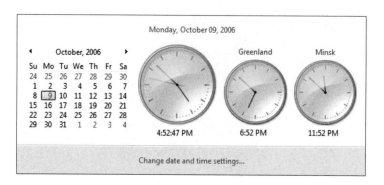

FIGURE 13-8   Displaying additional clocks in Vista.

the time in that time zone. Click Show This Clock for the second additional clock to display (this will be the third clock that shows on the clocks window). Set up the time zone and type in a display name for the clock. Click OK. When you click the clock on the taskbar, a window appears with your clocks and a calendar (see Figure 13-8).

Alternatively, you can tell Windows to update the time itself by synchronizing its clock with an Internet-based *time server*. (This feature is turned on by default.) To change this setting, click the Internet Time tab on the Date And Time dialog box. Click Change Settings to open the Internet Time Settings dialog box. The Synchronize With An Internet Time Server check box turns the feature on and off, and the Server box determines which time server you contact (the default is time.windows.com). Windows checks in with the time server every week and updates its clock.

TIP   *If your computer communicates through a firewall (other than the firewall built into Windows Vista), time synchronization may be blocked. Also, Windows doesn't update your time if the date is incorrect. If you find that Windows is setting your clock to the wrong time, check that the time zone is set correctly.*

Adding and Removing Hardware

Windows Vista lets you add new hardware to your computer relatively easily, but you still have a lot of details to get right. This chapter describes the general steps for installing hardware. It also discusses Plug and Play, the Device Manager, the types of hardware you may want to install, how to configure Windows to work with new hardware, troubleshooting hardware, and adding memory.

How Do You Add Hardware to a Windows Computer?

Most Windows-based computers let you add extra hardware to extend your computer's capabilities. Some hardware fits inside your computer; some plugs into existing connectors on the back of the computer; and some requires adding a card inside your computer, into which you plug external equipment. After you add the device, you need to configure Windows to use your new hardware.

> **TIP** *For the definitions of many hardware-related terms and acronyms, see the Velocity Micro web site at www.velocitymicro.com/hw.php.*

Adding hardware is a three-step process:

1. Set any switches and jumpers on the new equipment as needed. For example, if you install a second hard drive in your computer that you plan to use as a secondary disk, you must use jumpers to set it up as the non-boot drive (sometimes referred to as the "slave" drive).

2. If the card or drive goes inside the computer, turn off and unplug the computer, open it up, install the card or drive, and put the computer back together. Plug in any external equipment.

3. Turn on the computer and tell Windows about the new equipment.

> **TIP** *Before adding new hardware, make a backup of your important files, in case you can't restart your computer (see Chapter 10).*

What Is Plug and Play?

Plug and Play (PnP) is a feature of Windows and some hardware that allows Windows to configure itself automatically when the hardware is installed. Windows 95 was the first version of Windows to include Plug and Play, and Microsoft has been improving the feature with each new version. *Universal Plug and Play (UPnP)* was added in Windows Me to simplify configuring network devices. If your hardware is Plug and Play, Windows notices when you install a new device and tries to install and configure a driver for the hardware automatically.

What Is the Device Manager?

To see a list of your computer's hardware, you use the *Device Manager* window, shown in Figure 14-1. The Device Manager lists all the devices that make up your computer and enables you to see and modify their configuration. If the Add Hardware Wizard detects a device conflict, it starts the Device Manager automatically.

To see the Device Manager, choose Start | Control Panel, click System And Maintenance, and click Device Manager. You can view devices by type or by connection; by connection is usually better for driver debugging, since it displays each connected device separately. If hardware is having trouble, Windows displays the devices listed by type, with the type of the problematic device expanded.

> **NOTE** *Another way to see the Device Manager is within the Microsoft Management Console. Click Start, right-click Computer, and choose Manage from the shortcut menu to see the Microsoft Management Console. Then click Device Manager in the left pane of the window (see "The Device Manager" in Chapter 37).*

What Types of Hardware Can You Install?

IBM-compatible computers, having evolved for over 30 years, offer numerous, often complicated, ways to attach new kinds of equipment. The details of PC hardware are beyond the scope of this book, but Table 14-1 describes the basics of PC hardware that you need to know to get a recalcitrant Windows driver installed, including older types of PC components, in case you are upgrading an older computer. See Chapter 34 for more information about configuring hard disks. Chapter 12 describes how to configure your display, and Chapter 15 talks about how to print once you've installed a printer.

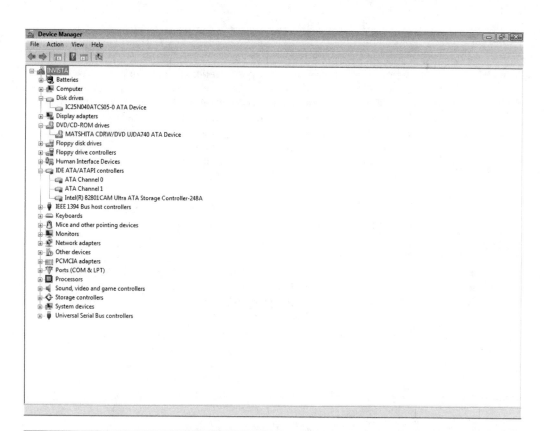

FIGURE 14-1 The Device Manager lists the hardware in your computer.

NOTE *The system requirements for Windows Vista are steep, so upgrading an older computer may not be worth the expense and trouble. Carefully weigh the costs of upgrading versus purchasing new (especially with the prices of new systems so low). Keep in mind that you may be required to completely replace everything inside the case to satisfy Windows Vista, so keeping the old system might actually be more useful than upgrading it to Vista. See the Microsoft Windows Hardware Quality Labs (HCL) web site at www.microsoft.com/whdc/hcl/default.mspx to find out whether your hardware has been approved by Microsoft for use with Windows Vista. Keep in mind that lots of hardware that Microsoft hasn't gotten around to testing also works.*

Hardware Parameters

Every card in your PC needs a variety of hardware parameters to be set, so that the CPU can communicate with the card reliably and without interfering with other cards. For the newest kinds of connections, such as PCI, USB, and FireWire, most—if not all—of these parameters are set automatically by Windows' Plug and Play feature; but older cards require manual tweaking.

Hardware Term	Description
Universal Serial Bus (USB) port	The USB port is the most popular port on computers. It is a faster and simpler alternative to legacy ports (serial and parallel ports), as well as for low- to moderate-speed devices such as cameras, network devices, modems, printers, media devices, external hard drives, sound cards, backup drives, and more. The USB uses a small rectangular connector. USB lets you connect a *USB hub* to your USB port, so you can have a desk full of USB devices. With USB you can *hot swap* USB devices—you don't have to turn off the computer, plug in the device, and restart the computer; just plug the device in and turn it on.
Network port	Some PCs come with a built-in network adapter to enable the computer to connect to a local area network, DSL modem, or cable modem. Newer network ports have RJ45 jacks that look like phone jacks, only larger.
Telephone plug	A *modem* connects your computer to a phone line. If you have a dial-up (analog) modem (the kind of modem that connects to a normal, old-fashioned phone line), the modem has one or two *RJ-11* telephone plugs that are identical to the plugs on the back of a U.S. telephone. If there are two plugs, one is for the incoming phone line plugged into the wall, and the other is for a phone that shares the line with the modem.
Parallel port	Some PCs have a parallel port, a D-shaped socket with holes for 25 pins. Parallel ports are often used for older printers, and sometimes for other devices such as removable disk drives (such as ZIP drives). Most lower-cost PCs, however, do not have parallel ports and use USB ports instead. Parallel ports can communicate unidirectionally (for sending information to a printer) or bidirectionally (for smart printers that send information back to the computer).
PS/2 (keyboard and mouse) ports	Some older PCs that can run Windows Vista have two connectors for a keyboard and a mouse and usually two *PS/2 connectors.* The keyboard and mouse ports look identical—look at the little icons next to the connectors to determine which is which.
Display port	Display adapters, into which you plug your monitor, all use a 15-pin (*DB-15*) connector. All monitors made in recent years are compatible with almost all display adapters, at least at common resolutions. Resolutions you are likely to encounter are 800×600 (the minimum required for Windows Vista), 1024×768, 1400×1050, and 1600×1200. Most can display 16-bit High Color, 24-bit True Color, and 32-bit True Color.
Multiple displays	Windows Vista can support more than one display (screen or monitor), continuing the Windows desktop from one display to the next. You need a video display adapter for each display or a special multidisplay adapter card (see "Using Multiple Displays" in Chapter 12). Some laptop computers enable you to use the built-in LCD screen as one monitor and an external monitor as the second monitor.

TABLE **14-1** Common PC Hardware (*continued*)

Hardware Term	Description
FireWire port	Some computers also have FireWire ports, also known as *IEEE 1394* or *Sony i.Link*. They are faster than USB ports, and are typically used for digital video cameras, hard disk drives, and high-speed printers. FireWire can be hot-swapped—connected and disconnected—while the computer is running. FireWire is efficient, self-powered, flexible, and fast.
Audio and video jacks	Most PCs have connectors for speakers or headphones, and sometimes a microphone. The speaker connector is a standard 1/8-inch stereo mini-audio jack. The microphone connector is usually also a mini-audio jack, so you have to be careful not to confuse the two. If you plan to use your TV to display information from your computer, check whether your PC has a TV jack or *S-video* jack, to which you can connect a television. Alternatively, your PC may come with a video card that includes a TV In plug so you can watch TV on your computer monitor.
PC card slot	Laptop computers usually have one or two PC card slots (known as *PCMCIA* slots originally). A few desktop computers have them, too. These take credit-card–sized adapter cards of many varieties, including modems, networks, and disk and tape controllers. PC cards, unlike other adapter cards, can be added to, and removed from, your computer while it's running. Before removing a PC card, you should first tell Windows, so that it can stop sending data to, or receiving data from, the card. An icon for the card appears in the notification area of the taskbar.
Serial (Com) port	Some PCs have serial ports, which are D-shaped connectors with 9 or 25 pins. For the most part, USB ports have replaced the need for serial ports, but you can still use them for connecting external modems, serial mice, computer-to-computer cabling for "poor man's networking," UPS (uninterruptible power supply) devices, and occasionally printers.

TABLE 14-1   Common PC Hardware (*continued*)

To see a list of your computer's hardware, you use the Device Manager window (see Figure 14-1 earlier in the chapter). You can choose commands from the View menu to see listings by type of device or by how they are connected to the computer. To see listings of the interrupt requests (IRQs), input/output (I/O) addresses, direct memory access (DMA) channels, and memory addresses (see Figure 14-2), choose View | Resources By Type, then click the plus box to the left of each item.

Tip *Keep a logbook for your computer, listing all the cards installed in your computer and the hardware parameters you've set on them. This makes troubleshooting a lot easier.*

Table 14-2 lists and describes the hardware parameters that are common in most PCs.

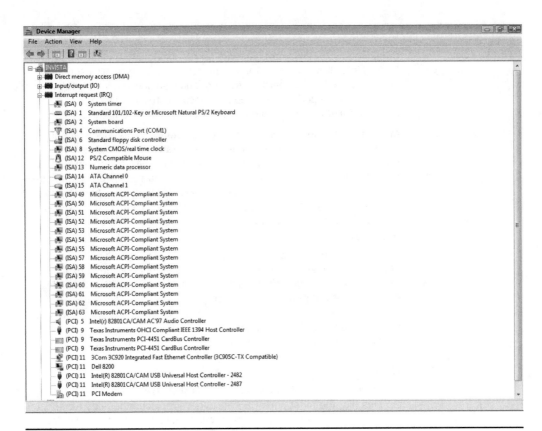

FIGURE 14-2 The Device Manager window.

Memory (RAM)

Memory, or *RAM (random access memory)*, is the temporary storage your computer uses for the programs that you are running and the files you currently have open. Most PCs have from two to four memory slots, and usually the computer is shipped with one or two of the four slots already containing memory. Memory comes in many different sizes, speeds, and types, so you must ensure that the memory you add is compatible with your particular computer (see the section "Adding Memory" later in this chapter). Memory chips are extremely sensitive to static electricity, so be sure to understand and follow the procedures needed to avoid static damage. (Some memory ships with an antistatic wrist strap and instructions on how to use it.)

What Are Drivers?

Many hardware devices—whether they come as part of your computer or are added later—require a *driver* or *device driver*, a program that translates between your operating system (Windows) and the hardware. For example, a printer driver translates printing requests from Windows (and through it, your applications) to commands that your printer can understand.

Windows comes with standard drivers for a wide range of monitors, printers, network adapters, modems, and other devices. When you buy hardware, you usually receive a CD

Parameter	Description
I/O address	Every device attached to a PC has at least one I/O address, a hexadecimal number that the CPU uses to communicate with the device. All I/O addresses on a given computer must be unique; address "collisions" are the most common reason that a new I/O device doesn't work.
IRQs	The PC architecture provides 15 IRQs, channels that a device can use to alert the CPU that the device needs attention. The IRQs are numbered 0, 1, and 3 through 15. (For historical reasons, IRQ 2 isn't available, and the few devices that used IRQ 2 on early PCs use IRQ 9 instead.)
DMA channels	DMA is a motherboard facility used by a few medium-speed devices. There are six DMA channels, of which the floppy disk (if available on your PC) always takes DMA 2. Some sound cards need a DMA channel, usually DMA 1. You set the DMA channel in the Properties dialog box for the device.
Memory addresses	Each byte of memory in your computer has a unique memory address. A few devices, notably screen controllers and some network cards, use a shared memory region to transfer data between the CPU and the device. Those devices need a range of memory addresses for their shared memory.

TABLE 14-2   Common PC Hardware Parameters

or DVD disc that contains the driver for the device, which you need to install during the configuring process to get the device to work with Windows. For some devices, Windows already has a driver on the Windows Vista DVD, so you never need to insert the driver disc. Many manufacturers provide updated device drivers on their web sites.

TIP *Many hardware components come with one set of drivers for use with Windows 9x and Me, and another set for Windows 2003 and XP. If a device doesn't have drivers for Windows Vista, try the Windows 2003 or XP drivers.*

To see information about the driver for a device, display its Properties dialog box—from the Device Manager window, right-click a device and choose Properties from the menu that appears. If there is a Driver tab, click it, as shown in Figure 14-3. Most Driver tabs contain a Driver Details button (for a list of files that make up the driver), Update Driver button (for installing a new driver), Roll Back Driver button (for reinstalling a previous driver), Disable (to deactivate the driver), and Uninstall (to uninstall the driver, leaving the device with no driver).

Configuring Windows for New Hardware

Plug and Play helps Windows Vista automatically detect and configure itself for a wider range of hardware devices. Follow these steps to install new hardware and configure Windows to use it (see the next section if you are installing a PC card):

1. Install your new hardware. This can involve opening up the computer and installing a card, inserting a card into a PC card slot, or just plugging a new external device into a port, such as a USB port, FireWire port, or other port. Follow the directions that come with the new hardware. (For USB and FireWire devices, you don't even have to turn off the computer before plugging them in.)

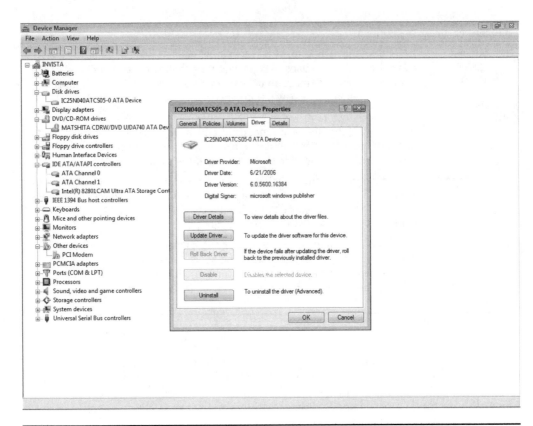

FIGURE 14-3 The Driver tab provides information about a component's hardware device driver.

2. Turn on the device (if external), and turn on and start up your computer. Some devices have a BIOS setup routine that you have to enter when you turn on the computer and run one time to do low-level configuration of your new device.

3. If you're lucky, Windows notices the new device as it starts and automatically configures it for you.

4. If you're less lucky, Windows just starts up. Run the Add Hardware Wizard, described in the next section.

5. If the new device came with a CD or DVD, put the disc into the CD or DVD drive and see what happens. If an installation program starts, follow its instructions to install the drivers and other software that the new device needs.

6. If you're unlucky, Windows doesn't start at all, or starts up in Safe Mode, and you have to figure out what's wrong (see "Troubleshooting Your Hardware Configuration" later in the chapter).

Installing and Uninstalling Hot-Swappable Devices

You can connect and disconnect hot-swappable devices, such as USB, FireWire, and PC card devices, without turning off your computer. For example, if you have a digital camera it probably has a port that enables you to connect it to your computer via a USB or FireWire cable (usually USB). You can connect the camera to your computer and download your photos from the camera's memory. Windows notices the device within a few seconds, and you can begin using it. Digital video cameras act the same way, but usually you want to get one that has a FireWire port because of the high-speed capabilities of that kind of port.

Before you remove the device, though, you should tell Windows that you are going to do so. Click the Safely Remove Hardware icon on the taskbar to see a list of the devices you can remove. Choose the one you are about to remove. Alternatively, right-click the icon to display the Safely Remove Hardware dialog box, as shown in Figure 14-4. Choose a device and click the Stop button. If you want to see the properties of a PC card, click the Properties button.

If a device doesn't appear in the Safely Remove Hardware dialog box, don't disconnect it without first shutting down Windows and turning off your computer.

Using the Add Hardware Wizard

The Add Hardware Wizard does a good job handling the details of installing new device drivers. After you've installed a new device, if Windows doesn't detect it, run the wizard by following these steps.

1. Choose Start | Control Panel, click Classic View on the left pane, and double-click Add Hardware. The Add Hardware Wizard starts.

2. Click Next. You are asked if you want Windows to locate and install any new devices automatically, or if you want to set them up manually.

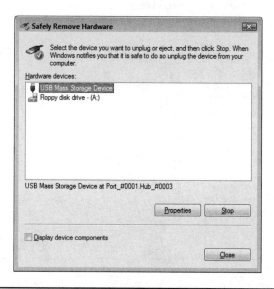

FIGURE 14-4 Checking the status of your PC cards and other hot-swappable devices.

3. Select to have Windows locate and set up any new devices automatically. Click Next.

4. If Windows finds a new device, it automatically sets up the device. However, if it cannot find any new devices, the wizard shows a screen telling you that it did not find any new devices. Click Next to select a device from a list of device types, as shown in Figure 14-5.

5. Select the hardware type from the list and click Next to see a list of manufacturers and models (see Figure 14-6). Sometimes it's difficult to guess which category a device falls into, so you might have to pick one category, look there, and then click Back and try another category or two before you find your device.

6. Choose the manufacturer and the model of your device. If your device came with a driver on a floppy disk and you want to use that driver, click Have Disk and tell Windows which drive contains the disk, which usually is drive D:. If you downloaded the driver from the manufacturer's web site, look for the driver in the files you downloaded from the manufacturer.

7. Click Next to see a summary page of what Windows will install (see Figure 14-7).

8. Click Next and Windows finishes installing your device. You might have to insert your Windows Vista CD-ROM if the device needs drivers that haven't been used before, and you might have to reboot Windows.

At this point, unless Windows has reported a configuration problem, your device should be ready to use.

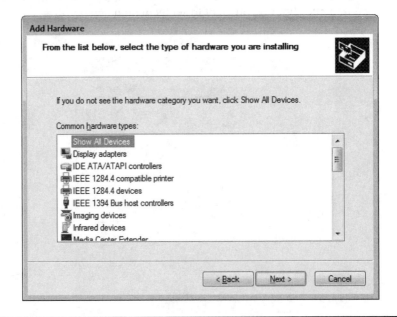

FIGURE 14-5 Select a device to install if the Add Hardware Wizard cannot find your new device.

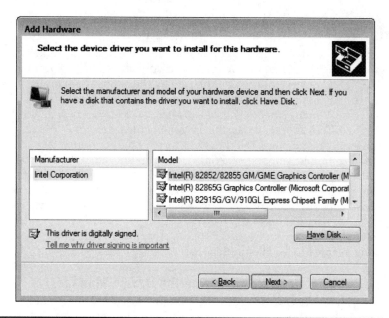

FIGURE 14-6   Adding non-Plug and Play devices.

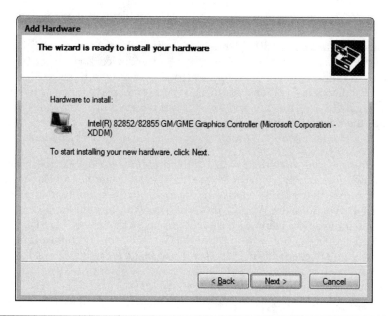

FIGURE 14-7   The Add Hardware Wizard getting ready to install a new device.

Troubleshooting Your Hardware Configuration

In a perfect world, every device installation would work the first time. In the real world, something goes wrong about one time in three, and you have to fix it. The most common problem is that an I/O device address or IRQ used by the new device conflicts with an older one (see "Hardware Parameters" earlier in the chapter).

In the worst case, Windows doesn't boot at all after you add your new device. Back in the old days of ISA and EISA adapter cards, this invariably meant that the settings on the card conflicted with an existing device. You'd have to turn off the computer, take out the new device, turn on the computer, and reboot. With Windows Vista you can use the Device Manger to see what addresses and IRQs are currently in use, and use the card's documentation to find out how to change jumpers to addresses and IRQs that are available (the next section describes how). Then reinstall the card and try again. However, newer cards almost never run into this problem because few have jumpers.

If you can't tell what the conflicts are, boot the computer in Safe Mode, described in the section "Booting in Safe Mode" later in this chapter.

Solving Configuration Problems by Using the Device Manager

You can use the Device Manager to deal with configuration problems by looking at the details of how Windows communicates with the device. The settings for each device are different, depending on the type of hardware and the specific model.

Display the Device Manager by choosing Start | Control Panel, clicking System And Maintenance, and clicking Device Manager. (Figure 14-1 near the beginning of this chapter shows the Device Manager window.) If a device has a problem, its icon appears with a red or yellow exclamation point next to it (or a red X over it).

To see information about a particular device, right-click that device, and click the Properties button to see the Properties dialog box for the device. Look at the General and Resources tabs for information about its status (try the other tabs, too, if you can't find the information). If a device has resource conflicts, Windows displays them, as in Figure 14-8. In this case, the conflict is that the device driver for this device is not installed. To resolve the problem, click the Reinstall Driver button.

Here are the two most common problems you can see in the Device Manager:

- **Something wrong with the driver**   If the driver for the device doesn't work with Windows or is missing, you can right-click the device in the Device Manager window and choose Update Driver Software from the menu that appears. The Update Driver Software Wizard runs and steps you through the process of installing a driver. If the device came with a CD-ROM or DVD, choose Search Automatically For Updated Driver Software and put the CD-ROM (or DVD) into your CD-ROM drive. Be sure to check the manufacturer's web site for new drivers. If you have a driver from a previous version of Windows, such as Windows XP or Windows 9x/Me, it may not work with Windows Vista.

- **IRQ conflict**   If two devices have an X on their icons in the Device Manager window, they may have conflicting IRQs (that is, they are both trying to use the same IRQ). Click the Resources tab on each device's Properties dialog box (if there is one) to see which IRQ the device uses to communicate with the rest of the computer.

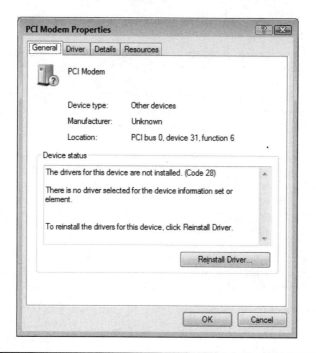

FIGURE 14-8   This modem has a hardware problem.

To see a list of IRQs and which device uses each one, choose View | Resources By Type in the Device Manager window and click the plus box by the Interrupt Request (IRQ) item. Change the IRQ for one of the conflicting devices, restart the computer, and see if the new setting works.

Booting in Safe Mode

Safe Mode provides minimal Windows functions by disabling all devices except the keyboard, screen, and disk. If you are in Windows and would like to restart in Safe Mode, restart the computer normally, but hold the CTRL key throughout the shutdown sequence. To cold boot (turn on your computer) into Safe Mode, start your computer normally, but watch the screen carefully. As soon as you see the Starting Windows message, press F8 repeatedly. You should see a menu of startup options, one of which is Safe Mode. (Other options include Safe Mode With Network Support, which you can use if you're 100 percent sure that the problem isn't a network device, nor any other device that might be conflicting with the hardware resources used by a network device.) See "Startup Modes" in Chapter 37 for more information on starting Windows in other modes.

Once you've booted in Safe Mode, you can use the Device Manager and other Windows facilities to figure out what's wrong.

To leave Safe Mode, reboot the computer normally.

Adding Memory

Adding memory is simple because no drivers are required. To add memory, follow these steps:

1. Shut down Windows, turn off and unplug the computer, open up the computer, and add the memory to available memory slots. Follow the instructions that came with your computer or with the memory.

CAUTION *Either use an antistatic wrist band (or a wire clipped to your metal wristwatch and the grounded metal frame) or, at the very least, touch a piece of the metal frame of the case to discharge static electricity before handling the delicate RAM, to prevent static shocks from damaging the RAM chips. You can even plug the computer back in while you are installing the memory chips, so that the third prong of the AC outlet connects your computer chassis to ground.*

2. Unplug the computer if you plugged it back in, close it up, plug it back in, and start it up. Most PCs do an internal memory test, notice that the amount of memory has changed, and possibly display a message before Windows starts.

3. If your computer complains, enter the computer's low-level configuration setup (also called *BIOS setup* or *CMOS setup*), and adjust the configured amount of memory to reflect the total now installed. Then reboot. When Windows starts, it automatically takes advantage of all memory installed in your computer.

TIP *The BIOS setup programs of most computers can be accessed during the bootup process by pressing the* DELETE *or* F1 *key, as instructed. If Windows doesn't accept your new memory, the RAM card may not be seated properly or may be defective. Reinsert the memory card and try again. If you have another computer, test the RAM in that computer also.*

Printing

Windows Vista has a sophisticated and powerful printer management system. Setting up a Plug and Play printer is almost effortless, and even printers without Plug and Play are not that difficult. Once they're configured, you can quickly and easily print from your programs by using any printer accessible to your computer and be confident that your printouts will look the way you want.

After your printer is installed, you can manage your print jobs from the Printers folder, which provides a way to view, pause, or cancel print jobs. You can change the printer configuration, including settings such as paper size and default fonts. If you run into printer trouble, you can use the Print Troubleshooter to find the problem (see "Diagnosing Problems Using Troubleshooters" in Chapter 37).

Windows handles the fonts that appear on the screen and on your printed pages. Windows itself comes with fonts, as do many application programs, and you can buy and install additional fonts.

What Is the Printers Folder?

The command center for printing is the Printers folder, shown in Figure 15-1. Each printer that your computer knows about has an icon in this folder, and you start the process of adding a new printer by clicking Add A Printer from the toolbar. The default printer (the HP DeskJet in the figure) has a check next to it. The number of documents in a device's queue is shown in the Documents column when you view the Printers folder in Details view (choose Views | Details). In Figure 15-2, the HP DeskJet has one document waiting to be printed, and the other printers and the fax devices are idle.

You can open the Printers folder from the Control Panel. Select Start | Control Panel | Hardware And Sounds | Printers. If you find that you access the Printers folder on a regular basis, you can add it to the Start menu as follows:

1. Right-click the Start button and select Properties from the shortcut menu. The Taskbar And Start Menu Properties dialog box appears (see "Changing Start Menu Properties" in Chapter 11).

2. Click the Customize button on the Start Menu tab. The Customize Start Menu dialog box appears.

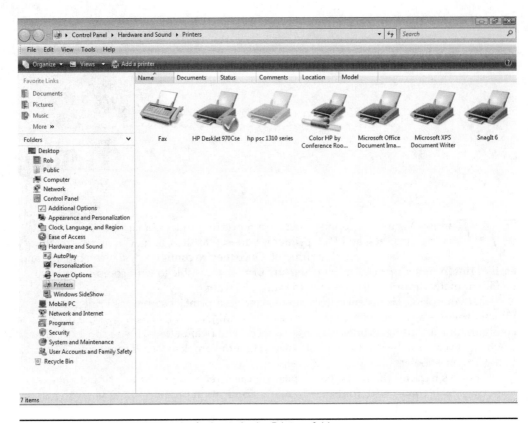

FIGURE 15-1   Windows keeps track of printers in the Printers folder.

3. Check the Printers option in the list of choices to add to the Start menu.

4. Click OK and then click OK again.

How Does Windows Handle Printers?

Printers come in three flavors:

- **Local printers**   Printers that are physically connected to a USB port of your computer (on older computers, printers can attach to parallel or LPT ports). Typically, a local printer is sitting right next to your computer.

- **Network printers**   Printers that may or may not be in the same room with you, but are connected to the same network as your computer (see Chapter 31).

- **Virtual printers**   Not really printers at all, but they show up as printing options in dialog boxes and as icons in your Printers folder. When you "print" a document to a virtual printer, it doesn't put ink on paper, but it may send a fax or create a file in some compact, widely readable format like Adobe PDF.

Each printer installed on your system has an entry in the Printers folder. When you print something from an application, a Windows *printer driver* (printer control program) for the

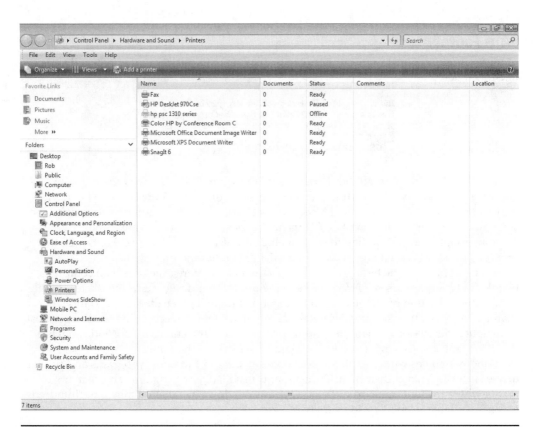

Name	Documents	Status	Comments	Location
Fax	0	Ready		
HP DeskJet 970Cse	1	Paused		
hp psc 1310 series	0	Offline		
Color HP by Conference Room C	0	Ready		
Microsoft Office Document Image Writer	0	Ready		
Microsoft XPS Document Writer	0	Ready		
SnagIt 6	0	Ready		

FIGURE 15-2   Use the Details view to see the number of documents in a printer's queue.

current printer formats the material for that particular printer. As far as printer limitations permit, documents look the same no matter what printer they're printed on.

You can have several printers defined on your system. They may be different physical printers or different modes on the same printer. For example, a few printers handle both the Hewlett Packard Printer Control Language (PCL) and the Adobe PostScript language. You can have two printer drivers installed, one for PCL and one for PostScript. If your printer can print on both sides of the paper, you can have two drivers installed, one for single-sided printing and one for double-sided printing. To see the installed printers, open your Printers folder.

At any particular moment, one of the printers is marked as the *default printer*. Anything you print goes to the default printer unless you specifically tell your program to use a different printer. You can make any of your printers the default by right-clicking its icon in the Printers folder and selecting Set As Default Printer from the shortcut menu.

Windows also provides *spooling*, a service that stores document data until the printer can accept it. When you print a document from an application, the information to be printed (the *print job*) is stored temporarily in the *queue* (storage for print jobs) until it can be printed. If you print a long document to a slow printer, spooling lets you continue working with your application while the printer works in the background. (Many years ago, "spool" stood for Simultaneous Peripheral Operation On-Line, but no one thinks of it as an acronym any more.)

What Are Fonts?

Modern computer screens and printers can display text in a variety of *typefaces* and sizes, as illustrated here:

> This is a sample of Times, a proportionally spaced
> This is a sample of 12-point Arial, another proportional
> This is a sample of 12-point Courier, a
> This is a sample of a small 6-point type
> This is rather large 18-point type.

In *fixed-pitch* typefaces, all the characters are the same width, as on a typewriter. In *proportionally* spaced typefaces, different characters are different widths. (The relative widths vary from one typeface to another.) Most typefaces are available in different sizes, with the sizes measured in printer's points, 1/72 inch. The most common sizes are 10-point and 12-point, roughly corresponding to sizes of elite and pica typewriter type. Fonts are often provided in several variations, such as normal, bold, italic, and bold-italic.

Typographers use the terms *font* and *typeface* with a bit more exactness than computer people. To typographers, a *typeface* refers to the underlying design of the characters, while a *font* is the collection of all the characters in a typeface of a given size and variation. For example, Arial is a typeface and Arial italic 12-point is a font. This precision usually gets lost in computer discussions, where *font* and *typeface* are used interchangeably. Windows refers to Arial as a font, and (having noted our objections) we will do the same.

Windows comes with a small but adequate set of fonts, but many programs and printer drivers include fonts of their own. Once a font is installed, any program can use it, no matter where the font came from. Thus, a typical Windows installation may have hundreds of fonts available, each in a wide variety of sizes.

NOTE *In addition to fonts that contain letters and numbers, Windows comes with several fonts of special characters. You can use the Character Map program to look at them and add them to your documents (see "Using Special Characters with Character Map" in Chapter 18).*

What Is TrueType?

Computer printers and screens print and display characters by printing or displaying patterns of black-and-white (or colored) dots. The size of the dots depends on the resolution of the device, ranging from 72 to 120 dots per inch (dpi) on screens, to 2400 or higher dpi on laser printers. In early versions of Windows, each typeface was provided as a *bitmap* (dot picture) of the actual black and white dots for each character, with separate bitmaps for each size. The bitmaps were available only in a small variety of sizes, such as Courier 10-, 12-, and 18-point.

This scheme does not produce very good-looking documents, because the dot resolution of printers is rarely the same as that for a screen. In the process of printing, Windows had to rescale each character's bitmap to the printer's resolution, producing odd-looking characters with unattractive jagged corners. Even worse, if you used a font in a size other than one of the sizes provided, the system had to do a second level of rescaling, producing even worse-looking characters.

TrueType solves both of these problems by storing each typeface not as a set of bitmaps, but essentially as a set of formulas the system can use to *render* (draw) each character at any desired size and resolution. This means that TrueType fonts look consistent on all devices, and that you can use them in any size.

Tip *Use only TrueType fonts in documents that you plan to print, to make your documents look their best.*

How Do Printers Handle Fonts?

Older printers had one or two fonts built in, and when you printed a document, those were the fonts you got. Modern printers can print any image that the resolution of the printer permits, so they can print all the fonts that are installed on your system.

Most printers have a reasonable set of built-in, general-purpose fonts, and some printers can accept font cartridges with added fonts. Occasionally, you may want to print a document that contains fonts your printer doesn't know, and then one of the following three things happens:

- Windows reverts to printing graphics, in effect turning your document into a full-page bitmap image that Windows can send to the printer.

- If your printer is smart enough (most laser printers that use PostScript and PCL5 are), Windows can send the printer all the fonts that a particular document needs. This delays the start of the print job a little, but as soon as the printing starts, it proceeds at a normal speed.

- To speed up printing, Windows uses *font substitution*, using built-in printer fonts where possible for similar TrueType fonts. For example, Microsoft's Arial font is nearly identical to the Helvetica font found in PostScript printers, so when Windows prints Arial text, it tells the printer to use Helvetica instead. This process of font substitution normally works smoothly, although occasionally on clone printers, the built-in fonts aren't exactly what Windows expects and the results can look a little off. (You can tell Windows to turn off font substitution if you suspect that's a problem.)

Setting Up a Local Printer

Setting up a local printer can be as simple as plugging it in, connecting it to your computer, and waiting for Windows to notice it (see "Configuring Windows for New Hardware" in Chapter 14). Or, you may need to answer a few questions for the Add Printer Wizard and insert the CD-ROM or DVD that came with your printer.

After the printer is set up, you may decide to share it over a network (see Chapter 31).

Note *If you have more than one user account on your computer, you need to install the printer from an account with administrator privileges (see Chapter 6).*

Adding a Plug and Play Printer

All new printers support Plug and Play, a Windows standard for the past several years, which makes installing printers very easy. If Windows Vista already has a driver for your printer, the process may be effortless: We installed an HP 1310 All-In-One printer just by plugging one end of a cable into the printer and the other into the appropriate port on our computer. Windows found the printer on its own and installed the appropriate driver in about the time that it took us to crawl out from under the desk. (Windows Help says to turn the printer on before connecting it to the computer, but we didn't even have to do that much.) If your printer connects wirelessly via infrared, turn the printer on and point its infrared port toward your computer's infrared port.

If Windows cannot identify your printer or find a driver for it, the Found New Hardware Wizard should appear. Answer its questions and be prepared to insert the CD-ROM or DVD that came with your printer if the wizard asks for it.

If Windows does not find your new printer at all, Plug and Play has fallen down on the job (or the printer is too old to support Plug and Play). See the instructions for installing a non-Plug and Play printer in the following section, or consult the instructions of the printer's manufacturer.

Adding a Printer Without Plug and Play

To add a non-Plug and Play printer, follow these steps:

1. Make sure the printer is plugged in and turned on.

2. Connect the printer to your computer. The instructions that came with your printer should tell you what cable to use and which computer port to connect it to. Newer computers usually do not have the older parallel ports (LPT ports); they have only USB ports for printer connections. If you have an older printer that you must use on a newer computer, contact a computer supply store for adapters that enable you to change a parallel port connection to a USB port. However, many times you are better off purchasing a low-cost printer that supports USB than you are trying to convert an older PC to work with a new computer (and Vista).

3. Open the Printers folder. You may be able to do this from the Start menu; if not, open the Control Panel and choose Printers in the Hardware And Sounds category.

4. Click Add A Printer from the Printers folder toolbar. The Add Printer Wizard opens. The first screen of the wizard asks whether the printer is local or is located on a network or wireless network.

5. Click an answer (we assume local for the rest of the steps).

6. Answer the questions the wizard asks. In particular, it will want to know what port you connected the printer to and the printer's manufacturer and model number. If you can't find the printer's make and model on the list the wizard gives, click the Have Disk button and insert the floppy or CD-ROM that came with your printer.

TIP   *If you have a disk for your printer, and your printer also appears in the Windows list, you have a choice to make. In general, you want to use the newest driver you can. So use the Windows driver, unless your disk is dated 2007 or later. If your printer isn't listed and you don't have a recent disk, check the printer manufacturer's web site for up-to-date drivers that you can download and install.*

FIGURE 15-3   Configure a printer from its Properties dialog box.

Configuring a Printer

After you install your printer or printers, you configure the driver to match your printer's setup. Some simple printers have little or no setup, while laser printers have a variety of hardware and software options.

To configure a printer, open the Printers folder either from the Start menu or from the Hardware And Sounds category of the Control Panel. Right-click the printer of interest and select Properties from the menu that appears. You see the Properties dialog box for the printer, as shown in Figure 15-3.

The settings for the printer are organized into groups, which you can display by clicking the appropriate tab. Not all printers have the same capabilities, so their Properties dialog boxes are not identical. (A black-and-white printer, for example, won't have a Color Management tab.) Commonly used tabs include the following:

- **General**   Add comments about the printer and click a button to print a test page.

- **Ports**   Select the network connection or printer port and change spooler settings.

- **Color Management**   For color printers, select how color profiles work (making printed colors match screen colors).

- **Paper**   Change the size of paper the printer is using, handle options such as double-sided, portrait, or landscape print orientation, and specify the number of copies of each page to print. (Some printers have a Printing Preferences button on the General tab that you use for setting paper size.)

- **Graphics**   Change the dots-per-inch resolution of printed graphics (higher dpi looks better, but prints slower); or use dithering, half-toning, and screening (techniques used to approximate shades of gray on black-and-white printers).

- **Fonts**   Change which font cartridges are in use, control font substitution, and control whether TrueType fonts are downloaded to the printer as fonts or graphics (which can be useful to work around flaky print position problems). Newer printers usually don't have a Fonts tab.

- **Device Options or Setup**   Change what optional equipment the printer has, such as extra memory, envelope feeders, and other paper-handling equipment, and change among various print-quality modes on ink-jet printers.

- **PostScript**   On high-end PostScript-compatible printers, select PostScript suboptions and control whether PostScript header information is sent with each print job (important on printers shared with other computers) or only once per session.

- **Sharing**   If your computer is on a local area network and this printer is physically connected to your computer, change whether other people on the network can share this printer (see Chapter 31).

- **Services**   Some printer drivers include procedures for maintenance, like cleaning print cartridges or aligning print heads.

After you have the properties for your printer set to your liking, you'll find that you seldom need to change the properties. For most printers, you never need to change them.

TIP   If you find that you frequently switch between two different sets of properties, such as single- and double-sided printing, install the printer twice, and configure one installation for single- sided and one for double-sided printing. Windows lets you configure single- versus double-sided printing in a dialog box, but switching "printers" is a lot easier.

Testing and Troubleshooting Your Printer

After installing a new printer or changing its configuration, it's a good idea to print a test page. To do this, right-click the printer's icon in the Printers folder and choose Properties from the shortcut menu. When the printer's Properties dialog box appears, click the Print Test Page button.

After sending the test page to the printer (but before the printer has had enough time to do much with it), Windows asks you how the test page came out. Wait for the page to finish printing, and click OK if it looks good. If the page either does not print or looks wrong, click the Troubleshoot Printer Problems link to launch the Troubleshoot Printer Problems Help feature. You can also launch the Troubleshoot Printer Problems Help feature without printing a test page as follows:

1. Choose Start | Help And Support to display the Windows Help And Support window (see Chapter 4).

2. Type **Printers** in the search box and press ENTER.

3. Click Troubleshoot Printer Problems from the list of help topics that are returned. The Troubleshoot Printer Problems screen appears.

The Troubleshoot Printer Problems area lists help articles to common problems users tend to have when setting up, configuring, and using printers. Click the links to see if the information can help you solve your printer problems. As with all such systems, the Troubleshoot Printer Problems feature is hit-or-miss. With luck, your problem is one that the Troubleshoot Printer Problems feature addresses.

Setting the Default Printer

The default printer is the printer that Windows uses when you give a Print command without specifying a particular printer. In the Printers folder, the current default printer is identified with a tiny check mark in the corner of its icon. You can make any printer the default printer by right-clicking the printer's icon in the Printers folder and selecting Set As Default from the shortcut menu. Or, select the printer and choose File | Set As Default Printer from the menu bar.

Deleting a Printer

If you want to remove an installed printer, just right-click the printer's icon in the Printers folder and choose Delete from the menu that appears. Or, select the printer and press DELETE.

Printing a Document

The simplest way to print a document is to find its icon in an Explorer window (or on the desktop), right-click it, and select Print from the shortcut menu. Windows opens the document in its default application and sends it to the printer using the default settings of that application. You have a short time in which to click a Cancel button while the document is being sent to the printer. (If you miss this opportunity, you can still cancel the job from the Printer Control window.) This technique works for some file types (such as those used by Microsoft Office), but not all (see "Pausing or Canceling Print Jobs" later in the chapter).

If Print does not appear on the file's shortcut menu, or if you want to make some choices about how the document is printed, open the document and issue the Print command from within the document's application. (Typically File | Print works, or you may find a Print icon on a toolbar.) Depending on the application, you may be able to see a preview of the printed document before giving the Print command. You can do this in Word or Internet Explorer, for example, by selecting File | Print Preview.

Choosing Printing Options

After you give the File | Print command, the Print dialog box appears. Which options this dialog box presents depends on the application and on the properties of your printer, so your Print dialog box may not look exactly like the one shown in Figure 15-4. Some of the choices you may be offered include:

- **Printer name**   The default printer is listed, but a drop-down list allows you to choose any of the printers whose icons are in the Printers folder.
- **Pages range**   You can print the entire document, specific pages, or a range of pages.

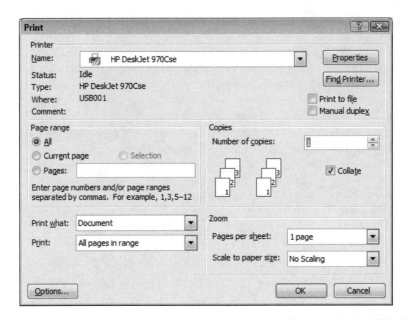

FIGURE 15-4   The Print dialog box

- **Copies**   The dialog box in Figure 15-4 contains a Collate check box. If the box is checked, copies of the entire document are printed one by one. Otherwise, all the copies of a single page are printed before moving to the next page.
- **Print quality**   Low-quality printing is faster and uses less ink or toner.
- **Black-and-white or color**   You can choose to print documents in color or as black and white (if your printer supports color printing).
- **Orientation**   Portrait orientation is longer than it is wide, while landscape orientation is wider than it is long.
- **Paper tray**   If your printer has more than one paper tray, you can choose which to use.
- **Order of pages**   The default is to print page one first, but you may print in reverse order so that the document comes out properly ordered in the printer tray. You may also be able to choose to print only even or odd pages, which is handy if you are doing two-sided printing.

When you have made your choices, click OK to send the document to the printer.

Printing to a File

When Windows prints a document, it first converts it into a form that the printer can understand. You can decide to capture this printer-ready form of the document in a file (and not send it to a physical printer) so that you can print it later or transport it via e-mail or a CD/DVD disc to a printer not connected to your computer. This is called *printing to a file.* You can do this in three ways:

- From the Print dialog box
- By changing the properties of an existing printer
- By creating a new printer icon

If you are printing only a single document to a file, and will want to print subsequent documents directly to paper, issue the Print command from within the document's application, and look for a Print To File check box in the Print dialog box. (Figure 15-4 has one, but yours may be in a different place or may be absent entirely. If you can't find it, you can still print to a file by changing the printer properties.) Make whatever other choices you want in the Print dialog box, and then click OK. A Print To File dialog box appears to let you choose what to call the file and where to save it. Click OK to begin producing the file.

If you are temporarily disconnected from your printer and want to print a series of documents to files, you may find it more convenient to change the printer properties so that documents sent to that printer go to a file automatically. To do this, find your printer's icon in the Printers folder, right-click it, and select Properties. When the Properties dialog box appears, look for the tab on which the printer port is set. (In Figure 15-3 you would choose the Ports tab, but your printer's Properties dialog box may be different.) Choose File from the list of possible ports. Make a note of the port that the printer was connected to before you changed, so that you can change back.

If you frequently print to a file, create a new printer icon and choose File as its port. Follow the instructions for installing a non-Plug and Play printer (see "Adding a Printer Without Plug and Play" earlier in the chapter).

Managing Printer Activity

Most print jobs don't require any management on your part: You tell your computer to print a document, it sends the job to a printer, and you pick up the printed pages after they are done. Occasionally, however, you want to communicate with a printer while it is in the act of printing. For example, you may realize that you have told the printer to print a full hundred-page document when you only intended to print one page of it. Or you may have queued several print jobs and realize that you want them printed in a different order, or that you want to cancel a job and send it to a different printer.

You deal with these situations from the printer's Print Control window, shown in Figure 15-5. Open this window by opening the printer's icon in the Printers folder. (Or, if you are displaying the Control Panel as a menu, you can open the printer by selecting Start | Control Panel | Printers | *printer name.*) The Print Control window shows you what job is currently printing, how that job is progressing, and which jobs are waiting to be printed.

Pausing or Canceling Print Jobs

To suspend the current print job until you can figure out what you want to do with it, choose Printer | Pause Printing from the menu of the Print Control window (or right-click the document in the Print Control window and choose Pause Printing from the shortcut menu).

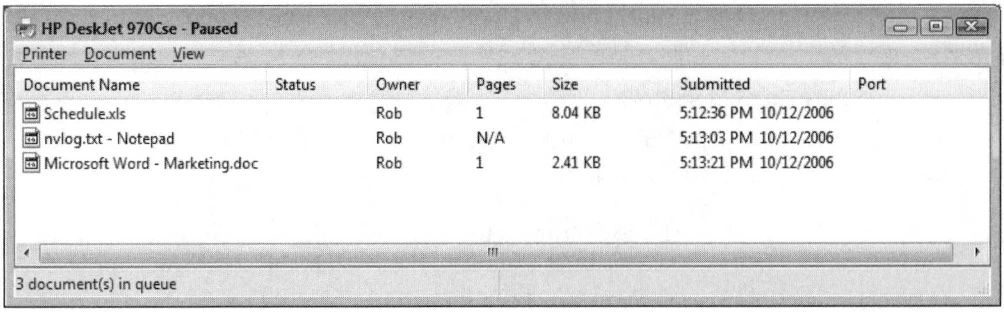

HP DeskJet 970Cse - Paused

Printer   Document   View

Document Name	Status	Owner	Pages	Size	Submitted	Port
Schedule.xls		Rob	1	8.04 KB	5:12:36 PM 10/12/2006	
nvlog.txt - Notepad		Rob	N/A		5:13:03 PM 10/12/2006	
Microsoft Word - Marketing.doc		Rob	1	2.41 KB	5:13:21 PM 10/12/2006	

3 document(s) in queue

FIGURE 15-5   The Print Control window

To resume the job where you left off, select Printer | Pause Printing again (or right-click anywhere in the Print Control window and choose Pause Printing). To delete a particular print job, right-click the job in the Print Control window and choose Cancel from the shortcut menu that appears. To get rid of everything waiting for that printer, choose Printer | Cancel All Documents.

Changing the Order in Which Jobs Are Printed

By default, print jobs are executed in a first-in, first-out manner. However, print jobs also have priority settings, and the highest-priority jobs move to the front of the queue. If you are printing a number of jobs and want to move one of them in front of the others, change its priority as follows:

1. Open the printer's icon in the Printers folder. The Print Control window appears, as shown in Figure 15-5. The jobs waiting to be printed are listed.

2. Right-click the print job whose priority you want to change and select Properties from the shortcut menu.

3. The default priority is 1, which is the setting for the least-important jobs. (This takes some getting used to, as we usually think of "first priority" being the most important.) Move the Priority slider to the right to raise the job's priority.

4. Click OK.

Scheduling a Print Job

If you have a very large print job that is going to take a long time, you can schedule it to print in the middle of the night, or some other time when the printer is unlikely to be needed by anyone. To do this, submit your job to the printer as usual, but then do the following:

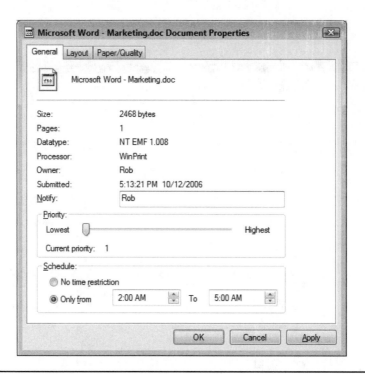

FIGURE 15-6 Set the print job to start during off-peak times.

1. Open the printer's icon in the Printers folder. The Print Control window appears, as shown in Figure 15-5.

2. Right-click the print job you want to schedule and select Properties from the shortcut menu. The Document Properties dialog box appears.

3. Click the Only From *xx* To *xx* radio button (as shown in Figure 15-6).

4. Select times from the drop-down lists so that the radio button corresponds to a complete sentence. For example: Only From 2 A.M. To 5 A.M.

5. Click OK.

TIP *If you have scheduled a large print job for a time when the printer is unattended, make sure that it has plenty of paper and a fresh cartridge of ink or toner.*

Installing and Using Fonts

Windows provides a straightforward way to install and use fonts. To see which fonts you have installed, open the folder C:\Windows\Fonts in Windows Explorer (assuming that Windows is installed on drive C:).

TrueType fonts have a TC icon, Open Type fonts have an O icon, and older fonts have an A icon. You can open any font to see its description and samples of the font in a variety of sizes.

TIP   *Windows can handle up to 1000 fonts, but to avoid slowing down your applications, don't install more than 200.*

Installing Fonts

To install new fonts from a CD/DVD or network, follow these steps:

1. View the C:\Windows\Fonts folder in Windows Explorer (or the Fonts folder of whatever folder Windows is installed in).

2. Choose File | Install New Font. The Add Fonts dialog box appears, as shown on the next page.

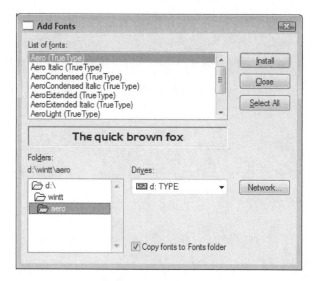

3. In the Drives and Folders boxes, select the drive and folder in which the files are located for the new font or fonts. Click the Network button if the font files are on a network drive that is not mapped to a drive letter on your computer. Windows displays the fonts it finds.

4. In the List Of Fonts box, select the font(s) you want to install.

5. Normally, Windows copies the font files into its Fonts folder (C:\Windows\Fonts). If you are installing fonts from a networked folder, you can uncheck Copy Fonts To Fonts Folder to use the fonts where they are located, which saves space in exchange for some loss in speed.

6. Click OK, and Windows installs the fonts you want.

Tip *You can also drag font files from the install disk or folder to the C:\Windows\Fonts folder.*

Deleting Fonts

To delete a font or fonts, display the C:\Windows\Fonts folder in Windows Explorer. Then select the fonts you want to get rid of and choose File | Delete. However, don't delete a font unless you are sure that none of the programs on your system use it. To be safe, move the fonts to a temporary folder for a few days to see if any programs display error messages when they try to use them. If no errors appear, then delete the fonts.

Finding Similar Fonts

Windows offers an occasionally useful "font similarity" feature that lets you look for fonts that are similar to a particular font. When viewing the Fonts folder, choose View | Group By | Font Type. The font similarity feature depends on special information in the font files, so older fonts without this information aren't ranked for similarity.

Running Windows Vista on Laptops

Many people use laptops—it's convenient to be able to pick up your computer, with all its data and software, and take it anywhere. But laptops have disadvantages, too, and Windows Vista addresses many of them. This chapter is full of suggestions about how to make the most of your laptop, including these:

- You can use the Windows Mobility Center to help you quickly configure your laptop when you work in different locations.

- You can coordinate files with those on a desktop or network by using offline files and the Sync Center.

- You can print a document, even when you aren't attached to a printer, by deferring printing until a printer is available.

- You can use Remote Desktop Connection to access your computer remotely through a LAN or the Internet.

- You can use power management to make your battery last longer.

- If you use a docking station to connect your laptop to desktop devices, you should know about docking and undocking and hardware profiles.

You also may want to explore connecting to a network or another computer to use its resources when you don't have a network card by using a dial-up connection—this topic covered in Chapter 29.

Using Windows Vista Mobile PC Tools

Windows Vista provides some tools to help you customize and use your laptop computer to work on the road or in the office. Laptops provide a great computing option for those who travel a lot, move from office to boardroom to conference room during the day, or just take their work home each night. One problem with laptops, however, is that as conditions or locations change, users can spend several minutes reconfiguring Windows each time they boot up their computer. For example, a marketing representative who shows presentations three times a week must set up her laptop for those situations (for example, turn off the screen saver and show a standard desktop image). With Vista, she can set up those options once and then just turn on the Presentation Settings tool when she begins her presentation.

Vista Mobile PC tools include the Windows Mobility Center, Presentation Settings, Tablet PC Settings, Pen and Input Settings, and Sync Center.

Using the Windows Mobility Center

A new tool available with Windows Vista is the Windows Mobility Center, shown in Figure 16-1. It has a set of tiles that provides quick access to different mobility features and provides a centralized location for managing and adjusting your laptop configuration depending on the situation you are in. For example, if you travel with your laptop and you constantly find that you are adjusting the brightness setting for different locations (office buildings, airports, cafes, and so forth), the Mobility Center has a control for quickly reducing or increasing the screen brightness. Similarly, if the laptop's volume needs tweaking, the Mobility Center has a setting for that as well.

Of course, you can find individual controls for these types of settings in other places in Windows, but the Mobility Center places these settings in one place. That's the idea of having a centralized location for these controls. But not only can you adjust screen brightness and volume, you also can check wireless network connections, search for projectors in your area, set up external displays (such as a widescreen television to display a presentation or video), change your screen's orientation, and more.

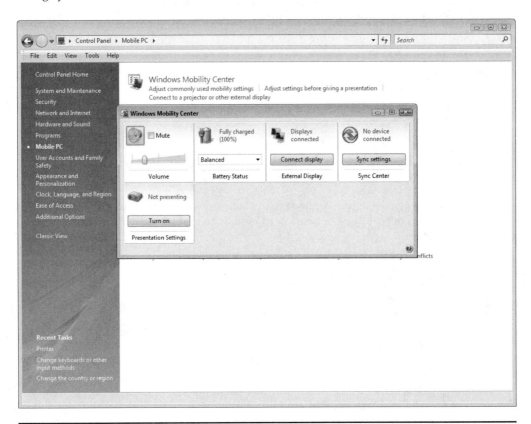

FIGURE 16-1 Windows Mobility Center

The type of settings on your laptop's Mobility Center depends on the laptop configuration and the types of controls put there by your laptop's manufacturer. Manufacturers can add to the list of settings that appear in the Mobility Center. The following list is some of the controls your laptop's Mobility Center may have:

- Sound adjustment and mute
- Battery level and power scheme settings
- External displays
- Brightness adjustment
- Status of wireless networks in your area
- Setting screen orientation from landscape to portrait
- Sync Center settings
- Presentation settings

The Mobility Center is located in the Control Panel. To display it, do the following:

1. Choose Start | Control Panel.
2. Click Mobile PC to display the Mobile PC icons.
3. Click Windows Mobility Center. The Mobility Center window appears, which was shown in Figure 16-1.

To use a feature on the Mobility Center, click the control for that item and change the settings. For example, the Battery Status tile lets you choose which type of power plan you want to use, such as Balanced, Power Saver, or High Performance. With the Presentation Settings tile, you can turn on or off the Presentation Settings tool (see the next section) when you start and end a presentation.

Windows Vista can be configured by laptop manufacturers to provide different tiles on the Mobility Center window. The tiles that are shown on your system, as well as which settings you can change for each tile, may be different from those shown here.

Changing Presentation Settings

Many users that travel to trade shows, client locations, training seminars, and similar destinations use laptops to present slide shows to a group of people. With Windows Vista, you can use the Presentation Settings tool to quickly set up Vista for a presentation session. You can set up the way you want Vista to look and behave every time you show a presentation, and then just click the option telling Windows you are giving a presentation for those settings to be active.

You can set the following presentation settings:

- Turn off screen savers
- Set the volume to a specific level
- Show a different background image or none at all
- Set which displays you use for your presentations

In addition to the preceding manual settings, Windows automatically disables the following when you turn on the presentation settings:

- Sleep mode, so your computer stays awake during idle times
- System notifications, so you are not shown notifications such as update settings, Windows Firewall messages, and the like

To use the Presentation Settings tool, do the following:

1. Choose Start | Control Panel.
2. Click Mobile PC to display the Mobile PC icons.
3. Click Adjust Settings Before Giving A Presentation. The Presentation Settings dialog box appears, as shown in Figure 16-2.

Most of the controls are self-explanatory (such as Turn Off The Screen Saver and Set The Volume To). For the Connected Displays settings, however, set up a second monitor (see "Using Multiple Displays" in Chapter 12 for information on how to do this) and then click the Connected Displays button. On the Current Displays dialog box, select the configuration you use for your presentations. Click OK.

FIGURE 16-2   Set your presentation settings prior to slide shows.

After you set up your Presentation Settings options, leave the I Am Currently Giving A Presentation check box cleared (unless you are giving a presentation right now). Click OK to exit the Presentation Settings dialog box and to save your settings. When you are ready to give a presentation, open the Windows Mobility Center (see the previous section) and click the Turn On button in the Presentation Settings tile. Vista applies your presentation settings (such as changes the background image and turns off the screen saver) and changes the Mobility Center tile to read Presenting. When you finish your presentation, click the Turn Off button in the Presentation Settings tile.

Changing Tablet PC Settings

Tablet PCs are flat computers that have a display, a few buttons, and a stylus or electronic "pen" to input information or make screen choices. They differ from ordinary laptops and desktop computers in that they don't have the traditional keyboard, mouse, monitor, speakers, and other devices hanging off of them. Tablet PCs are handy for users who spend most of their working time away from a desk, but who need some form of computer device to input or access digital information. Medical professionals, delivery persons, law enforcement officers, and construction workers are just a few professions who use tablet PCs in their daily life.

Windows Vista provides the Tablet PC Settings tool in the Control Panel to help you set up your Tablet PC. To use these settings, follow these steps:

1. Choose Start | Control Panel.

2. Click Mobile PC to display the Mobile PC icons.

3. Click the Tablet PC Settings option to display the Tablet PC Settings dialog box, shown in Figure 16-3.

On the General tab, you have the following options:

- **Handedness**   Lets you set where the menus appear on the screen for ease of access. If you are right-handed, set the Right-Handed option so menus appear on the left side of the screen, for example.

- **Calibration**   Lets you use the Digitizer Calibration Tool to calibrate the tablet pen to locate items on the screen better.

The Handwriting Recognition tab includes the following options:

- **Use The Personalized Recognizer**   Helps to improve the handwriting recognition settings.

- **Automatic Learning**   Turns on the Vista automatic learning feature that enables the handwriting recognizer to learn your handwriting style. It also stores data about the vocabulary you use so that it can interpret your chicken scratches into digital data.

On the Display tab, you can set the screen orientation, such as landscape or portrait, to suit how you best work with the tablet PC.

The Other tab is for configuring pen and input settings, which is covered in the next section. The Other tab may also include other settings and options provided by the manufacturer of your tablet PC.

PART III

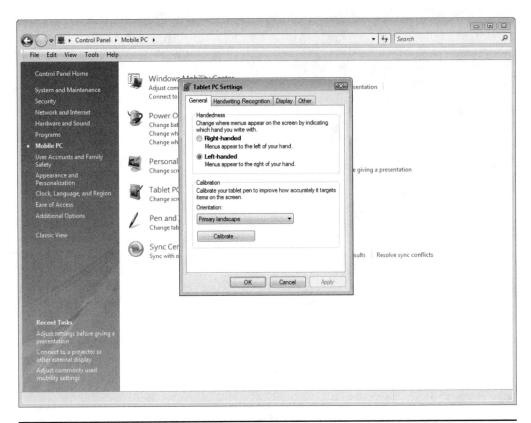

FIGURE 16-3 Set tablet PC settings with this dialog box.

Changing Pen and Input Settings

Tablet PCs use a pen or other digital stylus to allow users to input information, select screen icons or menus, and click/double-click items. You also can use pens for desktop or laptop computers if you perform tasks that require handwriting or drawing input that a mouse or trackball cannot achieve. To set the pen and input options for these devices, use the Pen And Input Devices dialog box.

To access this dialog box, do the following:

1. Choose Start | Control Panel.

2. Click Mobile PC to display the Mobile PC icons.

3. Click the Pen And Input Settings option to display the Pen And Input Devices dialog box, shown in Figure 16-4.

The Pen Options tab includes the following options:

- **Pen Actions** Lets you configure how your pen can perform common mouse actions, such as click, double-click, and right-click. Users can tap, double-tap, or press and hold the pen point to perform actions. Click the Settings buttons to further refine your action settings.

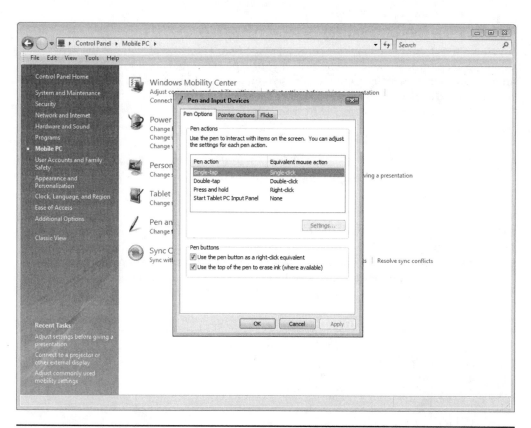

FIGURE 16-4   Control digital pens and other input devices using this dialog box.

- **Pen Buttons**   Some pens have pen buttons that can be set to display context menus (those menus that display when you right-click with a mouse). The top of the pen can also be set to perform "erase" functions.

The Pointer Options tab sets the following:

- **Dynamic Feedback**   Lets you set up visual cues when you perform pen actions, such as tapping.

- **Pointer Options**   Displays a pen cursor on the screen instead of the standard mouse cursor.

Finally, on the Flicks tab, you can set the different navigational actions when you use the flick feature of your pen or input device. For instance, if you flick the pen in a downward motion, the action is to scroll down a document page or web page. Another action could be to go back a page during web surfing if you flick the pen to the left. Other options are available by clicking the Customize button on the Flicks tab.

Coordinating Your Laptop Files

If you use files from more than one computer on a regular basis, you can use the Sync Center to keep track of files that you use on your laptop but that are normally stored on another computer. The Sync Center enables you to set up offline files if you usually access files from a network.

The Sync Center can be accessed by doing the following:

1. Choose Start | Control Panel.
2. Click Mobile PC to display the Mobile PC icons.
3. Click Sync Center to display the Sync Center window, shown in Figure 16-5.

Deferring Printing from a Laptop

One frequent problem with traveling with a computer is that you rarely have access to a printer. Even portable printers add more weight and cost to your electronic carryall than most people are willing to bear. So, instead, you survive without a printer.

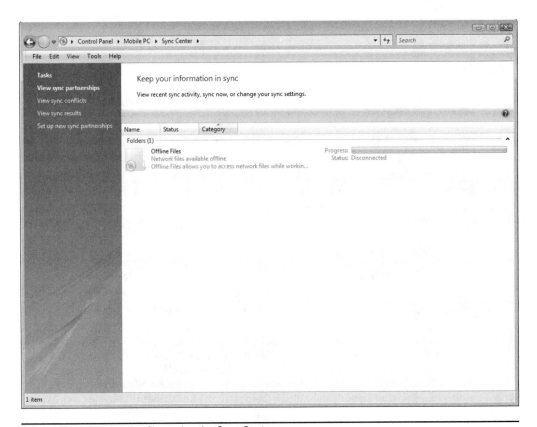

FIGURE 16-5   Synchronize files using the Sync Center.

You can print in several ways when you're away from home: you can connect to someone else's computer (using a network card, direct cable connection, or a dial-up connection) and print on its printer; you can sit at a computer with a printer and connect to your laptop with Remote Desktop and print; you can fax your document to the nearest fax machine (assuming you have fax software and a fax modem); or, you can go ahead and give the command to print the document, taking advantage of the Windows deferred printing feature.

NOTE *See Chapter 15 for more information about printing from Windows.*

Printing in Offline Mode

When a printer is set up but not currently attached to your computer, you can still give the command to print a document. You see a message telling you the printer isn't available and telling you the printer will be put into *offline mode*, which means files intended for the printer will, instead, be stored on your disk. When you next connect to the printer, you see a message that print jobs are waiting—you can then print or cancel the documents.

TIP *If you have problems printing while offline, try this: display your Printers folder, right-click the printer, and choose Use Printer Offline.*

If you don't see the message asking whether you want to print, when you are reconnected to a printer, follow these steps:

1. Open the Printers folder by choosing Start | Control Panel | Hardware And Sound | Printers.
2. Right-click the offline printer (grayed-out printers are offline).
3. Choose Use Printer Online to put the printer online. The print jobs waiting in the print queue start to print. The menu option will now read Use Printer Offline.

Printing on a Different Printer

If you want to print your queued documents using a printer other than the one you usually use, you can temporarily change the printer. If the printer's drivers were included on the Windows Vista DVD, Windows can probably find it because Windows copies most of its files to your hard disk. If your printer's drivers aren't included with Windows (if you installed them from a CD or DVD that came with the printer), you might need to insert that CD or DVD when changing printer descriptions.

TIP *If you use a wide variety of printers, you might want to install the Generic printer driver on your laptop to give you a basic printing option, no matter what kind of printer you're using.*

Follow these steps to change the description of a printer temporarily:

1. Open the Printers folder by choosing Start | Control Panel | Hardware And Sounds | Printers.

2. Double-click the printer you printed to (the printer appears grayed-out to indicate it is offline). You see the Printer window with all your print jobs listed.

3. Choose Printer and then choose Properties from the menu that appears. You see the Properties dialog box for the printer. See Figure 16-6.

4. If necessary, change the port on the Ports tab.

5. On the Advanced tab, choose the driver you need. If the printer you have available isn't listed (because you haven't used it before), click the New Driver button to choose the kind of printer you do have.

6. Close all the dialog boxes. You may be asked for your Windows Vista DVD.

7. If you change the driver for the printer, you need to repeat the preceding steps to change it back when you return to the office and connect to your regular printer.

FIGURE 16-6   A printer's Properties dialog box

TIP *Windows uses a single driver for a variety of similar printers. If you already have a printer defined that's similar to the one you want to use, you'll probably find that you can define the new printer and Windows won't need any extra files.*

Accessing Other Computers with Remote Desktop Connection

Remote Desktop Connection allows you to have access to the desktop of one computer while you are running another. Not only can you see and use all the files on the remote computer, you can actually see the desktop and run programs as if you were sitting in front of the remote computer.

NOTE *You can also access a computer remotely using Remote Assistance (see "Responding to an Invitation for Remote Assistance" in Chapter 4).*

Remote Desktop Connection uses a LAN, a virtual private network (VPN), or the Internet to access the remote computer—the speed of the response will depend on the speed of your connection.

The *server* is the computer that you will be taking control of from a remote location. Usually, the server computer in the Remote Desktop Connection application is the computer on your desk—the one that you will not be taking with you. The *client* computer is the one that you will use while you are away to see the desktop of the server computer.

Before you leave the computer you want to access remotely (the server), get Remote Desktop Connection configured and working—you should also test it before you leave. For example, if you want to be able to use your office desktop computer remotely while you are traveling, be sure to configure it for Remote Desktop Connection before you leave on your trip.

Configuring the Server for Remote Desktop Connection

To gain access using Remote Desktop Connection, you specify one or more user accounts on the server computer to which you want remote access. The user accounts must have passwords, so as not to leave your system open to hackers. If you normally do not use a login password, create a password for your user account or create a new user account with a password solely for the purpose of using Remote Desktop Connection (see "Creating, Modifying, and Deleting User Accounts" in Chapter 6). When you configure the Remote Desktop Connection server (as described in the next section), you type the user account name when Windows asks for the Object Name in the Select Users dialog box. If you are using Remote Desktop Connection over a domain-based LAN, you can connect using a user account on any computer on the LAN.

NOTE *Microsoft discourages you from using an administrative user account in situations where there is a security risk. Instead, Microsoft recommends that you use a non–administrative user account when logging in remotely. Make a new user account and add it to the Remote Desktop Users group (see Chapter 6).*

Configuring the Server for Remote Desktop Connection

If you plan on using Remote Desktop Connection, follow these steps to configure the server computer for access by you or others:

1. Display the System Properties dialog box by choosing Start | right-click Computer | Properties | .

2. Click the Remote Settings link in the Tasks pane.

3. Check the Allow Connections From Computers Running Any Version Of Remote Desktop check box in the Remote Desktop section of the dialog box.

4. Click the Select Users button to display the Remote Desktop Users dialog box. Users with administrative accounts are automatically given access, and you can add other users.

5. Click Add to display the Select Users dialog box, shown in Figure 16-7. User accounts have three identifiers: object type, location, and name.

6. To specify a user account from the computer you are sitting at, leave the Select This Object Type box set to Users, and type an account name in the Enter The Object Names To Select box. To specify a user account from another computer on a domain-based LAN, click the Locations button and choose the domain before you specify the user account name.

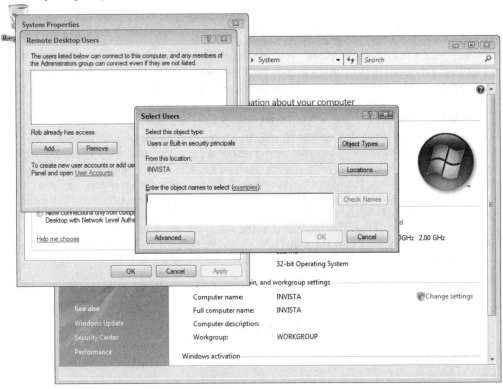

FIGURE 16-7   Choose users who can access the computer remotely.

NOTE *An* object type *is nothing mysterious—it specifies the type of resource, user account, or group account for which you want to establish remote access. To give a user account remote access, leave the Select This Object Type box set to Users. Other types are Computers, Printers, and groups of users, computers, and printers. The entry in the From This Location box is also simple, though the name is rather misleading. The location does not describe the physical place that another computer inhabits, but is the name of that computer. To allow a user from another computer access to your computer, you type the other computer's name. In the Enter The Object Names To Select box, you can type* computername\username *to specify a user account on that computer (for example, SOLARIA\Rima Regas or DELL8100\Margy Levine Young).*

7. Click Check Names. Windows replaces the name using the form it needs (*computername\username*).

8. Click OK. The Remote Desktop Users dialog box displays the user you added. To add another user, repeat Steps 5–8.

9. Click OK to close the Remote Desktop Users dialog box and click OK again to close the System Properties dialog boxes.

NOTE *If the computer you will be accessing is protected by a firewall, make sure that the firewall allows remote connection traffic (see Chapter 33).*

Configuring the Client Computer for Remote Desktop Connection
The client computer you will use to connect to your server computer must be running Remote Desktop Connection. You can use a computer running Windows Vista (of course) or Windows XP Professional. For greater success with the latter option, use a computer running Windows XP Professional with Service Pack 2 installed.

Connecting to the Remote Computer with Remote Desktop Connection
Once you have completed the necessary setup tasks, you are ready to test Remote Desktop Connection. Make sure that the server machine is on and working and connected to whatever network you will use to access it—usually the Internet or a LAN (obviously, you need to do this before you leave). Sit at the client machine—that is, the computer that you will have with you wherever it is you are going.

Start Remote Desktop Connection on the client computer by following these steps:

1. Choose Start | All Programs | Accessories | Remote Desktop Connection. You see the Remote Desktop Connection window:

2. Select the name of the server computer from the Computer drop-down list, or enter the computer name or IP

address. If no computer names appear in the drop-down list, choose Browse For More to see the available computers in your domain or workgroup—only computers that you have configured for remote access appear.

NOTE *To discover a computer's IP address, open a Command Prompt window and run the ipconfig program (see "Checking Your TCP/IP Address" in Chapter 30).*

3. Click Connect.

4. Enter your name and password in the Windows Security window: type the user account name and password that you use on the server computer. Click OK.

5. You see the remote desktop, such as the one in Figure 16-8. Notice the special toolbar at the top of the window—you can use it to minimize, restore, or close the Remote Desktop Connection window. (Click the Restore or Minimize button if you want to work on the client computer, but then return to the server computer.) Clicking the pushpin icon locks the menu open.

You're ready to work on the server computer.

Using the Remote Desktop Connection

Once you have established the remote desktop connection, you can work as if you were working on the server computer. You can also combine the capabilities of the remote server computer with the local client computer in the following ways:

- **Cut-and-paste**   You can cut information from the Remote Desktop Connection window and paste it into an application on the local computer.

- **Use local files in the remote session**   When using the Remote Desktop Connection program, local drives appear in the Computer folder. They also appear in Open and Save dialog boxes in applications.

- **Use a local printer in the remote session**   When you print while you are using Remote Desktop Connection, the print job automatically goes to the default local printer if the printer driver is available on the server computer.

Other Remote Desktop Connection Options

When you connect to a computer using Remote Desktop Connection, you see the Remote Desktop Connection dialog box (previously shown in the "Connecting with Remote Desktop Connection" section). You can click the Options button to see a larger version of this dialog box with many additional options, as shown in Figure 16-9. Table 16-1 lists and describes several of the options.

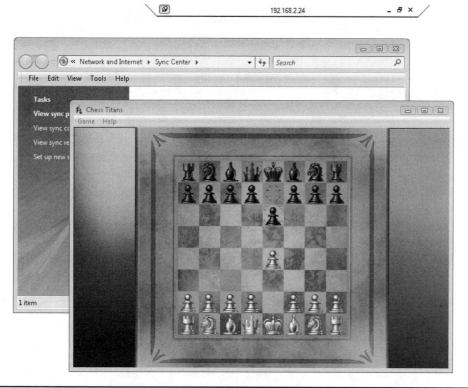

FIGURE 16-8   The remote desktop appears on your screen—notice the special toolbar at the top.

FIGURE 16-9   Setting the options for your remote connection

Tab	Setting	Description
General	Connection Settings	Saves your Remote Desktop Connection session as a Remote Desktop File (RDF). You can open saved session files later to streamline connecting to a Remote Desktop Connection session.
Display	Remote desktop size and colors	Selects the size and color depth of the Remote Desktop window on your screen.
Local Resources	Remote computer sound	Specifies whether to play the sounds that the other computer would make on your computer instead.
Local Resources	Keyboard	Specifies whether ALT- key combinations apply to the local computer or the remote computer.
Local Resources	Local Devices and Resources	Specifies which devices on the remote computer you connect to automatically.
Programs	Start the following program on connection	Runs a program automatically when you connect to the remote computer, and specifies which program.
Experience	Choose your connection speed to optimize performance	Specifies the speed of your connection to the remote computer.
Experience	Allow the following (Desktop background, Show contents of window while dragging, Menu and window animation, Themes, and Bitmap caching)	Specifies which desktop features appear in your Remote Desktop window. Deselect items to improve performance, especially if you have a slow connection.
Advanced	Server Authentication	Specifies authentication settings to verify that the computer you connect to is the correct computer.
Advanced	Connect From Anywhere	Enables you to configure Terminal Services Gateway so that you can connect to remote computers that are secured behind a firewall.

TABLE 16-1   Settings on the Remote Desktop Connection Dialog Box

TIP *Once you have configured the settings for your remote desktop connection, you can save them with a name by clicking the Save As button on the General tab of the Remote Desktop Connection dialog box. The next time you want to use these settings, click the Open button.*

Managing Your Computer's Power

If you often use your laptop when it isn't plugged in, you probably have had a battery die before you finished your work. Windows and some applications support power management, which eases this problem without actually solving it. Windows supports the Advanced Configuration and Power Interface (ACPI) power management standard.

TIP *The most power-hungry component of your laptop system is the monitor. Turning off the monitor using the Sleep or Hibernate feature when you won't be using it for several hours saves energy, in exchange for the relatively minor inconvenience of waiting a few seconds for it to come on again when you're ready to go back to work.*

Most laptops support Sleep Mode, in which the disks stop spinning and the screen goes blank, but the memory and CPU continue to run, using much less power than full operation. Vista saves any work that you are currently working on, and restores your previous work session when you awaken your laptop from sleep. Sleep can be enabled by setting Vista to place your computer to sleep when you shut the laptop lid or during idle work times. You also can click Start, the power button (right arrow), and then Sleep.

Some laptops (and some desktops) also support hibernation, in which the computer stores the contents of its memory in a temporary file on your hard disk and then shuts itself down completely, so it stops using power. When you reopen the laptop, click the computer's power button, and press keys or move the mouse, the computer wakes up again, restoring the contents of its memory from the temporary file. If your computer supports Hibernate Mode, the power plan settings includes a Hibernate option. When hibernation is enabled, an additional choice—Hibernate—appears when you choose Start and then a power option.

You use the Power Options available from the Control Panel to set your power plan. (Windows used to call these Power Schemes in previous editions.) To set up a plan, do the following:

1. Choose Start | Control Panel.
2. Click the Mobile PC item.
3. Click Power Options to display the Select A Power Plan window, shown in Figure 16-10. Select one of the following plans:
   - **Balanced** Sets the battery charge and performance settings on an even scale
   - **Power Saver** Extends battery life, but decreases system performance
   - **High Performance** Keeps system performance high (about the same as if you run on AC/DC), but drastically reduces the charge on the battery
4. Click Change Plan Settings under a plan if you want to modify its configuration. The Change settings for the plan window appears.
5. In the Change settings for the plan window, change the sleep and display settings for when you are running your laptop on battery and when you are running it while plugged in. For instance, if you want Vista to put the computer to sleep after

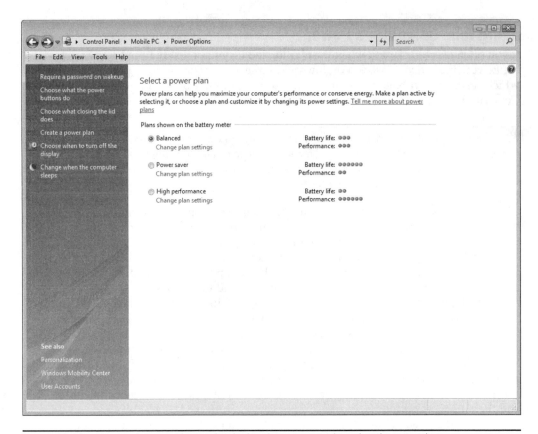

FIGURE 16-10   Manage how your laptop (or desktop) uses power by using these settings.

15 minutes of idle time when you are running on battery, select 15 Minutes under
the On Battery icon next to the Put The Computer To Sleep option.

6. Click Save Changes when you are finished modifying the power plan.

TIP   *Many laptop manufacturers add extra power management drivers to take advantage of special*
power-saving features—such as running the CPU slower when the computer is working on
batteries than when it's plugged in, or turning off serial and parallel ports when you're not
planning to use them. Consult your laptop's documentation to see whether your computer has
any extra features you can enable.

Using a Docking Station

Docking stations enable laptop users to avoid resource limitations that most laptops have.
A docking station lets you connect to a better monitor, a real mouse, a full-sized keyboard,
and possibly a network. Some docking stations give you access to additional hardware, such

as a hard drive or CD-ROM/DVD drive. In addition to these resources, docking stations are convenient—by simply clicking the laptop into the docking station, you have access to these additional resources, without having to plug cables into the laptop.

NOTE Port replicators *are a kind of simple docking station that contain no resources except additional ports. A port replicator can be used to give you immediate access to a full-sized screen, keyboard, mouse, printer, and network connection, without having to plug each cable in separately. Port replicators don't have hard drives or other internal resources.*

If your hardware supports it, you can plug your laptop into its docking station *without turning off the laptop* and gain access to the additional resources provided by the docking station. You can usually undock it by choosing Start | Eject PC. Windows automtically adjusts to the change in hardware, notifying you of open files and loading or unloading any necessary drivers. When you're ready to dock the laptop again, simply put it in the docking station. Windows again adjusts automatically to the change in hardware. Some laptops support hot docking, but no Eject PC command appears on the Start menu.

If your laptop doesn't support hot docking (check the laptop's manual or online help to find out for sure), you need to shut down Windows and turn the laptop off before docking or undocking. You can benefit from creating two hardware profiles—one to use when the laptop is docked, and one to use when you work away from the docking station. Multiple hardware profiles can save you time. When you undock your laptop, you needn't change each hardware setting that needs to be changed; instead, you can choose the correct hardware profile when the machine boots.

Ease of Access Center

Like previous versions of Windows, Windows Vista includes a number of options to help people who have disabilities that make using a computer difficult. In some cases, people without disabilities may also find the Ease of Access features useful. The options include settings for your keyboard, sound, display, and mouse.

To set your Ease of Access features, you can use the new Ease of Access Center, described in this chapter. After you set your options, you can turn them on and off by using the Ease of Access Center or the icons that appear in the notification area on your taskbar. Also, Internet Explorer (Microsoft's web browser) has additional Ease of Access features.

What Ease of Access Features Are Available in Windows Vista?

Windows includes the Ease of Access Center for people who have difficulty typing, reading the screen, hearing noises the computer makes, or using a mouse.

Keyboard aids for those who have difficulty typing include

- **Mouse Keys** Enables you to use the numeric keypad to move the mouse around.

- **Sticky Keys** Enables you to avoid pressing multiple keys by making the CTRL, WINDOWS, SHIFT, and ALT keys "sticky"—they stay in effect even after they have been released.

- **Filter Keys** Filters out repeated keystrokes. Good for typists who have trouble pressing a key once briefly.

- **Toggle Keys** Sounds a tone when the CAPS LOCK, SCROLL LOCK, and NUM LOCK keys are activated.

- **On-Screen Keyboard** Displays a keyboard on the screen that enables you to type by using your mouse.

TIP *For sloppy typists of all abilities (and for those with small laptop keyboards), Toggle Keys can be convenient to guard against accidentally pressing CAPS LOCK and typing capitalized prose by mistake.*

> **Do Applications Use the Windows Accessibility Settings?**
> Although Ease of Access features are built into the Windows operating system,
> software applications must be designed to work with them. Microsoft maintains
> standards, including standards for accessibility, that developers must meet to put the
> Designed for Windows logo on their product. The standards include support for high-
> contrast and enlarged displays, keyboard use with a single hand or device, adjustable
> timing for the user interface, and keyboard-only operation. If you need to use Ease of
> Access features with new software, make sure the software supports Windows Ease
> of Access features before you buy. Microsoft maintains an accessibility web site at:
> www.microsoft.com/enable.

Visual translation of sounds for those who have difficulty hearing include

- **Sound Sentry**   Displays a visual warning when the computer makes a sound.
- **Caption**   Displays a text caption when the computer makes a sound.

Display options for those who have trouble reading the screen include

- **High Contrast**   Uses a high-contrast color scheme and increases legibility wherever
  possible.
- **Cursor Options**   Makes the cursor easier to see.
- **Magnifier**   Displays a window that magnifies part of the screen.
- **Narrator**   Reads text on the screen aloud.

Mouse options for those who dislike or have trouble using a mouse or trackball include

- **Mouse Keys**   Enables you to use the numeric keypad to control the pointer.

Using the Ease of Access Center to Turn Features On or Off

In general, you probably want to turn on whichever Ease of Access features you find useful,
and leave them turned on, but if you share your computer, you may want the capability to
turn them on and off easily.

Windows Vista has a new way to turn on and off the Magnifier, Narrator, High Contrast
Settings, and On-Screen Keyboard: the Ease of Access Center. Press WINDOWS-U to see it (see
Figure 17-1).

You can also start the program by choosing Start | All Programs | Accessories | Ease Of
Access | Ease Of Access Center. Another way is to use Start | Control Panel | Ease Of Access |
Ease Of Access Center.

At the top of the Ease of Access Center are the following options you can select:

- Start Magnifier
- Start On-Screen Keyboard
- Start Narrator
- Set Up High Contrast

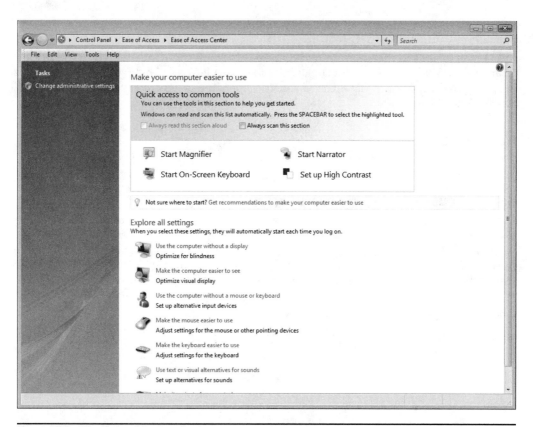

FIGURE 17-1   The Ease of Access Center

Other Ease of Access options you can set up or access using the Ease of Access Center include the following:

- Use the computer without a display
- Make the computer easier to see
- Use the computer without a mouse or keyboard
- Make the mouse easier to use
- Make the keyboard easier to use
- Use text or visual alternatives for sounds
- Make it easier to focus on tasks

Each of the preceding options displays a window from which you can select related Ease of Access features. Some features appear in more than one window, such as Narrator, which can be found by clicking either Use The Computer Without A Display or Make The Computer Easier To See.

Making the Keyboard More Accessible

Most of the options to change the way the keyboard accepts input are found by clicking the Change How The Keyboard Works link under the Ease Of Access Center category in the Ease of Access Center. The Make The Keyboard Easier To Use window appears, as shown in Figure 17-2.

NOTE *Other keyboard settings, including character repeat settings and language settings, are available in the Keyboard Properties dialog box (see "Configuring Your Keyboard" in Chapter 13).*

Setting Mouse Key Ease of Access Features

If you have difficulty using a mouse or other pointing devices, if your pointing device is broken, or if you don't like to use it, turn on Mouse Keys. If you have trouble using a keyboard and mouse for input, you can let Windows know you use an alternative input device. Windows also includes a number of keyboard shortcuts for giving commands from the keyboard (see the "Useful Keyboard Shortcuts" sidebar toward the end of the chapter).

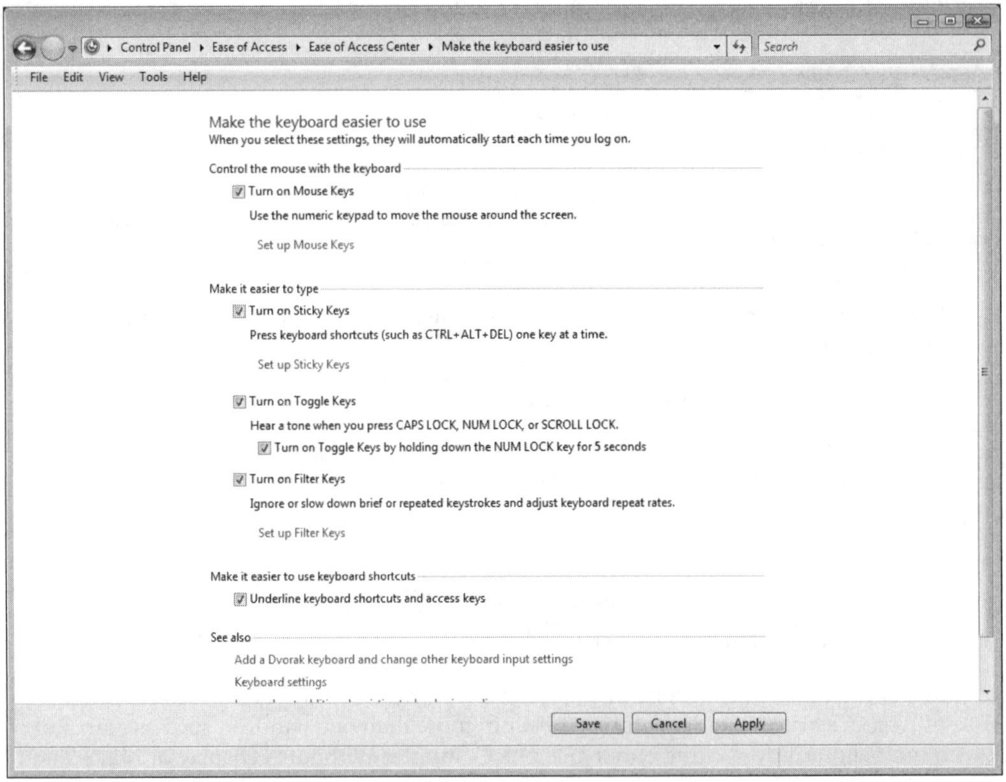

FIGURE 17-2   Ease of Access keyboard features

NOTE *Other mouse settings—including button configuration, double-click speed, and mouse pointer speed—are available in the Mouse Properties dialog box (see "Configuring Your Mouse" in Chapter 13). See Chapter 14 for information on installing other pointing devices.*

Changing Color and Size of Mouse Pointers

To help you see mouse pointers easier, you can change the size and color of them using the Make The Mouse Easier To Use Ease of Access feature. Choose Start | Control Panel | Ease Of Access | Change How Your Mouse Works. At the top of the window appears the Mouse Pointers area. Here you can choose from white, black, or inverted color for mouse pointers. Likewise, you can select Regular, Large, or Extra Large mouse pointer sizes.

Controlling the Pointer by Using the Number Pad

Mouse Keys enables you to control the mouse pointer by using the numeric keypad on your keyboard. The regular mouse or other pointing device continues to work as well. To turn on Mouse Keys, choose Start | Control Panel | Ease Of Access | Change How Your Keyboard Works, and select the Turn On Mouse Keys check box. To configure its settings, click the Set Up Mouse Keys link to display the Set Up Mouse Keys window, shown in Figure 17-3. You can set these options:

- **Keyboard Shortcut**   Turns Mouse Keys on or off when you press LEFT ALT-LEFT SHIFT-NUM LOCK (hold down the ALT and SHIFT keys that appear on the left side of the keyboard near the *X* and *Z* keys, and also press the NUM LOCK key). When you turn Mouse Keys on using the keyboard shortcut, Windows can display a warning message that it is being turned on. Also, you can set up Windows so that it plays a sound when you turn on or off Mouse Keys.

- **Top Speed**   Sets the pointer's top speed when you hold down keys to move it.

- **Acceleration**   Sets the speed at which the pointer accelerates when you hold down a key to move it. A faster rate of acceleration means the pointer reaches its top speed sooner.

- **Hold Down CTRL To Speed Up And SHIFT To Slow Down**   Gives you more ways to control the speed of the mouse pointer. When this option is selected, you can hold down CTRL when you want the pointer to move in big jumps across the screen, and hold down SHIFT when you want the pointer to move in smaller-than-usual increments.

- **Use Mouse Keys When NUM LOCK Is On/Off**   Determines when the number pad keys move the mouse pointer—when NUM LOCK is on or off. If you choose the Off setting, then you can enter numbers by using the number pad when NUM LOCK is on. However, you need another set of arrows to move the cursor. (Most keyboards have a separate set of cursor motion keys.)

 - **Display The Mouse Keys Icon On The Taskbar**   Displays a small graphic, shown here, in the notification area on the taskbar to the left of the time.

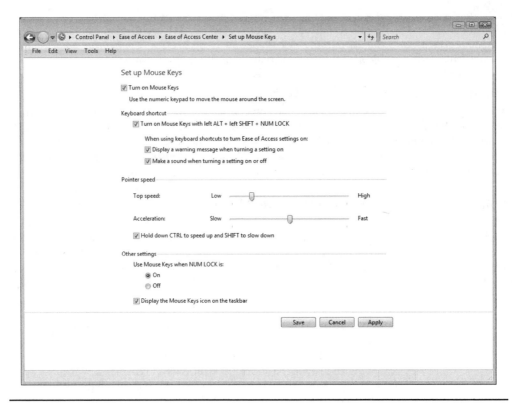

FIGURE 17-3 The Set Up Mouse Keys window

The following list shows how to use the number pad to control the pointer when Mouse Keys is on (be sure to use the keys on the numeric keys, not the equivalent keys elsewhere on your keyboard):

- Press the ARROW keys to move the pointer.
- Press the – key to set Mouse Keys to click the right mouse button whenever you press the 5 key.
- Press the / key to set Mouse Keys to click the left mouse button whenever you press the 5 key.
- Press the * key to set Mouse Keys to click both mouse buttons whenever you press the 5 key.
- Press the 5 key to click (with left or right mouse button, depending on whether you last pressed – or /) whatever the pointer is on.
- Press the + key to double-click whatever the pointer is on.
- Press the 0 or INSERT key to begin dragging (the equivalent of holding down the mouse button). Move the item by pressing the ARROW keys on the number pad. Drop the item (release the mouse button) by pressing the . (period) or DELETE key.

After you configure Mouse Keys, click Save.

Making Your Keys Stick

If you have trouble holding down two keys at once, activate *Sticky Keys*, which enables you to press the keys separately and still get the same effect. When Sticky Keys is on, you can save a document (for instance) by pressing the CTRL key, and then pressing the *s* key—you needn't press them at the same time. Pressing a second key turns off (or unsticks) the first key. Sticky Keys works only with the *modifier keys*: SHIFT, WINDOWS, CTRL, and ALT.

TIP *The* ALT *key is sticky all the time—to choose a command from a menu bar, you can press and release the* ALT *key before you press the letter for the command.*

To turn on Sticky Keys, select the Use Sticky Keys check box on the Make Your Keyboard Easier To Use window of the Ease of Access Center (choose Start | Control Panel | Ease Of Access | Make The Keyboard Easier To Use). Then, click the Settings button to see the following options that define exactly how Sticky Keys works:

- **Keyboard Shortcut**   Turns Sticky Keys on or off when you press SHIFT five times. You can set it so Windows displays a warning message when you turn on Sticky Keys. Also, you can set a sound to play when you are turning Sticky Keys on or off.

- **Lock Modifier Keys When Press Twice In A Row**   Lock on a modifier key when you press it twice. Turn off the key by pressing it once again.

- **Turn Off Sticky Keys When Two Keys Are Pressed At Once**   If two keys are pressed at once, Sticky Keys turns off. To make a modifier key sticky again, Sticky Keys must be turned on again by using the shortcut (if the Use Shortcut option is selected). This option can be annoying if you ever want to press two keys at the same time.

- **Play A Sound When Keys Are Pressed**   Beeps when a modifier key is struck. This is particularly useful when the previous option is turned on—it lets you know when Sticky Keys is turned off.

 - **Display The Sticky Keys Icon On The Task Bar**   Displays a small graphic, shown here, to the left of the time in the notification area of the taskbar.

The four blocks represent the four modifier keys: SHIFT at the top, CTRL at the bottom left, WINDOWS in the bottom middle, and ALT at the bottom right. When a modifier key is stuck, its block is shaded on the diagram. Double-click the icon to display the Set Up Sticky Keys configuration window. When Sticky Keys is off, the diagram is removed from the taskbar.

After you configure Sticky Keys, click Save.

Hearing When a Toggled Key Is Pressed

Toggle Keys is useful if you accidentally press keys that change the behavior of the keyboard. When Toggle Keys is turned on and you press CAPS LOCK, NUM LOCK, or SCROLL LOCK, a tone sounds—a high-pitched tone when you turn CAPS LOCK, NUM LOCK, or SCROLL LOCK on, and a low-pitched tone when you turn it off.

To turn on Toggle Keys, select the Turn On Toggle Keys option on the Make Keyboard Easier To Use window of the Ease of Access Center (choose Start | Control Panel | Ease Of Access | Make The Keyboard Easier To Use). Click the Turn On Toggle Keys By Holding Down The NUM LOCK Key For 5 Seconds option to turn on the Toggle Keys shortcut. This enables you to turn Toggle Keys on or off by holding down the NUM LOCK key for five seconds.

Filtering Out Extra Keystrokes

If you have trouble typing each letter only once, you may want to turn on *Filter Keys*—which "filters out" extra keystrokes—rather than spending time editing them out yourself. You can configure Filter Keys to ignore repeated keystrokes repeated too quickly and to slow down the repeat rate (the rate at which a character is repeated when a key is held down).

To turn on Filter Keys, select the Use Filter Keys check box on the Make Keyboard Easier To Use window of the Ease of Access Center (choose Start | Control Panel | Ease Of Access | Make The Keyboard Easier To Use). Then, click Set Up Filter Keys to define exactly how Filter Keys works:

- **Keyboard Shortcut** Turns Filter Keys on or off when you hold down the right SHIFT key for eight seconds. You can specify that Windows displays a warning message when you turn on Filter Keys. Also, you can specify that Windows plays a sound when you turn on or off Filter Keys.

- **Turn On Bounce Keys** Ignores keys repeated without a sufficient pause (called *Bounce Keys*). When you choose this option, click the button next to it, and then define the interval within which repeated keys should be ignored. Getting the right interval is crucial to avoiding frustration.

- **Turn On Repeat Keys And Slow Keys** This option enables features called Slow Keys and Repeat Keys. *Slow Keys* enables you to filter out keys that are pressed only briefly. When Slow Keys is on, you must type more methodically, but Windows ignores keys touched lightly or quickly. *Repeat Keys* enables you to change the way keys are repeated (see "Changing Keyboard Properties" in Chapter 13)—normally, if you hold down a key, it repeats at a certain rate after it has been held down for a certain interval. Click the Set Up Repeat Keys And Slow Keys link to configure settings for Slow Keys and Repeat Keys. Options include telling Windows how long holding down a key causes it to repeat; if so, after what interval and at what rate should it repeat; and how long a key should be held down to register.

- **Beep When Keys Pressed Or Accepted** Tells Windows to beep when a key is pressed, and beep again when a key is accepted.

- **Show Filter Key Status On Screen** Displays a small graphic, shown here, to the left of the time on the system tray.

You can double-click the icon to display the Set Up Filter Keys window and make changes to your settings. When Filter Keys is off, the icon is removed from the taskbar.

Displaying the On-Screen Keyboard

If using the mouse or other pointing device is easier for you than typing on the keyboard, Windows can display a picture of a keyboard on the screen. You can use a mouse, joystick, pointing stick, or other pointing device to choose characters from the On-Screen Keyboard:

To display the On-Screen Keyboard, choose Start | All Programs | Accessories | Ease Of Access | On-Screen Keyboard.

You can type by choosing the keys on the On-Screen Keyboard with your mouse in one of three ways (typing modes):

- **Click To Select**   Click an onscreen key.

- **Hover To Select**   Rest the mouse pointer on the onscreen key for the specified period of time. You can choose the amount of time the mouse pointer must "hover" before the key types by choosing Settings | Type Mode.

- **Joystick Or Key To Select**   Windows automatically moves the highlight from key to key on the On-Screen Keyboard, cycling endlessly across the keys. When the highlight gets to the key you want, press a key, click the mouse, or activate the joystick to select that key. You can choose how fast the highlight moves, what key or click chooses the selected key, and how your selection device is connected to the computer. Choose your typing mode by choosing Settings | Typing Mode from the menu bar at the top of the On-Screen Keyboard window.

The characters you "type" using the On-Screen Keyboard appear in the active window—be sure to select the window into which you want to type first. When you choose the "shft" button on the screen, it remains on until you choose the next button (for example, choose "shft" and then *a* to type a capital *A*).

You can choose the following options by using the On-Screen Keyboard menus as specified:

- Whether the keyboard appears "on top" of other windows that it overlaps, by choosing Settings | Always On Top

- Whether the onscreen "keys" make a sound when chosen, by choosing Settings | Use Click Sound

- What font appears on the keys of the On-Screen Keyboard, by choosing Settings | Font

- Whether to display the standard or enhanced keyboard (the enhanced keyboard includes the numeric keypad and more cursor movement keys), by choosing Keyboard | Enhanced Keyboard or Keyboard | Standard Keyboard

- Whether to arrange the keys like a real keyboard, or in a grid, by choosing Keyboard | Regular Layout or Keyboard | Block Layout

- How many keys to display, by choosing Keyboard | 101 Keys, Keyboard | 102 Keys (which adds a backslash key to the left of Z), or Keyboard | 106 Keys (which adds Japanese-language characters)

Setting Sound Ease of Access Features

Windows includes options to help translate the sounds programs make for people who have difficulty hearing. The sound Ease of Access features don't work for all sounds, but they do work for most sounds generated by Windows and for some sounds generated by applications. The options are found in the Use Text Or Visual Alternatives For Sounds window of the Ease of Access Center, as shown in Figure 17-4. Choose Start | Control Panel | Ease Of Access Features, and then click Use Text Or Visual Alternatives For Sounds.

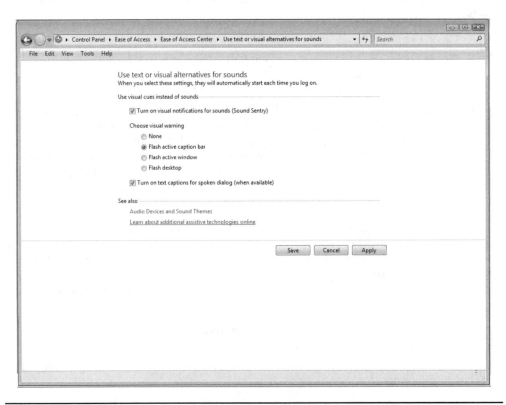

FIGURE 17-4   Use the Use Text Or Visual Alternatives For Sounds Ease of Access features to turn on tools for the hearing impaired.

You can set the following:

- **Turn On Visual Notifications For Sounds (Sound Sentry)**   Tells Windows to use a flashing element on the screen to tell the user a sound has been made. Under Choose Visual Warning, set Windows to display a visual cue. For example, we recommend choosing either the Flash Active Caption Bar or the Flash Active Window option— otherwise, it's impossible to determine which application caused the sound.

- **Turn On Text Captions For Spoken Dialog (When Available)**   Tells Windows to display text captions instead of playing audio to indicate a Windows action. For example, some programs announce that a document is printing or a new e-mail message has arrived. If your program supports this option, you can have Windows display a text message instead of playing a sound for that action.

Setting Display Ease of Access Features

Windows has four features that make the screen easier to read: a high-contrast color scheme, Narrator (which reads the screen out loud), Magnifier (which can magnify part of the screen), and configurable cursor appearance. To display the Ease of Access window for these features, choose Start | Control Panel | Ease Of Access | Make The Computer Easier To See. The window shown in Figure 17-5 appears.

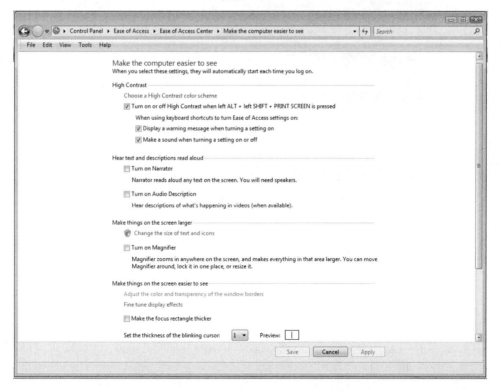

FIGURE 17-5   Set Display Ease of Access options from here.

NOTE *Other display settings—including colors and fonts—are available in the Display Properties dialog box (see "What Are Display Properties?" in Chapter 12).*

Displaying in High Contrast

The High Contrast feature, which you enable by choosing the Turn On Or Off High Contrast When Left ALT+Left SHIFT+PRINT SCREEN Is Pressed check box, changes the Windows color scheme and increases legibility wherever possible, often by increasing font sizes. Not every program uses font sizes controlled by Windows, so not everything on the screen gets bigger.

You can also choose a color scheme by clicking Choose A High Contrast Color Scheme. This displays the Appearance Settings dialog box, from which you can choose a color scheme such as High Contrast White, High Contrast Black, High Contrast #2, or High Contrast #1.

When High Contrast is on, your screen looks like Figure 17-6—the High Contrast White (Large) color scheme is shown. (High Contrast Black is the default, but the White version is

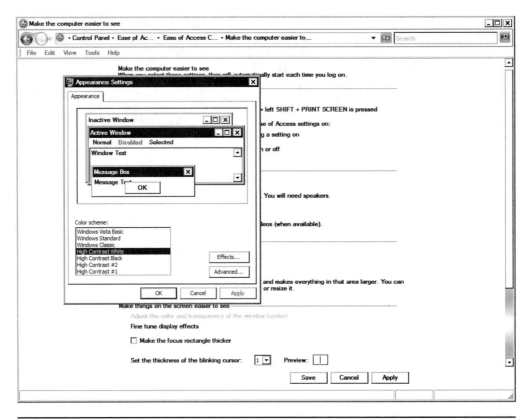

FIGURE 17-6 A dialog box and window shown in High Contrast

more readable when printed in this book.) Using bigger fonts results in less information fitting on the screen, so you see more scroll bars than usual. Also, the different color scheme may take some getting used to.

Listening to Microsoft Narrator Read the Screen Out Loud

For vision-impaired users, a screen-reader can be the best way to find out what's on the computer display. Windows Vista comes with a screen-reading program called Microsoft Narrator. Narrator is designed to work with most parts of Windows Vista itself, but may not work with other programs. The program says the items in the active window, including text, buttons, lists, and other things, using a computer-generated voice.

To turn on Narrator, display the Make The Computer Easier To See windows (see Figure 17-2) and select Turn On Narrator. The Microsoft Narrator dialog box appears, as shown in Figure 17-7.

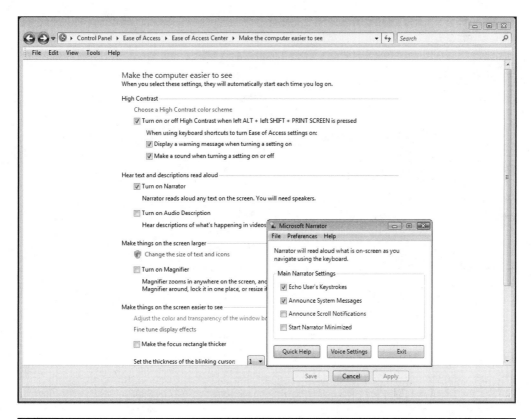

FIGURE 17-7   Use the Microsoft Narrator dialog box to set Narrator's reading options.

You can control these aspects of Narrator from the Narrator dialog box:

- **Echo User's Keystrokes**   Select the Echo User's Keystrokes check box to hear what you type and select Announce System Messages to hear background events, such as notifications and prompts.
- **Announce System Messages**   Specifies that Narrator announces system messages that display onscreen.
- **Announce Scroll Notifications**   Specifies that Narrator announces when the screen scrolls.
- **Start Narrator Minimized**   Specifies that the Microsoft Narrator dialog box starts minimized when you turn on Narrator or start Windows the next time.
- **Voice Settings**   Click this button to choose which preprogrammed voice to use and how fast, high, and loud the voice speaks.

You can also use the following keyboard shortcuts with Narrator:

Keyboard Shortcut	Action
CTRL-SHIFT-ENTER	Hear information about the active item.
CTRL-SHIFT-INSERT	Hear details about the active item.
CTRL-SHIFT-SPACEBAR	Hear all the information in the active window.
ALT-HOME	Hear the title bar of the active window.
ALT-END	Hear the status bar of the active window. (This feature does not work for all programs).
CTRL	Silence Narrator.

Once you have Narrator configured as you like it, select the Start Narrator Minimized check box in the Narrator dialog box to minimize it in the future. Also take a look at the "Useful Keyboard Shortcuts" sidebar later in this chapter.

Listen to Video Action

In the Make The Computer Easier To See window, you can select the Turn On Audio Description option to listen to descriptions of video action. This is not available with all video, but can be helpful for those who have difficulty seeing the contents of a video being played back on Vista.

Magnifying the Screen

The Magnifier is an alternative to High Contrast mode—it enables you to magnify only a part of the screen at a time. One section of the screen (usually a strip along the top of the screen) shows a highly magnified version of one area of the screen—the area where you are working.

Turn on Magnifier by choosing Start | All Programs | Accessories | Ease Of Access | Magnifier. You see the magnification window at the top of your screen and the Magnifier dialog box, as shown in the following illustration.

You can control the magnification level, which part of the screen is displayed in the magnification window, its color scheme, and its location on the screen:

- **Scale Factor**   Determines how much larger things appear in the magnification window. Use the Scale factor setting on the Magnifier dialog box to adjust magnification. The larger the level, the more the contents of the magnification window are magnified.

- **Invert Colors**   Controls colors in the magnification window. Click the Invert Colors check box to use the opposite of the colors in the rest of the screen. Inverted colors make it easier to see that the magnification window is a special part of the screen, but they may also make the display more confusing.

- **Docked and Dock Position**   You can change the size of the magnification window by dragging the lower window border up or down. You can change the position of the window by clicking inside the window and dragging. You can "dock" the window along any edge of the desktop or put it somewhere in the middle of the screen. If the magnification window appears as a window rather than a wide border, you can control its size and position in the same way you'd change them for any window. Your ideal magnification window may be a small square near one corner of the screen. The magnification window always appears on top—it cannot be covered by another window.

- **Tracking**   Determines what part of the screen is shown in the magnification window. You can choose to Follow Mouse Cursor, Follow Keyboard Focus, and Follow Text Editing. These three options are not mutually exclusive—if you select all three, the display in the magnification window is determined by what you are currently doing; in other words, Windows does its best to display the part of the screen you're working with in the magnification window.

When you have adjusted the settings in the Magnifier dialog box, click its Minimize button to shrink it to a button on the taskbar. (You may want to select the Minimize On Startup check box first, to tell Windows to minimize the Magnifier dialog box whenever you start Magnifier.) Don't click the Close button unless you want to stop seeing the magnification window on your screen.

Fine-Tuning the Display for Ease of Access

In the Make Things On The Screen Easier To See section of the Make The Computer Easier To See window (partially shown at the bottom of Figure 17-4), you can fine-tune some display elements to make the display easier to read. The following are the options you can choose:

- **Make The Focus Rectangle Thicker** Displays a thicker rectangle around areas that have the current focus

- **Set The Thickness Of The Blinking Cursor** Shows the blinking cursor larger to make it easier to see onscreen

- **Remove Background Images (Where Available)** Enables you to remove background images, such as any displayed in windows

Useful Keyboard Shortcuts

If you prefer using the keyboard to the mouse, you may want to try the following key combinations, which many but not all programs support:

ALT-SPACEBAR	Displays the system menu, from which you can choose to close, minimize, restore, maximize, or move the current window.
ALT-F4	Closes the current program.
ALT-TAB or TAB	Switches to another running program. Keep pressing TAB or ALT-TAB to cycle through all the programs that are running.
CTRL-C	Copies the selected information to the Clipboard.
CTRL-V	Copies the current contents of the Clipboard to the current position of the cursor.
CTRL-A	Selects all the information in the window.
CTRL-F4	Closes the current window. CTRL-W performs the same task in some programs.
SHIFT-F10	Displays the shortcut menu (the same menu you would see if you right-clicked at the current position of the mouse).
ESC	Cancels the current dialog box (the same as clicking the Cancel button).
ENTER	Works the same as clicking the currently selected buttom.
WINDOWS or CTRL-ESC	Displays the Start menu.
WINDOWS-L	Locks the computer.
WINDOWS-U	Displays the Ease of Access Center.

Making Internet Explorer Accessible

Internet Explorer 7.0, which comes with Windows Vista, has additional accessibility features you can use:

- **Keyboard**   Press TAB and SHIFT-TAB to cycle among the active parts of the Internet Explorer window, including links and buttons. The selected item is highlighted with a dotted-line box.

- **Display**   Internet Explorer can use the font sizes and formatting you choose, even if they are different from those specified in the web page (see "Choosing Fonts" in Chapter 25).

To choose other Ease of Access features, choose Tools | Internet Options on the Internet Explorer menu bar and click the Advanced tab. In the list of settings that appears, you can select or deselect these settings:

- **Always Expand ALT Text For Images (Accessibility section)**   Turn this setting on to display the entire ALT (alternative) text supplied on some web pages as captions for pictures, so a screen reader can read the caption.

- **Move System Caret With Focus/Selection Changes (Accessibility section)**   Turn this on so that the cursor moves along with the mouse pointer and a screen-reading or magnifier program can read or display the right part of the Internet Explorer window.

- **Enable Page Transitions and Use Smooth Scrolling (Browsing section)**   Turn these off to make screen readers and voice recognition programs work better.

- **Play Animations In Web Pages, Play Videos In Web Pages, Show Pictures (Multimedia section)**   Turn these off if your vision is impaired and you want to speed up web browsing.

- **Play Sounds In Web Pages (Multimedia section)**   Turn this off if sounds are annoying or interfere with your screen-reading program.

- **Print Background Colors And Images (Printing section)**   Turn this off for clearer printouts.

PART III

IV
PART

Working with Text, Pictures, Sound, and Video

Working with Documents in Windows Vista

Although word processing isn't glamorous, it is, and probably forever will be, one of the most popular uses for a computer. Windows Vista comes with two tools for working with text documents—the first is the unsophisticated Notepad, and the second is the surprisingly powerful WordPad. This chapter discusses both.

This chapter also covers two other useful utilities: Calculator and Character Map. The Calculator provides all the scientific functions you may need from a calculator, and Character Map gives you access to a variety of special characters.

Reading Text Files with Notepad

Notepad is a holdover from Windows 3.0. Back in the Windows 3.0 era, configuration information was stored in text files that regularly needed to be edited, and Notepad could edit those files. In subsequent releases of Windows, editing configuration files has become a task more often done either automatically by installation programs or manually by system administrators and hackers than by people simply trying to make their computers work the way they want.

Notepad, however, remains available in Windows Vista, and using it is the simplest way to edit a text file (also called an *ASCII file*)—that is, files that contain only letters, numbers, and special characters that appear on the keyboard. Sure, you can use a full-fledged word processor, but doing so is often more trouble than it's worth. Notepad can't format your text with bold, italics, or anything else pretty, but we've been known to use Notepad to edit web pages, and it's invaluable for storing little snippets of text you might need later.

Running Notepad

To run Notepad, choose Start | All Programs | Accessories | Notepad. (Or, you can choose Start | All Programs Accessories | Run to display the Run dialog box, and then type **notepad** and press ENTER.) Notepad looks like Figure 18-1: just a window with a menu.

The following sections offer some information about and tips on using Notepad.

FIGURE 18-1   Run Notepad when you need to edit a text file.

Copying, Moving, and Pasting Text

You can copy or move text to or from the Windows Clipboard using the Edit | Copy, Edit | Cut, and Edit | Paste commands (see "Cutting, Copying, and Pasting" in Chapter 5).

Document Settings

To change the setup of the document when you print it, choose File | Page Setup (this command isn't available if you haven't installed a printer in Windows). Use the Page Setup dialog box (shown in Figure 18-2) to change margins, page orientation, and paper size. (In the Orientation box, Portrait prints on paper in the usual way; Landscape prints sideways on the page, with the lines of text parallel to the long edge of the paper.) If you have more than one printer, you can select the one to use. Use the Header and Footer text boxes to add headers and footers to your documents. You can type plain text, or you can use the codes in Table 18-1.

File Types

Choose File | Open to see the Open dialog box. Change the Files Of Type option to All Files if the file you want to open does not have the .txt extension.

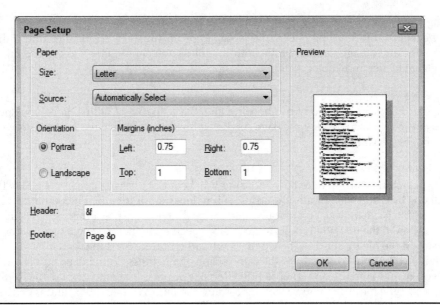

FIGURE 18-2   Notepad options for printing a text file

Fonts

Notepad normally uses a fixed-pitch font to display text files. You can change the font by choosing Format | Font to display the Font dialog box and then setting the font, style, and size.

Log Files

Create a log file by typing **.LOG** in the top-left corner (the very beginning) of your Notepad file (be sure to include the period and use capital letters). Each time you run Notepad and open the file, Notepad enters the current time and date at the end of the file. You can then type an entry for that time and date.

Code	Meaning
&f	Displays the name of the file
&p	Displays the page number
&d	Displays the current date
&t	Displays the current time
&&	Displays an ampersand
&l	Left-justifies the text after this code
&c	Centers the text after this code
&r	Right-justifies the text after this code

TABLE 18-1   Header and Footer Codes in Notepad

Printing

Print the text file by choosing File | Print. Notepad prints the file with the filename at the top of each page and a page number at the bottom, unless you choose File | Page Setup and change the Header and Footer settings.

Saving Files

Save the text file you are editing by choosing File | Save. To save it with a name you specify, choose File | Save As to display the Save As dialog box (see "Open, Save As, and Browse Dialog Boxes" in Chapter 2).

Searching for Text

You can search for a string of text by choosing Edit | Find or pressing CTRL-F to display the Find dialog box, and then typing the string you're looking for into the Find What text box. Click the Match Case check box if you want Notepad to find only text that matches the capitalization of the text you typed. You can also specify whether to search forward or backward in the file by clicking the Up or Down radio button. Start the search by clicking the Find Next button. To search for the same string again, press F3 or choose Edit | Find Next.

If you want to replace text, choose Edit | Replace or press CTRL-H to display the Replace dialog box. Type the string you're looking for into the Find What text box, and type the string you want to use as the replacement in the Replace With text box. Click Find Next to find the first instance of the string. You can replace all occurrences by clicking Replace All, or you can pick and choose by clicking Replace (if you want to replace the text) or Find Next if you want to skip an instance. The Replace dialog box, like the Find dialog box, provides a check box to use if you want to match the case of the Find What and Replace With strings.

Moving Around Text Files

You can move quickly through a large file by using the Go To option—choose Edit | Go To or press CTRL-G to display the Go To Line dialog box. Enter the line number that you want to go to and either click OK or press ENTER. The dialog box disappears, and the cursor moves to the specified line.

If you want to know where you are in a document, you may find the status bar useful—it displays the cursor position in lines and columns (Ln 4, Col 6 is the sixth character on the fourth line in the document). Display the status bar by choosing View | Status Bar.

Time and Date

You can insert the current time and date (according to your computer's clock) at the cursor by choosing Edit | Time/Date, or by pressing F5.

Undo

If you make a mistake, you can reverse your last edit by choosing Edit | Undo or pressing CTRL-Z.

Word Wrap

As you work with a document, you might want to turn on *Word Wrap*, so that Notepad breaks long lines to fit in the Notepad window. When Word Wrap is off, each paragraph appears as a single long line (unless it contains carriage returns). Turn on (or off) Word

Wrap by choosing Format | Word Wrap. Notepad then wraps lines the way a word processor wraps lines, so no line is wider than the Notepad window. The Notepad Word Wrap feature doesn't add carriage return characters to the text file when you save it and it doesn't affect the way the file appears when printed.

Files You Can Edit with Notepad

The standard file extension for text files is .txt. When you click or double-click a text file in Windows Explorer, Windows runs Notepad to view the file.

Windows associates a number of other types of files with Notepad, too, because these files contain only text and are usually small enough for Notepad to handle. These file types include:

- Configuration files, such as files with the extension .ini (see "Windows Initialization Files" in Chapter 39)
- Log files, such as the logs that the Backup program creates
- Log files, with the extension .log, which many housekeeping programs create
- Setup information files, which come with many installation programs and have the extension .inf

Taking Advantage of Free Word Processing with WordPad

WordPad is a great little word processor if your needs are modest—and the price can't be beat! Open WordPad by choosing Start | All Programs | Accessories | WordPad. (Or, you can choose Start | Run to display the Run dialog box, type **wordpad**, and press ENTER.)

WordPad (shown in Figure 18-3) does not offer many of the advanced features that you get in Microsoft Word or Corel's WordPerfect—notably missing is a spell check. But WordPad does offer many of the formatting tools you need to create a spiffy letter, memo, or essay. Many of the commands and keyboard shortcuts are the same as those in Microsoft Word, which makes them easy for many people to remember. The version of WordPad that comes with Windows can open documents created by versions of Word up through Word 2002 (Word 10). And, because WordPad is a small program, it loads quickly.

TIP Display WordPad online help by pressing F1 when WordPad is open.

Opening and Saving Files with WordPad

With WordPad you can open and edit a document that is saved in any one of a variety of formats, including documents saved with Word 97, 2000, and 2003 (WordPad cannot preserve all of Word's formatting, however). To open a document, choose File | Open, and use the Files Of Type drop-down option on the Open dialog box to choose the type of document you want to open.

When you save a document to pass on to a friend or coworker, choose File | Save to use the existing filename, or choose File | Save As to specify the filename. Be sure to save the

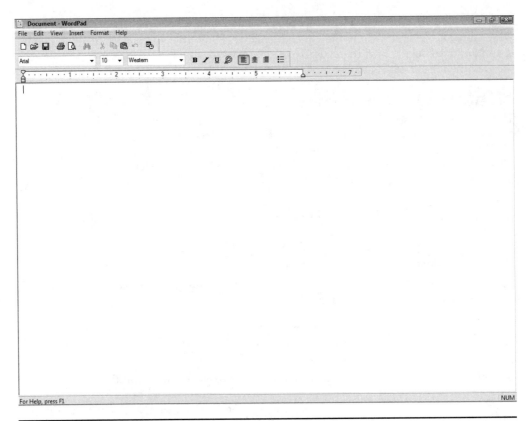

FIGURE 18-3 WordPad offers many of the features of a word processor—free.

document in a format that your friend's or coworker's software can open. Here's a rundown of the file formats WordPad can use to save a document:

- **Rich Text Format** If you want to preserve any formatting you've done in your WordPad document, save it in Rich Text Format (extension .rtf), which is compatible with just about anything.

- **Text Document** When you save a file in text format (with the extension .txt), you lose all formatting, but you preserve all text in the *ANSI* character set (a standard set of codes used for storing text).

- **Text Document—MS-DOS Format** When you save a file in MS-DOS text format (also with the extension .txt), you lose all formatting, but you preserve all text in Microsoft's extended ASCII character set, which includes various accented characters and smiley faces. Use this format only if you want to use the text in a Windows or DOS application, but not if you plan to send the file to a Mac, UNIX, or other non-Microsoft system.

- **Unicode Text Document** *Unicode* enables you to use characters from practically every language on Earth, from Latvian to Japanese. But make sure your recipient has a Unicode-compatible program before you save Unicode documents.

Formatting with WordPad

Use the options on the format bar (the row of buttons below the toolbar) to format a document in WordPad. If you don't see the format bar (or WordPad's other bars—the toolbar, ruler bar, or status bar), use the View menu to display them.

Formatting in WordPad works like this:

1. Select the text you want to format, using your mouse. Or, choose Edit | Select All (or press CTRL-A) to select the entire document.

2. Click the button or give the command for the type of formatting you want to apply.

The following sections describe some of the formatting options in WordPad.

Bullets

To format a paragraph with a bullet, click anywhere in the paragraph and click the Bullets button at the very end of the format bar, or choose Format | Bullet Style. To format more than one paragraph, select the paragraphs before clicking the Bullets button.

Indents

To indent a paragraph, click in the paragraph (or select several paragraphs) and choose Format | Paragraph to display the Paragraph dialog box. You can type a measurement from the left or right margin, or for the first line only. You can also specify that the paragraph is left aligned, right aligned, or centered. When you click OK, the margin indicators on the ruler bar move to show the current margins for the paragraph in which your cursor is located.

Tabs

You can set tab stops by clicking the ruler bar. If the ruler bar isn't already displayed, choose View | Ruler to display it. Be sure to select the text for which you need the tabs (press CTRL-A to select all text in the document) before you create tabs, because the tabs you create only apply to the paragraph the cursor is in if no text is selected. To set tab stops, click the ruler where you want a tab stop. L-shaped markers appear at each tab stop. Drag the L-shaped tab markers left or right on the ruler bar to adjust the tab stops. To delete a tab stop, drag it down off the ruler bar.

Alternatively, choose Format | Tabs to display the Tabs dialog box. Set a tab stop by typing a measurement from the left margin and clicking the Set button (if you're not sure what to use, every 0.5 inch is pretty standard). The tab stop appears on the list of tab stops that are set for the current position in the document. Type additional measurements from the left margin and click Set to set more tab stops. To delete a tab stop, select it from the list and click the Clear button. When you click OK, little L-shaped tab indicators appear on the ruler bar to show the location of tab stops.

Text: Fonts, Size, and Color

To change the font, font size, or color of the selected text, click the Font or Font Size box on the format bar and choose the font or font size from the list that appears. Or, choose Format | Font to display the Font dialog box, shown in Figure 18-4. Choose the font, font size, color, and whether you want the text to be bold, italic, underlined, or struck out. If you have installed multilanguage support, you can also choose the script (alphabet). Then click OK.

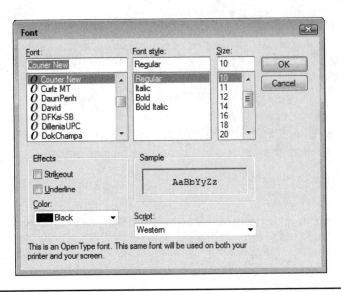

FIGURE 18-4 Choose the font for the selected text.

You can also choose settings from the Font dialog box without selecting text, before you type the text you want to format; use the Font dialog box again to turn the formatting off.

You can also format text by using keystroke combinations: CTRL-B to bold, CTRL-I to italicize, and CTRL-U to underline. You can use these keystrokes after you select text or before you type the text you want to format (press the key combination again to turn off the formatting).

Printing Your WordPad Document

To print your document, click the Print button (the fourth button on the toolbar), choose File | Print, or press CTRL-P. You see the Print dialog box, in which you can select the printer, which pages to print, and the number of copies.

You may want to preview the document before you print it so you'll know exactly how it will look on paper. To preview your document, click the Print Preview button (the fifth button on the toolbar) or choose File | Print Preview. The WordPad window shows approximately how the printed page will look. You can click the Zoom In button to get a closer look, click Print to begin printing, or click Close to return to the regular view of your document.

You can also format the page by choosing File | Page Setup to display the Page Setup dialog box. Use the Page Setup dialog box to change margins, paper orientation, and paper size.

WordPad Extras

WordPad has a few additional features you may find useful.

Copying, Moving, and Pasting Text

Use the Windows Clipboard to copy and move text within WordPad, and between WordPad and other applications (see "Cutting, Copying, and Pasting" in Chapter 5). Choose Edit | Copy, click the Copy button on the toolbar, or press CTRL-C to copy selected text to the Clipboard. Choose Edit | Cut, click the Cut button on the toolbar, or press CTRL-X to move selected text to the Clipboard. Choose Edit | Paste, click the Paste button on the toolbar, or press CTRL-V to copy information from the Clipboard to the current cursor location. If you are pasting information other than text into your document, choose Edit | Paste Special to choose how the information should appear.

Date and Time

Insert the current date and time into your document by clicking the Date/Time button, the last button on the toolbar, or by choosing Insert | Date And Time. The Date And Time dialog box appears, from which you can choose the format for the date, time, or both.

Inserting Objects

Insert an object (such as a picture) into a WordPad document by doing any of the following:

- Dragging the object into the WordPad window from Windows Explorer
- Using Insert | Object and choosing the type of object you want to insert
- Pasting an object from the Windows Clipboard

You can see the properties of an object by clicking the object and choosing Edit | Object Properties, or by pressing ALT-ENTER. If you insert a picture, you can use WordPad's simple graphic editing commands by double-clicking the picture; the annotation toolbar appears at the bottom of the WordPad window. You can also move an object in your document by clicking-and-dragging it to a new location.

Searching for Text

You can search for text by clicking the Find (binoculars) button on the toolbar, by choosing Edit | Find, or by pressing CTRL-F. Use the options of the Find dialog box to find only the whole word, or to match the case of the contents of the Find What text box. To search for the same information again, press F3, click the Find button, or choose Edit | Find Next. You can leave the Find dialog box open while you edit the document—click the document once to keep the found text selected; double-click to put the cursor where you click. Then, when you need the Find dialog box again, simply click it.

Replacing Text

You can replace specific text with other text throughout your document by choosing Edit | Replace or pressing CTRL-H. You see the Replace dialog box. In the Find What box, type the text to be replaced. In the Replace With box, type the text to be inserted. You can select the Match Whole Word Only and Match Case check boxes to tell WordPad which instances of the text to match. Click Find Next to find the next instance of the text in the Find What box, and then click Replace to replace this instance with the Replace With text. To replace all the rest of the instances in your document, click Replace All.

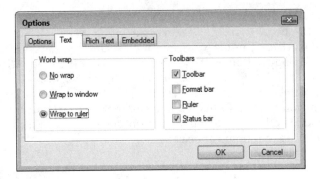

FIGURE 18-5   WordPad's Options dialog box

Undo

Undo your last action by clicking the Undo button, the second-to-last button on the toolbar, by choosing Edit | Undo, or by pressing CTRL-Z.

Setting WordPad Options

You can configure WordPad by choosing View | Options to display the Options dialog box (shown in Figure 18-5). The tabs that display depends on what type of document you have open. For example, Figure 18-5 shows four tabs. Five tabs that can possibly show on this dialog box—the Text, Rich Text, Word, Write, and Embedded tabs—all have the same options. Choose the tab for the type of document you're editing—most likely, Word, Rich Text, or Text. Use the Options tab to choose measurement units and automatic word selection. WordPad knows what kind of document you are editing based on the type of file you open.

Using Calculator

The Windows Calculator is actually two calculators: the unintimidating Standard Calculator that does simple arithmetic, and a more complicated Scientific Calculator. To use either of them, choose Start | All Programs | Accessories | Calculator. Switch from one calculator to the other by using the View menu.

You can enter numbers into the calculator by clicking its buttons or by typing the numbers using the keyboard. If you misenter a digit, click the Calculator's Backspace button or press BACKSPACE on the keyboard. The CE button stands for Clear Entry (clear the current entry) and the C button stands for Clear (clear the current calculation).

You can use cut-and-paste to copy numbers from a document into the Calculator, do a calculation, and then cut-and-paste the result back into a document (see "Cutting, Copying, and Pasting" in Chapter 5).

Using the Standard Calculator

The Standard Calculator (which you switch to by choosing View | Standard) adds, subtracts, multiplies, divides, takes square roots, calculates percentages, and finds multiplicative inverses. It has a one-number memory.

Performing Arithmetic

To perform an arithmetic calculation, enter the calculation as you would type it, left to right, as in

3 + 5 =

To compute a percentage, make the percentage the second number in a multiplication and don't use the equal sign. For example, to figure 15 percent of 7.4, enter

7.4 × 15%

The $1/x$ button computes the multiplicative inverse of the displayed number.

Storing Numbers in Memory

The four buttons on the left side of the Standard Calculator control its memory. To store the currently displayed number in the memory, click the MS (memory store) button. An *M* appears in the box above the MC button to show the memory is in use. The memory holds only one number, so storing another number causes the calculator to forget the previously stored number. Clicking MC (memory clear) clears the memory. To recall the number stored in memory, click MR (memory recall). Clicking the M+ button adds the displayed number to the number in memory and stores the result in the memory.

NOTE *Use the memory to transfer a number from the Standard to the Scientific Calculator or vice versa. The current display is cleared when you switch from one calculator to the other, but the memory is not cleared.*

Using the Scientific Calculator

The Scientific Calculator (shown in Figure 18-6) is considerably larger, more powerful, and more complex than the Standard Calculator. Switch to it by choosing View | Scientific. Anything you can do on the Standard Calculator works exactly the same way on the

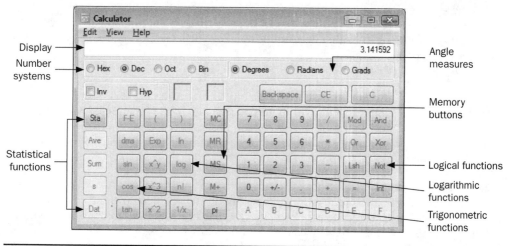

FIGURE 18-6   The Scientific Calculator displays a big piece of pi.

Scientific Calculator, except the Scientific Calculator has no % or sqrt buttons. (Compute square roots by clicking x^2 when the Inv box is checked.) In addition, you can perform calculations in a variety of number systems, do logical operations, use trigonometric functions, and do statistical analyses.

Why Don't All the Buttons Work?

Some buttons on the Scientific Calculator only make sense in certain situations; in other situations, they are grayed out and clicking them does nothing. For example, the A–F buttons are numbers in the hexadecimal number system, so they don't work unless the Hex radio button is selected. The hexadecimal, octal, and binary number systems are set up for whole number calculations only, so the trigonometric function buttons are grayed out when one of the Hex, Oct, or Bin radio buttons is selected. The statistics buttons are grayed out when no data is loaded in the statistics box.

Number Systems and Angle Measures

The Scientific Calculator can work in Dec (decimal, the default), Bin (binary), Oct (octal), or Hex (hexadecimal) number systems. Choose among number systems by using the radio buttons on the left side of the top row. When you are working in the decimal number system, you can use the radio buttons just to the right of the number-system buttons to choose among the different ways of measuring angles: degrees (the default), radians, and gradients. When using degrees, the DMS button converts a decimal number of degrees into degrees-minute-seconds form. To convert back, check the Inv box and click DMS again.

When you are working in the binary, octal, or hexadecimal number systems, the radio buttons just to the right of the number-system buttons enable you to select the range of whole numbers with which you will work. (In geek terms, this is the register size.) The choices are Byte (from 0 to 255, or 8 bits), Word (16 bits), Dword (double word, or 32 bits), and Qword (quadruple word, or 64 bits). The arithmetic in these systems is modular, so in hexadecimal with Byte register size

$2 - 3 =$

yields the answer FF rather than –1.

The F-E (fixed-exponential) button toggles between fixed-point notation and scientific notation. When entering a number in scientific notation, click the Exp button before entering the exponential part.

Trigonometric Functions

Trigonometric functions are computed with the Sin, Cos, and Tan buttons. Use the Inv and Hyp check boxes to compute inverse or hyperbolic trigonometric functions. The pi button (below the memory buttons) enters the first 32 digits of π. Because trigonometric functions almost never yield whole numbers, these buttons are grayed out in any number system other than decimal.

Logarithmic Functions

The Ln and Log buttons compute natural logarithms and base-10 logarithms, respectively. The Exp button *does not* compute exponentials. (It is used for entering numbers in scientific notation.) Compute exponentials by using Ln with the Inv box checked.

Statistical Functions

To use the statistical functions of the calculator, you must first enter a list of numbers, which constitutes the data. To enter a data list:

1. Enter the first number in the calculator display.
2. Click the Sta button. The statistics buttons are activated and a statistics box opens.
3. Click the Dat button. The number in the calculator display appears in the statistics box.
4. Enter the rest of the data, clicking Dat after each entry.

Once you enter a data list, clicking Ave computes the average of the entries, clicking Sum computes their sum, and clicking S computes their standard deviation.

You can see the statistics box at any time by clicking Sta. To edit the data list, use the buttons at the bottom of the statistics box: LOAD copies the highlighted number back to the calculator display, CD deletes the highlighted number from the data list, and CAD clears the data list.

Logical Functions

When the Bin radio button is chosen, the calculator works in the binary (base-2) number system and the buttons And, Or, and Not perform the bitwise logical operations their names suggest. The Xor button does exclusive or, and Lsh does a left shift. Perform a right shift by clicking Lsh with the Inv box checked.

Other Functions

The Int button finds the integer part of a number. When Inv is checked, the Int button finds the fractional part of a number.

Compute squares and cubes with the X^2 and X^3 buttons. Compute other powers with the X^y button.

The N! button computes factorials of integers. If the displayed number has a fractional part, N! computes a gamma function.

The Mod button does modular reductions; for example: 12 Mod 5 = 2

Using Special Characters with Character Map

Do you need to use unusual characters, like Æ, Ö, or ☎? The Character Map accessory can help you find them. Open Character Map by choosing Start | All Programs | Accessories | System Tools | Character Map. You see the Character Map window, shown in Figure 18-7.

To use a character from the Character Map:

1. Select a font from the Font list. The characters available in that font appear in the Character Map window, arranged in a 20-column grid.
2. Double-click the character you want to use; or single-click it and click Select. The selected character is magnified and a copy of it appears in the Characters To Copy box.

FIGURE 18-7   The Character Map lets you use unusual characters.

3. When you have displayed all the characters you want from this font in the Characters To Copy box, click Copy. Character Map copies the characters to the Windows Clipboard (see Chapter 5).

4. Paste the characters into a document using a command in the program you use to edit that document. (Most programs use Edit | Paste or CTRL-V to paste from the Clipboard.)

You can remove characters from the Characters To Copy box by clicking in the box and either backspacing over the characters or deleting them.

Another way to use many unusual characters is to select them in Character Map and notice the keystroke notation in the bottom-right corner of the Character Map window. Once you know this notation, you can produce the character in any document without running Character Map. For example, using the information in Figure 18-7, you could type a Œ character in any document as follows:

1. Open the document in a word processing program.

2. Set the font to Times New Roman.

3. Press the NUM LOCK on your keyboard.

4. While holding down the ALT key, type **0140**.

NOTE   *To use the Unicode number in WordPad and Microsoft Office Word, use the same digits as those here, but do not include the leading 0's. Also, you need to type the number (such as 152) first, then press ALT-X. So, for the preceding example, you would type 152 ALT-X to enter the Œ character.*

Working with Graphics

Windows provides many tools for working with pictures and other images. This chapter tells you how to use these tools to view images on your monitor; add information to the images; snap entire screens or portions of your display; create or edit image files; and download images from digital cameras or scanners and print them.

How Do Computers Handle Images?

For a computer to display, edit, or otherwise work with an image, that image has to be represented as data and stored in a file. In general, this is done by transforming the image into an array of small rectangles called *pixels*. Each pixel has only one color. If the pixels are small enough, the human eye doesn't notice this transformation, but if the rectangular components are visible, the image is said to be *pixelated*. A number can represent the color of each pixel, and the list of all these numbers is then turned into a file.

A file created in this way is very large, but fortunately much of this information is redundant. (Very often, for example, pixels next to each other have similar colors.) This fact allows an image file to be compressed into a smaller file from which a computer can re-create the original image file when needed. This compression can be done in a variety of ways, depending on whether the purpose of the compression is to create the smallest possible file, to represent the image most accurately, or to perform the compression as quickly as possible. Each compression method produces a different image file format. The most popular image formats are BMP, PCX, GIF, JPEG, and TIFF.

What Tools Does Windows Provide for Working with Images?

Windows Vista gives you more tools for working with images than any previous version of Windows:

- **Pictures folder**   The natural place in the Windows filing system to keep digital photos, pictures, graphics, and other images. Microsoft has preconfigured the viewing options in the Pictures folder (a subfolder of Documents) to make it easy for you to sort through pictures.

- **Windows Photo Gallery**   The default application for viewing image files (see "Looking at and Fixing Images with the Windows Photo Gallery"). It is new with Windows Vista. You can use the Fix pane to change colors, adjust brightness and contrast, crop images, and remove red eye.

- **Windows Snipping Tool**   A new program with Windows Vista that enables you to capture parts of or the entire computer screen. This is helpful for creating in-house documentation, snapping a screen to send to a help desk person for support issues, or if you need to show an example of a screen during a slide show you create.

- **Microsoft Paint**   An application for drawing and coloring (see "Creating and Editing Images with Microsoft Paint"). It also allows you to crop photos or transform images from one file format to another.

- **Scanner And Camera Wizard**   Sets up Windows to work with a scanner or digital camera (see "Downloading Images from Digital Cameras"). This wizard starts automatically when you plug a digital camera into your computer's USB or other port.

Viewing Images on Your Computer

Windows gives you two ways to view images: inside Explorer windows and using the Windows Photo Gallery.

Viewing Images in an Explorer Window

It is typically very hard to identify an image file by its name, especially if the name was assigned to the file automatically by a digital camera or scanner. Even if you rename the files yourself, the name seldom captures enough information to uniquely identify a single photo from, say, your Hawaiian vacation. For this reason, Explorer windows have two types of views that are much more convenient for examining folders of image files: Icon views and Slide Show view. Either can be selected from the Explorer window toolbar.

Icon views display small thumbnail views of the images. Although Vista provides a seemingly infinite number of choices between Small Icons and Extra Large Icons, the standard ones are Small Icons, Medium Icons, Large Icons, and Extra Large Icons. The Large Icons and Extra Large Icons views are probably the two best Icon views to view your pictures. Figure 19-1 shows sample photos viewed using the Extra Large Icons view.

Slide Show view is a new view in Windows Vista. As the name suggests, this view displays the images in the current folder as a full-screen slide show. When you click Slide Show, Vista displays each picture for a few seconds and then displays the next one in the folder. You can press ESC to close Slide Show and return to the Explorer window, or just wait for the last picture in the folder to display and Slide Show will quit automatically.

TIP *If you want to use an image as your desktop background, right-click its icon in an Explorer window and select Set As Desktop Background.*

FIGURE 19-1   Extra Large Icons view

Looking At and Fixing Images with the Windows Photo Gallery

Unless you have installed other graphics applications that have claimed image file types as their own, Windows opens image files using the Windows Photo Gallery program, shown in Figure 19-2. Windows Photo Gallery is a new program included with Windows Vista. It enables you to do the following:

- Manage photos and pictures in a number of image formats (file extensions in parentheses): bitmap (.bmp), Tagged Image File Format, or TIFF (.tif), Joint Photographic Experts Group, or JPEG (.jpg), Portable Network Graphics, or PNG (.png), Graphics Interchange Format, or GIF (.gif), and PCX (.pcx)
- View thumbnails of pictures
- Open picture files for larger views of them
- Fix a few problems with the image, such as remove red eye from photographs
- Print images
- E-mail images to other users

FIGURE 19-2   Windows Photo Gallery

- Burn a CD or DVD data disc (such as for backup or archiving) or burn a video DVD for playback on a DVD drive or player
- Create a movie of your photos using Windows Movie Maker
- Open images in a different program such as Microsoft Paint

Changing What You See

Windows Photo Gallery gives you several tools to help you examine an image. To start Windows Photo Gallery, choose Start | All Programs | Windows Photo Gallery. When you first open Windows Photo Gallery, you see a gallery view of all the pictures Windows Photo Gallery locates in your Pictures folder. At the bottom of the Windows Photo Gallery window is a set of controls similar to those you can find on the Windows Media Player (which plays music and video files). By clicking the middle button, you can play a slide show of your images, just like you can with Windows Explorer.

Double-click a picture to open it in Windows Photo Gallery. Figure 19-3 shows an example of a picture in Windows Photo Gallery. On the bottom toolbar, you can click one of the following tools:

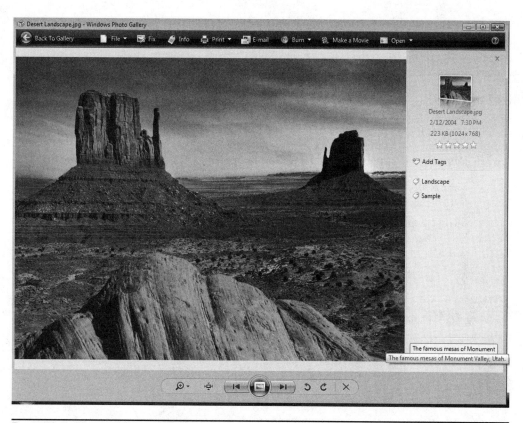

FIGURE 19-3   Viewing a picture in Windows Photo Gallery

- **Magnifying Glass**   Displays a zoom setting that enables you to zoom in or out on the picture.
- **Fit To Window**   Enlarges the picture to fit the entire Windows Photo Gallery window.
- **Previous**   Displays the picture in Photo Gallery that precedes the current one.
- **Slide Show**   Displays your pictures as a slide show.
- **Next**   Displays the next picture in Photo Gallery.
- **Rotate Counterclockwise**   Turns the picture 90 degrees to the left (counterclockwise). Unlike the Zoom tool, the Rotation tool changes the image itself, not just your view of it. If you rotate an image and then move to a new file (or exit Windows Photo Gallery), the image is saved automatically and will be rotated the next time you open the file.
- **Rotate Clockwise**   Turns the picture 90 degrees to the right (clockwise). Again, any change you make here is saved automatically when you move to a new picture or leave Windows Photo Gallery.
- **Delete**   Removes the picture from your computer.

Before you make any changes, you may want to make a copy of the current picture. This enables you to have at least one good copy of the picture in case you modify the picture beyond recognition. To do this, choose File | Make A Copy at the top of Windows Photo Gallery. In the Make A Copy dialog box, enter a new name for the image and click Save.

Fix Operations

Probably the most useful features of Windows Photo Gallery are the Fix tools. Click the Fix menu on the toolbar. The Fix pane appears on the right side of the Windows Photo Gallery window, as shown in Figure 19-4.

The follow list identifies each tool and briefly describes what it does when you click it:

- **Auto Adjust**   Automatically adjusts the color, brightness, and contrast of the picture. Sometimes this is all you need to do to get your picture looking better.

- **Adjust Exposure**   Displays controls for setting brightness and contrast. You can move each of the controls' slider bar to the left to decrease brightness or contrast, or to the right to increase brightness or contrast.

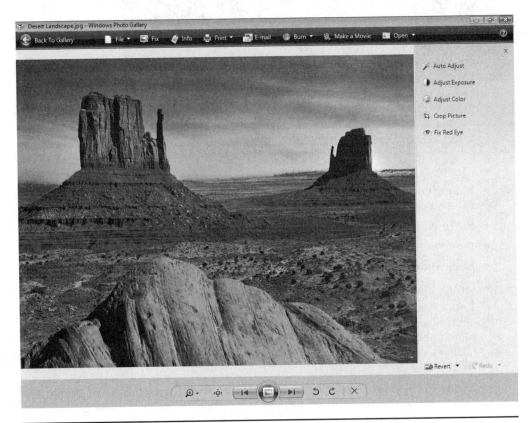

FIGURE 19-4   Windows Photo Gallery Fix pane

- **Adjust Color** Displays controls for changing a picture's color temperature, tint, or saturation.

- **Crop Picture** Displays the crop frame, which enables you to crop (remove) part of a picture. The area you enclose in the crop frame is the part that you will see after you click the Apply button. Click the Undo button if you want to return to the uncropped image. Also, you can use the Rotate Frame button to change the frame from a landscape to portrait position. Use the Custom button to see other frame sizes, such as 8×10.

- **Fix Red Eye** Removes those strange alien-looking eyes some people have in photographs. You draw a rectangle around the eye you want to fix and Windows Photo Gallery takes care of the rest.

As you read in the description of the Crop Picture tool, you can use the Undo button at the bottom of the Fix pane to remove changes you have made to your picture. The Redo button undoes the Undo, returning it back to the way you had it edited before you clicked the Undo button.

Advanced Windows Photo Gallery Items

You can use Windows Photo Gallery to perform other tasks besides viewing or editing a picture. Table 19-1 describes these tasks.

Button	Description
Info	Enables you to add filename tags for searching.
Print	Enables you to send the picture to a printer attached to your computer or your network. If you click the Order Prints command, the Order Prints dialog box appears with names of companies that can print professional-quality prints of your digital images. Select the company and then click Send Pictures. You will need to set up an account with the company, arrange payment transactions with the company (usually via credit card), and have an Internet connection.
E-mail	Attaches your picture to an e-mail message that you can then send to another person. You must have an e-mail program installed (such as Microsoft Windows Mail) and an e-mail account set up. You can specify the size of the picture file that is attached, including Original Size, Smaller, Small, Medium, or Large.
Burn	Includes two choices. Data Disc enables you to burn a picture to a CD-RW or DVD-RW drive. The Video DVD option enables you to burn a DVD using the Windows DVD Maker software.
Make a Movie	Starts the Windows Movie Maker software and import the current picture to a Movie Maker project. You can add the picture to a movie that you create.
Open	Displays a list of other photo-editing and photo-viewing programs on your computer. Click one of those programs to open your current picture in that program.

TABLE 19-1 Windows Photo Gallery Advanced Tasks

Using the Windows Snipping Tool

The Windows Snipping Tool is another new program to Windows Vista. It enables you to select something on your screen and take a snapshot of it. This is called a *screenshot* or *screen capture*. The images in this book, for instance, are screen captures that were taken to illustrate different parts of Windows or related software.

Capturing Screenshots

To start the Snipping Tool, choose Start | All Programs | Accessories | Snipping Tool. The Snipping Tool window appears, as shown in Figure 19-5. When you start it, the Snipping Tool is ready to go. Draw a rectangle around the area you want captured, such as the Welcome Center window shown in Figure 19-5. After you draw the rectangle, the Snipping Tool creates a screenshot of your selection. An example is shown in Figure 19-6.

If you are not ready to capture a screenshot when you initially start the Snipping Tool, but you still want the tool open, click the Cancel button. This takes the focus off the Snipping Tool, removes the selection pointer from the screen, and enables you to work on something else (such as setting up a dialog box or window you want to capture).

Click the New button to start the capture process.

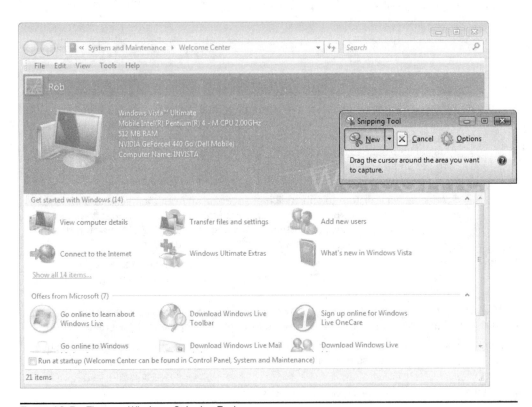

FIGURE 19-5   The new Windows Snipping Tool

FIGURE 19-6   A screen capture in the Snipping Tool window

To adjust some Snipping Tool settings, click the Options button to display the Snipping Tool Options dialog box (you also can display this from the Snipping Tool window after you capture a screenshot—choose Tools | Options). Some of the options include hiding instruction text, adding URLs (web addresses) below screenshots of web pages, and selecting a different color for the capture rectangle. Click OK to close the Snipping Tool Options dialog box.

Saving, Annotating, and Sharing Screenshots

When you have a screenshot displayed in the Snipping Tool window, you can do a couple of different things with it. First, you can save the screenshot to a file. Click the Save Snip button on the toolbar, or choose File | Save As. The Save As dialog box appears. Save the file with a name and file type. You can save the file in PNG, GIF, JPG, and MHT. The latter file type is a HTML document that displays as a web page file in Internet Explorer.

In addition to saving a screenshot, the Snipping Tool enables you to annotate a screenshot. This provides a way for you to mark up the screenshot with notes, instructions, or other messages. You use the Pen tool (which has Red, Blue, Black, and Custom settings from which to choose—you can set up a custom pen with different pen points and colors from the Customize command) or Highlighter to mark up the screenshot. Use the Eraser to remove annotations.

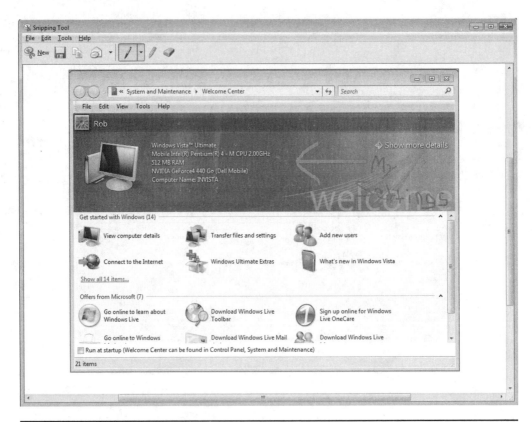

FIGURE 19-7   Annotating a screenshot

For example, Figure 19-7 shows the example screenshot after it has been annotated.

When you finish annotating or saving a screenshot, you might want to send it to another person via e-mail. This is handy for times you want to point out a specific setting on your computer, show another user what you are displaying on your computer, or send a screen capture for documentation. To send a snip in an e-mail message, click the down arrow next to the Send Snip button. With the E-mail Recipient command, you insert the snip into an e-mail message and the snip becomes part of the message (if your e-mail program supports inserting graphics). The E-mail Recipient (As Attachment) command adds the snip as an e-mail attachment that the recipient will have to save to his or her system and then view.

Choose File | Exit to close the Snipping Tool when you finish with it.

Adding Information to Digital Images

For as long as people have been taking photographs, they've also been writing on the backs of their prints so that they can keep track of information such as where and when the picture was taken, who the people in the picture are, and so on. You can't write on the back

FIGURE 19-8   Typing information into the Details tab of an image file's Properties dialog box is like writing on the back of a print.

of an image file, but Windows enables you to add extra information to a digital image: You can include this information in the file's properties.

Like any file, an image file has a Properties dialog box that you can open by right-clicking its icon and selecting Properties from the shortcut menu. The General tab of the Properties dialog box contains the same kind of information that is in any file's Properties dialog box: the file's name, type, size, and so on. But the Details tab of an image file's Properties dialog box contains spaces you can use to record other important details about the picture (see Figure 19-8). Click next to a label, such as Camera Maker or Camera Model, and type in the information you want saved with the file.

Creating and Editing Images with Microsoft Paint

Microsoft Paint is to images what WordPad is to text documents—a simple but versatile tool for creating and editing files. You can use it to make diagrams for presentations or to crop your online vacation photos; your five-year-old can use it as a coloring book, or your ten-year-old can use it to draw moustaches on the Mona Lisa.

Note *For more advanced editing of image files, as well as for converting files to different graphics formats, we recommend Corel Paint Shop Pro (www.corel.com), Adobe Photoshop (www.adobe .com), or Serif PagePlus (www.serif.com). These programs are not free, but they do offer trial versions that you can download and use for short periods of time until you must decide to purchase them or not.*

To run Paint for the first time (or for the first time in a while), choose Start | All Programs | Accessories | Paint. Depending on how your file system is set up, Paint may be the default application for BMP files or other image files. If so, Paint runs whenever you open one of these files. Figure 19-9 shows the parts of a Paint window.

The toolbar buttons are labeled with shapes that suggest their use. For example, the button that draws lines has a line on it. When the cursor passes over a tool button, a short description of the tool appears on the status bar.

Opening and Saving Files

Paint works with only one document at a time. Opening a file or creating a new one automatically closes whatever file you had open in Paint previously. Paint opens files in most

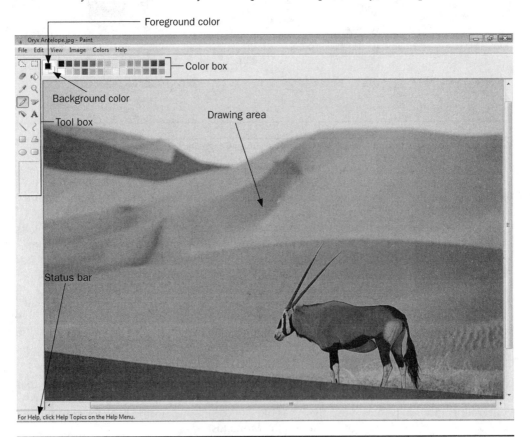

Figure 19-9   The anatomy of a Paint window

popular image formats, including BMP, TIFF, JPEG, Icon (ICO), PNG, and GIF. Files created or edited by Paint can be saved as bitmap files in a variety of color schemes (monochrome, 16 color, 256 color, and 24-bit color), as well other image formats.

NOTE *By default, most image file types open in Windows Photo Gallery. Even if you have just created a file in Paint, opening its icon will open it in Windows Photo Gallery. To open an image file in Paint, right-click its icon and select Open With | Paint from the context menu.*

By default the File | Save command saves new files in the Pictures folder inside Documents, and it saves other files to the location from which they were opened. To save elsewhere, choose File | Save As.

Selecting Objects

With the Select tool chosen (by clicking the dotted-rectangle button in the Toolbox), you can select objects inside the drawing area, just as you select objects inside an Explorer window: by enclosing them in a rectangle. Move the pointer to one corner of the rectangular area that includes the objects you want to select, hold the mouse button down, move to the opposite corner of the area, and release the mouse button.

The Free-Form Select tool (the top-left- button in the Toolbox) enables you to select objects and parts of objects inside a region of any shape. Drag the cursor to trace out any shape. Either close up the shape, or Paint closes it up automatically with a straight line. The enclosed region is now selected, and can be moved by dragging-and-dropping or copied by cutting-and-pasting—useful for creating repeated patterns.

Magnifying and Enlarging

To magnify the objects in your drawing, or zoom in on a portion of the drawing area, click the Magnifier tool (the magnifying-glass button in the Toolbox). A rectangle appears in the drawing area, which represents the portion of the drawing that will be visible after magnification. Position the rectangle to enclose the area you want to zoom in on, and then click. The portion of the drawing that was inside the rectangle now fills the entire viewing area. To zoom back out, click the Magnifier tool again, and then click anywhere in the viewing area.

When the Magnifier tool is selected, the Options box displays four magnification levels: $1x$, $2x$, $6x$, and $8x$. The current level of magnification is highlighted. To change to another level of magnification, click that option in the Options box.

To enlarge or shrink the drawing area (the "sheet of paper"), drag its corners.

Drawing Lines and Curves

Clicking with the Line tool (the straight-line button in the Toolbox) nails down one end of a line; the other end moves with the cursor. When the line is where you want it, click again to fix the other end. To make a curved line, click the Curve tool (the wiggly-line button in the Toolbox) and begin by drawing a straight line, as you would with the Line tool. Then, click-and-drag a point on that line to make a curve. You have the option of dragging a second point to make another kink in the curve.

When the Line or Curve tool is selected, different line thicknesses appear in the Options box, just below the Toolbox. Select a new thickness by clicking the line thickness you want.

When you click with the left mouse button, the Line and Curve tools draw in the foreground color. To draw lines and curves in the background color, use the right mouse button.

Drawing Freehand

Paint has four tools in the Toolbox that make freehand marks as you drag them: Pencil, Brush, Spray Can, and Eraser. Pencil makes thin lines, Brush makes thick lines, and Spray Can sprays a pattern of dots. You can choose among three densities of Spray Can dot patterns by clicking the pattern you want in the Options box. As its name suggests, the Eraser erases anything in its path, replacing it with the background color.

Making Shapes

These four tools in the Toolbox make shapes: Ellipse, Rectangle, Rounded Rectangle, and Polygon. The simplest shape to make is a rectangle:

1. Click the Rectangle tool (the solid—not the dotted—rectangle button).
2. Click in the drawing area where you want one corner of the rectangle located.
3. Drag to where you want the opposite corner of the rectangle located. When you release the mouse button, Paint creates the rectangle.

You use the Ellipse and Rounded Rectangle tools in a manner similar to the Rectangle tool. The Polygon tool makes figures with any number of sides:

1. Click the Polygon tool (the L-shaped polygon button).
2. Click inside the drawing area where you want one corner of the polygon located.
3. Each click defines the next corner of the polygon. For the first side, you must click-and-drag; for subsequent sides, just click.
4. Double-click the last corner. Paint closes up the polygon automatically.

Coloring Objects

Control the colors of objects by using the Color box at the bottom of the Paint window. The two colored squares at the far left of the Color box show the current foreground and background colors, with the foreground square on top of the background square. Any object you construct using the left mouse button has the foreground color, whereas objects made using the right mouse button have the background color.

To choose a new foreground color, left-click the square of the new color in the Color box. To choose a new background color, right-click the square of the new color. You can match the color of any object in the drawing area by using the Pick Color tool (the eyedropper button in the Toolbox). Select the tool, and then click the object whose color you want to match. Left-clicking changes the foreground color to match the object; right-clicking changes the background color to match the object.

To color within an outlined area, such as a rectangle or an ellipse, select the Fill With Color tool (the tipped-paintcan button), and click within the area. Right-click to fill with the background color. Using the Fill With Color tool on an area that is not outlined colors the whole "sheet of paper"—the area outside of any enclosed region.

Changing the foreground or background color does not change the color of objects already created. To change an object to the new foreground (background) color, select the Fill With Color tool and click (right-click) the object whose color you want to change. You can invert the colors in a region (that is, make a negative of the original) by selecting the region and choosing Image | Invert Colors.

Adding Text

Click the Text tool (the *A* button) and drag across the part of your picture where you want the type to appear. Paint displays a rectangular text box for you to type in. A font selection box appears above the text box so you can select the font, size, and style of the text. The color of the text is the foreground color. Click inside the text box and type. Click outside the text box when you are done typing.

The Options box below the Toolbox gives two choices for using the Text tool. The top choice makes a solid background for the text box, using the background color. The bottom choice makes a transparent background.

Flipping, Rotating, and Stretching

Commands on the Image menu flip, rotate, or stretch the entire image or a selected part of the image. Choosing Image | Flip/Rotate opens a dialog box from which you can choose to flip the image horizontally or vertically, or you can rotate it by any multiple of 90 degrees. Choosing Image | Stretch/Skew opens another dialog box from which you can stretch the image horizontally or vertically by any percentage, or slant it by any number of degrees.

Elements that you add to a flipped, stretched, slanted, or rotated drawing are normal. This feature allows you to mix elements of various types in a single drawing.

Cropping Images

You can crop an image—remove unwanted material around the edges of a picture. To crop an image, use the Select tool to enclose the area of the image that you want to keep. To save the selected area as a new file, choose Edit | Copy To. Type a new filename and click Save. The original image is unaffected.

Working with Digital Cameras and Scanners

From a user's point of view, scanners and cameras have little to do with each other. It would never occur to you, for example, to point your scanner at the Grand Canyon. But to a computer, scanners and digital cameras are very similar: both turn visual information into image files. This is why these two types of devices share a Control Panel icon (Scanners And Cameras, which lives inside the Hardware And Sounds category) and a wizard (the Scanner And Camera Installation Wizard) for installing them.

Setting Up a Scanner or Digital Camera

In order to work with a scanner or digital camera, Windows needs to have a driver program that tells it how to communicate with the device (see "What Are Drivers?" in Chapter 14).

Windows Vista comes with drivers for most popular devices, so your installation process may be as simple as plugging your scanner or camera into the appropriate port (usually a USB port), turning it on, and waiting for Windows to notice it. Installing an Olympus Camedia camera was just this easy when we tried it; Windows noticed the camera immediately and had it ready to go in less than a minute.

If the plug-in-and-wait technique doesn't work with your camera or scanner, put the CD or DVD that came with the camera or scanner into your CD/DVD drive and see whether a program runs that steps you through installing the drivers and related software.

If you still don't have drivers installed, try this:

1. Open the Scanners And Cameras icon from the Hardware And Sounds category of the Control Panel.

2. Select Add Device from the Scanners And Cameras dialog box. The Scanner And Camera Installation Wizard starts.

3. Click Next. The wizard asks you for the names of the manufacturer and model of your camera or scanner. If you can't find your camera or scanner on the wizard's list, click the Have Disk button and be prepared to insert the CD or DVD that came with your hardware.

4. Click Next. Type a name you want to use for the device.

5. Click Next.

6. Click Finish. You may have to tell the wizard which port the device is connected to. The rest of the installation happens automatically. You may have to restart the computer before using your device.

You can test your scanner or digital camera by clicking its entry in the Scanners And Cameras window, clicking the Properties button, and then clicking the Test Scanner Or Camera button.

Many cameras and scanners come with additional software, beyond the drivers needed to allow Windows to work with the device. These additional programs may provide a "front panel" for the device (one of our scanners comes with a program that looks like the front of a photocopying machine) or graphics editing. You usually don't need this additional software to use your camera or scanner: you do need the drivers.

NOTE *Even after you install your scanner or digital camera and it works fine, the Scanners And Cameras icon may not appear in the Control Panel. If you open the Scanners And Cameras window, your scanner or camera may not appear in the list of installed devices, either. The device may appear, however, in other areas of Vista. For example, some appear as drives in Windows Explorer or as sync devices in Media Player. You also can see them in Device Manager. Choose Start | Control Panel | System And Maintenance | System and click the Device Manager link in the Tasks pane to display the Device Manager window (see "What Is the Device Manager?" in Chapter 14). Look down the list of all installed devices—scanners and cameras appear in the Imaging Devices category or the Portable Devices category. Older cameras and scanners may not be on the list.*

Downloading Images from Digital Cameras

A digital camera is also a disk drive in disguise. As you take pictures, the image files are stored on some device like a CompactFlash card, internal memory, DVD, or a memory stick. When you connect the camera to your computer, Windows assumes you want to do something with the files the camera is holding, so it displays the default program for accessing the images. For example, for the Olympus Camedia camera, a Windows Explorer window appears, with Large Icons view of the images, as shown in Figure 19-10.

Depending on the camera you use, the application that appears may not be Windows Explorer, which appears with my Olympus camera. In fact, if I were to install the software that came bundled with the camera, that software would be the default application for managing my digital camera. Other cameras open the Scanner And Camera Wizard, which helps you download the pictures to a folder on your computer.

The Scanner And Camera Wizard takes you through the process of selecting which pictures to download and what folder to store them in. You can tell the wizard to automatically delete the pictures from the camera after you download them, or you can leave them on the camera and deal with them later. After the pictures have been downloaded, you can edit them in

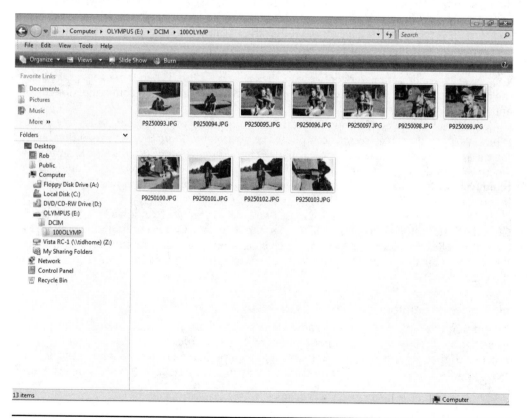

FIGURE 19-10 View your photographs taken with your digital camera.

Windows Photo Gallery, Paint, or a third-party program that you may have installed on your computer. Some digital cameras come bundled with photo-editing software.

TIP *If you're on the road with nothing but a laptop and a digital camera, you can use the camera as a disk drive to back up a few important files. Strange, but true!*

Downloading Images from Scanners

When you first connect your scanner to your computer, you may see the AutoPlay dialog box, asking what you want Windows to do with images that arrive from the scanner. The preceding section also describes how you can use the Scanner And Printer Wizard to copy files from your scanner to your computer.

Alternatively, graphics programs can use your scanner to create images. Most scanners come with a *TWAIN* driver that adds an Acquire command to your graphics editor (for example, the Paint Shop Pro program gains a File | Import | TWAIN | Acquire command after you install a scanner driver). You can issue this command to bring information from the scanner or camera into the program.

To scan a document or picture from your scanner, you can use the Windows Fax and Scan program or your favorite graphics editor (including Microsoft Paint, which now supports TWAIN). If you use a program other than Windows Fax and Scan, check the program to be sure it can acquire pictures directly from a scanner. Some programs start scanning as soon as you give the command, whereas others display a dialog box in which you can set scanner parameters before you click a Scan button. When the scanner finishes, the picture appears on your screen. Use the graphics program's usual commands to edit and save the scanned image.

Windows Fax and Scan, shown in Figure 19-11, is a new program that comes free with Windows Vista. It enables you to scan photos or documents, store those scanned files, send the files as an e-mail attachment, or fax them. Scanned images are stored in the Scanned Documents folder inside your Documents folder. You can open the scanned image from the Scanned Documents folder by using a photo-editing program like Windows Photo Gallery if you want to edit the image.

To start Windows Fax and Scan, choose Start | All Programs | Windows Fax And Scan. Click the Scan button on the left pane to open the scan area. Or to start scanning a picture or document, click the New Scan button, which starts the scanning process. After you scan a file, you also can delete the file, print it, or save it to a different location using commands on the File menu.

Linking Your Scanner or Digital Camera to a Program

In addition to graphics programs, some other types of programs accept digital graphic information directly from a scanner or camera. For example, a database program may accept a digital picture of a person for storage in a personnel database, and pressing the button on the camera can send the picture directly into the database. If both your scanner or

FIGURE 19-11   Windows Fax and Scan lets you scan photos or documents.

camera and your program support this feature, you can tell Windows to run a program whenever you scan an image or take a digital picture. Follow these steps:

1. Display the Scanners And Cameras window (see "Setting Up a Scanner or Digital Camera").

2. Click the device and then click the Properties button to display the Properties dialog box for that scanner or camera. (If the Events tab does not appear, your scanner or digital camera does not support linking to programs.)

3. In the list of events to which the camera or scanner can respond, click an event.

4. In the Start This Program box, click the name of the program that will receive the image from the scanner or camera. Only programs that can accept digital images appear on the list.

5. Click OK.

PART IV

Working with Sound

Early PCs weren't equipped to work with audio data, but since about 1998, most computers sold have come with a sound board and speakers, and some with a microphone. Like Windows 9x, Me, NT, 2000, XP, and 2003 Server, Vista contains built-in support for audio devices—hardware that enables your computer to record and play sounds. In addition to better drivers for audio devices, Windows comes with Windows Media Player 11, which enables you to rip music, burn CDs or DVDs, and record or play audio and video files or discs.

This chapter provides an introduction to audio file formats, with instructions for configuring Windows to work with sound, using Windows Media Player, and using the older Sound Recorder. Chapter 14 describes how to install hardware, including audio hardware; this chapter explains how to configure and use these devices.

How Does Windows Work with Sound?

Almost all new computers come with a *sound board*, an adapter board inside the computer that lets you connect a microphone and either speakers or headphones to your computer for audio input and output or similar functions already on the computer's system board. Some computers actually include the sound card as an integrated piece of the motherboard, rather than having a separate adapter card inserted into the PC.

Many programs use sound to alert you to events, like the musical snippets that you may hear when Windows starts or shuts down. You need sound capabilities to participate in Internet phone and voice chats and to listen to sound clips on the Web.

Windows plays sounds when certain events occur. You can associate a sound with a new event, or change the kind of sounds Windows plays, as described in the next few sections of this chapter. You can also play and record sounds by using the Sound Recorder or Media Player programs and play an audio CD or DVD in your CD-ROM or DVD player by using the disc-playing components of Windows Media Player.

What Are Common Sound File Formats?

For Windows to be able to save, edit, or play sound, it must be able to store audio information in files. Table 20-1 lists the most commonly used file formats for audio data.

Medium	Input Device	Output Device	File Extensions for Popular Formats
Audio	Microphone, MIDI keyboard, synthesizers, line input	Speakers, headphones	.wav, .mp3, .m3u, .asx, .wax, and .wvx
Streaming audio	Microphone, MIDI keyboard, synthesizers, line input, usually downloaded from the Internet	Speakers, headphones	.ram, .ra (for RealAudio files), .asf, and .asx (for Advanced Streaming Format files)
MIDI	MIDI-compatible instrument	MIDI-compatible instrument, speakers, headphones	.mid, .midi, or .rmi

TABLE 20-1 Audio Devices and File Formats

To see the properties of any audio file, right-click the filename and choose Properties from the menu that appears. You see a Properties dialog box like the one shown in Figure 20-1.

The General and Details tabs include information pertinent to the audio features of the file. The information on the General tab parallels that provided for almost any file: type, size, and attributes. The Details tab displays the bit rate, audio sample size, and other formatting information.

What Is the Music Folder?

Windows Vista comes with a folder called Music in your Documents folder. The idea is for you to store your music files there for replay with Windows Media Player. The folder can contain subfolders for different types of music—Windows Media Player automatically creates new folders when you copy sound files from audio CDs. When you display the Music folder in an Explorer window, the toolbar includes two tools just for sound files:

- **Play All**   Plays all the music in the folder (or just the selected files).
- **Burn**   Opens your CD-R or DVD-R drive's tray for you to insert a writeable disc, and displays the Burn To Disc dialog box. You can then burn an audio disc based on the music you select in the Music folder.

What Is Streaming Audio?

Streaming audio is audio stored in a format for use over the Internet. When you want to play a streaming audio file over the Internet, your computer can start playing the file after downloading only the beginning of the file, and can continue to play the audio while the rest of the file downloads—optimally, downloading stays a step ahead of the player (the audio yet to be played is stored in a *buffer*). To play streaming audio files from the Internet, run Windows Media Player (see "Playing Sound Files with Windows Media Player 11" later in the chapter). For instructions for playing video files, see the next chapter.

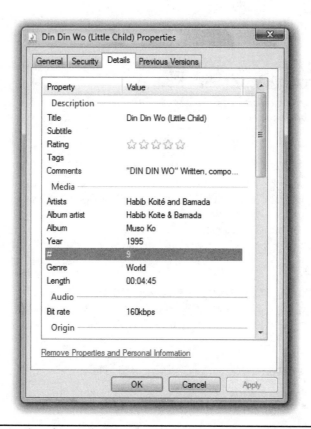

FIGURE 20-1 The properties of an audio file.

One of the most popular streaming audio formats is RealAudio (with either the .ra or .rm file extension). You can download the RealPlayer program for free from the Real.com web site at www.real.com; this program works with your web browser to play both RealAudio and RealVideo files from the Internet. Microsoft has its own streaming format, called Advanced Streaming Format (ASF), which Windows Media Player can play.

What Is MIDI?

A specialized type of audio data is called *MIDI* (Musical Instrument Digital Interface), a format for transmitting and storing musical notes. MIDI devices are musical instruments or recording devices that have digital inputs and outputs and can transmit, store, and play music using the MIDI language. For example, if you connect a MIDI keyboard to your computer, you can view the music you play on the MIDI keyboard on your computer screen and hear it on your speakers. Data from MIDI devices is stored in MIDI files. Windows includes software that can "play" MIDI files; that is, software that can translate the musical notes in the files into sound that can be played through speakers or headphones.

PART IV

Windows Media Player can play MIDI files. You need additional MIDI software to edit and mix MIDI inputs.

Configuring Windows to Work with Sound

Many applications, particularly games, have built-in sound. Those programs automatically take advantage of your system's sound card, speakers, and microphone, once Windows is configured to work with them.

Displaying the Status of Your Audio Devices

To see all the audio devices installed on your system, choose Start | Control Panel, click Hardware And Sound, and then click Sound. You see the Sound dialog box. Sound devices that are installed show up on the Playback tab (see Figure 20-2). Those working correctly show Working in the short description for each device.

To display or change the settings for some devices, click the device and click the Properties button.

Choosing and Configuring Audio Input and Output Drivers

When you install sound equipment, Windows usually configures itself automatically to use the proper sound drivers. If you need to tell Windows which sound drivers to use, or

Figure 20-2 The Sound dialog box.

choose settings for your audio devices, including voice, you can configure Windows in the Sound dialog box. This dialog box has tabs for configuring when Windows plays sounds and which drivers Windows uses to play and record sounds. You can also use this dialog box to display the properties of all your audio and video devices. Follow these steps:

1. Choose Start | Control Panel, click Hardware And Sound, and then click Sound. You see the Sound dialog box.

2. Click the Playback tab, shown in Figure 20-2, if it's not already selected.

3. Click a device.

4. Click Properties to open the Properties dialog box for that device.

5. Click Properties on the General tab and then click the Driver tab on the resulting dialog box. The driver used to play sounds by selecting the device from the list of available devices in the Sound Playback section of the Audio tab.

6. Click the Advanced tab. For some systems, you can adjust the sample rate and bit depth of your sound cards (you can set some sample rates on the Supported Formats tab). Also, if you play games or other sound-intensive applications, make sure the Exclusive Mode options are selected. Click OK.

7. Tell Windows more about your speakers or headphones by clicking the Speakers item on the Playback tab of the Sound dialog box (see Figure 20-2). Click Properties. Each tab on the Speakers Properties dialog box provides settings for your speakers. For example, on the General tab (see Figure 20-3) you can select the type of speaker jack you use to plug in your speakers to your computer.

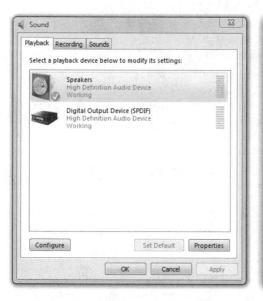

FIGURE 20-3   Use the General tab to set speaker jack information.

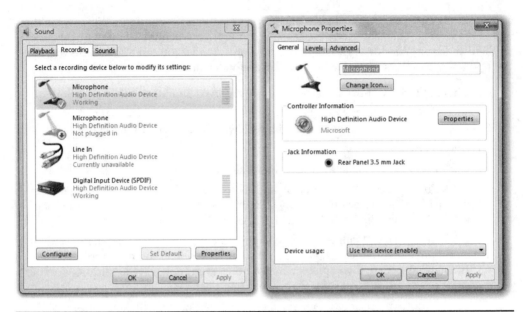

FIGURE 20-4 Set microphone options in the Microphone Properties dialog box.

8. Click OK to return to the Playback tab of the Sound dialog box. Click Speakers in the list of devices and click Configure. Choose your computer's arrangement of speakers or headphones. Click Next and work through the Speaker Setup wizard. You can specify the position of your speakers, types of speakers (such as subwoofers), and if you have satellite speakers in surround-sound setup.

9. To control the volume of your speakers or headphones, click the Properties button on the Sound dialog box and click the Levels tab. Move the Speakers control to the right to increase volume, to the left to decrease volume. Click OK.

10. Click the Recording tab on the Sound dialog box. Choose a recording device, such as a microphone you might use to record audio notes for a business document. Click Properties to open the Microphone Properties dialog box (see Figure 20-4). You can change the icon for the microphone, configure device driver settings (click the Properties button on the General tab), set jack information. You can set sound settings on the Levels tab, and sample rates on the Advanced tab. Click OK.

11. Click OK to save your changes and exit the Sound dialog box.

TIP *If you have trouble getting sounds to play, try the Troubleshoot Sound Problems Help articles (see "Finding Topics" in Chapter 4).*

Controlling the Volume and Balance

You can control the volume and balance of the sound that goes into your microphones and comes out of your computer's speakers or headphones. You can also choose to mute (suppress) the sound for any audio device. You can use the Volume icon (a little white

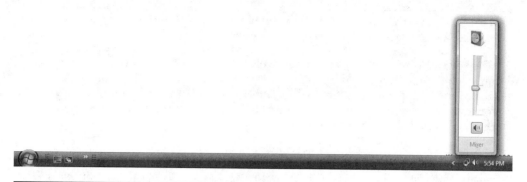

FIGURE 20-5   Use the Volume icon for adjusting audio volumes.

loudspeaker icon) in the notification area on your taskbar to set the volume of sounds and music that play back through your computer.

To adjust the volume of your speakers, click the Volume icon on the taskbar once; you see a Volume slider (see Figure 20-5) and speaker icon.

Drag the Volume slider up for louder volume or down for softer volume. Click the speaker icon to suppress audio output completely (such as when you are using your laptop on a train). Click outside the window to make it disappear.

To adjust the volume and balance of any audio device, click the Volume icon and click Mixer. You see the Volume Mixer window, shown in Figure 20-6. Depending on the sophistication of your sound system, you may see more controls and mixer items here.

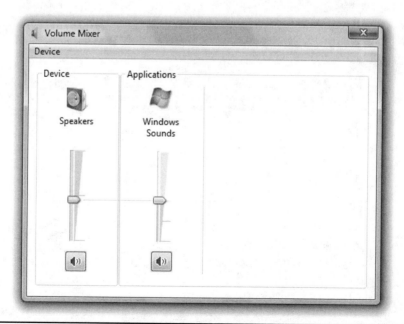

FIGURE 20-6   Use the Volume Mixer to adjust device and application volumes.

NOTE *Some sound cards come with their own mixer application. To use all of the features of your installed device, use the mixer program that comes with the sound card.*

The Volume Mixer lets you set volume levels for different devices or applications. For example, you can control Windows sounds using the Windows Sounds Volume Mixer element. That way, if you want Windows sounds (such as clicks and dings when you perform specific Windows actions) to be lower than other sounds (such as music you play), you can adjust that sound lower.

TIP *If your speakers or headphones have a physical volume control knob, it's generally simpler to leave the Windows volume set fairly high, sending a strong signal through the wires, and just turn the knob to change the volume. Similarly, laptops usually have volume controls on the keyboard to let you quickly mute, turn up, or turn down the volume.*

Choosing What Sounds Windows Makes

Windows comes with an array of sounds that it makes when certain *events* (Windows operations) occur. When you start Windows, for example, a rich, welcoming sound occurs; however, you might prefer the sound of a friend yelling "Hello!" You can control which sounds Windows plays when specified events occur by clicking the Change System Sounds link in the Hardware And Sound Control Panel. The Sounds tab of the Sound dialog box displays, as shown in Figure 20-7.

FIGURE 20-7 Associating sounds with Windows events.

The Program box lists all the events that you can associate with a sound, including events that happen in Windows and other programs that use sound, such as Windows Explorer. If an event has no speaker icon to its left, no sound is currently assigned to that event. To change the sound for an event:

1. Click the event name in the Program box.

2. Below Sounds, click the drop-down arrow and choose a sound stored in a WAV file on your computer. You see a list of the sounds that come with Windows Vista. Click the Browse button to find other WAV files, such as the ones you recorded yourself (see the following section). To assign no sound to an event, choose (None) from the Sounds list.

3. To test out the sound, click the Test button in the Sounds area.

The list of sounds in the Sound area is the list of WAV files (with extension .wav) in the C:\Windows\Media folder (assuming that Windows is installed on C:). You can also test sounds in the Browse For New Complete Navigation Sound dialog box that you see when you click the Browse button. Select any sound that appears in the window, right-click a sound, and click Play. Windows Media Player opens and plays the sound.

You can save the set of sound associations as a *sound scheme*. Windows comes with a Windows Default sound scheme, which associates sounds with many events, and a No Sounds sound scheme, in which no sounds are associated with events. You can create your own sound schemes, too; simply associate the sounds you want to hear with the events that you want to prompt those sounds and click Save As.

Playing and Recording WAV Sound Files with Sound Recorder

To play or record WAV files (with the extension .wav), you can use the built-in Sound Recorder program. Choose Start | All Programs | Accessories | Sound Recorder. You see the Sound Recorder window, shown in Figure 20-8. If you are used to the program in earlier versions of Windows, you will be surprised. The latest version does not include as many "bells and whistles" as those versions. You can click the Start Recording button, speak your part, click Stop Recording, and save the sound file. If you click Stop Recording and click Cancel in the Save As dialog box, you can then click Resume Recording in the Sound Recorder window to add to your sound file.

To play back a sound you recorded, open Windows Explorer, locate the sound, and double-click it. Windows Media Player plays back the sound.

Figure 20-8 Playing and recording sounds using the Sound Recorder.

Playing Sound Files with Windows Media Player 11

Another program that can play sound files, and many other types of files, is Windows Media Player, recently updated to version 11.0 and touting some new features. Start Windows Media Player by choosing Start | All Programs | Windows Media Player or by clicking the Windows Media Player icon on the Quick Launch toolbar (if it appears on your taskbar). You see the Windows Media Player window, shown in Figure 20-9. When it starts, Windows Media Player displays the Library tab, which displays the audio and video files on your computer.

To play a sound file, choose File | Open, set the Media Files box to Windows Audio File (to skip other types of files, such as video files), choose a file, and click Open. Windows Media Player loads the file and starts playing it. When it's over, you can click the Play button to play the sound file again. You can stop playback by clicking the Stop button near the bottom of the window.

NOTE *See "Playing Video Files with Windows Media Player" in Chapter 21 for details about playing video files with Windows Media Player.*

FIGURE 20-9   The Windows Media Player window.

The Windows Media Player Window

The new Windows Media Player window has tabs across the top of the window. What displays in the main Media Player window depends on the tab you click. The tabs are as follows:

- **Now Playing**   Displays the currently loaded file. If the file is a video, it appears on the video screen. If an audio file is loaded, you see a visualization of the music.

- **Library**   Enables you to organize your audio and video files.

- **Rip**   Enables you to copy music from an audio CD or DVD inserted in your disc drive.

- **Burn**   Enables you to copy audio files to a CD or DVD, if you have a CD or DVD burner.

- **Sync**   Enables you to move audio files to and from a portable audio player.

- **Media Guide (URGE is the default)**   Connects to online media stores (URGE is the MTV online store) from which you can purchase and download music, videos, and other files.

- **Sign In**   Enables you to log into Media Guide sites to which you have subscribed.

Playing Audio Files Stored on Your Computer

To play a file on your computer or on a shared drive on a LAN, choose File | Open and choose the filename. (If you don't see the menu bar, press CTRL-M on your keyboard.) Windows Media Player can play sound files in a variety of formats, including WAV, MIDI, SND, and streaming audio files.

   Click the Now Playing button on the toolbar to see the video that goes with the audio (see Figure 20-10). If the file you are playing doesn't include video images, Windows Media Player creates them for you. As the music plays, the video screen shows *visualizations*, graphical representations of the sound. Windows Media Player provides several visualizations (approximately 50 of them)—all are interesting, and some are positively mesmerizing. You can change the visualization that appears by clicking the small gray arrow buttons underneath the visualization. The name of the visualization appears to the right of the buttons. You can also surf through them all by right-clicking in the Now Playing window and choosing from the Alchemy, Bars And Waves, and Battery menus.

   You can add other information to the video screen by choosing View | Enhancements. Some of these enhancements include:

- Color Chooser
- Graphic Equalizer
- SRS WOW Effects

Organizing Your Audio Files into a Media Library

Windows Media Player includes the Media Library, a storehouse for all of your audio and video files (see Figure 20-9). To organize your audio and video files (also called *tracks*, as on an audio CD), Windows Media Player can search your drives (local and shared network

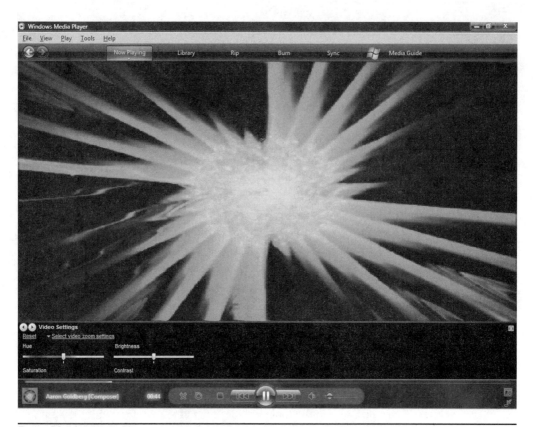

FIGURE 20-10 Media Player can show visualizations as your audio files play.

drives) for files. It organizes them into lists of audio files, video files, and the addresses of radio stations on the Internet. You can then organize the files into playlists, described in the next section.

To add files to the Library tab, do the following:

1. Choose Files | Add To Library. You see the Add To Library dialog box, shown in Figure 20-11.

2. Select the folders you want Windows Media Player to examine to add media files to the Library tab. For example, you can click the My Personal Folders option to allow Media Player to monitor your User folders for any files that Media Player supports (audio, video, and sound). To add a custom folder, click Add, navigate to that folder using the Add Folder dialog box, select the folder, and click OK. This is handy if you store media files in folders that are not in your User folders.

3. Click OK to close the Add To Library dialog box.

The list on the left of the Library tab, called the Navigation Pane, shows your media files by category, playlists, and Now Playing. Click an item in the Navigation Pane to show individual albums or songs. For example, when you rip music from a CD or DVD, those

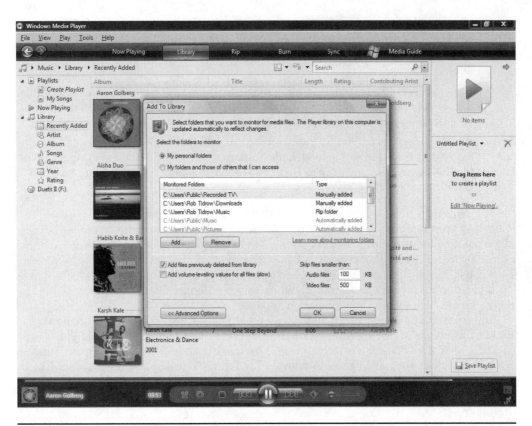

FIGURE 20-11   Add media to the Library tab using the Add To Library dialog box.

songs are added to the Recently Added library folder. That way you can quickly find them after you rip them. Click that item in the Navigation Pane to see each song categorized by the album from which the song was ripped.

The Navigation Pane displays your media in two major categories: Playlists and Library. Playlists are discussed a little later in this chapter. The Library category lists these subcategories:

- **Recently Added**   Displays files you recently added to your collection.

- **Artist**   Displays audio files by artist. If you have songs from more than one album by a single artist, the albums appear as sub-subcategories.

- **Album**   Displays audio files by the album of which they are a part (if any). Windows Media Player identifies albums by information from audio CDs (see the next section) or from the MP3 ID3 tags, for MP3 format files.

- **Songs**   Displays audio files alphabetically by album. Each song on that album that is saved to your computer displays next to the album from which it was downloaded or ripped.

- **Genre**   Displays audio files by genres and styles. Since genres and styles are primarily determined by personal taste, this can be an unreliable way to sort music—unless you go through each album and assign each album to the genre where you think it belongs.

- **Year**   Displays audio files according to the year in which they were released. If this data is not known for an album, Windows Media Player displays that album in the Other category at the bottom of window.

- **Rating**   Displays audio files based on the star rating system. It seems that all albums are given a three-star rating by default. You can change this by right-clicking an album (do this in another view, such as Recently Added or Album), clicking Rate, and then choosing a star value.

You can click a file to play it and the files that follow it on the list. Windows Media Player can keep track of lots of information about each file—use the status bar at the bottom of the window to see the artist that is playing. To see additional information about a song, right-click it and choose Properties. Click the Content tab of the Properties dialog box to see Title, Artist, Album, Composer, Genre, Copyright, Rating, and Descriptions.

If you don't want a file to appear anywhere in your Media Library, right-click it and choose Delete from the shortcut menu that appears.

You can also update the information about a file. Right-click a piece of information about a file and choose Edit. Windows Media Player enables you to edit the field you clicked (this feature doesn't work on all fields). To make changes to more than just visible fields, right-click a song and choose Advanced Tag Editor. This displays the Advanced Tab Editor, shown in Figure 20-12. Here you can modify several properties of your media file, including Subtitle, Original Album, Subgenre, Artist Info, and the picture that displays with the album.

If you want to synchronize lyrics with your songs, click the Lyrics tab. Enter the lyrics in the Text box and click Synchronized Lyrics. In the Synchronized Lyrics dialog box (see Figure 20-13) use the Time and Value columns to sync up music with your lyrics. Click OK twice to save your lyrics and sync times. As you play your song, the lyrics display on the Now Playing tab.

Creating and Editing Playlists

A *playlist* is a set of audio files that you plan to play as a group. You can create a playlist, give it a name, and put audio (or video) files into it. Then you can play that group of files any time, either in the order in which they appear on the playlist or in random (shuffled) order.

Click the Library button on the toolbar to see, create, and edit playlists. In the list of categories on the Navigation Pane (it appears on the left side of screen), one category is Playlists.

To create a new playlist, click the Create Playlist item in the Playlists list. Type a name for the new playlist and press ENTER. Windows Media Player adds your new playlist to the Playlists category and shows it in the List pane on the right side of the screen.

To add files to a playlist, open the Library tab in Windows Media Player and drag-and-drop files to the List pane. The songs are automatically added to the new playlist.

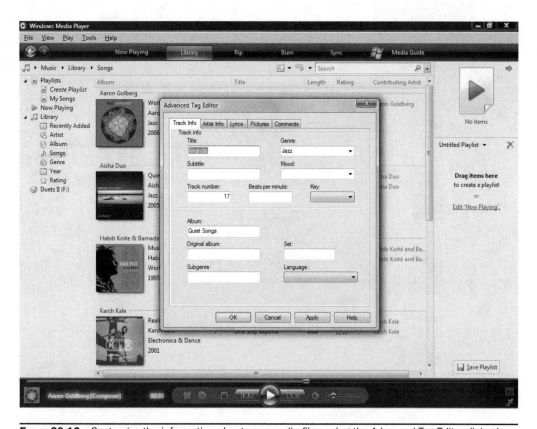

FIGURE 20-12 Customize the information about your media files using the Advanced Tag Editor dialog box.

If you want to add songs to a different playlist, or if a playlist is not showing in the List pane, right-click a file (or select a group of files and right-click it) and choose Add from the shortcut menu that appears. A submenu appears with the names of all your playlists. Select the playlist to which to add the song.

When you add a file to a playlist, Windows Media Player doesn't copy the file to the playlist—the audio file remains where it is stored. Instead, it creates a shortcut to the file. This capability allows you to include one file in many playlists. When you delete a file from a playlist, Windows doesn't delete the audio file; it just deletes the shortcut to the file from the playlist. To delete a file from a playlist, right-click the file and choose Remove From List from the shortcut menu that appears.

You can adjust the order of the files in the playlist by dragging them up and down the list. Or, right-click a file in the list and choose Move Up or Move Down.

Click the Save Playlist button when you finish adding songs to it.

NOTE *With some digital audio devices, playlists can be synced to the device to make it easy to pick songs you want to play back on your devices.*

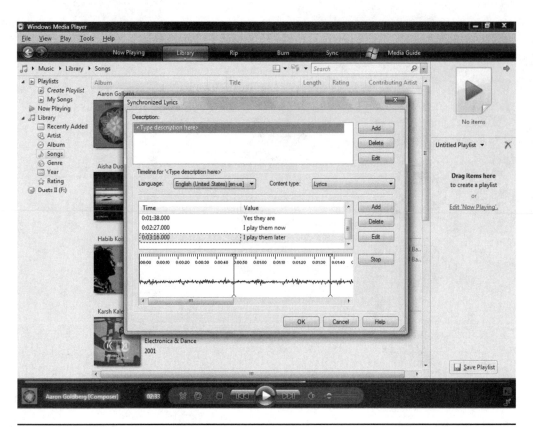

FIGURE 20-13   Synchronize lyrics with a song.

Playing Audio CDs

Every audio CD has a serial number that identifies the artist, album title, and the list of tracks (songs) on the CD. These serial numbers are stored in a database called the *Compact Disc Database* or *CDDB*, which is accessible over the Internet. The CDDB began as a cooperative effort of the community of music lovers, entering information about their CDs, but has since become a commercial venture.

When you insert an audio CD into your CD-ROM drive, the Windows Media Player program runs automatically. If AutoPlay is turned on, the music begins playing. Windows Media Player reads the number from the audio CD and sends that number to the CDDB over the Internet. If the audio CD number is in the CDDB, the list of songs and artists is usually already in the CDDB, unless you have a truly obscure album. Windows Media Player downloads this information to your computer automatically. The list of tracks appears in the playlist that appears when you click the Now Playing or CD Audio button. If the CD is not in the CDDB database, then you have the option to type the titles of the tracks in yourself (do so—as a public service).

To play a specific track, double-click a song title, right-click a song title and select Play, or select the song title and click the Play button at the bottom of the window. You can edit the information about a CD track the same way you edit information about a track in a playlist: right-click information about the track and choose Edit from the shortcut menu that appears; or, select a group of tracks, right-click the information about one track, and choose Edit Selected to make the same change to all the selected tracks. For more information about a track, right-click it and choose Properties.

You can change the order in which Windows Media Player plays the tracks on the CD. Right-click a track and choose Move Up or Move Down from the shortcut menu, or simply drag them up or down with the mouse. A gray line tracks your movement, indicating where the track will be placed when you let go. Click the Turn Shuffle On button along the bottom of the Windows Media Player window to play the files in random order.

To see a visualization of the music, click the Now Playing button and choose a visualization.

Windows Media Player includes several configuration settings for audio CDs (see Figure 20-14). Choose Tools | Options. The Options dialog box includes tabs for changing Player settings, how Windows Media Player rips music to your computer, which devices are audio and video capable, CD and DVD burn settings, and more.

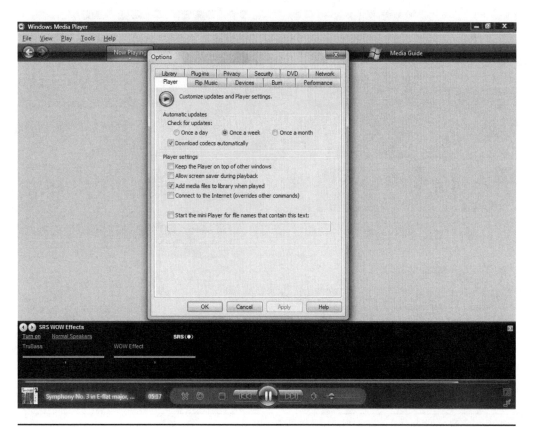

FIGURE 20-14 Use the Options dialog box to control how your audio files play, sync, and rip in Media Player.

Playing Streaming Audio Files from the Internet

If you know the exact URL of an audio file on the Internet, choose File | Open Location and enter the URL of the file to play it. However, it's usually easier to use the Media Guide button to help you find the file you want.

When you click the Media Guide button, the program connects to Microsoft's Windows Media site at www.windowsmedia.com. This site, as shown in Figure 20-15, usually includes information about television, movies, or new music, and often has neat stuff to look at or listen to.

Windows Media Player's Media Guide feature acts like a web browser to show you the Windows Media home page, which you can also view with Internet Explorer. The pages have Back and Forward links in the upper-right corner of the display that allow you to move about with a modicum of the ease you get in your web browser. Some links may display pages in your browser rather than on the Windows Media Player's video screen.

If your PC connects to the Internet through a firewall, you might not be able to use Windows Media Player's Media Guide or Radio Tuner buttons. The port numbers used when connecting to streaming audio material on web sites aren't standard, and the system

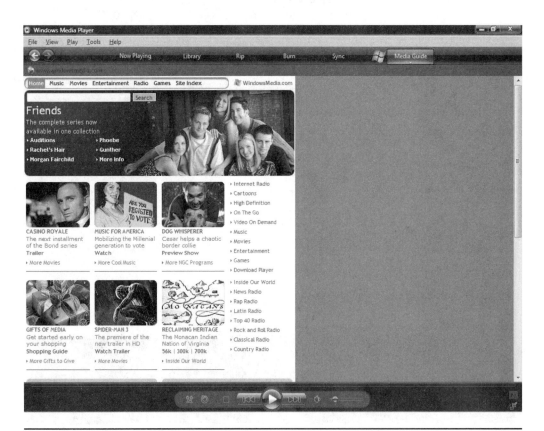

FIGURE 20-15   Microsoft's Media Guide web site.

that connects your LAN to the Internet might not be configured to handle them. If you have a problem, choose Tools | Options to display the Options dialog box. The Network tab controls how the program communicates over the Internet:

- **Protocols**   Defines which network access protocols the program uses to communicate with servers and (optionally) which ports to use (useful if you communicate with the Internet through a firewall).

- **Proxy Settings**   Specifies whether your PC communicates with the Internet over a LAN, using a proxy server program (see Chapter 32). The default is not to use a proxy server. If your PC connects to the Internet over a LAN, get the configuration information from your LAN administrator.

Adjusting Volume, Graphic Equalization, and Other Sound Settings

If you want to adjust how your audio files sound, choose View | Enhancements and click Graphic Equalizer from the submenu that appears. A small equalizer appears at the bottom of the screen.

Several other tools may appear in this area. You can right-click the area to choose items, or use the View | Enhancements submenu. Some of the tools you can use include the following:

- **SRS WOW Effects**   Includes several special effects: TruBass, WOW Effect, SRS WOW Effect, and Speakers. TruBass adds more bass to your music the farther to the right you slide it. WOW Effect adds more separation between the stereo channels. The Turn On/Turn Off link enables or disables all these effects. Clicking the SRS logo takes your web browser to the SRS WOWcast.com web site at mediaplayer.srswowcast.com, in case you are interested in files that use the SRS WOW technology.

- **Graphic Equalizer**   Enables you to adjust the treble and bass balance and left and right speaker balance. The ten vertical sliders adjust the volume of the high treble notes (at the right end) through the low bass notes (at the left end). The Turn On/ Turn Off link enables or disables the effects of any modifications you make to the equalizer. Turning it off means you get the sound exactly as it was recorded. Rather than setting them individually, you can click the down arrow next to the Default link to show a list of settings that work for many common musical genres (see Figure 20-16). If you like to adjust the equalizer yourself, the three buttons on the left end of the controls define whether you can adjust each frequency individually, adjust them in a loose group, or adjust them in a tight group.

- **Video Settings**   Enables you to control the color and brightness of the video images.

Syncing Files to and from Portable Players and Other Devices

Portable MP3 players and personal CD players are quite popular. The portable digital music machines of today are small and can hold several hours' worth of digital music. Others can hold up to thousands of hours and take up no more room than a cell phone or key chain.

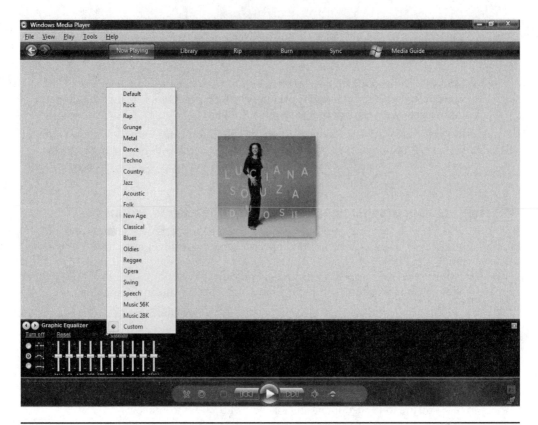

FIGURE 20-16 Use Media Player's preset graphic equalizer settings, or make your own with the Custom setting.

NOTE *Some portable CD players can play CD-R/RW discs only if they were burned in the same format as standard audio CDs. Others have the ability to see and play back MP3 and WMA files from a CD-R/RW. A typical 640 MB or 700 MB CD-R can hold much more music than a 74- or 80-minute audio CD. For example, the average audio CD recorded at 128 Kbps takes up 60 to 80 MB of space. That means that a 700 MB CD-R can hold an average of ten complete CDs.*

It's easy to copy music from your PC to a portable device or CD-R by using Windows Media Player. Here's how:

1. Make playlists of all the music you want to copy.

2. Click the Sync tab.

3. Drag your playlist to the List pane. In Figure 20-17, the List pane now includes an icon of a portable device and tells you to Connect A Device and Drag Items Here.

4. Drag individual files to the List pane (if they are not part of a playlist and you want them on the device).

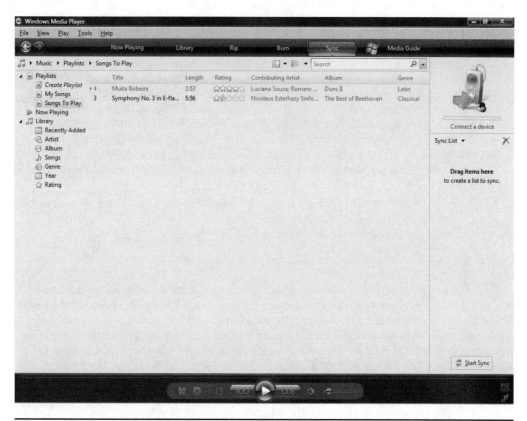

FIGURE 20-17 Sync your portable devices using Media Player.

5. Connect your device to your computer.

6. Click Start Sync. Windows Media Player displays the Sync page and shows the progress of copying files to your media device. When finished, you return to the Sync tab and you can disconnect your player and listen to your songs.

You can control how Windows Media Player copies files to portable players—choose Tools | Options and click the Devices tab of the Options dialog box to see a listing of your devices. If a device you have does not appear, then it is either not supported or not installed.

Customizing the Windows Media Player Window

Several years ago, WinAmp, a popular shareware MP3 player, popularized the ability to *skin* an application—that is, offer a variety of user interfaces so that you can choose among a number of window, menu, and button designs (or even create your own). In a complete turnaround from Microsoft's typical functional look, the company had integrated skins into Windows Media Player. In the past few editions of Media Player, colorful skins were included. Now, however, you can apply skins to Windows Media Player but you have to download them from the Internet first.

Licensing Issues for Digital Music

To protect music transferred from audio CDs or the Internet from being copied, Microsoft has integrated some protection features that prevent you from copying *unsigned* files to a portable device. A file is *signed* if you copied the music from an audio CD using Windows Media Player. When you copy music from an audio CD, Windows Media Player assumes that the music is licensed to you to use at your discretion (as long and you don't resell it or otherwise misrepresent the media to the general public). All files that you copy are encoded in Microsoft's proprietary WMA format by default, so you need a device that can play WMA files. You can also get signed music files by buying and downloading them from the Windows Media web site or other sites where music is offered legally.

NOTE *You are fairly safe from getting improperly licensed music from unknown online sources as long as you patronize the Windows Media web site (and maybe a few select partners). Any music purchased through the Windows Media site or from one of its partners is likely to be properly licensed.*

When you run Windows Media Player, it appears in Full mode, with all the buttons and controls we've described so far. To switch from Full mode to Skin mode, choose View | Skin Mode. Media Player includes two skins with Windows Vista: Corporate and Revert. Corporate appears like the Media Player window of old—a small rectangular box with few controls and no tabs. Revert is a tiny window that is handy for playing music, but not for showing videos. The screen is about a 2 inch by 2 inch square, as shown in Figure 20-18.

To see the skins, choose View | Skin Chooser. Click a skin and then click Apply Skin. To download skins, click More Skins. Internet Explorer opens to the Skins For Windows Media Player web page. Scroll down through the pages to find skins you like, and click the appropriate link to download the skin to Windows Media Player 11 for Vista.

CAUTION *Changing skins changes the locations of all the controls and the overall appearance of Windows Media Player, often drastically. Don't try changing the program's skins until you feel confident with the application as a whole. If you do get stuck, click the large Windows Media logo button that appears in a floating window.*

Skins are stored in files with the extension .wmz in the C:\Program Files\Windows Media Player\Skins folder (assuming that Windows is installed on C:).

TIP *Some skins consume lots of memory. If your computer's performance slows when you are using Windows Media Player, switch back to the default skin.*

Not only can you change Media Player's look and feel with skins, you also can configure a number of other settings. You can configure Windows Media Player by choosing Tools | Options to display the Options dialog box. The Player tab of the Options dialog box controls the program itself:

- **Automatic Updates** Specifies how often you want Windows Media Player to check the Microsoft web site for updates. You can also enable or disable automatic codec downloads.
- **Player Settings** Specifies how Windows Media Player looks when it starts.

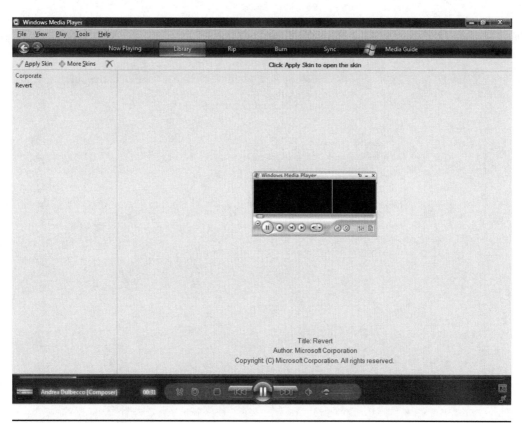

FIGURE 20-18   You can apply the Revert skin to make Media Player small.

Using Windows Vista Speech Recognition

Windows Vista includes a new technology to enable you to control your computer by voice commands. The tool is called Windows Speech Recognition. With a microphone attached to your computer and your voice, you can instruct Windows to perform several tasks, such as transcribe text, click buttons, and start programs.

To start using Windows Speech Recognition, do the following:

1. Choose Start | All Programs | Accessories | Ease Of Access | Windows Speech Recognition. The Set Up Speech Recognition wizard appears.

2. Click Next.

3. Select the type of microphone you have connected to your computer. Figure 20-19 shows some examples.

4. Click Next. You now must set up your microphone so that it is positioned optimally for your speech.

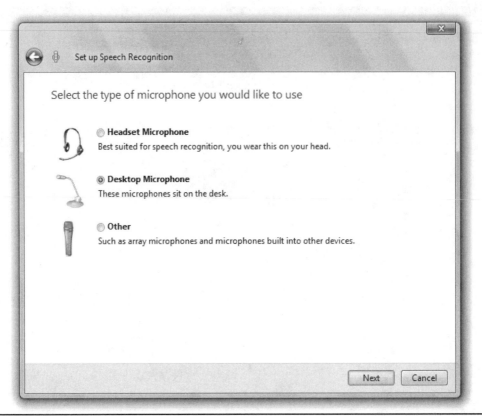

FIGURE 20-19   Specify your microphone type here.

5. Click Next. You now must speak into your microphone to set its volume level. You want to speak so that the voice indicator stays in the green area of the bar, as shown in Figure 20-20 (although it is in black and white in the book, you will know onscreen where the green area starts and ends). If your voice is too low, the indicator falls in the yellow; if your voice is too loud, the indicator goes to red. As you use the Windows Speech Recognition tool, try to keep your voice level the same all the time. You will get better results from the tool that way.

6. Click Next and then Next again.

7. Specify if you want Windows Speech Recognition to monitor your documents and e-mail creations to better recognize the type of language you use. This will help as you begin dictating documents.

8. Click Next. You can print a list of commands that Windows Speech Recognition recognizes by clicking the View Reference Sheet. For example, to double-click the Computer icon on your desktop, the command you give is "double-click computer."

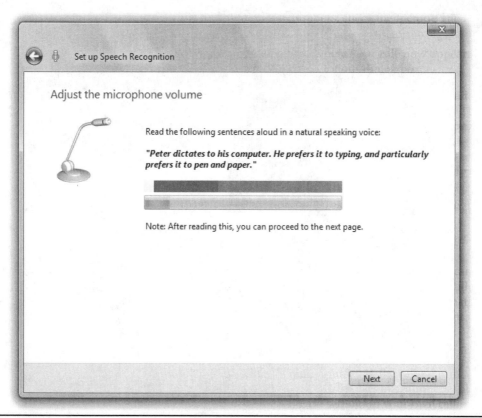

FIGURE 20-20 Set your volume level for using Windows Speech Recognition here.

9. Click Next. Make sure the Run Speech Recognition At Startup option is selected.

10. Click Next.

After you set up Windows Speech Recognition, take a few moments to walk through the tutorial. If you have never used a speech recognition tool, you will learn a lot about how to speak to control your computer properly. Click Start Tutorial to begin learning (see Figure 20-21).

In the tutorial, you learn the following:

- Basics of Windows Speech Recognition
- How to dictate to Windows to create documents and e-mails
- Ways to command Windows to perform tasks such as switching between windows and clicking buttons
- How to work inside windows to scroll, open files and programs, and navigate a window

PART IV

FIGURE 20-21   Use the Windows Speech Recognition Tutorial to learn how to speak to your computer.

When you finish your tutorial, start using Windows Speech Recognition in your daily computing life. The Windows Speech Recognition tool appears at the top of the screen. To begin, say "start listening."

Working with Video

Computers have been able to handle video data for decades—after all, when you use a computer you are already sitting in front of a video screen. Windows Vista supports video output on the screen, and video input if you add the necessary hardware to your computer. This chapter describes what formats video data is stored in, how to play video files using Windows Photo Gallery and Windows Media Player, and how to make your own video files using the Windows Movie Maker program. You are also shown how to view DVDs using Media Player.

NOTE *You can learn how to burn DVDs to make your own movies to play back on a home entertainment center, DVD player, or DVD computer drive in Chapter 22.*

How Does Windows Work with Video Data?

You can use various *video capture* devices, such as digital video cameras, to get video information into your computer. See Chapter 14 for instructions on how to install video capture devices. To display video, Windows uses your screen, and to play the accompanying audio, it uses your sound board and speakers.

Because the amount of data coming from a digital video camera is so immense, your computer can't process and store it fast enough. Instead, video data is compressed on its way into the computer from the camera and is then stored in a compressed format. A very fast *DSP* (*digital signal processor*, a kind of specialized computer) chip in your video capture hardware does the actual compression. Windows comes with a number of *codecs*, programs for video compression and decompression, so that it can decompress and recompress video data when you want to display or edit it. Windows also includes *DirectX*, a feature that enhances video playback. Windows stores most video in *AVI files* or *WMV files*, files with the filename extension .avi or .wmv. Other popular formats for video files are QuickTime (.qt) and MPEG (.mpg).

To see a list of your installed video capture devices, choose Start, then right-click Computer and choose Properties. Click Device Manager and double-click the Imaging Devices item. A list of your video cameras, digital cameras, and other imaging devices appears. To see a list of codecs that are available, open Media Player, choose Help | About Windows Media Player, and click the Technical Support Information link. A web page

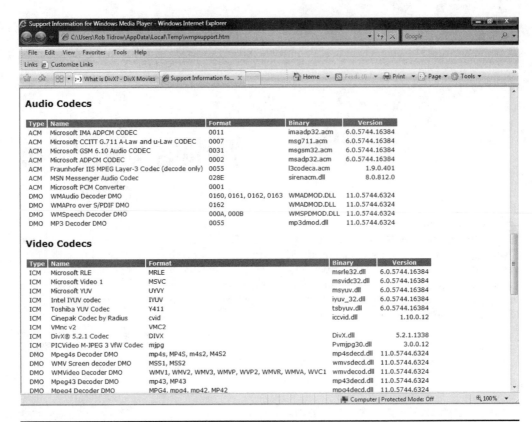

Figure 21-1   View your installed video and audio codecs on this Windows Media Player troubleshooting web page.

appears (see Figure 21-1) that lists files used with Windows Media Player. Scroll down the list to view tables named Audio Codecs and Video Codecs.

Playing Video Files with Windows

Windows provides three ways to view videos on your computer:

- Windows Photo Gallery
- Windows Media Player
- Windows Media Center

We discuss Windows Media Center in Chapter 22, and we discussed Windows Photo Gallery in Chapter 19. In this chapter, we do show how to start videos in Windows Photo Gallery, but we focus on Windows Media Player for much of the chapter.

Playing Video Files Using Windows Photo Gallery

Probably the easiest way to manage your video is with the new Windows Photo Gallery application. In this program you can do the following tasks with your videos:

- View your videos in the Windows Photo Gallery window.
- Add tags to videos to help you organize videos and search for them.
- Rename and delete videos.
- Organize videos into subfolders.
- Send your videos to someone else using e-mail.
- Burn a movie to a CD or DVD.
- Use the video in Windows Movie Maker 6 to create your own movie.
- Open the movie in Windows Media Player or another program.

To start Windows Photo Gallery, choose Start | All Programs | Windows Photo Gallery. You see a window similar to the one shown in Figure 21-2. On the left is the Navigation

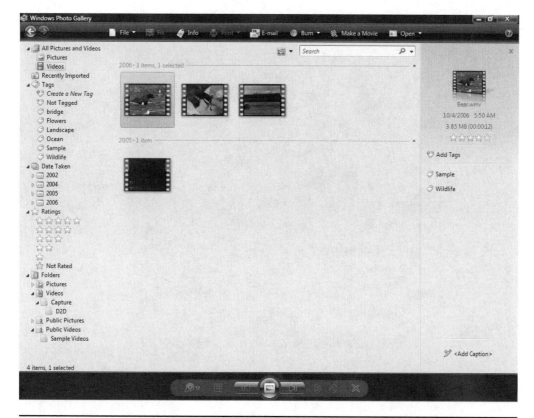

FIGURE 21-2   You can use Windows Photo Gallery to organize and view videos on your computer.

Pane that includes folders, tags, and other items to help you organize and sort your files (videos and pictures).

To view a video, select it from a folder that includes videos. For example, when you install Windows Vista, you are given some sample videos that are stored in the Videos folder. At the top of the Windows Photo Gallery Navigation Pane there is a selection called All Pictures And Videos, with a subfolder called Videos. Click that subfolder to see what's inside it. Your samples may be called something like Bear, Butterfly, and Lake. You can see the name of a video file by clicking it and viewing the name in the Info pane on the right side of the Windows Media Player window, as shown in Figure 21-3.

Playing Video Files Using Windows Media Player

Another way to view your videos is with the Windows Media Player. This is the primary way to view videos if you insert a disc containing a video file, launch a video from your hard drive (such as in Windows Explorer), or run one from an e-mail message or an Internet site. To start Windows Media Player, choose Start | All Programs | Windows Media Player, choose Start | Windows Media Player (if the program is on your Start menu), or click the Windows Media Player icon on the Quick Launch toolbar on the taskbar (if your taskbar

FIGURE 21-3   Windows Photo Gallery can play back your videos.

includes this toolbar). In addition, when you configure Windows AutoPlay to play DVDs or movie files using Windows Media Player, Media Player starts when you insert DVDs or discs with movie files on them. Figure 21-4 shows Windows Media Player playing a video.

NOTE *Windows Media Player can't play all types of video files. To play Apple QuickTime files (.qt), you need the QuickTime viewer, available at www.apple.com/quicktime. Windows Media Player, however, can play the popular MPEG format.*

Playing Video Files from Your Hard Disk

To play a video file that does not appear on the Windows Photo Gallery Navigation Pane, open Windows Explorer and double-click the video file. The default program for playing videos (usually this is set to Windows Media Player when you install Windows Vista) opens and plays back your video. If you are already in Windows Media Player and want to display a video from your hard drive (or other drive), choose File | Open from the Windows Media Player menu bar, or press CTRL-O. In the Open dialog box that appears, navigate to your video file and click Open.

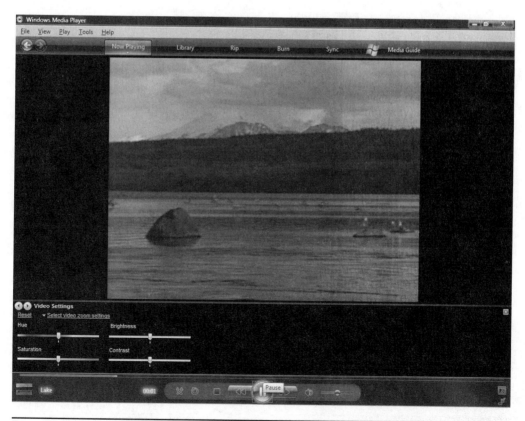

FIGURE 21-4   Windows Photo Gallery can play back your videos, too.

NOTE   Make sure to set the Media Files drop-down list to Media Files (All Types) to see all types of video files.

You can also drag a video file (or any multimedia file) from the desktop or an Explorer window into the Windows Media Player Now Playing tab. This causes Windows Media Player to play back the video. (If you drag a file to the Windows Photo Gallery window, the file is moved there but does not play.)

When you open a file, Windows Media Player loads the video file, switches to the Now Playing tab, and displays the video in the video screen part of the Windows Media Player window. If it's not already playing, click the Play button to start the video, which appears in the video screen (middle) section of the Windows Media Player window.

While you are playing a video file, you can also perform these actions:

- Stop the video by clicking the Stop button.
- View the image full-screen by pressing ALT-ENTER or by choosing View | Full Screen from the menu bar (see Figure 21-5). To return from full-screen display, press ESC.

FIGURE 21-5   View a video in full-screen mode in Windows Media Player.

- Move forward or backward in the file by clicking the Rewind and Fast Forward buttons (the VCR-style buttons along the bottom of the window) or by dragging the Position slider.

- Adjust the volume by clicking and dragging the Volume slider or by choosing Play | Volume from the menu bar.

If you are experiencing video problems and suspect your video card is the cause, you can change your acceleration setting. Choose Tools | Options from the menu and click the Performance tab, as shown in Figure 21-6. Clear the Use Video Smoothing and Turn On DirectX Video Acceleration For WMV Files options. Click OK and run your video again.

Playing Streaming Video Files from the Internet

Video files tend to be huge because each frame of a video requires many thousands of bytes of information. Viewing video over the Internet can involve long waits for video files to complete downloading. The advent of streaming video improved matters: you can begin playing a streaming video file after only a portion of the file has arrived (see "What Is

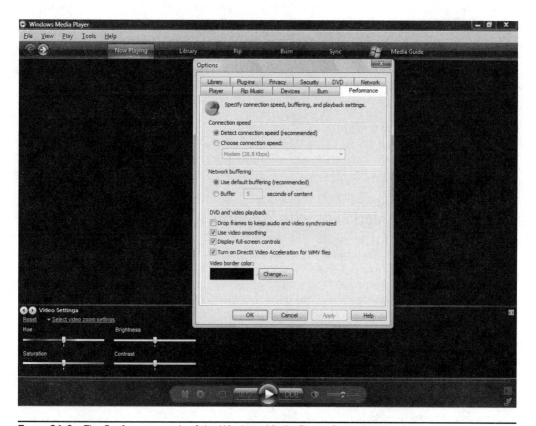

FIGURE 21-6   The Performance tab of the Windows Media Player Options dialog box.

Streaming Audio?" in Chapter 20). Usually the video plays inside a web browser to let you enjoy the video without leaving the browser window. The streaming video player continues to receive parts of the file at the same time that it is playing earlier parts. As long as the program can receive information at least as fast as it can play it, you see uninterrupted video. Streaming audio files and players work the same way.

One of the most popular streaming video formats is RealVideo (with extension .rv). You can download the RealPlayer program for free from the Real web site at www.real.com; this program works with your web browser to play RealAudio and RealVideo files from the Internet.

Microsoft has its own streaming video format, called *Advanced Streaming Format (ASF)*. Files in this format have the extension .asf or .asx. *ASF files* with the .asf extension contain the actual streaming video data. *ASX files* with the .asx extension contain a single line of text, with the URL of a continuously updating video newsfeed. Windows Media Player can play both ASF and ASX files. Normally, Windows Media Player runs automatically inside your web browser (Internet Explorer, for instance) when you start to download an ASF, ASX, or other supported streaming file from the Internet. You can also run Windows Media Player and then open the streaming file by choosing File | Open URL from the menu.

When you see a link on a web page for a video file that you want to play, click the link. Depending on how your web browser is configured, you may see a message asking whether to open the file or save it; choose to open the file. Your browser downloads the first section of the file, runs a Windows Media Player applet in your web browser, and begins to play the file. The video may appear in your browser window (see Figure 21-7) or in a separate window. Some video files may also display a separate window in which the video plays.

You can use the Stop, Pause, and Play buttons to stop and start the video. When you are done playing the video, close the Windows Media Player window if it remains open. If you started viewing the video by clicking a link in your web browser, the browser window is probably still open where you left it.

To find video to watch on the Internet, you can use the Media Guide button on the Windows Media Player toolbar, as shown in Figure 21-8 (see "Playing Streaming Audio Files from the Internet" in Chapter 20).

Creating and Editing Video Files with Windows Movie Maker 6

Windows Movie Maker 6 is an upgrade to Movie Maker 2 that was delivered as part of Windows XP, Service Pack 2. It enables you to edit graphical, audio, and video files into movies that are stored in video files that you can play with Windows Media Player. Although Movie Maker 6 includes many of the same features of earlier versions, plus a few nice enhancements, there is one main difference between the versions: your computer must be capable of running the Windows Vista Aero interface in order to run Movie Maker 6. For Movie Maker 6, you need a system that has the following specifications:

- Processor that is rate at 1 GHz or higher
- 1 GB of random access memory (RAM) or more
- Graphics adapter that has at least 128 MB RAM
- Graphics adapter that supports DirectX 9

FIGURE 21-7   View videos on a web page using the Windows Media Player applet.

If your system does not meet the preceding requirements, Windows displays the message shown in Figure 21-9 when you attempt to start Windows Movie Maker 6.

After you upgrade your system to meet the Aero requirements, or purchase a computer that does, you can run Movie Maker 6. When you use Movie Maker to create movies, you first create a file called a *project*, with the extension .mswmm. Each project can contain one or more *collections*, which are lists of items to include in the movie. A collection contains *clips*, which can be video, audio, or still-graphics files. Information about your collections is stored in your Videos folder by default, which is in your Documents folder. You can, however, save the information in any folder or network folder you have access to. Once you've created your movie, you can publish it as a video file in Windows Media format with the extension .wmv. Movie Maker also allows you to publish it to different mediums, including saving it to your hard drive, sending it as an e-mail attachment, recording it to a video tape, burning it to a DVD, or burning it to a CD.

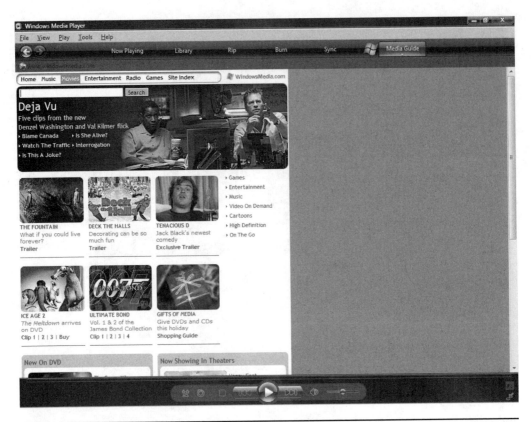

FIGURE 21-8 The Media Guide button offers links to online video—some appear in the Windows Media Player window, but most play in your browser.

The Windows Movie Maker Window

To open Windows Movie Maker, choose Start | All Programs | Windows Movie Maker. The Windows Movie Maker window has four areas and several toolbars, as shown in Figure 21-10. The parts of the window follow:

- **Collections list**   Lists the collections in this project.
- **Clips**   Shows icons for each clip in the currently selected collection. Clips can include graphics files, audio files, or video files. For graphics files, you see a small version of the file (a *thumbnail*). For audio files, you see a speaker icon. For video files, you see a thumbnail of a scene from the video.
- **Monitor**   Displays the current clip or movie as you work on it. If you click a graphics file clip, the graphic appears in the monitor. If you click a video clip, the clip plays in the monitor. If you click an audio clip, that clip plays in the monitor. As you create your movie using the workspace (described next), you can view your movie in the monitor. Below the monitor are VCR-style buttons to play the current clip.

FIGURE 21-9   Windows Vista displays a warning message when your system cannot run Movie Maker 6.

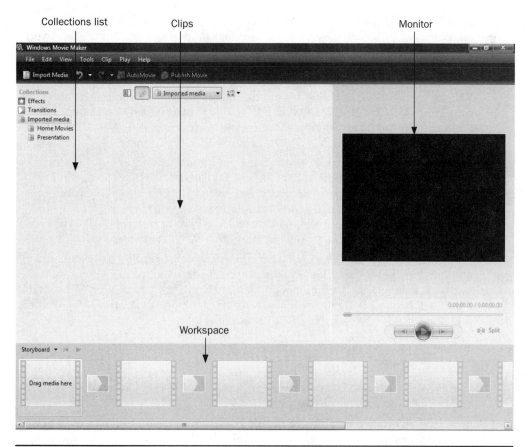

FIGURE 21-10   The Windows Movie Maker editor window, where you compose the next Oscar winner.

- **Workspace** Displays the timeline or storyboard of your movie, as explained in the section "Composing Your Movie" later in this chapter.

If you've already been working on a movie, Windows Movie Maker opens the last project you opened. You can open any existing project by choosing File | Open Project from the menu.

Importing Files

Before you can create a movie, you need to import video, audio, and graphic information with which to make the movie. Depending on where your picture, sound, and video information comes from, you need the appropriate hardware or access to get that information onto your computer. The following are the three types of information you can import:

- **Video** Movie Maker lets you import video from CDs, DVDs, Internet downloads, removable drives, or video recorders. The easiest way to import your own video is to capture it on a digital video recorder and then transfer it to your computer via a FireWire port, USB port, or other input port that supports video file transfer. If you want to import video from an older video camera (such as an 8 mm or VHS tape), you need a video capture card. Both ATI (ati.amd.com) and Creative Labs (us. creativelabs.com) make reasonably priced video capture cards. Finally, for older VHS tape you may have laying around the house, some video equipment stores can copy your videotapes to CD-ROM or DVD, which you can then import into Windows Movie Maker. Windows Movie Maker can import ASF, AVI, MLV, MP2, MP2V, MPE, MPEG, MPG, MPV2, WM, and WMV video format files.

- **Audio** You can capture audio with your computer by using Windows Media Player to capture music from audio CDs and DVDs (see "Playing and Recording WAV Sound Files with Sound Recorder" in Chapter 20). Other sources include digital music devices (such as an MP3 player), removable drives, Internet downloads, and network drives. Windows Media Player can import AIF, AIFC, AIFF, ASF, AU, MP2, MP3, MPA, SND, WAV, and WMA audio files.

- **Still pictures** You can use a digital camera or scanner to capture still pictures in graphics files (see Chapter 19). You can also create drawings or titles using Microsoft Paint or another graphics editor (see "Drawing Pictures with Microsoft Paint" in Chapter 19). Windows Movie Maker can import BMP, DIP, EMF, GIF, JFIG, JPE, JPEG, PNG, TIF, TIFF, and WMF graphic files.

Once you have graphic, audio, or video files, you can import them into Windows Movie Maker. Follow these steps:

1. Run Windows Movie Maker and open your project, if it's not already open. To create a new project, choose File | New Project.

2. Select the collection into which you want to import the files. You can create a new collection for them by selecting the top-level collection (Collections) and choosing File New | Collection Folder.

3. Choose File | Import Media Items or press CTRL-I to import media files you have stored on your hard drive (or another disk location). You see the Import Media

Items dialog box. (To import from a video camera, choose File | Import From Digital Video Camera to start the Import Video wizard. See the next section for more information.)

4. Select the file or files to import. You can select more than one file by holding the SHIFT or CTRL key while selecting files.

5. Click Import. The files are added to the active collection.

TIP   *Another way to import files is to drag-and-drop them into the Windows Movie Maker window.*

After you import information into the program, Windows Movie Maker shows each clip as a little icon in the current collection. You can find out more about any clip by right-clicking it and choosing Properties from the shortcut menu that appears. To play a single clip, select it and click the Play button on the VCR-style buttons just below the monitor (the leftmost button).

You can organize your clips into collections by dragging the clips from one collection to another, or by using cut-and-paste (CTRL-X to cut and CTRL-V to paste).

NOTE   *If you don't have any video, just place all of your still pictures in a collection and make a slide show with still pictures and a soundtrack or narration.*

Importing Videos

To import video from a video camera to use in Movie Maker 6, you use the Import Video tool. The Import Video tool enables you to import an entire tape or select parts of it to import. As it imports the video, Movie Maker creates clips and displays them in the Clips area of the Movie Maker window. When you choose to import the entire tape, Import Video rewinds the tape to the beginning, starts the import process, and goes until the tape ends. If you choose to select only parts of the video, you can control the starting place of the import (for example, fast forward the tape to a specific position), and then stop the import manually or tell the Import Video tool to stop after so many minutes.

If your video camera is connected to your computer already, you can start the Import Video tool by choosing Tools | Import From Digital Video Camera from the Movie Maker menu bar. The Import Video window appears, in which you can specify a name for the clips that will be imported, the location of the clips, and the format (AVI or WMV format). Click Next. You then choose to import the entire tape or only part of the tape to your computer. Click Next. The Import Video window appears, as shown in Figure 21-11. We selected to import only parts of the video, so we are given controls to position the video to the starting point we want, which may or may not be the beginning of the tape. Use the Digital Video Camera Controls at the top of the window to move the tape to where you want to start importing. Another handy feature of the Import Video tool involves the Stop Importing After (Min) option. This lets you specify how many minutes of recording you want to import.

NOTE   *The Import Video tool also launches when you connect your video camera to your computer and the AutoPlay setting is set to Launch Import Video. Video clips are automatically imported to the Videos subfolder in your user folder.*

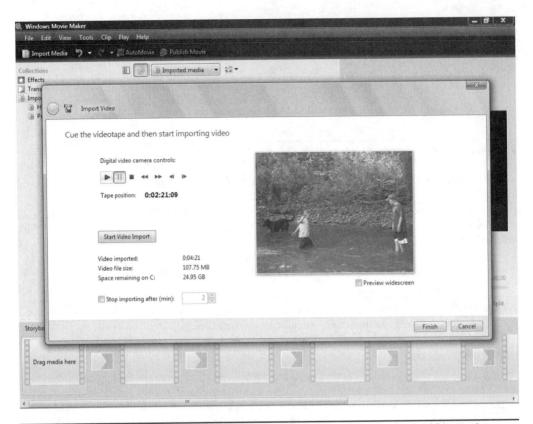

FIGURE 21-11   Import your home movies from digital video cameras using the Import Video tool.

After you set up your tape settings, click Start Video Import. The Import Video tool begins importing the video to your computer. You can then click Stop Video Import (the Start Video Import button changes to Stop Video Import as the import process begins) when the portion you want to import has completed. Cue up the next portion to import and click the Start Video Import button again. Repeat the start and stop process as many times to import sections of your tape.

Click Finish when you have finished importing your video. Movie Maker imports the video clips into your current collection and displays them in the Clips area, as shown in Figure 21-12.

TIP   *When you import a video file, Windows Movie Maker automatically breaks it into clips, based on where it thinks the scenes start and end.*

Composing Your Movie

The Workspace area at the bottom of the Windows Movie Maker window displays either the Storyboard or the Timeline. To create a movie out of your clips, you drag them to the Storyboard or Timeline in the order that you want them shown.

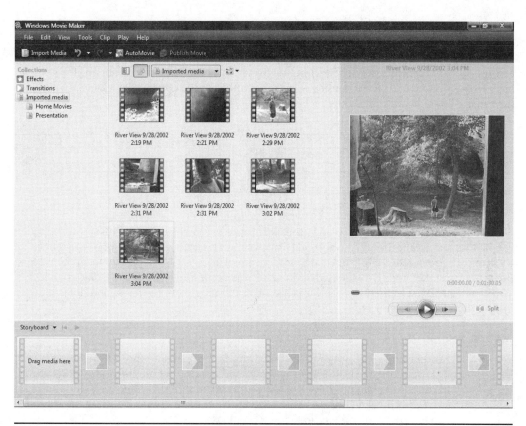

FIGURE 21-12 Movie Maker shows imported clips in the Clips area.

The *Storyboard* is like a book, in which each blank square is like the page of a book, and you decide what appears on each page and in what order. Find the first clip—either video or graphic file—and drag it to the first space in the Storyboard. This clip becomes the first page of your story, and the first part of your movie. Continue dragging video and graphic clips to the Storyboard in the order in which you want them to appear. You can always switch the order later. With clips, the Storyboard looks like this:

TIP *To move clips around after you've placed them in the Storyboard, just drag them left or right. When a line appears between the clips where you would like to place the clip to be reordered, drop it.*

The *Timeline* gives you another view of the same movie. Display it in the Workspace area by clicking the Storyboard drop-down arrow at the left side of the Workspace and clicking Timeline (switch back to the Storyboard by clicking the Workspace drop-down arrow). You also can choose View | Timeline from the menu (View | Storyboard takes you back to the Storyboard). The Timeline shows the timing of the clips in the movie, displaying how many seconds each clip takes:

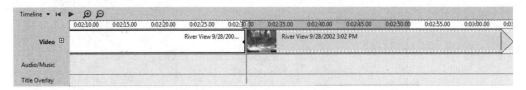

You can add, delete, and rearrange the clips (only video or graphics clips; audio clips can be inserted on the Timeline only) on either the Storyboard or the Timeline—the effect is the same. If you delete a clip from the Storyboard or Timeline, it disappears from the movie, but remains in the project, available for reuse. If you don't think you'll use a clip after all, you can delete by selecting it in the Clips area and pressing DELETE—this action deletes the information from the project.

Adding Sound

To provide a soundtrack, you can drag an audio clip to the Timeline (not the Storyboard). The audio clip runs along the bottom of the Timeline, showing where the audio starts and ends. You can control the balance between the sound portion of the video clips and of the audio soundtrack by choosing Tools | Audio Levels from the menu and sliding the slider between Audio From Video and Audio/Music:

You can record a narration to go with your slide show or video. The idea is to synchronize what you're saying with what's appearing on the screen. (Note: Your computer needs a working microphone to record the narration.) Follow these steps:

1. Choose Tools | Narrate Times to display the Narrate Timeline window.

2. When you're ready, click the Start Narration button. Be prepared—as soon as you click the Record button, Windows Movie Maker begins recording and playing the video at the same time.

3. Talk along with the movie.

4. When you're finished, click the Stop Narration button. Windows Movie Maker prompts you to save your narration and imports it into your project.

5. Click Close to close the Narrate Timeline window and return to the main Movie Maker window.

TIP *Run through your video a few times, clicking Pause and making some notes. Then spend some time rehearsing. Don't try to be James Earl Jones, but you'll gain appreciation if you do a well-timed job.*

Previewing Your Movie

After you add the clips for your movie, you can see how it looks. Choose Play | Play Storyboard/Timeline from the menu, or right-click the Storyboard or Timeline and choose Play Storyboard/Timeline from the shortcut menu that appears. You can also play a section of the movie by selecting a series of clips from the Storyboard and clicking the Play button below the Monitor. Or, select all of the clips on the Storyboard (right-click any clip and choose Select All) and then click the Play VCR button below the Monitor.

Editing Your Movie

Windows Movie Maker includes many commands for editing your movie. Here are a few neat things you can do:

- **Slide shows**   If you put a graphic file in your movie, Windows Movie Maker shows it for five seconds. You can make a good-looking slide show that you can send to people through e-mail, just by adding your still photos to the Storyboard of a movie. You can change the five-second length to speed up or slow down your slide show. On the Timeline, select the clip for the still photo. A double-sided arrow appears. Click-and-drag to the right to add time to the clip, or to the left to subtract time from it.

- **Transitions**   You can create a fading transition from one video or picture to the next. Click the first clip of the pair. A pair of triangles appears along the top of the clip. Drag the right triangle into the next clip, so the clips appear to overlap:

The wider the overlap, the longer the transition will be.

NOTE *Windows Movie Maker includes integrated transition effects as well. Click the Transitions collection in the Collections pane to choose a transition.*

Movie Maker 6 also includes a number of built-in transitions. To use these, click Transitions in the Collections area. The Clip area changes to show you the built-in effects, such as Bars Horizontal, Circle, Heart, and more. To add one to your movie, drag it to the Timeline or Storyboard between the clips at the place you want the transition to occur.

- **Effects**   Movie Maker includes effects that change the look of your clips. For example, one of the effects is called Film Grain. This changes the clip in the movie so that it appears old and grainy. The effects do not change the clip itself, just how that clip appears in that portion of your movie. To add an effect, you must be in Timeline view and click the Effects item in the Collections area. Drag an effect from the Clips area to the Timeline of your movie. To remove an effect, right-click the clip in which the effect appears, and click Effects to display the Add Or Remove Effects dialog box. Select the effect in the Displayed Effects pane, and click Remove. Click OK. You can also use this dialog box to add effects to your clip.

- **Titling**   Windows Movie Maker includes a nice feature to let you add titles and credits to your movies. Click Tools | Title And Credits to display the title window (see Figure 21-13). This window includes links for creating titles and credits. Click one and enter the title or credit information (such as Director—Your Name), click

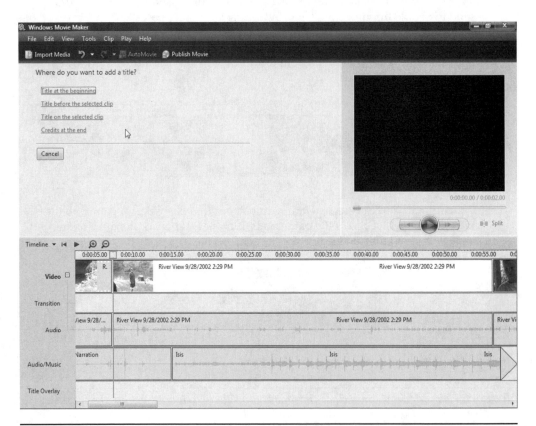

FIGURE 21-13   You can also add titles and credits to your movie using Windows Movie Maker.

the options if you want to change how the title or credit text appears, and click Add Title. You can choose to add titles to the beginning of the movie, before a selected clip, or on a selected clip. Credits go at the end of the movie.

Saving Your Project

You can save your project so that you can return to it later and make edits to it. To do this, choose File | Save Project. If this is the first time you have saved the project, enter a filename and click Save. Movie Maker saves it as an MSWMM file.

Publishing Your Movie

Once your movie shines, click the Publish Movie button on the toolbar or choose File | Publish Movie from the menu. You see the Publish Movie dialog box. You can choose which delivery medium you want to use to publish your movie:

- This computer
- DVD
- Recordable CD
- E-mail
- Digital video camera

Click a choice based on your output needs and then click Next. The next screen asks you to give the movie a filename. Click Next. Now choose the settings for the movie. Here you can set the compression ratio of your movie to limit its file size. As you compress the movie, you decrease the overall quality of the movie as well as the playback size of the movie. For this reason, you may want to use the This Computer option to publish your movie to, select a compression rating, and then experiment with the setting at different sizes. You will, however, need to open your original project file, click the Publish Movie button, provide a new filename (to distinguish it from the first file), and click This Computer to set up different quality settings.

When you are ready to publish the movie, click Publish. Depending on the choices you have made, such as the medium to which you want to publish the movie, the Publish Movie wizard guides you through each step. For example, if you choose to send the movie via e-mail, Movie Maker creates the movie and then displays your default e-mail program's new message window with the complete movie attached to the message. You just have to address the message, add a subject, enter some body text for the message, and click Send.

Playing Video Disks (DVDs)

A *DVD* (*Digital Versatile Disk* or *Digital Video Disk*) is like a large CD—it's a digital disk that can contain video material. If you buy movies on DVDs and you have a DVD drive connected to your computer, you can play DVDs on your computer by using the Windows Media Player program or Windows Media Center. To read more about Media Center, see the next chapter.

NOTE *You cannot play a DVD movie with just a DVD drive and a disc. You must also have a decoder, either built into the drive, on a separate card (or integrated into your system's video card), or from a software package like WinDVD or PowerDVD. Windows Vista includes a DVD decoder program built into the operating system files when you install Windows. Your DVD player may have come with its own player program that you can use for playing DVDs—you don't have to use the Windows Media Player program.*

Playing a DVD with Windows Media Player

To play a DVD, insert the DVD in your DVD drive, and Windows Media Player starts automatically. When you are playing a DVD, the Windows Media Player works like a VCR (as shown in Figure 21-14). Additional controls may appear for the advanced features that a specific DVD offers: consult the DVD itself. These advanced features may play video clips, alternative edits, different endings, or the ever-popular outtakes. Windows Media Player has a few added DVD interface options. Right-click the movie and choose DVD Features. This shows the features available for that movie, such as Root Menu, Title Menu, and Camera Angle.

FIGURE 21-14   Windows Media Player playing a DVD.

Controlling Rated Movies

One popular feature with parents is playback restrictions, which is amazingly simple and effective. The playback restrictions feature uses the already existing and well-established MPAA ratings system. Each DVD movie has a lot of additional information encoded into the DVD, including the movie's rating, so the decoder software can tell a G-rated movie from an NC17-rated movie.

Before you can use playback restrictions, you must set up user accounts for yourself and other users of the computer (see Chapter 6). Assuming that you are a parent, give yourself and other adults administrative user accounts, and make any children's accounts limited user accounts. Once you set a maximum DVD rating in Media Player's playback restrictions, only administrative users can play DVDs with higher ratings.

To control which DVDs people can play on Windows Media Player, choose Tools | Options and click the DVD tab (shown in Figure 21-15). Click the Change button under DVD Playback Restrictions. From the drop-down list in the Change Rating Restriction dialog box, select the highest rating that you want nonadministrative users of the computer to be able to play.

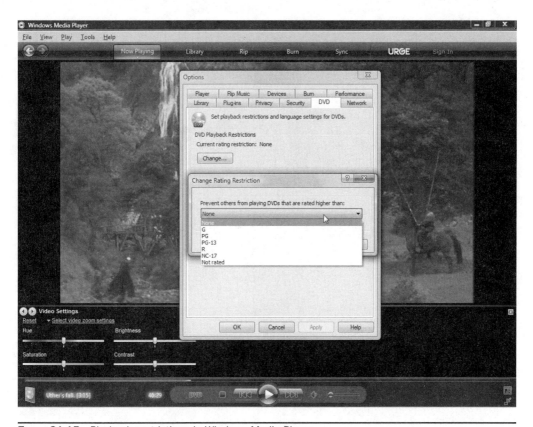

FIGURE 21-15 Playback restrictions in Windows Media Player.

Working with Windows Media Center

Computers are now everywhere, even in people's kitchens and garages. Many users find that they want to control their home entertainment systems using the power of their computer. Now they can with Windows Media Center. It includes many multimedia features that let users control TV shows, record and play back TV shows, view slide shows of their pictures, burns DVDs, and perform other tasks using their computer and a TV. With Media Center, user can use a Media Center Remote Control and Receiver device or a Media Center Keyboard to navigate the Media Center interface while they relax in the comfort of their living room. This chapter introduces the features of Media Center.

NOTE *Media Center includes a number of options and features that are beyond the scope of this chapter and this book. Consult a separate title that discusses Media Center in detail to learn all about its features.*

What Is Media Center?

When Microsoft released its first version of Media Center, it was a separate operating system users could install to replace their current operating system. With Windows Vista, however, Media Center has become a part of the operating system, essentially an application users can launch. Windows Media Center provides a centralized entertainment hub to let you control other home entertainment devices. For example, one feature of Media Center is the Live TV tool, with which you can watch TV shows using Windows Vista and a TV tuner installed in your computer. Along with watching TV shows, you also can record shows to watch at a later time (see Figure 22-1), or pause, rewind, and fast forward shows as you watch them. By connecting your computer's TV tuner to a TV set (it becomes the display by which you view your computer output), you can view the TV shows on your regular TV set but have it controlled by Windows Media Center.

FIGURE 22-1   Record, watch, and pause live TV using Media Center and a TV tuner card.

NOTE *A TV tuner is a hardware device that you can install in your computer or connect via USB port that enables you to receive TV signals on your computer. TV tuners come in varying designs and capabilities, but most of them support cable, satellite, and antenna hookups. Many of the newer ones also support HDTV (high-definition television) standards. To learn more about TV tuner hardware, visit Pinnacle Systems at www.pinnaclesystems.com and Hauppague Computer Works at www.hauppauge.com/index.htm. These companies produce and sell TV tuners compatible with Windows Vista.*

The idea behind Media Center is to allow you to integrate your PC into your everyday entertainment life. The features of Media Center include the following:

- **Pictures + Videos**   Organize, play back, and delete photographs and videos. You also can watch a slide show of your pictures. Media Center stores images in the Picture Library and stores videos in the Video Library.

- **Music**   Play music stored on your computer in the Music Library, play back all your music by clicking Play All, tune into radio stations using an FM tuner (a hardware device you must have on your computer) or Internet radio software, and search for music in your Music Library.

- **TV + Movies**   Record and play back TV shows, watch TV shows live, access the Program Guide to get a listing of upcoming shows and to set up Media Center to record future shows, access the Movies Guide for a listing of upcoming movies that will be showing on your local TV stations, play DVDs, and search for shows and movies listed in the Program Guide, Movies Guide, or saved on your computer.

- **Online Media**   Access the Program Library, which enables you to access online media tools and files, such as online games, news and sports reports and shows, lifestyle segments, and more. You also can share pictures with other users, download movies, and find and download online music.

- **Tasks**   Set up and configure Media Center for it to work with your TV tuner, allow it to locate and monitor videos and images to add to the Picture and Video Libraries, burn CDs or DVDs, synchronize digital devices, set up Windows Media Center Extender devices, and more.

Setting Up Media Center

To start Media Center, choose Start | All Programs | Windows Media Center. The first time you start Media Center, you are prompted to set it up. Media Center provides options to set up your version of Media Center: Express Setup and Custom Setup. Express Setup is more automatic than Custom Setup. With Custom Setup, you walk through each step of the configuration process to set up all features of Media Center. This includes specifying the type of display you use (TV set, computer monitor, digital projector, and so on), which folders you want Media Center to use to build your Pictures Library and Video Library, the type of Internet connection you have, and more.

After you finish setting up Media Center, you can modify the settings using the Settings window (see Figure 22-2).

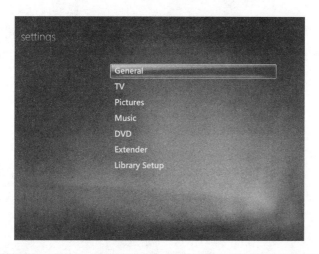

FIGURE 22-2   Use the Setting window to configure settings after you initially set up Media Center.

Viewing the Media Center Interface

When first start using Media Center, you may be taken aback by its predominate use of blue and white colors. An important feature of Windows Media Center is its interface. The interface uses highly contrasting colors to help you read and pick options on the screen. Microsoft designed Media Center to be displayed on TVs that are viewed from several feet away, such as from across your living room or home theatre room.

In addition to its color, the interface uses large buttons and controls. This makes it easy to pick the items you want onscreen. Users sitting in front of their computer will use a mouse to pick buttons and items on the Media Center screen. Users that have an optional wireless Media Center Keyboard or Remote Control and Receiver device find that picking items onscreen easier when the buttons are large like this.

NOTE *Microsoft manufactures the Media Center Keyboard and Media Center Remote Control and Receiver devices. You can learn more about these products and find retailers for them by visiting the Windows Marketplace web site at www.windowsmarketplace.com. You also can choose Start | All Programs | Windows Marketplace to open Internet Explorer to that site.*

Figure 22-3 shows examples of the large buttons and items you can click on a typical Media Center window. Notice how each item in the Pictures list has large check boxes and radio buttons. When using the Media Center Remote Control, you can navigate through these options easily using the directional buttons, and then press ENTER to select an item. Also, as you move the mouse over an option, the option becomes darker so that you know which item you are selecting.

Navigating Media Center

To navigate inside Media Center, you start at the main Media Center window. The main Media Center window includes the primary tools from which you can select a feature to start. You select an item by displaying it in the center selection box and then clicking it. The primary

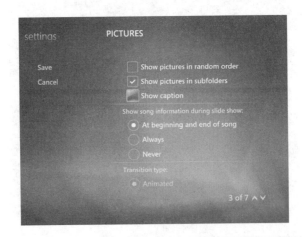

FIGURE 22-3 Windows Media Center uses large text and buttons to make it easy to read and select onscreen items.

Figure 22-4   Media Center provides a handy way to select the tool and feature you want to use.

tools (TV + Movies, Online Media, Tasks, Pictures + Videos, and Music) appear in a vertical list in the center of the main Media Center window. You can click one of these items to cause the list to scroll one item at a time. Click until the feature you want is highlighted above the center selection box. For example, in Figure 22-4 the Picture Library tool is selected.

Another way to move items through the selection box is with the directional arrows. When you select an item, up and down arrows appear above and below the list of tools. Hover the mouse over one of these arrows and Media Center scrolls through the list of tools one at a time until you move the pointer away from the arrow.

Features for each of the primary tools display horizontally. Select one of these to have it display in the selection box. For example, in Figure 22-4 the Picture Library feature displays inside the center selection box. You can click it to start it, or click another feature (such as Play All) to start that feature. Some tools include several features, while others may have only one or two.

As you start moving from one window to the next, you may want to jump back a window, or jump all the way back to the starting window. To do this, use the controls that briefly appear at the top left of each window. There is a left arrow and a Media Center icon. The left arrow moves you back to the previous windows. Move the pointer for these controls to appear on the window. The Media Center icon returns you to the main Media Center window. If you are still viewing a movie, watching a show, playing music, or performing other tasks, those tasks continue to play in the background even as you jump from one window to the next.

Watch and Record Television with Media Center

One of the most popular features of Media Center is its Live TV feature. With it you can watch TV through a TV tuner, record TV shows to your hard drive, play back shows, pause live shows, and use the Program Guide to find shows of interest.

NOTE *You must have your TV tuner installed and configured to watch and record TV shows.*

To start watching live TV, select the TV + Movies tool and then click Live TV. Media Center displays the Live TV window. You can change channels by using the Media Center Remote Control and Receiver device or by clicking the onscreen controls that appear when you move the pointer. They appear at the bottom right of the screen. Press + to move up one station or – to move down. The current station, the name of the program, the running time of the program, and the current time display in a small window, as shown in Figure 22-5.

Another way to access TV shows is to use the Program Guide (shown in Figure 22-6). This is an electronic "TV guide" that offers you listings of shows in your area for a two-week block of time. You can access it by clicking Guide when choosing TV + Movies from the main Media Center window. The Program Guide downloads and is stored on your hard drive. Updates are downloaded daily automatically by Media Center. To view a show in the Program Guide, click it.

You also can right-click a show to get a menu of commands such as Program Info, Record, Record Series, Categories, and Settings. If you click Program Info from this menu, you see a Program Info screen like the one shown in Figure 22-7. You can read the program description, set up recording tasks, and see when the show is scheduled to appear again (click Other Showings for that information).

The Program Guide also lets you view listings by station. Click a station in the left column. A listing for that station appears with the next six time blocks displaying. If you want to see listings organized by categories, return to the Program Guide main window and click the Categories button on the far left. Media Center lets you list programs by the following categories:

- Most Viewed
- Movies
- Sports
- Kids
- News
- Special

Click a category to see the type of show you want to watch.

To record a show, right-click a listing and click Record. If the show is on now, Media Center begins recording the show (even if you want to watch another show at the same time). If the show is scheduled for another time, keep your computer running, make sure Media Center is started, and Media Center will record the show for you.

> **26 The Game**
> WBDT 6:00 PM - 6:30 PM   6:17 PM

FIGURE 22-5 Media Center displays information about the current show.

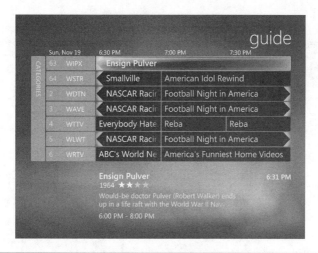

FIGURE 22-6   Use the Program Guide to find a show to watch on TV.

To play back a recorded show, return to the main Media Center window (click the Media Center icon at the top left of a window). Choose TV + Movies and click Recorded TV. A window appears with your recorded TV shows. Click a show and then click Play to begin playing it back. Media Center gives you three snippets of sample shows as well.

NOTE *Another feature of Media Center is the Movies Guide. Its function is similar to the Program Guide, but it looks a lot different. Movies Guide lists all the movies that are scheduled to be shown on TV in your area. Each movie includes a picture of its DVD or videotape box, the time of the showing, and other information. Figure 22-8 shows the Movies Guide.*

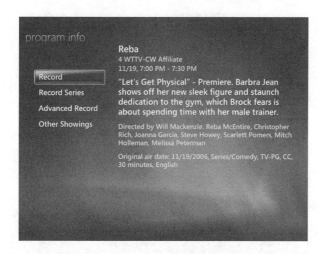

FIGURE 22-7   Get more information and set up to record a show from the Program Info window.

Figure 22-8 The Movies Guide lists the movies that are scheduled to appear on TV in your area.

Play Music in Media Center

The Music Library in Media Center stores a list of the music you have on your computer. When you click Music and then Music Library from the main Media Center window, the Music Library window appears (see Figure 22-9). From here, you can click a music album to see the individual songs on the album (shown in Figure 22-10). You can click Play Album to play back all the songs on the album, or click a song to play it back now.

Figure 22-9 The Music Library shows the music stored on your computer.

FIGURE 22-10   See details about an album when you click the album in the Music Library.

Also, you can burn a song to a DVD or CD, click the Edit Info button to change information about an album, or add songs to a queue of songs you play later.

View Pictures Using Media Center

Media Center makes it easy to view your saved pictures on your computer. This makes it nice to show family and friends the photographs you have taken over the years. Click Pictures + Videos and then Picture Library to display the Picture Library windows (see Figure 22-11).

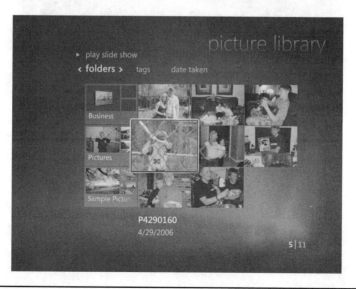

FIGURE 22-11   Show your family pictures using the Picture Library tool.

To view a picture, click it. The picture appears full screen. Click the Play button and Media Center turns your collection of pictures into a slide show that streams across the screen. You can click the Close button to stop the slide show and return to the Picture Library window. While there, you can click the Play Slide Show button to launch the slide show again.

In the Picture Library window, you can organize the pictures according to folders, tags, or date taken. For example, to see pictures taken on a specific day, click Date Taken. Media Center displays pictures in folders named after the months of the year that a picture was taken. Click a folder to see all the pictures for that month. Likewise, if you prefer to see pictures organized by descriptive tags, click the Tags button.

Play Your Videos Using Media Center

Media Center provides a way to play back the videos you have stored on your computer. Video formats that Media Center supports include all those that Windows Media Player can play, including AVI and WMV. To play back your videos, choose Pictures + Videos and then click Video Library. The Video Library window appears, as shown in Figure 22-12.

Click a video to launch it in the full-screen video player. Use the video controls to fast forward, rewind, pause, stop, and play your video. When you finish viewing your video, click the Stop button. While you're watching a video, you can right-click it to choose Video Details, Burn, Zoom, and Settings. The Video Details option displays your video in a thumbnail view and displays file, creation date, and running time information. Click the Play button to resume in full-screen mode.

The Burn command burns the video to a CD or DVD disc. See the next section for more details.

FIGURE 22-12   Use Media Center to play back your videos on your TV or projector.

Burn DVDs and CDs from Media Center

If you have content that you are viewing from Media Center and want to make a DVD or CD from it, send it to the DVD Maker while in Media Center. To burn a CD or DVD, you must have a DVD burner or CD burner installed on your computer, and have a blank CD or DVD disc inserted in the burner. Next, use Media Center to open the content you want to burn, such as a picture library, recorded TV show, or video. Right-click the content and choose Burn. The playback of a video or TV show stops and you are presented with the Select Disc Format window. Figure 22-13, for example, includes the format for burning items to a DVD. If you are burning a movie, video, or recorded TV show, click Video DVD. For pictures, select Data DVD.

Click Next and name the disc. Click Next. The Review & Edit List window appears. You can click Burn DVD to start the burning process. Or, to add additional items to the disc, click the Add More button. You can select to browse for more media content, such as the Recorded TV or Video Library areas. Select the content to add to the disc and click Next. Again you are shown the Review & Edit List. Repeat what you just did to add more content, or click Burn DVD (or Burn CD if you are creating a CD) if you are ready.

When you do click the Burn DVD button, the Initiating Copy window appears. Click Yes to continue, and Media Center burns a copy of the media content to your disc. When finished, Media Center displays a message asking if you want to continue burning additional discs using the same choices, or to end the burning process. Your disc is now ready to be played in another disc player.

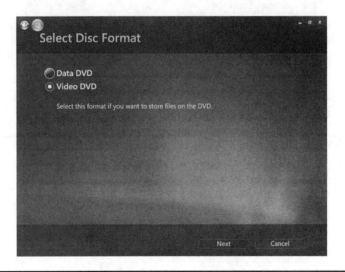

FIGURE 22-13 Select a format for burning a DVD or CD from Media Center.

Another way to start the burn process is to click the Burn CD/DVD tool on the main Media Center window after choosing Tasks. This displays the Select Disc Format window. Select a format; your choices may include options in addition to those shown in Figure 22-13. For example, when starting the burn process from the main Media Center window, you also are shown an option for creating a DVD (or CD) Slide Show. Click Next after selecting your format. The Name This DVD window appears. Enter a name and click Next. You can then browse for the media to add to the disc; for example, if you are burning a DVD video disc, you can browse the Recorded TV or Video Library locations. Click Next after you select an option. Next you can choose the videos or other media to add to the disc. Click Next. The Review & Edit List window appears, as show in Figure 22-14.

As described earlier, you can click the Add More button to select additional media files to include on your disc. When you are ready to burn, click Burn DVD (or CD) to display the Initiating Copy window. Click Yes to start the burn process. When done, you can burn another copy using the same files or you can finish the process.

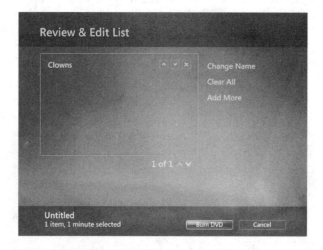

Figure 22-14 View the list of media files you selected to burn to disc.

PART

V

Windows Vista on the Internet

Configuring Windows to Work with Your Modem

Before you connect to the Internet (or any other computer) using a modem, you must install your modem, whether you use a conventional modem and phone line, or a high-speed *broadband* DSL (digital subscriber loop, or line) line, cable modem, or satellite line.

Once your modem is installed, you're ready to read Chapter 24 to sign up for a new Internet account or set up Windows to connect to an existing account.

NOTE *If you connect to the Internet over a local area network (LAN) rather than by using a modem, contact your LAN system administrator. If you are the system administrator, see Chapter 32.*

If you use a dial-up modem (with a regular or ISDN line) with a laptop, you may want to set up a dialing location for each telephone line from which you dial, so that Windows knows when to dial 1 and the area code. If you charge the cost of your calls to a telephone calling card, you can configure Windows to dial the digits to charge your calling card automatically.

Configuring Windows to Use Your Dial-Up Modem

Up until a few years ago, the most common way to connect to the Internet had been via a dial-up modem that attaches to a regular phone line (or via a LAN, for computers in large organizations). Now, high-speed Internet options that are available through cable companies, wireless grids, electrical utilities, satellite companies, and other sources provide most of the Internet access for business, schools, and regular consumers. However, some users (such as those with low bandwidth needs—e-mail for example) still opt for dial-up connections to the Internet. They are much slower than high-speed alternatives, but they are also usually much less expensive.

When setting up your modem for dial-up Internet accounts, Windows needs to know exactly which make of dial-up modem you have, so it can send the appropriate commands.

You can also tell Windows from which area code you usually dial, from what other locations you make calls (if you have a portable computer), and to which calling cards you want to charge your calls.

What Does Windows Know About Your Modem?

When you install a modem, Windows either determines what kind of modem it is or asks you. Windows installs a *modem driver*, a small program that usually comes with the modem (Windows comes with modem drivers for many popular modems; see Chapter 14, "Configuring Windows to Work with Your Hardware").

You can look at or change your modem configuration settings by choosing Start | Control Panel, clicking Hardware And Sound, and then clicking Phone And Modem Options. (If Windows doesn't know you have a modem, the Add Hardware Wizard runs. If your modem is external, make sure it is turned on, and then follow the wizard's instructions to set up the modem.)

You see the Phone And Modem Options dialog box. Click the Modems tab to see a list of the installed modems, as shown in Figure 23-1. Select the appropriate modem from the list,

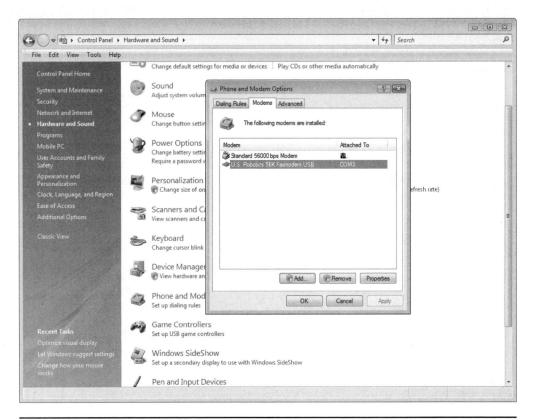

FIGURE 23-1   The Phone And Modem Options dialog box.

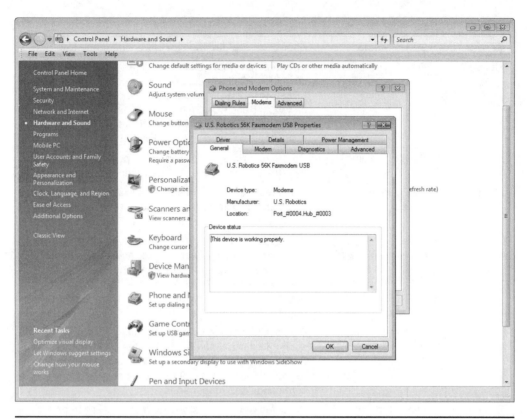

FIGURE 23-2 The Properties dialog box for a modem.

and then click the Properties button to see the Properties dialog box for the modem, shown in Figure 23-2. (The exact appearance of the dialog box depends on which modem driver you select.) To find out which modem driver Windows uses for your modem, click the Driver tab in the modem's Properties dialog box.

Table 23-1 lists the modem properties that appear in the Properties dialog box for most modems. Table 23-2 shows additional settings that appear in the Default Preferences dialog box for the modem, which you display by clicking the Advanced tab in the modem's Properties dialog box, and then clicking the Change Default Preferences button. Except where noted, don't change these settings unless you are sure your modem is configured incorrectly. Most people never have to change these settings except in consultation with their modem manufacturer, communications software publisher, or Internet service provider.

TIP *You can also display your modem's Properties dialog box from the Device Manager: select the modem and click the Properties button on the toolbar.*

Tab	Setting	Description
General	Device status	Shows whether the modem is working properly or not.
Modem	Port	Specifies how your modem is connected to your computer. PCs have serial communications ports named COM1, COM2, COM3, and COM4 (most PCs come with only COM1 and COM2), or your modem may connect to a USB port. Even if your modem is internal (installed inside the computer), it is assigned a port.
Modem	Speaker volume	Specifies how loud the modem's speaker is set, or how loud the system speaker plays modem sounds.
Modem	Maximum Port Speed	Specifies the maximum speed at which your modem can communicate over the cable to your computer (not over the phone to another modem), in *bits per second* (*bps*, usually 115,200 bps).
Modem	Dial Control	Specifies whether to wait for the modem to detect a dial tone before sending commands to dial; if the modem can't detect a dial tone, this should be deselected. Outside North America, many modems require this to be deselected.
Diagnostics	Modem Information	Displays identifying information about your modem, such as its serial number. Click Query Modem to see the responses to standard modem commands (refer to your modem's manual for the meanings of the commands and responses).
Diagnostics	Append to Log	Specifies whether to store information sent to and from the modem in a log file—usually in C:\Windows\ Modemlog_*modemname*.txt. The log file is useful for troubleshooting; to see the log file, click View Log.
Advanced	Extra initialization commands	Lists additional commands to send to your modem after Windows sends the standard initialization commands. Consult your modem's manual for a list of commands your modem understands.
Driver	Driver Provider, Driver Date, Driver Version, Digital Signer	Displays information about the software driver for the modem. Click Driver Details for more information, including the names and locations of the driver files. Click Update Driver to install a new driver. Click Roll Back Driver to reinstall a previously installed driver. Click Disable to keep the modem installed and set up, but disable it for troubleshooting purposes. Click Uninstall to remove the driver.
Details	Property	Displays a number of modem properties in the Value list when you select an item from the Property drop-down list.

TABLE 23-1 Modem Properties in the Properties Dialog Box

Tab	Setting	Description
General	Disconnect a call if idle for more than *xx* mins	Specifies whether to hang up the phone connection if no data is transmitted for a specified number of minutes (usually not selected). Choose this setting if you want to avoid leaving the phone off the hook when you remain online by accident.
General	Cancel the call if not connected within *xx* secs	Specifies whether to time-out after this number of seconds if no connection occurs (usually selected, with a time-out period of 60 seconds).
General	Port speed	Same as the Maximum Port Speed in the modem Properties dialog box (see Table 23-1).
General	Data Protocol	Specifies what type of error correction to use. Removing error correction may allow modems to make a connection, but may make the connection less reliable.
General	Compression	Specifies whether to compress data before transmitting it (usually enabled). Not all modems support data compression, and the modem to which it is communicating must also support it.
General	Flow control	Specifies whether to use a system of *flow control* to control the flow of data between your modem and your computer. If selected, you have two options: Xon/Xoff or Hardware (preferred).
Advanced	Data bits	Specifies the number of *data bits*, the number of bits of information included in each byte sent (must be 8 bits).
Advanced	Parity	Specifies whether the modem uses *parity*, which means the modem sends an error-detection bit as the eighth bit of each byte; and, if so, which type of parity (usually None).
Advanced	Stop bits	Specifies how many extra *stop bits* are sent after each byte (must be 1 bit).
Advanced	Modulation	Specifies the *modulation*, which is how your modem converts the digital information from your computer into analog "sound" information for transmission over the phone.

TABLE 23-2   Modem Properties in the Default Preferences Dialog Box

PART V

Troubleshooting Your Modem

If you have trouble getting your modem to connect, here are some things to check:

- **Make sure the correct modem driver is installed**   Look on the Modems tab of the Phone And Modem Options dialog box to make sure the correct modem is listed. Remove any modems that are no longer installed. If the wrong modem is listed, select it and click Remove. Then click Add to run the Add Hardware Wizard and install the correct modem.

- **Make sure the modem driver is enabled**   Choose Start, right-click Computer, choose Manage, and choose Device Manager from the list at the left side of the

Computer Management window. Choose View | Devices By Type, and then click the plus (+) sign next to the Modems entry on the list of devices. Your modem should appear in the list: if it appears with an exclamation point or X on it, something is wrong. Click it and click the Properties button to display the Properties dialog box for the modem. On the General tab, make sure that Device Usage is set to Use This Device (Enabled).

- **Make sure the modem is connected to the correct port**   Display the Properties dialog box for the modem, as described in the preceding paragraph. On the Modem or General tab, check that you see the port to which the modem is connected.

- **Make sure the modem speed is right**   On the Modem tab in the Properties dialog box for the modem, check the Maximum Port Speed setting. Choosing a lower speed may solve your connection problem.

TIP   *If you have an external modem, be sure the modem is turned on.*

Configuring Windows for Dialing Locations

If you have a laptop computer, you may connect to the Internet or other dial-up service from different locations using different phone numbers. Windows enables you to define one or more dialing locations so that Windows knows from what area code you are calling and can dial numbers appropriately.

What Is a Dialing Location?

A *dialing location* defines a location from which you use your modem. Windows stores information about the area code and phone system from which you are dialing, including whether to dial extra digits to get an outside line. It also remembers whether the phone line at that location uses *call waiting*, a phone line feature that beeps when another call is coming in on the line. The call waiting beep disrupts most modem connections, so you should tell Windows to turn off call waiting before dialing the phone, if you don't want your online session interrupted.

You can use dialing locations when connecting to Internet accounts via dial-up connections (explained in the next chapter).

Displaying Your Dialing Locations

To define or change your dialing locations, choose Start | Control Panel, click Hardware And Sound, and click Phone And Modem Options. In the Phone And Modem Options dialog box that appears, click the Dialing Rules tab (if it's not already selected), which lists your existing dialing locations, as shown in Figure 23-3.

The Dialing Rules tab enables you to create area code rules to tell Windows when to dial 1, and enables calling card definitions to tell Windows the access number, account number, and PIN you use when charging phone calls to a calling card.

Creating a Dialing Location

To make a new dialing location, follow these steps:

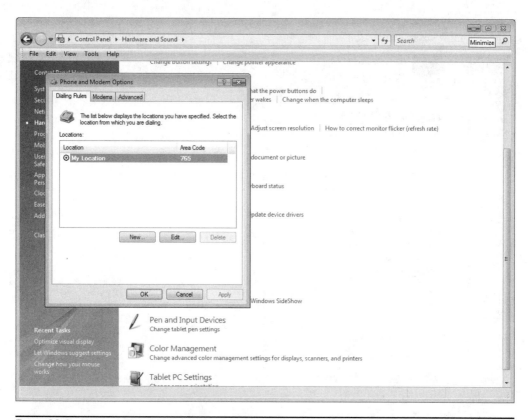

FIGURE 23-3   Your existing dialing locations.

1. Click the New button on the Dialing Rules tab of the Phone And Modem Options dialog box. You see the New Location dialog box, shown in Figure 23-4. (If this is the first dialing location you create, you can skip this step and edit the New Location dialing location that already appears.)

2. Type a name for the dialing location in the Location Name box (using any name you'll find helpful), choose the country from the list, and type the area code or city code from which you are dialing.

3. If you need to dial extra digits before dialing local or long-distance phone numbers, type the digits into the two To Access An Outside Line boxes.

4. The Use This Carrier Code To Make Long-Distance Calls/International Calls boxes are rarely used.

5. If the phone line has call waiting (that is, if incoming calls cause a beep on the phone line), select the check box to disable call waiting and select the number to disable it. (Check with your phone company if you are unsure.)

6. If your phone doesn't accept tone dialing, set Dial Using to Pulse.

PART V

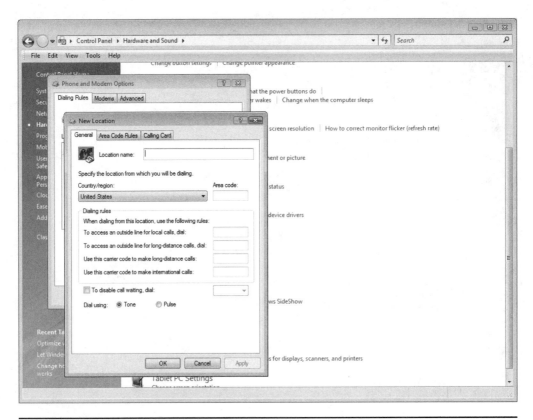

FIGURE 23-4   Creating or editing dialing locations.

7. If you have to dial 1 and the area code for some exchanges in this area code, or if you have to dial 1 and the area code for all exchanges—even in your own area code—click the Area Code Rules tab to tell Windows exactly what to dial (see "Setting Up Area Code Rules" later in the chapter).

8. If you use a calling card to charge the calls made from this phone line, click the Calling Card tab to select a card (see "Configuring Windows to Use Calling Cards" later in the chapter).

9. Click OK to return to the Phone And Modem Options dialog box, where your new location appears.

To delete a dialing location, choose the dialing location from the Locations and click Delete.

Setting a Default Dialing Location

Before you exit from the Phone And Modem Options dialog box, select the dialing location you use most often, so that a dot appears in the radio button to its left. Windows displays this dialing location in dial-up connections and Windows Fax and Scan as the default dialing location.

TIP *When you go on a trip and arrive at your destination, create a dialing location for the phone from which your computer will be dialing. Select this dialing location before exiting the Phone And Modem Options dialog box to make this location the default. When you return from your trip, display the Phone And Modem Options dialog box again, select the dialing location for your home or office, and click OK. This resets the default to your usual dialing location.*

Using Dialing Locations

Dialing locations come in handy when connecting to the Internet and when sending faxes., as explained in the following points:

- **Dial-up Internet connections**   You can use dialing rules when calling your ISP with a dial-up connection. In the Connect dialog box, you select your dialing location by clicking the Properties button to display the properties of the dial-up connection, clicking the Use Dialing Rules check box, clicking the Dialing Rules button, and choosing another location (see "Dialing the Internet Manually" in Chapter 24).

- **Sending faxes**   The Windows Fax and Scan program uses dialing locations when sending a fax (see "Working with Fax and Scan" in Chapter 19).

Setting Up Area Code Rules

You can configure Windows to dial 1 and the area code automatically when necessary, but not to dial it for local calls.

What Are Area Code Rules?

In the old days, you probably had to dial 1 and the area code only for numbers outside your own area code. Now, you may have to dial 1 and the area code for some or all phone numbers, even within your own area code. You can tell Windows exactly when it has to dial what numbers, so when you type a phone number to dial, Windows can dial the correct sequence of digits. Windows stores this information as an *area code rule*, which defines what Windows should dial when calling from one dialing location to one area code (for example, when dialing 617 area code numbers from your Lexington, Mass. dialing location).

Creating Area Code Rules

To tell Windows the dialing rules for an area code:

1. Choose Start | Control Panel, click Hardware And Sound, and click Phones And Modem Options. In the Phone And Modem Options dialog box that appears, click the Dialing Rules tab (if it's not already selected), as shown in Figure 23-3.

2. Choose the dialing location for which you want to create area code rules, click the Edit button to display the New Location dialog box (shown in Figure 23-4), and

then click the Area Code Rules tab. You see a list of the area code rules that apply to calls made from that dialing location (the list starts out empty).

3. Click the New button. You see the New Area Code Rule dialog box, shown in Figure 23-5.

4. Type the area code to which this rule applies (that is, Windows follows this rule when dialing numbers in this area code from this dialing location).

5. In the Prefixes section, specify whether the rule appears to all numbers in the area code or only to certain prefixes (or exchanges—that is, the three digits that come after the area code). If the rule applies to certain prefixes, click Add and type the prefixes.

NOTE *You can't tell Windows that a rule applies to all prefixes except the ones you list (which would be handy in some area codes).*

6. If you must dial 1 (or another set of digits) for these phone numbers, click the Dial check box and type the digit (usually 1, which already appears there).

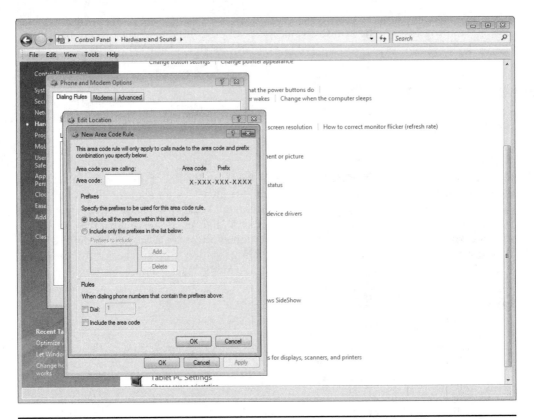

FIGURE 23-5   The New Area Code Rule dialog box tells Windows when to dial 1 and the area code.

7. If you must dial the area code for these phone numbers, check the Include The Area Code check box.

8. Click OK to return to the Edit Location dialog box, where your rule now appears. Click OK again to return to the Phone And Modem Options dialog box.

You can change an existing area code rule (or delete it) by selecting the dialing location to which it applies from the Dialing Rules tab of the Phone And Modem Options dialog box, clicking Edit, clicking the Area Code Rules tab of the Edit Location dialog box that appears, clicking the area code rule, and clicking Edit or Delete.

Configuring Windows to Use Calling Cards

If you use a telephone calling card to charge your phone calls, especially when you are away from your home or office, Windows can dial all the extra digits for you.

What Is a Calling Card?

A *calling card* is a telephone credit card to which you charge toll calls. To use a calling card, you dial several series of digits in addition to the phone number you want to call, usually including some digits to identify your calling card account. Windows can store information about your telephone calling cards; so when you need to connect to an Internet account via a calling card, Windows can dial the special digits for you.

Windows needs to know the following to place calls using a calling card:

- **Account number**   The number you dial to identify yourself to the calling card company. Windows pre-defined calling cards don't use the account number at all, so we recommend leaving this box blank unless you are setting up your own calling card.

- **Personal ID Number (PIN)**   The number that identifies you to the calling card company, usually your phone number plus four additional digits.

- **Long-distance access number**   The digits you dial to connect to your calling card company before you dial the phone number you want to call or your calling card number. Windows doesn't let you type punctuation, such as dashes—just the digits to dial. For example, to use AT&T from most locations in the United States, you dial 10288, followed by 0; so you would type **102880**. You can also include pauses to wait for a prompt from the calling card company.

- **International access number**   The digits you dial to connect to your calling card company when you want to place an international call.

- **Local access number**   The digits you dial to connect to your calling card number when you want to place a local call.

Setting Up Calling Cards

To create, edit, or delete your list of calling cards, Choose Start | Control Panel, click Hardware And Sound, and click Phones And Modem Options. On the Phone And Modem Options dialog box that appears, click the Dialing Rules tab (if it's not already selected), as shown in Figure 23-3. Choose the dialing location for which you want to work with calling cards, click

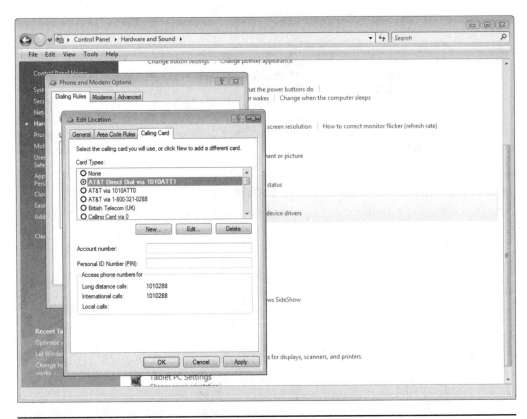

FIGURE 23-6   Many calling cards are predefined in Windows.

the Edit button to display the New Location dialog box, shown in Figure 23-4, and then click the Calling Card tab. You see a list of the calling cards you can use from this dialing location (see Figure 23-6). Windows comes with calling cards for the major phone companies predefined.

Windows already knows about dozens of widely used calling cards, including their access numbers and the sequence of numbers to dial when placing a call. To set up a calling card that Windows already knows about, choose it from the Card Types list. Windows displays the default properties for that type of calling card. Only the Account Number and Personal ID Number (PIN) boxes are blank; you must type these numbers before Windows can use the calling card. Also check that the access numbers are right (these are the numbers that Windows tells your modem to dial when making long-distance, international, and local calls using the calling card). When you click OK, you return to the Phone And Modem Options dialog box.

Creating a New Type of Calling Card

If your calling card doesn't appear on the Calling Card tab of the Edit Location dialog box for your dialing location, you can create one. You need to know not only the access numbers, account number, and PIN number, but also in what order to dial them and how long to wait between them. The standard set of steps for dialing a calling card number is as follows:

1. Dial the access number.
2. Wait for a moment (10 seconds is usually enough).
3. Dial the PIN.
4. Wait a moment more (about 5 seconds).
5. Dial the area code and phone number that you want to call.

When setting up a new calling card, you tell Windows what to dial and when to pause. Follow these steps:

1. Make a note of what you dial and what you wait for when you place a call by hand. If you dial your PIN (phone number plus four extra digits), followed by the number you want to dial, that's all you have to enter. But if there are additional steps, with additional prompts, make a note of them so you can tell Windows how to follow the same steps.

2. In the Edit Location dialog box for the dialing location, click the Calling Card tab and click the New button. You see a dialog box that looks like Figure 23-7. The settings for a new calling card are blank, so you have to enter them.

3. Type the name of the calling card, your account number (if your calling card uses one—most don't, so you can leave it blank), and your PIN (usually your phone number followed by a four-digit number).

4. Click the Long Distance tab (shown in Figure 23-8), in which you tell Windows the sequence of steps to follow when dialing a long-distance number using the calling card. Each step includes dialing a number or pausing for a prompt.

5. In the Access Number For Long Distance Calls box, type the digits you would dial, omitting any punctuation (Windows allows only digits in this box).

6. Consult the notes you made in Step 1, then click the button in the lower part of the dialog box to indicate what Windows should do first when dialing the number. For most calling cards, this usually means dialing the access number you typed in Step 5, so click Access Number. The step appears in the Calling Card Dialing Steps box.

7. Continue clicking buttons to specify what to dial, or how long to wait. If Windows needs to wait before continuing to dial, click Wait For Prompt, and specify whether to wait for a dial tone, wait for a message to play, or wait for a specific number of seconds. Each step you specify appears in the Calling Card Dialing Steps box. If you enter a step by mistake, remove it by selecting the step and clicking Delete. You can also change the order of the steps by selecting a step and clicking Move Up or Move Down.

8. When the series of steps looks right, click the International tab to see an identical dialog box for specifying how to dial international calls with the calling card. Then click the Local Calls tab to specify how to dial local calls.

9. Click OK to save all the sequences of steps for the calling card.

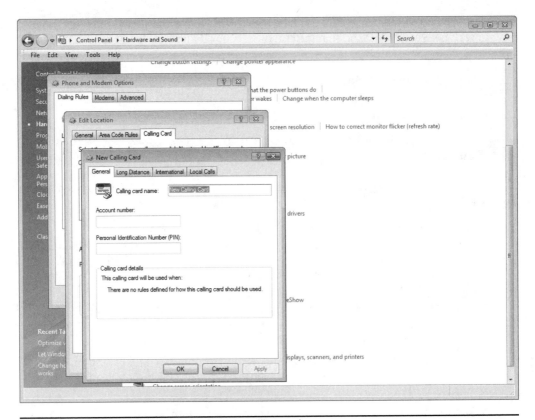

FIGURE 23-7 Entering information about a new calling card.

If your calling card *does* appear but the access numbers or other information is wrong, you can change the information by selecting the calling card and clicking Edit on the Calling Card tab. You see the Edit Calling Card dialog box with the same settings as the New Calling Card dialog box.

Deleting a Calling Card

To delete a calling card, choose the calling card you no longer want to use from the Edit Location dialog box for the dialing location, and then click Delete.

CAUTION *Don't delete the standard calling cards that come with Windows. You might want to use one again later, and losing all the specifications of that type of calling card would be a shame.*

Using Calling Cards

When placing calls using a dial-up connection, in the Properties dialog box for the connection, click the Use Dialing Rules check box, click the Dialing Rules button, choose a dialing location, click Edit, click the Calling Card tab, and choose a calling card to use (see "What Are Network Connections?" in Chapter 24).

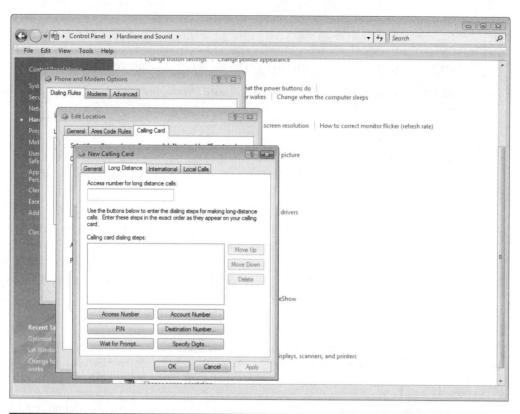

FIGURE 23-8   The Long Distance tab shows the steps for dialing long-distance numbers using the calling card.

Connecting to a DSL Line

A *DSL* (*digital subscriber line* or *digital subscriber loop*) *line* is a special phone line that communicates digitally. With a dial-up phone line, your modem converts the digital information from your computer into an analog signal for transmission. At the other end, another modem converts the analog signal back into digital information. Along the way, your phone company may perform additional conversions. With a DSL line, your digital information never has to be converted. Unlike dial-up lines, DSL lines stay connected all the time—there's no waiting for your computer to connect. Data transmission is also much faster than on a dial-up line: downstream (downloading) speeds range from 384 Kbps to 8 Mbps, and upstream (uploading) speeds range from 90 Kbps to 640 Kbps. Some DSL lines support simultaneous computer and voice use.

DSL comes in several varieties:

- **ADSL**   Asymmetric DSL, because it downloads faster than it uploads
- **SDSL**   Symmetric DSL
- **IDSL**   ISDN (Integrated Services Digital Network) emulating DSL
- **HDSL**   A modern replacement for a T1 line

ADSL, the most common type of DSL line, supports faster communication to your computer (downloading) than from your computer (uploading), which matches the way most people use the Internet. When people talk about DSL, they usually mean ADSL.

There are two ways that your PC can connect to the Internet using your DSL line:

- **DHCP (Dynamic Host Configuration Protocol)**   Your computer is online all the time, with a numeric IP address assigned to you by your ISP's DHCP server (a server computer that issues IP addresses as needed; see "How Does TCP/IP Work?" in Chapter 30).

- **PPPoE (PPP over Ethernet)**   Your computer must log on each time you want to use the Internet, as if you were dialing in. Once you log in, your ISP issues to your computer a numeric IP address that works until you log out (or the connection times out).

Which method you use depends on your DSL provider; you don't get to choose. Windows Vista can work with either method. You can find out more about DSL from the xDSL web site at http://en.wikipedia.org/wiki/dsl.

TIP *Because DSL is high-speed, it's well suited for allowing a LAN (like a group of networked computers in a home or small office) to share one Internet account (see Chapter 32).*

Getting DSL

DSL is not available from all phone companies. Prices and speeds vary. You can call your local phone company for pricing and availability in your area. Better yet, call your ISP and ask them to order the DSL line for you. You may also be able to get a DSL line from a third-party provider.

To connect your computer to a DSL line, you need a *DSL modem*. DSL modems may be internal or external, and external DSL modems may connect either to a network adapter or to a USB port. Order the DSL line from your ISP when you check whether it offers DSL service; your ISP can probably order the line for you from your phone company. Ask for the phone company or ISP to provide the DSL modem, too—some phone companies don't support DSL modems purchased elsewhere. If the DSL modem requires a network adapter (network interface card, or NIC), get one from a computer store and install it in your computer before the installer arrives (see "Network Ports" in Chapter 13). The ISP or phone company should provide the software and instructions for configuring Windows to work with the DSL modem. Your phone company or other DSL provider usually installs the DSL modem and configures your computer to use it. It usually configures your NIC to work with the cable modem.

CAUTION *Not all DSL modems work with all DSL lines. Get your DSL modem from your phone company or ISP. If you already have a DSL modem, check with your DSL provider to find out whether the modem will work with its phone lines or not.*

Configuring Windows for DSL

To see your DSL configuration, choose Start | Network and right-click your DSL connection. Choose Properties to see the Properties dialog box. Click Internet Protocol (TCP/IP) and click the Properties button to see the configuration for the connection. Don't change the settings without information from your phone company or ISP.

CAUTION *In the Properties dialog box for the DSL connection, make sure that neither the Client For Microsoft Networks check box nor the File And Printer Sharing For Microsoft Networks check box is selected. If either is selected, deselect it—otherwise, you may be giving other people on the Internet access to your files and printer!*

Connecting to a Cable Modem

Many cable television companies offer *cable Internet accounts*—cable connections to the Internet over the same cable that your television uses. Many refer to this service as *broadband* service. Downloading speeds can be fast, although the more people in your neighborhood who are using the cable, the slower transfers go. Cable Internet accounts have several advantages over dial-up Internet accounts:

- **Speed**   Cable modems can communicate much faster than dial-up modems. Expect downloading speeds of 1 to 2 Mbps or more, and uploading speeds of between 500 Kbps and 1 Mbps.

- **Separate line**   If you use a cable account, you don't tie up your regular phone line. If you currently pay for a separate phone line for your Internet connection, the cost of a cable Internet account won't be much more (depending on the phone and cable rates in your area).

Call your local cable company to find out if it offers an Internet service.

Getting Connected

To connect your computer to the cable system, you use a *cable modem*. It connects to a NIC (also used for connecting to a LAN—see "Chapter 29) or (less commonly) to a USB port. Your cable company usually supplies the modem, along with the software and instructions for installing the cable modem and configuring Windows to use it. Some cable companies let you buy or lease the cable modem; consider leasing, because cable modem failure rates are reported to be high. As prices fall and quality improves, buying will eventually become more advantageous. The cable installer usually configures your NIC to work with the cable modem.

Configuring Windows for a Cable Modem

When your cable installer connects your PC to the cable modem, she usually also configures Windows to work with the cable modem. Windows communicates with the cable modem using the TCP/IP networking protocol, which you can configure. Choose Start | Network, right-click your cable Internet connection, and choose Properties to see the Properties dialog box. Don't change the settings without information from your cable company.

CAUTION *In the Properties dialog box for the cable Internet connection, make sure that neither the Client For Microsoft Networks check box nor the File And Printer Sharing For Microsoft Networks check box is selected. If either is selected, deselect it—otherwise, other people in your neighborhood with cable Internet accounts may have access to your files and printer!*

Connecting to an ISDN Line

An *ISDN (Integrated Services Digital Network) line* is an all-digital phone line that is less widely used in the United States, but quite common, for example, in Europe, where an ISDN line is typically cheaper than two analog phone lines. The type of ISDN service for residential customers is Basic Rate Interface (BRI). BRI consists of two 64 Kbps (or 56 Kbps on some older systems in the United States) channels, each of which can be used independently for phone, fax, or data connections. Both channels can be combined (bundled) in a single data connection, allowing you to connect at 128 Kbps, over twice the speed of a fast dial-up line (at the cost of being unable to make or receive phone calls over the ISDN line for the duration of the bundled connection). Unlike DSL and cable modems, ISDN is not connected directly to the Internet, but rather to the telephone network, so you connect to the Internet by making a phone call to an ISP that offers ISDN access.

TIP   *If your phone company offers DSL, choose it over ISDN, as DSL delivers higher speeds than ISDN, is usually cheaper, and usually lacks a per-minute charge. In the United States, ISDN lines are usually priced with a monthly charge that includes a base number of minutes of usage, plus a per-minute charge if you use the line for additional minutes.*

For more information about how ISDN works, see the ISDN Zone web site at www.isdnzone.com.

Getting ISDN

You can order an ISDN line from your local telephone company, but you should call your ISP first to confirm that it can also provide ISDN service. ISDN lines are more expensive than normal phone lines, and not all phone companies can provide them. Even companies that do provide ISDN lines often have trouble installing them correctly; so if your ISP can arrange to set up the line, order it through your ISP.

You also need an *ISDN terminal adapter* (also called an *ISDN adapter, ISDN TA,* or *ISDN modem*) to connect your computer's serial port to the ISDN phone line. Better yet, get an external ISDN TA with a USB (Universal Serial Bus) interface or an internal ISDN adapter card that installs inside your computer for faster communications (external ISDN adapters that connect to the serial port are limited by the 115 Kbps speed of the serial port). Your ISP (or whatever computer you are connecting to) must have ISDN phone numbers for you to connect to (see "Internet (PPP) Accounts" in Chapter 24).

Configuring Windows for Your ISDN Adapter

Your telephone installer usually installs the ISDN adapter and configures Windows to use it, but here is information about how to do so yourself. See Chapter 14 for how to install an internal ISDN adapter. If you have an external ISDN adapter that connects to the serial port, connect its serial cable to a serial (COM) port on your PC (shut down Windows and turn your PC off first). If you have an external USB ISDN TA, plug it into a free USB connector on your PC (you don't have to turn off your PC first).

When you turn your PC back on or when you plug in an USB ISDN TA, Windows should detect the new hardware and run the Add Hardware Wizard automatically. If it doesn't, choose Start | Control Panel, and click the Classic View link on the left pane. Double-click the Add Hardware icon and walk through the Add Hardware Wizard to set up your ISDN adapter.

When Windows has installed the drivers for the ISDN adapter, you (or your telephone installer) configure Windows to use it. The Add Hardware Wizard usually displays a dialog box asking for configuration information: if it doesn't, choose Start, then right-click Computer, click Properties, and then click the Device Manager link in the Tasks pane. Your ISDN adapter appears in Modems if it is external or Network Adapters if it is internal. Right-click the ISDN adapter and choose Properties from the menu that appears. Click the ISDN tab and select the Switch type or D-channel protocol your phone company uses (ask your phone company for this information). Then click the Configure button and enter the requested information, which you need to get from your phone company or ISP:

- **Phone Number**   The phone number(s) of your ISDN line for U.S. and Canada switch types. Your ISDN line may have one or two phone numbers.

- **Service Profile Identifier (SPID)**   Your ISDN phone number, plus a few extra digits that identify the type of ISDN switch. SPIDs are generally used only in the United States and Canada.

- **Multi-Subscriber Number (MSN)**   The phone number(s) of your ISDN line for European ISDN (DSS1)—this has nothing to do with MSN, Microsoft's ISP. European ISDN allows multiple phone numbers on an ISDN line. You only need to enter the MSNs you actually intend to use with your computer—the MSNs you want your computer to accept calls for, and the MSN to which you want outgoing calls to be billed. Note that outgoing calls you make with your computer will be billed to the first MSN in the list, which will always be the lowest number, since Windows sorts the list. If you enter no MSN, the calls will be billed to the primary MSN of your line.

TIP   *You must be logged on using an administrator account to configure your ISDN adapter.*

Two-Way Satellite Connections

A new option for connecting to the Internet is by two-way satellite. For example, StarBand (at www.starband.com) and HughesNet (at www.hughesnet.com) offer a satellite dish, satellite modem, Internet account, and optional satellite television service. It's more expensive to install than DSL or cable Internet, but it's available anywhere in the continental United States where you can see the Southern sky.

The satellite dish mounts on your roof, and connects using a coaxial cable and a satellite modem to either the USB or network adapter on your computer. A StarBand or HughesNet installer does the installation of both the dish and the modem.

Connecting to the Internet

Once your modem is installed (as described in the previous chapter), you need to configure Windows Vista to work with the account. How you connect depends on the type of account. Windows can have network connections to dial-up, ISDN, DSL, satellite, and cable Internet accounts as well as connections to local area networks (LANs).

If you don't already have an Internet account, you will need to find one in your area before running the Connect To The Internet Wizard. If you have an account, this wizard can create a network connection for the account. Once created, you can configure, copy, or delete the network connection manually. Then you can connect to and disconnect from the Internet manually, or configure Windows to connect automatically when you request information from the Internet.

If your computer is connected to a LAN, you can connect to the Internet over the LAN if another computer serves as an Internet gateway. If you have a small LAN at home or in a small organization, Windows Vista comes with a program called Internet Connection Sharing (ICS) that allows a computer running Windows to act as an Internet gateway for all the computers on the LAN (see Chapter 32).

TIP *If you dial in to your Internet account, you can tell Windows either to dial direct or use a telephone calling card, and you can specify whether to dial the area code or not (see Chapter 33).*

To What Types of Internet Accounts Can Windows Connect?

To connect to the Internet, you can use one of several types of accounts: Internet PPP accounts (using a dial-up, ISDN, or DSL line), cable Internet accounts, or online services. Cable Internet accounts are described in "Connecting to a Cable Modem" in Chapter 23.

NOTE *If you use America Online (AOL), you must use the software that AOL provides—you can't use the Windows network connections. AOL connection software may come with your Windows Vista installation (as it has with previous versions of Windows).*

Internet (PPP) Accounts

A *PPP* (*Point-to-Point Protocol*) account is an Internet account that uses the PPP communications protocol. (PPP is not the same as PPPoE, which is *PPP over Ethernet* for use with DSL or cable modems.) PPP is the most popular type of Internet account because the most popular software—Internet Explorer, Mozilla Firefox, Windows Mail, Opera, and other programs—is designed to work with PPP accounts. This book refers to PPP accounts as *dial-up Internet accounts*.

An *Internet service provider (ISP)* is a company that provides Internet accounts, usually PPP accounts. All ISPs provide dial-in accounts using regular phone lines, and many also provide ISDN and DSL connections.

Dial-Up Internet Accounts, Including ISDN

To connect to an Internet account over a dial-up phone line, you need a PPP-compatible communications program, such as the built-in Windows Network Connections program (see the upcoming section "What Are Network Connections?"). Windows Network Connections can dial the phone by using your modem, connect to your ISP, log into your account by using your username and password, and then establish a PPP connection, so your computer is connected to the Internet. While connected, you can use a variety of Internet-compatible programs to read your e-mail, browse the Web, and access other information from the Internet. When you are done, you tell Windows to disconnect from your Internet account. You configure your network connection by using the Dial-Up Connection wizard (see "Creating a Dial-up Connection").

ISDN phone lines are a high-speed type of dial-up line; see the section "Connecting to an ISDN Line" in Chapter 23 for instructions on how to configure Windows to connect to an ISDN line. Then see "Creating a Network Connection for an ISDN Line" later in this chapter.

TIP *You can have several network connections on one computer. For example, your laptop computer might have one network connection for the DSL account you use at home and another for the national ISP you dial into when you are traveling.*

DSL Accounts

If you want to use a high-speed Internet account, check with local and national ISPs to find out which ones offer DSL in your area. If your ISP offers ISDN or DSL accounts, they can work with your telephone company to get the high-speed phone line installed and tell you the type of ISDN or DSL modem you need. See the section "Connecting to a DSL Line " in Chapter 23 for how to configure Windows to work with a high-speed account.

Cable Internet Accounts

With a cable Internet account, your cable television company is your ISP, and you connect to the Internet over your cable. Contact your cable company to find out whether it offers

---

What Is TCP/IP?

TCP/IP is the acronym for Transmission Control Protocol/Internet Protocol, which is the protocol computers use to communicate with each other on the Internet. All Internet accounts use TCP/IP. Windows Vista also uses TCP/IP for communication over LANs.

Internet accounts. If it does, sign up to open an account. The monthly fee usually includes the rental of a cable modem. See "Configuring Windows for a Cable Modem" in Chapter 23 for an explanation of how to configure Windows to work with a cable Internet account.

Online Services

An *online service* is a commercial service that enables you to connect and access its proprietary information system. Most online services also provide an Internet connection, e-mail, access to the Web, and sometimes other Internet services. Some online services usually require special programs to connect to and use your account.

One of the most popular online services in the United States is AOL. AOL is available in the United States, Canada, and the United Kingdom, with other countries being added. The latest version of the AOL software (as of 2006) is 9.0. To sign up for an AOL account, install and run the AOL software. Download the software from the AOL web site, if you haven't already received it on a CD-ROM bound into a magazine, a new computer, or in a direct mail solicitation. Windows Vista may come with the AOL software pre-installed, especially if you buy a computer with Windows Vista preinstalled. The program steps you through connecting to AOL using an existing account, or signing you up for a new one.

What Are Network Connections?

A *network connection* tells Windows how your computer is connected to another computer, whether over the phone or via a cable. Windows supports these types of network connections:

- **Dial-up connection**   Connection using a modem and phone line, either a regular phone line or an ISDN line. Dial-up connections to the Internet are described throughout this chapter.

- **LAN connection**   Connection over a cable or wireless LAN adapter to other computers in the same building. LAN connections are described in Chapter 30. DSL and cable Internet accounts usually appear as LAN connections, because they don't have to dial in.

- **Virtual private network (VPN) connection**   Connection to a private LAN over the Internet. See Chapter 29 for details.

To see network-related tasks you can perform, such as creating and editing network connections, display the Network And Sharing Center window shown in Figure 24-1 by choosing Start | Control Panel | Network And Internet | Network And Sharing Center. You also use this window to manage your LAN connections, as described in Chapter 30.

To see your existing Internet and LAN connections, click the Manage Network Connections link in the Tasks pane to display the Network Connections window, shown in Figure 24-2. The Network Connections window lists every way that your computer connects to other computers: LAN, cable Internet, and DSL connections are listed in the LAN Or High-Speed Internet section and dial-up connections (including ISDN connections) are listed in the Dial-Up Connection section. You can right-click a connection in the Network Connections window and choose Properties from the menu that appears to see or change the properties for that LAN or Internet connection.

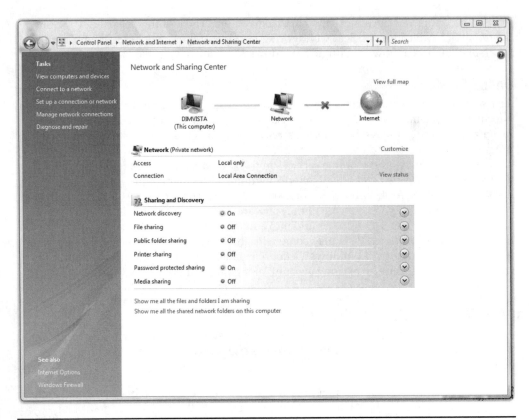

FIGURE 24-1 The Control Panel's Network and Sharing Center window.

Signing Up for a New Account

We recommend that you choose an ISP by talking to people you know and determining which ISP your friends and coworkers are most satisfied with. You also can look in your local telephone directory to find listings for ISPs. Look under Internet, Internet Service Providers, World Wide Web, or similar listings.

Running the Connect To The Internet Wizard

To set up an Internet connection manually, use the Connect To The Internet Wizard. To start this wizard, choose Start | Control Panel | Network And Internet | Network And Sharing Center and click Set Up A Connection Or Network link in the Tasks pane. The Set Up A Connection Or Network window appears (see Figure 24-3).

Choose Connect To The Internet and click Next to move from screen to screen. The next two sections describe how to use the wizard to sign up for an Internet account.

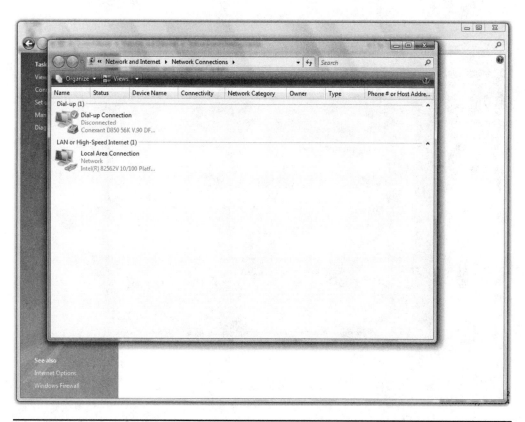

FIGURE 24-2   The Network Connections window shows both Internet and LAN connections.

Creating a Network Connection for an Existing Account

To create a new network connection to a dial-up Internet account, you use the Connect To The Internet Wizard. For ISDN accounts, see "Creating a Network Connection for an ISDN Line" later in this section. For DSL accounts, your DSL installer should already have set up Windows to work with your account: some DSL accounts appear as dial-up connections in the Network Connection window, and you use this connection to log in.

TIP   *If you installed Windows Vista, the Setup Wizard may have created a network connection for your Internet account during Windows setup. Check the Network Connections window to find out.*

Creating a Dial-up Connection

The Connect To The Internet Wizard can create a network connection, using easy-to-follow straightforward questions. Run it by following the instructions in the section "Running the Connect To The Internet Wizard" earlier in this chapter. If you know you want to set up

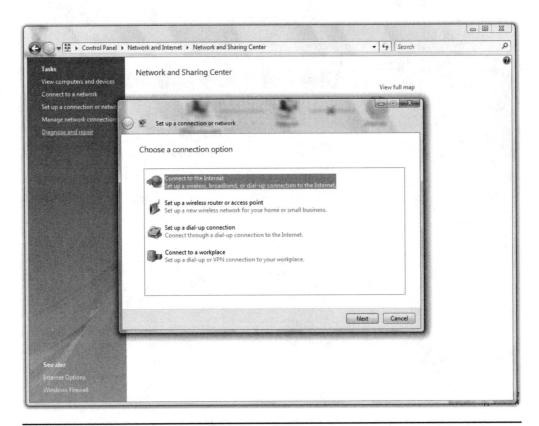

FIGURE 24-3   The Set Up A Connection Or Network window.

a dial-up account, simply click the Set Up A Dial-Up Connection link when you see the Choose A Connection Option window. Click Next to move from screen to screen and answer the following prompts:

- **Choose A Connection Type**   Choose Connect To The Internet.
- **Do You Want To Use A Connection That You Already Have?**   Choose Create A New Connection, if the Do You Want To Use A Connection That You Already Have? window appears. This enables you to create a new connection even if you have an existing one set up.
- **How Do You Want To Connect?**   Choose the type of connection you use, broadband or dial-up. For this example, use the Dial-Up option.
- **Type The Information From Your Internet Service Provider (ISP)**   Type the ISP's access phone number, your username and password, and a name that you want to use for this connection. It doesn't have to be your ISP's name—it's the name that Windows will assign to the connection icon. Click Connect after you fill out this window. Windows connects to your ISP. If it cannot find the ISP, or if you do not have your modem connected to a phone line yet, when the Internet Connectivity Test Was Unsuccessful window appears, click Set Up The Connection Anyway.

- **The Connection To The Internet Is Ready To Use**   Click Close when you see this window, to indicate that you are finished setting up the new dial-up account.

The wizard creates a new icon in the Network Connections window.

Creating a Network Connection for an ISDN Line

To create a dial-up connection for an ISDN line, run the Connect To The Internet Wizard by following the instructions in the section "Running the Connect To The Internet Wizard" earlier in this chapter. Click Next to move from screen to screen and answer the following prompts:

- **Choose A Connection Type**   Choose Connect To The Internet.

- **Do You Want To Use A Connection That You Already Have**?   Choose Create A New Connection, if the Do You Want To Use A Connection That You Already Have? window appears. This enables you to create a new connection even if you have an existing one set up.

- **How Do You Want To Connect?**   Choose the type of connection you use, broadband or dial-up. For this example, use the Dial-Up option.

- **Type The Information From Your Internet Service Provider (ISP)**   Type your username and password, and a name that you want to use for this connection. It doesn't have to be your ISP's name—it's the name that Windows will assign to the connection icon. If you want to share your broadband connection, click Allow Other People To Use This Connection. Click Connect after you fill out this window. Windows connects to your ISP. If it cannot find the ISP, or if you do not have your modem connected to a phone line yet, when the Internet Connectivity Test Was Unsuccessful window appears, click Set Up The Connection Anyway.

- **The Connection To The Internet Is Ready To Use**   Click Close when you see this window, to indicate that you are finished setting up the new dial-up account.

The wizard creates a new icon in the Network Connections window.

The wizard creates the dial-up connection for the ISDN line. Now you can configure the ISDN line type to use. The following procedure shows how to configure your ISDN adapter (note that your adapter may have different settings than the ones described here):

1. Right-click the dial-up connection icon in the Network Connections window. Choose Properties from the menu that appears. You see the Properties dialog box for the ISDN connection.

2. On the General tab, select the ISDN channel that you want to configure. Click the Configure button to display the ISDN Configuration dialog box.

3. Set the Line Type, Negotiate Line Type, and other settings according to the instructions you receive from your phone company or ISP.

TIP *Some phone companies charge "data" calls by the minute, while "voice" calls are free. For that reason, some ISPs allow you to connect with the 56 K Voice line type, which disguises the connection as a "voice" call to the phone company. This method is called* Data over Voice (DoV).

If you create a multilinked ISDN connection that bundles both of your ISDN channels, you can also configure the bundling. Click the Options tab of your dial-up connection's Properties dialog box and select the bundling behavior under Multiple Devices:

- **Dial Only First Available Device**   Uses only the first free ISDN channel and leaves the other one available, so you can still make or receive phone calls.

- **Dial All Devices**   Creates a "static" 128-kbps connection that uses both ISDN channels all of the time.

- **Dial Devices Only As Needed**   Allows dynamic use of the ISDN channels, which you can configure by clicking the Configure button. With this setting, Windows initially uses only one ISDN channel, and starts using the second one when you fully exploit the bandwidth of this channel for an extended time period (for example, when you start downloading a big file). When the download is finished, Windows automatically disconnects the second ISDN channel again.

Changing Your Dial-Up Connection Settings

Once you have used the Connect To The Internet Wizard to create a dial-up Internet connection, you can change its settings, copy it, rename it, or delete it. You can also choose which network connection is the default for connecting to the Internet.

NOTE   *Versions of Windows prior to Windows XP didn't come with TCP/IP (the communications protocol used on the Internet) preinstalled. Instead, you chose it from a list of popular network protocols. Windows XP and Vista come with TCP/IP installed, and you can't uninstall it. (It's unlikely that you'd want to do so, since TCP/IP is used for both the Internet and LANs!)*

To configure a dial-up Internet connection or to change an existing connection's configuration, open the Network Connections window by choosing Start | Control Panel | Network And Internet | Network And Sharing Center and click Manage Network Connections. Right-click the icon for the connection and choose Properties from the menu that appears. You see the Properties dialog box for the network connection. Different types of connections display different Properties dialog boxes. Figure 24-4 shows one for a dial-up connection, and Table 24-1 lists dial-up connection properties.

You can set a few more items by clicking the Configure button on the General tab of the Properties dialog box for the connection: you see the Modem Configuration dialog box. Most of the settings on this dialog box are the same as the settings in the modem's Properties dialog box (see "What Does Windows Know About Your Modem?" in Chapter 23).

CAUTION   *Make sure that file and printer sharing are not enabled for your Internet connection, unless you want to allow everyone on the Internet to access the files on your computer. On the Networking tab of the Properties dialog box for your Internet connection, make sure that the check boxes are not selected for these two components:*

- *File and Printer Sharing for Microsoft Networks*
- *Client for Microsoft Networks*

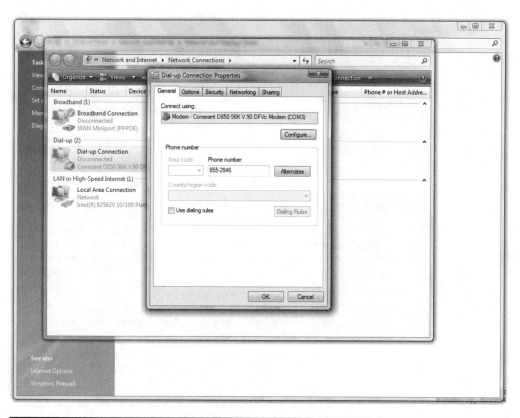

FIGURE 24-4   The Properties dialog box for a dial-up connection.

Configuring a TCP/IP Connection

For a connection to an Internet account, you may also need to configure the TCP/IP protocol. In the Properties dialog box for the connection, click the Networking tab, select Internet Protocol Version 6 (TCP/IPv6) or Internet Protocol Version 4 (TCP/IPv4) in the list of components, and then click the Properties button. Most current ISPs use Internet Protocol Version 4 (TCP/IPv4), but some have started using the newer Internet Protocol Version 6 (TCP/IPv6) protocol. You may want to configure each setting to ensure connectivity. You see the Internet Protocol Version 4 (TCP/IPv4) Properties dialog box, shown in Figure 24-5.

When your computer is connected to the Internet using TCP/IP, it has its own *IP address* (*IP* is the acronym for Internet Protocol). An IP address is in the form of *xxx.xxx.xxx.xxx*, where each *xxx* is a number from 0 to 255. (That is, an IP address consists of four 8-bit numbers.) An example of an IP address might be 204.71.16.253.

In addition to IP addresses, computers on the Internet have *domain names*, alphanumeric names like www.microsoft.com or http://net.gurus.com. A *domain name server* or *DNS* is a computer on the Internet that translates between domain names and numeric IP addresses.

Tab in Properties Dialog Box	Setting	Description
General	Connecting using	Specifies which modem to use to connect. Click the Configure button to check or change the configuration of the modem (see Chapter 22).
General	Phone number	Specifies the phone number your computer dials to connect to the account. Composed of the area code, telephone number, and country code (you choose from a list of countries). Click the Alternates button to enter additional phone numbers. Select the Use Dialing Rules check box to use area code dialing rules and calling cards (see "Setting Up Area Code Rules" in Chapter 22).
Options	Display progress while connecting	Specifies whether to display the Connection dialog box, which shows whether Windows is dialing or verifying your username and password before the connection is made.
Options	Prompt for name and password, certificate, etc.	Specifies whether to display a dialog box that prompts for your username and password (or other security information if your account requires it) before connecting.
Options	Include Windows logon domain	Specifies that if the preceding check box is selected, Windows also prompts for your logon domain. This setting isn't used by most ISPs.
Options	Prompt for phone number	Specifies whether to include the phone number in the Connect dialog box displayed before connecting to the account. This setting allows you to check or change the phone number each time you dial the account.
Options	Redial attempts	Specifies how many times Windows redials the connection if it can't connect.
Options	Time between redial attempts	Specifies how long Windows waits before dialing again.
Options	Idle time before hanging up	Specifies whether Windows disconnects if the connection is idle for a specified length of time. Choose Never to disable auto-disconnect.
Options	Idle threshold	Specifies the idle time when your Internet connection automatically disconnects.
Options	Redial if line is dropped	Specifies whether Windows reconnects if the connection is lost (for example, if the ISP hangs up).
Options	PPP Settings	Displays the PPP Settings dialog box, in which you can configure PPP settings for your dial-up account.

TABLE 24-1   Settings for a Dial-Up Connection (*continued*)

Tab in Properties Dialog Box	Setting	Description
Security	Validate my identity as follows	Specifies how your ISP determines who you are. For most ISPs, choose Allow Unsecured Password (that is, passwords are sent unencrypted). For corporate networks, you may need to choose Require Secured Password or Use Smart Card.
Security	Automatically use my Windows logon name and password (and domain if any)	Specifies what username and password to use (available only if you set the preceding setting to Require Selected Password or Use Smart Card). Usually not selected for Internet accounts.
Security	Require data encryption (disconnect if none)	Specifies that the computer to which you are connecting must support encryption for all information transmitted, and to disconnect otherwise (available only if you set the preceding setting to Require Selected Password or Use Smart Card). This setting is rarely used.
Security	Advanced (custom settings)	Click the Settings button to display the Advanced Security Settings dialog box, in which you can specify EAP (Extensible Authentication Protocol) or other advanced protocols, if your ISP supports them.
Security	Show terminal window	Specifies whether to display a terminal window that shows the interaction between the network connection and the account while the logon script is running. During debugging, select this setting so you can see the terminal window.
Security	Run script	Specifies the name of the file containing the logon script for this connection (see "Creating and Using Logon Scripts" later in the chapter). Click Edit to edit a script file or click Browse to select an existing file.
Networking	This connection uses the following items	Specifies the network connection services, protocols (such as TCP/IP), and clients that are installed for your Internet connection. These settings specify how to communicate over the network. Most connections use TCP/IP and QoS Packet Scheduler (see the sidebar "What Is TCP/IP?" earlier in the chapter) See Chapter 30 for information about other protocols.
Sharing	Allow other network users to connect through this computer's Internet connection	Specifies whether to run ICS on this PC, allowing other computers on the LAN to access the Internet through your connection (see Chapter 32).

TABLE 24-1   Settings for a Dial-Up Connection (*continued*)

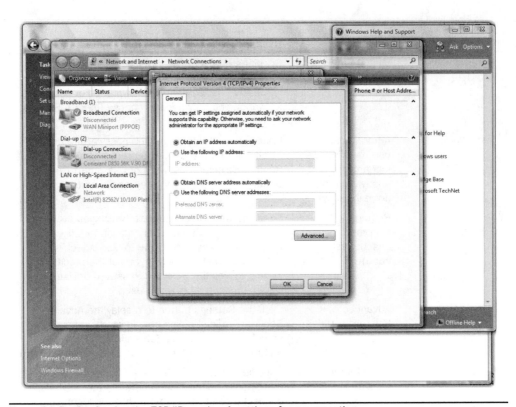

FIGURE 24-5   Configuring the TCP/IP version 4 settings for a connection.

Your ISP usually provides two DNS servers (one is in case the other one breaks down).
In the Internet Protocol (TCP/IP) Properties dialog box, make these entries:

- **Your IP address**   Ten years ago, when you signed up for an Internet account, your
  ISP assigned you a static IP address (see the sidebar "What Is TCP/IP?" earlier in
  the chapter)—an IP address that never changed. Now, almost all ISPs assign you a
  temporary IP address when you connect, so choose Obtain An IP Address
  Automatically unless your ISP has given you a static IP address (unlikely).

- **DNS Server Address**   Until a few years ago, you needed to choose Use The
  Following DNS Server Addresses and type the addresses in. Now most ISPs can tell
  Windows the DNS addresses when you connect, so choose Obtain DNS Server
  Address Automatically unless your ISP tells you otherwise.

NOTE *For more settings, click the Advanced button to see the Advanced TCP/IP Settings dialog box. Few ISPs require you to change these settings.*

Creating and Using Logon Scripts

Windows tries to log on to your dial-up account automatically. Most accounts follow a standard series of steps: they transmit your username and your account password, and then receive confirmation that you are logged in so that communications can begin.

If your account uses a nonstandard dialog box for logging in, Windows can't log in automatically. You can automate logging in by creating a *logon script*, a text file containing a small program that tells Windows what prompts to wait for and what to type in response. For example, if your ISP's computer uses a nonstandard prompt to ask for your password, or requires you to type a command to begin a PPP session, you can write a script to log on for you. If your ISP uses the standard series of transmissions, you don't need a logon script. Logon scripts have the file extension .scp.

To use a logon script, follow these steps:

1. Log on manually, making notes about which prompts you see and what you must type in response to those prompts. To log in manually, you can use your network connection with a *terminal window*, which enables you to see the session and type commands to your ISP. To tell Windows to open a terminal window while connecting, click the Security tab of the Properties dialog box for the connection and select the Show Terminal Window check box.

2. Create a logon script by using a text editor, such as Notepad (see "Reading Text Files with Notepad" in Chapter 21). A sample script file, named SWITCH.INF, provides some information on writing scripts. Usually your ISP has ready-made scripts that it can provide to set up scripts on your computer.

3. Tell Windows about the logon script by selecting the Run Script check box on the Security tab of the Properties dialog box for the connection and typing the filename in the box to its right.

4. Test the script, editing it with your text editor and viewing the results in a terminal window.

5. You can deselect the Show Terminal Windows check box when your script works, if you are tired of seeing the terminal window each time you connect.

Setting Additional Dial-Up Options

You might think all the properties of a dial-up connection would appear on the connection's Properties dialog box (shown earlier in the chapter in Figure 24-4), but they don't. Most of the settings on the (ill-named) Internet Properties dialog box pertain to your web browser rather than to your Internet connection, but a few additional settings appear on its Connections tab. (This dialog box is called Internet Options when you display it by choosing Tools | Internet Options from Internet Explorer.)

To display the Internet Properties dialog box, choose Start | Control Panel | Network And Internet and run the Internet Options program. Figure 24-6 shows the Connections tab

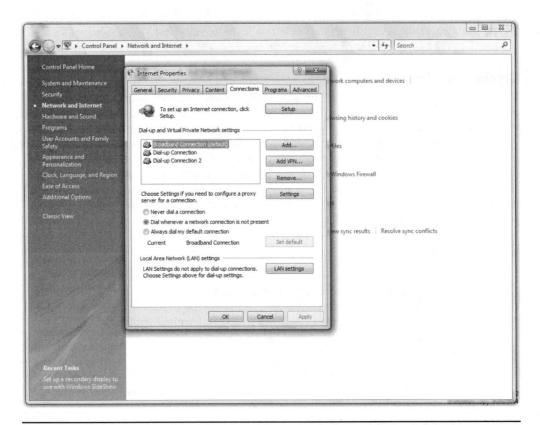

FIGURE 24-6   The Connections tab of the Internet Properties (or Internet Options) dialog box.

of the Internet Properties (or Internet Options) dialog box. The other tabs of this dialog box apply to using a web browser, and are covered in Chapter 26. Most of the settings on the Connections tab control your Internet connection:

- **Dial-up And Virtual Private Network Settings**   Lists your dial-up connections, so you can enable those to use, disable those not to use, configure them, and set the default connection.

- **Never Dial A Connection, Dial Whenever A Network Connection Is Not Present, and Always Dial My Default Connection**   Specify what Windows does when a program tries to connect to the Internet (for example, an e-mail program tries to connect to a mail server, or a web browser tries to retrieve a web page).

- **Current**   Displays the name of the connection Windows uses unless you specify another connection. To change the default, select a connection from the Dial-Up **And Virtual Private Network** Settings list and click the Set Default button.

Click the Setup or Add button to create a new connection: both buttons run the Connect To The Internet Wizard, but you see a different series of screen (it looks like two slightly different wizards with the same name!). The Settings button displays a Settings dialog box (shown in Figure 24-7) that contains settings for the selected connection: you see the same

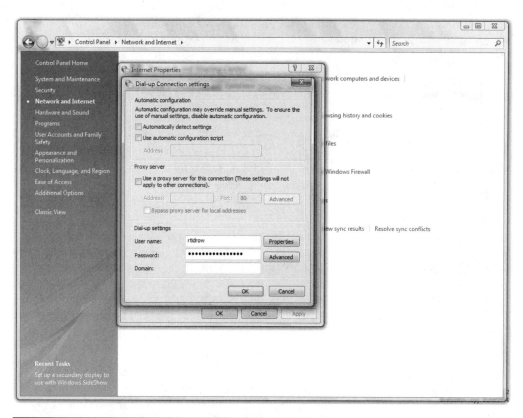

Figure 24-7 Settings dialog box for a dial-up connection.

settings that appear in the Properties dialog box for the connection, but arranged differently. A few items on the Settings dialog box pertain to connecting to the Internet over a LAN. Clicking the LAN Settings button on the Connections tab of the Internet Properties (or Internet Options) dialog box displays the LAN Settings dialog box, which also contains LAN-related settings (see "ICS Server Configuration Details" in Chapter 32).

Renaming, Copying, or Deleting a Network Connection

You can rename a network connection by clicking Rename This Connection from the Network Connection window. You also can right-click the connection and choose Rename from the menu that appears. This action changes the name that appears on your computer for the connection; it doesn't change any of the information sent to the ISP.

Sometimes you may want two or more versions of the same dial-up connection. For example, you might dial into your ISP from different numbers depending on where you take your laptop. To copy a connection, right-click its icon in the Network Connections window and choose Create Copy. A new icon appears. Rename the new copy and change its settings by right-clicking it and choosing Properties.

If you don't expect to connect to a particular account in the future, delete its connection from the Network Connections window by selecting the icon for the connection and clicking

Delete This Connection from the Network Connections window. Or, you can press the DELETE key (or right-click the connection icon and choose Delete). Be sure you also delete any shortcuts to the connection.

Connecting to Your Account

You can tell Windows to connect to your Internet account automatically when a program asks for information from the Internet, or you can tell Windows when to connect.

NOTE *Some Internet connections, such as many DSL and cable Internet connections, are connected all the time, so you don't need to connect—you're online all the time.*

Dialing the Internet Automatically

What happens if you aren't connected to the Internet and you tell your e-mail program to fetch your mail, or you ask your web browser to display a web page? Windows usually tries to dial up and connect to your Internet account automatically when you request Internet-based information.

To set Windows to connect automatically, follow these steps:

1. Choose Start | Control Panel | Network And Internet | Internet Options (or choose Tools | Internet Options from Internet Explorer) to display the Internet Properties (or Internet Options) dialog box, shown earlier in Figure 24-6.

2. Click the Connections tab and make sure the Always Dial My Default Connection setting is selected. (If your computer is sometimes connected to the Internet over a LAN, choose Dial Whenever A Network Connection Is Not Present instead.)

3. Click the dial-up connection you want to use and then click the Set Default button to make this connection the one Windows will use.

4. With the dial-up connection still selected, click Settings to display the Settings dialog box for the connection (see Figure 24-7).

5. In the Dial-Up Settings part of the dialog box, type your username and password.

6. Click the Advanced button to display the Advanced Dial-Up dialog box.

7. Set the number of times to try to connect, how long to wait between dialing attempts, whether to disconnect if the Internet connection has been idle, and whether to disconnect when the program that originally triggered the connection exits.

8. Click OK to dismiss the Advanced Dial-Up dialog box and click OK again to dismiss the Internet Properties dialog box.

When you use an Internet program and Windows detects you are asking for information from the Internet, Windows dials your default connection. You don't see anything at all if you have configured the connection not to display the progress of the connection (using the Display Progress While Connecting check box on the Options tab of the Properties dialog box). If the connection is configured to display its progress, you see a Connecting dialog box, which displays the progress of your connection.

The dialog box displays messages as it dials, connects, and logs into your Internet account using the information in the Dial-Up Settings dialog box.

Automatically dialing the Internet can be annoying, too. For example, if you are reading your e-mail offline and open a message that contains a link to the Web, you might not want your computer to dial into the Internet. If you no longer want Windows to connect automatically to the Internet, display the Internet Properties (or Internet Options) dialog box, click the Connections tab, and click the Never Dial A Connection option.

Dialing the Internet Manually

Usually, Windows connects to the Internet automatically (as described in the preceding section). However, you can also tell Windows to dial in, by following these steps:

1. Display the Network Connections window (see "What Are Network Connections?" earlier in the chapter). Then click the connection icon (or double-click it, depending on how Windows is configured). If a connection icon appears on your desktop, you can run it instead. You see the Connect dialog box, shown in Figure 24-8.

2. If the username, password, or phone number doesn't appear, fill it in. (See "Configuring Windows for Dialing Locations" in Chapter 23 for instructions on how to set up dialing locations, if you use a laptop computer in more than one location.)

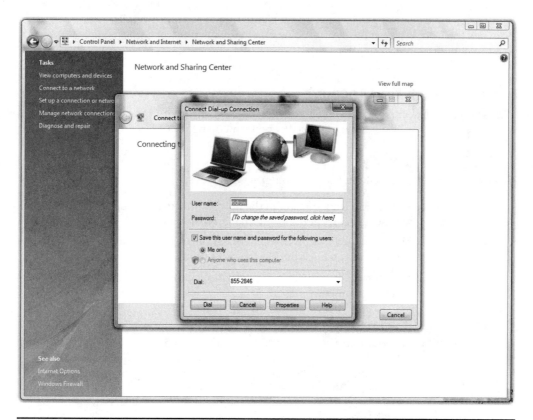

FIGURE 24-8   Dialing up a network connection.

3. Unless you are worried about someone else using your computer to connect to your account, select the Save This User Name And Password For The Following Users check box so you needn't type your password each time you connect. Choose whether Windows saves this information only for when you are logged into the computer or for all user accounts (see Chapter 6).

4. Click the Dial button. Windows dials your account and logs in. You may see a window telling you that you're connected to the account.

TIP *If you see a window confirming that you are connected, click the Do Not Display This Message In The Future check box, so you needn't see this confirmation dialog box each time you connect to the Internet.*

5. Click the Close button.

While you are connected, the dial-up connection icon—two overlapping computer screens—may appear in the notification area at the right end of the taskbar. (It appears if you have selected the Show Icon In Notification Area When Connected check box on the General tab of the Properties dialog box for the connection.) Move the mouse pointer to the icon (without clicking) to see the name of the connection, your connection speed, and how many bytes have been sent and received. Click the icon to see more details.

Click the Details tab on the status dialog box to see the modem name, connection type, IP address, and other information.

Disconnecting from Your Account

When you are done using the Internet, you can disconnect. Or you can configure Windows to disconnect automatically when the connection isn't being used.

Disconnecting Manually

You can disconnect your Internet connection in several ways:

- If a dial-up connection icon appears in the notification area of the taskbar, right-click it and choose Disconnect from the menu that appears.
- Click the dial-up connection icon in the notification area to display the status dialog box for the connection and click the Disconnect button.
- Choose Start | Connect To and choose the dial-up connection to display its status dialog box. Click Disconnect.

Disconnecting Automatically

If you are connected to your Internet account and don't use it for a while (usually 20 minutes), Windows or your ISP may disconnect you automatically. You may see a dialog box asking whether you want to disconnect. You can't control whether your ISP hangs up on you after a period of inactivity, but you can configure Windows to set whether and when to disconnect. Follow these steps:

1. Choose Start | Control Panel | Network And Internet Connections | Internet Options (or choose Tools | Internet Options from Internet Explorer) to display the Internet Properties (or Internet Options) dialog box, shown earlier in Figure 24-6.

2. Click the Connections tab.

3. Click the dial-up connection for which you want to configure auto-disconnection and click the Settings button. You see the Settings dialog box for the connection.

4. Click the Advanced button to display the Advanced Dial-Up dialog box.

5. To tell Windows to hang up after a specific time during which no information is transmitted, select the Disconnect If Idle For *xx* Minutes check box and set the number of minutes.

6. To tell Windows to hang up when no Internet programs are running, select the Disconnect When Connection May No Longer Be Needed check box.

7. Click OK three times to dismiss all the dialog boxes.

Using Windows Mail for E-mail

The most popular use of the Internet is to send and receive messages from other Internet users. Windows Vista comes with Windows Mail (previously named Outlook Express), Microsoft's free e-mail and newsreading program. You can also install and use any number of mail and newsreading applications, whether they are Microsoft products or not. Windows Vista also comes with Windows Contacts for keeping track of names, addresses, e-mail addresses, or whatever information you happen to have about people.

This chapter describes how to use Windows Mail to send and receive e-mail messages, and organize the messages you decide to keep. This chapter also describes how to use Windows Contacts, both with and without Windows Mail.

Should You Use Windows Mail?

If you are a happy user of Microsoft Office Outlook, Mozilla Thunderbird, Yahoo! Mail, Google Mail (Gmail), or another e-mail program, Windows Mail doesn't contain any gotta-have features that would make you want to switch. The hassle of importing your messages (which never seem to come through perfectly) isn't worth it. However, if you are a new user who doesn't have a lot of message files, or if you have used other e-mail programs and have been unhappy with them, Windows Mail is worth a try.

The case for using Windows Mail gets a little better with each new version. Windows Mail has a number of advantages: it's free, already installed, and easy to use; it has a nice collection of features for handling e-mail and newsgroups; it lets you import messages and addresses from most other popular e-mail programs; and it works well with Office Live Mail (also called Hotmail), Microsoft's free web-based e-mail provider.

Windows assumes that Windows Mail is your *default e-mail program* (the program that runs when another program tells Windows that you want to send e-mail). If you install another e-mail program, its installation program usually asks whether to make it the default e-mail program. If you plan to use it regularly to send and receive e-mail, choose Yes.

How Does E-mail Work?

Oversimplifying the process somewhat, e-mail works like this:

1. Using an e-mail program, such as Windows Mail, the sender creates a message and decides who the recipients should be.

2. At a designated place at the beginning of the message, the sender lists the e-mail addresses of all the recipients. (The sender can specify a long list of recipients, but for simplicity, we'll pretend there is only one.) An *e-mail address* specifies two things: a computer on the Internet on which a recipient receives mail (called an *incoming mail server*), and the name that the incoming mail server uses to designate the mailbox of the recipient. So, for example, the e-mail address president@whitehouse .gov specifies the incoming mail server whitehouse.gov and a mailbox on whitehouse.gov called president.

3. The sender connects to an *outgoing mail server*, a computer connected to the Internet (usually a computer owned by the sender's Internet service provider, or ISP) that runs a mail-handling program that supports the *Simple Mail Transfer Protocol (SMTP)*, which is used for Internet mail). These servers are usually called *SMTP servers*. The message is sent from the sender's computer to the outgoing mail server.

4. From the outgoing mail server, the message is passed across the Internet to the recipient's incoming mail server.

5. The recipient's incoming mail server files the message in the recipient's *mailbox*, a file or folder containing all the messages that the recipient hasn't downloaded to her own computer yet.

6. Using an e-mail program (which need not be the same as the one the sender used to create and send the message), the recipient looks for new mail by logging into the incoming mail server. Incoming mail servers use one of three protocols for receiving mail: *Post Office Protocol 3* (abbreviated *POP3* or *POP*), *Internet Message Access Protocol (IMAP)*, or *Hypertext Transfer Protocol (HTTP)*. The incoming mail server uses POP or IMAP to deliver the message to the recipient's computer, along with any other messages that may have arrived since the recipient last checked for mail.

NOTE *Windows Mail does not support HTTP servers, such as those used for Hotmail. If you try to select the option for setting up an HTTP incoming mail server, you see a message to the effect that you must set up a different e-mail type (POP3 or IMAP).*

---

7. The recipient uses the e-mail program to read the message.

Every e-mail message consists of a *header* (lines containing the address, the return address, the date, and other information about the message) and a *body* (the text of the message).

TIP *To send messages right away to people who are logged in at the same time you are, and receive answers in seconds, use an instant messaging program like Windows Messenger (see "Chatting Online with Windows Live Messenger" in Chapter 27).*

What Are Attached Files?

Sometimes when you write e-mail, you want to send more than just a message; you want to send files that the recipient can use with an application on her computer. For example, if you are working on a Word document with someone, you don't just want to talk about the document in your e-mail, you want to send revised versions of the document back and forth.

Attached files (or *attachments* for short) are files that you send along with an e-mail message. The recipient can save the files on their own computer system and/or use them with their own applications. See "Attaching a File to a Message" later in this chapter for directions on how to attach files to e-mail messages.

How Do E-mail Viruses Work?

E-mail viruses are computer viruses—rogue programs that hackers write to do mischief on other people's computers—that spread by e-mailing copies of themselves to other computers. (Technically, such programs are *worms*, not viruses, but the popular press does not usually make this distinction.) If an e-mail virus gets into your computer, it may try to send infected e-mail to everyone in your address book (Windows Contacts). The e-mail sent will look like it is coming from you—which won't make you popular with the people in your address book.

The most common (but not the only) way for e-mail viruses to spread is through file attachments, especially attachments that are executable (EXE) files or that invoke powerful applications such as Java or ActiveX. The text of the message is a lure to get you to open the attachment. (Remember: the message comes to you from someone who has you in his address book, so it looks like your good friend Bob has sent you a mysterious attachment with a message saying something like "Try this. It's fun.") Once you open the attachment, your computer is infected.

By default, Windows Mail is set up to reduce the number of security problems with incoming messages. However, if you decide to disable security features in Windows Mail, it can be vulnerable to viruses, both because it is widely used and because it can automatically run programs that arrive attached to e-mail messages. To decrease your risk of getting e-mail viruses, see the section "Protecting Yourself from E-mail Viruses" later in this chapter. For more about viruses in general and what you can do to protect your system, see "Protecting Your System from Viruses and Worms" in Chapter 33.

What Are Newsgroups?

Newsgroups provide another way for you to use your computer and the Internet to communicate with the outside world. Newsgroups are called Microsoft Communities by Microsoft. Unlike e-mail, however, a newsgroup is a public medium. When you send a message to a newsgroup, the message is available to anyone who wants to look at it—it's as if you have tacked up a notice on a public bulletin board. You never know who—if anyone—reads your message. The Internet-based system of newsgroups is called *Usenet*.

Newsgroups are organized by topic. Because there are tens of thousands of newsgroups, topics can be very specific. When you have something to say about the topic of a newsgroup, you can use a *newsreading program*, such as Windows Mail, to compose a message (which may be many pages or only one line) and send it to your *news server*, a computer on the Internet that supports the *Network News Transfer Protocol (NNTP)*, which makes your message available to other news servers. People who want to read the recent contributions to this newsgroup (including your message) can use a newsreading program (not necessarily the same as yours) to download messages from their own news servers.

Getting Started with Windows Mail

To begin using Windows Mail, choose Start | All Programs | Windows Mail. When you run Windows Mail for the first time, you may be greeted with a dialog box asking if Windows Mail should be your default e-mail client. In other words, should Windows launch Windows Mail whenever you give a command to send mail from some other application (such as Internet Explorer or Windows Contacts)? Choose Yes or No. If you intend to choose No, uncheck the Always Perform This Check When Starting Windows Mail check box so that you are not nagged.

Working with the Windows Mail Window

The Windows Mail window, shown in Figure 25-1, resembles an Explorer window. At the top is a menu bar, with a toolbar underneath it. Below the toolbar, the window is divided into three panes. The upper-left pane is a folder list, similar to the left pane in an Explorer window. Local Folders is at the top of the list and has subfolders, such as Inbox, Outbox, and Sent Items. The right pane contains two panes: the upper pane shows a list of messages for the selected folder (in this case the Inbox folder); the lower pane shows the full text of a selected message.

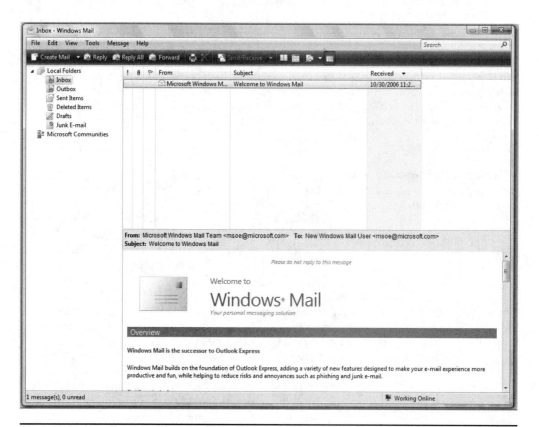

FIGURE 25-1   Your first view of Windows Mail.

The folders immediately beneath Local Folders on the folder list are necessary parts of the mail system:

- **Inbox**   Where Windows Mail puts the incoming messages that it downloads from your incoming mail server. The messages remain there until you delete them or move them to another folder.

- **Outbox**   Contains the outgoing messages that you have completed and chosen to send, but have not yet been sent. For example, you might complete and choose to send several messages while you are offline. Those messages wait in the Outbox folder until the next time your computer is connected to your outgoing mail server.

- **Sent Items**   Contains messages that you have sent. Messages remain in this folder until you delete or move them.

- **Deleted Items**   Contains the messages (both incoming and outgoing) that you have deleted. Like the Recycle Bin, it is a last-chance folder that gets unwanted messages out of the way, but from which they still can be retrieved. Windows Mail can be set up to clean out the Deleted Items folder automatically, or you can delete messages from it manually (see "Saving and Deleting Messages" later in the chapter). Windows Mail cannot retrieve messages deleted from the Deleted Items folder.

- **Drafts**   Contains unfinished messages that you have chosen to save and work on later. Any time you are composing a message, you can choose File | Save to save the message in the Drafts folder.

- **Junk E-mail**   Contains messages that you or Windows Mail considers junk mail based on who sends you the message.

As you begin sending and receiving messages, you can set up other folders to keep track of your correspondence (see "Organizing Your Correspondence" later in the chapter). You don't have to do so, but if you plan to keep copies of messages, they will be easier to find if you sort them into folders by topic or by correspondent.

Setting Up Your Accounts

Before Windows Mail can send or receive mail, or allow you to interact with newsgroups, you need to tell it what accounts you have and how it can access them. Have the following information handy:

- **The name you want attached to any message you send**   Do you want to be known as Johnny Public, Jonathan Q. Public, or by some nickname?

- **Your return e-mail address**   If people want to reply to your messages, where should the replies go?

- **The names of the servers your account deals with**   You provide two names: one server for incoming mail (a POP or IMAP server) and one server for outgoing mail (an SMTP server, for example). Your ISP should have given you this information—if you don't have it, check the ISP's web site or call them.

- **Your username and password (if any) for logging into the servers**   This information also comes from your ISP.

Once you have assembled this information, you need to tell Windows Mail. From the Windows Mail menu bar, choose Tools | Accounts. When the Internet Accounts dialog box opens, click the Add button and select the type of account you want to define: mail, news, or directory service. Choose Mail for an e-mail account.

You have to go through this process once for each account you want to establish. Windows Mail runs the mail setup wizard, which collects the necessary information about your e-mail account. When you complete the wizard for your new account, Windows Mail attempts to connect to your account and download new messages.

Importing Messages from Other Mail Programs

If you've been using e-mail for a while, your message files are an asset. Continuity can be an important reason to stay with whatever mail program you've been using. Windows Mail lets you convert your message files from these other mail programs:

- Microsoft Exchange
- Microsoft Outlook
- Microsoft Outlook Express 6
- Microsoft Windows Mail 7

TIP *If you decide that you don't like Windows Mail and want to go back to your old e-mail client, do not rely on that client's ability to import Windows Mail messages. If you plan to try Windows Mail for a few days before choosing between it and your old mail program, set Windows Mail to leave your incoming messages on your incoming mail server, and collect your mail using both programs until you make up your mind. Choose Tools | Accounts, click the mail account, and choose Properties. Click the Advanced tab and select the Leave A Copy Of Messages On Server check box. Above all, you should inspect your imported files for completeness before throwing away the originals, or just archive the originals somewhere.*

To import messages from one of these mail applications, select File | Import | Messages and then select the type of mail you want to import using the Windows Mail Import wizard, shown in Figure 25-2. The wizard needs to know the application from which it is importing, and where the files are located. If your old e-mail program isn't installed, you may need to install it for the import to work (for example, if are moving your e-mail files to a new computer).

Folders of imported messages show up in the Local Folders folder list, from which you can move them into whatever folders you like (see "Organizing Your Correspondence" later in the chapter). The imported folders retain their names and structure. For example, say you import a folder from Microsoft Outlook named People At Work, with subfolders Bob and Jenny. When it arrives in Windows Mail, it should still have the subfolders it contained, and those subfolders should contain all the messages they had in Outlook. (However, in our experience, subfolders don't always import correctly.)

Importing Addresses from Other Mail Programs

Windows Mail can import addresses in these formats:

- CSV (Comma Separated Values), which are text files with one line per entry and fields separated by commas

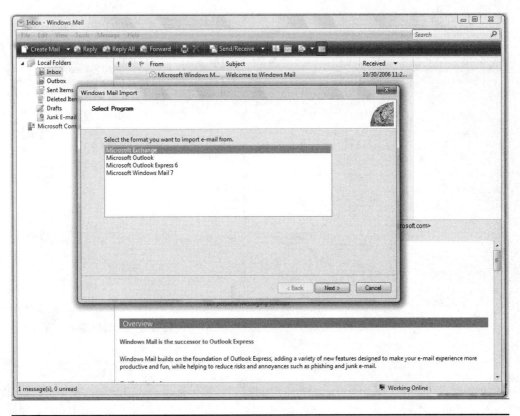

FIGURE 25-2   Importing messages from other e-mail programs into Windows Mail.

- LDIF (LDAP Data Interchange Format) directories
- vCard (VCF file) from Microsoft Office Outlook
- Windows Address Book File (Outlook Express contacts)

To import addresses into Windows Mail:

1. Select File | Import | Windows Contacts from the menu.
2. Answer the questions asked by the Import To Windows Contacts wizard.

If all goes well, the addresses wind up in Windows Contacts (see "Storing Addresses in Windows Contacts" later in the chapter).

Choosing a Layout for the Windows Mail Window

Like Windows Explorer, the Windows Mail window provides a number of features that you can choose to display or not display. When all the features are made visible, you get a busy, complicated window, as shown in Figure 25-3.

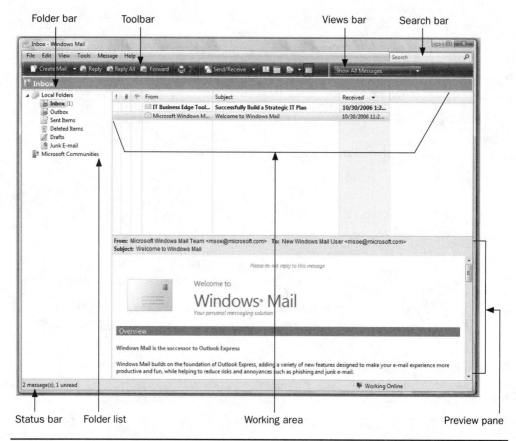

FIGURE 25-3 All the features of Windows Mail, if you choose to display them.

You can make any of these features (other than the working area) appear or disappear as you like. Choose View | Layout to display the Window Layout Properties dialog box, check the features that you want to have in your Windows Mail window, and click OK.

We recommend displaying the folder list, toolbar, status bar, and Search bar.

Sending and Receiving E-mail

After you set up one or more mail accounts, you can check your mail by clicking the Send/ Receive button on the toolbar or choosing Tools | Send And Receive | Send And Receive All or pressing CTRL-M. After you have clicked Send/Receive, Windows Mail goes through the following process automatically:

1. Connects to your mail servers. If you are on a local area network, this part of the process may happen so quickly that it is almost invisible to you. If you connect to the Internet over a modem, however, and are not already online, Windows Mail uses your default dial-up connection to dial up your ISP. Once an Internet connection is established, Windows Mail contacts your mail servers over the Internet.

2. Sends all the messages in your Outbox. Messages you aren't ready to send should be stored in the Drafts folder, not in the Outbox.

3. Downloads all the incoming messages from the server into your Inbox (or into other folders if you have defined message rules that sort your incoming correspondence; see "Filtering Your Mail with Message Rules" later in the chapter).

By default, clicking the Send/Receive button sends all queued messages and checks for mail in all of the e-mail accounts Windows Mail knows about. If you want to be more selective, click the drop-down arrow next to the Send/Receive button. A drop-down menu offers you the following choices:

- **Send And Receive All**   Sends all queued messages and checks for incoming mail in all known accounts. The default.

- **Receive All**   Checks for incoming mail in all known accounts, but doesn't send queued messages.

- **Send All**   Sends all queued messages, but doesn't check for incoming mail.

- **Individual Listings Of Your E-mail Accounts**   Choosing an account sends and receives for that account only.

The same choices are available from the Tools | Send And Receive menu.

While messages are downloading, a Windows Mail progress dialog box appears.

Table 25-1 shows some of the most important configuration options for sending and receiving messages. (We omit those that are self-explanatory.) Choose Tools | Options to display the Options dialog box that shows these settings.

Receiving Mail

New mail accumulates in your Inbox and stays there until you delete it or move it to another folder. To see your new mail, click Inbox in the folder list of the Windows Mail window. The window has three panes, as it does when you look at any mail folder: the folder list, the message list, and the selected message. You can drag the boundaries of these three panes to reallocate the space occupied by each. The three panes are the following:

- **The folder list view in the left pane**   The selected folder is highlighted. In Figure 25-4, Inbox is the selected folder.

- **The selected folder's message list in the upper-right pane**   Each message receives one line in the list. The line tells who the author of the message is, what the Subject line says, and when the message was received (or sent, if the message is outgoing). If the author rated the message as Urgent, an exclamation point (!) appears on the left side of its entry on the list. If the message has an attachment (a file attached to the message), a paper clip icon appears to the left of its entry. The currently selected message is highlighted. Unread messages have a closed-envelope icon next to them; read messages have an open-envelope icon.

- **A preview of the selected message in the lower-right pane**   The bar at the top of the lower-right pane lists the sender and receiver of the message, together with the Subject line. Below this bar is a scrollable window containing the full text of the message.

Tab	Setting	Description
General	Send and receive messages at startup	When you start Windows Mail, sends messages in your Outbox and downloads messages from your incoming mail server.
General	Check for new messages every *xx* minutes	Specifies how often Windows Mail connects automatically to the mail servers to download incoming messages and upload outgoing messages.
General	If my computer is not connected at this time	Specifies what to do if your computer is not connected to the Internet when Windows Mail tries to check for new messages. Your options are Do Not Connect, Connect Only When Not Working Offline, and Connect Even When Working Offline.
Read	Mark message read after displaying for *xx* seconds	Specifies that Windows Mail mark a message as read after displaying it in the Preview pane for the specified time.
Read	Fonts button	Enables you to set the fonts in which Windows Mail displays unformatted messages.
Receipts	Returning Read Receipts	Specifies how to process *return receipt requests* (tags attached to e-mail messages that request a receipt so that the sender knows that you've seen the message). Not all ISPs and e-mail programs support return receipts.
Send	Save copy of sent messages in the 'Sent Items' folder	Specifies that Windows Mail keep copies of your outgoing messages. You can move them from the Sent Items folder to another folder after the message is sent.
Send	Send messages immediately	Specifies that Windows Mail connect to your outgoing mail server and send messages whenever a message is in your Outbox (see "Sending Messages" later in the chapter).
Security	Select the Internet Explorer security zone to use	Specifies which security zone to use when deciding whether or not to let ActiveX controls and other potentially dangerous scripts and programs run (see "Internet Explorer's Zones" in Chapter 33).
Security	Warn me when other applications try to send mail as me	Stops a virus program from spreading itself via e-mail without your knowledge.

TABLE 25-1   Settings of the Options Dialog Box (*continued*)

Tab	Setting	Description
Security	Do not allow attachments to be saved or opened that could potentially be a virus	Refuses to open or save file attachments in formats used by most e-mail viruses.
Connection	Ask before switching dial-up connections	Should Windows Mail break an existing dial-up connection to use its default connection, or should it ask you what to do?
Connection	Hang up after sending and receiving	Specifies that after sending and receiving messages, Windows Mail disconnect from the Internet.

TABLE 25-1   Settings of the Options Dialog Box (*continued*)

Selected folder   Selected message

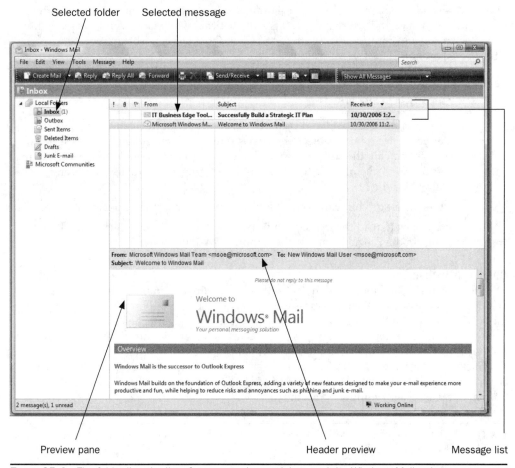

Preview pane   Header preview   Message list

FIGURE 25-4   The folder list, the list of messages in your Inbox, and the Windows Mail welcome message.

Customizing the Message List

To choose what columns are displayed in the message list, right-click the row of column headings and choose Columns from the shortcut menu. The Columns dialog box appears, listing the possible columns Windows Mail can display. Check the columns you want. You may also use this dialog box to rearrange the columns by selecting a column name and clicking the Move Up or Move Down button. You can switch the order of the columns by dragging the header left or right. You can use the Columns dialog box to fix the widths of the columns in the message list as well, but dragging the boundaries between the columns in the message list itself is simpler.

Sorting the Messages in a Folder

You can sort the messages in a folder according to any of the columns in the message list—just click the label above any of the columns. Click once to sort in ascending order, twice for descending order.

For example, clicking the From column label sorts the messages according to sender. The various senders appear in alphabetical order, but the program is not smart enough to recognize first names and last names, so it is alphabetical by the name as it is displayed. (Abe Zachary would come before Smith John.) Click From again to sort in reverse alphabetical order.

Reading the Messages in a Folder

To read the messages in any folder:

1. Click the name of the folder in the folder list of the Windows Mail window. If the folder you want is not visible, it either has scrolled off the edge of the folder list or is contained in another folder. Use the left pane scroll bar to look up or down in the folder list. Click the plus box next to a folder's name to see the list of folders contained inside it.

2. Find the message you want to read in the message list in the upper-right pane.

3. Double-click to read the message in its own window, or single-click to read the message in the Preview pane of the Windows Mail window.

Opening Attached Files

Messages with attached files are denoted with a paper clip icon in the message list of the Windows Mail window. When the message is selected, a larger paper clip icon appears in the title bar of the Preview pane. When the message is opened, attached files appear as icons just below the Subject line. Images from attached image files are appended to the bottom of the message automatically; you don't have to decide to open them.

Clicking the large paper clip icon produces a list of the attached files; selecting one of the files from this list opens the file. Similarly, selecting an attached-file icon from the bottom of the message window opens the file.

CAUTION   *Attached files are a major source of e-mail viruses. Don't open an attachment unless you know what it is.*

Protecting Yourself from E-mail Viruses

Because Microsoft Office Outlook and Windows Mail are so widely used, they are the most popular targets for the hackers who create e-mail viruses. Windows Mail contains several features for decreasing your vulnerability to e-mail viruses, including restricting attachments and warning you if any other program attempts to send e-mail from your computer using your identity. In addition, you have a choice of whether Windows Mail uses the rules of Internet Explorer's Internet zone or the much safer Restricted Sites zone (which we recommend; see "Internet Explorer's Zones" in Chapter 33). Finally, you can set up Windows Mail to direct possible junk mail to a Junk Mail folder, from which you can quickly delete messages you deem are from senders you do not want to bother even opening. (There are times, however, that Windows Mail is overzealous in sending things to the Junk Mail folder, including messages you may eventually deem fine. So you will have to check through the folder from time to time to ensure you get the messages you really want.)

These features and options are far from a panacea. The file types that are blocked are the most popular ones for e-mail viruses, but far from the only ones. Simply blocking HTML attachments does nothing to protect you from viruses that may be embedded in e-mail messages written in HTML. Whether you use these features or not, we recommend that you continue to be cautious: Do not open unexpected attachments from strangers, or even from friends if the accompanying message does not convince you that they are genuine.

Restricting Attachments

When you open a file attached to an e-mail message, the file is opened by the application appropriate to its file type, not by Windows Mail. In other words, if you don't know the file type of an attachment, you can't be sure what program will run when you open it. If the attachment is itself a program, opening the attachment turns the program loose to do whatever it was designed to do. Some types of files are more dangerous to open than others, because the applications that run them have the power to make fundamental changes to your system. In particular, executable (.exe extension) files, scripting files (such as .vbs for Visual Basic or .js for JavaScript), or files that contain links to other files that could contain executable code (like .htm or .url) are potentially dangerous.

CAUTION *Some viruses try to disguise the file type of their attachments by giving the files two extensions (for example, Loveletter.doc.vbs). If Windows is configured not to display all extensions, you might be fooled by the filename, which would appear without the last extension (for example, you'd just see the filename Loveletter.doc). To display all extensions, choose Start | Computer, choose Tools | Folder Options from the menu bar, click the View tab, and deselect the Hide Extensions For Known File Types check box.*

Windows Mail allows you to block attachments that it judges to be of a dangerous file type. To do this:

1. Select Tools | Options from the menu bar. The Options dialog box opens.
2. Click the Security tab.

PART V

3. Check the Do Not Allow Attachments To Be Saved Or Opened That Could Potentially Be A Virus check box.

4. Click OK.

To unblock all attachments, repeat these steps but uncheck the box in Step 3.

When the Do Not Allow Attachments To Be Saved Or Opened That Could Potentially Be A Virus box is checked, the paper clip icon still appears to tell you when a message has attachments. Clicking the icon reveals a list of attachments, but any attachments that are blocked appear dimmed, so that they cannot be selected. If you decide that you want to open or save these attachments, go back to the Security tab of the Options dialog box and uncheck the Do Not Allow Attachments To Be Saved Or Opened That Could Potentially Be A Virus box. You can then open or save attachments normally.

Note *Even if you are blocking some attachments, image file attachments still get through and are displayed appended to the end of the message they are attached to.*

Preventing Other Programs from Sending E-mail as You

By default, Windows Mail is set up to allow other programs to use it to send e-mail automatically. A virus program could use this feature to send itself to other people. You can alter this behavior so that Windows Mail will block such e-mail until you have confirmed that you want to send the message. Make this change as follows:

1. Select Tools | Options from the menu bar. The Options dialog box opens.

2. Click the Security tab.

3. Check the Warn Me When Other Applications Try To Send Mail As Me check box.

4. Click OK.

To undo this change, repeat these steps but uncheck the box in Step 3.

Choosing Your Security Zone

Windows Mail borrows its security zones from Internet Explorer. See "Internet Explorer's Zones" in Chapter 33 for more details about security zones and how to change the rules that apply to them. Windows Mail offers you a choice between the two most conservative zones: the Internet zone and the Restricted Sites zone. The Restricted Sites zone is more conservative (meaning more secure) and thus we recommend it.

To choose your security zone:

1. Select Tools | Options from the Windows Mail menu. The Options dialog box appears.

2. Click the Security tab.

3. Select the radio button of the security zone you want, and then click OK.

Composing Messages to Send

You create messages in three ways:

- **Compose a new message from scratch**   Click the Create Mail button on the Windows Mail toolbar

- **Reply to a message you have received**   Select a message from a Windows Mail folder (such as Inbox) and click either the Reply button or the Reply All button on the Windows Mail toolbar

- **Forward a message you have received**   Select a message from a Windows Mail folder and click the Forward button on the Windows Mail toolbar

Any of these three actions opens a message window, like this:

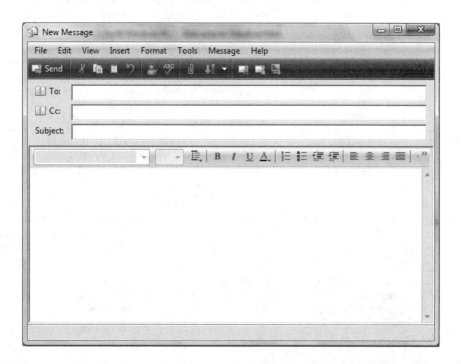

The message window has two main parts: a header and a body. The body is the window into which you enter the text of your message. Use it as you would use a word processor. If you are composing a plain-text message, you are limited (naturally) to plain text, but if you are composing in Rich Text (which is also HTML format), you can use different fonts, inserted images, and other fancy formatting. (If you use Rich Text, make sure your recipients use mail programs that can read HTML; otherwise they may see a mixture of text and HTML codes.) If you are composing a message from scratch, the body of the message window has nothing in it other than what you type. If you are forwarding a message, the text of the original message is included automatically. If you are replying, Windows Mail can be set up to either include or not include the original text (see "Including the Original Message in Your Reply" later in the chapter).

NOTE *When you reply to a message that has an attachment, the attachment is not included in the reply (because presumably the person doesn't want another copy of the file). When you forward a message with an attachment, the forwarded message includes the attachment.*

Table 25-2 shows the most important settings in the Options dialog box for composing messages. (Table 25-1, earlier in this chapter, listed other settings.) Choose Tools | Options to display the Options dialog box.

Tab	Setting	Description
Receipts	Request a Read Receipt for all sent messages	Specifies that your outgoing messages include return receipt requests so you know when the person opened the message. Not all e-mail programs respond to return receipt requests, and not all ISPs process them.
Receipts	Secure Receipts	Opens the Secure Receipts Options dialog box, from which you can specify whether your outgoing messages include a request for a *secure receipt* (return receipt for a digitally signed message) and how to respond to requests for secure receipts (see "Sending and Receiving E-mail Securely" in Chapter 33).
Send	Automatically put people I reply to in my Contacts list	Adds entries to Windows Contacts for each person to whom you send a reply (see "Storing Addresses in Windows Contacts" later in the chapter). If you reply to many messages from strangers to whom you are unlikely to write again, deselect this check box.
Send	Include message in reply	Specifies that replies contain the text of the original message in a quoted format (see "Including the Original Message in Your Reply" later in the chapter). Be sure to edit out the irrelevant parts of the original message.
Send	Reply to messages using the format in which they were sent	Composes replies to Rich Text–formatted messages using Rich Text (HTML) formatting, and composes replies to plain-text messages using plain text.
Send	Mail Sending Format: HTML/Plain Text	Specifies whether your e-mail messages are sent as HTML (Rich Text) or as plain text.
Compose	Compose Font: Mail	Specifies how unformatted messages appear on your screen when you are composing them.
Compose	Stationery: Mail	Specifies what stationery (standard formatting) your new messages will use. Rather than specifying mail stationery here, turn it on only for occasional messages (by choosing Format | Apply Stationery when composing a message).
Compose	Business Cards: Mail	Specifies that your virtual business card (vCard) be included when you compose new messages.
Signatures	Signatures	Enables you to create one or more *signatures*—a few lines of text that are appended to messages you send. Your signatures should contain your name and e-mail address, and should be no more than four lines long. Click New to create a signature, then type the text in the Edit Signature box.

TABLE 25-2 Message Composition Settings of the Options Dialog Box (*continued*)

Tab	Setting	Description
Spelling	Always check spelling before sending	Specifies that Windows Mail automatically run its spell checker when you send each message. Other settings on this tab control whether it suggests correct spellings and which words to skip.
Security	Digitally sign all outgoing messages	Adds a digital signature to all messages that proves that you sent the messages. Click Advanced to specify the type of digital signature.
Security	Encrypt contents and attachments for all outgoing messages	Encrypts (encodes) all outgoing messages so that they cannot be read unless the recipient has the encryption key. Click Advanced to specify the type of encryption.

TABLE 25-2   Message Composition Settings of the Options Dialog Box (*continued*)

Completing the Header

The header section of the message window consists of four lines (though Bcc may not appear unless View | All Headers is checked):

- **To**   Type the e-mail addresses of the primary recipient(s) of your message. If there is more than one recipient, separate the e-mail addresses with commas. Click the open-book icon to look up addresses in Windows Contacts (see "Storing Addresses in Windows Contacts" later in the chapter). This is the only line of the header that cannot be left blank (unless you enter addresses in the Cc or Bcc lines). If you generate the message window by choosing Reply, Windows Mail puts the address of the author of the original message on this line. If you use Reply All, Windows Mail lists the addresses of the author and the other recipients of the original message. You may add more addresses or delete some of them if you want to.

- **Cc (Carbon Copy)**   Type the e-mail addresses of secondary recipients (if any). If you opened this message window by clicking the Reply All button, Windows Mail uses the same Cc list as the original message. You may add to or delete from the list if you want to.

- **Bcc (Blind Carbon Copy)**   Type the e-mail addresses of other secondary recipients, if any. The recipients listed in the To and Cc boxes can see the list of other recipients listed in the To and Cc boxes, but not those listed in the Bcc box. If one of the To or Cc recipients replies to your message with Reply All, the recipients on your Bcc list will not receive the reply.

- **Subject**   Enter a word or short phrase to describe the subject of your message. The Subject line helps both you and your recipients to keep track of the message in your files. If you are replying to another message, Windows Mail automatically uses the original Subject line, preceded by Re. If you are forwarding, Windows Mail uses the original Subject line, preceded by Fw.

Including the Original Message in Your Reply

One advantage e-mail has over paper mail is that you can indicate exactly what part of an e-mail message you are responding to. To make Windows Mail automatically include the original message in any reply:

1. Select Tools | Options to open the Options dialog box.

2. Select the Send tab.

3. Check the Include Message In Reply check box and click OK.

By doing this, whenever you click the Reply or Reply All buttons, the body of the message window contains a divider, with the original message below the divider. The text of the original message is indented, with a > at the beginning of each line.

To remove the indentation or change the indentation character:

1. Open the Send tab of the Options dialog box, as just explained.

2. If Plain Text is selected as the Mail Sending Format, click the Plain Text Settings button to open the Plain Text Settings dialog box. If HTML is selected, click the HTML Settings button to open the HTML Settings dialog box.

3. Check the Indent The Original Text With check box at the bottom of the Plain Text Settings dialog box to indent the original text. The drop-down list next to the Indent The Original Text With check box lets you choose a different indentation character. With HTML messages, you can click the Indent Message On Reply option on the HTML Settings dialog box.

You can use the original text in two ways. You can either type your message at the beginning of the message, leaving the original message at the end for reference. Or, you can edit the original message, deleting the parts irrelevant to your reply, and then type your reply in parts (each part immediately below the portions of the message to which you are responding). If don't want to include any of the original text for a particular message in your reply (but don't want to change the option), just press CTRL-A to select all the text in the message body window and then either press DELETE or just start typing your message.

Inserting Text Files into a Message

If what you want to say is already contained in a text file, you don't have to retype the text or even cut-and-paste the text out of the file. Just follow these steps to incorporate the text into your message:

1. Move the cursor to the place in the text of your message that you want the text file inserted.

2. Select Insert | Text From File.

3. When the Insert Text File window opens, browse to find the text file you want.

4. Click Open.

The complete text of the text file is now inserted into the spot where the insertion point is located.

Attaching a File to a Message

You can use e-mail to send more than just text. Any file—a picture, a spreadsheet, a formatted text document—can be sent along with your message as an attachment (see "What Are Attached Files?" earlier in the chapter).To attach a file to a message, click the Attach File To Message button on the message window toolbar or select Insert | File Attachment. When the Open window appears, browse to find the file you want to attach, and click Open.

When sending plain-text messages, Windows Mail encodes file attachments using *Multipurpose Internet Mail Extensions (MIME)*, the most widely used method of attaching files to messages. Most e-mail programs can deal with MIME attachments. You can switch to a different encoding method called *uuencode*: select Tools | Options, click the Plain Text Settings button on the Send tab of the Options dialog box, and then click the Uuencode radio button in the Plain Text Settings dialog box.

TIP *If you are attaching a large file or several small ones, create a compressed folder (ZIP file) that contains the file(s) and attach the compressed folder instead (see "What Are Compressed Folders?" in Chapter 9).*

Saving and Deleting Messages

Windows Mail keeps the messages that you send and receive until you tell it to delete them. Messages that you receive are stored in your Inbox folder. Under the default settings, messages that you send wind up in your Sent Items folder and remain there until you either delete them or move them to another folder (see "Organizing Your Correspondence" later in the chapter).

Saving Messages

Even though Windows Mail saves your messages automatically, you need to be aware of four issues:

- *Windows Mail folders and the messages in them are separate from the overall filing system of your computer.* You may have a folder called Mom in Windows Mail, but no Mom folder exists on the folder tree you see in Windows Explorer. If you want a message to be a file in your computer's filing system, you have to save that message as a file. You can drag a message out of the Windows Mail window and drop it onto the desktop or into an Explorer window. Or, you can select the message in the Windows Mail message list window, select File | Save As, and give the new file a name. Either way, the message is saved in an EML file. To read these files on a system that doesn't have Windows Mail, use Notepad. You also can save message in TXT (text) or HTML format.

- *Unfinished messages are lost when you close Windows Mail unless you save them.* You don't have to start and finish a message in one sitting. If you want to put the message away and work on it later, select File | Save to save the message in your Drafts folder. If you want the unfinished message to be in a Windows Mail folder other than Drafts, save it to Drafts first, and then drag it to another folder.

- *Your mail files should be backed up as often as (or perhaps more often than) any other files on your system.* The simplest method is to back up the entire folder in which you told

Windows Mail to store your messages. The default folder is called Windows Mail and lies inside the C:\Users*username*\appdata\local\microsoft\windows mail\ *mailbox name* (*username* is your user account name, as described in Chapter 6).

- *You can prevent Windows Mail from automatically saving your outgoing messages.* Select Tools | Options to open the Options dialog box. Go to the Send tab and uncheck the Save Copy Of Sent Messages In The 'Sent Items' Folder check box.

Deleting and Recovering Messages

Delete a message by clicking it in the message list and pressing DELETE. The message is sent to the Deleted Items folder, which functions within the Windows Mail filing system as a kind of Recycle Bin.

You can still examine messages from the Deleted Items folder by opening them, and you can move them to another folder if you change your mind about deleting them. However, if you delete an item from the Deleted Items folder, it is gone permanently.

Windows Mail can be set up to empty the Deleted Items folder automatically when you exit the program:

1. Select Tools | Options. The Options dialog box appears.

2. Click the Advanced tab.

3. Click the Maintenance button and check Empty Messages From The 'Deleted Items' Folder On Exit.

4. Click OK twice.

Sending Messages

Once you are satisfied with the message you've composed, click the Send button in its message window. One of the following two things then happens:

- Windows Mail connects to your ISP, finds your outgoing mail server, and sends the message.

- The message is placed in your Outbox and is not sent until you click the Send/ Receive button.

To tell Windows Mail whether to send messages immediately:

1. Open the Options dialog box by selecting Tools | Options.

2. Select the Send tab.

3. Select or deselect the Send Messages Immediately check box.

4. Click OK.

You can undo this decision at any time by returning to the Send tab of the Options dialog box and changing the Send Messages Immediately setting.

Even if Send Messages Immediately is selected, you can move a message to your Outbox without sending it immediately to your outgoing mail server by selecting File | Send Later. This option is handy if you are temporarily unable to connect to the Internet—if you are traveling, for example, and your computer is not currently online.

As long as the message is sitting in your Outbox, you can still intercept it:

1. Select the Outbox folder from the folder list of the Windows Mail window.

2. Select the message from the Outbox message list.

3. Press DELETE or select Edit | Delete to get rid of the message completely. To put the message away to edit later, drag-and-drop the message from the upper-right pane into the Drafts folder in the folder list, or select Edit | Move To Folder and choose a folder in which to move the message. Alternatively, you can right-click the message and select Move To Folder from the shortcut menu.

Storing Addresses in Windows Contacts

One of the first things people did when personal computers were invented was store lists of addresses on them. It makes sense—the old-fashioned little black book quickly gets filled with scratch-outs as people move, change phone numbers, or get new e-mail addresses, and you always end up wishing you had left a little more space between Sloane and Smith.

The next good idea in address management was to make the address book into a system utility so that any program could access it. You shouldn't have to keep one list of addresses for your word processor, another for your e-mail program, and a third for your personal information manager. And you shouldn't have to wonder which list has Aunt Gertrude's new address.

Windows Contacts keeps track of almost anything you would want to keep track of; provides a space for notes; and is accessible from other Windows program, such as Windows Calendar.

Running Windows Contacts

You can access Windows Contacts either from another program or by choosing Start | All Programs | Windows Contacts. You see the Windows Contacts window, shown in Figure 25-5.

The window lists the people you have entered into the address book (which Windows Contacts calls *contacts*) with the name, e-mail address, and phone numbers for each person.

Sharing Contacts with Other People

Each user account has its own Windows Contacts program, with its own files of contacts. People who use the same user account access the same address book, but they can keep their contacts separate by defining different *identities*. To share a contact with another user, right-click the contact and choose Share. The File Sharing window appears. Type the name of the user you want to share with, click Add, and then click Share.

Entering Information into Windows Contacts

You can get information into Windows Contacts in several ways: importing information from an address book program (see "Importing Addresses from Other Mail Programs" earlier in this chapter), importing virtual business cards (VCF files) that have arrived by e-mail, capturing information automatically from Windows Mail, or entering information by hand. Once you have a list of contacts in Windows Contacts, you can organize the list into groups. To see the entries in your address book, click the Contacts folder in the left pane. The entries appear on the right side of the Contacts window.

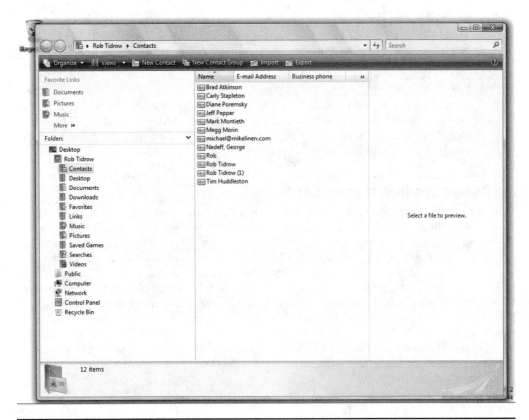

Importing Virtual Business Cards

Windows Contacts can import addresses from vCards (virtual business cards), which arrive as attachments to e-mail messages in files with the extension .vcf. Select Import from the Windows Contacts toolbar. Select the vCard (VCF file) option from the Import To Windows Contacts dialog box. Click Import. The Select a vCard File For Import window appears. Select the file to import and click Open. This converts the VCF file to the CONTACTS file format, which is the native Windows Contacts format.

Capturing E-mail Addresses from Windows Mail

If you use Windows Mail as your e-mail program, you can set it up to add names and e-mail addresses to Windows Contacts automatically whenever you reply to a message:

1. Open Windows Mail.

2. Select Tools | Options. The Options dialog box appears.

3. On the Send tab, check the box Automatically Put People I Reply To In My Contacts List.

4. Click OK.

Entering Information by Hand

To enter a new contact into Windows Contacts, click the New Contact button on the toolbar. A blank Properties dialog box appears, as shown in Figure 25-6. Type in any information you want recorded, and leave blank any lines you want left blank. To add or change information about an existing contact, select the contact in the address list and click the Open button. You also can double-click a contact. The Properties dialog box appears. Enter or edit information on any of its tabs.

To add more information to an existing contact's listing, double-click the contact in the contacts list. Enter the new information on the appropriate line and tab of the contact's Properties dialog box. Notice the Properties dialog box displays a Summary tab that you didn't see when you were entering a new contact. This tab is just for reference; each piece of information on this tab can be edited on some other tab. Any web page listed on the Summary tab is hot-linked: clicking this link opens your web browser and displays the web page.

Windows Contacts enables you to keep track of several e-mail addresses for a single person, with one of the addresses specified as the default. To add a new e-mail address, type it into the E-mail box on the Name And E-mail tab of the contact's Properties dialog box.

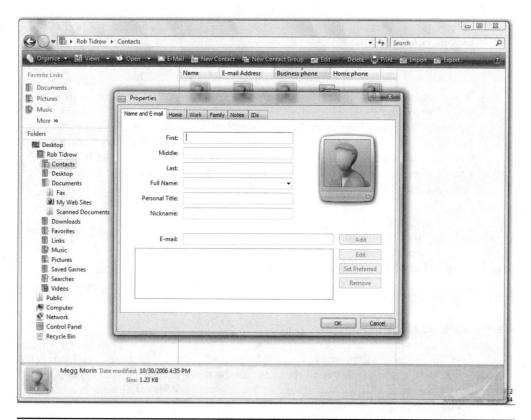

FIGURE 25-6 Creating a new contact.

Then click the Add button. The new e-mail address appears in the list just below the E-mail box.

To set one of a person's e-mail addresses as the default, select it from the list of e-mail addresses on the Name tab of the Properties dialog box associated with that person's name. Then click the Set Preferred button.

Defining Groups

Having your customers, your coworkers, and your child's piano teacher all on one big alphabetical list can be confusing. Windows Contacts enables you to give your contacts list some structure by defining groups of contacts that have something in common. An individual contact can appear in any number of groups.

To define a group:

1. Click the New Contact Group button on the Windows Contacts toolbar. A group Properties dialog box opens.

2. Type a name for the group into the Group Name box.

3. Click the Add To Contact Group button. The Add Members To Contact Group window appears.

4. Select names and click the Add button to add this name to the group. Use the CTRL or SHIFT key to select multiple contacts to add. You can add an entire group to the new group in the same way.

5. When you have finished selecting group members, click Add to return to the group Properties dialog box. The members you have selected are listed.

6. If you want to add new members to the group, click Add To Contact Group again. If you want to remove names from the list, select the names in from the Group Members list in the Properties dialog box and click Remove Selected Contacts. If you want to add people who aren't already in your contacts list, click Create New Contact and enter the information for a new contact. When you click OK to save the new contact, Windows Contacts automatically adds the new contact to the new contact group.

7. Click OK.

The new group appears in the Windows Contacts window.

Looking Up Information in Windows Contacts

When you open Windows Contacts, the first thing you see is the contacts list, as shown in Figure 25-5.

Viewing the Contacts List

Windows Contacts offers you the same choice of views that Windows Explorer does: Tiles, Details, List, Small Icons, Medium Icons, Large Icons, and Extra Large Icons. The icon views and List view use icons to display each contact with the name appearing. The Details view shows the name, e-mail address, and other contact information. The Tiles view uses an icon and shows the name and e-mail address.

Sorting the Contacts List

In Details view, you can list contacts according to name, e-mail address, home phone number, or business phone number. As in the Details view in Windows Explorer, click the head of any column to list contacts according to that column in ascending order. To list in descending order, click the column head a second time. To tell Windows Contacts whether the Name column should be ordered according to first name or last name, choose View | Sort By. (Click Organize | Layout | Menu Bar if the View menu is not showing.)

Looking Up Detailed Information

Each contact has a Properties dialog box associated with it, as shown in Figure 25-6. To view the Properties dialog box for a contact, double-click the person's entry in the contacts list. The entries on the IDs tab enable you to send and receive encrypted information from the person (see Chapter 33).

Finding People

If you have a lot of contacts in your Windows Contacts folder, you don't want to have to scan the whole list to find a particular entry. To search Windows Contacts, click in the Search bar on the toolbar. Type what you know about the person, and then press ENTER. Any fragment of information helps to narrow down the search. If, for example, you remember the phone number has a 456 in it somewhere, enter 456 in the Search bar. Or, if you can only remember a person's first name, enter that in the Search bar.

Contacting People

To send e-mail to a person or group on your contacts list, select the recipient(s) from the contacts list and click E-Mail on the toolbar. (To address a message to several people, choose them by holding down the CTRL key while you select them.) Your default e-mail program should display a new mail message window to the person that you selected.

Printing Information from Address Book

You can print information from Windows Contacts in three formats:

- **Memo**   Prints all the information Windows Contacts has about the selected contact(s).
- **Business Card**   Prints only the information from the Work tab of the contact's or contacts' Properties dialog box.
- **Phone List**   Prints a list of phone numbers of the selected contact(s).

To print information, follow these steps:

1. Select contacts from the contacts list. Select blocks of names by holding down the SHIFT key while you click the names. Select individuals scattered throughout the list by holding down the CTRL key while you click the names. Select a group by clicking its name in the contacts list (not the group list).
2. Click the Print button on the toolbar. A Print dialog box appears.
3. Select the Memo, Business Card, or Phone List from the Print dialog box.
4. Click OK.

To print addresses in any other format, export them (as described in the next section) to a database or word processing program that can print the format you want.

Exporting Names and Addresses from Windows Contacts

You can also export names and addresses from Windows Contacts in a comma-delimited text file (CSV) or as vCards:

- **Text file**   Click the Export toolbar button then select CSV (Comma Separated Values) from the Export Windows Contacts dialog box. The CSV Export wizard runs. Specify the name of the file in which you want to store the exported addresses, and then click Next. Select the information you want to include for each person, and then click Finish.

- **vCard (folder of VCF files)**   Select the person whose information you want to export, and then choose Export | vCard (folder of VCF files). Click Export. Specify the folder where you want to store the business card and click OK.

Organizing Your Correspondence

A mail program is more than just a way to read and write messages, it is also a filing system. Over time, the records of your correspondence may become a valuable asset. Although you can leave all of your mail in your Inbox, it's a lot easier to find messages if you file messages by sender or topic.

Windows Mail allows you to create folders and move messages from one folder to another.

Working with Folders

The Windows Mail filing system resembles the filing system that Windows itself uses, but the Windows Mail files and folders can't be seen by other programs (see Chapter 8)—you must use Windows Mail to manipulate them.

Creating and Deleting Folders

To create a new folder in Windows Mail:

1. Click the Local Folders icon in the folder list.
2. Select either File | Folder | New or File | New | Folder. The Create Folder window opens.
3. Type the name of your folder in the Folder Name line.
4. In the bottom half of the Create Folder window, select the folder into which you want to place the new folder.
5. Click OK.

To delete a folder, select it in the folder list of the Windows Mail window and select File | Folder | Delete.

Moving and Copying

To move or copy a message from one folder to another:

1. Select the folder that contains the message in the folder list of the Windows Mail window. You may need to expand some folders (by clicking the plus boxes in the margin) to find it.

2. Find the message in the message list and right-click it.

3. Select either Move To Folder or Copy To Folder from the right-click menu. A window appears displaying a folder list.

4. Select the folder into which you want the message moved or copied.

5. Click OK.

You can also move a message by dragging it from the message list and dropping it onto the icon of the target folder in the folder list.

To move a folder, drag-and-drop its icon on the folder list to the location you want it to be located. You can move several messages or folders at the same time by holding down the CTRL key while you select the items to move.

Finding Messages in Your Files

A filing system isn't worth much unless you can find what you put there. Windows Mail gives you a search tool that lets you search for messages based on

- The sender
- The recipient
- The subject
- A word or phrase in the message body
- Whether the message has attachments
- Whether the message is flagged
- The date received
- A folder containing the message

Begin your search by selecting Edit | Find | Message. The Find Message dialog box appears, as shown in Figure 25-7. You also can click the Find button on the toolbar and select Message. Enter as much information as you know about the message and click Find Now. Windows Mail lists at the bottom of the window all the messages that fit the description you've given. Open any message on this list by double-clicking it.

Type any string of characters into the From, To, Subject, or Message lines of the Find Message dialog box. This restricts your search to messages whose corresponding parts contain those character strings.

To specify the date of a message, check either the Received Before or Received After check box. Enter a date in MM/DD/YY format into the corresponding line or click the drop-down arrow to locate the date you want on a calendar. (Change months on the calendar by clicking the left or right arrows at the top of the calendar.) You can use Before and After together to specify a range of dates.

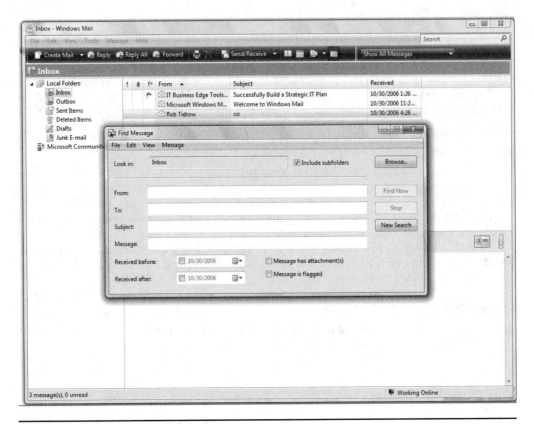

FIGURE 25-7   The Find Message dialog box.

The Look In box specifies a folder in which to search. Click the Browse button to locate a new folder to look in. The Include Subfolders check box does just what it says—if the box is checked, the search includes all the subfolders of the specified folder; if it is not checked, the subfolders are not included.

If the message you wanted didn't show up, check the View | Current View menu in the Find dialog box. Make sure it is set to Show All Messages.

Filtering Your Mail with Message Rules

Windows Mail can do some secretarial work to help you manage your POP e-mail messages automatically. It can do the following:

- File messages to the appropriate folders, rather than letting them pile up in the Inbox
- Forward messages to another e-mail address
- Send a stock reply message

TIP   *An easy way to delete messages from a particular person automatically is to add his or her name to your Blocked Senders list (see "Blocking a Sender" later in the chapter).*

You tell Windows Mail to do these things by establishing *message rules* or *mail rules*, which specify a kind of message and a type of action to take when such a message arrives. To establish a message rule for your e-mail, select Tools | Message Rules | Mail. The New Mail Rule dialog box appears, shown in Figure 25-8.

The upper portion of the New Mail Rule dialog box lists the rules you have created. A rule is active if its check box is checked, and inactive otherwise, so turning a rule on and off is easy. The lower portion of the dialog box gives a description of the currently selected rule. Some parts of the description are underlined in blue; these are links to other dialog boxes that allow you to edit these particular portions of the rule.

The New Mail Rule dialog box has four sections.

1. **Select The Conditions For Your Rule**   Enables you to define the messages that the rule should apply to. These conditions are vague, but you specify their details in the Rule Description section.

2. **Select The Actions For Your Rule**   Enables you to specify what Windows Mail should do when such messages arrive. As in the first section, these actions are also vague, but are spelled out in the Rule Description section.

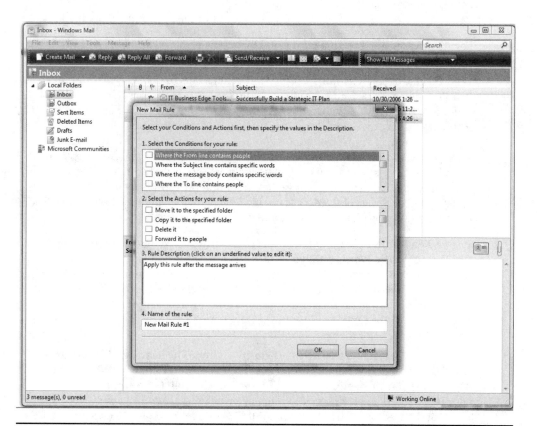

FIGURE 25-8   Defining a new message rule.

3. **Rule Description**   Gives a description of the rule as you have defined it so far; when more information is needed, the description contains a placeholder phrase that is linked to a dialog box for specifying the information. Clicking these phrases opens additional dialog boxes that allow you to specify which people, which words, and what message. The word "and" is also linked; clicking it opens the And/Or dialog box, described in the next section.

4. **Name Of The Rule**   Enables you to specify a name for your rule. Otherwise, the rule will be numbered, such as New Mail Rule #1, shown in Figure 25-8.

Defining Conditions for Message Rules

You define conditions for your message rules by checking the appropriate boxes in the Select The Conditions For Your Rule section of the New Mail Rule dialog box. As you check boxes, the text next to those boxes appears in the Rule Description section, in which you click the linked phrases to specify any additional information that the condition requires.

If you check more than one box, the conditions are connected with an "and"—in other words, all checked conditions need to be true before the action you specify is taken. You can change this "and" to an "or" by clicking an "and" in the rule description and selecting the Messages Match Any One Of The Criteria radio button. There is no way to create more complicated conditions than to mix "ands" and "ors."

You can choose from 12 conditions listed in section 1 of the New Mail Rule dialog box:

- **For All Messages**   The rule works on all messages.

- **Where The From Line Contains People**, **Where The To Line Contains People**, **Where The CC Line Contains People**, and **Where The To Or CC Line Contains People**   Any of these four conditions requires you to specify which people the condition applies to. Click the phrase "contains people" in the Rule Description section to display the Select People dialog box. Add people to your list either by typing their e-mail addresses into the top line and clicking the Add button, or by clicking the Address Book button and selecting them from your address book. By default, the rule applies to a message in which any of the selected people are included in the specified line. You can require that the condition apply only if *all* of the people are included or if *none* of the people are included by clicking the Options button and choosing the appropriate radio button in the Rule Condition Options dialog box.

- **Where The Subject Line Contains Specific Words** and **Where The Message Body Contains Specific Words**   Either of these conditions requires you to specify which words or phrases the rule is looking for. Click the phrase "contains specific words" in the Rule Description section. When the Type Specific Words dialog box appears, type a word or phrase and click the Add button. If you specify more than one word or phrase, click the Options button to specify whether all words/phrases must be present or just one of them.

- **Where The Message Is Marked As Priority**, **Where The Message Is From The Specified Account**, **Where The Message Size Is More Than Size**, **Where The Message Has An Attachment**, and **Where The Message Is Secure**   These five conditions require you to specify which priority, which account, what size, and what kind of security. Click the highlighted phrase in the Rule Description section and choose the appropriate radio button from the dialog box that appears.

Specifying Actions for Message Rules

By setting conditions in the Select The Conditions For Your Rule section of the New Mail Rule dialog box, you have picked out a particular class of messages. Now you need to tell Windows Mail what to do with those messages by filling out the Select The Actions For Your Rule section. Select actions by checking the check boxes. You may select as many actions as you like. You have 12 choices:

- **Move It To The Specified Folder** or **Copy It To The Specified Folder**   Either of these actions requires you to specify a folder to put the message into. Click the word "specified" in the Rule Description section and choose a folder from the dialog box that appears.

- **Forward It To People**   This action requires you to specify which people to forward the message to. Click the word "people" in the Rule Description section and enter an e-mail address into the Select People dialog box, or click the Contacts button to choose an address from Windows Contacts.

- **Delete It, Flag It, Mark It As Read, Do Not Download It From The Server**, and **Delete It From The Server**   These actions are self-explanatory. No highlighted words or phrases appear in the Rule Description.

TIP *Test a Delete rule using the Flag It action first to verify the rule works as expected. If the rule works fine by flagging messages you want deleted, change the rule to the Delete It action.*

- **Stop Processing More Rules**   If more than one rule applies to a message, the message may get processed twice, and may even be duplicated. If you find this happening, add Stop Processing More Rules to the rules that are causing the problem.

- **Highlight It With Color**   After you select this check box, click the word "color" in the Rule Description section and make your choice from the Select Color dialog box.

- **Mark The Message As Watched Or Ignored**   Click "watched or ignored" in the Rule Description section and choose the Watch Message or Ignore Message radio button. Windows Mail *watches* a message by displaying an icon (a pair of glasses) by it, and *ignores* a message by flagging it with the international "forbidden" icon.

- **Reply With Message**   This action requires you to tell it which message to use as your automatic reply. Click the word "message" and identify a message file when the Open dialog box appears. (Prior to defining the rule, you should compose your reply and select File | Save As to save it as an EML file.)

Blocking a Sender

You can't stop annoying people or organizations from writing to you, but you can have Windows Mail send their e-mail messages straight to the Deleted Items folder or refuse to display their newsgroup messages. Make this happen by adding their names to the Blocked Senders list as follows:

1. Select Tools | Junk E-mail Options from the Windows Mail menu bar. The Junk E-mail Options dialog box appears.

2. Click the Blocked Senders tab, shown in Figure 25-9.

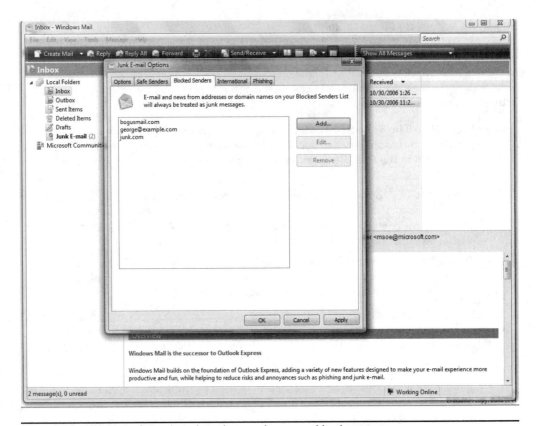

FIGURE 25-9   Blocking a few selected senders can lower your blood pressure.

3. Click the Add button. The Add Address Or Domain dialog box appears.

4. Enter the e-mail address that you want to block in the Address field. If you want to block all messages from an entire Internet domain (the part of the address after the @), type only the domain name.

5. Click OK. The Blocked Senders list now includes the new entry, with check boxes that say whether the blocking applies to the sender's e-mail or newsgroup messages.

TIP   *Spammers keep changing names and addresses, so adding them to the Blocked Senders list will work only once and eventually you'll fill up the Blocked Senders list. Use the Blocked Senders list to block addresses that regularly send you mail, such as from mailing lists that you cannot seem to get unsubscribed from or from an annoying Internet acquaintance who forwards you a lot of junk.*

Remove a sender from your Blocked Senders list by choosing Tools | Junk E-mail Options | Blocked Senders List tab, select the sender in the Message Rules dialog box, and click the Remove button.

Managing Your Message Rules

All your message rules are listed by name in the upper section of the Message Rules dialog box. Windows Mail only applies rules whose check boxes are checked, so you can turn rules on and off easily by checking or unchecking their boxes. When you click a rule's name, its description appears in the Rule Description section of the dialog box. You can edit any of the highlighted phrases in the rule description, or you can rewrite the rule completely by clicking the Modify button. The Edit Mail Rule dialog box appears; it behaves in the same manner as the New Rule dialog box.

You can put the rules into a different order by selecting rules in the Message Rules dialog box and clicking the Move Up or Move Down button. To get rid of a rule completely, select its name and click Remove.

Using Message Rules to Sort Old Messages

Message rules are applied automatically to new messages as they arrive, but you can also apply message rules to the messages stored in a folder. This technique can help you organize your correspondence. To do this:

1. Define a rule as described in the earlier section "Filtering Your Mail with Message Rules," or identify an already-defined rule that you want to apply.

2. If the Message Rules dialog box is not already open, select Tools | Message Rules | Mail to make it appear.

3. Select the rule you want to apply.

4. Click the Apply Now button. The Apply Mail Rules Now dialog box opens.

5. Select the folder that the rule should be applied to. Inbox is the default, but if you want to apply the rule to a different folder, you can click the Browse button and find the folder you want.

6. Click the Apply Now button. Windows Mail opens a confirmation box to tell you when it has finished.

Posting to Google Groups

One of the most popular areas on the Internet has been online social communities, such as Google Groups. Many other communities like Google Groups are available, including MySpace, YouTube, and Yahoo Groups. As an example, we focus on Google Groups here. With Google Groups, you can join others in restricted and public groups to discuss topics, share photos, communicate with friends, plan events, and perform other actions.

To access Google Groups, you must have an account established. Go to http://groups .google.com and click Sign Up For Google Groups. Fill out the Create An Account form and click the I Accept/Create My Account button at the bottom of the form. Once you create

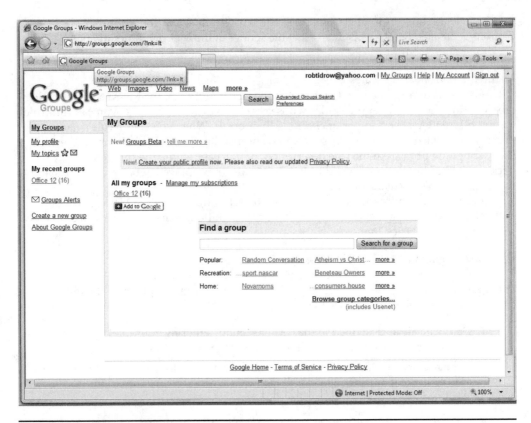

FIGURE 25-10   Google Groups enables you to set up your own profile.

your account, Google takes you to the My Groups page, shown on Figure 25-10. Here you can set up your profile, which enables you to manage your subscription to any group on the site.

To find groups to join, use the Find A Group search box at the bottom of the page. Enter a topic and click the Search For A Group button. Google returns a list of categories and groups that fall under your search term. For example, the term "fitness" might return categories called Science and Technology – Biology, News, and Society, and return groups called rec. sport.rowing and Sports Medicine Article Digest. Click a link to review the group and join it. To join it, click the Subscribe To This Group link (see Figure 25-11) at the top of the page.

Answer the questions on the subscription page and click the Subscribe To This Group button. Some groups will immediately return you to the previous page as a member of the group. Others may send you e-mail asking you to confirm that you want to be a member.

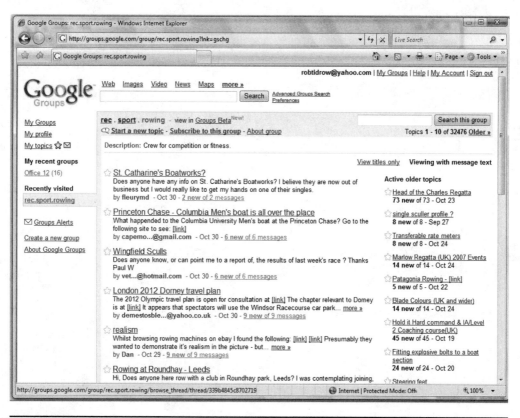

FIGURE 25-11   An example of a Google Group you can subscribe to.

While a member of a group, you can post messages to topics, read messages, create a new topic, view and post pictures (if the group supports them), and jump to related groups. To find out more about Google Groups, click the Help link at the top of a group page. This shows the Groups Help web page.

Browsing the World Wide Web
with Internet Explorer

Along with e-mail, the World Wide Web is the main reason most people bother with the Internet, and it is one of the most important reasons that people have home computers at all. Windows Vista includes Internet Explorer 7 (IE 7), the latest version of the world's most popular web browser.

This chapter explains some of the basic concepts of the World Wide Web and describes how to set up Internet Explorer and configure it according to your tastes. It then explains how to use Internet Explorer to browse web pages, search for new web sites, and remember your favorite sites, and how to use IE 7's new phishing and RSS features. We also explain how to tell Internet Explorer to fill in web forms automatically, how to set colors and set your start page, and how to control privacy settings.

What Is the World Wide Web?

The *World Wide Web* (usually just referred to as "the Web") is a collection of millions of files stored on thousands of computers (called *web servers*) all over the world. These files represent text documents, pictures, video, sounds, programs, interactive environments, and just about any other kind of information that has ever been recorded in computer files. It is probably the largest and most diverse collection of information ever assembled.

What unites these files is a system for linking one file to another and transmitting them across the Internet. HTML codes allow a file to contain links to related files (see the next section, "What Is HTML?") Such a *link* (also called a *hyperlink*) contains the information necessary to locate the related file on the Internet. When you connect to the Internet and use a web browser program like Internet Explorer, you can read, view, hear, or otherwise interact with the Web without paying attention to whether the information you are accessing is stored on a computer down the hall or on the other side of the world. A news story stored on a computer in Singapore can link you to a stock quote stored in New York, a picture stored in Frankfurt, and an audio file stored in Tokyo. The combination of the web servers, the Internet, and your web browser assembles this information seamlessly and presents it to you as a unified whole. This system of interlinked text, called *hypertext*, was first described in the 1960s by Theodor H. Nelson, but it took 30 years for it to be widely used in the form of the World Wide Web, which was invented in 1990 by Tim Berners-Lee at CERN, a particle physics lab in Geneva, Switzerland.

By following links, you can get from almost any web document to almost any other web document. For this reason, some people like to think of the entire Web as being one big document. In this view, the links just take you from one part of the document to another.

An *intranet* is an internal network that uses the same communication protocols as the Internet, but is limited to a specific group, usually the employees in one company. Some organizations create private versions of the Web on their intranets so that access to their web pages is limited to employees of that organization.

What Is HTML?

Hypertext Markup Language (HTML) is the universal language of the Web. It is a language for laying out pages that are capable of displaying all the diverse kinds of information that the Web contains. A web browser, at the most basic level, is a program that reads and interprets HTML.

While various software companies own and sell HTML reading and writing programs, no one owns the language HTML itself. It is an international standard, maintained and updated by a complicated political process that so far has worked remarkably well. The World Wide Web Consortium (W3C), at www.w3.org, manages the HTML standard.

What Is a URL?

When the pieces of a document are scattered all over the world, but you want to display them seamlessly to a person who could be anywhere else in the world, you need a very good addressing system. Each file on the Internet has an address, called a *Uniform Resource Locator (URL)*, also sometimes called an *Internet address* or *web address*. For example, the URL of the CNN web site is http://www.cnn.com. The first part of a URL (the part before the first colon) specifies the *transfer protocol*, the method that a computer needs to use to access this file. Most web pages are accessed with the *Hypertext Transfer Protocol (HTTP*, the language of web communication), which is why web addresses typically begin with http (or its secure, encrypted versions, https or shttp). The http:// at the beginning of a web page's URL is so common that it is assumed as the default protocol by modern browsers. If you simply type **www.cnn.coom** into the Address box of Internet Explorer, the browser fills in the **http://** for itself. Or, if you type in cnn.com, Internet Explorer fills in the *http://www.* for itself. In common usage, the http:// at the beginning of a URL is left out.

The rest of the address denotes the web page, but might not tell you where its files are actually located. Whether CNN's web server is in Atlanta, GA or Bangkok, Thailand, it is invisible from its URL. Information about which web server is responsible for answering requests for which URLs is contained in a huge database that the web servers themselves are constantly updating. As users, we don't need to deal with this level of detail, and that's a good thing. The Web would be much less usable if sports fans had to learn a new set of URLs every time CNN got a new computer.

What Are Web Pages and Web Sites?

A *web page* is an HTML document that is stored on a web server and has a URL so that it can be accessed via the Web.

A *web site* is a collection of web pages belonging to a particular person or organization. The *home page* is the "front door" of the site and is set up to help viewers find whatever is of interest to them on that site. The URL of the home page also serves as the URL of the web site.

For example, the URL of Microsoft's home page is www.microsoft.com. From the home page, you can get to Microsoft's web pages about Windows Vista at www.microsoft.com/windowsvista/.

What Is a Web Browser?

A *web browser* is a program that your computer runs to communicate with web servers on the Internet so that it can download the documents you ask for and display them. At a bare minimum, a web browser has to be able to understand HTML and display text. In recent years, however, Internet users have come to expect a lot more. A state-of-the-art web browser provides a full multimedia experience, complete with pictures, sound, video, active content, and 3-D imaging.

What Are Add-ons?

Add-ons, which are also called *plug-ins*, are programs that are independent of your web browser but "plug in" to it in a seamless way, so that you might not even be aware that you are using software that is not part of the web browser. Typically, add-ons arise when a software company develops a way to display a new type of data over the Web such as Adobe PDF files or streaming audio. Rather than create a whole new browser with this additional capability, the software company writes a plug-in for popular web browsers like Internet Explorer or Mozilla Firefox. Users who want to extend the capabilities of their browser in this particular way can install the plug-in, which then operates as if it is part of the web browser.

Typically, installing an add-on is fairly painless. Web pages that contain content requiring a special add-on usually include instructions for downloading and installing the plug-in. When you run Internet Explorer with its default security settings, the Information Bar (at the top of the page) displays a warning message that the page needs to install an add-on. You can click the Information Bar and then continue with the installation process. The main inconvenience is the length of time necessary to download the add-on (which is not even that long if you have a broadband Internet connection). Installing the add-on is usually a simple matter of clicking a few buttons and perhaps registering with the company that makes the plug-in.

As with any kind of software, downloading and installing an add-on requires faith in whoever created and distributed it. An add-on can introduce viruses into your system, modify files without your consent, or transmit data from your machine without your knowledge. Add-ons from reputable software companies are as safe as any other kind of Internet software, but you should be cautious about downloading plug-ins from web sites that you know nothing about.

With IE 7, you can manage add-ons using the Tools | Manage Add-ons menu option. The Enable Or Disable Add-On command displays the Manage Add-ons dialog box, where you can view installed add-ons, turn on or off installed add-ons, and delete add-ons. The Find More Add-ons command displays the Add-ons For Microsoft Internet Explorer web page, from which you can download add-ons.

What Is the Default Web Browser?

The *default web browser* is the application that Windows uses to open a web page when you haven't told it what browser to use—for example, when you click a web link in an e-mail message or choose a web page from the Favorites menu. Initially, Internet Explorer is the default web browser under Windows Vista, but you can choose another browser to be the default if you want.

You can, of course, open any web browser you want and use it to browse the web, whether it is the default browser or not. You can even have several browsers running at the same time—for example, Internet Explorer and Mozilla Firefox.

What Is Internet Explorer?

Internet Explorer is Microsoft's web browser. It intentionally resembles Windows Explorer, and it is an integral part of Windows Vista—Windows uses some of the same code for displaying the Control Panel, Help And Support Center, and other pages. Having Internet Explorer doesn't depend on any decisions you might have made during installation, and you couldn't uninstall it if you wanted to, because many other Windows programs use Internet Explorer's code to display HTML-formatted information. You can uninstall or delete the shortcuts to Internet Explorer from your desktop, taskbar, and Start menu, but the program remains installed.

Internet Explorer 7 is the version that comes with Windows Vista. It has some new features compared to previous versions, such as tabs, which we spell out in the remainder of this chapter. Fundamentally, though, if you have used earlier versions of IE, you won't have much trouble figuring out how to use IE 7.

Getting Started with Internet Explorer

Internet Explorer is installed automatically when you install Windows Vista. Its icon (a blue letter *e*) is not hard to find; look at or near the top of the Start menu, on the Quick Launch toolbar, or on the desktop. To run Internet Explorer, click one of these icons or choose Start | Internet Explorer.

Under the default settings, one of the following three things happens when you start Internet Explorer:

- Internet Explorer opens displaying its start page, which Microsoft has initially set as the MSN home page, www.msn.com.

- If you are not online and your start page is only available over the Internet, Internet Explorer tries to connect to the Internet. Depending on how your account is set up, this may happen automatically or you may have to enter a password into the Connect dialog box or some other connection software. If Internet Explorer succeeds in establishing an Internet connection, the start page appears. Otherwise it asks if you want to continue working offline. If you agree, it displays a blank start page.

- If you either do not have an Internet account or have not told Windows about the one you have, the Connect To The Internet Wizard starts (see "Running the Connect To The Internet Wizard" in Chapter 24).

Elements of the Internet Explorer Window

When all of the major components of the Internet Explorer window are made visible, it looks like Figure 26-1.

From top to bottom, it contains the following:

- **Standard Buttons toolbar**   Includes the Back and Forward buttons to enable you to move between web pages you have previously viewed.

- **Address bar**   Displays the URL of the currently displayed web page or the Windows address of the currently displayed local file.

- **Search bar**   Enables you to search for content on the Web using the Live Search tool.

- **Menu bar**   A row of menus you can use to access different IE commands. You can hide the Menu bar by choosing View | Toolbars | Menu Bar. You can move it to a different location in the window by clicking and dragging the handle (ridge) at its left end.

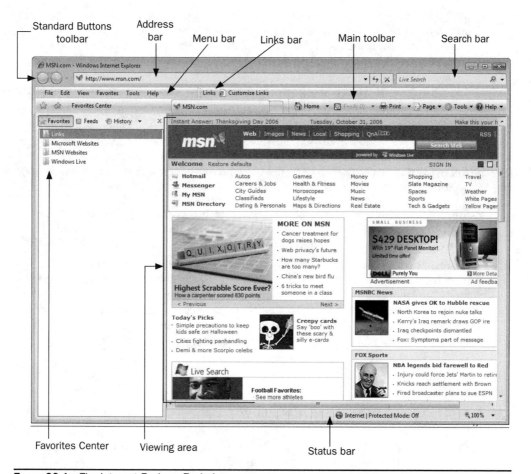

FIGURE 26-1   The Internet Explorer 7 window.

- **Links toolbar**   A row of icons that you can link to files on your computer or to web pages. Hide the Links toolbar by unchecking View | Toolbars | Links. Expand or shrink this toolbar by dragging the left boundary. (You might need to unlock the toolbars first by choosing View | Toolbars | Lock The Toolbars.)

- **Main toolbar**   Displays standard tools, including the Home button, RSS Feeds, Print, Page, Tools, and Help. The main toolbar remains on the Internet Explorer window permanently.

- **Favorites Center**   Displays the Favorites folder, RSS feeds, or the History folder so you can quickly access saved web sites, RSS information (which sends information to you automatically), or previously visited sites.

- **Viewing window**   Displays web pages. It can't be hidden, since otherwise there would be no point in running a browser. Maximize the viewing window by selecting View | Fullscreen or pressing f11. Return to the previous (unmaximized) state by selecting View | Fullscreen or pressing f11 again.

- **Status bar**   Displays a variety of useful information. When the cursor passes over a link in the viewing window, the URL of the link is displayed in the status bar. When Internet Explorer is looking for or downloading a web page, the status bar keeps you apprised of its progress. Hide the status bar by unchecking View | Status Bar.

Using the Standard Buttons Toolbar

The Standard Buttons toolbar has a few buttons for Internet Explorer that are different from those that it has for Windows Explorer, but several are the same, and in general you use the toolbar in the same way. You can display the toolbar in several ways, and you can customize it by choosing which buttons to display and what order to put them in.

The following buttons are new to Internet Explorer, in the sense that they are not part of the default toolbar for Windows Explorer:

- **Stop** (denoted by an X)   Active only when the browser is in the process of downloading a page from the Web; clicking it stops this process. The menu equivalent is View | Stop, and the keyboard equivalent is the ESCAPE key.

- **Refresh** (denoted by a document with two arrows)   Asks the server to send the most recent version of the page currently being viewed. When a web page is updated on the server, the new version is not automatically sent out to anyone who might be viewing an older version. Clicking Refresh makes sure that the scoreboard you are viewing has the latest scores, or the portfolio shows the most recent stock prices. The menu equivalent is View | Refresh, and the keyboard equivalent is the f5 key.

- **Home** (denoted by a house icon)   Linked to the home or start page. The menu equivalent is View | Go To | Home Page, and the keyboard equivalent is the home key.

- **Feeds**   Displays when a web page you are visiting includes an RSS feed subscription.

- **Print**   Opens the Print dialog box, which is the first step in sending the current page to the printer. It is equivalent to File | Print on the menu or CTRL-P on the keyboard.

The following buttons are not part of the default configuration, but you might find them useful:

- **Full Screen**   Maximizes the viewing area by stretching the Internet Explorer window to the full size of your monitor while shrinking all the other features of the Internet Explorer window. Click it again to return to the previous configuration. It is equivalent to View | Full Screen on the menu or F11 on the keyboard.
- **Print Preview**   Shows a page-by-page view of what you would get if you printed out the current web page. The menu equivalent is File | Print Preview.

Viewing Web Pages

The main purpose of a web browser is to display web pages. Those pages may actually be on the Web, or they may be on your own computer.

Browsing the Web

As soon as you open your first web page, like the MSN start page shown earlier in Figure 26-1, you can begin *browsing*—moving from one web page to another, depending on what you find interesting.

On a standard web page, text phrases that are links to other web pages are displayed in underlined blue type. If you have recently displayed the web page to which the text is linked, the text is displayed in maroon. When you are exploring a web site, this feature lets you know where you've been and keeps you from going in circles. In Internet Explorer you can also define the color that a link turns when the cursor is above it (the default is red). You can change these colors (see "Choosing Colors" later in the chapter).

When you pass the mouse pointer over a linked object (including a linked text phrase), the pointer changes from an arrow to a hand, and the URL of the web page that the object is linked to is displayed in the status bar of the browser window (if you have the status bar enabled). Not all links on a page are obvious; a small picture, for example, might just be an illustration, or it might be linked to a larger version of the same picture. Passing the mouse pointer over an object is the easiest way to tell whether it is linked.

While files are being downloaded to your web browser, the mouse pointer changes to an hourglass icon. However, it is still functional—you can click buttons or scroll the window with an hourglass pointer. Most important, you can use it to click the Stop button if a link is taking longer to download than you're willing to wait.

TIP *Try right-clicking items on web pages—Internet Explorer provides shortcut menus of useful commands. Shortcut menus are available for links, images, backgrounds, and other parts of web pages.*

Using Internet Explorer 7 Tabs

New with Internet Explorer 7 are tabs. Tabs enable you to open more than one web page at a time when you are browsing pages. You can, for instance, open a web page to MSN and then go to Google.com to start a keyword search. As Google performs a search, you can click a new tab and begin an entirely new browsing session, while having only one IE window open.

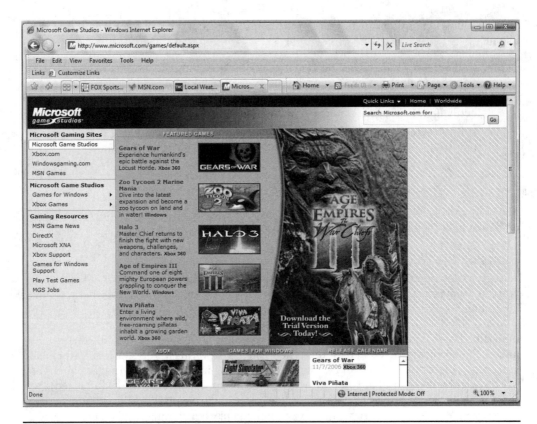

FIGURE 26-2   IE 7's new tabs make viewing multiple pages easy.

This is very handy when you want to browse several different pages but do not want to have multiple IE windows open and do not want to have to click the Back and Forward buttons to navigate to the page you want. Figure 26-2 shows four tabs with different web sites displayed: Fox Sports, MSN.com, Weather Channel, and Microsoft Game Studios.

IE automatically opens two tabs when you start the browser window. The top tab goes to your home page, while the second tab is empty. Click the tab to open that window and then type in a URL or click a Favorites link to visit that page. When you click the second tab, a third tab automatically appears under the second tab so you can quickly use the third tab for additional pages.

To close a tab, click the red Close Tab button on the tab.

Using IE 7 Quick Tabs and Tab List

Quick Tabs are another Internet Explorer 7 addition. When you have multiple pages open on your tabs, click the Quick Tabs button to the left of your first tab. It is a small button with four rectangles on it. When you click this tab, a window appears with thumbnail views of all the pages you currently are viewing on your tabs. Figure 26-3 shows an example of this.

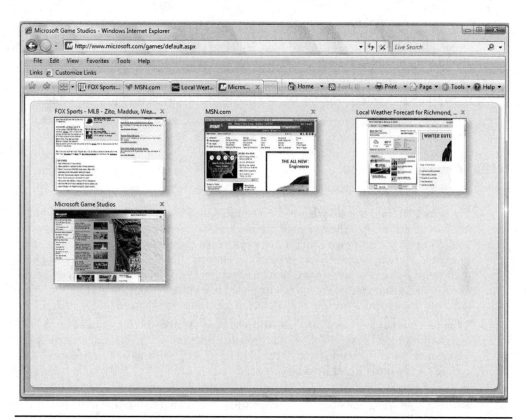

FIGURE 26-3   Using Quick Tabs in IE 7.

To display one of the pages in the Quick Tabs window, simply click that page. IE 7 displays that tab. Another action you can do is to close a tab in the Quick Tabs window by right-clicking the thumbnail of the page that you want to close and choosing Close. If a page in the Quick Tabs window appears to be outdated, right-click the thumbnail image and choose Refresh or Refresh All.

Just to the right of the Quick Tabs tool is the Tab List tool. Click this to see a list of the tabs and the name of the page showing for that tab. Select a page name to display that tab and page.

Opening Files on Your System

You can use Internet Explorer to view HTML files that are stored on your hard drive or elsewhere on your system. You can also view images stored in several different image formats, such as JPEG, GIF, or PNG:

1. Select File | Open or press CTRL-O in Internet Explorer and click the Browse button in the dialog box that appears. You see an Open dialog box almost identical to the Open dialog box of Windows Explorer.

2. Make sure that the Files Of Type line of the Open dialog box contains the type of file you want to open. Web pages are of type HTM, and pictures, depending on picture

format, are of type JPG, GIF, or PNG, If the Files Of Type line doesn't contain the file type you want to open, choose another type from the drop-down menu. If you can't find the right type, choose All Files.

3. Browse until you find the file you want to open.

4. Select the file by clicking its name. Its name then appears in the File Name line.

5. Click Open. You are returned to the Open dialog box, with the address of the file entered. Click OK.

Getting Around on the Web

You can open a web page in Internet Explorer by using any of the following methods:

- **Enter its URL into the Address box**   The most direct way is to type the URL; but if you have the URL in a file or a mail message, you can cut-and-paste it. The Paste command on the Edit menu might not work when the cursor is in the Address box, but you can always paste by pressing CTRL-V. Internet Explorer has an autocomplete feature that tries to guess what URL you are typing and finishes it for you, based on similar URLs that you've visited before. A list of its guesses appears under the Address box as you type. If one is correct, click it and press ENTER.

- **Type its Internet keyword into the Address box**   Many web pages have been assigned Internet keywords that you can substitute for their URLs. So, for example, you can arrive at the home page of the University of California at Los Angeles by typing **UCLA** into the Address box.

- **Select it from the list that drops down from the Address box**   The Address box remembers the last 25 URLs or keywords that you have typed into it.

- **Link to it from another web page**   The reason it's called a "web" is that pages are linked to each other in a tangled, unpredictable way. Click a link (usually underlined, blue text or icons) to see the web page it refers to.

- **Link to it from a mail message or newsgroup article**   Many mail and messaging programs, including Windows Mail and Microsoft Office Outlook, automatically link the URLs in a message to the corresponding web pages (see Chapter 25). Clicking the URL opens the default web browser, which displays the web page. If the browser can't find the page, try copying and pasting the URL into its Address box and making sure it looks right (remove spaces and line breaks from the URL, for example).

- **Select it from History**   Internet Explorer maintains records of the web pages you have viewed in the past 20 days (or as many days as you select). You can display these records and return to any of the web pages with a click (see "Examining History" later in the chapter).

- **Select it from the Favorites menu**   Accessing a Favorite from the Internet Explorer Favorites menu opens the target web page in Internet Explorer, no matter what the default browser is.

- **Open an Internet shortcut**   Opening an Internet shortcut from Windows Explorer starts the default browser (even if another browser is already running), connects to the Internet, and displays the web page to which the shortcut points.

> **Getting Help**
>
> Access Internet Explorer Help by choosing Help | Contents And Index. You can find what you want by looking through the table of contents on the Contents tab, seeing the topics listed alphabetically on the Index tab, or searching for particular terms on the Search tab. Clicking the Web Help button and clicking the Support Online link opens a browser window displaying the Microsoft Support web page at www.support .microsoft.com/default.aspx.

Remembering Where You've Been on the Web

Internet Explorer provides a variety of ways to remember which web sites you've already visited and how to get back to them. The Back menu keeps track of the last few web pages you've viewed and a drop-down list from the Address box shows the most recent URLs that you've typed. There's also a History feature that you can check when you find yourself saying "I know I saw that last week."

When you find a web page you like, you likely will want to look at it again sometime. Favorites and Internet shortcuts allow you to return easily to a web page without having to write down or remember the page's URL (see "Using Favorites, Links, and Internet Shortcuts" a bit later in the chapter).

Using the Back Menu

The Back button has a drop-down menu of the last several web pages you have looked at during the current session. To access this menu, click the arrow on the right side of the Back button.

Using the Address Box

If you remember the beginning of the URL you are looking for, start typing it into the Address box. As you type, Internet Explorer's autocomplete feature generates a menu of URLs, based on the URLs you have visited recently. If the URL you want appears, you can choose it from the menu.

In addition, Internet Explorer maintains a drop-down list of the last 25 URLs that you have typed into the Address box. You can select an entry off the drop-down list, and the browser fetches the corresponding web page.

Examining History

Internet Explorer keeps track of the web pages that you have accessed recently. This information is stored as Internet shortcuts inside a hierarchy of folders capped by the History folder. You can turn History off, wipe the History folder clean, or edit it selectively, removing only the web pages you don't want recorded.

Clicking the History Favorites Center button (it's a picture of a gold star) on the toolbar, pressing CTRL-H, or selecting View | Explorer Bar | History opens the View History pane, shown next.

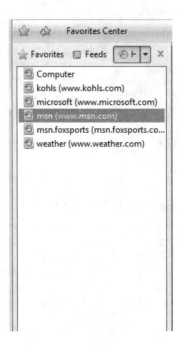

Covering Your Tracks and Tracking Others

If other people use (or are authorized to look at) your user account, you need to be aware of the privacy implications of the History folder, the Address box, and the Back menu. These features (especially the History folder) provide a trail that someone else can follow to see what you've been viewing on the Web. Conversely, you may examine the History folder to see what other people (your children, for example) have been viewing on the Web.

If you want to erase that trail, do the following:

1. Select Tools | Internet Options to open the Internet Options dialog box.

2. Click Delete on the General tab to display the Delete Browsing History dialog box.

3. Click the Delete All button.

4. Click Yes when you are asked to confirm. IE erases the files in your Temporary Internet Files cache, deletes downloaded cookies, deletes the history and the list of URLs that you have typed in the Address box, removes form data you have entered, and deletes any saved passwords you have entered.

5. Click OK.

6. If you just walk away from the computer at this point, the Back menu could still give you away, so exit Internet Explorer. This clears the Back menu.

Clicking the Close The Favorites Center button causes the History pane to disappear.

The History pane is organized into subfolders—one for each day of the current week and one for each previous week, going back 20 days. Selecting a closed folder expands the tree to show its contents; selecting an open folder compresses the tree to hide its contents. Each day's folder contains one subfolder for each web site visited. Inside the web site folders are Internet shortcuts to each of the pages viewed on that web site.

Delete a shortcut or a subfolder from the History folder by right-clicking it and selecting Delete from the shortcut menu.

To change Internet Explorer's History settings:

1. Select Tools | Internet Options. The Internet Options dialog box opens with the General tab on top.

2. Click Settings in the Browsing History area. The Temporary Internet Files And History Settings dialog box appears, as shown in Figure 26-4.

3. If you want to change the number of days that the History folder remembers a web page, enter a new number into the Days To Keep Pages In History box.

4. Click OK.

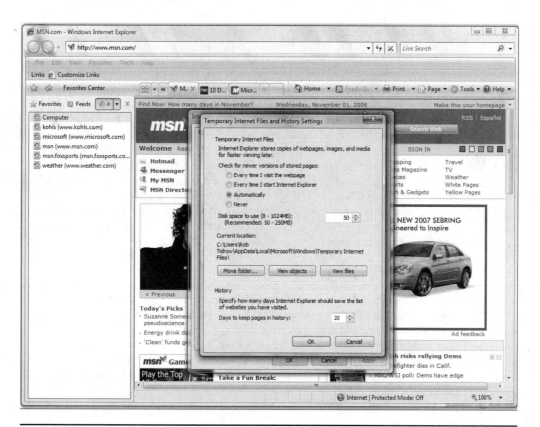

FIGURE 26-4 Change the days to keep history records in this dialog box.

History is subject to user accounts: each user has their own History folder with its own settings.

Using Favorites, Links, and Internet Shortcuts

Favorites and Internet shortcuts are ways to keep track of web sites that you think you will want to return to.

An *Internet shortcut* is a small file (with the extension .url) that contains the Internet address of a web page. Opening an Internet shortcut causes Windows to connect to your Internet service provider (if necessary), open your default web browser, and display the web page that the shortcut points to.

Favorites is a folder of Internet shortcuts. This folder is accessible from the Favorites Center in Internet Explorer (click the gold star to see it). To anchor the Favorites Center (that is, to keep it open), click the Pin The Favorites Center button after you click the Favorites Center button. The Pin The Favorites Center button appears as a small left-pointing arrow. You can add Favorites to the Start menu as well (right-click the Start button, click Customize, and then click Favorites Menu in the Customize Start Menu dialog box).

Selecting an entry from the Favorites menu has the same effect as opening an Internet shortcut that points to that web page. When Favorites are chosen from the Start menu, they open in the default browser, but choosing a web page from the Favorites Center of Internet Explorer opens the page in Internet Explorer, even if another browser is the default browser.

You can place items on the Links bar to help you navigate to sites you visit often.

Adding Favorites and Links

Adding a web page to the Favorites menu automatically creates an Internet shortcut pointing to that web page. If a web page is displayed in Internet Explorer, you can add it to Favorites by clicking the Add To Favorites button (it is a picture of a green plus sign and a gold star) and choosing Add To Favorites, which opens the Add A Favorite dialog box. Another way to open the Add A Favorite dialog box is to right-click a web page and click Add To Favorites. Click the Create In drop-down button to see a list of folders in which to place the shortcut. You also can click the New Folder button to create a new Favorites folder in which to place the shortcut. If you have the menu bar open, you can click Favorites | Add To Favorites as well.

To add a web page to the Links toolbar, either drag its icon from the Address box to the place on the Links bar where you want it, or click the Create In drop-down button in the Add A Favorite dialog box and select the Links folder.

Creating Internet Shortcuts on Your Desktop

To create shortcuts that appear on your desktop by using Internet Explorer, open the page to which you want to create a shortcut and choose File | Send | Shortcut To Desktop.

You can also create shortcuts in Windows Explorer or the desktop. From Windows Explorer, choose File | New | Shortcut. From the desktop, right-click and choose New | Shortcut. Either way, a Create Shortcut dialog box opens. Type the URL of the web page into the Create Shortcut dialog box or, if you have copied the command line from some other document, paste it into the Create Shortcut dialog box by pressing CTRL-V. Click Next. Give the shortcut a name. Click Finish.

Organizing Favorites

If you have picked out only a few web pages, your favorites don't have to be well organized, but as time goes by, favorites accumulate like knick-knacks. It saves time to reorganize them once in a while and toss out the ones that are obsolete.

The Favorites list is actually a folder (C:\Windows\Favorites, if you haven't established user profiles on your computer; C:\Users*username*\Favorites, if you have), and each of the entries on the Favorites list is a shortcut pointing to the URL of the corresponding web page. Consequently, one way to organize Favorites is to use the same techniques you would use to organize any other folder in Windows Explorer. You also can choose Favorites | Organize Favorites from the Internet Explorer window. An Organize Favorites dialog box opens. Move, rename, or delete entries on your Favorites list by selecting the entries and clicking the corresponding buttons in the Organize Favorites dialog box.

Importing and Exporting Favorites and Bookmarks

If the computer you upgrade to Windows Vista has another web browser installed (such as Mozilla Firefox), you can import your favorites from that browser to Internet Explorer 7. To import bookmarks, select File | Import And Export to start the Import/Export Wizard. This wizard provides the best way to convert between Internet Explorer's Favorites (a folder of Internet shortcuts) and FireFox's bookmarks (an HTML file of links).

Searching for Web Pages

Internet Explorer gives you three ways to search the Web:

- Simple convenient searches from the Address box
- More complex searches, using a variety of search engines, from the Search Companion Explorer bar
- Searches from the web site of whatever search engine you like

Searching from the Address Box

The simplest way to search the Web is to type a question mark followed by a word or phrase into the Address box and press ENTER. (Be sure to leave a space after the question mark.) By default, Internet Explorer uses the Microsoft Live Search tool for Address bar searches.

Using the Search Bar

The Search bar allows you to search not just for web pages, but for addresses, businesses, maps, words, pictures, and newsgroups. It is the same Explorer bar that you use to search for files and folders within Windows Vista and Windows Explorer. The general aspects of the Search bar are discussed in Chapter 9.

To look for a web page, type a question or some keywords into the Live Search box and click the Search button.

Changing Internet Explorer's Default Search Engines

By default, Internet Explorer uses the Live Search engine for searches from either the Address box or the Explorer bar. You can change search engines by clicking the drop-down arrow on the Live Search bar and choosing Find More Providers. IE searches for supported search providers and displays them in the IE viewing area. Figure 26-5 shows the search engines we found.

Click a search link (we like Google, so we clicked the Google link). The Add Search Provider dialog box appears. Click Add Provider. Continue clicking search links to add them to your search providers menu. If you want to set a search provider as a default, click Make This My Default Search Provider in the Add Search Provider dialog box. Or, when you finish, you can set a different default by clicking the drop-down arrow on the Live Search bar, choosing Change Search Defaults, selecting a search provider in the Change Search Defaults dialog box, and clicking Set Default.

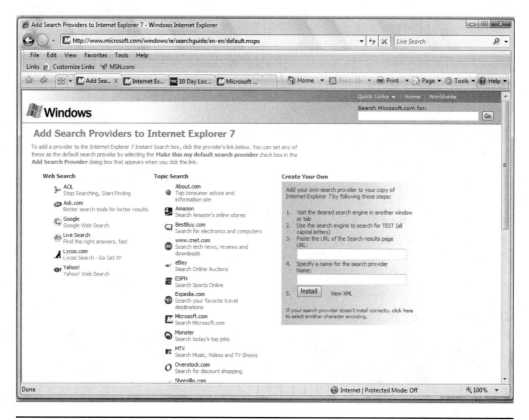

Figure 26-5 Finding additional search providers for IE.

TIP *No matter what search engine Internet Explorer wants to use, you can always go to the web site of your favorite search engine and use it directly—we like www.google.com.*

Interacting with Web Sites Automatically

Web sites that provide some personalized service typically ask you to fill out a registration form when you first establish a relationship with the site and to log in by giving a username and password when you return to the site in the future. Filling out forms and typing in passwords are precisely the kinds of repetitive, mindless work that computers are supposed to do for us, so Internet Explorer provides a way to do these small tasks automatically.

CAUTION *You should give some thought as to whether to let the browser remember passwords and which passwords to entrust to it. Once a browser has been allowed to remember a password for a personal account on a web site, anyone who uses your user account can get into that web account.*

If you want Internet Explorer to remember passwords automatically for you, do the following:

1. Choose Tools | Internet Options to open the Internet Options dialog box.
2. Go to the Content tab.
3. Click the Settings button in the AutoComplete area to open the AutoComplete Settings dialog box:

4. Check the User Names And Passwords On Forms check box. This setting means that Internet Explorer will insert the usernames and passwords it has memorized into the appropriate logon forms for web pages.

PART V

5. Check the Prompt Me To Save Passwords check box. This setting means that whenever you log into a site whose password Internet Explorer hasn't memorized, it will ask you whether you want it to memorize that password. If Internet Explorer already knows all the passwords you want it to know, leave this box unchecked.

6. Click OK in each of the open dialog boxes.

When these settings are in place, you will encounter the following dialog box every time you enter a new password:

Click Yes if you want IE to remember the password. Checking the Don't Offer To Remember Any More Passwords check box has the same effect as unchecking the Prompt Me To Save Passwords box on the AutoComplete Settings dialog box: Internet Explorer remembers and continues to use the passwords it knows but stops asking whether it should remember new passwords.

Occasionally, you may click Yes to remember the password and then later regret it. Unfortunately, there is no way to instruct Internet Explorer to forget one or two of your passwords but remember the others. If you want Internet Explorer to forget all the passwords it knows, open the Internet Options dialog box (as in the previous steps), click the General tab, and click Delete. On the Delete Browsing History dialog box, click Delete Passwords and click Yes.

Using Windows CardSpace

A new feature to Internet Explorer 7 and Windows Vista is the Windows CardSpace tool. CardSpace enables you to set up cards that let you log into web sites automatically, sort of like digital business cards. CardSpace includes the following features:

- Enables you to manage personal information on a card
- Enables you to set up multiple cards
- Provides a way for web sites to easily and consistently request information from you
- Lets you find the identity of a site you visit
- Enables you to double-check information you send to a site before actually sending it

Adding a CardSpace Card

You configure Windows CardSpace from Windows Vista Control Panel, not within IE 7. Do the following to set up a new card:

1. Choose Start | Control Panel | User Accounts And Family Safety.

2. Click the Windows CardSpace link. The Windows CardSpace —Welcome window appears, which describes CardSpace.

3. Click OK to clear the window and to display the Windows CardSpace window, as shown in Figure 26-6.

4. Click Add A Card in the Tasks pane. The Add A Card window appears.

5. Click Create A Personal Card. (The Install A Managed Card option is for installing cards you have been issued from businesses or other organizations that create managed cards for you, such as a credit card company.) The Edit A New Card windows appears, as shown in Figure 26-7.

6. Fill out the card.

7. Click Save to save your new card. The new card appears in the Windows CardSpace window.

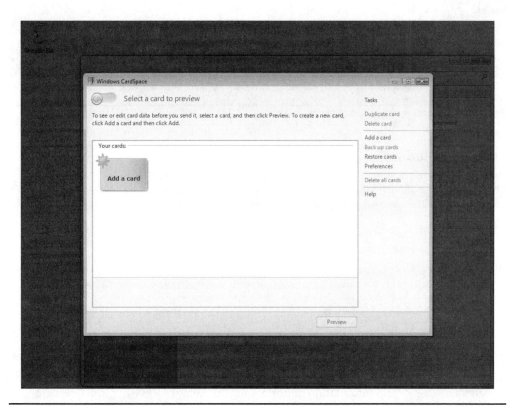

FIGURE 26-6 Use Windows CardSpace to manage cards for logging into secure sites automatically.

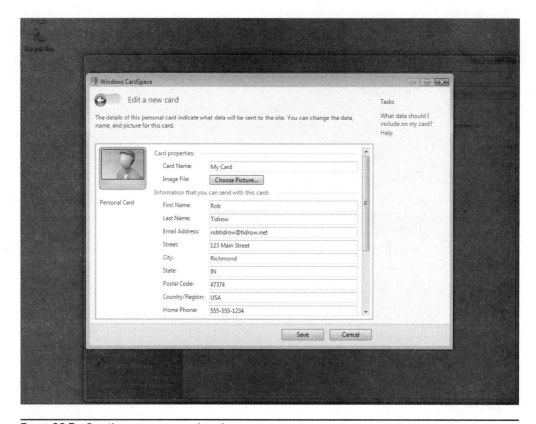

FIGURE 26-7   Creating a new personal card.

Applying a Card

As you use the Web, some sites use CardSpace features to enable you to input information or to request CardSpace information. You can specify the personal card or managed card (depending on the site and transaction) that you want to send to a site.

Configuring RSS Feed Settings

IE 7 supports RSS technology to allow you to receive headlines and updates automatically from your favorite web sites. Just so you know, RSS stands for any of the following:

- Really Simple Syndication
- Rich Site Summary
- RDF Site Summary

Regardless of which term you use, RSS is a convenient way to stay in touch and remain updated with topics and information important to you. Some of the ways RSS feeds are being used include:

- News sites offering up-to-the-minute events
- Sports sites sending scores and player happenings
- Entertainment and music sites providing actor and artist information
- Retailers promoting upcoming sales

These represent just a tiny fraction of the ways in which RSS feeds are used. In fact, your company may use RSS feeds to send you company information, new employee postings , and data on the latest quarterly results.

Adding RSS Feeds to IE 7

IE 7 makes it easy to identify which sites offer RSS feeds: the View Feeds icon on the main toolbar lights up when you hit a site with feeds. You can click the drop-down arrow on the View Feeds icon to see which types of feeds you can get (for instance, CNN has news feeds broken into U.S., Top Stories, and Recent Stories). You also can look for the orange and white RSS icon, an orange XML icon, or just text that says RSS. Some of the RSS feed icons are shown here:

When you see an RSS icon, click it to set up RSS feeds to your computer. You are shown the feeds page for that site. Click Subscribe To This Feed. Some sites take you to a separate page before the feeds page, from which you set up individual RSS feed settings. For example, the Weather Channel web site has the page shown in Figure 26-8. Here you can set up RSS feeds to deliver national and local weather, and the Weather Channel blog to your computer. Click the XML icon next to the feed you want to receive to see the feeds page, and then click Subscribe To This Feed.

The Internet Explorer window shown in Figure 26-9 appears. Click the Subscribe button to add it to your list of RSS feeds.

Viewing RSS Feeds

After you set up RSS feeds, you can view them by using the View Feeds pane in IE. Click the Favorites Center button and then click Feeds. A list of subscribed-to feeds appears, like the ones shown in Figure 26-10. Click a feed to display the feeds page for that RSS feed.

Most RSS feeds are short snippets of information, so you can't read the entire article on the feeds page. Instead you can click the Go To Full Article icon (a green right-pointing arrow). The full article page appears in the IE tab.

Configuring RSS Feed Settings

RSS feeds use the Feeds Property settings to determine how often feeds are updated, how they are denoted as being on a web page, and other settings. To modify them, right-click a feed in the Feeds pane and click Properties. The Feed Properties dialog box appears, as shown in Figure 26-11.

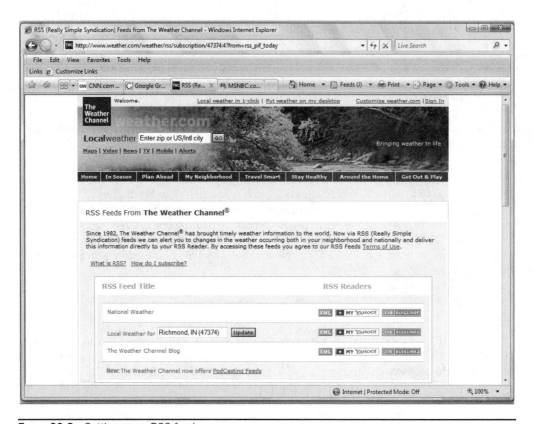

Figure 26-8   Setting up an RSS feed.

You can set the following items:

- **Name**   You can use the default name provided by the web site or enter another one of your own choosing.

- **Update Schedule**   By default, IE downloads updates once per day. This may not be often enough for sites that regularly update, such as news sites or intra-office sites. Click the Settings button to display the Feed Settings dialog box. Select a different update time from the Every drop-down list. You might try every hour, for instance. Usually this is enough time between checks (too many checks can overload the RSS site). Also, you can have the feed marked as read after reading it, turn on the feed reading view, and play a sound when a new feed is found on a web page. Click OK. If you want to use a custom schedule for a feed, select it from the Use Custom Schedule drop-down list. That particular site uses the custom setting, while others and new ones will use the default setting (which you set using the Feed Settings dialog box).

- **Automatically Download Attached Files**   Specifies that IE should automatically download any attached files to the RSS feed. These are placed in your Downloads folder in your User Accounts area (open the Documents folder to see the Downloads folder).

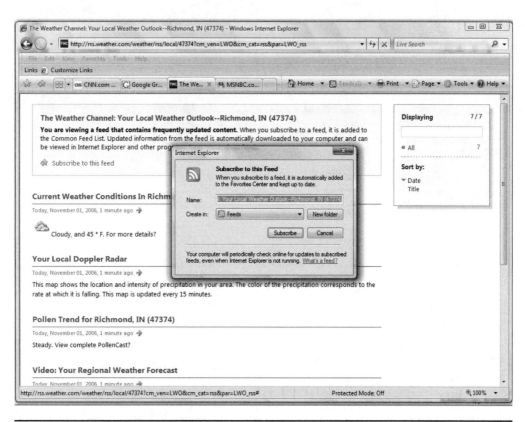

FIGURE 26-9   Subscribing to an RSS feed to appear in IE 7.

- **Archive**   Specifies the number of updates IE saves for each RSS. If you keep the maximum (2500) and you have a lot of RSS feed subscriptions, you will really be adding a lot of extra content to your system. Consider limiting this to the default, 200, or even fewer to keep your system free of them.

Click OK after you modify the RSS feed properties.

Changing How Web Pages Look

Internet Explorer allows you to change the fonts and colors that it uses to render web pages, and even the alphabets. You can also decide to save downloading time by telling Internet Explorer not to download pictures or other multimedia content.

These preferences are controlled from the Internet Options dialog box (shown in Figure 26-12), which you access by opening the Internet Options icon on the Control Panel (Start | Control Panel | Network And Internet | Internet Options) or by choosing Tools | Internet Options from Internet Explorer's menu bar. (Strangely, if you open it from the Control Panel, the dialog box is called Internet Properties, but it contains the same tabs, buttons, and settings.)

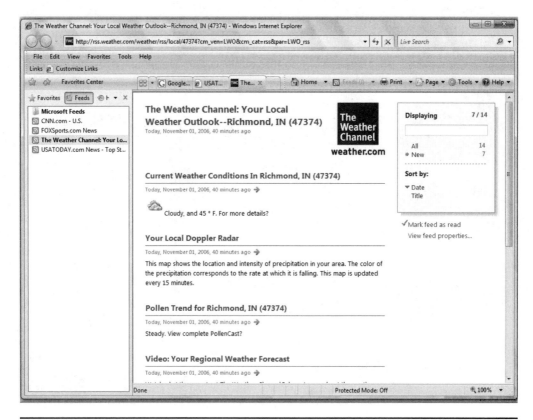

FIGURE 26-10 Viewing your RSS feeds in the Feeds pane.

CAUTION From its name, you might think that the Internet Options dialog box controls settings for any web browser or other Internet program, but it doesn't. Changes you make in the Internet Options dialog box only affect Internet Explorer.

Choosing Fonts

To make Internet Explorer display text in a different size, use the View | Text Size menu. There are five choices, from smallest to largest. The default size is Medium, which for the Latin-based alphabet means 12-point variable-width fonts and 10-point fixed-width fonts.

To make more fundamental changes in the fonts Internet Explorer uses, click the Fonts button on the General tab of the Internet Options dialog box. The Fonts dialog box opens, shown in Figure 26-13. This dialog box has two basic elements:

- **A drop-down list of alphabets** This list is labeled Language Script and the English language script is "Latin Based."

FIGURE 26-11   Setting RSS feed properties.

- **Two lists specifying the web page (or variable-width) font and the plain-text (or fixed-width) font for the selected alphabet**   Change either font by picking a new one from the corresponding list.

Sometimes a web page specifies a font, and that specification overrides the choices you make in the Fonts dialog box. To make your font choices override those of the web page, click the Accessibility button on the General tab of the Internet Options dialog box and check either the Ignore Font Styles Specified On Web Pages check box or the Ignore Font Sizes Specified On Web Pages check box.

Choosing Colors

You can change the colors that Internet Explorer uses to display text, backgrounds, and links. To change the color of the text and background, click the Colors button on the General tab of the Internet Options dialog box.

FIGURE 26-12 The Internet Options dialog box.

The default is to use Windows colors—that is, the colors defined in the Window Color And Appearance window (see "Choosing a New Color Scheme" in Chapter 12). If you don't want to use the Windows colors, take the following steps:

1. Remove the check from the Use Windows Colors check box.

2. Click the colored button next to the Text label or Background label. A palette of colors appears.

3. Click the color you want for the Text or Background and click OK to make the palette disappear. The button next to Text or Background should now be the color you selected.

4. Click OK to close the Colors dialog box.

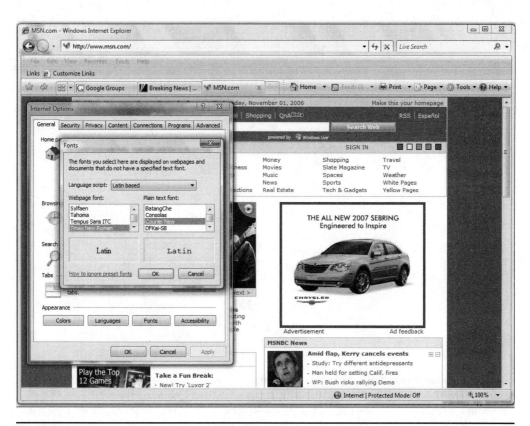

FIGURE 26-13 Internet Explorer's Fonts dialog box.

Changing the colors used for links is a similar process, except that you don't need to remove the check from Use Windows Colors. The Colors dialog box also allows you to define a *hover color*, a color that links change to when the cursor *hovers* over them.

TIP *We suggest you leave the colors alone, except perhaps for making the background color white (if it's not white already).*

Internet Explorer has other accessibility features for the visually impaired (see "Making Internet Explorer Accessible" in Chapter 17).

Changing Language Preferences

Some web pages are available in multiple languages, and your web browser picks the one that matches your preferences. To define or change your language preferences in Internet

Explorer, click the Languages button near the bottom of the General tab of the Internet Options dialog box to open the Language Preference dialog box:

The purpose of this dialog box is to maintain a list of favored languages in order, with your preferred language on top. Add a language to the list by clicking the Add button and selecting a language from the list that appears. Remove a language from the Language list by selecting it and clicking the Remove button. Reorder the Language list by selecting a language on the list and clicking the Move Up or Move Down button. When you are satisfied with the list of languages, click OK.

Choosing Whether to Download Images, Audio, and Video

Many web pages have pictures or other graphics on them. These are more time consuming to download than text, so if your connection is slow, you may decide not to bother downloading graphics. Multimedia content such as audio, video, or animation is even slower to download, and you can tell your browser to ignore them, too. To do this, go to the Advanced tab of the Internet Options dialog box, shown in Figure 26-14. Scroll down until you see the Multimedia heading. Remove the check from each box next to any type of content that you want to ignore.

Managing Internet Explorer's Behavior

Internet Explorer is intended to be simple enough for novice users. For this reason, most of what it does is invisible. Some choices that IE makes for you, however, have implications for your system's use of disk space or its security—implications that more advanced users may want to consider. Internet Explorer allows you some limited opportunities to "get under the

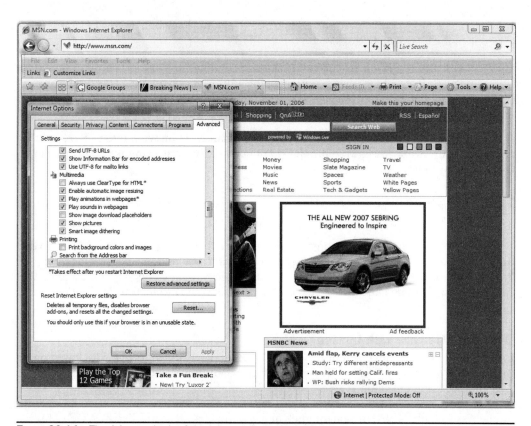

FIGURE 26-14   The Advanced tab of the Internet Options dialog box.

hood" and make choices for yourself about your start page, blocking offensive content, caching web pages, and the default mail and news applications. You can even decide that Internet Explorer should not be the default web browser.

Choosing and Customizing Your Start Page

Your browser's home page (also called a *start page*) is the web page that the browser loads when you open the browser without requesting a specific page. You can also see the browser's home page by clicking the Home button on its toolbar. (Don't confuse this use of "home page" with the home page of a web site.)

Microsoft promotes its MSN web site by making it the default home page of Internet Explorer. In general, this not a bad home page, and many people never change it. However, you can select any web page or file that you want to be your browser's home page.

To change Internet Explorer's start page, choose Tools | Internet Options to display the Internet Options dialog box with the General tab on top (as you saw in Figure 26-12).

You can type the URL of the new home page into the Home Page box on this tab or you can click one of the following buttons:

- **Use Current**   The page currently displayed by Internet Explorer becomes the home page. (If Internet Explorer is not open, this button is grayed out.) This can be any page on the Web, or even an HTML document on your hard drive.
- **Use Default**   You get a personalizable MSN home page at www.msn.com.
- **Use Blank**   The home page is blank. This is handy if you want Internet Explorer to start up as quickly as possible and don't necessarily want to invoke your Internet connection.

TIP *Setting your start page to be an HTML document on your hard drive makes Internet Explorer start up more quickly than if it has to download a start page from the Internet.*

You also can set up multiple home pages, each one displaying on a different tab. To do this, open multiple tabs with different pages you want to use as home pages. Click the drop-down arrow next to the Home button and choose Add Or Change Home Page. In the Add Or Change Home Page dialog box, click Add This Webpage To Your Home Page Tabs. Click Yes.

Blocking Offensive Web Content

Internet Explorer includes Content Advisor, which can block access to web sites based on their level of potentially offensive content. Unfortunately, this system does not work very well, and we cannot recommend it.

Content Advisor is based on a voluntary rating system devised by the Internet Content Rating Association (ICRA) for the Internet, at www.ircra.org. It works like this: web site managers add labels to their web pages to rate the content of the pages based on a number of different metrics, such as language, nudity, sex, and violence. These labels are attached to the web sites with codes that browsers can read, but usually do not display. When you set up Content Advisor, you specify the numerical ratings you will accept, and web sites with ratings beyond your specifications are blocked.

The ICRA rating system has been in place for several years now, and it has become clear that the vast majority of web sites (whether they contain potentially objectionable content or not) will never be rated. This leaves you with the following choice: You can block all unrated sites, which makes the Web almost useless to you, or you can allow access to unrated sites, many of which contain the kind of content you had hoped to block.

Using the Phishing Filter

New with Internet Explorer 7 is a tool called the *Phishing Filter*. The Phishing Filter blocks web pages that are deemed to be potential phishing sites. What is phishing? Phishing is a technique whereby a site is built to look like a legitimate site, such as a banking or shopping site, but really is designed to steal your personal information. When you enter data like your credit card, Social Security Number, and other confidential information, phishing sites store your information and sell it to other unsavory sites, or use it to steal your identity.

The IE Phishing Filter can identify sites that are potential phishing sites and display an icon in the Security Status bar (it is part of the Address bar) to identify the following types of sites:

Known
Phishing Site

Suspected
Site

You can access Phishing Filter tools and options by choosing Tools | Phishing Filter. You can choose from the following commands:

- **Check This Website**   Enables you to check the current web site against a list of potential phishing sites on the Microsoft.com web site.

- **Turn Off/On Automatic Website Checking**   Enables you to turn off the Phishing Filter if it is activated. If you have it off, you can turn it on here as well.

- **Report This Website**   Links you to the Microsoft Phishing Filter Report A Website page. Here you can submit the current page as a suspected phishing web site.

- **Phishing Filter Settings**   Displays the Advanced tab of the Internet Options dialog box. Scroll down to the Phishing Filter category to change whether IE enables the Phishing Filter when you start IE, keeps it turned off, or totally disables it.

NOTE *As you may suspect, using the Phishing Filter can slow down IE as it displays web pages. If you have a slow connection to the Web, consider turning it off and using the Check This Website tool to manually check sites you may suspect as phishing sites.*

Managing Caches of Web Pages

Internet Explorer stores some of the pages that you view so that they can be redisplayed quickly if you return to them. In general, this speeds up the browsing experience, but if you are running short of disk space, you may decide to limit or eliminate these caches. They are stored in a folder named Temporary Internet Files, which is inside the hidden folder C:\ User*your username*\Local Settings.

You control Internet Explorer's cache of web pages from the General tab of the Internet Options dialog box. Delete all these web pages by clicking the Delete button and then Delete Files in the Temporary Internet Files section. To set limits on the amount of disk space that can be devoted to temporary Internet files, click the Settings button on the General tab in the Browsing History section to open the Temporary Internet Files And History Settings dialog box. Set the Disk Space To Use box to raise or lower the amount of your hard drive that the Temporary Internet Files folder is allowed to use. Click OK to apply your changes. 50 MB is the default.

Managing Internet Explorer's Security and Privacy Settings

You should keep two risk factors in mind when you use the Web:

- Web sites may be collecting information about you and your browsing habits using small files called *cookies* that are stored on your computer.

- The scripts and applets that allow web sites to offer more complex content and services may also make your computer more vulnerable to viruses or hackers.

This section discusses the tools and options that Internet Explorer provides for dealing with these risks. Also see "Managing Which Files Internet Explorer Downloads" in Chapter 33.

Controlling Cookies

A *cookie* is a small (at most 4 Kb) file that a web server can store on your machine. Its purpose is to allow a web server to personalize a web page, depending on whether you have been to that web site before and what you may have told it during previous sessions. For example, when you establish an account with an online retailer or subscribe to an online magazine, you may be asked to fill out a form that includes some information about yourself and your preferences. The web server may store that information (along with information about when you visit the site) in a cookie on your machine. When you return to that web site in the future, the retailer's web server can read its cookie, recall this information, and structure its web pages accordingly.

Internet Explorer 7 gives you some control over cookies. Unfortunately, IE 7's privacy level settings (which are the same as the ones in IE 6) make the situation seem much more complicated than it is, and none of them is a very good cookie policy. The privacy settings are based on the Platform for Privacy Preferences (P3P), a voluntary standard that helps set privacy controls on the Web.

NOTE *To learn more about the policy that helps control privacy matters on the Web, you can visit the P3P web site at www.w3.org/P3P.*

How Does Internet Explorer Implement Privacy Policies?

The Privacy tab of the Internet Options dialog box contains a slider that you can set to one of six levels, from Accept All Cookies to Block All Cookies. The default level is Medium. The descriptions of these levels are phrased using technical terms like *personally identifiable information*, *implicit consent*, *explicit consent*, and *compact privacy policy*. What follows is our interpretation of what these levels actually mean:

- **Block All Cookies**   At this level you are unable to log in to access Hotmail, or a Yahoo home page, or to use a subscription to the online *Wall Street Journal*. You could make this setting tolerable if you could create exceptions for your favorite web sites, but Microsoft has disabled the exception-making capability for this setting.

- **High**   Cookies are only accepted from web sites that offer P3P information, and then only if that information says that they don't keep track of information that would identify you personally (like your name, for example, or your phone number) unless you've explicitly given them permission to do so. At this level we could log into Hotmail and Yahoo, but not *The Wall Street Journal*.

- **Medium High**   Same as High, except that first-party cookies are accepted from web sites that use personally identifiable information without your explicit consent, if they somehow allow you to opt out of this usage. (In general, we don't like opt-out processes. They require too much alertness and diligence on your part.) At this level we could see *The Wall Street Journal*.

- **Medium**   Allows third-party cookies that let you opt out of their use of personally identifiable information. Restricts first-party cookies that use personally identifiable information without letting you opt out. (We have no idea what the difference between "restrict" and "block" is.)

- **Low**   Accepts all first-party cookies. Restricts third-party cookies from web sites that don't offer P3P information or that don't let you opt out of their use of personally identifiable information.

- **Accept All Cookies**   Accepts all cookies without asking you.

What Is a Sensible Cookie Policy?

First we'll tell you what you don't want: You don't want to block all cookies, because you give up much of the functionality and convenience of the Web. You also don't want Internet Explorer to ask you what to do every time a web site wants to set a cookie, because you'll spend more time deciding about cookies than you'll spend reading web pages.

You *do* want to make a distinction between first-party and third-party cookies, because third-party cookies benefit only the advertisers, not you.

The cookie policy we'd like to have is Medium High for first-party cookies, and block third-party cookies altogether. This does not seem to be possible with Internet Explorer. Given that fact, we recommend the following policy: accept all first-party cookies and block all third-party cookies. This isn't one of the six levels on the slider, but you can configure Internet Explorer to do it.

Another reasonable option (but somewhat more difficult to set up) is to select the High level and then create exceptions for a few favorite web sites whose cookies are blocked. This policy allows a few more third-party cookies and a few less first-party cookies than the policy suggested in the previous paragraph. However, this option stops many shopping sites from working, because the sites use shopping-cart programs hosted on third-party web sites. (Another options is to use Netscape instead of IE, because of its more flexible cookie policies.)

Setting Cookie Policy

Cookie policy is controlled from the Privacy tab of the Internet Options dialog box. If you want one of the settings described in the previous section, move the slider to that setting and click OK.

If you want to set up our recommended cookie policy (allow first-party and block third-party cookies), do the following:

1. Select Tools | Internet Options to open the Internet Options dialog box.

2. Select the Privacy tab (see Figure 26-15).

3. Click the Advanced button on the Privacy tab. The Advanced Privacy Settings dialog box appears.

4. Check the Override Automatic Cookie Handling box.

FIGURE 26-15   Setting IE's privacy options.

5. Select the Accept radio button under First-Party Cookies and the Block radio button under Third-Party Cookies.

6. Click OK in both of the open dialog boxes.

If a particular web site is not working because its cookies are being blocked, you can choose to create an exception for it without changing your settings for other web sites. (For reasons that escape us, Microsoft has made this option unavailable if you have chosen the Block All Cookies setting.) Do the following:

1. Select Tools | Internet Options to open the Internet Options dialog box.

2. Select the Privacy tab.

3. Click the Sites button on the Privacy tab. The Per Site Privacy Actions dialog box opens.

4. Type the URL of the web site into the Address Of Web Site line.

5. Click the Allow button and click OK in both open dialog boxes.

If you want to block the cookies on a particular web site when your overall policy would allow them, do the previous steps, but click the Block button in Step 5.

Managing the Cookies You Have

Windows stores your cookies in two folders:

- C:\Users*username*\Cookies
- C:\Users*username*\Local Settings\Temporary Internet Files

Reading a cookie in WordPad or some other text program probably will not tell you much, though it may set your mind at ease to realize just how little information is there (see "Taking Advantage of Free Word Processing with WordPad" in Chapter 18). Delete individual cookies from your system by deleting the corresponding text files, or nuke them all by clicking the Delete button on the General tab of the Internet Options dialog box and then clicking Delete Cookies in the Delete Browsing History dialog box. Click Yes when asked if you are sure you want to delete them. Click OK twice.

Managing Scripts, Applets, and ActiveX Controls

Some web pages increase the amount of interactivity they can offer by downloading small programs to run on your computer. For example, rather than transmitting the individual frames of an animation over the Internet, a web server may send an animation-constructing program that runs on your computer. A financial web site may download a program that displays a scrolling stock ticker. Typically, this process is invisible to the user—the interaction or the animation just happens, without calling your attention to how it happens.

While these programs are useful, they also create security issues. If web sites can put useful programs on your computer and run them without informing you, precautions must be taken to make sure that they can't also put harmful programs on your computer. Internet Explorer takes certain precautions automatically and allows you the option to choose additional precautions.

What Are Java, JavaScript, VBScript, and ActiveX?

Java is a language for sending small applications (called *applets*) over the Web so that they can be executed by your computer. *JavaScript* is a language for extending HTML to embed small programs called *scripts* in web pages. *VBScript*, a language that resembles Microsoft's Visual Basic, can be used to add scripts to pages that are displayed by Internet Explorer. Anything that VBScript can do, JavaScript (which Microsoft calls JScript) can do, too, and vice versa.

ActiveX controls, like Java, are a way to embed executable programs into a web page. Unlike Java and JavaScript, but like VBScript, ActiveX is a Microsoft system that is not used by all browsers. When Internet Explorer encounters a web page that uses ActiveX controls, it checks to see whether that particular control is already installed; if it is not, IE asks whether you want to install the control on your machine using the Information Bar at the top of the IE Viewer area. Click the Information Bar and then click Install ActiveX Control to download and install the control.

CAUTION *ActiveX controls are considerably more dangerous than JavaScript or VBScript scripts or Java applets. Java applets and JavaScript scripts are run in a "sandbox" inside your web browser, which limits the accidental or deliberate damage they can do; and VBScript scripts are run by an interpreter, which should limit the types of damage they can do. However, ActiveX controls are programs with full access to your computer's resources.*

PART V

Security Zones

Internet Explorer has different security settings for its four zones: Trusted Sites, Local Intranet, Internet, and Restricted Sites. The default settings are Low in the Trusted Sites zone, Medium-Low in the Local Intranet zone, Medium in the Internet zone, and High in the Restricted Sites zone. These zones and settings are discussed Chapter 33.

The rules governing scripts and applets are set zone by zone on the Security tab of the Internet Options dialog box. To examine or change these settings:

1. Open the Internet Options dialog box by selecting Tools | Internet Options from the Internet Explorer menu bar.

2. Click the Security tab of the Internet Options dialog box.

3. Select the zone you want to examine or change.

4. If you want to change the security setting of a zone, move the slider on the Security tab of the Internet Options dialog box. (The slider doesn't appear if the zone has been given custom settings. To reset such a zone to one of the standard settings, click the Default Level button. When the slider reappears, you can move it to the desired setting.)

5. To see the nitty-gritty details of the current security settings for the selected zone, click the Custom Level button. The Security Settings dialog box opens.

6. If you want to change the security settings of the selected zone, scroll through the Security Settings dialog box until you see the item you want to change. Change an item by checking or unchecking its check box, or by selecting a different radio button than the current selection.

7. Click OK to close each open dialog box. Click Yes in the confirmation box that asks if you want to change the security settings.

Managing Java and JavaScript

The security settings that affect Java and JavaScript are in the Java and Scripting sections of the Security Settings dialog box. You may change what these applets and scripts are allowed to do on your computer, or even disable Java or JavaScript entirely. Follow the steps in the previous section.

Managing ActiveX Controls

We have never been big fans of ActiveX controls. They allow web sites to have too much power over your system and are hard to monitor. If you should happen to download and install a rogue ActiveX control by mistake, it could (on its own) download and install lots more rogue ActiveX controls—which would then be permanent parts of your software environment, even when you are offline. None of this would appear the least bit suspicious to any virus-detecting software you might own, because ActiveX controls aren't viruses: they have the same status as applications that you install yourself.

Disabling ActiveX controls is one option. However, if you frequent Microsoft web sites like MSN or MSNBC, you will be exposed to numerous temptations to turn them back on. We suggest the following compromise: Disable ActiveX controls everywhere but in the

Trusted Sites security zone. (Do this from the Security Settings dialog box, following the steps in the "Security Zones" section above.) When you find a Microsoft web site that offers some wonderful service involving ActiveX controls, move that site into the Trusted Sites security zone. See Chapter 33 for a discussion of security zones and trusted sites.

ActiveX controls are stored in the folder C:\Windows\Downloaded Program Files. If you use Internet Explorer, you should check this file periodically to see what applications Internet Explorer has downloaded. Dispose of an ActiveX control by right-clicking its icon and selecting Remove from the shortcut menu.

Displaying a Privacy Report about a Web Page

IE 7 includes the Privacy Report to help you determine how much information you are willing to give a particular site. It also enables you to determine what kind of information a site is storing on your computer and whether the site complies with its own privacy policy.

Accessing the Windows Privacy Report is easy. In Internet Explorer, choose View | Web Page Privacy Report from the menu. You see a list of the objects that are loaded on the page you are looking at, typically graphics, like this:

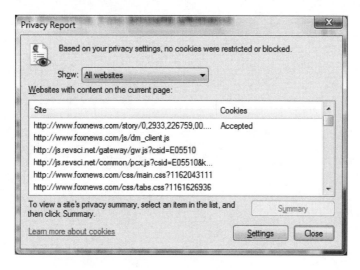

These connected objects may be on the same web server as the page itself or might have been loaded from other web servers. If any of the objects listed have placed a cookie on your computer, you see it listed in the column to the right.

Click the Settings button to see the Privacy tab of the Internet Options dialog box, which was covered earlier in this chapter. Clicking the Advanced button enables you to set how cookies are dealt with. Our favorite arrangement is to allow cookies from the originating server but to refuse them from any external servers. This almost globally allows cookies that are specific to your browsing while rebuffing those that are used for external tracking and advertising information gathering.

Internet Conferencing with Windows Live Messenger

Unlike previous versions of Windows, Windows Vista does not come with a built-in program for chatting and conferencing over the Internet. Prior version of Windows included Windows Messenger and Microsoft NetMeeting. You can, however, download and install the new Windows Live Messenger program. It provides an instant messenger program for chatting and communicating with your friends, family, and colleagues.

This chapter describes how to download Windows Live Messenger, how to install it, and how to start using it. You can download other Internet chat and conferencing programs from the Internet itself; Chapter 28 tells you how.

Setting Up Windows Live Messenger

Windows Live Messenger enables you to chat with family, friends, or coworkers who are online at the time that you want to chat. It's quicker than e-mail, and multiple people can take part in the conversation. Windows Live Messenger also enables you to speak to other users and send messages to pagers.

Downloading Windows Live Messenger

Windows Live Messenger must be downloaded from the Internet to begin using it. To download it, follow these steps:

1. Make sure you are connected to the Internet.

2. Choose Start | All Programs | Windows Live Messenger Download. Internet Explorer launches and connects to the Windows Live Messenger download page, as shown in Figure 27-1.

3. Click the Get It Free button. The File Download dialog box appears.

4. Click Save. If you want, you can click the Run button, but I prefer saving the file to my hard drive and then running the program from there. That ensures I have the program on my computer in case I have to reinstall it at a later date and don't want to bother downloading it again. The Save As dialog box appears.

FIGURE 27-1   Download Live Messenger.

5. Locate a place on your hard drive to which to save the file. The filename is Install_ Messenger.exe.

6. Click Save to start the download. It's a little over 16MB, so it will take a few moments to download on a broadband or LAN connection. With dial-up, you'll be here for a while.

7. After the file downloads, close Internet Explorer.

8. Double-click the Install_Messenger.exe file to launch the setup program.

9. Click Run. The Windows Live Messenger Setup Wizard appears (see Figure 27-2).

10. Work through the wizard to set up Live Messenger. On the third screen, you can deselect any optional program you do not want to install, such as MSN Home, Windows Live Toolbar, and Rhapsody Music Service. This chapter does not discuss those features. At the end, click Close to close the wizard.

The Windows Live Messenger signup window appears after you install it. The window is shown in Figure 27-3.

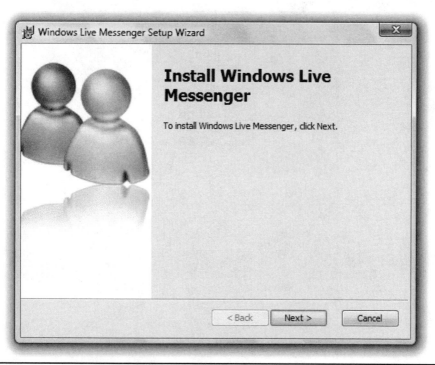

FIGURE 27-2   Work through the Windows Live Messenger Setup Wizard.

Signing In to Windows Live Messenger

If you haven't used Windows Live Messenger before, you need to establish a Microsoft Live ID. A Microsoft Live ID is the same thing as a Microsoft Passport, which was an ID you could use for Microsoft web sites and services. You also can acquire a Live ID if you use Microsoft Hotmail (also called Microsoft Live Mail). Getting an e-mail account with that service automatically grants you a Live ID. Finally, if you had an MSN Messenger account with previous Windows versions, you can use it as your Live ID.

If you need a Live ID, click the Get A New Account link at the bottom of the Live Messenger window. It is free. You are taken to the Get Your Windows Live ID page of the Windows Live Services web site, as shown in Figure 27-4.

When creating a new Live ID, you provide a password as well as a secret question and answer that you can use if you forget your password. You must also provide your location (country and state or province).

When you have created a Live ID for yourself, you can start filling out the Windows Live Messenger window (shown earlier in Figure 27-3). Fill out your e-mail address and password and set the other options accordingly. Some users, for instance, go ahead and select the options for Live Messenger to remember them on this computer, which makes logging in each time transparent. Click Sign In after you fill out the sign-in window.

Once you sign on, you see two windows like the ones shown in Figure 27-5. The one on the left is the main Live Messenger window in which you set up your contacts, create chat

FIGURE 27-3 The Windows Live Messenger signup window.

messages, read messages, and do other tasks. The window on the right is an information window that pops up when you sign on to Live Messenger. It includes Live Messenger information and other web pages that Microsoft sends to you. You can close this window by clicking its Close button. This helps tidy up your screen.

The window lists your contacts—those who are online and those who are not. Of course, if you've never used Windows Live Messenger, you don't have any contacts listed (yet).

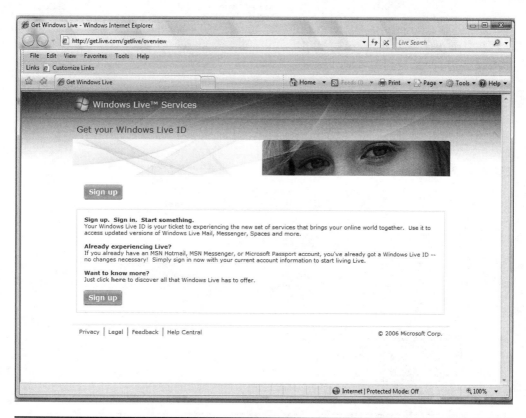

Figure 27-4   Sign up for a Live ID here.

Tip   *The Windows Live Messenger window includes an icon showing how many new e-mail messages are in your Live Mail (or Hotmail) account. Click the e-mail icon to display the Live Mail web site. There's no way to configure Windows Live Messenger to display how many messages are in mailboxes other than your Live Mail mailbox (Microsoft owns Live Mail and Hotmail, and it is using Windows to promote them).*

Telling Windows Live Messenger about Your Contacts

Before you can begin to chat, you have to have someone to chat with. The easiest way to find someone to chat with is to ask your friends if they use Windows Live Messenger and, if so, what their e-mail address is (at least, the e-mail address they use for messaging—some people use a different address to avoid getting messages at the regular e-mail address). Once you know a person's e-mail address, add it to your contacts by following these steps:

1. Open Windows Live Messenger.

2. Click Add A Contact on the toolbar next to the box that reads Find A Contact Or Number. You see the Windows Live Contacts – Add A Contact dialog box, shown in Figure 27-6.

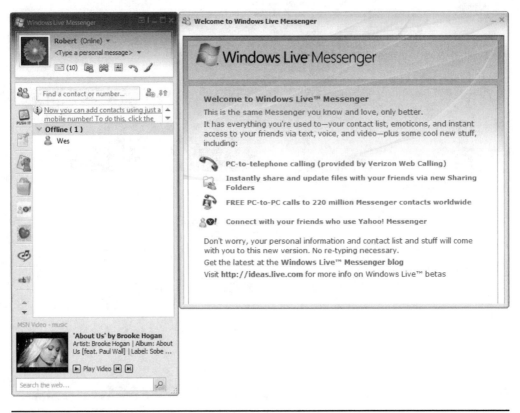

FIGURE 27-5 The Windows Live Messenger window.

3. Fill out the General page, including the person's e-mail address and nickname. A phone number is not required unless you plan to use Windows Live Messenger to make phone calls.

4. Click the other pages (Contact, Personal, Work, and Notes) to fill them out with information about your new contact. Of course, you may not know all this information, or may not care to put it in at this time. That's okay. You may, however, find the information useful sometime, but it's not required for you to use Windows Live Messenger.

5. Click Save when you create the user.

6. Windows Live Messenger adds the person to your contact list and searches to see if that person is online. Notice in Figure 27-7 that the new contact has just come online and a new message appears on the taskbar to indicate such. Also, the Windows Live Messenger window shows that the contact is now Online.

7. In case the person does not have a Live ID, you can send them an e-mail message telling them how to get up and running with Windows Live Messenger.

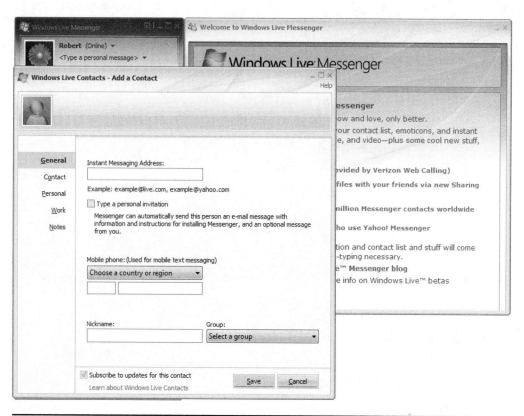

FIGURE 27-6   Adding a new contact.

When Someone Else Adds You as a Contact

When someone adds your e-mail address as a contact, the Windows Live Messenger system notifies you with a message that they want to add you as a contact. A window like the one shown here appears:

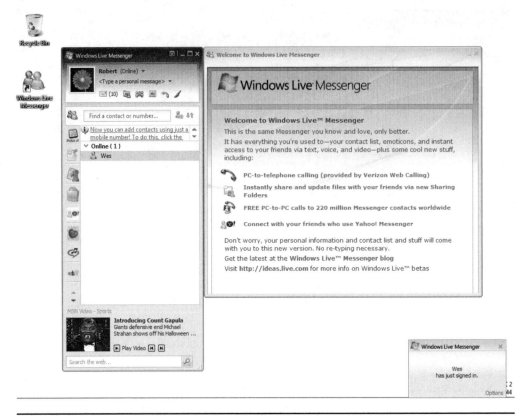

FIGURE 27-7 Windows Live Messenger with one contact online.

If you don't know the person (or are acquainted but don't want further contact), you can prevent him or her from knowing when you are online or from contacting you via Windows Live Messenger (see "Other Things You Can Do with Windows Live Messenger" later in the chapter). On the other hand, if the message is from a friend, family member, or coworker, you can add the person to your own contact list.

Starting a Windows Live Messenger Conversation

To exchange typed messages with a contact who is online, double-click his or her name in the Windows Live Messenger window. A Conversation window appears like the one shown in Figure 27-8.

FIGURE 27-8   The Instant Message window.

NOTE *To help clean up the screen a little, I shut the second Windows Live Messenger window. You can do this, too, by clicking its Close button in the upper-right corner of the window. You also can minimize that window as an alternative to closing it.*

To converse, type in the box at the bottom of the window and click Send or press ENTER. When another person is typing a response, you see a message to that effect on the status line (the bottom line) of the Conversation window. If you have a sound card, microphone, and speakers, and the person you're chatting with does also, click Call Computer to speak with them.

When someone starts a conversation with you, a little box pops up from the notification area (right end) of the Windows taskbar, like this:

Click the box to switch to a Conversation window with the person. After a few seconds, this box disappears.

You can invite other contacts to join in the chat by clicking the Invite Someone To Join This Conversation button in the top-left corner of the Conversation window. You can block the person you are talking to from contacting you by clicking Block This Contact From Seeing Or Contacting You. (If you want to unblock someone, right-click the person's name in your contact list and select Unblock.)

Holding Voice Conversations

Once you have opened a Conversation window with someone, you can switch to a voice chat, assuming that you and the other person have microphones and speakers attached to your computers. The first time you click Call Computer in the Conversation window, Windows runs the Audio And Video Setup Wizard to check your microphone and speakers. Follow its instructions.

When you click Start Talking in the Conversation window (or click a contact name in the Windows Live Messenger window and click Call), Windows Live Messenger sends an invitation to the other person to have a voice conversation. They must click the Answer link to answer the phone. When they do, you can start conversing. Windows Live Messenger displays the tools shown here on the Conversation window to let you adjust volume and other features:

When you are finished with the phone call, click the Hang Up link in the Conversation window. As you talk, you also can send text messages back and forth to each other.

Video Conferencing

If your computer has a video camera, you can use it to transmit a picture to the person with whom you are having a conversation. Click the Start Or Stop A Video Call button in the Conversation window to start receiving video images from the other person. The video image appears in the upper-right part of the Conversation window. Click Start Or Stop A Video Call to stop receiving video data.

Sharing Files with Others in a Conversation

To share a file with someone with whom you are having a conversation, click Share Files in the Conversation window. Click Create A Sharing Folder to set up a folder in which to share multiple files, or click Send A Singe File to send just one file at a time. Otherwise, right-click the name of the contact in the Windows Live Messenger window and choose Send Other | Send A Single File, or click Create A Sharing Folder. If you send a file, select a file in the Send A File To *contact* dialog box, and then click Open. The contact has to accept the file for the transfer to occur.

When you receive a file, Windows stores it in the Received Files subfolder of your Documents folder.

Other Things You Can Do with Windows Live Messenger

You can use Windows Live Messenger in a few other ways, too:

- **Blocking someone from calling you**   Right-click a contact and choose Block.
- **Changing the way your name appears to others**   Click the drop-down arrow next to your name at the top of the Windows Live Messenger window and click Personal Settings. In the My Display Name area, change your name.
- **Adding a personal message**   Right below your name on the Windows Live Messenger window, type a short personal message.

- **Changing other configuration settings**   Click the drop-down arrow next to your name at the top of the Windows Live Messenger window and click Personal Settings. The Options dialog box that appears contains settings that control what information other people can see about you and how the program runs.

- **Preventing Windows Live Messenger from running when Windows starts up**   Click the drop-down arrow next to your name at the top of the Windows Live Messenger window and click Personal Settings, click General, and deselect the Automatically Run Windows Live Messenger When I Log On To Windows check box.

- **Playing games**   Some new Internet-based games are designed to work with Windows Live Messenger, and can send invitations to other Windows Live Messenger users to join a game. Click the Play Games With A Friend icon on the Windows Live Messenger window and then select from the list of games from the MSN Games site that appears in the Windows Live Messenger window. You may need to download and install new software, such as an ActiveX control, to run the games.

- **Getting help with your computer**   If you choose See A List Of Activities in the Conversation window and click Request Remote Assistance, Windows runs the Remote Assistance program, described in Chapter 4.

- **Adding emoticons to messages**   These are the small smiley face characters you see on many messages your teenager writes to emote feelings. Click the Select An Emoticon button in the Conversation window to add one of several emoticons (see Figure 27-9) that Windows Live Messenger provides.

NOTE *You can uninstall Windows Live Messenger by choosing Start | Control Panel | Uninstall A Program. Choose the Windows Live Messenger item in the Uninstall Or Change A Program window and click Uninstall. Follow the steps to remove the program. If you do this, however, all your contacts and any saved conversations are lost.*

- **Changing background**   Click the Select A Background For Your Conversation Window button in the Conversation window to select from a number of different images you can place in your background. What you pick for your background can also be shared by your contact. If he or she clicks Accept, then your background becomes their background. If he or she clicks Deny, then your background stays as the new background, while their background remains what they have selected.

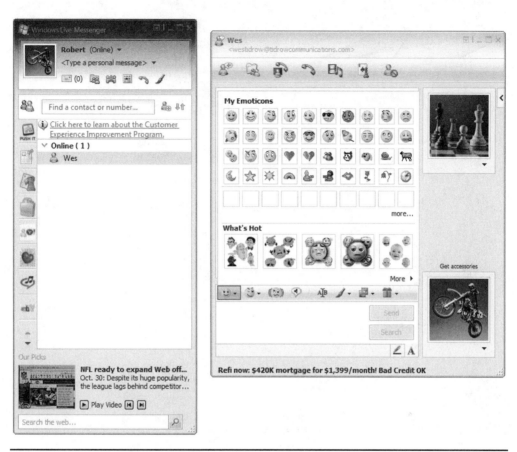

FIGURE 27-9   Use emoticons (but sparingly please) in your messages.

Other Internet Programs That Come with Windows Vista

Windows Vista comes with lots of Internet-related programs. In addition to the new Internet Explorer 7, the Connect To The Internet Wizard, and dial-up connections (all described in Chapter 24), you get lots of Internet applications—which are described in the other chapters in this part of the book.

Windows also comes with these other useful Internet programs:

- **Telnet**   Lets you do terminal emulation over the Internet
- **Ftp**   Lets you transfer files to or from FTP servers

This chapter describes how to use these programs. You can download other Internet programs from the Internet itself; we recommend some programs that complement those that come with Windows and suggest where to find the programs on the Web.

Logging into Other Computers Using Telnet

Telnet enables you to log into a remote computer over the Internet and emulate that you are a workstation on that computer's network. It lets your powerful Windows computer—loaded with RAM, hard disk space, and other hardware—pretend to be a dumb terminal. Telnet is useful for connecting to computers that are designed to talk to terminals, including UNIX shell accounts and bulletin board systems. The computer you connect to by using Telnet is called the *remote computer* (as opposed to your own *local computer*).

If you have an Internet account (or other TCP/IP-based connection), you can use Telnet to connect to the Internet by using a dial-up connection or broadband. For example, you can look up books at the U.S. Library of Congress by making a Telnet connection to the library's mainframe system and using its text-only interface. You tell HyperTerminal to connect using TCP/IP, along with the port number and host address of the computer to which you want to connect. The standard *port number* (a number that tells an Internet host computer whether you are connecting for e-mail, the Web, Telnet, or another Internet service) is 23. The *host address* is the Internet hostname of the computer you want to telnet into; for example, the host address of the U.S. Library of Congress is locis.loc.gov.

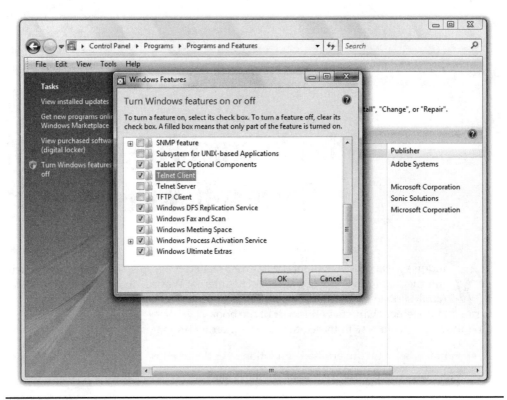

FIGURE 28-1 You must install Telnet before using it.

Installing Telnet

Windows Vista requires that you first install Telnet before using it. Follow these steps to install it:

1. Click Start | Control Panel | Programs.
2. Click Turn Windows Features On Or Off. The Uninstall Or Change A Program window appears.
3. Click Turn Windows Features On Or Off from the Tasks pane. The Windows Features dialog box appears, as shown in Figure 28-1.
4. Click Telnet Client.
5. Click OK.

Running Telnet

To run the Windows built-in Telnet program:

1. Choose Start | All Programs | Accessories | Run.
2. Type **telnet**, and click OK. You see the Telnet window, shown in Figure 28-2.
3. To see the list of commands shown in Figure 28-2, type **?** and press ENTER.

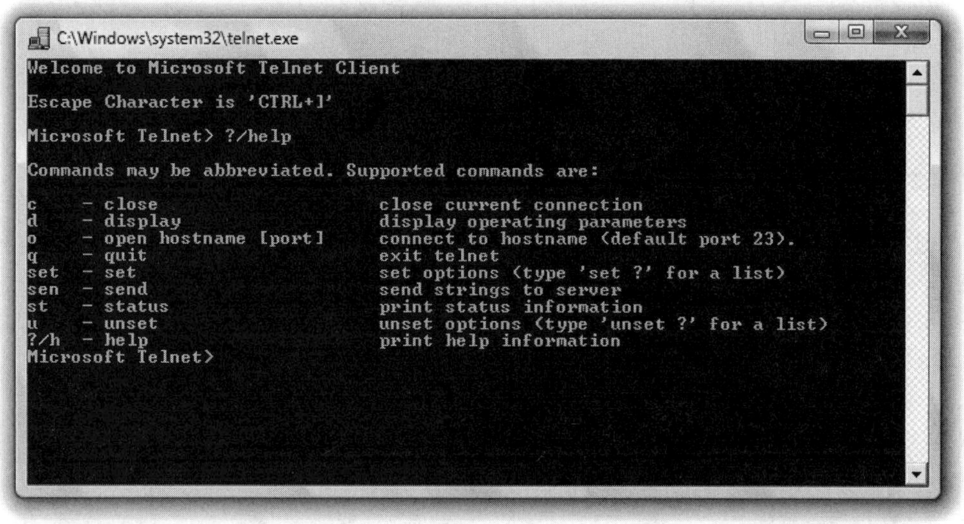

FIGURE 28-2   The Telnet window.

Most of the time when you use Telnet, you are connecting to a server inside your company, organization, university, or research facility. To get specific instructions on how to navigate the system you telnet into, contact the network administrator for that system. They will have detailed commands you need to use for that computer. For example, to log into the Library of Congress Information System, type the following commands at the Telnet prompt:

```
o locis.loc.gov and press ENTER
```

A screen like the on shown in Figure 28-3 appears.

From this screen you can type a number to access one of the listed areas. For example, enter 1 to access Copyright Information.

Working with FTP

File Transfer Protocol (FTP) is a system for transferring files over the Internet. An *FTP server* stores files, and *FTP clients* can log into FTP servers either to upload (transfer) files to the FTP server or (more commonly) to download files from the FTP server. To use FTP, you must have an FTP client program.

Most web browsers, including Internet Explorer and Mozilla Firefox, include an FTP client program that you can use to download and upload files. Web editors, including Microsoft FrontPage, include an FTP program for uploading your finished web pages to a web server.

Versions of Windows prior to Windows XP had an FTP client (described next), but Windows XP and Windows Vista have an FTP client built into Windows Explorer.

Transferring Files Using FTP

To transfer files to or from an FTP server, you use Vista's separate FTP client program. Windows Vista comes with a basic command-driven FTP client program called Ftp. If you

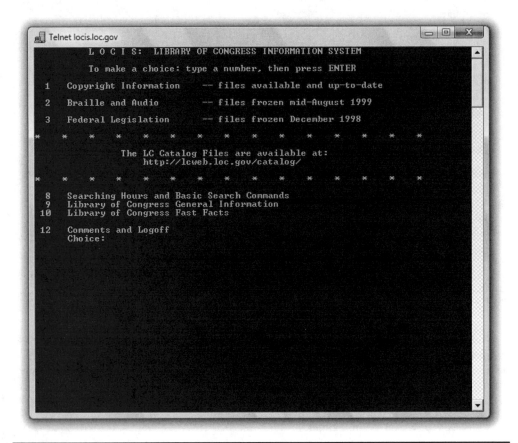

FIGURE 28-3 Telnetting into the Library of Congress computer.

plan to do much file transfer, especially uploading, you'll want to use a better FTP client program, such as WS_FTP (see "Downloading, Installing, and Running Other Internet Programs" later in the chapter), or use the Internet Explorer feature called Open FTP Site In Windows Explorer.

Basics of FTP

To run the Windows Vista FTP program, choose Start | All Programs | Accessories | Run. Type **ftp** *serverhost*, where *serverhost* is the hostname of the FTP server, and click OK. If you are not connected to the Internet and you see your dial-up connection window, click Connect. You see the Ftp window, shown in Figure 28-4.

To connect to an FTP server, you specify the hostname of the server (for example, rtfm.mit.edu) and then log in. You have two choices:

- If you have an account on the FTP server, log in with your username and password. You can access all the files that your username gives you permission to use.

C:\Windows\system32\ftp.exe

```
Connected to PENGUIN-LUST.mit.edu.
220 (vsFTPd 1.2.2)
User (PENGUIN-LUST.mit.edu:(none)): anonymous
331 Please specify the password.
Password:
230 Login successful.
ftp>
```

Figure 28-4   The Ftp window.

- If you don't have an account on the FTP server, the server may accept connections from guests. Connection without an account on the FTP server is called *anonymous FTP*. To use anonymous FTP, type **anonymous** for the username and your own e-mail address as the password. Thousands of FTP servers on the Internet allow you to use anonymous FTP to download files, although some are so busy that it may be hard to get connected.

NOTE   *UNIX, the operating system of choice among Internet servers, is sensitive to the case of the names of files, unlike Windows. Be aware of capitalization in filenames.*

Once you are connected to an FTP server, it displays lots of messages to let you know what's going on. These messages start with three-digit numbers, which you can ignore. For example, when you have transferred a file, you see the message "226 Transfer Complete."

When you transfer a file—by either uploading or downloading—you must choose between two modes:

- **ASCII mode**   When transferring text files, use ASCII mode. Different computer systems use different characters to indicate the ends of lines. In ASCII mode, the Ftp program automatically adjusts line endings for the system to which the file is transferred.

- **Binary or Image mode**   When transferring files that consist of anything but unformatted text, use Binary mode. In Binary mode, the Ftp program does not make any changes to the contents of the file during transfer. Use Binary mode when transferring graphics files, audio files, video files, programs, or any kind of file other than plain text.

TIP *At the ftp prompt, type **?** to see a listing of the commands that Ftp can perform.*

Navigating the Folder Trees

The following are the most common FTP tasks:

- To see a list of files and subdirectories in the current directory on the FTP server, type **dir**. The exact format of the listing depends on the FTP server's operating system. Figure 28-5 shows a typical listing. You can use wildcards (*) to limit the list. If you want to see filenames only, with no other information, you can use the **ls** (list) command.

- To change directories, type **cd** (for "change directory"), followed by the name of the directory to which you want to move.

- To find out the name of the current directory, type **pwd** (for "print working directory").

On many publicly accessible FTP servers, all the downloadable files are in a directory called pub. Here are a few tips for moving to the directory you want:

- To move to the parent directory of the current directory, type **cd ..** (that is, the **cd** command followed by a space and two dots).

- To move to the top-level directory on the FTP server, also called the *root* directory, type **cd /** (that is, the **cd** command followed by a space and a forward slash). Most FTP servers run the UNIX operating system, which uses forward slashes (as opposed to the backslashes used in Windows).

- You can move directly to a directory by typing its full pathname, starting at the root; the full pathname starts with a / to represent the root directory.

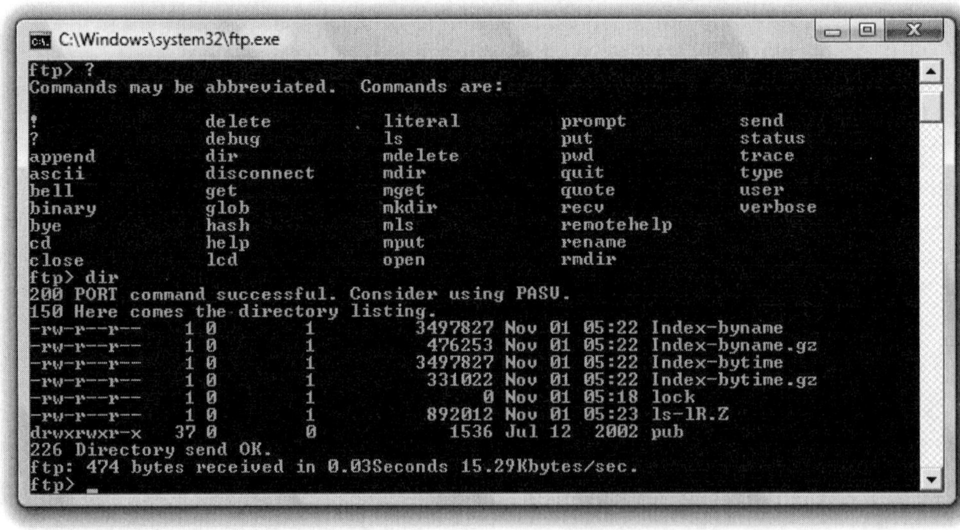

FIGURE 28-5   A directory list from an FTP server.

- If the FTP server runs the UNIX operating system, capitalization is important. When typing directory names or filenames, be sure to use the correct capitalization—most names use lowercase.

- To change the current local directory (the folder from which Ftp can upload files and to which it can download files), type **lcd** (local directory), followed by the name of the folder on your computer. If the pathname of the folder contains spaces, enclose the pathname in quotes. To move to the parent folder of the current folder, type **lcd ..** (the **lcd** command followed by a space and two dots).

- When you have finished transferring files, type **quit** or **bye** to disconnect from the FTP server. A message confirms that you have left the FTP server.

TIP *If you want to disconnect from the FTP server and connect to a different server, you don't have to exit the Ftp program. Instead, type **close** or **disconnect** and press ENTER to disconnect from the FTP server. Next, type **open**, followed by a space, and then the hostname of another FTP server; and press ENTER to connect to the other server.*

Uploading Files

You use the **put** command to upload the files. To upload a group of files, you can use the **mput** (multiple put) command.

NOTE *You can upload files only if you have write permission in the directory on the FTP server. Most anonymous FTP servers don't accept uploads, or they accept them into only one specific directory. Read the welcome message to find out the rules for the FTP server you are using.*

To upload a file, follow these steps:

1. Connect to the FTP server, move to the directory on the FTP server in which you want to store the file, and set the current local directory to the folder on your computer that contains the files you want to upload.

2. If the file or files you want to upload contain anything but unformatted ASCII text, type **binary** to select Binary mode (see "Basics of FTP" earlier in the chapter). To switch back to ASCII mode to transfer text files, type **ascii**.

3. Type **put**, a space, the filename on your computer, a space, and the filename to use on the FTP server. Then press ENTER. For example, to upload a file named draft13.doc and call the uploaded version report.doc, you would type **put draft13.doc report.doc**.

4. You see a series of messages; the message Transfer Complete appears when the file transfer is done.

CAUTION *If a file with the name that you specify already exists on the FTP server, the put command may overwrite the existing file with the uploaded file. You can use the dir or ls command to check for the existence of a file with the same name.*

5. If you want to check that the file is really on the FTP server, type **dir** to see a listing of files in the current directory.

You can copy a group of files to the FTP server by typing **mput**, followed by a wildcard pattern that matches the names of the files you want to upload. The pattern * indicates that all files in the current directory on your computer should be copied. For example, to upload all the files with the extension .html, you would type **mput *.html**.

As it copies the files, **mput** asks you about each file. Type **y** to upload the file or **n** to skip it.

TIP *If you don't want* **mput** *to ask you about each file before uploading it, type the* **prompt** *command first before giving the* **mput** *command. The* **prompt** *command turns off filename prompting.*

Downloading Files

To download files from the FTP server to your computer, follow these steps:

1. Connect to the FTP server, move to the directory on the FTP server that contains the file that you want to download, and set the current local directory to the folder on your computer in which you want to store the files you download.

2. If the file or files you want to download contain anything but unformatted ASCII text, type **binary** to select Binary mode (see "Basics of FTP" earlier in the chapter). To switch back to ASCII mode to transfer text files, type **ascii**.

3. Type **get**, a space, the filename on the FTP server, a space, and the filename to use on your computer. Then press ENTER. (You can't use filenames with spaces.) For example, to download a file named bud9812.doc and call the downloaded version budget.dec1998.doc, the command is **get bud9812.doc budget.dec2001.doc**.

4. You see a series of messages; the message Transfer Complete appears when the file transfer is done. To interrupt the file transfer, press CTRL-C. Sometimes that doesn't work, and the only way to interrupt the transfer is to close the FTP window.

5. If you want to check whether the file is really downloaded, use Windows Explorer to see a listing of files on your computer.

You can copy a group of files to the FTP server by typing **mget**, followed by a wildcard pattern that matches the names of the files that you want to download. The pattern * means that all files in the current directory on your computer should be copied. For example, to download all the files whose names start with *d*, you would type **mget d***.

As it copies the files, **mget** asks you about each file. Type **y** to download the file or **n** to skip it.

TIP *If you download a nontext file that is unusable, you probably forgot to issue the* **binary** *command before downloading the file.*

Using Windows Explorer to View an FTP Site

Another way to access FTP sites for uploading and downloading is to use Windows Explorer and Internet Explorer. Start Internet Explorer and connect to your FTP site. In the Address bar, use ftp:// instead of http:// for the preface of the site. This instructs IE that the site you want to visit is an FTP site. Once you access the site, you are presented with a logon screen. Enter a username and password and click OK. A screen like the one shown in Figure 28-6 appears.

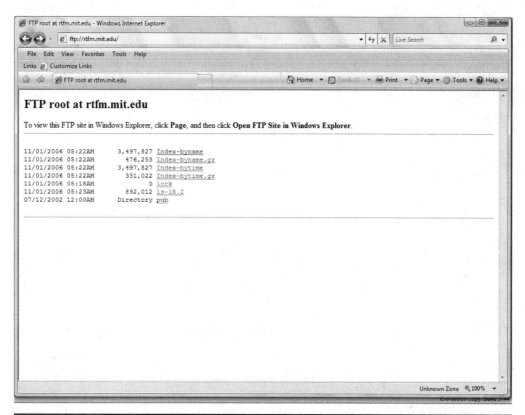

FIGURE 28-6   An FTP site shown in Internet Explorer.

Once in, you can navigate the FTP site using IE. However, to make uploading and downloading files easier, use Windows Explorer. To do this, choose the Page menu from IE and click Open FTP Site In Windows Explorer. Windows Explorer starts and shows the directory structure of the FTP site in its window just as if it were from your local hard drive, similar to the one shown in Figure 28-7. You can now drag-and-drop files from the FTP site to your computer to download them, or drag-and-drop files from your computer to the FTP site to upload them. On slow FTP connections, the file transfers may take awhile. Also, sometimes your uploads and downloads may quit in the middle due to transmission problems or other reasons (the FTP server was shut down, for instance). In these cases, reconnect to the FTP site and try again.

Downloading, Installing, and Running Other Internet Programs

Once you have established a connection to the Internet, you can run many Internet-compatible programs. Although Windows comes with a few good Internet applications, you can supplement (or replace) them with other programs. For example, the Ftp program that comes with Windows is not particularly powerful or easy to use; we vastly prefer the excellent shareware

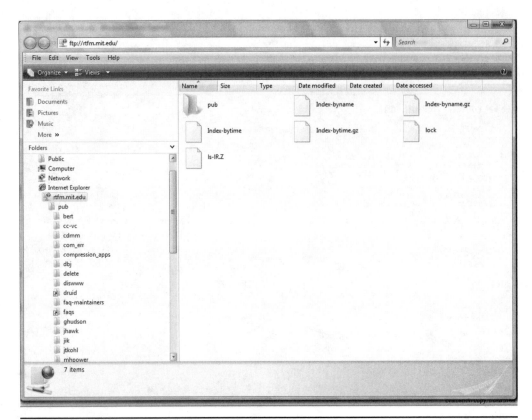

FIGURE 28-7   An FTP site shown in Windows Explorer.

WS_FTP program, which shows you the contents of the local and remote directories, and lets you transfer files by clicking buttons rather than typing commands. (Read on to find out how to get WS_FTP.)

Where to Get Internet Programs

Lots of Internet programs are available for downloading from the Internet itself. Some are *freeware* programs that are entirely free to use; some are *shareware* programs that require you to register the program if you decide that you like it; some are demo programs that let you try a partially disabled version of the program before you decide whether to buy the real program; and some are commercial programs that ask you to pay before downloading.

Many web-based libraries offer all types of programs. Here are our favorites:

- **Tucows, www.tucows.com**   Classifies programs by operating system and type. It has lots of mirror sites (identical web sites) all over the globe, so it's rarely a problem to begin downloading even very popular programs. It's particularly easy to browse a long list of programs of a given type (browsers or e-mail programs, for example) and compare reviews.

- **WinPlanet, http://cws.internet.com**   This is the original Winsock library (software that is Windows and Internet compliant), and it is still excellent. Forrest Stroud set up this site when shareware and freeware Internet software first started to become available.

- **CNET Shareware.com, www.shareware.com**   Offers lots of non-Internet-related programs.

- **CNET Download.com, www.download.com**   Has thousands of downloadable programs organized by category.

Installing and Running Internet Programs

Once you've downloaded a program from the Internet, it's a good idea to check it for *viruses*, self-replicating programs that may infect other programs on your computer. Windows doesn't come with a virus checker, but you can download a good one from any of the software libraries in the preceding section (see "Preventing Infection by Viruses" in Chapter 33). We like McAfee's and Symantec's Norton antivirus programs, too (commercial software that is downloadable from McAfee's web site at www.mcafee.com and Symantec's web site at www.symantec.com).

Most downloaded programs arrive as self-installing files; in Windows Explorer, run the file you downloaded. The program usually installs itself, asking you configuration questions along the way. Most programs either add themselves to the Start | All Programs menu or add an icon to the desktop (or both). Other downloaded programs arrive in ZIP (compressed) files, which the Windows compressed folders feature can uncompress (see "Working with Compressed Folders" in Chapter 9).

The first time you run a program, you might need to configure it further; check any documentation files that are installed along with the program. Look for a Tools | Options command or an Edit | Preferences command, as these usually display configuration or preferences dialog boxes.

VI

PART

Networking with Windows Vista

29 CHAPTER

Designing a Windows-Based
Local Area Network

A local area network (LAN) is a necessity for small offices and home offices with more than one computer who want to share a DSL or cable broadband modem.
Windows Vista provides all the features needed to connect your computer to a LAN—no other software is required (although you will probably need some hardware). This chapter introduces LANs, including what a network is and why you might want one. Most new networks use Ethernet technology, either with cables or WiFi. This chapter also describes what you need to do to install a LAN.

This chapter provides the background for the specifics covered in the rest of the chapters in Part V, configuring Windows for a LAN (Chapter 30), sharing drives and printers (Chapter 31), connecting your LAN to the Internet (Chapter 32), and network security (Chapter 33).

NOTE *This chapter covers setting up your network from scratch. However, if you are adding a Windows Vista computer to an existing peer-to-peer network or upgrading a computer on a network from an earlier version of Windows to Windows Vista, the steps you need to follow are also found in this chapter (see the sidebar "Adding or Upgrading a Computer on an Existing Network").*

Purposes of Networks

A network provides a connection between computing resources, a way to share hardware and files, and a paperless way to communicate. A *local area network (LAN)* is a network limited to one building or group of buildings. A LAN is a necessity in a small office/home office (SOHO) with two or three computers. LANs are already standard in large offices. Today's LANs can include computers wired via Ethernet cabling, via Wi-Fi, or a combination of both networking technologies.

Wide area networks (WANs) connect computers that are geographically dispersed, and the Internet—the biggest network of them all—is a worldwide network of interconnected networks, including LANs and WANs.

Wireless networks are also gaining in popularity in home offices and corporate offices, and even large cities are rolling out municipal Wi-Fi networks (think citywide wireless WAN), enabling local city businesses and citizens to access the Internet for free or a low fee from anywhere in the city that is covered by the Wi-Fi network.

Sharing Hardware

Without a network, each *resource* (hard drive, CD-ROM drive, printer, scanner, external hard drive, or other device) is connected to only one computer. You may have a hard drive on which your small company's main database or your family's music collection is stored, the color printer everyone wants to use, and the CD-RW drive on which nightly backups are made. Without a network, you can use a resource only from the computer to which the resource is attached. With a network and sufficient security access privileges, anyone using a computer attached to the network can print to the color printer or open the database, and the computer with the external backup drive can access all the hard disks on various machines that need to be backed up.

The low-tech way to share resources is what some techie types call *sneakernet*—take removable storage media like a USB thumb drive, copy the file you need to print or share, and walk it over to the computer with the printer or the person who needs to use the file. But sneakernet isn't very efficient—in the long run, you save time and hassle ("Dude, where did I leave my thumb drive?") with a network. In a SOHO, using a network and only one printer—to which everyone can print—is more cost effective.

Sharing Files

If you want to share files without the danger of creating multiple versions, you need a network, so every person who accesses the file uses the same copy. Some software (notably database software) enables multiple users to use one file at the same time. Other software warns you when a file is being used by someone else on the network and may even notify you when the file is available for your use.

When you work with files that are too large to fit on a floppy disk, moving them to other computers can be cumbersome without a network (unless both computers have a CD-R or CD-RW drive or you have a USB thumb drive with sufficient memory).

Sharing an Internet Connection

If everyone in your SOHO wants to access the Internet—to send and receive e-mail, browse the Web, or access Internet applications—all your computers need a connection to your cable or *digital subscriber line (DSL)* modem or business-class Internet connection (like a fast T1 line). This is where a specialized device called a router comes into play, which connects your LAN to an Internet connection. Chapter 32 describes how to use Windows Vista Internet Connection Sharing to connect a LAN to the Internet.

Peer-to-Peer vs. Domain-Based Networks

Peer-to-peer (P2P) and client-server are the predominant networking topologies in use in many of today's networked SOHOs. The following sections explain both networking technologies.

Client-Server Computing

Client-server computing is a long-time mainstay of corporate computing. In a *client-server network*, server computers provide resources for the rest of the network, and client computers (*also called workstations*) use these resources. Client-server networks typically are more difficult and expensive to set up and administer than peer-to-peer networks, but they also have many advantages: they can handle more computers, they provide more-sophisticated administration and security options, and all resources are managed centrally on dedicated servers.

Client-server networks require a *network operating system (NOS)*—Windows .NET Server, Windows 2000 Server, Windows NT, Linux, and UNIX are common NOSs—as well as a greater initial outlay of time and money for setup and equipment, and a network administrator to create and maintain user IDs and permissions.

Microsoft's client-server network system uses domains to organize the large numbers of computers that can be on corporate networks. A *domain* (when used in reference to Microsoft LANs) is a group of user accounts administered together. Microsoft calls a client-server network a *domain-based* network.

A *client* is a computer that uses resources on the network. A printer client, for instance, is a computer that uses a network printer. A *server* is a computer (or a device with a computer hidden inside) that has resources used by other devices on the network. For instance, a file server is a computer that stores files used by other computers; a print server is a computer with a printer attached to it—the print server lets other computers on the network send print jobs to the printer. The server makes a resource available to the network, and a client uses the resource. It's possible and often useful for a computer to act as both a client and a server—for example, sharing files on its large disk but using a printer on another computer.

Windows Peer-to-Peer Networking

Windows Peer-to-Peer Networking is a Windows Vista component enabling you to create P2P applications for computers running Windows XP SP 2, Windows XP Professional x64 Edition, and the Advanced Networking Pack for Windows XP, or Windows Vista.

Peer-to-Peer Networking is a worthy solution for SOHO networking where you may not have a server residing on the network but still share applications, files, and network peripherals among the network PCs.

Versions of Windows since Windows for Workgroups 3.11, including Windows XP Home Edition, have included support for peer-to-peer networks. Microsoft calls a group of computers on a peer-to-peer network a *workgroup*, and the network itself a *workgroup-based* network. When you configure Windows to connect to a workgroup-based LAN, you tell it the name of the workgroup (we like to use the name WORKGROUP).

In a *peer-to-peer network*, all computers are equal and can function as both clients and servers. Security and permissions are administered from each computer in the network. Each computer in a P2P network can both request resources from other computers and share its own resources with other computers in the network. You can also configure the network so that some computers only share their resources and others only use resources. Even in this situation, however, the network is still a P2P network because each computer on the network is administered individually.

PART VI

A P2P workgroup-based network is relatively easy to set up—any SOHO with more than one computer can create a small P2P network by using Windows to share printers and files. Only a small amount of hardware is required. The rest of this chapter explains how to choose, install, and configure the hardware to create a P2P network, and Chapter 30 describes how to configure Windows Vista for a LAN.

NOTE *Windows Vista Home Basic is limited to connecting up to six computers, so a P2P LAN with Windows Vista Home Basic computers is limited to seven computers, unless not all computers need to communicate with each other. For example, you might need to install Windows XP Professional on the computer with the large hard disk and fast printer so that more than six Windows Vista Home Basic computers can share its hard disk and printer.*

Client-Server vs. Peer-to-Peer Networking

When setting up a SOHO network, you may have cause to consider a P2P network versus a client-server network depending on your networking requirements.

Your networking requirements should balance the number of computers you intend to put on your network, network-based applications (if any), and network connection to the Internet (cable broadband modem, DSL modem, Verizon FiOS, or a corporate-grade Internet connection like a T-1 line).

Table 29-1 lists differences between P2P and client-server networks. To set up your Windows computer on an already-existing Windows network, contact your LAN administrator.

Factor	Peer-to-Peer (Workgroup-Based)	Client-Server (Domain-Based)
Size	Good for small networks (under 12 computers, depending on the uses for the network). Keeping track of available resources and passwords for each resource becomes difficult on a large P2P network.	Good for medium-to-large networks. Because administration of network resources is central, the user can access all available resources with only one password (more passwords may be necessary if the network has more than one server).
Hardware	No dedicated file server is needed.	At least one computer must be a server.
Operating system	Windows Vista Home Basic, Windows Vista Home Premium, or Windows XP Home SP2.	Requires a NOS on the server. Workstations can run Windows Vista Business, Windows Vista Enterprise, Windows Vista Ultimate, or Windows XP Professional SP2.
Administrator training	Little training needed for users to administer their own computers' resources for all users on the network.	System administrator must be trained.

TABLE 29-1   Differences Between Peer-to-Peer and Client-Server Networks

Steps for Setting Up a Peer-to-Peer LAN

Setting up a network consists of the following major tasks:

- Purchasing a Vista Capable PC or practically any PC today means it has a network interface card.

- Choosing and buying the hardware (see "Buying Network Hardware" later in this chapter).

- Configuring Windows to use the network (see Chapter 30).

While you needn't be a network engineer to set up a small P2P network, you do need to have some knowledge about your computer. You need to be able to use Windows Vista to configure each computer to communicate on the LAN.

Choosing Between Cabled and Wireless LANs

Before you buy hardware for your network, you need to decide how to connect the computers on your network. The majority of LAN installations use Ethernet because it has become a ubiquitous standard. Today's Vista Capable desktop PCs and laptops ship with an Ethernet network interface card (NIC) installed.

If you are setting up a new network, you need to choose between regular Ethernet cabling and Ethernet-based wireless equipment.

Ethernet Cable and NICs

There are three speeds of Ethernet. Original Ethernet has a speed of 10 Mbps (megabits per second). *Fast Ethernet* has a speed of 100 Mbps. An even faster version, *Gigabit Ethernet*, is available and can transmit data at a maximum speed of 1 Gbps (gigabits per second), or ten times the Fast Ethernet standard.

The *topology* of a network determines the pattern of cabling you use to connect the computers. In a *star topology* network, each computer is connected by a cable to a *hub*, the computer in the center of the star. One end of the cable plugs into a computer's NIC, and the other end plugs into the hub, which provides a central connection point for the network cabling.

> **Adding or Upgrading a Computer on an Existing Network**
>
> If you're adding a computer to an existing network, you can skip the sections regarding choosing a network technology and a topology—someone has already made those choices for you. Also, if no leftover cable is on hand, buy the correct kind of cable for your network. Once you've done these things, you can dive into the section "Installing Your Network Hardware" later in this chapter.
>
> If you are upgrading the operating system of a computer on an existing network from an earlier version of Windows to Windows Vista, you may find that your network works right away—open the My Network Places icon on the desktop to see whether other computers on the network appear. If your computer doesn't appear to be communicating on the network, skip ahead to Chapter 30.

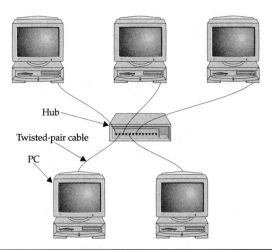

FIGURE 29-1   Star topology (with twisted-pair cable).

Hubs vary in size (with different numbers of ports), and more advanced hubs can connect both 10- and 100-Mbps Ethernet. Ethernet *switches* serve the same function as hubs but offer higher network performance by permitting several data transfers to occur simultaneously. Figure 29-1 shows a diagram of a network using star topology.

In the past, you chose either star or bus topology. However, most new networks use star topology. This configuration uses more cable and more hardware than a bus topology network, but it's easier to manage and less likely to fail. Star topology is easy to set up, and the network is easier to troubleshoot than a bus network because a damaged cable affects only one computer.

The cable used in Ethernet star topology is usually *unshielded twisted-pair*, or *UTP* (also called *Category-5* or *Cat-5*). The connectors on the ends of the cables are *RJ-45 connectors*, which look like large phone connectors. You can also use *Cat-5e* (enhanced), which is rated for higher speeds.

Wireless LANs

In a *wireless LAN* there are no network cables. Instead, each computer has a wireless network adapter, allowing the computers to communicate via radio waves. Wireless LANs enable you to put computers as far as 300 feet away from each other, depending on what walls and furniture are between them. The adapters include scrambling or encryption to prevent other computers from listening in on your data transmissions or adding themselves to your LAN.

A wireless LAN can be arranged as either an *infrastructure* LAN or an *ad hoc* LAN. An infrastructure LAN is a star topology LAN, with an *access point* as the hub of the star. The access point is a box that contains a radio transceiver, hardware and software for communications and encryption, and an Ethernet port that lets you connect it to a cabled LAN, if you have one. The rest of the computers on the LAN have wireless LAN adapters that contain a radio transceiver, which communicates with the access point. An ad hoc wireless LAN has no access point, just the adapters in each computer. Ad hoc LANs save the cost of the access point but require that every computer in the LAN be within radio range of every other, usually in a single room, while with an infrastructure LAN the access point is put in a central location and each computer need only be within radio range of the access point, not of the other computers.

Wireless LAN standards are opening up as networking companies spend research and development dollars to satisfy corporate and consumer needs for ever faster wireless network connectivity. These standards exist to ensure that wireless adapters from different manufacturers can communicate with each other. The most popular is *802.11g*, also known as *Wi-Fi*, which uses the 2.4-GHz radio band and can communicate at 54 Mbps. For instructions for configuring Windows to work with your wireless LAN, see the section "Adding Your Computer to a Wireless LAN" in Chapter 30.

Emerging Wireless Networking Standards

Other emerging wireless LAN standards are pushing the speeds of wireless connectivity past 802.11g. The standards include multiple input multiple output (MIMO) and 802.11N.

MIMO is a wireless communications technology exercising multiple antennas at both the source (transmitter) and the destination (receiver). MIMO antennas at each end of the communications circuit are combined to minimize errors and optimize data speed. MIMO wireless routers for SOHOs are available from D-Link (www.dlink.com), Linksys (www .linksys.com), and NETGEAR (www.netgear.com).

Another emerging wireless networking standard going through approval is 802.11n. This standard is designed to increase wireless network speed and reliability. It's also designed to extend the operating distance of wireless networks. It's speed is expected to reach as much as 600 Mbps (more than ten times the throughput of 802.11g).

Making the Choice—or Choosing More than One

The cabling technology you choose determines the hardware you buy. Each standard has advantages and disadvantages. However, if you are starting a network from scratch, choose the cheaper and more common Fast Ethernet. Wireless networking is a consideration if your SOHO has mobile workers that travel or you want your computer users to have the flexibility to take their laptop away from the desk. Then again, if you don't want to bother with cabling, then a Wi-Fi network is the option for you.

You may decide that you need several types of networks. For example, within your home office, you may need to connect your three computers with cables for reliability and speed. Nevertheless, you may also want to install a wireless access point on one of the office computers to communicate with laptops in the rest of your house, so your kids can get online (see Figure 29-2 for an example of what this might look like). On the other hand, you might have wired network hubs in two parts of the house.

If your networks don't already have hubs that you can cable together, you can buy devices called *bridges* that connect two kinds of Ethernet into one network. Or, Windows XP can connect several Ethernet networks together via software *bridging*. Chapter 29 describes how to bridge networks.

From here on, this chapter discusses setting up an Ethernet network. However, the steps outlined here don't differ much for setting up a wireless network—instead of buying NICs, cabling, and a hub, you buy wireless LAN adapters and a wireless access point.

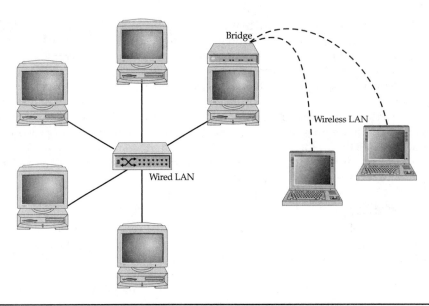

FIGURE 29-2   You can bridge a cabled LAN to a wireless LAN to create a single LAN.

Buying Network Hardware

You need the following hardware to set up your network:

Cabled LAN	Wireless LAN
A NIC for each computer in the network.	A wireless LAN adapter with an antenna for each computer in the network.
A connection among all the computers, most commonly, copper wires, but can also be fiber-optic cable, infrared, radio waves, or deploy a mix of Cabled/Wireless LAN. The amount and type of cable you need depends on the topology you choose for your network.	No cabling is needed.
A hub.	A wireless access point for one computer.

NOTE *If you are connecting only two computers and have no plans to add additional computers, you may not need a hub or access point. You can use a crossover cable to connect the two computers. The crossover cable takes the place of a hub and two network cables.*

Take inventory of every computer that will be on the LAN. For cabled LANs, check whether they have an RJ-45 jack or built-in wireless adapter. If they do not, make a note of the type of slot each has available—you have to buy a NIC or wireless LAN adapter that fits a slot in each computer. The easiest way to determine slot types is to check the documentation for each computer. PCI slots are most common for desktop computers. Laptops usually have PC Card slots (also called PCMCIA slots) that look like they fit a credit card. Both laptops and desktops may have Universal Serial Bus (USB) ports (a narrow rectangular plug) that may be used for some models of network cards, especially wireless NICs. You may be able to tell what kind of slot your computer has by taking the cover off and looking, and then describing the slot to your local computer store expert. However, it's safer to check your documentation for the type of architecture the motherboard has for each computer that will be on the LAN. You can (and probably will) mix cards of different slot types so long as the network type is consistent.

Networking a SOHO today is easier than it was five years ago because today's Vista Capable desktop and laptop PCs include a NIC as part of the standard specification. Prices for wired and wireless routers and hubs are also dropping, even as SOHO networking vendors add 802.11n and MIMO technologies to their product line-ups.

Buying a Hub

If you've blown out the ports on your SOHO router, you need a *hub*, a small box with lots of cable connectors. Buy a hub with enough connections for all the computers on your network. You may want a few extra connections, so you can add additional computers or network peripherals like printers to the network later. Hubs are widely available with 4, 8, 16, or 24 ports.

Buying Wireless LAN Adapters and Access Points

If you are planning a wireless LAN, decide whether you need the cheaper and more popular 802.11g Wi-Fi. Wi-Fi adapters are available as PCI cards (for desktop computers), PC Cards (for laptops), or USB (for desktop or laptop computers). We've had good luck with all three, but as a general rule, the larger the antenna on the adapter, the greater its range. An infrastructure wireless LAN needs one access point (base station) as its hub. An access point costs around $100 and each computer's wireless LAN adapter costs from $50 to $80.

Buying Ethernet Cable

For a standard cabled Ethernet network, you need twisted-pair or Cat-5 cable (as shown in Figure 29-1). The ends of these cables have RJ-45 connectors, which look like telephone cord connectors (the ones that plug into a telephone wall jack) but are about twice as big. When using twisted-pair cable, plug one end of each cable into a NIC installed in a PC and plug the other end into the hub that's at the center of the star topology.

A general rule is not to run a cable more than 150 meters between computers (although the actual specifications for different types of cable in different types of networks may be greater). If you are connecting computers that are not close to each other, you need to do some research on how to create a network over medium distances.

To determine how much cable you need, decide where you are going to place the hub, and then measure from each computer to the hub's location. Remember to allocate extra cable to go around furniture and out of the way of office traffic, and add some slack to allow you to move the computer around—like pulling it away from the wall for repairs.

NOTE *When you buy your cable, remember to string it so that people don't trip over the cable. Measure carefully and allow extra—you can always hide cable that's too long. If your cable is too short, you'll have to go shopping again.*

Installing Your Network Hardware

Now that you have all your parts—a NIC or wireless LAN adapter for each computer, enough cabling (or none, for a wireless LAN), and a hub (or wireless access point), you're ready to put it all together to create the physical network. This procedure is best done when the computers aren't in use and when you have a good chunk of time to devote to it—on a weekend.

Installing the Hub, Switch, or Wireless Access Point

Put the hub, switch, or wireless access point in a location where it won't be disturbed. It doesn't have to be near any computers—in a house, you might want to put a hub in the basement or attic, because it's easy to run all your cables there. You can have more than one hub, too; you might want one hub in the basement, with a cable from each room to the basement, and another hub in the office, to connect all the computers in the office. (This is more efficient than running a separate cable from each computer in the office to the basement.) You can *cascade* hubs by connecting one of the jacks on one hub to the uplink port of the other hub.

A wireless access point should be in a central location to minimize the distance and the number of walls between it and each of the computers with which it has to communicate. If you have a large house or office, you can have multiple access points and cable them all to a hub.

TIP *Be sure to label each cable, so that when you are troubleshooting later, you can tell which cable goes to which computer. We use indelible laundry marker: paper labels may rip, mold, or fall off. When you buy your Ethernet cable, you can choose different-colored cables.*

Stringing Cable

For a cabled network, once the NIC and its driver are installed, you can connect the cabling. The computers can be turned on when you connect the cables.

Cabling can be a simple job or an extravagant one, depending on your needs and how much time, effort, and money you're willing to invest. A home office network that consists of two computers close together probably means cables running on the floor around the edge of the room and behind furniture. Cabling for an office probably means cables hidden by conduit, running inside walls, and running above dropped ceilings. You may want to hire someone if you have many computers to connect and want it done neatly. If you put cable inside ceilings or walls, be sure the installation conforms to fire and electrical codes.

When planning your wiring job, plan for the future. If you're wiring your office, add extra cables while the walls and ceiling are open. Put network jacks in the walls of any room that you think might have a computer in it some day. Plan your network cabling in the same manner you would plan phone extensions. Doing all the wiring now can make adding a computer to your network much easier in the future.

Home office cabling can be a bit more free form, especially if all the PCs are within close proximity of your broadband connection and router. However, it's prudent to manage your cabling nonetheless to prevent a spider's nest of network cables running under your desks or across the floor. Such nests of cabling can cause hazards to children, pets, and even the inattentive SOHO worker who trips over a loose cable.

Connecting the cables to the hub and to the computers is easy—just plug the cable into the RJ-45 jacks on the NIC and the hub as you would plug a phone wire into a phone jack.

CAUTION *Don't run twisted-pair cable in a bundle with electrical power cable, because the electromagnetic interference (EMI) can adversely affect the network—a short-circuit between power and network cables could cause injury or fire.*

Once you complete the construction phase, you need to sit at each computer and configure Windows so it knows about the network, as described in the next chapter.

Configuring Windows for a LAN

I f your home or office has up to six computers and they all run some version of Windows, you can set up a peer-to-peer local area network (LAN) using Windows as your network operating system. You don't need a separate server: Windows Vista Home Basic and all previous versions of Windows back to 3.11 contain all the networking software you need.

Once you connect your router to your broadband modem, you'll need to configure Windows Vista for networking. You need to make sure that Windows' networking components are installed, and then configure the components. The easiest way to configure your computer to communicate over a LAN is usually to run the Network Setup Wizard, and then to test your network connection using the Ping program and the My Network Places window. Windows comes with some network troubleshooting tools, described at the end of this chapter. Once your computer can communicate over the LAN, read the next chapter to learn how to share folders and printers with other computers.

If you are looking for additional information about Windows networking, check out PracticallyNetworked.com (www.practicallynetworked.com) and SmallNetBuilder (www .smallnetbuilder.com).

What Windows Components Are Needed for a Network?

To configure Windows for a peer-to-peer LAN, you use these network components:

- **Client** Specifies the type of network to which you are attaching—a Windows-compatible peer-to-peer network.

- **Protocol** Identifies the way information is passed between computers on the network. TCP/IP is the protocol used by the Internet, for example. The most commonly used protocols are described in the next section.

- **Service** Enables you to share resources on the computer (for example, file or printer sharing).

What Is a Network Protocol?

The *protocol* is the language your computer uses on the network. More than one protocol may be installed on a single computer, because computers can speak more than one language. Windows networks usually use one of these three protocols:

- **TCP/IP (Transmission Control Protocol/Internet Protocol)**   The language spoken by computers on the Internet. Any computer using the Internet through a direct connection needs to have TCP/IP installed. Microsoft is standardizing on this protocol for all networking. See the next section for more details.

- **IPX/SPX (Internetwork Packet eXchange/Sequenced Packet eXchange)**   Used primarily by Novell in its NetWare operating system. IPX/SPX also works well for peer-to-peer networks. Using IPX/SPX, rather than TCP/IP, for sharing files on networks that connect to the Internet provides more security.

- **NetBEUI (NetBIOS Extended User Interface)**   Microsoft's older peer-to-peer networking product. NetBEUI is fast and requires almost no configuration—it's by far the simplest protocol to use and configure. That simplicity has a drawback, however. NetBEUI is *nonroutable*, which means it works only on simple networks where routing devices aren't used to connect multiple segments of networks. On previous versions of Windows, NetBEUI was the default protocol.

Generally, you can use TCP/IP for everything, eliminating all other protocols from your network. However, if you are adding a new computer to an existing NetBEUI- or IPX/SPX-based network, you may not want to reconfigure all the other computers: instead, you can install these additional protocols on your Windows Vista computer.

IP Addressing

When you use TCP/IP on a LAN, the network interface card (NIC) in each computer on the LAN has an IP address on the LAN. IP addresses are in the format *xxx.xxx.xxx.xxx*, where each *xxx* is a number from 0 to 254. IP addresses are used on the Internet to identify Internet host computers and on LANs to identify the computers on the LAN. When you connect directly to the Internet, you also use TCP/IP, and your computer has an IP address to identify it to other computers on the Internet.

On a LAN that uses TCP/IP, computers usually use "private" IP addresses that are not used on the Internet. Several ranges of IP addresses have been set aside for private use. The most commonly used private IP addresses are in the format 192.168.0.*xxx*, where *xxx* is a number from 1 to 253. If one computer on the LAN provides a gateway to the Internet, that computer has the address 192.168.0.1, and the rest of the computers have addresses from 192.168.0.2 up to 192.168.0.253. Figure 30-1 shows a LAN with an IP address assigned to each computer.

How are IP addresses assigned? You can use one of three methods:

- **Static IP addressing**   You can assign the IP addresses yourself, using addresses in the format 192.168.0.*xxx*. You need to keep track of which addresses you've assigned, so that you don't give two computers the same address. Another problem is that ICS doesn't always work with static IP addressing.

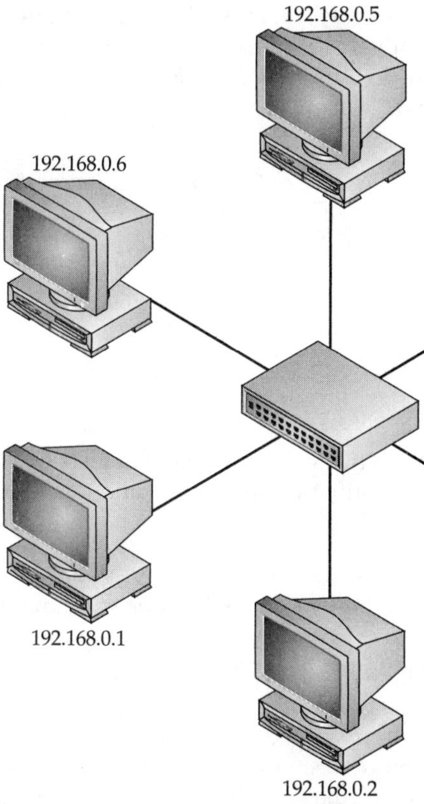

FIGURE 30-1   Assigning IP addresses to computers on a LAN.

- **Automatic private IP addressing (APIPA)**   This Windows system assigns IP addresses to the computers on a LAN automatically (called *dynamic addressing*). The addresses are in the format 169.254.*xxx.xxx*, where each *xxx* can be a number from 1 to 253. You can't use APIPA addresses with ICS or on LANs that use DHCP addressing.

- **DHCP (Dynamic Host Configuration Protocol) addressing**   A *DHCP server* is software that assigns IP addresses for the LAN. Like APIPA, DHCP assigns an IP address to your computer automatically, but it is designed to work with much larger LANs. ICS, which is part of Windows Vista, includes a DHCP server. Most Internet routers include a DHCP server, too. Microsoft's TCP/IP networking systems generally use DHCP addressing.

When you connect directly to the Internet, you don't have a choice about your address; your ISP assigns it for you. In the early days of dial-up connections, ISPs issued a static IP address with each Internet account. Now, most ISPs run DHCP-like servers that issue to your computer an IP address each time you connect.

When setting up a LAN that uses TCP/IP, you must choose among these IP addressing methods. Use static addressing only for very small LANs (with fewer than ten computers) that don't use ICS. If you plan to share an Internet connection using ICS or a router, it includes a DHCP server (see Chapter 31).

NOTE *If your computer has more than one TCP/IP connection, it needs more than one IP address. For example, your computer might have a NIC that connects it to the LAN and another card that connects to a DSL modem that connects to the Internet. Each network interface has one TCP/IP address.*

The section "Configuring the TCP/IP Protocol" later in this chapter describes how to configure Windows to communicate using TCP/IP.

Identifying the Computer

For your computer to communicate with the other computers in your workgroup, you need to give the computer a unique name, identify the workgroup, and, optionally, provide a description:

- **Computer name**   Naming your computer lets the users of other computers refer to your computer by name. Each computer on the LAN needs a unique name. If you are adding your computer to an existing LAN, check the names of the other computers and choose one that's not already in use.

- **Workgroup**   The *workgroup* is a group of computers on your network. Large LANs may have a different workgroup for each department, but on a small LAN (fewer than 20 computers), all the computers on the LAN need to have the same workgroup name. For a new LAN, the default name is MSHOME (although we prefer to use WORKGROUP as the name).

- **Computer description**   Optionally, you can enter a description of the computer. Windows doesn't use this description during logon, but it does display it in the My Network Places window.

For example, five computers comprising a small network may all belong to the same workgroup called WORKGROUP. Within the workgroup, the computers might be named Office, Playroom, WillsRoom, JuliesRoom, and Kitchen, for example, or Accounting, Sales, Marketing, Administration, and Shipping. We recommend not using people's names as computer names, because people tend to switch computers, or move desks, or go off to college and get new computers. It's confusing when Ted regularly uses a computer named Mary.

NOTE *Larger networks use domains to centralize network administration, and require a server running Windows 2003 Server or Windows 2000 Server. Windows Vista Home Basic Edition can't connect to server-based (domain-based) networks.*

When you configure your LAN using the Network Setup Wizard (described in the next section), the wizard asks you for the computer name, workgroup, and computer description. You can also change these settings later (see "Changing the Computer Name, Workgroup, or Domain" later in this chapter).

Windows Vista Basic Edition and Domain-Based LANs

Windows Vista can connect to a domain-based corporate LAN, but Windows Vista Home Basic Edition cannot. If your office uses the Microsoft Exchange Server for e-mail, you can use Microsoft Outlook Web Access to read your mail. Check with your company's LAN administrator for instructions. Windows Vista Home Basic Edition can also connect to an Exchange server by using Outlook to send and receive mail without logging into the domain.

Configuring and Viewing Your LAN Connections

Windows Vista offers upgraded networking tools, enabling you to better manage your PC's network access whether it be your home network, the Wi-Fi hotspot at your favorite coffee place, or your employer's LAN.

What Is the Windows Vista Network Center?

The Windows Vista Network Center is a central network-monitoring console that informs you about the your network connection and whether your PC can successfully reach the Internet (see Figure 30-2). In today's mobile computing age, being able to manage your network connectivity is a necessity for many users.

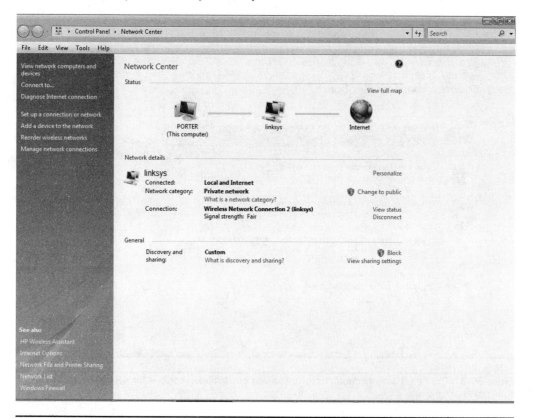

FIGURE 30-2   The Windows Vista Network Center enables you to Manage your Network Connectivity.

The Network Center graphically represents your network connectivity status in the Network Map so that you can diagnose network outages and then use Network Diagnostics to help determine the cause of the problem and get a suggestion for a solution.

The Windows Vista Network Center also enables you to set up a new connection or network, add a device such as a printer or external hard drive to your network, reorder wireless networks, and manage your network connections.

Connecting to a SOHO Network

After attaching a cable to connect your computer to your SOHO LAN, follow these steps:

1. Begin network setup by choosing Start | Network to open the Network Center. Click Network And Sharing Center to open the Network And Sharing Center window.

2. Click Set Up A Connection Or Network to open the Set Up A Connection Or Network dialog box, shown in Figure 30-3.

3. Choose one of the following options:
   - Connect to the Internet
   - Set up a wireless router or access point
   - Manually connect to a wireless network

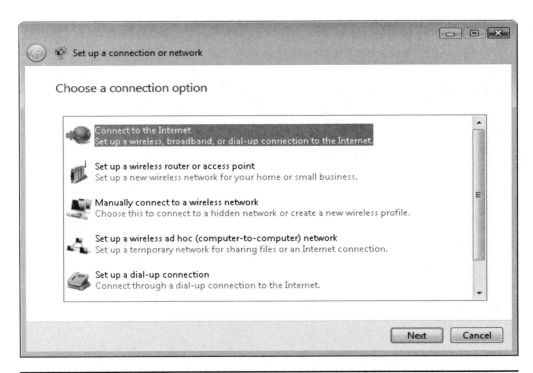

FIGURE 30-3 The Setup a connection or network dialog box includes options for setting up a Internet connection or network.

- Set up a wireless ad hoc (computer-to-computer) network
- Set up a dial-up connection
- Connect to a workplace

4. After choosing the connection option that meets your needs, click it and follow the directions presented in the wizard.

Viewing Your Network Connections

To configure the network, you use the Network Connections window, shown in Figure 30-4. Choose Start | Control Panel, click Network And Internet, and click Network And Sharing Center. From the Network and Sharing Center, click Manage Network Connections.

The Network Connections window displays your LAN and Internet connections and lists network-related tasks.

Running the Network Setup Wizard on Windows 2000 and XP Systems

You can use the Network Setup Wizard to configure computers on your LAN even if they don't run Windows Vista. If you created a Network Setup Disk when you ran the Network

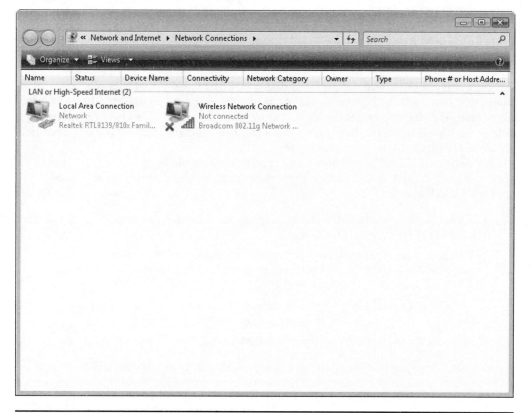

FIGURE 30-4   Network Connections window.

Setup Wizard, you can run the Network Setup Wizard on Windows 2000 or XP computers on your LAN by putting the floppy disk in the drive, choosing Start | Run, typing **a:setup** in the Open box, and clicking OK. The wizard configures the computers to use TCP/IP, and may need to restart each computer after it runs.

If you didn't create a Network Setup Disk, you can run the wizard from the Windows Vista DVD. Follow these steps:

1. Put the Windows Vista DVD in your computer's DVD drive. If the Welcome To Microsoft Windows Vista window doesn't appear, choose Start | Run and type *d*: **setup** (where *d* is the letter of your DVD drive) to display it.

2. Choose Perform Additional Tasks.

3. Choose Set Up A Home Or Small Office Network.

4. Follow the wizard's instructions, clicking Next to move from window to window.

Installing and Configuring Network Components

Running the Network Setup Wizard is usually all you need to do to set up a TCP/IP-based peer-to-peer network or attach your PC to an existing LAN. However, if you are connecting to a NetBEUI- or IPX/SPX-based network, or if your network connection isn't working properly, you may need to install, configure, or uninstall network components yourself.

For each networking connection listed in the Network Connections window, you can see its properties by right-clicking the connection and choosing Properties from the menu that appears.

The Local Area Connection Properties dialog box lists the NIC that connects your computer to the LAN. It also lists the clients, protocols, and services used for this network connection. The NIC appears at the top, in the Connect Using box. The clients, protocols, and services are listed in the This Connection Uses The Following Items box, with icons that identify the different types of components.

For a standard TCP/IP LAN, these four components should be installed (they should appear in your Local Area Connection Properties dialog box) and enabled (each check box contains a check mark):

- **Client For Microsoft Networks**   Client that enables the computer to communicate with other Windows computers.

- **File And Printer Sharing For Microsoft Networks**   Service that shares files and printers. This service should be enabled only on a LAN connection, not on an Internet connection. The Internet Connection Firewall blocks this service.

- **QoS Packet Scheduler**   Service that determines the precedence of information packets on the LAN based on quality of service (QoS) standards.

- **Internet Protocol (TCP/IP)**   Protocol used on the Internet and many LANs.

If your LAN connection has these four components and your LAN uses TCP/IP, you probably don't need to install any other network components. Skip ahead to the section "Checking Your Network Connection" later in this chapter.

Installing a Client

The next step is to install the client component, which identifies the type of network on which your computer will be located. When you configure your network connection (or when Windows finds your Plug and Play NIC), Windows also installs the Client for Microsoft Networks. If a client is installed, it appears in the This Connection Uses The Following Items dialog box in the Local Area Connection Properties dialog box.

Because you are installing a peer-to-peer Windows network, the Client for Microsoft Networks is the one you need. If you mistakenly deleted your Client for Microsoft Networks, follow these steps:

1. Display the Local Area Connection Properties dialog box (by clicking Start, right-clicking My Network Places, choosing Properties, right-clicking Local Area Connection, and choosing Properties). Click the General tab (if it's not already selected).

2. Click the Install button. You see the Select Network Component Type dialog box.

3. Select Client as the type of network component you want to install and click the Add button. You see the Select Network Client dialog box.

4. Choose the network client. If you have a floppy disk or CD with software for another type of client, insert it now and click Have Disk.

5. Click OK. You return to the Local Area Connection Properties dialog box, with the client you just defined listed. You may be prompted to insert the Windows Vista DVD.

6. Click OK to save your changes.

Installing a Protocol

When you install Windows, it automatically installs the TCP/IP protocol, in case you want to use TCP/IP for Internet communication. We recommend that you use TCP/IP if you are setting up a new network, since it's the standard. Windows Vista also comes with support for NetBEUI (Microsoft's older protocol) and NetWare's IPX/SPX protocol.

Copying NetBEUI Files

Before you can install the NetBEUI protocol, you need to follow these steps to copy the files from the Windows Vista DVD:

1. Put the Windows Vista DVD in the drive. Choose Perform Additional Tasks from the menu that appears, and then Browse This DVD.

2. In the Explorer window that appears, locate the Valueadd\msft\net\netbeui folder on the DVD.

3. Copy the Nbf.sys file into the C:\Windows\System32\Drivers folder (assuming that Windows is installed in C:\Windows).

4. Copy Netnbf.inf into the C:\Windows\Inf folder.

After copying the files, you can install NetBEUI, as described in the next section.

NOTE *You may need to configure Windows Explorer to display hidden files in order to see the copied files. In an Explorer window, choose Tools | Folder Options, click the View tab, and select the Show Hidden Files And Folders check box in the Advanced Settings list.*

Installing NetBEUI or IPX/SPX

Installing a protocol is similar to installing other network components. Follow these steps to install NetBEUI or IPX/SPX:

1. Display the Local Area Connection Properties dialog box (by clicking Start, right-clicking My Network Places, choosing Properties, right-clicking Local Area Connection, and choosing Properties). Click the General tab (if it's not already selected).

2. Click the Install button to display the Select Network Component Type dialog box.

3. Select Protocol and click the Add button. You see the Select Network Protocol dialog box.

4. Select the protocol and click OK. (For IPX/SPX, select NWLink IPX/SPX/NetBIOS Compatible Transport Protocol.)

5. You return to the Local Area Connection Properties dialog box, with the protocol you just defined listed and enabled for this local area connection. You may be prompted to insert the Windows Vista DVD.

6. Click Close to save your changes.

Setting the Order of Your Protocols

When you install a protocol, Windows "binds" the new protocol to all the clients and services you have available—usually File And Printer Sharing For Microsoft Networks and Client For Microsoft Networks. A *binding* tells Windows to use a specific protocol with a specific client or service.

You might not want to use all of your installed protocols to work with all your installed clients and services. You can control which protocols work with which clients and services, and which protocol Windows should try first, by opening the Network Connections window (choose Start | Network, click Manage Network Connections, and choose a Network Connection) and choosing Advanced | Advanced Settings from the menu bar. Click the Local Area Connection in the Connections box (if it's not already selected). The lower part of the Adapters And Bindings tab shows your client and services for that connection, with your installed protocols listed under each client or service.

You can switch the order of the protocols, so that the one you plan to use most often appears first. Click the protocol and click the up- or down-pointing arrow button to move it. If you don't plan to use a protocol with a particular service, deselect the check box by the protocol.

TIP *If you connect to the Internet through a hub or router that doesn't provide a firewall between your computers and the Internet, don't use TCP/IP for your file and printer sharing. Instead, on each computer on your LAN, install the NetBEUI or IPX/SPX protocol, as described in "Installing a Protocol" earlier in this chapter. Then use the Advanced Settings dialog box on each computer to disable Internet Protocol (TCP/IP) for File And Printer Sharing For Microsoft Networks. Leave NetBEUI or IPX/SPX enabled, so that all the computers can use that protocol for file and printer sharing. Leave TCP/IP installed for communications with the Internet.*

Configuring the TCP/IP Protocol

On a TCP/IP-based LAN, you need to assign an IP address to your computer's NIC, using static addressing or DHCP (see "IP Addressing" earlier in this chapter). For a laptop, you can also use an alternate configuration, for when the computer isn't connected to its regular network. Follow these steps:

1. Display the Local Area Connection Properties dialog box (by clicking Start, right-clicking My Network Places, choosing Properties, right-clicking Local Area Connection, and choosing Properties). Click the General tab (if it's not already selected).

2. On the list of network components that the connection uses, select Internet Protocol (TCP/IP).

3. Click Properties. You see the Internet Protocol (TCP/IP) Properties dialog box.

4. To assign a static IP address, click Use The Following IP Address. In the IP Address box, type the IP address you've chosen. Windows supplies the dots that separate the four parts of the address.

5. In the Subnet Mask box, type **255.255.255.0**.

6. To use DHCP or APIPA (systems that assign an IP address to your computer when Windows starts up), select Obtain An IP Address Automatically. If your LAN has a DHCP server, Windows will get IP addresses from the server each time you start Windows. If not, Windows will assign itself an address.

7. If you have a laptop that connects to a LAN in a different way when you are not at your desk, click the Alternate Configuration tab. Your IP addressing choices are Automatic Private IP Address (APIPA) or User Configured (a static address).

8. Click OK in each dialog box.

On rare occasions, the TCP/IP protocol installation may get damaged. You can reset TCP/IP by following these steps:

1. Open a Command Prompt window by choosing Start | All Programs | Accessories | Command Prompt (or Start | Run, type **cmd**, and press ENTER).

2. Type the following command and then press ENTER:

```
netsh int ip reset ipreset.log
```

3. If you want to read the contents of the log file created by the command, you can type the command **type ipreset.log** and press ENTER.

4. Type **exit** and press ENTER to close the Command Prompt window.

Installing a Service

A service is the last network component you install. It also is the only optional component. Your network can work fine without a service, but no one on the network will be able to share resources, such as hard disks, DVD drives, files, or printers. If you don't want to share resources, don't install any services.

On a peer-to-peer network of Windows computers, you need the File And Printer Sharing For Microsoft Networks service. The Network Setup Wizard installs this service automatically. If you need to install it (or another service) yourself, follow these steps:

1. Display the Local Area Connection Properties dialog box (by choosing Start | Network | Manage Network Connections). Choose Properties.
2. Click the Install button to display the Select Network Component Type dialog box.
3. Select Service and click the Add button. You see the Select Network Service dialog box.
4. Select the service you want and click OK.
5. You return to the Local Area Connection Properties dialog box, with the protocol you just defined listed. You may be prompted to insert the Windows Vista DVD.
6. Click Close to save your changes.

Changing the Computer Name, Workgroup, or Domain

To see or change your computer's name and which workgroup or domain it is in, follow these steps:

1. Click Start, right-click My Computer, and choose Properties from the menu that appears. You see the System Properties dialog box.
2. Click the Computer Name tab.
3. Type a description of the computer in the Computer Description box. This description appears in the My Network Places window.
4. To change the computer name or workgroup, click the Change button to display the Computer Name Changes dialog box.
5. In the Computer Name box, type a unique name for the computer.
6. In the Workgroup box, type the workgroup name. Use the same workgroup name used for the other computers in the LAN.
7. Click OK. You may see a message telling you to restart Windows for your changes to take effect.

Checking Your Network Connection

The Network Setup Wizard usually installs and configures your network components correctly. This section describes how to discover your computer's IP address and how to try rudimentary network communication.

Checking Your TCP/IP Address

Windows can display your computer's IP address and other TCP/IP settings. In the Network Connections window (choose Start | Control Panel, click Network And Internet Connections, and click Network Connections), right-click a connection and choose Status from the menu that appears.

You can also see where the IP address came from (in this example, it was assigned by a DHCP server). For details, click the Details button. You can click Repair to re-request an IP address from the DHCP server.

Another way to see your IP address and other information is by running the Ipconfig program. Choose Start | All Programs | Accessories | Command Prompt to open a Command Prompt window. Then type **ipconfig /all** and press ENTER. You see a listing like this:

```
Windows IP Configuration

        Host Name . . . . . . . . . . . . . : inspiron7000
        Primary Dns Suffix  . . . . . . . :
        Node Type . . . . . . . . . . . . : Hybrid
        IP Routing Enabled. . . . . . . . : No
        WINS Proxy Enabled. . . . . . . . : No

Ethernet adapter Local Area Connection:

        Connection-specific DNS Suffix  . : mshome.net
        Description . . . . . . . . . . . : EtherFast 10/100 PC Card
        Physical Address. . . . . . . . . : 00-E0-98-04-47-15
        Dhcp Enabled. . . . . . . . . . . : Yes
        Autoconfiguration Enabled . . . . : Yes
        IP Address. . . . . . . . . . . . : 192.168.0.4
        Subnet Mask . . . . . . . . . . . : 255.255.255.0
        Default Gateway . . . . . . . . . : 192.168.0.1
        DHCP Server . . . . . . . . . . . : 192.168.0.1
        DNS Servers . . . . . . . . . . . : 192.168.0.1
        Lease Obtained. . . . . . . . . . : Tuesday, July 31, 2001
        Lease Expires . . . . . . . . . . : Wednesday, August 01, 2001
```

The Dhcp Enabled line tells you whether your computer got its IP address from a DHCP server and, if so, the Lease Obtained line tells when your computer got the address. If your computer uses ICS, the Default Gateway, DHCP Server, and DNS Servers entries are 192.168.0.1.

Testing Your TCP/IP Connection

Once you've installed and configured the network components for a computer, you need to see whether your network works. Sit down at any of the computers on the network and follow these steps:

1. Use the Ping program to ping yourself—that is, ping your own computer's IP address. In the Network Connections window (choose Start | Control Panel, click Network And Internet Connections, and click Network Connections), right-click your LAN connection, choose Status, and click the Support tab to find out your own computer's IP address. If this step doesn't work, TCP/IP isn't correctly installed on your computer, or it's not getting an IP address.

2. Ping another computer on the LAN to see whether information can travel from your computer to another. Follow the instructions in the previous section first to determine the IP address of a computer on the LAN to ping. (Try pinging your

PART VI

default gateway, which is frequently at 192.168.0.1.) If this step fails, your LAN cable or connection may not work.

3. Open the My Network Places window (choose Start | My Network Places) to see what appears. Shortcuts to shared folders on the other computers should appear automatically. Otherwise, you can click Add A Network Place to add shortcuts to folders. If this step doesn't work, your workgroup name may not be set correctly.

4. If you don't see shortcuts in the My Network Places window, there's another way to connect to other computers on the LAN. Click View Workgroup Computers in the Tasks pane of the My Network Places window. You see the names of all the computers in the workgroup. Open an icon (click or double-click it, depending on how you have Windows configured) to see the folders and printers that are available on that computer. If you see Entire Network as an entry, open it. Then open Microsoft Windows Network, and then open your workgroup. The computers in your workgroup should appear.

5. If you still don't see icons for the other computers on the network, read through the section "Troubleshooting Your Network" later in this chapter to find and fix the problem. If you see only your own computer in the workgroup, or the Entire Network window is blank, communication has broken down with the other computers. It could be physical, like a bad cable, or it could be a problem with your software configuration, such as using the wrong protocol.

Once your network is working, the next step is to use it to share resources (see Chapter 31).

Viewing LAN Resources with the net Command

You can see a list of the shared resources of a computer on the LAN by using a command-line program called NET VIEW (actually, it's the NET program with the VIEW command-line argument). Open a Command Prompt window by choosing Start | All Programs | Accessories | Command Prompt. Then type **net view //computername** and press ENTER. Replace *computername* with the name of a computer on the LAN. For example, the command **net view \\dell8100** might produce this listing:

```
Shared resources at \\dell8100

Dell Dimension 8100

Share name    Type     Use as    Comment
-------------------------------------------
D             Disk
SharedDocs    Disk
PRINTER       Print
The command completed successfully.
```

If the computer has no shared resources, you see the message "There are no entries in the list." If you don't have permission to view the shared resources on that computer, you see the message "Access is denied." If you see the message "System error 53 has occurred," the computer name is wrong, the computer is not on the LAN, or File And Printer Sharing For Microsoft Networks isn't running on that computer.

You can see a list of all the shared resources on your own computer by typing **net share**.

NOTE *The NET VIEW command works with all installed protocols. Ping works only with TCP/IP.*

Viewing LAN Usage

If you are worried that your LAN is slowing down because it can't handle the volume of data, Windows can display a graph of LAN utilization. Press CTRL-ALT-DELETE to see the Windows Task Manager window. Click the Networking tab.

The graph shows network usage over time, as a percentage of the amount of data that it could carry. Unless you are copying huge files (for example, if you do backups over the LAN), the percentages usually stay amazingly low.

Troubleshooting Your Network

Although Windows networking generally works well, you may have trouble with one computer or all of the computers on the network, especially when you first set up the network. This section recommends some steps to take to solve your problems.

If you have trouble with the IP addresses on the LAN, use the Networking (TCP/IP) Troubleshooter. Choose Start | Help And Support, click Fixing A Problem in the Pick A Help Topic list, click Networking Problems, and click Home And Small Office Networking Troubleshooter. Another useful program is Network Diagnostics. To use it, type **Network Diagnostics** in the Help And Support Center window's Search box and press ENTER.

The solutions to some common problems and solutions follow:

- **The "Local Area Network: A Network Cable Is Unplugged" message appears**   If you see this message in a pop-up window from the notification bar of the taskbar, the message is probably right—the cable from your computer to the LAN hub is unplugged or damaged, or for a wireless LAN, the SSID or network key is wrong. When you fix the connection, the message goes away.

- **Computer can't log onto a domain**   You can't log onto a domain-based LAN if you use Windows Vista Home Basic Edition; only Windows Vista Business or Windows Vista Ultimate Edition can log onto a domain.

- **Computers do not appear in My Network Places**   If a computer doesn't appear in your Network Connections window when you click View Workgroup Computers, it may have a loose cable connection, a bad cable, or a NIC that isn't working properly. Check all of the cable connections. Occasionally, cables become damaged, so you might want to try replacing a suspect length of cable with one you know is good. Use Ping to see if the computer can communicate.

- **Shared folders don't appear in Network**   The Network Connections window contains shortcuts to shared folders on the LAN, but these shortcuts can be deleted. If a shared folder you need doesn't appear in My Network Places, click Add A Network Place in the Tasks pane. Try searching for the computer name by choosing Start | Search and choosing Computers Or People at the What Do You Want To Search For prompt (if you don't see that prompt, click More Advanced Options and then Other Search Options).

PART VI

- **Bad or missing protocol**   A protocol may be missing or incorrectly configured. Check to see that your computer is speaking the same language as all the others. If the other computers are using NetBEUI and you are using TCP/IP, you will not be able to communicate with them. Open the Network Connections window, right-click the Local Area Connection icon, and choose Repair from the menu that appears. Windows will try to reinstall any missing components. Also, check which protocols the other computers are using to communicate, and install that protocol on the computer that is incommunicado.

- **Network interface card problem**   You may have a hardware conflict. Use the Device Manager to see whether there's a problem with the NIC. If the NIC appears with a yellow exclamation point, the card isn't working properly. Check the installation instructions for your card.

- **Password problems**   If Windows asks for a password when you try to use a shared folder or printer, you may need to find out the password for that resource or have your user account name added to the list of users who can address the resource.

Sharing Drives and Printers on a LAN

The true power of your SOHO LAN is the ability to share resources like printers and network drives. Perhaps you have three computers and only one printer and one Internet connection. Perhaps several people use a database from different computers, and you want to make sure that they're always working with updated information. Whatever the reason, your LAN isn't much good if you don't know how to share your hardware and files.

This chapter tells you how to share disks and folders on your own computer, use shared disks and folders on other computers, and choose which of your own disk drives to make available to other people on your LAN. We also describe how to share the printers on your system and how to use printers on other people's systems.

NOTE *This chapter assumes that you have connected your computer to a workgroup-based LAN and have installed file- and printer-sharing services.*

Network drives (also called *shared drives*) are disk drives that have been configured to be available for use from other computers on the LAN. Similarly, *shared folders* are folders that have been configured to be usable by other computers on the LAN. For a disk drive or folder to be shared by other people on a LAN, it must be configured as sharable. Once a drive or folder is sharable, other people can read and write files on the disk drive or in the folder. Microsoft makes sharing a whole drive a little more difficult than sharing just a folder because of the security risks involved.

Enabling Hardware Sharing

To share your hardware—disk drives and printers—with others on the LAN, you need to make sure that sharing is enabled.

Installing file and printer sharing does not automatically share your printer and disk drives—that could compromise security. Instead, you choose exactly which resources to share on your computer by using the commands covered in this chapter.

TIP You can't share files or printers through a network connection that uses the Internet Connection Firewall. You should enable ICF on any connections to the outside world, so outsiders can't snoop on your network, but do not use ICF on connections to your LAN, which would prevent sharing resources with other computers on the LAN. If you use the Network Setup Wizard to configure your LAN, it automatically enables ICF on external connections but not on internal ones.

User Accounts and LAN Security

Chapter 6 describes how you can set up user accounts on a computer to allow several people to be able to use the computer, storing separate settings for each person. The section "Keeping Your Files Private" describes how to set up public and private folders for each user.

User accounts are also useful on a peer-to-peer LAN, even if each computer is normally used by only one person. Windows Vista Home Basic Edition doesn't support the security provided by Microsoft's domain-based LANs. However, you have the following security options:

- **Read-only drives and folder files** When you share a drive or folder on the LAN, you can designate it to be read-only, so that people on other computers can't change your files. For example, on a home LAN you might have a folder that contains your family's photos. You might want to share the folder with family members on other computers but set it as read-only so that other people can't accidentally delete pictures (or deliberately delete pictures in which their hair looks funny).

- **Nonshared drives** You can set some drives not to be accessible over the LAN. We recommend that you separate your programs and documents into two separate partitions, and share only the documents partition. (Few programs run off of partitions on other computers, so there's no point sharing your Windows and program partition.)

- **Private folders** You can use Windows Vista's user accounts to create private folders (see "Keeping Your Files Private" in Chapter 6).

Using Shared Drives from Other Computers

You can access a shared drive or shared folder in one of two ways:

- If you use the drive or folder only occasionally, you can use Network window to access the drive.

- If you use the drive or folder frequently, you can *map* the drive or folder, which means that you assign the drive or folder a letter so that it appears on the drop-down list of drives in Open and Save As dialog boxes, and as a disk in My Computer.

Using Network Drives with Network Window

You can see a list of the shared drives and folders to which you have access. The Network window, shown in Figure 31-1, lists *network shortcuts* to all the shared drives and folders available to you on the LAN. Choose View | Details to display all the information about each shared drive.

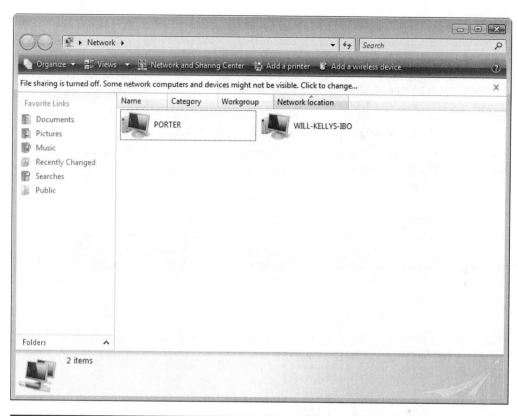

FIGURE 31-1   The Network window showing shared drives and folders on the LAN.

The name of each shared drive or folder appears, along with its UNC (Universal Naming Convention) address—the pathname you use when referring to that shared drive or folder. The UNC address consists of two backslashes, the name of the computer, another backslash, and the share name of the drive or folder (see "Sharing Your Disk Drives and Folders with Others" later in this chapter).

To display the Network window, choose Start | Network. If you don't see a list of shared folders, consider troubleshooting your network (see "Troubleshooting Your Network" in Chapter 30). If one or two shared folders are missing, click Add A Network Place in the Task pane to add it. This command is also useful for adding web servers and FTP servers to your Network window (see "Working with FTP and Web Servers Using Web Folders").

Another way to see all the shared folders on the system in the My Network Places window is by clicking the Entire Network plus box, the Microsoft Windows Network plus box, and the plus box for your workgroup (which is usually named MSHOME). You see a list of the computers on the LAN. Click a computer's plus box to see its shared drives and printers.

> **TIP** *You can change the name of a shared drive or folder as it appears on your computer. For example, if a drive appears as "data drive on Surfrider" and you'd rather see the name "Accounting Data," you can rename it by right-clicking the shared drive or folder in an Explorer window and choosing Rename from the shortcut menu that appears. Renaming a shared drive or folder on your computer doesn't change its real name on the computer on which it's stored, just how it appears in your Explorer windows.*

Opening and Saving Files on Shared Drives and Folders

You can see the folders and files on a shared drive by opening the drive or folder in the Network window. Once you see the drive, you can work with it as you do any drive on your own computer.

Mapping a Shared Drive or Folder to a Drive Letter

If you use a shared drive or folder frequently, you can assign it a drive letter. When you want to find or save a file to the shared drive or folder, you don't have to spend so much time navigating through Network to find it. For example, if you frequently use files in a shared folder on another computer, you can map drive letter S to that folder. Drive S: appears as a disk drive on your computer, even though it's actually on the server.

Here's the easiest way to map a shared drive or folder to a drive letter:

1. Run Network (choose Start | My Network) to display the Network window.

2. Choose Connect To Network from the menu bar. You see the Connect To A Network dialog box:

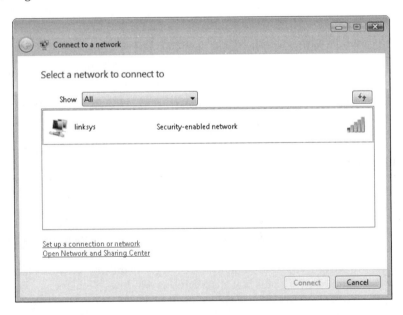

3. Choose a drive letter, clicking the Show drop-down list to see the available letters. Letters that are mapped to drives on your own computer don't appear. Letters that

are already mapped to shared drives or folders appear with the name of the resource to which they are mapped.

4. In the Folder box, type the UNC address of the shared drive or folder you want to map. Better yet, click the down-pointing arrow at the right end of the Folder box and choose from the UNC addresses that appear or click the Browse button and navigate to the drive or folder. The list includes all the drives and folders on the LAN that have been configured to be sharable.

5. If you want to continue to map this drive or folder to this drive letter each time you restart Windows, leave the Reconnect At Logon check box selected.

6. Click Finish to close the dialog box. If the shared drive or folder requires a password, Windows prompts you to type it.

Once you have mapped a drive, it appears in the folder tree with your local drives, and in the Computer window. You can access a mapped network drive in the same way that you access a local drive from any dialog box.

NOTE   *To map a drive letter to a folder, the folder itself must be defined as shared. It is not enough to share the drive on which the folder resides.*

You can map a drive letter to a shared folder on a domain-based corporate LAN if the server has a fixed IP address or domain name.

Tips for Mapping Shared Folders and Drives

When you map a drive letter, you map it for only one computer at a time. If you want the drive letter mapped for other computers on the LAN, you need to sit down at each of them and repeat the steps in the preceding section. That is, if you want all the computers in your home or small office to be able to use the drive letter F to refer to the Family Finances folder on the Kitchen computer, you must map the Family Finances folder to the F: drive on each computer on the LAN.

If you use a shared drive or folder from more than one computer, you might want to spend a moment considering which drive letter to use. You will find it more convenient if the shared network drive has the same drive letter on each computer on the LAN—that way you won't have to refer to "the C: drive on the computer in the corner near the door—the one called XFiles." Instead, you can just call it the F: drive (the exception, of course, is the person who uses the computer called XFiles, for whom it's just the C: drive). Choose a letter that people can remember—for example, map the disk drive on the playroom computer to drive P:, or the drive with your accounting data to drive Z:. Before you assign the drive letter, make sure that letter is available on the other computers on the LAN (letters up to about G are frequently already occupied by hard disks, CD-ROM drives, Zip drives, and other devices).

Unmapping a Drive Letter

If you want to "unmap" a drive letter, you can do so by disconnecting it: right-click the drive in Computer and choose Disconnect from the shortcut menu, or choose Tools | Disconnect Network Drive, choose the drive to disconnect, and click OK. The drive remains accessible through Network, but a drive letter is no longer mapped to it. (To make a drive inaccessible even through My Network Places, you must disable sharing from the computer that owns the resource.)

Sharing Your Disk Drives and Folders with Others

You might want to share the files stored on your computer's disk drives in a number of ways. You might want to permit all the computers on the LAN to access an external storage drive, or NAS (network attached storage). You can permit other people to read files in specific folders on your hard drive. For instance, you can give read-only access to the folder that contains your family's collection of digital photos and music, so that you don't waste space on each computer saving the same files (and time updating numerous copies of the files). Maybe there is one shared folder on your hard drive that you want other people to be able to use. Maybe you just want to share everything—you want to allow everyone on the LAN to read and write to your hard drive.

Before anyone else can read or write files on your disk drives, you must configure either the entire drive or specific folders as sharable. You choose a *share name* for the drive or folder—the name that you want to appear in Computer as *name* on *computer name*. For example, if your computer is named Laptop, and you share your CD-ROM (your drive D:) with the share name CD-ROM Drive, it appears as "CD-ROM Drive On Laptop" in Network on other people's computers. You can provide a comment to further identify a shared drive or folder. The comment is visible only when the properties are displayed.

When you make a drive or folder sharable, you also decide what access to specify, within the limits of what Windows Vista Home Basic allows. There are alternatives to sharing a whole drive with full read and write access:

- You can share just a folder.
- You can specify read-only rights.

By default, Windows Vista enables *Simple File Sharing*, which means that when you share a drive or folder, you share it with everyone in your network workgroup.

NOTE *If you need more flexible security, enabling specific people to have read and write access to specific folders, consider upgrading to Windows Vista Ultimate and setting up a domain-based LAN, which has more powerful LAN security features. In Windows Vista Ultimate, you can disable Simple File Sharing to display a Security tab in file and folder Properties dialog boxes, on which you can specify permissions for individual users.*

Sharing Drives

Follow these steps to share a drive or folder:

1. Run Computer (choose Start | Computer) and display the name of the drive or folder you want to share with others.

2. Right-click the drive or folder you want to share and choose Share from the shortcut menu. You see the Properties dialog box for the drive or folder, with the Sharing tab selected. If you have chosen to share a whole drive, you will see a link warning you that sharing the root of the drive is risky. Click the link to see Figure 31-2.

FIGURE 31-2   Sharing a disk drive.

3. In the File Sharing dialog box, type the name of the person you want to share files with and then click Add.

4. Click the arrow to the right of the text box (if your PC is on a Windows domain). Next, click Find. Type the name of the person you want to share files with. Click Check Names, and then click OK.

5. Click the arrow located to the right of the text box (if your computer is on a domain), click Everyone to share the files with everyone on your network. Next, click Add.

6. Sometimes, if your computer is on a workgroup, you might not see the name of the person you want to share files with in the list. Click the arrow to the right of the text box. Next, click Create a new user to create a new user account for the user you cannot find. The name of the person or group that you selected appears in the list of people you want to share files with.

7. Next, you need to set permission levels. Click the arrow next to the permission level for that person or group, and give them one of the following permission levels:

- **Reader**   To restrict the selected user to viewing files in the shared folder.

- **Contributor**   To enable the user to view all files, add files, and change or delete the files that they add.

- Co-owner   To enable the user to fully manipulate (view, change, add, and delete) files in the shared folder.

8. Click Share if Vista prompts for an administrator password or confirmation. Type the password to provide confirmation.

9. After you receive confirmation that your folder is shared, you should send a link to your shared files to the people you are sharing them with, so they know the files are shared and how to access them. Next, you have the option to click the E-mail link to open a Windows Mail e-mail message, including a link to your shared files. Otherwise, you can copy-and-paste the link displayed on this screen into an e-mail message.

If you make a folder sharable, the shared folder looks like a whole drive from other computers on the LAN, but other people can see and use only the shared folder.

TIP   *To hide shared folders, add a dollar sign ($) to the end of the share name (for example, type* Docs$ *in the Share Name box). Other people can still use this shared folder by mapping it to a drive letter.*

Controlling Access to Files and Folders on NTFS Volumes

If a shared folder is on an NTFS volume, you can set individual files and folders to be read-only even if the folder is read-write. You can also mark files and folders as hidden so they don't normally appear in Explorer windows. Right-click the file or folder, select Properties, and check or uncheck the Read-Only or Hidden check box. When you close the Properties dialog box for a folder, Windows asks whether you want the changes to apply to the files and folders within the folder, or just to the folder itself.

Sharing Printers on a LAN

Sharing a printer on a LAN has two steps. First, you sit at the computer that is directly attached to the printer and configure the printer to be a *network printer* or *shared printer* so that other computers on the network can print to it. Then you configure the other computers on the LAN so that they know about the network printer—with luck, Windows on each computer automatically detects the existence of the newly sharable printer and installs the new printer driver itself.

CAUTION   *Not all printers come with printer drivers that work for sharing the printer on a LAN.*

Making Your Printer Sharable

If you want other people on the LAN to be able to print on your printer, first install the printer on your own computer and make sure that you can print to it. Once the printer is correctly installed, you can share it.

The computer that the printer is attached to is called a *print server*. The print server can also be someone's PC, the usual arrangement on a small network, or a computer that does nothing else. You give the printer a share name, the name that other people will see when they connect to the printer. The share name can be the type of printer (for example, HP1100A), the group that uses the printer (for example, Accounting), or some other name. A straightforward name makes it easier for others on the network to figure out which printer they are using.

To share the printer so that other computers on the LAN can print to it, follow these steps:

1. Click Start | Control Panel | Network And Internet | Network And Sharing Center.

2. Choose Printer Sharing, click the arrow button to expand the section, and click Turn On Printer Sharing. Next, click Apply. Your printer is now available for sharing on the network. If you are prompted for an administrator password or confirmation, type the password or provide confirmation.

3. Select Turn Off Printer Sharing to discontinue sharing the printer.

Printing to a Network Printer from Another Computer

When Windows detects a shared printer on another computer on the LAN, it tries to install the printer's driver automatically. When you print from an application, check the list of available printers—the list may already include shared printers on other computers. To see the list of printers you can use, choose Start | Control Panel | Hardware And Sound | Printers to display the Printers folder. The icon for a shared printer has a cable beneath it.

If the printer doesn't appear on the list, you need to install a driver for the printer. Here's how:

1. Open the Printers window.

2. Click Add A Printer. You see the Add Printer Wizard. The wizard asks the following:

   - **Whether you're installing a local or network printer**   You're installing a network printer.

   - **The network path for the printer**   Unless you can type the path for the printer from memory, use the Browse button to find it. To find the printer, first find the computer to which it is attached by expanding the My Network Places hierarchy; click My Network Places, then Entire Network, then the computer to which the printer is attached, and then the name of the printer.

   - **Which driver to install**   If you already have a driver installed for this type of printer, the wizard asks whether you want to keep the existing driver or install a new one (one of these options will be recommended). If you don't have a driver installed, the wizard prompts you to install one—you'll probably need your Windows Vista CD-ROM or a printer driver from another source (many can be found at the printer manufacturers' web sites).

   - **What name you want to call the printer**   This should be a name that enables you to identify the printer. If you have three DeskJets on your network, you probably don't want to call it just "DeskJet"—instead, you might want to call it "Cindy's DeskJet" since it's attached to Cindy's machine. That way, when you print to this printer, you'll know where to go to pick up your printout.

- **Whether you want this printer to be your default printer**   If you want to print automatically to this printer every time you print, then the answer is Yes. If you usually want to print to another printer, choose No.

You can print to the shared printer from this computer any time you want. If you defined the shared printer as your default printer, then anything you print automatically goes to that printer. If you didn't define the network printer as the default printer, then you have to choose it from the list of defined printers before you print. This is usually done in the Print dialog box of the application you are using.

If the network printer is unavailable, any print jobs will be held on your computer until the printer is again available.

TIP   A quick way to connect to a network printer is by using the Run dialog box. Choose Start | Run and type the UNC path of the printer. For example, if the printer is called DeskJet900 and it's attached to a computer called Inspiron8000, type \\Inspiron8000\DeskJet900 as the UNC path. When you click OK, your computer connects to the printer.

If you need to print to a network computer from DOS programs, you can type the NET USE command in a Command Prompt window. At the command prompt, type:

```
net use lp2 \\computername\printername
```

This command maps the LP2 (second parallel printer) port to the printer you specify.

Connecting Your LAN to the Internet

Connecting PCs to the Internet via a broadband Internet connection has driven the emergence of LANs in home offices and small business. By connecting the LAN to the Internet, all the PCs on the LAN can share one Internet connection. Large companies have connected their internal networks to the Internet for years, and small offices and home LANs can do the same. A home office network is also useful for connecting to your employer's VPN and web-based mail applications like Outlook Web Access.

For the PCs on a LAN to use the Internet, you must configure each PC to communicate using TCP/IP, the Internet's communication protocol (see "IP Addressing" in Chapter 30). Then a program or device must route the TCP/IP information between the LAN and the Internet; you can use a dedicated device (a router) or a gateway program running on a PC.

Even if you are only connecting one PC in your home office to a broadband modem, a complete Internet security solution to protect your PC from Internet attacks includes a hardware router along with a software firewall, antivirus software, and antispyware software.

NOTE *Virtual private networking is a system that lets your organization extend a private LAN over the Internet. Windows comes with a virtual private networking program that enables your computer to connect to a VPN (see Chapter 27).*

Methods of Connecting a LAN to the Internet

Communication on the Internet uses the TCP/IP protocol; messages are addressed to other computers using numeric IP (Internet Protocol) addresses. To share an Internet connection, the computers on your LAN must be able to communicate with TCP/IP. The computers can also communicate on the LAN with another protocol (for example, a LAN might use NetBEUI for file and printer sharing on the LAN and TCP/IP for Internet Connection Sharing).

The device or program that connects your LAN to the Internet acts as a *gateway*, passing messages between the computers on the LAN and computers on the Internet, and possibly controlling what types of information can pass.

What Does a Gateway Do?

Your home office router acts as a gateway to manage Internet traffic to and from your PC and can perform the following tasks:

- **Route packets of data between the LAN and the Internet** The most basic function of a gateway is to pass packets of data from computers on your LAN out to the Internet and vice versa.

- **Translate between the IP address on the LAN and the IP addresses on the Internet** Computers on a LAN usually use private, LAN-only IP addresses, assigned by a Dynamic Host Configuration Protocol (DHCP) server on the LAN. Computers on the Internet use publicly visible IP addresses that are usually assigned by your ISP. A gateway accepts packets (messages) from the LAN, replaces the private IP address with its own ISP-supplied IP address, and passes the packet along to the Internet. When a reply returns, the gateway figures out which computer on the LAN the reply is intended for, replaces the gateway's address with that of the real destination, and sends the reply along to the computer that made the request. To the rest of the Internet, all packets from the LAN appear to be from the gateway. This service is called *Network Address Translation (NAT)*. All gateways to networks that use private addresses must perform this task.

- **Address assignment** NAT gateways invariably include a DHCP server to assign private addresses to the other computers on the LAN.

- **Control the types of information that can flow between the Internet and your LAN** The gateway can act as a *firewall* and control what services on internal computers are visible to hosts on the Internet . This adds an important level of security, since outsiders cannot exploit security holes in services that they can't see. Computers on small LANs usually offer no services at all to outside users. A few peer-to-peer applications such as online chat require that the user's computer act as a server to its peers; you'll have to adjust the firewall settings if you use them.

- **Caching** The gateway can store information that has been requested from the Internet so that if a user requests the same information, the gateway can provide it without having to get it from the Internet again.

- **Log usage of the Internet** The gateway can log all packets that pass between the LAN and the Internet so that you have a record of who has access to your LAN from the Internet and what Internet services your LAN users have used.

ICS provides address translation and DHCP, and can optionally use the Windows XP Internet Connection Firewall. Other gateway programs, called *proxy servers*, also provide caching (storing web pages and other information for reuse) and logging (so you can track what people are using the Internet for).

Devices That Can Act as Gateways

Two kinds of devices are commonly used as gateways, connecting LANs to the Internet:

- **Routers**   Routers are hardware devices that connect your small office/home office (SOHO) LAN to the Internet via a digital subscriber line (DSL), cable broadband modem, or Verizon FiOS (http://www22.verizon.com/content/ConsumerFiOS/). NAT, DHCP, and firewall software is built into some routers, which also include phone jacks for VoIP (Voice over IP) telephones. All you have to do is cable the router to your LAN, connect your modem, plug it into power, and your LAN is on the Internet. Routers are the simplest and most effective way to connect your LAN to the Internet. You connect your Internet connection (DSL, cable, or FiOS) to the router and run a LAN cable from the router to the LAN's hub or switch.

- **UNIX or Linux systems**   Because the Internet was built on UNIX systems, lots of excellent TCP/IP communication software comes with most UNIX and Linux systems. Some commercial-grade routers like those routing your ISP's network traffic are actually computers running UNIX or Linux.

NOTE *Just because your home router has a built-in firewall doesn't mean you can get away with not using a software firewall. The router's firewall is just part of your overall security solution.*

Choosing Your SOHO Router

Several vendors, such as Linksys and D-Link, sell dedicated routers for the SOHO market. These physically resemble network hubs, with one Ethernet jack for the connection to the outside world (cable modem or DSL) in addition to the Ethernet jacks for the computers on your LAN.

Walk into the home networking section of your local computer store or big box electronics store and it's hard not to trip over a plethora of wired and Wi-Fi routers designed for the SOHO market.

If you are purchasing a router for the first time, it's best to do some research up front and walk into the store with some general requirements you are seeking in a router. Some general requirements to consider:

- How many PCs are you planning to put on the network?
- Are you planning to put your employer's Wi-Fi-enabled laptop on the network?
- Do you have a Wi-Fi-enabled DVR like a Tivo or Windows Media Center PC that needs access to your network?

Wired vs. Wi-Fi Routers

We recommend a hardware router even if you are only connecting one PC to a broadband Internet connection for a complete Internet security solution. Wired routers are less expensive but lack the flexibility, and it's safe to say that these routers may get left by the wayside as consumers and small to medium-sized businesses pour their money into the latest Wi-Fi router technology.

To reach the broadest audience, we are focusing on Wi-Fi routers in the following sections because they offer users the most expandability options. However, many of the points about router configuration remain the same if for some reason you choose a wired router.

Choosing the Right Wi-Fi Router

Networking your SOHO via Wi-Fi can be a productivity boost because you have freedom to roam around your office. Also, going Wi-Fi means you can skip the intricacies of running network cable throughout your house.

Here are some considerations for choosing the right router:

- Shoot for the latest wireless standard support in your router of choice. While at the time of press, 802.11g is the popular Wi-Fi standard, is supported by the major Wi-Fi router vendors, and even entry-level laptop PCs include 802.11g Wi-Fi cards, the standards are always evolving. Staying on or a little bit ahead of the wireless standards curve offers you speed and flexibility in the future as you swap desktop PCs and laptops in and out of your network. Wi-Fi speed is always a good thing!

- Look for routers that include autoconfiguration software because nobody is expected to be a network engineer. Such router configuration software is wizard-driven and requires basic information to configure your router, such as your PC name and home network name.

- Check out the router vendor technical support sites to gauge their level of help content. While these router vendors do offer telephone technical support, viewing the web sites will help you to build your body of home-networking knowledge and help alleviate some of the frustration navigating the telephone support phone tree and divining exactly what the support rep is reading from the script on their PC. While home networking has become an easier proposition than years ago, a little bit of networking knowledge is power.

- While many Wi-Fi routers come with four network ports, consider expandability options for the future. Is VoIP, such as SunRocket or Vonage, in your future? How about additional network storage? These plans can dictate how many PCs you wire into your Wi-Fi router and how many PCs you equip with Wi-Fi network cards.

Broadband ISPs and Home Networking

As home networking has grown more popular for SOHOs, broadband ISPs have gotten into the act by bolstering their support for SOHO routers through help content and even fee-based add-on services where the ISP will send a technician to your office or home to set up your router and home network for you.

Many major cable broadband providers like Cox Communications, Comcast, and Time Warner Cable offer home networking as an add-on service for their customers.

While going through your broadband ISP to get your SOHO network installed and running may be attractive to some, you do have to weigh the pros and cons of letting your ISP inside your home network. The plus side is outsourcing networking issues that you may not want to trouble yourself with. The minus side is allowing a stranger access to your personal and business data.

These same router vendors also offer hubs for plugging into your router if you have more PCs and peripherals, like networked-attached storage (NAS) devices and print servers, than you do router ports.

Managing Your SOHO Router

You don't have to be a certified network engineer to manage your SOHO router, but these routers still require proper care and feeding. Router vendors like Linksys and D-Link have synthesized all the necessary management tools you need in one easy-to-use web interface. For the most part, they're self-configuring, but you can control them through your browser if you need to adjust security settings or other router features. The router's built-in software provides many of the same features as corporate-level routers, including NAT, DHCP, firewall, and even PPP over Ethernet (PPPoE) if your DSL line requires it.

NOTE *Some of the new fiber-optic Internet offerings like Verizon FiOS require a specially configured and tuned router available only from the ISP.*

Setting Up and Managing Your Wi-Fi Network Router

Even if you have no intention of being a "road warrior," a Wi-Fi router is an ideal router choice for SOHOs because it offers you the best possible future-growth opportunities—and if you can get out of your home office with your laptop to sit out on your porch on a nice day, why not take advantage of the technology that enables you to do so and still connect to the Internet? In fact, in many stores the Wi-Fi routers handily outnumber the wired routers.

The following sections provide general guidance on setting up and maintaining your Wi-Fi network router.

Connecting Your Router to Your PC(s)

The first step to connecting your Wi-Fi router is to power it up, so it's smart to place your router near a power outlet. Plug the router's power supply into the nearest power outlet and turn on the router. Once your router is powered up, you should be able to find your new Wi-Fi router via the Windows Vista Network Center.

Configuring Your Router

While many SOHO routers include an automated setup CD that does the decision making and other heavy lifting during your router's configuration, it's always good to understand the basics of SOHO router configuration since routers serve as the first line of defense against Internet attacks.

Prior to configuring your router, visit your router vendor's support web site to see if any Windows Vista updates exist for the router's software or firmware. Threats on the Internet change rapidly and, again, your router is the first line of defense for your PC and its data against attackers.

Your router's management console has its own IP address accessible via your web browser. Most mass-market Wi-Fi routers like those from Linksys and D-Link use http://192.168.1.1/ or http://192.168.0.1/. Your router documentation will include the proper IP address for your Wi-Fi router's management console.

The following settings changes are at a general level; depending on your Wi-Fi router brand, the terminology may be different and organized differently on the user interface. After you access your Wi-Fi router's management console, you should change the following default settings:

1. Change the wireless SSID name from the manufacturer's default name to a name of your own choosing. Be sure to not use any obvious identifying information, like your last name, as the SSID. Also, keeping the vendor's SSID is a sure sign of an easy target for hackers seeking an open Wi-Fi router.

2. You can also adjust your wireless network mode settings to best support the Wi-Fi devices on your network. Most router wireless network mode settings include B-Only, G-Only, or Mixed. If you have all 802.11g devices on your SOHO's Wi-Fi network, then it's safe to go with G-Only. If your SOHO network is going to have users with a mix of Wi-Fi network cards, then stick with Mixed as the setting. Going with Mixed means users still using 802.11b can access the Internet from your network if given the appropriate permissions.

3. Turn on the security encryption. This is not a step to skip or go back to at a later date! Type in a passphrase and click Generate. The Key fields fill in with a passphrase automatically. Write it down on a piece of paper that you'll keep near the router. If your Wi-Fi network is supporting other Wi-Fi-enabled peripherals like the Series II Tivo (www.tivo.com) then your security encryption settings are limited to the lowest level of security settings supported by that device. As Wi-Fi routers mature (and, depending on the router model, their level of security), encryption could include Wireless Encryption Protocol (WEP, offering a 40-, 64-, or 128-bit security) or Wi-Fi Protected Access (WPA). Be prepared to consult your router's help documentation to delve deeper into specific security settings.

4. Once you complete configuring your Wi-Fi router, unplug the cable from your computer to the router. Next, plug it back into the router. Choose the name you chose for your access point from the Windows Vista Network Center. You should be prompted for a password. Enter the password, and you should be online and seeing the Internet.

Securing Your Router

There are two opposing camps when it comes to securing your Wi-Fi router. There is a vocal minority that believes in open Wi-Fi access points for everyone (even if open Wi-Fi access points violate their broadband ISPs' terms of service). While this may sound like the socially conscious thing to do, let's look at the risks for not securing your Wi-Fi router:

- An open Wi-Fi access point is an invitation to hackers and leaves your network and its data vulnerable to attack.

- Although Wi-Fi law is still largely up for varied interpretations, some legal critics and pundits foresee a future where people running open Wi-Fi access points could conceivably be held accountable for activities carried out on their networks even by unauthorized users. Network security experts have long known that open Wi-Fi access points can be accessed maliciously and used to cover a user's online tracks.

In fact, in the post-9/11 world some legal critics have gone as far to ponder the potential of open Wi-Fi access points aiding and abetting terrorists' communications.

Real-World Wi-Fi Security

Wi-Fi security is becoming a hot topic of debate because of the rising numbers of mobile workers in corporate America today. While Wi-Fi usage can open up the home network, it can also open up corporate networks to potential attack.

The rise of Wi-Fi access both on corporate networks and on the public Internet means that Wi-Fi users have additional reasons to be conscious about security—both their own data and the data of their employer may be open to attack.

Mobile computing and Wi-Fi have impacted corporate networking, especially network remote access, so much that some early adopters are moving to an "inverted network" model where every Wi-Fi-enabled computer is viewed as a "guest" and thus requires authentication at the application level. The traditional model has been the inside/outside the firewall model, which corporations have followed since they took their businesses online.

If your employer issues you a Wi-Fi-enabled laptop, you may find yourself having to attend security training, especially if you are a mobile worker accessing corporate resources from your home Wi-Fi network, a coffee shop Wi-Fi hotspot, or your hotel room after a long day on a client site. Common sense should rule your approach to Wi-Fi security. Here are some tips:

- Never log onto a Wi-Fi hotspot blindly. Look for Wi-Fi hotspot documentation, including login and fee information.

- Run a personal firewall and updated antivirus software on your laptop at all times.

Chapter 34, which is about security, delves into what you need to protect your PC from attack. You shouldn't venture online with a Wi-Fi-enabled PC unless it is equipped with a software firewall, antivirus software, and antispyware.

Network, Internet, and Web Security

Communication security ensures that the data you transmit and receive through the Internet or an intranet is sent to and received from the actual systems with which you intend to communicate, as opposed to another system impersonating the desired system. Communication security also ensures that messages are sent and received without being intercepted or spied upon.

This chapter discusses viruses and how to avoid catching them, how to control what Internet Explorer downloads when you browse the Web, browsing secure web sites, and how to send and receive secure e-mail messages. Windows Vista includes an Internet Connection Firewall that you can turn on to protect your computer from malicious intruders (see Chapter 22).

NOTE *User accounts and passwords for multiple people using the same computer are described in Chapter 6. Security settings for people sharing files over a LAN are described in Chapter 30.*

For more information about Windows security, see the Microsoft Security web site at www.microsoft.com/security and the Microsoft TechNet Security Center web site at www .microsoft.com/technet/security. Another valuable Windows Vista security web site is www.microsoft.com/technet/windowsvista/security/ and the Windows Vista Security Team blog at http://blogs.msdn.com/windowsvistasecurity/.

Protecting Your System from Viruses and Worms

A *virus* is a self-reproducing malicious program that can infect files on one computer but needs help in order to find other systems to infect (like filesharing programs). A *worm* is a self-reproducing program that can send itself to other systems (e-mail viruses are actually worms). Some viruses and worms are just annoying, taking up space on your system or displaying an annoying message, but many others are destructive, deleting or altering files or clogging up Internet e-mail systems with thousands of unwanted messages. The upcoming sidebar "How Viruses Spread" contains more information.

The Microsoft Baseline Security Advisor

Microsoft has written a program that can check your computer for incorrect security settings. Go to www.microsoft.com/technet/security/tools/mpsa.mspx to download the Microsoft Baseline Security Advisor (MBSA). Or go to Microsoft's support site at http://support.microsoft.com and search for article Q320454. The program is small—about 2.5 MB. It can scan the computer on which it is running or other computers on a LAN or the Internet. It displays a security report like this:

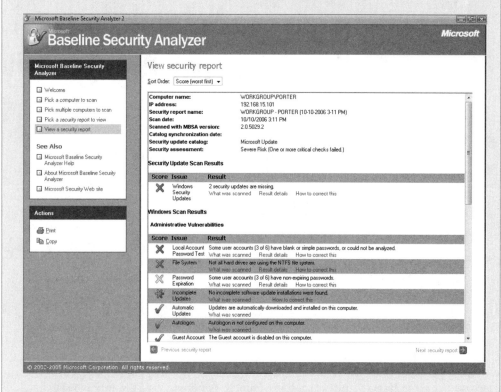

The report includes security information about user accounts, file systems, Windows updates, Internet Explorer settings, and other configuration options.

Many SOHO PC users have their own *secret sauce* for protecting their PCs from viruses and worms. Said sauce typically includes Microsoft Windows Vista security features bolstered by third-party antivirus, firewall, and antispyware solutions.

Types of Virus Files

Viruses and worms can be stored in several types of files:

- **EXE, COM, BAT, MSI, MSO, and PIF program files, scraps, or shortcuts**   These viruses and worms run when they are opened (clicked or double-clicked in Explorer or Windows Mail, for example). If Windows is configured not to show file extensions, you may not be able to tell easily which files have these extensions. Tell Windows to display filename extensions by choosing Start | Control Panel. From the Control Panel, type **Folder** in the Search field to bring up the Folder Options icon. Click Folder Options to open the Folder Options dialog box. Click the View tab, and clear the Hide Extensions For Known File Types check box.

- **DOC (Word document), XLS (Excel spreadsheet), and MDB (Access database) files** These files may contain viruses and worms written in Microsoft Word, Excel, or Access macro languages. The macros (customized automation instructions) usually run when you open the file. Because Word and Excel are the most popular programs that run macros, Word documents and Excel spreadsheets are the most common macro virus carriers.

- **VBS (VBScript) files** These viruses and worms are written in Visual Basic and run when you click or double-click them. Visual Basic is a programming language used, among other things, to write macros for the Office suite of applications, including Outlook 2002.

For a more complete list of file types that might contain viruses, see article OL2000, "Information about the Outlook E-mail Security Update," in Microsoft's Knowledge Base: go to http://support.microsoft.com and search for the article number.

CAUTION Scraps, a Windows file type created by cut-and-paste operations, can contain executable files (including viruses and worms) that appear to be other types of (harmless) files. An article on this issue, "Scrap Files Can Tear You Up," is at http://pc-help.org/security/scrap.htm.

Preventing Infection by Viruses

The best prevention for viruses is to avoid getting infected in the first place (practice safe computing). If you do get infected, tools are available to clean your system.

How Viruses Spread

The commonly cited psychological reasons for individuals to open suspicious e-mails are fear, greed, and sex. The notorious Melissa worm by David Smith was started simply by being posted to the alt.sex newsgroup. Smith asked that the file not be circulated, so of course it was. That single posting to a newsgroup was the only action that Smith performed to spread his worm throughout the world, causing millions of dollars in damages and, in some cases, days of mail server downtime for some major companies.

So, the moral of the story is: If you receive a message from someone you don't know, or from someone you know but didn't expect to receive a file from, approach it with caution. If it has an attachment, just delete it. If you're not sure, let it sit unopened in your inbox for a few days, while you check the antivirus and e-mail hoax web sites. A one-day delay in opening an attachment might be enough for you to hear about the danger of the virus.

Avoiding Getting Infected

The generally accepted method of preventing viruses from successfully attacking your computer is the use of antivirus software that detects known viruses before they run and infect your computer. Of course, there is the tried-and-true method of not downloading or opening anything that you cannot verify, validate, or otherwise determine its source.

NOTE *The Internet isn't the only way to catch viruses. If you commonly move files from one place to another using removable media (for example, USB thumb drives, DVDs, or CD-ROMs), then you need to be careful. The data on a disk, whether it be from school, office, or library, likely came from the Internet. This simple fact makes it possible for the disk to contain a virus. Office networks are typically more secure, because your LAN administrator is running a firewall, intrusion-detection software, and antivirus software, but don't take that for granted. School networks are often less secure because of insufficient staffing resources and budgets. Public access points like ones in libraries, copy shops, or cyber cafés are a mixed bag. Your best bet is to be wary of any data coming to your computer from the outside. Even commercial software has been known to be a transmission source for viruses.*

Practicing Safe Computing Online

If you regularly work with others across the Internet and use file attachments regularly to collaborate on projects, then you need to be especially astute about viruses. You should institute a PC security regimen that includes an antivirus program (with autoupdates to download the latest antivirus signatures) and a firewall (software like McAfee Firewall and a hardware firewall on your home office router). Awareness and common sense are also integral to a security regimen. Here are some tips to help you stay aware:

- Never open a file attachment from an unknown sender.

- If one of your usual e-mail correspondents deviates from their usual e-mail communications style and the message includes a file attachment, call the person to verify they are sending you a file attachment. A number of e-mail viruses work by infecting one user, then culling their Outlook or Windows Mail address book to propagate the virus to other PCs.

- Do not download files from sources you are not familiar with. Stick to known, reputable web-based software libraries like CNET's Download.com (www .download.com), Tucows (www.tucows.com), and WinPlanet (cws.internet.com), and the web sites of well-known hardware and software manufacturers. Many pornography sites require you to download a viewer program: think twice, since these programs have been known to contain dangerous viruses.

- Do not accept any file that is offered unsolicited. If you receive an e-mail notifying you that you have won a contest and you can click a URL in the message to download your prize, think again. Did you sign up for a contest? Legitimate sources invariably draw from an existing customer base and rely on word of mouth and advertising campaigns to get new customers, not random free give-aways.

- Use a software firewall in conjunction with your SOHO network router's hardware firewall to protect your PCs and SOHO network.

- Back up your PCs on a regular basis to an external backup drive or an online backup service like Xdrive (www.xdrive.com), backup.com (www.backup.com), IBackup (www.ibackup.com), or EVault (www.evault.com).

- Secure your instant messaging (IM) client by staying on top of client software updates. Additionally, you may want to consider third-party IM security software like ZoneAlarm IMsecure or IMsecure Pro (www.zonelabs.com). Small to medium-sized businesses (SMBs) should look to enterprise IM solutions like AIM Pro (http://aimpro.premiumservices.aol.com/) or Microsoft Office Communicator (www.microsoft.com/office/communicator/prodinfo/overview.mspx).

Using Antivirus Programs

A strong antivirus program is a *must* in today's Internet-connected computing world. An antivirus program can't prevent infection if it's not running. Buying and installing an antivirus application is a small price to pay compared to losing all of your work for a week, all of your carefully collected bookmarks, the hours that you spent making all of your CDs into MP3 files, your priceless photos of your first time abroad—whatever your most treasured files include. Here are some of the most popular and effective antivirus programs:

- **Symantec Norton AntiVirus, at www.symantec.com/home_homeoffice/ products/**   Norton AntiVirus is a complete antivirus solution. You can go with the simple Norton AntiVirus, or pop for the complete Norton Internet Security suite of security applications—a particularly good deal that includes a personal firewall that is well suited to protecting broadband (cable, DSL, and Verizon FiOS) users.

- **McAfee VirusScan, at www.mcafee.com**   McAfee has migrated many of its security programs into software as service (subscription-based) offerings. McAfee's online security offerings are updated daily (or even more often) with the latest virus signatures, making them a proactive tool to protect your PC from the latest virus du jour.

- **Windows Live OneCare, at www.windowsonecare.com**   Microsoft's subscription-based entry into antivirus and online security is part of its Windows Live strategy and is a complete online security tool that includes antivirus, antispyware, firewall, performance tune-ups, and automatic backups.

When deciding on an antivirus program, look to subscription-based services like Microsoft Windows Live OneCare or McAfee VirusScan (and keep the subscription up to date!) because the automated download tools (once installed and configured) pay attention to the latest antivirus updates, meaning you don't have to worry.

Once you have an antivirus program installed, configured, and running, the antivirus program scans all incoming files (via e-mail and web downloads) for viruses. For example, the antivirus program might display a dialog box while you are retrieving your e-mail, reporting that a message contains a worm and offering to delete it for you. Some antivirus programs also scan your hard disk regularly to look for viruses that might have sneaked through. If the program sees a virus, it displays a message telling you what to do.

Knowing When You're Infected

You may find out that your system is infected when you see a strange message telling you that you're a victim. Some other ways of telling are as follows (although all but the last can be signs of other Windows problems):

- Your system slows down (especially programs loading)
- Files disappear
- Programs crash unexpectedly

Dealing with an Infected Windows System

If you have already been infected with a virus, follow these steps:

1. If an unfamiliar dialog box, error message, or something else unfamiliar appears, make a note of the message or other symptom. Unplug the modem or network cable, and then shut down the computer. Continuing to use an infected computer is a bad idea for several reasons. Depending on what type of virus or worm you have, additional damage can be done. With the speed of today's systems, a virus or worm can delete or write over gigabytes of data in a matter of minutes.

2. Do not try to repair or otherwise contain the damage or effects of a virus or worm using software that was not specifically designed to do so. In other words, don't run Norton Speed Disk to try and solve the problem.

3. Do not install antivirus software *after* you discover a virus or worm. Unless you are sure that the virus is nondestructive, leave the computer turned off until you find out how to get rid of the specific virus that your system has contracted.

4. Locate a computer that is not infected. Go to a virus resource web site and find out how to fix it. Try the web site of one of the most popular antivirus programs (listed in a previous section) or one of the virus information sites listed in the next section. Look for step-by-step instructions for removing the virus. Companies like Symantec and McAfee often develop scripts that aid in the removal of recently discovered viruses and publish the details about what that virus has done or can do, so that they can be safely removed.

5. Once you know which virus you have, follow the steps to disinfect your system (that is, remove the virus). If the virus has deleted or overwritten files, it might not be possible to get the files back, but you can at least prevent further damage to your system and infection of other systems.

6. If you can't identify the virus or find a procedure for getting rid of it, call technical support for your computer (or your office's technical support person). Explain to them what happened and that you would like some assistance in removing the virus, or at least in taking steps to minimize the damage. You may have to pay a fee for this service if you go through your computer's manufacturer.

7. Once you are sure that the virus is gone, buy and install an antivirus program. Don't make the same mistake twice!

Another approach is to back up all your data files (but none of your programs), reformat your hard disk, reinstall Windows and your applications, restore your data files, and buy and install an antivirus program to prevent reinfection. However, leaving your computer running while you make the backups can give the virus time to delete more files.

Tip *After you have cleaned up a virus, back up, reformat, and reinstall your system. Many viruses and the resulting repairs leave your system unstable, and parts of virus files may still be lying around.*

If you make regular backups, check the backups that you made within at least 72 hours of discovering the infection (see Chapter 9). Your system may have been infected for days (or longer) before you realized it.

Protecting Your System with Windows Firewall

Windows Internet security had long been the domain of third-party security companies like McAfee and Symantec until the launch of Windows XP Service Pack 2, in which Microsoft added Security Center to the Windows Control Panel. That's when pundits and even critics began to see Microsoft as a potential contender in the PC security realm.

The introduction of the Security Center in Windows XP SP2 meant that Microsoft Windows finally had a native security monitoring tool that governed the Internet firewall, software/operating system updates and patches, and virus protection.

The Security Center eventually seeded the launch of Windows Live OneCare (www .windowsonecare.com/), a full security suite that includes firewall, antivirus, and automated backup software.

What Is Windows Firewall?

Windows Vista includes Windows Firewall (see Figure 33-1) to help protect your PC (including your data and personal information) from malicious online threats, including hackers, viruses, and worms that try to reach your computer while you are online. Windows Firewall checks information incoming from the Internet to your PC and either blocks the information or accepts it depending on your security settings.

Cutting past Microsoft marketing, Windows Firewall should be seen as a lower-end security firewall solution. It's fine for when you are just getting your PC set up with the latest Microsoft Windows security patches and service packs. However, be security conscious and shop for a firewall from one of the major security vendors like McAfee (www.mcafee.com), Symantec (www.symantec.com), or Zone Labs (www.zonelabs.com).

The next few sections show you how to set up Windows Firewall to protect your PC. This is also a good primer to demonstrate the typical steps you need to take to set up a software firewall.

Enabling/Disabling Windows Firewall

You can enable and disable Windows Firewall from the Windows Control Panel, depending on the group policies that are set on your PC. Perform the following steps to enable Windows Firewall:

1. Click Start | Control Panel to open the Windows Control Panel.
2. Click Security to open the Security Options windows.
3. Click Turn Windows Firewall On Or Off to open the Windows Firewall dialog box.

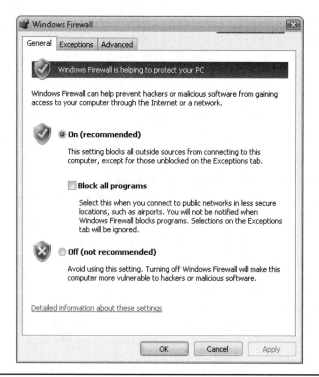

FIGURE 33-1   Windows Vista includes Windows Firewall for protecting your PC from malicious attackers.

4. Click On to turn Windows Firewall on. This is the recommended setting. You also have the option Block All Programs, which effectively seals your PC from any incoming application downloads. Click Off to turn Windows Firewall off.

NOTE   *You should turn Windows Firewall off once you install a third-party firewall on your PC, because running two software firewalls can hamper system performance. You can run a software firewall in conjunction with a hardware firewall (like those included in home network routers) without such issues.*

Setting Inbound and Outbound Rules

If you have appropriate security policies, you can have control over the inbound and outbound rules for Windows Firewall. Think of setting inbound and outbound rules as being "the gatekeeper," because you are blocking and unblocking applications' passage through your firewall to the public Internet. Perform the following steps to set inbound and outbound rules:

1. Click Start | Control Panel to open the Windows Control Panel.

2. Click Security to open the Security Options window.

3. Click Allow A Program Through Windows Firewall to open the Exceptions tab in the Windows Firewall dialog box.

4. To unblock a program or service, select it in the Program Or Service drop-down list.

5. Click OK to confirm the change.

Other inbound and outbound management options include adding programs and ports. Click Add Program to open the Add A Program dialog box, in which you can add programs to your Windows Firewall rules. If the program you want to add doesn't appear in the Programs list, you can click Browse to browse to the program's executable file on your local hard drive.

Click Add A Port to open a new firewall port in Windows Firewall. Adding a new port to your firewall doesn't require a network engineer. However, in absence of said network engineer, you should always consult the program's documentation to find the port number and protocol you need to open on Windows Firewall in order for the program to be able to access the Internet.

Protecting Your System with Windows Defender

Windows Defender is another new Microsoft online security tool that launched with Windows Live OneCare and was later included in Microsoft Windows Vista.

What Is Windows Defender?

Windows Defender (see Figure 33-2) enables you to apply another level of security over your Windows Vista PC. It guards your PC from spyware and other malicious software that can install itself on your PC without your knowledge or express consent.

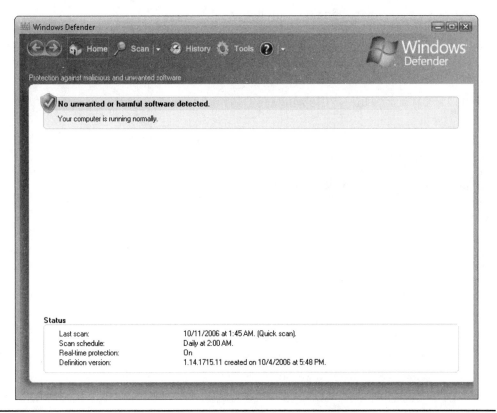

FIGURE 33-2   Windows Defender is your first line of defense against spyware.

Spyware protection via Windows Defender offers real-time protection when spyware or other unwanted software attempts to install itself on your PC. It also alerts you whenever an application attempts to alter important Windows settings.

Windows Defender also ties into the Microsoft SpyNet community, an online resource for tracking how Windows Defender users respond to software that has yet to be classified as spyware, malware, or other sort of risk.

Spyware scanning can be run automatically by Windows Defender, acting as a first line of defense against spyware and other malicious files that might be installed on your PC without your consent or knowledge.

Windows Defender runs two types of scans:

- Quick scan, which scans just the important Windows system components
- Full system scan, which scans your entire hard drive

Opening Windows Defender

Windows Defender is available from the Control Panel. First, you need to open Windows Defender:

1. Click Start | Control Panel to open the Control Panel.
2. Click Security | Windows Defender to open Windows Defender.

Keeping Windows Defender Definitions Up to Date

It's imperative that you keep Windows Defender up to date to stave off the latest spyware and malware floating around the Internet. Windows Defender includes automatic scanning as one of its settings. When setting up Windows Vista for the first time, you should perform the following setup to keep your Windows Defender definitions up to date:

1. Click Tools | Settings. The Windows Defender Tools And Options dialog box appears.
2. Click Options, and then select Check For Updated Definitions Before Scanning.
3. Click Save to save the new settings.

Turning On Windows Defender Real-Time Protection

Automating security like antispyware and antivirus protection is one of the keys to defending your PC and home network from attacks.

Real-time protection against spyware and malware is a boon to home and SOHO PC users because it means you can focus on your work at hand and not have to obsess over the security of your PC. However, it's always good to review the settings and status of your security software (like Windows Defender) on a regular basis, especially as the service packs and patches for Windows Vista multiply during the first year after the product's launch.

To set your Windows Defender scanning settings:

1. Click Tools | Options. The Options dialog box appears.
2. Choose Automatically Scan My Computer.
3. Choose your scan frequency from the Scan Frequency drop-down list. Daily is the default selection. You can also choose to scan your PC on a particular day of the week.

4. Choose the time of day you want the scan to run. The default time for Windows Defender is 2:00 A.M.

5. Choose the type of scan you want to run from the Type of scan list. By default it's set to Quick Scan, but you can also select Full System Scan.

6. Click Save once you have finished configuring your Windows Defender scan settings.

TIP *Full System Scan can be time consuming and thus you may want to run full system scans after you suspect your PC has been attacked, late at night when you are sleeping, or as part of your normal PC maintenance regimen.*

Sources of Antivirus Information

Here is a quick list of applications and sites that you should investigate long before you need them:

- **Antivirus Software, at http://antivirus.about.com**   This About.com site is a clearinghouse about the latest antivirus software and virus news.

- **Download Squad, at www.downloadsquad.com/category/security/**   This popular web log covering all things software includes antivirus and security coverage.

- **Doug Muth's Anti-Virus Help Page, at www.claws-and-paws.com/virus**   A fantastically deep collection of information regarding computer viruses with lots of helpful papers, reports, and links to additional resources. One thing that makes this site great is that it's not tied to any commercial concern.

- **Symantec Security Response at www.symantec.com/security_response/index. jsp**   Symantec Security Response is a launching point to Symantec security solutions for consumer and corporate customers.

- **McAfee Avert Labs Threat Library, at http://vil.nai.com/vil**   This encyclopedic listing of viruses is one of the first places you should look to get help or find out what's going on.

Managing Which Files Internet Explorer Downloads

Internet Explorer can retrieve a wide variety of files and objects, ranging from innocuous plain text files and images to potentially destructive executable programs. Many entertainment and business web sites take advantage of interactive technologies like Adobe Flash, Java, JavaScript, and ActiveX. While these programs are useful, they also create security issues. If web sites can put useful programs on your computer and run them without informing you, precautions must be taken to make sure that they can't also put harmful programs on your computer. Internet Explorer takes certain precautions automatically, and gives you the option to choose additional precautions.

Internet Explorer's downloaded-object security allows you to decide, based on both the web site where an object came from and the type of object, whether to retrieve an object and, once it's retrieved, what to do with it. Internet Explorer defines three levels of object access (low, medium, and high) to give varying amounts of access to your computer. You can also define custom access permissions, if the three standard settings don't meet your needs.

Java, JavaScript, VBScript, and ActiveX

Java is a language for developing small applications (called *applets*) that can be downloaded over the Web, so that they can be executed by your computer. *JavaScript* is a language for embedding small programs called *scripts* in web pages. *VBScript*, a language that resembles Microsoft's Visual Basic, can be used to add scripts to pages that are displayed by Internet Explorer. Anything that VBScript can do, JavaScript (which Microsoft calls JScript .NET) can do, too, and vice versa.

ActiveX controls, like Java, are a way to embed executable programs into a web page. Unlike Java and JavaScript, ActiveX is a Microsoft system that is not used by Mozilla Firefox except in some work done by the Mozilla ActiveX Project (www.iol.ie/~locka/mozilla/mozilla.htm). When Internet Explorer encounters a web page that uses ActiveX controls, it checks to see whether that particular control is already installed; if it is not, Internet Explorer installs the control on your machine.

CAUTION *ActiveX controls are considerably more dangerous than JavaScript or VBScript scripts or Java applets. Java applets and JavaScript scripts are run in a "sandbox" inside your browser, which limits the accidental or deliberate damage they can do; and VBScript scripts are run by an interpreter, which should limit the types of damage they can do. However, ActiveX controls are programs with full access to your computer's resources.*

Internet Explorer's Zones

Internet Explorer's security policy is based on trust, and the decisions that you make involve who to trust and who not to trust. For example, when a web page wants to run an ActiveX control on your machine, Internet Explorer verifies who wrote the control (Microsoft, for example) and that it hasn't been tampered with. It doesn't consider what the control intends to do or what privileges it requests on your system (rewriting files, for example). Instead, it asks you whether you trust its author.

To determine who to trust, Internet Explorer divides the world into four *zones*:

- **Internet**   Includes all sites that are not in one of the other three zones. Objects from this zone generally are given the medium level of access to your computer.

- **Local Intranet**   Contains computers on your local network. They're usually considered fairly trustworthy, and objects are given a medium level of access to your computer.

- **Trusted Sites**   Includes the sites that you or Microsoft have listed as trustworthy. Objects from this zone generally are given the highest level of access to your computer.

- **Restricted Sites**   Includes the sites that you have listed as untrustworthy. Objects from this zone are given the lowest level of access to your computer. Don't change the access level of this zone to grant higher access.

Downloaded ActiveX controls and other executable objects can and should be signed by their authors, using a certificate scheme similar to that used for validating remote servers.

For each of the four zones into which a web page can fall, you can set the security to high, medium, medium-low, or low. For each zone, you can set exactly which remote operations you're willing to perform. To prevent downloading and running software that might infect your system with a virus, see the section "Preventing Infection by Viruses" earlier in this chapter.

Controlling Your Download Security

The rules governing scripts and applets are set zone by zone on the Security tab of the Internet Options dialog box. To examine or change these settings:

1. Open the Internet Options dialog box by selecting Tools | Internet Options from the Internet Explorer menu bar.

2. Click the Security tab of the Internet Options dialog box (as shown in Figure 33-3).

3. Select the security zone you want to examine or change. The rest of the information on the Security tab changes to show the settings for that zone.

4. If you want to change the general security setting of the zone without specifying how to handle specific web page elements, move the slider on the Security tab of the Internet Options dialog box. (The slider doesn't appear if the zone has been given custom settings. To reset such a zone to one of the standard settings, click the Default Level button. When the slider reappears, you can move it to the desired setting.)

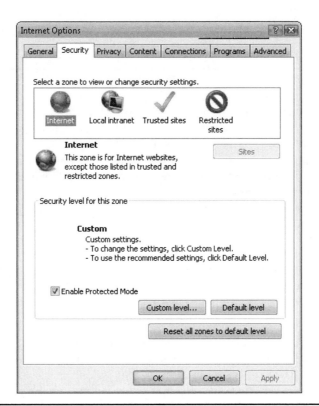

FIGURE 33-3   Security tab of the Internet Options dialog box.

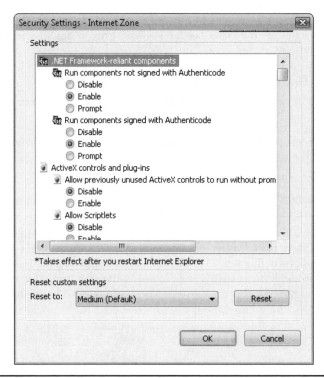

Figure 33-4   Enabling and disabling web page elements for a security zone.

5. If you want to specify how to handle specific web page elements, click the Custom Level button to display the Security Settings dialog box, shown in Figure 33-4. Scroll through the settings until you see the item you want to change. Change an item by selecting or deselecting its check box or by selecting a different radio button from the current selection.

6. Click OK to close each open dialog box. Click Yes in the confirmation box that asks if you want to change the security settings.

Controlling Which Web Sites Are in the Local Intranet Zone

The Local Intranet zone normally contains sites on your own LAN and is set up that way by your network administrator when he or she sets up the network. When you click the Sites button on the Security tab, Windows displays the Local Intranet dialog box, with these three check boxes:

- **Include All Local (Intranet) Sites Not Listed In Other Zones**   Select this check box to include all other sites on the same LAN in the Local Intranet zone. This check box is usually checked.

- **Include All Sites That Bypass The Proxy Server**   Many organizations have a *proxy server* that mediates access to sites outside the organization. Select this check box to include sites outside your organization to which your organization lets you connect directly in the Local Intranet zone. You can see a list of the sites that bypass the proxy server by displaying the Internet Properties or Internet Options dialog box, clicking the Connections tab, and clicking the Advanced button.

- **Include All Network Paths (UNCs)**   Select this check box to include all the sites with UNC (Universal Naming Convention) addresses, which apply only to computers on your LAN.

You can also click the Advanced button to add sites individually, as you can for the Trusted Sites and Restricted Sites zones. See Chapter 31 for more information on how networks connect to the Internet.

Controlling Which Web Sites Are in the Trusted Sites and Restricted Sites Zones

The Trusted Sites and Restricted Sites zones start with no web sites listed; you must specify the web sites to include in these zones. To specify sites, select the zone to which you want to add sites and click Sites on the Security tab of the Internet Options dialog box. You see the Trusted Sites or the Restricted Sites dialog box, the first of which is shown in Figure 33-5. To add a new site, type its full address, starting with **http://** or **https://**, into the Add This Website To The Zone box and click Add. The web site appears in the Websites list. To remove a site, select it in the Websites list and click Remove. You can require a verified secure connection to all sites in this zone by clicking the Require Server Verification (https:) For All Sites In This Zone check box at the bottom of the dialog box; when selected, this setting prevents you from adding any sites that don't support HTTPS, which is described in "Securing Your Web Communication with Encryption and Certificates" later in this chapter.

FIGURE 33-5   Adding sites to the Trusted Sites zone.

Managing Java and JavaScript

The security settings that affect how Internet Explorer deals with Java and JavaScript programs are in the Microsoft VM and Scripting sections of the Security Settings dialog box. Follow these steps:

1. On the Security tab of the Internet Options dialog box, click the zone for which you want to change or see the settings.

2. Click the Custom Level button to display the Security Settings dialog box. You may change what these applets and scripts are allowed to do on your computer, or even disable Java or JavaScript entirely, by choosing Disable (Internet Explorer does not run this type of program downloaded from this zone), Enable (Internet Explorer does run this type of program downloaded from this zone), or Prompt (ask before running the program).

Managing ActiveX Controls

We have never been big fans of ActiveX controls. They allow web sites to have too much power over your system and are hard to monitor. If you should happen to download and install a rogue ActiveX control by mistake, it could (on its own) download and install lots more rogue ActiveX controls—which would then be permanent parts of your software environment, even when you are offline. None of this would appear the least bit suspicious to any virus-detecting software you might own, because ActiveX controls aren't viruses: they have the same status as applications that you install yourself.

Disabling ActiveX controls is one option, as described in the previous section. However, if you frequent Microsoft web sites like Office.microsoft.com and Windowsupdate .microsoft.com, you will be exposed to numerous temptations to turn them back on. We suggest the following compromise: Disable ActiveX controls everywhere but in the Trusted Sites security zone. (Do this from the Security Settings dialog box, following the steps in the previous section.) When you find a Microsoft web site that offers some wonderful service involving ActiveX controls, move that site into the Trusted Sites security zone.

ActiveX controls are stored in the folder C:\Windows\Downloaded Program Files (if Windows is installed in C:\Windows). If you use Internet Explorer, you should check this file periodically to see what applications Internet Explorer has downloaded. Dispose of an ActiveX control by right-clicking its icon and selecting Remove from the shortcut menu.

Securing Your Web Communication with Encryption and Certificates

Browsers store *certificates*, cryptographic data that can identify your computer to remote computers or vice versa. Certificates are issued by *certificate authorities*, each of which has its own certificate. Internet Explorer comes with about 30 *authority certificates* that you can use to check that the certificates presented to your computer by other sites are, in fact, issued by known certificate authorities. To provide secure communication with a remote web site, Internet Explorer uses Secure Sockets Layer (SSL) to provide a variation of the standard HTTP web protocol, called *HTTPS*. Web servers that use HTTPS are called *secure servers*.

You can also acquire a *personal certificate* to use to identify yourself when Internet Explorer or another browser contacts a web site. The most widely used authorities for personal certificates are VeriSign, at www.verisign.com, and Thawte (which is owned by VeriSign), at www.thawte.com. See RSA Data Security's list of questions and answers at its web site at www.rsasecurity.com/rsalabs/faq for more information about certificates.

New applets usually are digitally signed by their authors; that is, each applet includes certificate information that identifies the applet's author and verifies that the applet wasn't tampered with since the author signed it. Unfortunately, the cost of Microsoft's certification process means that many perfectly safe applets won't be signed and will trigger a warning message when you install them.

Browsing the Web Securely

Internet Explorer handles communication security by using SSL to encrypt messages sent to and from remote servers and by using certificates to verify who the party is at the other end of a connection. For example, you use this type of security when you place a credit card order with a web-based retailer that uses a secure web server. For the most part, SSL works invisibly, with all the security validation happening automatically.

You can tell whether the current page is secure in the following ways:

- Look at the URL for the page in the browser's Address or Location box to see whether the page's address starts with https:// (secure) rather than http:// (insecure).

- Look at the status bar at the bottom of the browser window to see whether a little lock icon appears, indicating that the connection is secure.

Whenever your browser opens an HTTPS connection to a server that supports SSL, the server presents a certificate to your computer. If the certificate is validated by one of the authority certificates known to your browser, and the name on the certificate matches the name of the web site, the browser uses the connection and displays web pages as usual. If either of those checks fails, the browser warns you and gives you the option to continue. You see a Security Alert or similar dialog box when your browser can't validate a remote site's certificate. If you trust the source of the file that you are downloading, you can tell Windows to continue and use the connection despite the warning.

Using Object Certificates when Downloading Files

Whenever Internet Explorer retrieves a web page that uses a hitherto unknown ActiveX control or Java applet, Internet Explorer checks to see whether your download security settings permit you to download it (see "Controlling Your Download Security" earlier in this chapter). If your settings don't permit the download, Internet Explorer warns you and doesn't download the file.

Unless a site is in the Trusted Sites zone (in which case Internet Explorer accepts the applet without question), Internet Explorer checks the certificate with which the program is signed and displays the Security Warning dialog box. You see who the signer is and who verified the signature. If the signer is someone you're inclined to trust, such as a large reputable organization or someone you know personally, click Yes to accept the applet. If you expect always to accept applets from this signer, click the Always Trust Content From *This Signer's Name* check box at the bottom of the dialog box to tell Internet Explorer not to ask about signatures from this signer in the future. (If you check the box and later change your mind, the list of signers you've checked is in the Internet Properties dialog box; click the Content tab and click Publishers to examine and change the list.)

Managing Certificates from Certificate Publishers

If you expect to download many programs (or display web pages that contain applets), you will end up with a collection of certificates with which Internet Explorer can verify the sources of the programs.

In Internet Explorer, choose Tools | Internet Options to see the Internet Options dialog box. Clicking the Content tab and then the Publishers button displays the Certificates dialog box with the Trusted Publishers tab selected. The dialog box lists certificates for software publishers that you have told your browsers to trust. New certificates are added when you download authenticated software from the Internet. You can delete a certificate from this list by selecting it and clicking Remove.

Managing Your Personal Certificates

You can get your own certificate to identify yourself to secure remote web servers that demand user certificates for identification. See "Getting a Certificate" later in this chapter for how to get your own certificate for use both on the Web and in sending and receiving secure e-mail.

To see what personal certificates are installed in Internet Explorer, choose Tools | Internet Options, click the Content tab, and click the Certificates button to display the Certificates dialog box with the Trusted Root Certification Authorities tab selected, shown in Figure 33-6. You see a list of the certificates you have installed on your computer that you can use to identify yourself.

If you receive a certificate and store it on your disk, click Import to read the certificate and include it on the list in this dialog box. Windows can read certificates stored in personal

FIGURE 33-6   The Certificates dialog box showing your own certificates.

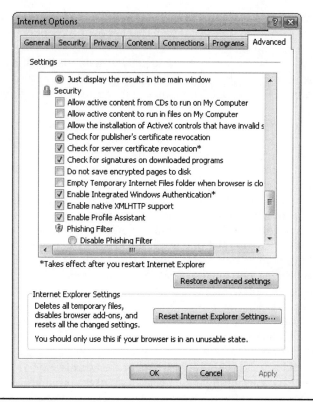

FIGURE 33-7   Additional security settings in Internet Explorer.

certificate files (with the extension .pfx). You can export a certificate and its associated information to a personal certificate file; select the certificate from the list in the Certificates dialog box and click Export.

Tip   *If you get a certificate in Internet Explorer, you can export it to a file and then import the certificate from that file into any other certificate-capable web browser (like Mozilla) or vice versa.*

Other Internet Explorer Security Settings

A few additional security settings appear on the Advanced tab of the Internet Options dialog box (choose Tools | Internet Options in Internet Explorer, click Advanced, and scroll down to the Security section of the list of settings, shown in Figure 33-7).

Sending and Receiving E-mail Securely

E-mail programs offer two kinds of security: signatures and encryption. Both depend on certificates that serve as electronic identity keys. The security system that Microsoft provides with Windows Mail, *S/MIME*, uses certificates issued by third parties, such as

PART VI

VeriSign and Thawte. Another popular security system, *Pretty Good Privacy*, better known as PGP (www.pgp.com), lets each user generate his or her own encryption keys. Both are forms of *public-key cryptography*.

Each certificate consists of a *public key* (or *digital ID*), a *private key*, and a *digital signature*. You keep your private key and digital signature secret, while you provide your public key to anyone with whom you exchange secure mail, either directly or via a generally available key server.

Signatures allow you to add to your mail a *signature block*, generated with your private key, that verifies the author is indeed you, and that the message was not modified in transit. Anyone who wants to validate your signature can check it by using your public key. The signature is added as an extra block at the end of the message, without modifying the other contents, so that the recipient can read your message, whether he or she validates your signature or not.

Encryption scrambles a message so that only the recipient can decode it. A message encrypted with someone's public key can be decrypted only with that person's private key. You encrypt a message with the recipient's public key, and the recipient uses his or her private key to decode it. Anyone else looking at the message would see only unreadable gibberish. It's possible both to *digitally sign* and encrypt the same message, so that only the designated recipient can decode the message and the designated recipient can then verify that the message is really from you.

Mail security depends on a *key ring* of keys. On your key ring, you need your own private key and digital signature and the public key of everyone with whom you plan to exchange secure mail. Windows Mail security keeps your private key and digital signature as one of the properties of your Mail account and keeps other people's public keys in the Address Book.

Windows Mail and Microsoft Outlook 2007 provide a certificate-based system (called S/MIME) for signing and encrypting mail. *Signed* mail uses your own certificate to prove to the recipient that the author of the message is you and that the message arrived without tampering (these are the same type of certificates described in the preceding sections for authenticating material you download from the Web). *Encrypted* mail uses the recipient's certificate to protect the message's contents so that only the intended recipient can read the messages. A single message can be both signed and encrypted.

NOTE *For more information about encryption and signatures, see RSA Security's web site at www.rsasecurity.com and the PGP Corporation's Pretty Good Privacy web site at www.pgp.com. These sites describe how to use encryption with various e-mail programs.*

Getting a Certificate

The only source of certificates is a certificate authority, and for a certificate to be useful, the authority has to be one that is widely accepted. The best known certificate authority is VeriSign, at www.verisign.com, which also owns Thawte, at www.thawte.com. VeriSign provides a variety of certificates at various prices, usually including a free two-month trial of a personal certificate suitable for signing e-mail. The certificate authority's web site walks you through the process of getting a certificate. Details vary, but, generally, the steps include the following:

1. You enter basic information, including your e-mail address, into a form on the authority's web site.

2. Your browser automatically downloads your private key, part of the security information from the authority.

3. The authority e-mails a confirmation code to the address you give. This ensures that the address you provide is really yours.

4. You run Windows Mail and receive the message. It contains the URL of a page that will finish the registration and a unique code to identify yourself when you get there. Use the Windows cut-and-paste tool to copy the code from your mail program to the browser window, rather than trying to retype it.

5. The authority generates the public key that matches your private key and downloads it as well.

NOTE *This process of obtaining a certificate only verifies your e-mail address, not any other aspect of your identity. VeriSign offers more secure certificates with more careful identity checks, but the vast majority of certificates in use are the simplest kind.*

Sending Signed Mail

Once you have a certificate, sending signed mail is simple. While you're composing a message in Windows Mail, click the Encrypt Message button to tell Windows Mail to sign the message as it's sent.

Sending Encrypted Mail

Sending encrypted mail is only slightly harder than sending signed mail. The difference is that before you can send signed mail to someone, you have to have that recipient's digital ID (public key) in your Windows Address Book (see "Storing Addresses in the Address Book" in Chapter 23). Once you have the digital ID, create the message as usual in Windows Mail and click the Encrypt Message button (the envelope with the little blue lock) before sending the message. The encrypted mail icon looks like this:

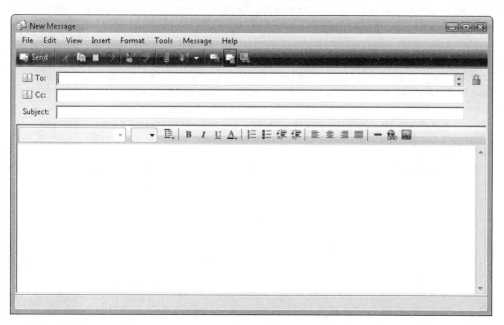

There are three common ways to obtain someone's digital ID: from a signed message he or she sent, from an online directory, or from a file obtained elsewhere, such as a web-based lookup system.

Getting a Digital ID from Incoming Mail

Any time someone sends you a digitally signed message, you can get that person's digital ID from the message and add it to your Address Book. (Note that the digital ID is the equivalent of the sender's public key; the corresponding private key is not disclosed.) Open the message, select File | Properties, and click the Security tab; you see the View Certificates tab. Assuming that the signature is valid, click Add To Address Book. The Address Book opens, creating a new entry for your correspondent (if one does not already exist). Click the Digital IDs tab and observe that a digital ID is listed; then click OK to update the Address Book.

Getting a Digital ID from a File

Digital IDs can be stored in certificate files, usually with the extension .cer (see "Securing Your Web Communication with Encryption and Certificates" earlier in this chapter). Someone can mail you a third party's ID as a file, or you might download the file from a web-based search system.

To add the digital ID to your Address Book, open the Address Book and create an entry for the person, including his or her e-mail address. (The e-mail address has to match the one to which the certificate is assigned.) Then click the Address Book's Digital IDs tab. Click the Import button and select the file containing the ID. The Address Book reads the digital ID and adds it to the Address Book entry.

If you want to store someone's digital ID in a file to transfer it to another computer or send it to a third person, open the Address Book entry for that person, click the Digital IDs tab, click Export, and specify the file to create.

CAUTION *Don't try to export your own digital ID this way; bugs in Windows keep it from working. Remember, you can send anyone your digital ID by sending a signed e-mail message.*

Receiving Encrypted or Signed Mail

Windows Mail and Microsoft Outlook 2007 automatically handle incoming encrypted or signed mail. Signed messages have a little orange seal at the right end of the Security line of the message headers; encrypted messages have a little blue lock. When you open the message, Windows Mail automatically validates the signature or decrypts the message. The first time it does so, it displays a special window in place of the actual message, telling you what it did. Scroll down and click Continue to see the actual message. If you'd rather not see the special window in the future, a check box above the Continue button lets you opt to avoid the window in the future.

VII
PART

Windows Housekeeping

Formatting
and Partitioning Disks

H ard disks can be *partitioned*—divided into one or more logical sections—using Disk Management or a compatible program. (Most disks have only one partition.) Both hard disks and removable disks must be formatted with a *file system*, the information that keeps track of which files are stored where on the disk. Windows Vista supports three file systems: FAT (File Allocation Table, the file system used in DOS and Windows 95), FAT32 (the file system introduced with Windows 95 OSR2 and used in Windows 98, 98SE, and Me), and NTFS 5.0 (New Technology File System, the latest version of the file system designed for Windows NT/2000).

On computers with Windows preinstalled, the hard disk has already been partitioned (usually into a single large partition) and formatted. However, if you install an additional hard disk or replace the original hard disk, you have to format and perhaps partition the new disk. Some disks (both hard disks and removable disks) come preformatted and some don't. Whether or not a disk is preformatted, you can reformat it to remove any existing files and make it a "clean" empty disk.

Each disk drive, including CD drives, DVD drives, and other removable media like USB thumb drives or external hard drives, has a drive letter assigned to it by Windows, but you can change these letters, or assign drive letters to folders, if you must. You can also check how much free space is on any disk and look at the properties of a disk.

This chapter describes how to partition and format hard disks; how to decide whether to use FAT, FAT32, or NTFS (and how to convert partitions to NTFS); how to assign drive letters to disk drives; how to check for free space; and how to control the way in which Windows uses DVDs and CD-ROMs. It also covers how to format and copy floppy disks.

Partitions, File Systems, and Drive Letters

Partitions and file systems determine how and where Windows stores information on your hard disk. *Drive letters* refers to the various disks on your computer. Before you can decide which file system to use on your partitions, you need to know the differences among FAT, FAT32, and NTFS.

Hard Disk Partitions

A *partition* is a section of a hard disk. Normally, a disk is set up as a single large partition spanning the entire disk, but sometimes using more than one partition makes sense. When you partition a disk, you allocate a fixed amount of space to each partition.

TIP *If your disks contain only one partition each, you can use the terms "disk drive" and "partition" interchangeably. Neither CDs nor DVDs can contain multiple partitions.*

Types of Partitions

The partitions used by Windows have historically been called *primary partitions* and *extended partitions*. One disk drive can store either four primary partitions, or three primary partitions and one extended partition. An extended partition can contain many *logical drives*, which are also partitions—extended partitions provide a way to have more than four partitions on a disk. An extended partition can also contain free space, which isn't allocated to a logical drive. Disks can also contain unallocated space, which doesn't belong to any partition. Other operating systems, such as Linux and Apple Macintosh OS X, have their own types of partitions.

When you are running Windows Vista, it also designates partitions as system, boot, and active:

- **System partition**   Has the files needed to start up the computer, stored in the root (main) folder. May be FAT, FAT32, or NTFS. For a multiboot system with Windows Me/9x, the system partition must be FAT or FAT32. The system partition can be small because only a few files are needed. The files needed to start the computer are Ntldr (the NT boot loader, the most important startup file), Boot.ini (which contains the operating system menu for multiboot systems), and Ntdetect.com.

- **Boot partition**   Has the files that contain the Windows Vista operating system. Windows Vista uses the NTFS (recommended) file system. The boot partition must be large enough for the Windows Vista program files and lots of extra space, since other programs usually install in the same partition and Microsoft encourages users to store data there, too—your boot partition should be at least 2GB. If you have other operating systems installed on your computer, each one has a separate boot partition containing its system files.

- **Active partition**   The current boot partition. If you have several operating systems installed on your computer, each one has a boot partition. You can mark a partition as active so that the next time you restart your computer, this partition will be used as the boot partition (see "Selecting the Active Partition" later in this chapter). The active partition must be on disk 0 (the first hard disk attached to the computer).

NOTE *We find it confusing that your computer* boots *off the system partition, while the operating system is stored in the* boot *partition. Just remember that the names are backward.*

The system and boot partitions can be the same partition, or they can be different. If you have one hard disk with one partition, it's both the boot and system partition. If they are different, the computer reads the files from the system partition first when it starts up, then switches to the boot partition to load Windows Vista.

You can see what partitions your hard disks contain, what types of partitions they are, and which are your system, active, and boot partitions, by using the Disk Management program (see "Displaying Information about Drives and Partitions" later in this chapter).

NOTE *Windows also refers to partitions as* volumes. *Volumes can be disk partitions or they can be on storage media other than hard disks, such as tape drives.*

The Master Boot Record (MBR)

When your computer starts up, the computer's BIOS (Basic Input/Output System, which is stored on ROM chips on the system board) performs various self-tests. Then it searches for the very first sector on your hard disk(s)—cylinder 0, head 0, sector 1 of the first hard disk—which contains the *master boot record (MBR)*.

The MBR tells the computer where your active partition is stored. The computer reads the first sector of the active partition (the *boot sector*) to look for a *boot loader*, a program that begins loading an operating system (like Windows or UNIX). For Windows Vista, the boot loader is stored in the Ntldr file. When your computer runs Ntldr, it begins to load the Windows Vista program from the boot partition.

Partitions for Multiple Operating Systems

If you run more than one operating system on your computer, you can create a partition for each operating system and then start the computer from the partition that contains the operating system you want to use (see "Creating Dual-boot Installations" in Appendix A).

Managing Partitions with Norton PartitionMagic

Norton PartitionMagic is a program from Symantec (www.symantec.com/home_ homeoffice/products/overview.jsp?pcid=sp&pvid=pm80) that enables you to create, resize, move, and delete all types of partitions. The Windows Vista setup program can set up a separate partition for Windows Vista, and the Windows Disk Management window can create and delete partitions, but it still can't do everything that we use PartitionMagic for, such as expanding, shrinking, copying, and moving partitions. Also, PartitionMagic can move and resize partitions without losing the data stored in the partitions: Windows Vista loses your files when you make changes to partitions.

Because all of our data is stored separately on drive D:, backups can be smaller and faster, including only data and not programs. Backing up is easy when all you have to do is specify all files on D:.

However, because application compatibility problems arose during Vista beta testing, you should confirm application compatibility with Symantec prior to purchasing PartitionMagic.

With Windows Me/9x, using multiple partitions to switch between different Windows versions was hard, because they all started from the same primary partition. (Norton PartitionMagic, a program you can purchase separately, enables you to install more than one version of Windows.) Windows NT and 2000 included the NT boot manager, which made dual-boot systems easier to set up (see the sidebar "Managing Partitions with Norton PartitionMagic").

Windows Vista has partitioning built in, and its setup program can create a separate partition for it, leaving other versions of Windows alone. It can display a list of the installed operating systems (each in its own boot partition). However, PartitionMagic is still useful for moving and resizing partitions.

The NTFS File System

A *file system* is the information that keeps track of which files and folders are stored where in a partition, and what disk space is free. The Windows file system includes a *FAT (File Allocation Table)* or *Master File Table*, which stores information about each *sector*, or physical block of storage space, on the disk.

NTFS is a more mature version of FAT32 that was originally designed for use with Windows NT and Windows 2000 for server applications. Partition size can be from 520 MB to 2 terabytes (larger sizes are possible, but not recommended). Files are limited only to the size of the partition. Windows Vista uses NTFS 5.0 (it was called 5.1 during product testing), a very slight upgrade from the version used in Windows 2000. Recommended for systems with security needs, large hard disks, and LAN connections.

Each partition on a hard disk and each removable disk must be formatted with FAT, FAT32, or NTFS, but it's possible (and often desirable) to have some disks with one format and some with the other format on the same system. Both FAT32 and NTFS are designed for large partitions and disks and offer no significant benefits when used on smaller disks. However, with Windows Vista's rather significant system requirements, it will be unlikely to see a system available with less than 10GB of hard drive space, making FAT largely useless.

NTFS 5.0 offers all of the advantages of FAT32 as well as the following:

- **More efficient use of space**   NTFS can allocate as little as 2KB of disk space to a file, reducing wasted disk space.

- **On-the-fly compression**   Individual files can be compressed and decompressed as needed. Entire drives can be reduced in size without affecting overall performance.

- **Encryption**   In Windows Vista, files and folders can be encrypted with a user's password (see "File and Folder Attributes" in Chapter 8). However, Windows Vista Home Edition doesn't support file and folder encryption.

Why Divide Your Hard Disk into Partitions?

Most often, you allocate all the space on a hard disk to one partition, which Windows treats as a single logical disk drive using a single drive letter (drive C: for the first hard disk). You can also allocate some of the space to the primary partition and some to an extended partition, which can, in turn, be subdivided into multiple logical disks.

As a general rule, a single partition is all you ever need. However, here are circumstances where more than one partition will be useful:

- **Scratch areas** In some cases, it's useful to have a separate partition to use as a scratch area that you can quickly reformat to wipe out its contents and start fresh.

- **Multiboot systems** The boot manager built into Windows (or PartitionMagic) can dynamically reassign active partitions so that you can effectively have more than one operating system on a large drive (see the sidebar "Managing Partitions with Norton PartitionMagic").

- **Data partitions** We recommend creating a separate partition for your data—all your documents, spreadsheets, databases, and other files. You should back up your data partition regularly. You needn't back up your programs as often because you can restore them from your program CDs.

- **Quotas** You can set quotas for each user, limiting the amount of space that each user can use on a partition (see "Setting Quotas for Disk Usage" in Chapter 6).

We recommend that you set up two partitions: one primary NTFS partition (which appears as drive C:) for Windows Vista and one primary or extended partition (drive D:) for data. Use drive C: for Windows and programs, and use drive D: for data—all documents, spreadsheets, e-mail, and other files that you create or edit. You can configure Windows to store your Documents And Settings folder on D: . You can also configure your programs (where possible) to store their program configuration files on D:—for example, Microsoft Word's template files and or Mozilla's bookmark files.

Keeping all your data and personal configuration settings in a separate partition has several advantages:

- **Backups** Making backups is easier when all your files are stored together. Whether you use Windows Explorer, the Backup Utility, or another backup program, it's easy to specify that you want to back up all the files on D: (see Chapter 10).

- **Reinstalling Windows** If Windows starts acting oddly or you decide to start fresh when you upgrade to a new version of Windows, you can reinstall Windows without disturbing your data files. (Make a backup of all your data before reinstalling or upgrading Windows, though, just in case!) You can wipe out the files on C: without deleting the files on D:.

- **Multiboot systems** If you need to switch between two operating systems (for example, Windows Vista and Linux), you can access your data files from either one. You might want to store Windows Vista on C:, Linux on D:, and your data on E:.

TIP *Don't slice your disk into too many partitions—we rarely use more than three. Unlike folders, when you create a partition, you must decide in advance how much disk space to devote to that partition. You are bound to run out of space in one partition while you still have plenty of space in another.*

Partition and Drive Letters

Every partition, logical drive, and removable disk available to Windows has a *drive letter*. Whether your computer has floppy drives or not, drives A: and B: are reserved for floppy disk drives. Hard disk partitions and drives for *removable disks* (such as CD-ROMs, CD-R/W drives, and USB thumbdrives) and external hard drives are assigned letters starting with C:. Any remaining letters can be used for network drives.

NOTE *Windows Vista has an annoying habit of assigning drive letters in the order in which drives and partitions are added to the system, so that the drive containing Windows Vista itself may not be C:, and hard disk drive letters may follow CD-ROM drive letters. You can reassign drive letters if necessary (see "Choosing Your Own Drive Letters" later in this chapter).*

Displaying Information about Drives and Partitions

Windows Vista stores a set of properties for each installed disk drive and partition, and allows you to manage those properties from the Computer window. This windows includes drop-down menus and icons for each of your drives and partitions. You can also look at the properties of individual drives and partitions by right-clicking the drive and choosing Properties.

The Computer Window

Click Start | Computer. In the Computer window that appears (see Figure 34-1), you have the following options just below the menu bar to get a better view of your drives and partitions:

- **Organize** Click Organize to open the Organize drop-down menu, where you can find options for better viewing your drives via the Computer window, including window layout and folder options.

- **Views** Click Views to alter how you view the drives appearing in the Computer window.

- **Properties** Click Properties to view basic information about your PC, including system information, computer name, domain, and workgroup settings.

- **Change Or Remove A Program** Click Change Or Remove A Program to remove software from one of your PC's drives.

- **Change A Setting** Click Change A Setting to change drive settings.

The Computer window lists all disks, drives, and partitions that are loaded, mounted, and recognized by Windows Vista. You have the following options for working with your drive information:

- **Name** Sort your drives alphabetically or by group

- **Type** Sort your drives by (drive) type including CD drive and local disk and stack

- **Free Space** Sort your drives by their free space in increments of 10% free, 50% free, and 90% free

Properties of Drives and Partitions

Each item on your system with a drive letter—each hard disk partition, floppy disk, and removable disk—also has properties. You can display these properties from the Computer window (choose Start | Computer); right-click the drive and choose Properties from the menu that appears. Figure 34-2 shows the Properties dialog box for a partition (the dialog boxes for other kinds of disk drives look similar, but may have different tabs).

The tabs that appear on the Properties dialog box for a disk drive or partition include the following:

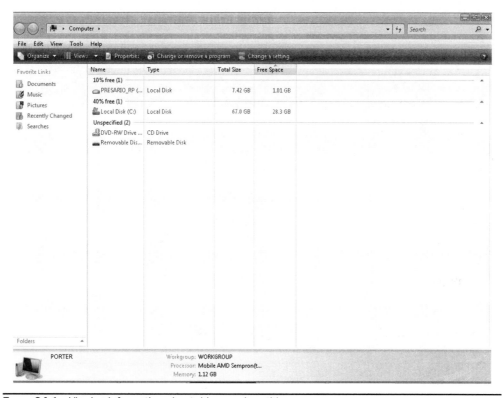

Figure 34-1 Viewing information about drives and partitions.

- **General**   Appears for all drives and partitions, showing used and free disk space, type, and file system.
- **Tools**   Contains buttons for error checking, defragmenting, and backing up the drive. This tab doesn't appear for disks you can't write on, such as CD-ROM drives.
- **Hardware**   Lists disk drives and displays the manufacturer, location, and status for the selected drive. You can click the Troubleshoot button on the Hardware tab for device-specific troubleshooting, and the Properties button for the drive's properties.
- **Sharing**   Enables you to share the drive or partition with other computers on a LAN.
- **Previous Versions**   Enables you to view a previous version of a folder.
- **Quota**   Provides settings for disk quotas for user accounts.
- **AutoPlay**   For CD-ROM, CD-R, and CD-RW drives, controls what happens when you put a CD into the drive, depending on the type of files it contains.
- **Recording**   For CD-R and CD-RW drives, displays the write speed and location of the temporary files used during CD burning (see "Configuring CD-R and CD-RW Drives" later in this chapter).

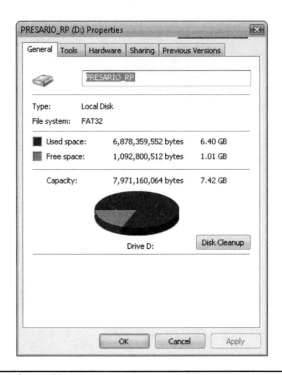

FIGURE 34-2 Properties of a partition.

If you have installed a hard-disk housekeeping program like Norton Utilities, additional tabs may appear.

Partitioning a Disk Using Disk Management

When you buy a new computer or hard disk, you receive it ready for use—already partitioned (usually with one partition) and formatted. If you are adding new unformatted, unpartitioned disk drives, or if you want to create a computer system that can run one of several operating systems—such as switching between Windows Vista and Linux—you may need to partition a disk yourself. However, formatting destroys the data in the areas of the disk it partitions, so be sure to make a backup copy of all the information on your disk before formatting a disk or partition (see Chapter 10).

CAUTION *Most of the commands in this chapter are available only to users who have administrator user accounts—user accounts that give them permission to make changes to the system itself (see Chapter 6). Before working with partitions and drives, be sure to back up the important files on your system (as described in Chapter 10).*

To partition a hard disk, you need to run Disk Management. Choose Start | Control Panel | System And Maintenance | Administrative Tools. Choose Computer Management from the System And Maintenance options. When you see the Computer Management window, click the Disk Management item listed underneath the Storage heading. You then see the main Disk Management pane in the right side of the Computer Management window.

Many computer systems have only one hard disk and one CD-ROM drive (CD-R/RW, DVD, or what have you), which appear as Disk 0 and CD-ROM 0 in the left column of the lower pane. Figure 34-1 shows two hard disks, Disk 0 and Disk 1, and two removable storage drives, CD-ROM 0 (which is actually a DVD drive) and CD-ROM 1.

NOTE   *The Disk Management program replaces the Fdisk program that was part of previous versions of Windows.*

Creating a New Partition

If you have unallocated space (which appears as an Unknown Partition in the Disk Management window), you can create a new partition in some or all of that space. To create a new partition, right-click the part of the window that represents the unallocated space (unallocated space has a black stripe running along the top), and choose New Partition from the menu that appears. To create a new logical drive in an extended partition that contains free space (free space has a light-green strip along the top), right-click the free space and choose New Logical Drive from the menu that appears. Either way, you see the New Partition Wizard.

The New Partition Wizard asks you to specify the following:

- **Type**   Primary, extended, or logical partition. A disk drive can contain up to four primary partitions, or three primary partitions and one extended partition. The logical partition type is available only if you choose to create the new partition in an extended partition with some free space. Choose a primary partition if you are creating a partition in which you will install an operating system (an unusual situation). Choose an extended partition if you plan to create several logical partitions within it.

- **Size**   The wizard displays the minimum and maximum size for the partition, based on its type and the space where it will be stored. You can use the entire available space, or leave room for other partitions. Windows Vista doesn't provide a way to resize partitions later, but you can use a third-party program like PartitionMagic to do so (see the sidebar "Managing Partitions with Norton PartitionMagic" earlier in the chapter).

- **Drive letter or path**   The wizard offers the next available drive letter, but you may select any unused letter. To use the Mount In The Following Empty NTFS Folder option, you must have an NTFS partition with a drive letter on the same machine. If you plan on installing more than one operating system on your computer, you may select the Do Not Assign A Drive Letter Or Drive Path option, and let Windows assign a letter later. We usually take the default drive letter assignment.

- **File system**   The default is NTFS, but you can feel good about using FAT32 as well. Both efficiently utilize space on large drives, but NTFS has more security features, better recovery capabilities after a crash, and file-level compression built in. If you select NTFS, you are also given the option to enable compression. Leave the Allocation unit size as Default.

- **Label**   Type a name for the partition, indicating what you will use it for.

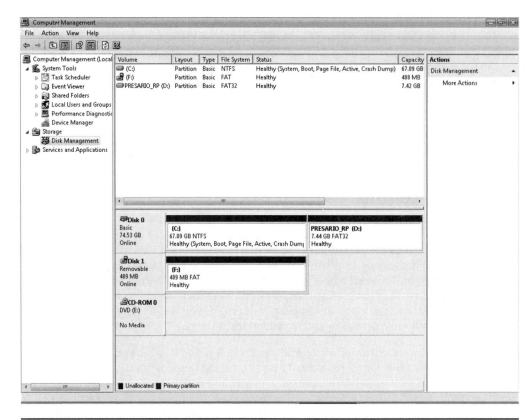

FIGURE 34-3   Creating a new partition with Computer Management.

Figure 34-3 shows the Computer Management screen, summarizing your choices before Windows creates the partition. Formatting a new partition can take several minutes (see "Formatting a Disk" later in this chapter).

Selecting the Active Partition

If you partition your disk among multiple operating systems, one of the partitions is the active partition, the partition from which your computer starts. If you run Windows only, the primary partition is always active. In Windows Vista you can change this behavior manually by selecting another partition as active using the Disk Management pane in the Computer Management window. Right-click the disk or partition that you want to make active and select Mark Partition As Active from the menu that appears. You can only make this change to primary partitions. Extended partitions and logical drives cannot be made active. Only one partition is active at a time—and make sure it's a partition that contains a bootable operating system!

Deleting a Partition

You can delete a partition using the Disk Management pane of the Computer Management window. Right-click the partition and choose Delete Partition (for a primary or extended partition) or Delete Logical Drive (for a logical drive). If you want to delete an extended partition, you first have to delete all the logical drives in the partition.

CAUTION *When you delete a partition, all the files and folders on the partition are deleted for good—they don't go to the Recycle Bin. There's no way to get them back (unless you have a backup copy).*

Repartitioning a Disk

Repartitioning a disk with Windows Vista can be a dark art. Windows can only create and delete partitions—it can't move, resize, or copy them, and converting them requires using a DOS command. To rearrange the partitions on your system using only the Windows Disk Management program, you must delete all the data on the partition, then delete the partition, and then create new partitions. Follow these steps:

1. Back up all the files on the partitions that you need to delete (see Chapter 10).

2. Open the Disk Management pane in the Computer Management window—choose Start | Computer | Administrative Tools. From Administrative Tools, choose Computer Management. In the Computer Management window, click Disk Management under the Storage heading. You see the Disk Management pane shown in Figure 34-3.

3. Delete the partitions that are in the wrong place or are the wrong size by right-clicking each one and choosing Delete Volume or Delete Logical Drive from the menu that appears.

4. Create new partitions by right-clicking the unallocated space (or free space in an extended partition) and choosing New Volume or New Logical Drive from the menu that appears.

5. Reload the backed-up data.

Third-party disk utilities, such as PartitionMagic, make this process safer and easier and permit many kinds of changes without backing up and reloading everything. PartitionMagic can move, copy, and resize partitions without deleting them (it's amazing, actually). Utilities such as Drive Image make it easy to create a copy of a partition so you can reload it later. If you plan to use multiple partitions, we recommend you look into third-party partitioning programs (see the sidebar "Managing Partitions with Norton PartitionMagic" earlier in this chapter).

Converting Partitions to NTFS

Windows comes with a Convert command that can convert a FAT or FAT32 partition to NTFS (the Convert command can't convert anything to FAT or FAT32). To convert a partition to NTFS (after backing it up!), follow these steps:

1. Choose Start | All Programs | Accessories | Command Prompt to open a Command Prompt window (see "Starting and Exiting DOS Programs" in Chapter 4).

2. Type **convert** *n***: /FS:NTFS** and press enter, replacing *n* with the drive letter of the partition you want to convert. If you want verbose mode, in which you see extra explanatory messages, type **/v** at the end of the command.

TIP *If you need to convert to a file system other than NTFS, try PartitionMagic. Be sure to get the latest version, since earlier versions don't support NTFS 5.0.*

Choosing Your Own Drive Letters

Windows assigns a drive letter to each partition, logical drive, and removable disk that it can read. Whenever possible, we recommend you use the drive letters Windows assigns (see "Partition and Drive Letters" earlier in this chapter). If you can't (for example, you are using an antiquated program that expects files to be on certain drives or you install an application that reassigns drive letters willy-nilly), you have a few options: change the letters, assign letters to folders, or assign pathnames to drives or partitions.

When assigning or changing drive letters, you can use any unassigned letter from C: to Z: (inclusive). Letters A: and B: are reserved for floppy disk drives. If a program is using the files on a drive or partition when you try to change its letter, Windows displays an error message.

Changing Drive Letters

You can tell Windows to assign different drive letters to most of your drives and partitions. You cannot, however, change the drive letter of the boot partition (the one that contains the Windows Vista program files). You can alternately add new drive letter assignments or, if you're using NTFS, assign special folders to act as conduits to drives.

To change the drive letter for a partition, follow these steps:

1. Choose Start | Control Panel | Administrative Tools | Computer Management. In the Computer Management window, click the Disk Management item under the Storage heading (as shown in Figure 34-3 earlier in the chapter). The Disk Management pane appears in the right part of the Computer Management window.

2. Locate the partition whose letter you would like to change in the upper-right pane of the Computer Management console (the volume list) or the lower-right pane (the list of drives and the diagram of partitions on each drive).

3. Right-click the partition and select Change Drive Letters And Paths from the menu that appears. You see the dialog box shown in Figure 34-4.

4. Click the Change button to modify the existing letter assignment. You see this dialog box:

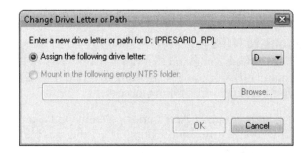

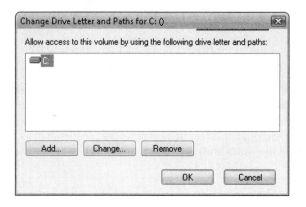

FIGURE 34-4   Changing the drive letter of a partition, or assigning a pathname to a partition.

5. Click the Assign The Following Drive Letter radio button, type or choose a letter in the box to the right, and click OK. You return to the Computer Management window, with updated drive letters for the partition.

You can't add a second drive letter to a partition—each partition has only one drive letter at a time. You can remove the drive letter, though, by clicking the Remove button in the Change Drive Letter And Paths dialog box. Windows warns you not to proceed if the drive letter is in use. If you click the Add button, Windows assumes that you want to assign a pathname to the partition, as described in the next section.

CAUTION   *Don't change the drive letters of the boot partition (which contains Windows Vista itself—Windows Vista shouldn't allow you to, anyway). Watch out when changing the drive letter of a partition that contains programs. With a different drive letter, existing references to the program files on that partition would be wrong. Changing the drive letter does not update references to the files on that partition.*

Assigning Pathnames to Partitions

You can assign a pathname—like C:\My Documents or D:\Budget Workarea—to a partition. The partition still has its usual drive letter (unless you remove it), but it also has a second name—a pathname. This technique is called *mounting a partition*.

NOTE   *Any space allocated to a specific file system is called a partition, whether it is a small partition on a large drive or a single partition that takes up an entire drive.*

Before you mount a partition (that is, assign it a pathname), you choose two things:

- **The partition to mount**   It continues to have its original drive letter, unless you delete the drive letter. The partition can contain files and folders, which will not be disturbed by assigning a pathname to the drive.

- **The pathname to assign to the partition**   The pathname must refer to an existing, empty folder on an NTFS partition. After you assign the pathname to the partition (mount the partition), Windows will redirect references to that folder to the partition instead.

For example, rather than storing all your user's settings and files in the C:\Documents And Settings folders and their subfolders, you might want to store them on a separate partition. You could format a partition with NTFS for this purpose. Move the entire contents of C:\Documents And Settings to the new partition, and mount this partition at the pathname C:\Documents And Settings.

CAUTION *Be sure to empty the folder in which you are about to mount a partition. In the C:\ Documents And Settings example, move the contents of C:\Documents And Settings before issuing the command to mount the partition at the pathname. After issuing the command, you won't be able to access those files and folders—Windows will redirect all requests to the new partition.*

To assign a pathname to a partition or drive, follow these steps:

1. Create an empty folder (choose New | Folder) in a partition formatted with NTFS. Or, empty out an existing folder. If you have a blank NTFS partition, you can use the root folder. (In the C:\Documents And Settings example, you might use a partition currently named D:.)

2. Choose Start, right-click Computer, and choose Manage from the menu that appears. In the Computer Management window, click the Disk Management item under the Storage heading (as shown in Figure 34-3 earlier in the chapter).

3. Right-click the partition that you want to mount and choose Change Drive Letter And Paths from the menu that appears. You see the dialog box shown in Figure 34-5. (In our example, right-click the D: partition.)

4. In the Mount In The Following Empty NTFS Folder box, type the pathname that you want to assign to the partition, or click the Browse button and navigate to the empty folder you identified in Step 1. (In our example, browse to C:\Documents And Settings.)

5. Click OK.

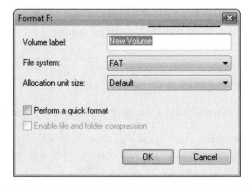

FIGURE 34-5   The Format dialog box.

> **NOTE** *You can also assign a drive letter to a network drive or a folder stored on a network drive (see "Mapping a Shared Drive or Folder to a Drive Letter" in Chapter 30).*

Assigning Drive Letters to Folders

You can use the DOS SUBST command to assign new drive letters that correspond to folders on existing disks. Follow these steps:

1. Open a Command Prompt window by choosing Start | All Programs | Accessories | Command Prompt.

2. Type the SUBST command in the following format (press ENTER after typing the command):

   ```
   SUBST N: C:\MYAPP
   ```

   This command makes the drive letter N a synonym for the folder C:\Myapp. You can use any unused drive letter and the address (pathname) of any folder.

3. Type **exit** to close the Command Prompt window.

The new substituted drive letter is available immediately.

> **CAUTION** *If the path of your folder uses long names, then in the SUBST command, you have to use the MS-DOS name equivalent, as shown by the DOS DIR command (see "DOS Filenames" in Chapter 4).*

To disconnect a substituted drive letter, type the following:

```
SUBST N: /D
```

Formatting a Disk

Formatting a disk writes the file system, the low-level structure information needed to track where files and folders will be located on the disk. Generally, you need to format disks only when you want to clean off a floppy disk or other removable disk for reuse, if you repartition your hard disk and create a new partition, or if you have a disaster with Windows and want to reinstall it from scratch. CD-R and CD-RW disks don't need to be formatted before use.

> **CAUTION** *Formatting a disk—hard disk or removable—deletes* all *the information from the disk, so proceed with care!*

Formatting a Hard Disk

Before formatting your hard disk (or one partition on a hard disk), be sure you make a backup copy of any files you want to keep (see Chapter 9). To format a hard disk, follow these steps:

1. Open the Computer window and locate the drive you want to format.

2. Right-click the icon for the drive and choose Format in the menu that pops up. You see the Format dialog box, shown in Figure 34-5. Almost none of the fields in the window, except for the volume label, apply to hard disks—leave them with their default settings.

3. Type a drive label in the Volume Label box (if the box is blank or if you want to change the existing label) and click the OK button in the Format dialog box.

4. If the drive contains files or folders, Windows asks whether you really want to reformat the disk, because existing files will be lost. Assuming you want to format the disk, choose Yes to do so. Formatting can take several minutes—the process involves reading the entire disk to check for bad spots.

NOTE *You can't format the disk from which you are running Windows; Windows displays an error message saying the disk contains files that Windows is using. You can't format a CD-ROM either.*

Formatting a Removable Disk

Formatting a removable disk (like a CD or DVD) is like formatting a hard disk, except more format options are available. If you only want to erase the files on a previously formatted disk without rechecking for bad spots, select Perform a Quick Format in the Format dialog box shown in Figure 34-5. Then click the Start button in the Format dialog box.

When you format a disk, Windows may report bad sectors on the disk. Windows marks the sectors as unusable, to prevent programs from trying to write information there. If a floppy disk has any bad sectors, throw it away and use a new one—floppy disks are too cheap for you to fool around with the possibility of losing data.

Checking Free Space

You can easily see how much free space is available on any partition. Choose Start | Computer and select the partition (or drive). Right-click the partition or drive and select Properties from the menu that appears. You see a Properties dialog box with a pie chart like the one shown in Figure 34-2 earlier in the chapter (if the General tab isn't selected, click it).

Configuring DVD and CD Drives

Because DVDs (data or video), CD-ROMs (data CDs), and audio CDs (CDs containing sound, or CD-DAs) are prerecorded, no preparation is needed to use them. Just insert them in the drive, and Windows recognizes them. If a CD-ROM contains an *AutoRun* program (that is, a file named Autorun.inf in the root folder of the CD-ROM, containing instructions for what program to run), Windows runs it. For audio CDs, Windows usually runs the Windows Media Player application automatically, turning your computer into a CD player (see "Playing Audio CDs" in Chapter 19)—useful if you like background music while you work.

TIP *If you don't want the AutoRun program on a CD-ROM to run, or you don't want Windows to start playing an audio CD, open the drive, insert the disk, and hold down the SHIFT key while closing the drive—keep the SHIFT key pressed down until you are sure no program has started.*

If the CD-ROM that you insert contains audio or video files (i.e., MP3 or AVI video), a dialog box may appear asking what you would like to do with the media contained on the disk. Your options are to either play the files or open an Explorer window displaying the items.

Checking the Always Do The Selected Action check box causes Windows to either play or display the files for that disk.

You can control what happens when you put an audio or data CD in the drive:

1. Open the Computer window, right-click the CD drive, choose Open AutoPlay, and click Set AutoPlay Defaults in the Control Panel. The AutoPlay Options window appears, as shown in Figure 34-6.

2. Set the Select Content Type drop-down menu to the type of files on the DVD or CD. For audio CDs, choose Audio CD.

3. Choose the action that you want Windows to perform when it detects this type of CD in the drive (see Figure 34-7). The list of actions depends on the type of CD you chose in the previous step.

4. Alternatively, you can choose the Prompt Me Each Time To Choose An Action option. This setting tells Windows that each time you put a DVD or CD in the drive, you want to see a dialog box with this list of options.

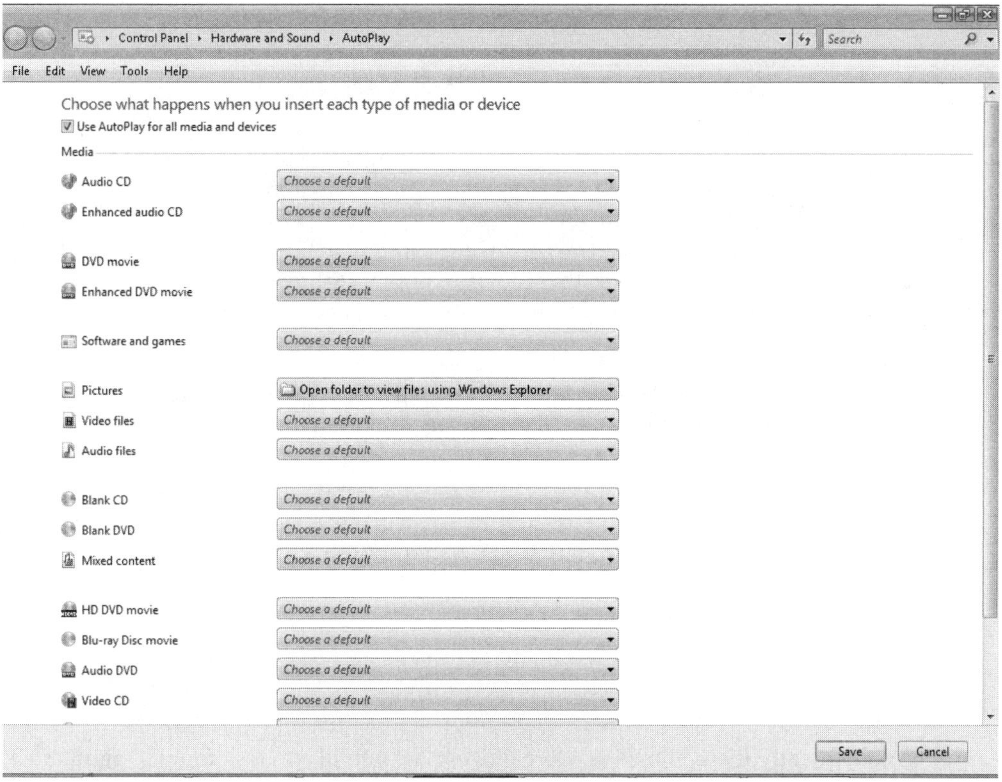

FIGURE 34-6   The AutoPlay Options window.

FIGURE 34-7   Specifying what to do when you put a DVD or CD in the drive.

Configuring DVD-R, DVD-RW, CD-R, and CD-RW Drives

Recordable disks include DVD-Rs and CD-Rs (which can be recorded once) and DVD-RWs and CD-RWs (which can be written, erased, and written again). See the section "Making Your Own CDs" in Chapter 8 for how to burn data CDs, and section "Creating Your Own Music CDs" in Chapter 19 for how to burn music CDs.

Most DVD or CD burners are read/write drives, which can burn both types of media. Some older systems have CD-R drives that can burn only CD-R disks. The Properties dialog box for a CD-R or CD-RW drive includes the Recording tab, shown in Figure 34-8. It enables access to the following settings:

- **Enable CD Recording On This Drive**   Normally, this check box is selected. If you have more than one CD-R or CD-RW drive on your system, only one can be enabled.

- **Select A Drive Where Windows Can Store An Image Of The CD To Be Written**   Before burning a CD, Windows copies all the files to a temporary storage space, converting file formats as necessary for the CD. Normally, this drive is the one where Windows is installed, but you can switch to another drive with more free space. An audio CD can take up to 70 MB of disk space, while a data CD can use up to 700 MB.

- **Select A Write Speed**   This setting defaults to Fastest (the fastest speed that the CD-R or CD-RW drive supports). However, if you have trouble with the CDs that you burn, try setting this to a lower speed.

- **Automatically Eject The Disc After Writing**   If you like to test your CD right after you burn it, you may want to turn this off. We like to select this check box, because the sound of the CD drawer opening is our signal that the CD is finished.

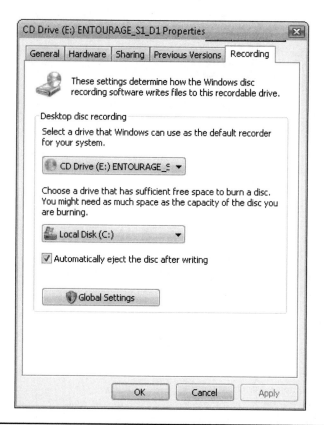

FIGURE 34-8   Configuring a DVD or CD drive.

TIP *If you have trouble burning CDs, or if the CDs you burn can't be played in CD players or other computers, see "Troubleshooting Burning CDs" in Chapter 8 for ideas. For audio CDs, see "Troubleshooting Audio CDs" in Chapter 19.*

Keeping Your Disk Safe

In addition to the files and folders on a disk, some of the space on each disk is used to store the structure of the disk, including a table of the parts of the disk that are free (available for storing new information), a table of the files and folders on the disk, and a list of which blocks on the disk store the information in which file.

If this structural information gets corrupted, you can lose some or all of the information on the disk. It's wise to check the structure of the information on each hard disk regularly by using a Windows program called ChkDsk, which not only checks the disk structure, but can also fix most of the errors that it finds.

Another disk problem arises when you create and delete many files over a long period of time. Files are stored in a series of sectors on your disk, and the sectors are not necessarily next to each other. While this is more of a problem for FAT32 partitions, NTFS partitions can also become fragmented after time. To fix this problem, you can run the Disk Defragmenter utility that comes with Windows. Disk Defragmenter moves the information on your disk around to speed up access.

Many programs create temporary or backup files, which are not always deleted when they are no longer needed. The Disk Cleanup program can delete stale temporary files for you.

NOTE *If you need to restore your Windows system files to the way they were before you installed an upgrade or before your system started having problems, try the System Restore program. For information about your system and repairing Windows system files, see "Returning Your System to a Predefined State with System Restore" in Chapter 37.*

Testing Your Disk Structure with ChkDsk

The ChkDsk (Check Disk) program can both diagnose and repair errors on a wide variety of devices, including hard disks, floppy disks, RAM drives, removable disks, and laptop memory cards. ChkDsk doesn't work on CD-R or CD-RW discs. ChkDsk can check the physical surface of disk drivers for bad sectors and possibly recover lost data, and it checks the file allocation table (FAT), the directory structure, and the long filenames associated with many files.

NOTE *If Windows crashes or you turn off the computer without shutting down, Windows typically runs ChkDsk when you restart, to check your hard disk for errors resulting from the unexpected termination. There are some occasions when ChkDsk will not run.*

Windows File Protection

Windows Vista comes with a feature called *Windows File Protection*, or *WFP*. WFP is running whenever Windows is running, monitoring the files that make up Windows itself. Whenever a program replaces one of the Windows system files, WFP checks whether the new file was accompanied by a "signed" (verified and encrypted) file from Microsoft. If not, or if an earlier version of a file has replaced a later version, WFP replaces the file with its own copy (from the WFP collection of duplicate files at C:\Windows\System32\dllcache, if Windows is installed on C:).

You don't have to turn WFP on, and there's no way to turn it off. WFP doesn't display any messages when it decides to replace a system file with its own version, but it may prompt you to insert the Windows Vista CD-ROM to reinstall a file.

Running ChkDsk

Certain ChkDsk functions, like fixing disk errors and recovering lost sectors, are not accessible while Windows is running. This is because the repairs cannot be completed while there are open files on the disk to be fixed. When you try to run ChkDsk, Windows might need to schedule the program to run the next time you restart Windows instead.

To run ChkDsk, follow these steps:

1. Right-click the disk drive in the Computer window and choose Properties.

2. In the Properties dialog box for the disk, click the Tools tab and click the Check Now button. You see the Check Disk dialog box:

3. Select both check boxes to perform a full disk check and click Start. You usually see a message saying that Windows can't run the program until the next time you start Windows.

4. Click Yes. The next time Windows starts, you see a message that the disk check has been scheduled, and displaying the results as the program runs, which can take several minutes (depending on the size of the disk). When ChkDsk runs, you see its results before Windows displays your logon screen or desktop.

TIP You can also run ChkDsk at the DOS command prompt (see "The Command Prompt Window" in Chapter 4). Choose Start | Run and type **chkdsk** *at the command prompt. Then press* ENTER. *To tell ChkDsk to fix any errors it finds, type* **chkdsk /f** *instead.*

Other ChkDsk Options

ChkDsk can do a number of other things if you run it at the command prompt. To see your options at the command line, type the following at the prompt in a Command Prompt window:

```
chkdsk /?
```

or type **help chkdsk**. When you press ENTER, you see information about ChkDsk's options, which are also listed in Table 35-1. Some switches work only on NTFS partitions, and some work only on FAT32 partitions.

Switch or Argument	FAT32 Partitions	NTFS Partitions
Volume	Specifies the drive to be acted on. Enter the drive letter as the letter and a colon (e.g., c:, d:, x:) or as a volume name (e.g., CRUNCHY, DRV012).	
Filename	Specifies specific files to be checked for fragmentation.	Not used.
/F	Fixes errors on the specified disk. If no disk is specified, ChkDsk checks the boot disk and fixes it as needed.	
/V	Displays the full filename and path of every file on the disk. This is not recommended, unless you have a lot of free time.	Not used.
/R	Locates and attempts to recover the data in lost sectors. This command also implicitly applies an /F command.	
/L:size	Not used.	Changes the file size of the operations log to the specified amount (in KB: 1 MB = 1024 KB).
/X	Causes a mounted volume to be forcibly dismounted before performing the implicit /F command. This switch cannot be used on the boot volume.	
/I	Not used.	Performs a less complete index check.
/C	Not used.	Skips checking directory structure cycles.

TABLE 35-1 ChkDsk Command Switches

Defragmenting Your Disk

Windows stores information on your disks in sectors, which can be anywhere from 2 to 32 kilobytes (KB) in size. Files are stored in as many sectors as required to fit (for example, a 64 KB file would take two sectors on a disk with 32 KB sectors). These sectors do not need to remain sequential: Windows keeps track of which sectors are used for which files, no matter where they are on the disk. Sectors for a single file can be located just about anywhere on the disk.

Fragmentation occurs when you add and remove files from your computer. When you delete a file, Windows marks the sectors as available, and uses them the next time you create a file. If a file gets larger and contiguous space isn't available, Windows uses other available sectors to store the new part of the file. As you continue to use your computer, your files can become more and more fragmented. When you save a new file, if no contiguous space is large enough, Windows writes the new file using sectors that aren't together—the file is fragmented right from the start.

Fragmentation slows down your disk access and, subsequently, your computing efficiency, because Windows has to spend more time finding the parts of each file. The more chunks a file is split into, the slower Windows accesses the file, because the file system has to move all over the disk to find pieces of the file.

Fortunately, Windows comes with a program that moves the contents of files around on your hard disk so that each file is stored as one contiguous string of sectors—Disk Defragmenter. Run the Disk Defragmenter utility when you plan on not using your computer for some time, because it can take an hour or so, and has to restart if you change any files.

In this day of ultra-cheap, gargantuan drives (80 GB and beyond) with superfast access times (7200 RPM standard and 10,000 RPM becoming more common), fragmentation doesn't affect speed nearly as much as it did on older hard disks. One reason is that newer disks read an entire *track* (concentric circle of information) at a time from the disk into the disk's buffer memory, so it matters less if the sectors of the track contain information in the wrong order. If your disk has lots of free space, your files are less likely to be badly fragmented.

NOTE *Even though Disk Defragmenter moves data about on your drive, no files or folders appear to move. How you organize your files and such is really an illusion anyway. Which folder you put your copy of the next Great American Novel in has nothing to do with where it's stored in the disk itself.*

Running Disk Defragmenter

Follow these steps to run Disk Defragmenter:

1. Right-click the disk drive in the Computer window and choose Properties. In the Properties dialog box for the disk, click the Tools tab and click the Defragment Now button. You see the Disk Defragmenter window, shown in Figure 35-1.

2. Click Defragment Now. Disk Defragmenter starts to work and displays the results of its analysis.

3. When Disk Defragmenter is done, a message asks whether you want to exit the program; click Yes.

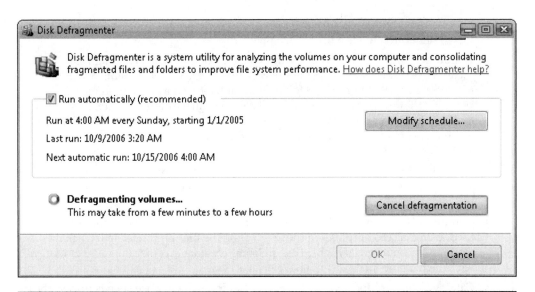

Figure 35-1   Disk Defragmenter analyzing your disk for file fragmentation.

Deleting Temporary Files with Disk Cleanup

When Windows notices that there's not much free space left on the disk on which Windows is installed (usually C:), it offers to run Disk Cleanup, a program that can delete unneeded temporary files from your hard disk. Some programs create temporary files and then don't delete the files when they are through with them. If a program, or Windows itself, exits unexpectedly (or "crashes"), temporary files can be left on your hard disk. Deleting these files from time to time is a good idea, not only because they take up space, but also because their presence can confuse the programs that created them.

Types of Temporary Files That Disk Cleanup Can Delete

Disk Cleanup may suggest deleting these categories of unnecessary files:

- **Downloaded Program Files**   These files are downloaded when you browse the Web and encounter web pages that include ActiveX controls or Java applets. If you need these files again, your browser will download them automatically, so it's safe to delete them. You can click the View Files button to see a list of filenames.

- **Temporary Internet Files**   This *cache* includes web pages you've viewed recently. Your browser stores them in case you want to view the same page again. They are always safe to delete. You can click the View Files button to see a list of filenames.

- **Offline Web Pages**   Your browser can store web pages so that you can look at them when you are offline (not connected to the Internet). You can click the View Pages button to see a list of web pages.

- **Old ChkDsk Files**   When ChkDsk finds misallocated disk sectors, it put them in files. Unless you plan to look in these files for missing information, go ahead and let Disk Cleanup delete them.

- **Recycle Bin**   Disk Cleanup can empty the Recycle Bin for you. You can click the View Files button to see a list of filenames.

- **Temporary Files**   Always include this category of files when running Disk Cleanup. Windows stores most temporary files in the C:\Documents And Settings\ *username*\Local Settings\Temp folder, although a few may end up in the C:\ Windows\Temp folder (if you installed Windows in a different folder, they are in the Temp folder wherever Windows is installed). Windows can become confused if this folder contains lots of temporary files that should have been deleted automatically but weren't.

- **WebClient/Publisher Temporary Files**   These are temporary files created when you use Web Folders (see "Working with FTP and Web Servers Using Web Folders" in Chapter 26). They are seldom large.

- **Compress Old Files**   On NTFS disks, Windows can compress files that you rarely used, using NTFS compression (not ZIP files). The files aren't deleted. Click the Options button to specify what files are compressed: you enter the number of days within which the files must not have been accessed.

- **Catalog Files For The Content Indexer**   The Indexing Service speeds up searches for files, but creates temporary files in the process. You can safely delete them.

CAUTION Disk Cleanup may recommend deleting files that haven't been used in months, without regard to type. When you click some categories in the Disk Cleanup dialog box, a View Names button appears. Take a look at the names of the files it recommends deleting to make sure that they don't include important documents that you haven't used in months but want to keep.

Running Disk Cleanup

Here's how to run Disk Cleanup any time, not just when Window notices that space is running low:

1. Right-click the disk drive in the Computer window and choose Properties. In the Properties dialog box for the disk, click Disk Cleanup on the General tab. The Disk Cleanup program runs and asks which disk you want to clean up. Choose a disk drive and click OK. The Disk Cleanup program checks the disk for unnecessary files and displays a window, shown in Figure 35-2, that tells you how much disk space you can reclaim by deleting temporary files right now. Of course, this may include temporary files that your programs are currently using!

2. Click the box for each type of temporary file you want Disk Cleanup to delete. For more information on a type of temporary file, click the description; the program displays an explanation of what the files are and what folders Disk Cleanup will delete them from.

3. For additional options, if you have administrator privileges and are choosing to clean everyone's files, click the More Options tab. Three buttons provide other ways to free up disk space, including deleting Windows components you don't use, uninstalling programs, and reducing the amount of space used by the System Restore program (see "Returning Your System to a Predefined State with System Restore" in Chapter 37). Click the corresponding button to try any of these methods.

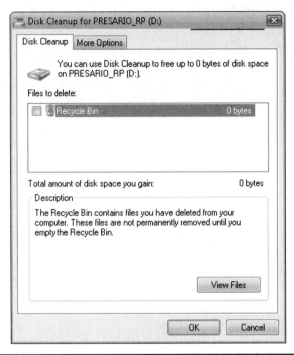

FIGURE 35-2 The Disk Cleanup's list of temporary files to delete.

4. If you want to see the names of the files that will be deleted (in a separate Explorer window), select the type of files to be deleted and click the View Files button.

5. To begin deleting files, click OK. The program asks whether you are sure you want to delete files. Click Yes.

NOTE *The programs shown on the More Options tab that can free up disk space are one-time operations. If you schedule the Disk Cleanup program to run on a regular basis (using Scheduled Tasks), these other programs do not run (see "Running Programs on a Schedule Using Scheduled Tasks" in Chapter 37).*

Disabling Low Disk Space Notification

If your Windows disk is chronically close to full and you don't want Windows to check for low disk space, you can turn this service off. You'll need to edit the Registry to make this change. After backing up your Registry, open the HKEY_CURRENT_USER/Software/ Microsoft/Windows/CurrentVersion/Policies/Explorer key. Set the value of the NoLowDiskSpaceChecks key to 1. If there is no key by that name, right-click the Explorer key, choose New | DWORD Value from the menu that appears, name the new key **NoLowDiskSpaceChecks**, and press ENTER. Double-click the new key and type **1** for its value. Restart Windows to complete the change.

Tuning Windows Vista for Maximum Performance

Windows Vista automatically sets itself up to give you adequate performance. However, as with the launch of any new operating system, to get maximum performance on your PC hardware, you need to tune Windows Vista. Several tools enable you to enhance performance, primarily disk performance:

- **Performance Options dialog box**   Shows you display, processor, and memory settings that affect performance
- **Task Manager**   Displays the system resources of your computer
- **System Monitor**   Displays graphs of system usage

Another important way to speed up Windows is to tune your hard disk to speed up disk access. Finally, be sure to check what programs Windows is running automatically on startup—you may be running AOL Instant Messenger and Quicken BillMinder, for example, without knowing it, slowing down your system.

TIP   Don't make a lot of performance changes at once. Change one or two settings and then wait a day to judge the effects.

On the other hand, in our experience, few tuning techniques make a noticeable difference on a balanced system with adequate memory and disk, although they do make some difference on small systems with slow disks. The best ways to improve system performance are to add more memory and a faster disk, in that order. As with the tradition of Microsoft marketing recommendations about memory, always take the memory requirements you see in the Microsoft marketing collateral and multiply it by two. For example, while writing this chapter, Windows Vista Ultimate specifications read 512 MB minimum. However, we recommend with 1 GB of RAM minimum.

New Tuning Tools in Windows Vista

Windows Vista adds a number of new and powerful tools that users with sufficient privileges can use to tune the performance of their Windows Vista system:

- **Resource view**   Enables you to monitor the usage of CPU, disk, network, and memory resources in real time and to identify which processes use which resources.

- **Reliability Monitor report**   Tracks changes to the system (including application installation, operating system updates, and driver updates) against an overall stability index that recognizes operating system crashes, application crashes, driver failures, and hardware failures as reductions in reliability.

- **Data Collector Set**   Groups data collectors into reusable elements for use with different performance monitoring scenarios.

- **Unified property configuration**   Enables you to configure all data collection, including scheduling.

- **Performance Logs and Alerts features**   Include scheduling of log collection, with improvements to security and reusability of configurations.

- **Server Performance Advisor features**   Include a view of all system performance diagnosis reports.

Inside the Windows Vista Diagnostic Console

The Windows Vista Diagnostic Console controls all Windows Vista performance-tuning and diagnostic tools. The console is set up like a dashboard, with the Resource Overview pane presenting four dynamic graphs. These dynamic graphs present the real-time usage of performance-sensitive system resources, including CPU, hard disk, network, and memory resources on the local computer.

You can drill down into the scrolling graphs by clicking the drop-down arrow beside one of the four expandable sections that provide more detail about each resource's performance.

Accessing the Performance Monitor

While the Windows Performance Monitor is a valuable utility, you aren't going to have access to the system mysteries it divines unless you are a member of your PC's Administrators group.

Perform the following steps to access the Performance Monitor:

1. Log onto the computer using an account that is a member of the Administrators group.

2. Choose Start | All Programs | Accessories | Command Prompt.

3. At the command prompt, type **perfmon**. Press ENTER. The Reliability and Performance Monitor appears.

Viewing the Graphs

The four graphs in the Resource Overview pane are powerful tools, even to the non-PC technicians out there. While you may be locked out of the Resource Overview pane on your employer's PC due to restrictions on administrator privileges, you should have access to the console on your personal PC (unless you are sharing the PC and don't have administrator privileges for some reason or another).

Even if you consider yourself a "non-techie," you can easily get an interesting picture of the inner workings of your PC by periodically viewing the graphs in the Resource Overview pane. The next few sections delve a bit deeper into the contents of the Resource Overview pane's graphs.

CPU Graph

If your PC's central processing unit (CPU) slows down, your overall computing experience is going to suffer. The Resource Overview pane's CPU graph encapsulates the total percentage of CPU capacity chugging along in your PC. CPU usage is broken down by the following graphical elements:

Element	Description
Image	Delineates the application using CPU resources
PID	Displays the process ID of the application instance
Threads	Shows the number of threads currently active from the application instance
CPU	Shows the number of CPU cycles currently active from the application instance
Average CPU	Displays the average CPU load resulting from the application instance expressed as a percentage of the total capacity of the CPU

Disk Graph

Poor hard disk performance is another drag on system performance. The Disk graph displays the total current disk I/O, broken down as follows:

Element	Description
Image	Shows the application using disk resources
PID	Displays the process ID of the application instance
File	Shows the file being read and/or written by the application instance
Read	Displays the current speed at which data (in bytes/min) is being read from the file by the application instance
Write	Shows the current speed at which data is being written to the file (in bytes/min) by the application instance
Total	Displays the current disk I/O (in bytes/min) in use by the application instance

Network Graph

The Network graph displays the current total network traffic (in Kbps). The Network graph includes the following information:

Element	Description
Image	The application using network resources
PID	The process ID of the application instance
Address	The network address with which the local computer is exchanging information; may be expressed as a computer name when referring to other computers on the same LAN, as an IP address, or as a fully qualified domain name
Send	The amount of data (in Kbps) the application instance is currently sending from the local computer to the address
Receive	The amount of data (in Kbps) the application instance is currently receiving from the address
Total	The total bandwidth (in Kbps) currently being sent and received by the application instance

Memory Graph

The Memory graph displays the current hard faults per second and the percentage of physical memory currently in use. The Memory graph includes the following information:

Element	Description
Image	The application using memory resources.
PID	The process ID of the application instance.
Hard Faults	The number of hard faults currently resulting from the application instance.
Working Set	The number of pages currently resident in memory for the application instance

Tuning Your Computer's Performance with the System Properties Dialog Box

To look at and change settings that affect Windows performance, you use the Performance Options dialog box. Click Start, right-click Computer, and choose Properties to display the System Properties, containing information about many aspects of your computer system. Click the Advanced System Settings link (shown in Figure 36-1) and then click Change Settings. You see the System Properties dialog box.

Tuning Your Display Settings

The Display Settings options of the Personalization window list about a dozen effects that make your screen display look snazzy but that also require processing power almost every time your computer updates the screen. The top part of the dialog box shows four options:

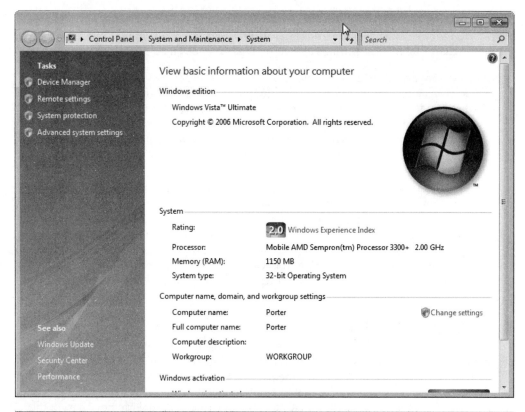

FIGURE 36-1   The System Properties dialog box.

- **Let Windows Choose What's Best For My Computer**   Windows decides which effects to make active (or inactive) based on the system resources you have available. Newer, faster systems have most, if not all, effects selected.
- **Adjust For Best Appearance**   Turns all effects on.
- **Adjust For Best Performance**   Turns all effects off, possibly speeding up your system.
- **Custom**   Enables you to select which effects you want active.

The list of screen effects appears in the lower part of the dialog box with check boxes to show which effects are active. If you select Custom, you can override Windows settings. Most of the effects do exactly what their names say they do, but two names defy comprehension:

- **Use Common Tasks In Folders**   Toggles on and off the Tasks pane that appears by default in all Explorer windows. (We find the Tasks pane useful, so we leave this check box selected.)
- **Use Visual Styles On Windows And Buttons**   Toggles on and off the default Windows Vista appearance.

Tuning Your Processor and Memory Settings

A few settings affect how Windows allocates its resources. Click Settings to open the Setting Properties dialog box. These settings appear on the Advanced tab:

- **Processor Scheduling** Controls how Windows allocates processor time to processes. You can elect to favor either Programs (applications) or Background Services (processes that Windows runs behind the scenes). If your computer provides file, printing, or Internet connection services for other computers on a network, you may wish to select Background Services to give requests from other computers higher priority. Otherwise, leave it at Programs. You can use the computer even if Background Services is selected, though your programs may run slowly.

- **Memory Usage** This setting, which controls how Windows allocates your computer's memory, is interesting. Normally, leave this setting at its default, Programs, to give your programs as much memory as they need. However, if you tend to load a few applications and then run them without loading other applications, you may be better served by selecting the System Cache option. Specifically designed for Web and network servers, this setting can also assist users who frequently access large files. The system cache has priority over the disc cache, and is faster.

Tuning Your Swap File Size

Windows automatically manages program storage by using *virtual memory*, which moves chunks of program and data storage between disk and memory automatically, so individual programs don't have to do all their own memory management.

Normally, Windows manages virtual memory automatically, but in a few cases you may want to change its parameters. Click the Change button in the Virtual Memory part of the Advanced tab of the System Properties dialog box to see the Virtual Memory dialog box. You can specify the disk drive on which Windows stores its *swap file* (the file to which virtual memory is copied), along with the minimum and maximum sizes of the swap file. Click a drive to see the settings for any swap file stored on it.

You might want to set your own virtual memory settings in two cases:

- If you have more than one disk, Windows normally puts the swap file on the boot partition (the partition or drive from which Windows loads). If you have another partition or drive that is larger or faster, you might want to tell Windows to store the swap file there, instead.

- If you are extremely short of disk space, you can decrease the amount of virtual memory and, hence, the disk space that Windows allocates. If you decrease virtual memory too far, programs may fail as they run out of memory. Generally, there's no advantage to increasing the amount of virtual memory beyond the default because extra virtual memory doesn't make the system run any faster.

You can also disable virtual memory altogether, which is usually a bad idea unless you have an enormous amount of RAM.

Tracking System Resources

To keep Windows running smoothly, it helps to know when your system resources are running low. Windows Vista deals with *system resources*—memory used by Windows applications—on a much more sophisticated level than Windows Me/9x. Because it is based on Windows 2000/ NT, Windows Vista inherits its foreparents' technological edge in memory management and does not succumb to the same resource limitations as Windows Me/9x.

Windows Vista runs each application in its own protected memory space. If a program crashes, Vista is far more likely to be responsive than Windows Me was, because other programs and Windows itself are not affected by the crash. The protected memory space also allows you to restart a crashed application safely, which rarely worked in Windows Me/9x. Of course, Windows Vista has its own liabilities.

If you push Windows Vista to the limit of its resources—by running too many programs at the same time—it behaves unreliably, just as Windows Me/9x did. This is because Windows Vista requires access to global system resources just like all other versions of Windows, so the benefits of protected memory do not apply in the event of a general system overload. If you only have a 512 MB system but have 2 GB appetites, your system will operate unreliably, if at all. The best thing to do is to monitor your system to see where your computer's cycles are going. (A *cycle* is a process in which the CPU completes one string of instructions.)

Monitoring System Use with the Task Manager

Windows, like any computer system, can monitor many aspects of its own operation, including CPU use, the software disk cache, disk operations, serial port operations, and network operations. Sometimes, when system performance is unacceptable, you can monitor key aspects and determine where the bottleneck is occurring. This helps determine whether the most effective improvements would be through software reconfiguration or a hardware upgrade, such as adding more memory. The Task Manager is a utility that comes with Windows and displays performance data, running applications, system-level processes, and network operability (see Figure 36-2).

You can run the Task Manager by right-clicking the taskbar and selecting Task Manager, or by pressing CTRL-ALT-DEL and then clicking Start. The Task Manager loads a small icon in the notification area of the taskbar, with bars that indicate at what percentage the CPU is being used.

The Processes tab lists all the processes that are currently running. If you want to see only your applications, rather than all the Windows-related background processes that take up most of the Processes list, click the Applications tab. The Networking tab displays information about your network connection, if any (see Chapter 29). The Users tab (which doesn't appear if Fast User Switching is disabled) shows what user accounts are in use (see Chapter 6).

The Performance tab, as shown in Figure 36-3, reveals a plethora of technical information, the same as the equivalent tab in Windows XP.

The important item to note is the CPU Usage bar graph in the top-left corner. Even when the computer is idle (meaning that no applications are doing anything significant), you still see some activity. However, if the meter spikes and mouse movement is sluggish, a culprit application is probably causing havoc. Switch to the Processes tab and look in the CPU column. (You can click a column heading to sort by the values in that column—click the CPU heading twice to list the highest CPU values at the top of the list.) The System Idle

FIGURE 36-2   The Task Manager.

Process item should have a number from 0 to 99 in the CPU column. If a process is using a lot of CPU cycles, try closing the program that created it. You can also end (kill) a process by selecting it and clicking End Process. If that doesn't work, you may be forced to shut down and restart the computer to stop the rogue process.

Viewing Performance Information and Tools

Previous versions of Windows came with a program called System Monitor, which graphed various measures of system performance. Windows Vista includes Performance Information and Tools to rate your Vista system's performance. You can run it by choosing Start | Control Panel | System And Maintenance | Administrative Tools and clicking the Performance Information And Tools icon. Windows Vista rates your computer's performance, as shown in Figure 36-4.

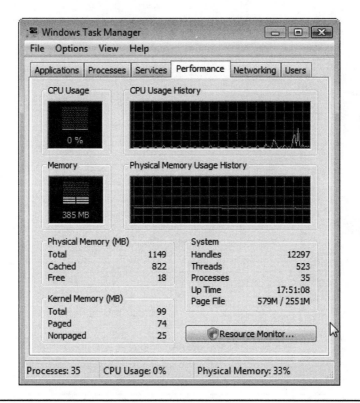

FIGURE 36-3   The Performance tab of the Task Manager.

Tuning Your Hard Disk's Performance

The most effective way to speed up most Windows systems, short of adding extra memory or a faster drive, is to optimize your hard disk. Try these two Windows utilities:

- **Disk Defragmenter**   The most important Windows tuning program is the Disk Defragmenter. As it defragments your disk, this program can also rearrange your executable programs so they can start and run faster.

- **Disk Cleanup**   As time passes, your computer's hard disk gathers junk (such as unneeded files). Windows slows down and may act strangely if too many of these unneeded files have accumulated, especially if they are in your temporary storage folder (usually C:\users*username*\Local Settings\Temp). The Disk Cleanup utility deletes these troublesome files.

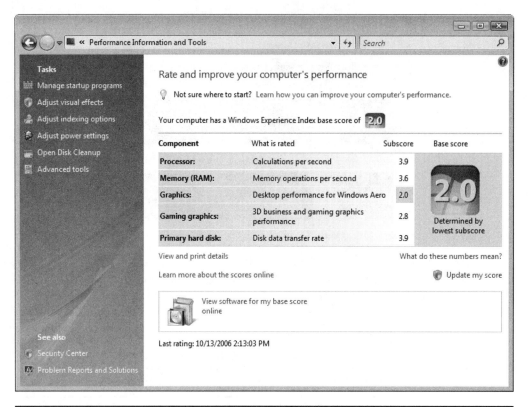

FIGURE 36-4 Performance Information and Tools.

TIP *The biggest space waster of the bunch is Internet Explorer, which is usually configured to occupy as much as 100 MB of your hard disk with temporary files. Two options can help to reduce this waste. First, reduce the amount of space that Internet Explorer uses for its temporary files. Choose Start | Control Panel | Network And Internet Connections and click the Internet Options icon. Or choose Tools | Internet Options from the Internet Explorer menu bar. You see the General tab of the Internet Properties or Internet Options dialog box. In the Temporary Internet Files section of the dialog box, click the Settings button and reduce the space allocation to something more reasonable, like 50 MB. Click OK. Second, click the Advanced tab of the Internet Properties or Internet Options dialog box and scroll down to the Security section of the settings. Select the Empty Temporary Internet Files Folder When Browser Is Closed check box to tell Internet Explorer to remove all old files automatically.*

Disabling Unnecessary Services

Windows has dozens of *services*—special programs running in the background that other programs (including Windows itself) rely on. Most of the services are vital parts of the operating system, but some aren't. For example, if your computer isn't on a LAN, you don't need to run the Computer Browser service, which maintains an updated list of the computers on your LAN.

To see and configure the services running on your computer, choose Start | Control Panel | System And Maintenance | Administrative Tools and click the Services icon. Or, choose Start | Accessories | Run, type **services.msc**, and press ENTER. Either way, you see the Services window. Maximize the window and enlarge the columns so you can read the names and descriptions of the services. Click the Extended tab at the bottom of the window if it's not already selected, so that you see information about the selected service. To read all the information about a service, double-click it so that its Properties dialog box appears.

Services that don't say "Started" in the Status column aren't running, so skip them. Look at each service that is running. If you don't understand what it does, don't stop it.

If a process on the Processes tab of the Windows Task Manager window is taking large amounts of CPU time, a program may be running out of control. To check whether it's a service, note the name of the program and search the Services window for the program name (it appears in the Path To Executable box in the service's Properties dialog box).

You can stop or pause a service by double-clicking the service and clicking the Stop or Pause button on the General tab of the Properties dialog box that appears. To restart a stopped service, click the Start button. Click Resume to restart a paused service. You can also control when the service starts by setting the Service Type on that General tab to Manual (you have to start the service), Automatic (the service starts when Windows starts), or Disabled (the service never starts).

To disable a service so that it doesn't restart when you restart Windows, set its Service Type to Manual. Or, use the System Configuration Utility: choose Start | Accessories | Run, type **msconfig**, and press ENTER. Click the Services tab to see a list of services. To disable a service whenever you start Windows, clear its check box.

Troubleshooting Windows Vista

As with the launch of any new operating system like Windows Vista, you can expect the need to troubleshoot issues, and the news about the Windows Vista betas and release candidates included reports of application compatibility issues and other problems. Even looking at it optimistically, Windows Vista represents a significant upgrade that is going to encounter issues as it gets out of the gate.

If you are a corporate user of Windows Vista, your IT department likely will handle troubleshooting of Windows Vista on your PC. However, if you are a SOHO user, chances are you are on your own when it comes to troubleshooting.

Windows Vista includes some powerful troubleshooting tools, including:

- **Microsoft Management Console (MMC)**   Includes a number of Windows, application, and networking troubleshooting tools for users with administrative privileges over their Windows Vista PC

- **System Restore**   Restores your Windows Vista PC to the last restore point after a catastrophic failure

At the time of writing, Microsoft as an internal document is still keeping the list of incompatible applications, so it is safe to expect application incompatibilities with older applications as Vista reaches the market. So stay informed about the latest Vista news and put some of the web resources documented in Chapter 38 into your RSS (Really Simple Syndication) feed or visit the sites regularly as you transition to Windows Vista.

The Microsoft Management Console

The MMC is a powerful Windows Vista administration and troubleshooting tool available to users with sufficient security privileges. The MMC enables you to administer PC hardware settings, specific areas of Windows, and network components.

The MMC also has snap-ins (small applications) available from Microsoft and third-party application providers. Here is a sampling of MMC snap-ins available by default in the Microsoft Windows Vista Business, Enterprise, and Ultimate editions:

- ActiveX Control
- Authorization Manager
- Certificates
- Components
- Computer Management
- Device Manager
- Disk Management
- Event Viewer
- Link to Web Address
- Local Users and Groups
- Shared Folders
- Task Scheduler
- Windows Firewall and Advanced Security on Local Computer

The Event Viewer

The Event Viewer is your window into errors that sometimes plague Windows Vista. Moreover, with the inevitable application compatibility issues with Windows Vista that may erupt in the weeks and months after the product launch, being able to track system events is going to be key to troubleshooting.

The Event Viewer is available from the Windows Vista Control Panel. The user interface is split into three columns. The far-left column enables access to custom views, Windows Logs, Applications and Services Logs, and subscriptions. The middle column has more of a dashboard look and feel to it with a summary of administrative events by Event Type, Event ID, Source, Log, and Time (Last Hour, 24 Hours, 7 Days, and Total). The far-right column is reserved for actions, including Open Log File and Create Custom Views.

Performance Logs and Alerts

In the and months after the launch of Windows Vista, real people are going to have to get Windows Vista performing under real-life conditions in corporate office and home offices, unlike the pundits and journalists who have been tinkering with the operating system during its beta and release candidates within controlled environments on the latest hardware.

The MMC includes performance logs and alerts that can help you home in on application performance issues that you may encounter with Vista.

Device Manager

Device Manager lets you determine which devices are running on your PC. You can also use Device Manager to update driver software for your devices, check whether hardware is functioning properly, and modify your hardware settings.

Click Start | Control Panel | System and Maintenance | Device Manager to open Device Manager.

NOTE *Access to Device Manager requires you to have administrator privileges to your PC.*

Returning Your System to a Predefined State with System Restore

System Restore can be a life saver if your PC suffers a catastrophic failure. The System Restore feature is available in the Windows Vista Backup and Restore Center, which provides a central interface to all the backup and recovery features available in your edition of Windows Vista. The major backup tools are easily accessible.

System Restore (introduced with Windows XP) enables you to restore your PC to a previous state without losing any of your personal data. It works by creating easily identifiable restore points, which you can use to revert your system to the way it was at a previous time. You can create restore points both at the time of significant system events and periodically. You can also create and name restore points at any time.

Windows Vista offers some performance enhancements over Windows XP System Restore, including the recovery from a greater range of changes.

Automatic Restore Points

When you request a restore point in Windows Vista, Windows creates a shadow copy of a file or folder. This shadow copy is a previous version of the file or folder captured at a specific time.

You can configure Windows Vista to request restore points automatically (recommended) or manually. When you run a restoration, files and settings are copied from the shadow copy to the live volume used by Windows Vista.

Running System Restore

System Restore is turned on by default on all volumes on your PC. The System Restore function regularly tracks changes to your computer's hard disk volumes and creates restore points. You can select which volumes have System Protection turned on.

Be cautious when turning off System Protection on a volume, because this action deletes all of the restore points for that volume. You cannot restore the volume until you turn System Protection on and it creates a new restore point.

You can only turn System Restore on and off if you have administrator access to your PC. Additionally, if your PC resides on a corporate network, Group Policy settings might prevent you from turning system restore on and off.

The following are the steps to turn System Restore on and off:

1. Choose Start | Control Panel | System and Maintenance | System.

2. Click System Protection on the left pane.

3. Select or clear the volume you want to configure under Create Restore Points Automatically On The Selected Volumes. Click OK.

Creating a Restore Point

Microsoft defines a restore point as "a representation of a stored state of your computer's system files." System Restore creates restore points at specific intervals and when it detects the beginning of a change to your computer. You can create a restore point manually at any time as well.

To create a restore point manually:

1. Choose Start | Control Panel | System And Maintenance and then click System.

2. Choose System Protection. The System Protection tab appears.

3. Click Create.

4. Type a description for the restore point in the System Protection dialog box, and then click Create.

Windows Update, Windows Ultimate Extras, and Other Windows Vista Resources

M icrosoft updates Windows constantly to accommodate new hardware and software, to enhance features already found in the system, and to secure the OS against the latest security threats. To stay up to date with these changes, you can run the Windows Update program to scan your system and look for outdated drivers and programs, or you can configure the Microsoft Updates program to download and install updates automatically.

This chapter explains how to update your computer by using Windows Update and Automatic Updates, and how to locate information about Windows from Microsoft and other sources.

However, if you are using Windows Vista on a corporate PC residing on a network, many of the features we mention in this chapter are probably going to be locked down and inaccessible unless you have administrator privileges on your PC.

Updating Your Computer with Windows Update with Windows Ultimate Extras

If your computer is on the Internet, Windows Update can examine your computer and give you a list of device drivers and other files that can be updated based on information from Microsoft's Internet-based servers. When the scan is complete, it presents a list of available updates, and you can choose which update(s) you want to install.

You can run Windows Update with Windows Ultimate Extras at any time to see whether new updates are available. It is especially important to run Windows Update with Windows Ultimate Extras after you install a new piece of hardware or a new software program to be sure you have the drivers and files that you need on your system.

NOTE *You must be logged in with an administrator user account to use Windows Update or Auto Update.*

Windows Update uses a wizard that guides you through the screens to complete the setup. The first time you run Windows Update with Windows Ultimate Extras, you may be asked to register as a Windows user and supply some personal information, such as your name, location, and e-mail address. Windows Update with Windows Ultimate Extras uses Internet Explorer and your Internet settings to connect you to the Microsoft update site on the Web. Before you start Windows Update, be sure your computer is connected or is ready to connect to the Internet. Also, close all your other programs, since some updates require restarting Windows.

To run Windows Update and update your Windows installation, follow these steps:

1. Choose Start | Windows Ultimate Extras, or run Internet Explorer and choose Tools | Windows Update. The Help And Support Center home page has a link to Windows Update, too. Or, choose Start | Control Panel, run Add Or Remove Programs, click Add New Programs, and click the Windows Update button.

2. If your computer is not already connected to the Internet, you may receive an error message saying you are offline; if so, click Retry to attempt reconnecting to the Internet. Windows Update connects to the Microsoft server over the Internet and displays a screen like the one shown in Figure 38-1. The Windows Update with Windows

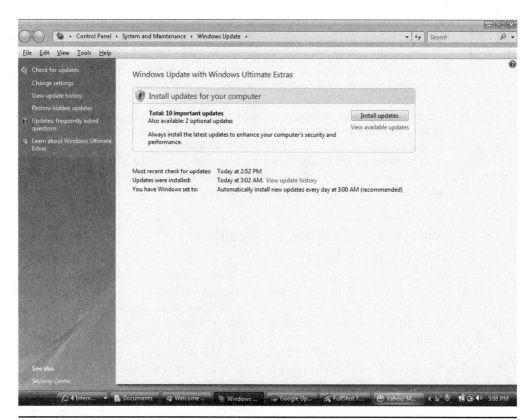

Figure 38-1   Windows Update with Windows Ultimate Extras.

Ultimate Extras page shows options that include your Windows update history, FAQs about the update process, and information about Windows Ultimate Extras.

NOTE *Windows Update works only with Internet Explorer, not with other browsers.*

3. Click the Check For Updates link to check for updates. You see a total number of available updates from which you can choose those appropriate for your system.

4. For each update you want to download, click the Add button.

5. Click Install Updates to install the available Windows updates. If an update requires you to agree to a license, you see a dialog box with the license agreement. Click Accept if you agree to the license agreement.

6. Windows displays a status dialog box to let you know about its progress.

7. Click Restart Now to restart your PC to complete the installation of the downloaded Windows updates.

TIP *To see a list of the updates that you have installed, go to the Windows Update web site as described in Step 1 and click View Update History.*

Updating Your Computer Automatically with Automatic Updates

When you install Windows Vista, within a few days it displays an Update Reminder balloon above the notification area on the taskbar, asking you to configure Windows to update itself automatically over the Internet. This message comes from Automatic Updates, a Windows feature that contacts Microsoft over the Internet, checks for Windows updates, downloads them, and installs them. You can configure Automatic Updates to ask your permission before downloading or installing updates.

If your computer is residing on a corporate network, your network administrator probably has an established Windows Update regimen in place of Automatic Updates via network management tools.

Configuring Automatic Updates

You have two ways to configure Automatic Updates:

- If the Automatic Updates icon or balloon appears in the notification area of the taskbar, click it to see the Windows Update With Windows Ultimate Extras dialog box. Then click Change Settings to Install updates automatically (recommended), Download updates but let me choose whether to install them, Check for updates but let me choose whether to download and install them. You also have the option to include recommended updates when downloading, installing, or notifying me about updates for my computer.

- Choose Start | Control Panel | System And Maintenance and click Windows Update to open the Windows Update With Windows Ultimate Extras dialog box. Click Change Settings, as shown in Figure 38-2.

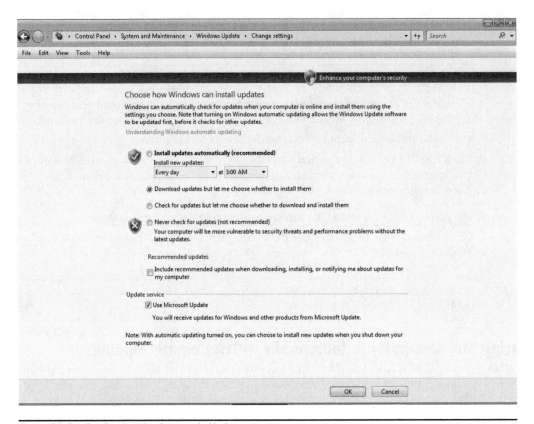

FIGURE 38-2 Configuring the Automatic Updates system.

You see a check box that enables Automatic Updates, and four notification options:

- **Install Updates Automatically (Recommended)** Windows checks to see whether updates are available. If they are, an icon appears in the notification area of the taskbar, and a reminder box asks whether you want to download and install them, as described later in this section. Double-click the icon to see the Windows Update With Windows Ultimate Extras dialog box, and click Install Updates.

- **Download Updates But Let Me Choose Whether To Install Them** When Automatic Updates downloads a group of updates, you can choose which ones to install.

- **Check For Updates But Let Me Choose Whether To Download And Install Them** When Automatic Updates downloads a group of updates, you have the option of which updates to download and install.

- **Never Check For Updates (Not Recommended)** This option leaves Windows vulnerable and should be avoided as a security risk.

CAUTION *We can't recommend the first option strongly enough. Automating the installation of your updates with an overnight installation time is the safest way to keep your machines updated against the next security issue.*

Uninstalling Updates

You can uninstall most updates (the Read More window about each update explains whether it can be uninstalled, and how). For most updates, choose Start | Control Panel, and click Uninstall Programs to open the Change Or Remove A Program dialog box.

Ultimate Extras

If you are using Windows Vista Ultimate, then Microsoft offers Ultimate Extras to help you customize and extend your Windows Vista computing experience.

What are Ultimate Extras?

With the launch of Windows Vista, Microsoft introduces Windows Ultimate Extras, a collection of tips, tricks, programs, and services for maximizing your experience with Microsoft Windows Vista Ultimate.

Windows Vista Ultimate encompasses the following:

- **Windows Ultimate Programs**   Special Microsoft applications designed to enhance your Windows Vista experience, available for download only if you are a Microsoft Vista Ultimate user

- **Windows Ultimate Services**   Aimed at personalizing your Windows Vista Ultimate user experience

- **Tips and tricks**   Help you become a Windows Vista expert in no time as you face the learning curve that comes with all the changes in Windows Vista

Downloading Ultimate Extras

Open Windows Update by clicking the Start | All Programs | Windows Ultimate Extras. However, the Windows Ultimate Extras section of Windows Update only appears when new Windows Ultimate Extras downloads are available for public consumption.

Getting Remote Assistance

Every PC user at one time or another has had to get assistance on a PC issue. Windows Vista includes a remote assistance feature that enables a person you trust to take control of your PC remotely either over a network or the Internet and help resolve your issues.

Programs have been available for years that allow someone to control another computer over the phone or the Internet. Symantec pcAnywhere (at www.symantec.com/smb/products/overview.jsp?pcid=cli_mgmt&pvid=pca12) and Altiris Carbon Copy (at www.altiris.com/Products/CarbonCopySolution.aspx) are popular programs with support technicians. These programs allow the technicians to look at and fix a computer without having to visit the office where the computer sits. Windows XP comes with Remote Desktop, which provides this same functionality (see "Accessing Other Computers with Remote Desktop" in Chapter 16). Remote Assistance is a special version of Remote Desktop that enables you to invite someone to control your PC to help you solve a software problem.

With Remote Assistance, you invite a specific person to take control of your computer. You can contact the person via Windows Messenger or by e-mail. If the person agrees to help, then the helper can control the mouse pointer and type as if he or she were at your computer. You can also chat by typing or talking (if you have microphones and speakers) and send files.

Inviting a Friend to Help

To invite someone to take control of your PC:

1. Open the Help And Support Center window by choosing Start | Help And Support.

2. Click Remote Assistance under Ask Someone. Click Invite Someone You Trust to Help You in the window that appears.

3. Choose whether to contact your helper by using Windows Live Messenger (if installed) or e-mail, identify the person, and click Invite. Then type the message you'd like to send with the invitation (something more specific than "Help!" is useful). In the Set The Invitation To Expire box, specify how long to leave the invitation open.

4. Leave the Require The Recipient To Use A Password check box selected; otherwise, anyone who gets hold of the invitation can take complete control of your computer while the invitation is open. Type a password in the Type Password box that the helper will have to type when taking control.

5. Click Send Invitation.

6. If you use Outlook Express for your e-mail program and Outlook Express is configured to let you know whenever another program tries to send e-mail (a useful anti-virus feature), you see a warning about it—click Send (see Chapter 23, section "Protecting Yourself from E-mail Viruses").

7. Communicate the invitation password to your helper by Windows Messenger, e-mail, phone, or other medium.

8. Wait for your helper to get the invitation and to respond. When your helper receives the invitation and types in the password in response to your invitation, you see a dialog box with the helper's name and the message "Do you want to let this person view your screen and chat with you?"

9. Click Yes to proceed. You see the Remote Assistance window. The left side of the window is where you can chat with your helper.

10. Send a message explaining the problem to your helper by typing in the Message Entry area in the lower-left part of the Remote Assistance window.

Once Windows makes the Remote Assistance connection, you can do the following:

- **Share control of your computer**   When the helper clicks Take Control, you see a dialog box asking whether you want to let the helper share control of your computer. Click Yes to do so. While the helper is using your computer, keep your hands off the mouse and keyboard—it's terribly confusing when two people try to control the mouse pointer or type at the same time! Press Esc (or any key combination with Esc) to end sharing control, or click Stop Control.

- **Send a file**   Click Send A File and specify the filename.

- **Voice chat**   Click Start Talking, if you and your helper have speakers and micro-phones on your computers, to start a voice chat. Click Settings to set the audio quality. If the helper clicks Start Talking first, you see a message asking whether you'd like to start a voice chat.

Click Disconnect when you are done being helped, unless the helper disconnects first.

Responding to an Invitation for Remote Assistance

If you receive an invitation to help someone by using Remote Assistance, you get an e-mail or Windows Messenger message with the subject YOU HAVE RECEIVED A REMOTE ASSISTANT INVITATION FROM: *xx*. The message says something like this:

```
Fred H. would like your assistance. You can easily provide assistance from your
computer by following the instructions at: http://windows.microsoft.com/Remote-
Assistance/en/RA.htm Caution: * Accept invitations only from people you know and
trust. * E-mail messages can contain viruses or other harmful attachments. * Before
opening the attachment, review the security precautions and information at the
above address.
```

The message includes an attached file named rcBuddy.MsRcIncident. (The first part of the filename may be different.) Click the link in the message to read a web page about how Remote Assistance works. (This web page works only in Internet Explorer.)

Follow these steps when you receive an invitation and password from someone you know and want to help:

1. Make sure that you are either connected to the Internet or (if both computers are on the same LAN) to the LAN.

2. Open the attached file. Your e-mail program may display a warning that attached files may contain viruses. Go ahead and open the file. You see the Remote Assistance dialog box.

3. Type the password and click Yes to connect. Remote Assistance makes the connection over the LAN or the Internet. You see a Remote Assistance window but with an image of the other computer screen in the right side of the window. The left side of the window is where you can chat with the other person.

4. Type messages in the Message Entry area in the lower-left part of the Remote Assistance window, and click Send to send the message to the other computer.

TIP   If someone sends you an invitation to help from a computer that has a higher screen resolution than your computer has, you won't be able to see much of the other person's screen in your Remote Assistance window (if you click Scale To Window, it will be unreadable). Set your screen resolution as high as you can.

Once Windows makes the Remote Assistance connection, you can do the following:

- **Control the other person's computer**   Click Take Control and wait for the other person to give permission for you to proceed. When you see a message indicating that you are sharing control, click in the right side of the Remote Assistance window, where the image of the other person's computer screen appears. While your mouse pointer is in that part of the window, its movements also move the mouse pointer on the other computer. However, the other person can also use the mouse and keyboard, and it gets confusing if you both try to do so at the same time. You can click Scale To Window if the image of the other computer screen doesn't fit in the Remote Assistance window, but it usually becomes unreadable: click Actual Size to display the other computer screen at actual size. Press ESC (or any key combination with ESC) to end sharing control, or click Release Control.

- **Send a file**   Click Send A File and specify the filename.
- **Voice chat**   Click Start Talking to start a voice chat. If the other person clicks Start Talking first, you see a message asking whether you'd like to start a voice chat. Both computers need microphones and speakers.

Click Disconnect when you are done helping, unless the other person disconnects first.

NOTE   *If you can't make a connection, one of the computers may be behind a firewall, and you may need to ask the network administrator to enable the port used by Remote Assistance (port 3389).*

Microsoft Vista Support Resources

Microsoft provides a wealth of support information about Windows Vista, including Windows Help and Support, the Microsoft web site, and company-sponsored and hosted web logs.

The Windows Help and Support Center

The Help and Support Center is a set of online and offline help content about Windows and the programs and accessories that come with it. The pages appear in a special Internet Explorer window. Other programs you install may also come with their own online help.

To see the Help and Support Center window (shown in Figure 38-3), choose Start | Help And Support. The Windows Help and Support Center has a browser-like interface consistent with Windows Vista.

When the Help and Support Center window first appears, you can see browser-like controls including a Home button, Print button, Browse Help button, Ask Someone Or Expand Your Search button, and an Options drop-down list. The Windows Help and Support window is subdivided into the following sections:

- **Find Answers**   The Windows Help and Support Center offers help content for a wide range of users, including Windows Basics (for novice users), Maintenance (for advice on how to best maintain your Windows Vista PC), Windows Online Help (a web site with dedicated Windows Vista help content), Table Of Contents (links to a range of Windows Vista help content), Troubleshooting (help for troubleshooting Windows Vista), and What's New (information about all the new Windows Vista features).
- **Ask Someone**   As user assistance has become interactive, Windows Vista enables you to get help from other users via Remote Assistance, online communities where you post questions for other Windows Vista users, and an online contact option for Microsoft Support.

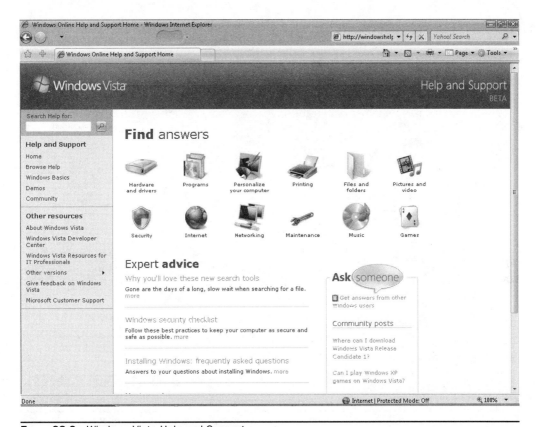

Figure 38-3   Windows Vista Help and Support.

- **Information from Microsoft**   With Windows Vista being such a big departure from previous versions, Windows Help and Support includes information about your file and folder locations, older program compatibility, and how to move your files and settings from your old PC.

You must be connected to the Internet to use the web-based resources accessible via Windows Help and Support.

TIP   *The Windows Vista Welcome Center includes complete information about your PC that can be useful when seeking help online.*

Microsoft Vista Support Sites

Microsoft maintains a number of useful web sites with information about Windows Vista:

- **Microsoft Product Support Services web site, at http://support.microsoft .com**   Site with support information for all Microsoft products (see Figure 36-4). Use the searchable Knowledge Base to find articles about problems and solutions,

FIGURE 38-4 The Microsoft Help and Support web site, where you can search the Microsoft Knowledge Base (MSKB).

known bugs, and overviews of how products work. You can also get to this page by clicking the Support link on the Windows Update web page. The Knowledge Base is a huge searchable database on articles, including bugs and fixes, about all Microsoft products. To search, type the product name and some keywords into the Search The Knowledge Base box (for example, "Windows Vista CD burning"). Each article has an article number consisting of the letter Q followed by a six-digit number; if you know the article number, search for it.

- **Windows Vista home page, at www.microsoft.com/windowsvista** A good resource for general announcements and information about Windows Vista. You can also check the general Windows site at www.microsoft.com/windows.

- **MSDN Vista site, at http://msdn.microsoft.com/windowsvista/** This resource serves as the central online resource for Windows Vista technical references, downloads, and support.

- **Microsoft TechNet, at www.microsoft.com/technet** Free technical support site with background articles for corporate IT (information technology) professionals.

- **Internet Explorer home page, at www.microsoft.com/windows/ie** Each component included with Windows has its own page at the Microsoft web site. The Internet Explorer 7 Home Page introduces the new features in Microsoft Internet Explorer 7.

Microsoft-Sponsored Windows Vista Blogs

Microsoft has embraced blogging as a conduit for its program managers and development teams to develop online dialogues with its customers. The Microsoft Windows Vista Team publishes the following blogs:

- **Windows Vista Team Blog, at http://windowsvistablog.com/blogs/windowsvista/ default.aspx**   This blog's mission is to provide "information on Windows Vista and associated products and technologies that you cannot otherwise get anywhere else."

- **Windows Vista Security, at http://blogs.msdn.com/windowsvistasecurity**   While this blog was just getting started at time of press, this blog has the potential to serve as an ideal dialogue vehicle about Microsoft Windows Vista security.

Related Microsoft Technology Blogs

As you upgrade to Microsoft Windows Vista, the following Microsoft blogs should make good reading:

- **IEBlog, at http://blogs.msdn.com/ie/**   The Microsoft Internet Explorer team uses this blog as a platform to highlight the technology developments in the new Internet Explorer 7, a significant Microsoft Explorer upgrade.

- **Microsoft Team RSS Blog, at http://blogs.msdn.com/rssteam/**   *Reallyl Simple Syndication* (RSS) is an integral part of Microsoft Internet Explorer 7, and the Microsoft Team RSS members detail their RSS development and support efforts on this blog.

- **UACBlog, at http://blogs.msdn.com/uac/**   The Microsoft Windows Vista User Account Control (UAC) Team offers insight into Windows Vista UAC security via this blog.

Other Windows Vista Web Resources

Windows is a popular topic on the Internet. The beta and launch of Windows Vista caused quite a stir on online media sites and the blogosphere. A number of third-party web sites and blogs focusing on Microsoft topics offer support for and analysis into Microsoft software and operating systems including Microsoft Windows Vista.

Third-Party Web Sites

These third-party web sites provide information on a variety of computer-related issues, including Windows:

- **CNET Download.com, at www.download.com**   This CNET site includes a number of popular Windows shareware and freeware software downloads.

- **CNET News.com, at www.news.com**   Current news about Microsoft, Microsoft Windows, and other happenings in the high-tech industry.

- **Microsoft Vista Ultimate, at www.vistaultimate.com**   While this site covers the gaming aspects of Microsoft Windows Vista, it does have well-rounded coverage and analysis of Microsoft Windows Vista news and releases.

- **Paul Thurrott's SuperSite for Windows, at www.winsupersite.com** FAQs (frequently asked questions and their answers), reviews, and news about upcoming Windows releases.

- **WinPlanet, at www.winplanet.com/winplanet** Articles, tutorials, and downloads of utilities and drivers.

Blogs Covering Microsoft Windows Vista

A number of third-party blogs have started covering Microsoft Windows Vista, including:

- **Download Squad, at www.downloadsquad.com** A sister site to the popular Engadget.com blog, Download Squad is an AOL online property covering Microsoft and Microsoft Vista, among a number of other popular software topics.

- **Lifehacker, at www.lifehacker.com** While best known for its posting about technology and "life hacks" (productivity tips), they extend their focus into Microsoft Windows Vista at www.lifehacker.com/windowsvista.

- **Windows Now, at www.windows-now.com/blogs/** This blog sponsored by Interscape Technologies has a mission to spread the word about Microsoft Windows Vista.

- **Tech Blogs on ZDNet, at http://blogs.zdnet.com** This network of blogs from venerable online publisher ZDNet.com (now part of CNET) covers Microsoft Windows Vista from productivity, technological, and technology industry angles.

Google Groups Covering Microsoft Windows Vista

While UseNet is a fading memory to many longtime Internet users, Google Groups (http://groups.google.com) has become an important interactive news and collaborative conduit for a myriad of topics, including Microsoft Windows Vista. Google Groups adds Google's rock-solid network infrastructure and web interface to the aging UseNet newsgroups model.

Google Groups about Windows Vista, including http://groups.google.com/group/WindowsVista and http://groups.google.com/group/windows-vista, were created during the Windows Vista Beta cycle. As Vista launches, it's safe to expect more Google Groups sprouting up to cover Windows Vista–related topics, especially related to tuning and troubleshooting.

VIII PART

Behind the Scenes:
Windows Vista Internals

Windows Vista Configuration Files

Windows stores its configuration information in a variety of files of different formats, including files for configuring Windows itself and files for running Windows and DOS programs. Windows comes with the System Configuration tool (or Msconfig, for short) to help make controlled changes to some of its configuration files. This chapter explains the configuration files used by Windows Vista, as well as how to run the System Configuration program.

What Kinds of Configuration Files Does Windows Vista Use?

Other than the Registry (described in Chapter 40), most of Windows' control information is stored in text files that you can open with Notepad or any other text editor. Although changing these files is usually a bad idea unless you're quite sure you know what you're doing, looking at their contents is entirely safe—and provides fascinating glimpses into how Windows works.

Making Configuration Files Visible

Most of the control information is stored in hidden, system, and read-only files (see "What Are Attributes?" in Chapter 9). Hidden and system files are like any other files, except that they don't normally appear in file listings when you use Windows Explorer to display a folder that contains them. (Any file can be hidden, but only a couple of required files in the root folder of the boot drive are system files.) Read-only files can't be changed or deleted.

You can tell Windows to show you all the hidden files on your computer. In an Explorer window, select Tools | Folder Options and click the View tab. The list of Advanced Settings includes a Hidden Files And Folders category. Click the Show Hidden Files And Folders check box so that a check appears. This setting reveals hidden files in all folders, not just the current folder. Hidden files appear listed with regular files, but their icons are paler than those of regular files. To reveal the hidden files that Windows considers "special," uncheck the Hide Protected Operating System Files (Recommended) check box. Click Yes in the warning dialog box. Click OK when you have finished making changes in the Folder Options dialog box to make the changes active.

You can change a file's hidden or system status by right-clicking the file and selecting Properties. Click the Hidden and Read-only check boxes at the bottom of the Properties dialog box to select or deselect these attributes.

TIP   *We recommend that you leave hidden and system folders and files hidden unless you plan to look at them. They can be distracting during normal work. If you do decide to display them, you can tell hidden and system files from normal files by their dimmed appearance.*

Windows Initialization Files

Since Windows 95, Microsoft has moved most Windows initialization information into the Registry, but Windows still uses two initialization files for 16-bit support: Win.ini and System.ini. Some Windows 3.1 applications stored their setup information in individual *INI files* (initialization files), such as Progman.ini for the Windows 3.1 Program Manager. Other Windows 3.1 programs used sections in the general-purpose Win.ini file.

All INI files have the file extension .ini, and nearly all reside in the folder in which Windows is installed (usually C:\Windows). All INI files have a common format, of which the following is a typical example (it contains configuration information for the WS_FTP file transfer program):

```
[WS_FTP]
DIR=F:\Program Files\WS_FTP
DEFDIR=F:\Program Files\WS_FTP
GROUP=WS_FTP Pro
INSTOPTS=4

[Mail]
MAPI=1
```

What Is %SystemRoot%?

You may see pathnames that include %SystemRoot% in a setting in a dialog box setting or in a configuration file. SystemRoot is a global system variable that tells Windows where the Windows program is stored. Windows replaces %SystemRoot% with the current location of Windows (usually C:\Windows).

Why is this useful? Because if you create a configuration file for your computer and then give it to a friend, your friend's Windows system may be installed somewhere else (for example, F:\Windows on a dual-boot system in which the C: partition is used by a previous version of Windows). Your Windows system could be installed on C: but theirs could be on F: or L: or Z:. Using %SystemRoot% in a configuration file's pathname allows it to work on any system, regardless of circumstance.

An INI file is divided into sections, with each section starting with a section name in square brackets. Within a section, each line is of the form *parameter=value,* where the value may be a filename, number, or other string. Blank lines and lines that start with a semicolon are ignored.

In general, editing the Win.ini or System.ini file is a bad idea, but if you need to do so, use the System Configuration tool (see "Configuring Windows with System Configuration" later in the chapter). You can take a look at the contents of the files using this program, too.

NOTE *While Windows may not make much use of the Win.ini and System.ini files, some third-party software publishers still use application-specific INI files to retain their programs' settings. Take a peek into the program folders for a few of your applications and you'll almost certainly find an INI file.*

The Win.ini File

In Windows 3.1, nearly every scrap of setup information in the entire system ended up in the Win.ini file in C:\Windows, meaning that if any program messed up Win.ini, the system could be nearly unusable. More recent versions of Windows alleviate this situation by moving most configuration information into the Registry, but Win.ini is retained to offer support for 16-bit applications. You'll typically find sections for a few of your application programs in Win.ini, plus a little setup information for Windows itself.

You can use Notepad to edit Win.ini, but it can be dangerous. Be sure to make a backup of the file first.

The System.ini File

In Windows 3.1, the System.ini file in C:\Windows listed all the Windows device and subsystem drivers to be loaded at startup. In Windows Vista the vast majority of the driver information is in the Registry, but System.ini still contains driver configuration information for 16-bit applications. You can edit the System.ini file in Notepad or similar ASCII text editor.

The Registry

The Windows Registry contains all of the configuration information that is not in an INI file, including the vast majority of the actual information used to control Windows and its applications. Use the Registry Editor to examine and manage the Registry (see "Editing the Registry" in Chapter 40).

Configuring Windows with System Configuration

Microsoft provides the System Configuration tool to help you make controlled changes to the various configuration files described earlier in this chapter. To run the System Configuration tool, choose Start | All Programs | Accessories | Run, type **msconfig** in the Open box, and click OK. You see the System Configuration window, shown in Figure 39-1.

The System Configuration window includes a tab for each configuration file, along with the Startup tab, which lists information from the Registry about programs to be run at startup time. Changes you make don't take effect until the next time Windows restarts, so when you close the System Configuration window, it asks whether you want to save the changes you've made; if you click Yes, it offers to reboot Windows for you.

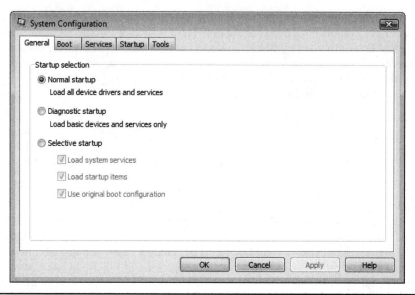

FIGURE 39-1   The System Configuration window.

Restarting Windows with Selected Startup Options

The General tab of the System Configuration window can help you restart Windows in a startup mode that helps diagnose problems. The three startup choices are as follows:

- **Normal Startup**   The default mode. You'll likely switch back to this if things are running smoothly.

- **Diagnostic Startup**   Essentially the same as Safe Mode. This option limits loading device drivers and system services that may interfere with normal operation.

- **Selective Startup**   Enables you to select which startup items to load. A good plan when you experience system instability is to turn all your startup items off, reboot, and then turn one on at a time. If that doesn't help, try different combinations.

If you want to restart Windows and tell it to process only specific configuration files, click the Selective Startup setting and choose the files to process. When you click OK, Windows asks whether you want to reboot your computer. Click Yes. Windows restarts and processes only the files you specified. To save your changes without restarting Windows, click Apply (the changes to the files are saved, but don't go into effect until you reboot).

Changing Your Services and Startup Settings

The Services and Startup tabs in the System Configuration window (Figures 39-2 and 39-3, respectively) show the services and applications that run when Windows starts up, including the startup programs listed in the Registry and the programs in your StartUp folder (usually stored in C:\Users*username*\Start Menu\Programs). You can disable loading a service or program at startup by deselecting its check box.

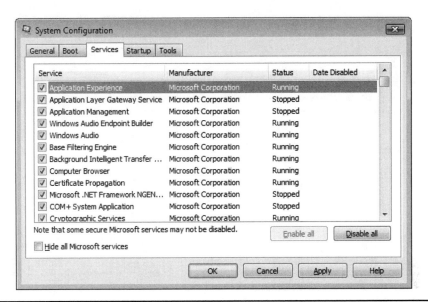

FIGURE 39-2 Editing your Services settings.

NOTE *We strongly suggest that you avoid modifying the Services tab at all. When installed as a workstation or home system, most of these services are already disabled, so unchecking them results in no change of functionality anyway. The Startup tab, which lists application programs, is where you should concentrate your debugging efforts.*

Launching System Tools

Windows Vista has added a new tab to the System Configuration tool: the Tools tab, as shown in Figure 39-4. On this tab you can launch several system configuration programs to help you diagnose, troubleshoot, and solve problems with your Windows installation. The tools include:

About Windows	Programs	Task Manager
System Information	Security Center	Disable UAC
Remote Assistance	System Properties	Enable UAC
System Restore	Internet Options	Command Prompt
Computer Management	Internet Protocol Configuration	Registry Editor
Event Viewer	Performance Monitor	

To start a tool, simply select it on the Tools tab and click Launch.

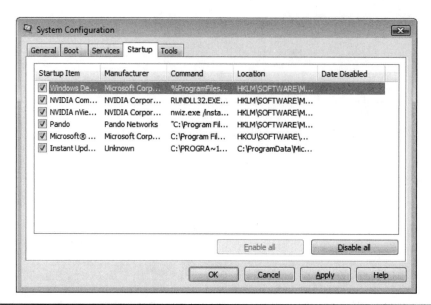

FIGURE 39-3   Editing the Startup settings.

Changing Your Environment Settings

DOS and early versions of Windows used *environment variables* to store some settings.
Environment variables can be changed while Windows is running by using the

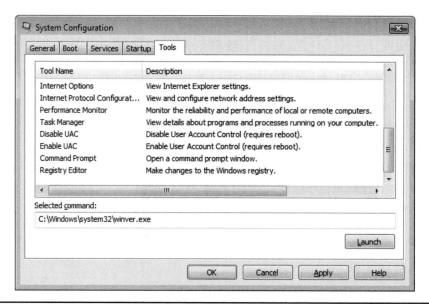

FIGURE 39-4   The Tools tab provides links to system tools.

DOS SET command. When Window or a DOS VM (virtual machine) start up, the variables must be *initialized* (that is, set to their initial values).

To see or set your environment variables, click Start, right-click Computer, and select Properties from the shortcut menu. In the System Properties window that appears, click the Advanced System Settings link on the Tasks pane, and then click the Environment Variables button. You see the Environment Variables dialog box (shown in Figure 39-5). The upper part of the dialog box shows user variables (which store information about the current user account). The lower part shows system variables (which store information about Windows itself).

The two default user variables are TEMP and TMP. Both define where Windows stores its temporary files. The default system variables, which you should not remove or modify, are as follows:

- **ComSpec**   Location of the Command Prompt program (usually C:\Windows\System32\Cmd.exe).

- **NUMBER_OF_PROCESSORS**   For single-CPU computers, 1.

- **OS**   The name of your operating system. Though a bit odd for more than one reason, Windows Vista's name appears as "Windows_NT."

- **PATH**   Where Windows looks for executable programs for launching applications from the command prompt (usually a list of pathnames, including C:\Windows\System32 and C:\Windows).

- **PATHEXT**   Shows which extensions are recognized as executable when launching from the command prompt (usually a list of extensions, including COM, BAT, CMD, VBS, VBE, JS, JSE, WSF, and WSH).

- **PROCESSOR_ARCHITECTURE**   Usually x86, the types of processors designed and sold by Intel.

- **PROCESSOR_IDENTIFIER**   Description of your computer's CPU. Ours shows x86 Family 15 Model 2 Stepping 7, GenuineIntel.

- **PROCESSOR_LEVEL**   Stepping level in the PROCESSOR_IDENTIFIER.

- **PROCESSOR_REVISION**   Revision number of the processor. Ours is 0207.

- **TEMP**   Where to store temporary files (usually C:\Windows\Temp).

- **TMP**   Where to store temporary files (usually C:\Windows\Temp).

- **USERNAME**   Shows what the username is. Ours shows SYSTEM.

- **WINDIR**   Location of the system directory (usually C:\Windows).

CAUTION *Do not remove or modify these system variables.*

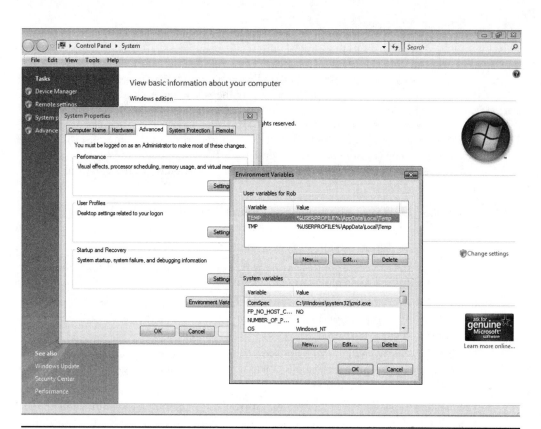

FIGURE 39-5   User and system environment variables.

40

Registering Programs and File Types

The Windows Registry stores configuration information about the programs you run, including which programs Windows uses to open, create, and edit each type of data file. It also includes configuration information for each user account you create on your system. You can use the Registry Editor program to edit the Registry, but do so with caution!

What Is the Registry?

Early versions of Windows scattered configuration settings among dozens of different files. Many settings were stored in C:\Windows\Win.ini and C:\Windows\System.ini, but programs were as likely to use their own INI files as the standard ones, and there was no consistency in the way that INI files were created and maintained. In Windows 95, Microsoft created the *Registry*, a single centralized database in which programs keep their setup information (see "Windows Initialization Files" in Chapter 39). The Registry contains all of the information that the INI files contained, as well as other settings from around the system. All subsequent versions of Windows store configuration information settings in the Registry, and the Win.ini and System.ini files remain only for backward compatibility with older programs.

The Registry contains configuration settings for Windows itself, as well as for most programs you have installed. It also includes user profile information, and information about each hardware component.

Most of the time, the Registry works automatically in the background, but in a few circumstances, you may want to edit it yourself.

Where Is the Registry Stored?

The Registry is stored in a group of files in your C:\Windows\System32\Config folder (assuming that Windows Vista is installed on C:). The files with no extension (Default, Software, System, Sam, Security, Userdiff) contain the actual Registry entries. The SAV files are copies of the corresponding files made when you installed Windows. User profile information is stored in files named Ntuser.dat in the user's folder in C:\Users.

> **NOTE** *Although Registry Editor looks and works the same as the Windows Me/9x Registry Editor, the location and format of the Registry files are quite different. The Windows Vista Registry system is based on Windows 2000/NT and is much larger than its Windows Me/9x equivalent.*

What Are Hives and Keys?

The Registry is organized much like the Windows file system. The Registry contains a set of *hives*, which are like folders, inside of which are stored *keys*. Additional keys can be stored within keys. Each key defines a setting or behavior for Windows or an installed application. Key pathnames are written with reverse slashes between them, much like filenames, so a typical key name is

```
HKEY_LOCAL_MACHINE\System\CurrentControlSet\Services\SysMain
```

This key is in the HKEY_LOCAL_MACHINE hive, which contains a key named System, which in turn contains a key named CurrentControlSet, which contains a key named Services, which contains a key named SysMain. Each key can have one or more *values*, each of which consists of a name, a data type, and some data. A key at any level can contain any number of values, so in the example, values can be associated with HKEY_LOCAL_MACHINE\ System\CurrentControlSet\Services or HKEY_LOCAL_MACHINE\System. (In practice, most of the values are stored at the lowest level or next lowest level.)

The data type of a value can be REG_BINARY (a series of binary or hexadecimal digits), REG_DWORD (4-byte numeric value, also called a *DWORD*), REG_EXPAND_SZ (variable-length *string*, or text), REG_SZ (fixed-length string), REG_MULTI_SZ (list of strings, separated by spaces, commas, or other punctuation), or REG_FULL_RESOURCE_DESCRIPTOR (larger grouping of information for storing a resource list, usually for a hardware driver). You never change the data type of a value: you change the data. (But only if you are *sure* you know what you are doing!)

The Top-Level Hives

The Registry comes with these hives at the top level of the tree structure (directly under the My Computer entry in the Registry):

- **HKEY_CLASSES_ROOT**   File associations for file types
- **HKEY_CURRENT_USER**   Configuration information for the current user account
- **HKEY_LOCAL_MACHINE**   Configuration information about the computer, for all users
- **HKEY_USERS**   Configuration information for all user accounts
- **HKEY_CURRENT_CONFIG**   Hardware profile information for the hardware profile that your computer uses at startup

Associating File Types with Programs

In Windows, every file has a *file type*, determined by the file extension (usually three letters) after the dot (see "What Are Extensions and File Types?" in Chapter 8). For example, My Proposal.doc has type DOC, so one usually calls it a DOC file. Every file type can be associated with a program or group of programs, so when you open a file of that type in an Explorer window (by clicking or double-clicking the file), the associated program runs automatically to process the file. Most programs associate themselves with the appropriate file types when you install the program, but in two circumstances, you may want to set your own associations:

- **Dueling programs**   When two or more programs can handle the same type of file, whichever one you installed most recently wins, unless you intervene. This problem is particularly common with graphics formats such as GIF and JPG, because both graphics editing programs (such as the Windows Photo Gallery that comes with Windows Vista) and web browsers (such as Internet Explorer) can display them. You can change the association to whichever program you prefer, and Windows Vista can display a list of the programs that should be able to open a file.

- **Nonstandard file extensions**   Many files with unknown types are, in fact, known types in disguise, or close enough to known types that a program you have installed can handle them. For example, most LOG files are actually text files that Notepad, WordPad, or any other text editor can read. Word processors can almost all read each other's files; for example, if you use WordPerfect rather than Word, you can associate DOC files with WordPerfect.

The Windows file association facility is complex and flexible. A file type can have several programs associated with it to do different actions, such as viewing and editing a file.

To see or change the details of a file association or to create a new association, open the Default Programs tool by choosing Start | Default Programs. Choose Associate A File Type Or Protocol With A Program. Highlight an extension and click Change Program to choose a different program to run when you open that type of file. Windows lists the programs that it recommends for handling this type of file, along with other programs that it knows can open them. You can also browse to other programs that are not listed. (See "Associating Files with Programs by Using the Default Programs Option" in Chapter 3.)

Tip   When you try to open a file from the Explorer window but the filename extension isn't associated with any program, Windows opens a dialog box explaining that it can't open the file. It offers two choices: downloading a program from the Internet, or using the Open With window to choose an application that you have on your computer. If you do not see the application you want to use, click the Browse button at the bottom of the dialog box and find the file that contains the program. You can also create a file association for this file type by entering a short description of the file type and selecting the appropriate application from the Programs list. Unless you uncheck the Always Use The Selected Program To Open This Kind Of File box, Windows saves the association.

Editing the Registry

The Windows Registry contains a great deal of information beyond the file associations discussed in the previous section. For the most part, you won't need to do any editing yourself, but occasionally, a bug fix or parameter change requires a change to the Registry, so you need to be prepared to do a little editing now and then. If you're interested in how Windows works, you can also spend as much time as you want nosing around the Registry with the Registry Editor program.

CAUTION *Never make changes to the Registry without first making a backup! Better yet, include the Registry in your daily backups (see Chapter 10).*

Restoring the Registry

If the Registry is damaged, you can restore it from a backup. Follow these steps:

1. Save your files and close all your programs.
2. Choose Start | Shut Off. Windows shuts down.
3. Restart the computer.
4. When you see the message Please Select The Operating System To Start, press F8. Windows displays a list of options (see Chapter 37).
5. Press the UP-ARROW or DOWN-ARROW until you highlight the Last Known Good Configuration option, and press ENTER. (If the ARROW keys don't work, press NUM LOCK to enable them.)
6. Choose the operating system (such as Windows Vista Ultimate). Windows then restores your most recently backed-up values for the HKEY_LOCAL_MACHINE\ System\CurrentControlSet hive in the Registry and restarts Windows.

If the Registry entries for an application get damaged, consider uninstalling and reinstalling the program. If restoring a backup of the Registry still doesn't fix your problem, you may have to back up your data, reformat the disk (or partition) on which Windows is installed, and reinstall Windows and all your programs.

NOTE *System Restore can also restore a previous version of the Registry (see "Returning Your System to a Predefined State with System Restore" in Chapter 37).*

Running Registry Editor

Registry Editor (Regedit for short) lets you edit anything in the Registry. To run Registry Editor, select Start | All Programs | Accessories | Run, type **regedit**, and press ENTER. This chapter describes Registry Editor version 6.

CAUTION *Registry Editor has almost no built-in checks or validation, so be very sure that you make any changes correctly. It does not have, for instance, an Undo command. Incorrect Registry entries can lead to anything from occasional flaky behavior to complete system failure. We suggest that you export the keys that you plan to edit before making any changes, so that you can reimport them if the changes cause problems.*

Finding Registry Entries

Registry Editor has a two-part window, shown in Figure 40-1, much like Windows Explorer. Each key is shown as a folder in the left pane of the Registry Editor window. When you select a key in the left pane, the name and data of each of its values appear in the right pane. You can expand and contract parts of the name tree by clicking the + and – icons in the key area. Select any key to see the names and data of the values, if any, associated with that key.

If you know the name of the key you want, you can navigate through the key names similar to the way you navigate through files in Windows Explorer.

If you don't know the name of the key, you can search for it by choosing Edit | Find (or pressing CTRL-F). You can search for any combination of keys, value names, and value data. For example, if you mistyped your name at the time you set up Windows and want to correct it, search for the mistyped name as value data. Press F3 to step from one match to the next.

TIP *As you edit Registry entries, Registry Editor makes the changes right away—there's no Save, Cancel, or Undo command. You can edit the Registry and leave the Registry Editor window open while you check whether your changes produce the desired effect. Some programs aren't affected by Registry changes until they are restarted; others reflect the changes immediately.*

When you run Registry Editor again, it displays the key that you were looking at when you last exited the program, so it's easy to continue making changes to the same key.

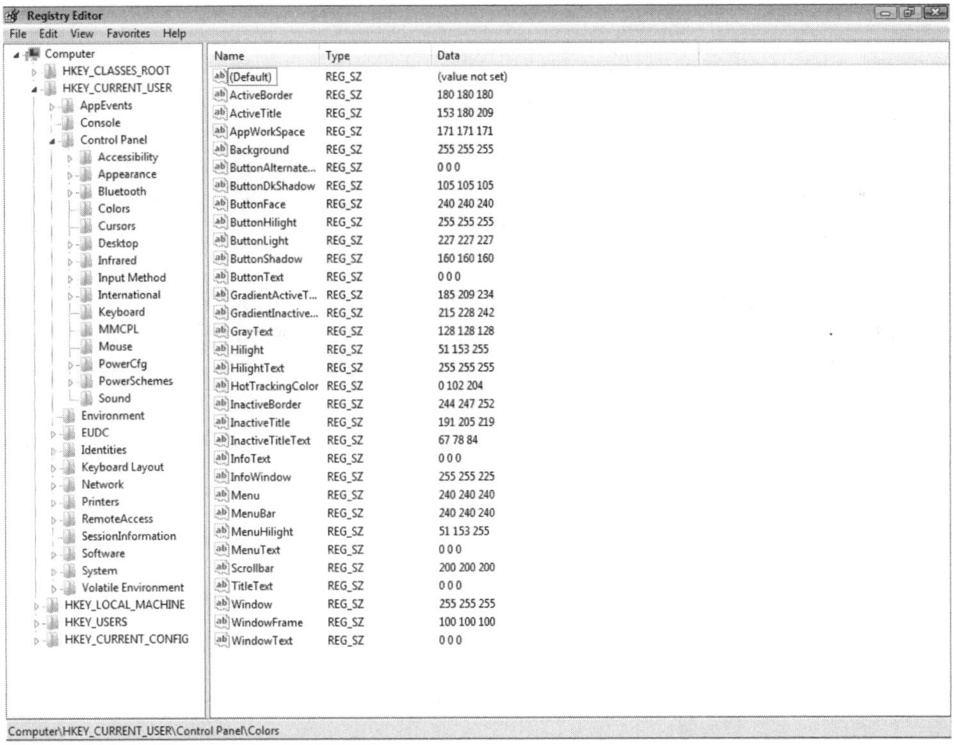

FIGURE 40-1   Looking at the Registry.

Adding and Changing Registry Entries

You can add, edit, and delete Registry entries (but be sure you back them up first):

- **Changing the data of a value**   Double-click the name of the value (in the Name column of the right pane of the Registry Editor window). Registry Editor displays a dialog box in which you can enter the new data for the value. You see the Edit String dialog box, which looks different depending on the data type of the value you are changing:

You can't change the type of a value, so you have to enter a text string, a numeric value, or a string of hexadecimal digits, depending on the type of the data.

- **Renaming a key or a value**   Right-click its name and choose Rename from the menu that appears. (Don't rename a value that Windows or another program uses, because Windows won't be able to find the key under its new name.)

- **Creating a new key**   Right-click the folder (key) into which you want to add the new key and choose New | Key from the menu that appears. As in Windows Explorer, the new key is created with a dummy name. Type the name you actually want and press ENTER.

- **Creating a new value**   Right-click the key in which you want store the new value, choose New from the menu that appears, and choose the type of value (String Value, Binary Value, or DWORD). Once you've created a value, double-click the value's name to enter its data.

- **Deleting a value or key**   Select the value or key and press DELETE.

TIP *If you're not absolutely sure about deleting a key, rename it. Add an underscore or number to the end, so that the Registry doesn't recognize it but you will if you need to change it back later.*

You can also rename and delete keys and values by using the Edit menu.

TIP *If you want to remember the name of a Registry key—or tell a friend about it—you can copy it to the Clipboard. Select the key whose complete name you want, and choose Edit | Copy Key Name.*

Editing the Registry as a Text File

Another way to edit the Registry is to export all or part of the Registry to a text file, edit the text file, and then import the changed values back into the Registry. You can export and import the entire Registry or one "branch" of the Registry's tree of keys. Registry Editor stores the exported Registry entries in a *registration file* with the extension .reg.

A registration file consists of a series of lines that look like this:

```
[HKEY_CLASSES_ROOT\.bfc\ShellNew\Config]
"NoExtension"="Temp
```

The first line is the name of the key (enclosed in square brackets) and the lines that follow are the values in the key, in the format *"name"="value"*.

NOTE *Windows Vista (like Windows XP) exports the Registry using Unicode rather than plain text. You can't export keys from the Windows Vista Registry and import them into a Windows Me/9x Registry.*

Follow these steps to edit the Registry by using a text editor:

1. Select a hive or key in the left pane, choosing one that contains all the keys that you want to edit. To export the entire Registry, select the Computer item at the root of the Registry tree.

2. Choose File | Export to write the text file. Registry Editor asks you for the folder and filename to use for the registration file. Then it writes the data into the new file, which may take a few minutes.

3. Edit the registration file in any text editor. (Notepad works fine.) Right-click the REG file in Windows Explorer and choose Edit from the shortcut menu that appears. Notepad runs (or another text editor, if you choose it). Make as few changes as possible to the file and save the file.

4. In Registry Editor, choose File | Import to read the edited file back into the Registry. The keys and values in the imported file replace the corresponding keys and values in the Registry. Note that if you delete a key or value in the text file, importing the file doesn't delete the key or value in the Registry.

TIP *The Registry is quite large—an exported version of the whole thing can be 50MB or more. If you do plan to edit it, just export the branch you plan to work on.*

Running Programs on Startup

You can tell Windows to start a program automatically when Windows starts up by including a shortcut to it in the Startup folder of your Start menu (see "Starting Programs when Windows Starts" in Chapter 2). However, there are two other ways to run a program automatically when Windows starts: lines in the Win.ini file and keys in the Registry.

The Win.ini file (which is stored in C:\Windows, assuming that Windows in installed on C:), can include lines like this:

```
run=program
load=program
```

Replace *program* with the pathname of the file that contains the program. To stop a program from running, remove this line from the Win.ini file, or add a semicolon at the beginning of the line.

Two places in the Registry can contain entries that run programs at Windows startup. Look in these two keys:

```
HKEY_LOCAL_MACHINE\Software\Microsoft\Windows\Current Version
HKEY_CURRENT_USER\Software\Microsoft\Windows\Current Version
```

These keys can contain keys named Run, RunOnce, or RunOnceEx, which contain values that start programs when Windows starts. To stop the program from running, remove or rename the key.

Installing or Upgrading to Windows Vista

If you didn't buy a computer with Windows Vista already installed, you face the task of installing Windows Vista—either installing it on a blank hard disk or upgrading your existing operating system. This appendix explains your installation options and how to install or upgrade to Windows Vista. The Install Windows wizard runs for several hours (depending mainly on the speed of your DVD drive). You'll also find out what Windows Vista's hardware requirements are.

During installation, Microsoft's product activation system requires you to check in with Microsoft so that your copy of Windows Vista can be "locked" to your particular computer. If you are replacing an old computer with a new one, you may want to use the Files And Settings Transfer Wizard to help you move your files to Windows Vista after the installation process completes.

What Versions Are Available?

Windows Vista comes in several different versions. The installation DVD includes all these versions. However, you must have the proper product activation key to unlock the version you purchased. For example, if you purchase Windows Vista Basic and you install Windows Vista Ultimate, your product activation key will not work.

The following describes each version:

- **Windows Vista Starter** is available in 119 emerging markets and includes features that help new users use their computer. Microsoft does not plan to sell this version in the United States, Canada, the European Union, Australia, New Zealand, and other world markets that have high income levels.

- **Windows Vista Home Basic** includes basic features, such as features allowing you to easily set up Internet connections, features to set up parental controls, and ways to create documents. Many of the advanced Windows Vista features, however, are not included with Home Basic.

- **Windows Vista Home Premium** provides your computer with Media Center so you can turn your computer into a media hub. Home Premium includes the new Vista Aero design.

- **Windows Vista Business** is primarily suited for the business user. It includes security tools and Microsoft Backup. However, it does not include the media tools, such as Windows Photo Gallery.

- **Windows Vista Ultimate** includes everything, including business tools, multimedia features, and Aero. Vista Ultimate is a hybrid of Vista Business and Home Premium. It lets you use your computer as a media center, but has the enhanced business features, too.

- **Windows Vista Enterprise** boasts drive encryption and other high-end features, such as compatibility mode.

What Are the Windows Vista Installation Requirements?

To install Windows Vista, you need the following:

- A Windows Vista DVD and product activation key.

- A DVD drive.

- A Pentium III, Celeron, or compatible CPU running at a speed of at least 800 MHz. You must have at least a 1 GHz processor for the Aero features to function.

- At least 512 MB of RAM memory, but at least 1 GB of RAM for Aero features.

- A hard disk with a capacity of 40 GB and 15 GB of free space.

- A graphics card that supports DirectX 9 and WDDM (Windows Display Driver Model), and has 128 MB of graphics memory for the Aero features.

- A Super VGA or better monitor.

- A keyboard and mouse (or other pointing device).

What Are Your Installation Options?

You can install Windows in one of the following ways:

- **From scratch**   Install Windows on a blank, formatted hard disk or on a blank partition of a hard disk.

- **Upgrade**   Install Windows Vista over Windows XP.

Because Windows Vista does not use the Boot.ini file as did previous versions of Windows, dual-boot configurations are not officially supported. Once you install Windows Vista on a computer that also includes Windows XP, you will not be able to start XP again. There are, however, some programs and configuration settings that you can find that will help you create dual-boot setups. This book, however, does not cover them.

How Does Product Activation Work?

In addition to entering a 25-character product key, Microsoft now requires you to *activate* your copy of Windows. Microsoft requires product activation for Windows Vista, Microsoft Office 2007, and most of their new or upgraded software. Windows Vista allows you 30 days of use before requiring activation. When the 30 days expires, if you haven't activated Windows, it won't let you log on until you activate it.

How does activation work?

Many of the components inside any computer have unique serial numbers that are routinely read by the operating system. The Install Windows wizard collects data about the hardware components of your computer as it installs drivers for the hardware you have installed in your system. It then creates an individually identifiable *activation ID* that it applies to your computer. When you activate Windows Vista, Windows sends your activation ID to Microsoft's databank, where the information is stored, and Microsoft's activation server "unlocks" (activates) your copy of Windows. (If your computer isn't connected to the Internet, you need to call Microsoft to send your activation ID.) Each time you reinstall Windows Vista, you must reactivate it, and Microsoft checks that the activation ID hasn't changed.

NOTE *Product activation does not limit the number of times you can reinstall Windows Vista on a single machine.*

You can't install the same copy of Windows Vista on several different computers, because they have different hardware serial numbers. If you try, when the activation ID is checked against your original activation ID, they won't match, so Microsoft won't allow you to activate Windows Vista. This is how Microsoft's product activation prevents casual piracy. For example, if you forget about activation and loan your copy of Windows Vista to a friend, when he installs it on his computer it will create a different activation ID. The problems will begin when your friend tries to activate Windows on his computer and this new activation ID does not match the activation ID of the previously installed version. Even after Windows is activated, you can run into trouble, because Windows periodically checks the activation ID with the activation servers at Microsoft. (Yes, your computer will periodically report to Microsoft's activation servers, and no, you will not be asked permission beforehand.)

Preparing to Install Windows

Here are some tips, including suggestions from Microsoft, for a smoother installation:

- **Check compatibility**   Run the Check Compatibility tool when you are upgrading from Windows XP to Windows Vista. You will see this tool when you run the Install Windows program from the Windows Vista DVD. It finds any problems with hardware and software on your computer before you even start the installation process. For software that is incompatible with Windows Vista, consider uninstalling it before you launch the installation program. After Windows Vista installs, reinstall the software and things may work okay. If not, you can check online for updates or steps to help solve the compatibility problem. In some instances, you will have to upgrade to a newer version of that program.

- **Virus checking**   Run a virus checker on your system before installing Windows, so that no viruses interfere with the installation. You can download one of several good virus checkers from the Internet, including those from McAfee (www.mcafee.com)

and Symantec (www.symantec.com). Then disable your virus checker before installing Windows.

CAUTION   *Some computers have antivirus programs stored in the computer's BIOS. In this case, the Install Windows wizard won't run. If you see an error message reporting an antivirus program, check your system's documentation for instructions on how to disable virus checking.*

- **Disk errors**   Run ScanDisk or ChkDsk (if you use Windows) to clean up any formatting errors on your hard disk.

- **Backups**   Make a complete backup of your system. If that's not possible, make a backup of all of your data files.

- **Program installation disks**   Make sure that you have the program disks (CDs or DVDs) for all the programs you want to install. If you downloaded programs, make backups of the installation files.

- **Disk space**   Make sure that you have enough free space on the hard disk on which your Windows program folder will be stored. Windows needs 15GB of free space.

- **Hardware problems**   If you have problems with hardware or software on your system, fix the problems first or uninstall the hardware or software.

- **Other utilities**   Uninstall any non-Microsoft disk-caching programs, such as the caching programs that come with the Norton Utilities and PC Tools. Turn off other utilities that might interfere with installation, such as CleanSweep (which monitors software installations). Exit from all programs.

- **Network information**   If your computer is on a network, contact your network administrator before upgrading to Windows Vista. Ask whether the computer is part of a domain and, if so, ask for the domain name and your computer's name on the domain. If your network uses static IP addresses (your network administrator will know), ask for your computer's IP address. If your computer isn't part of a domain (that is, it's a peer-to-peer network, as described in Chapter 30), ask for the name of the workgroup. Make sure that your computer is connected to the network during installation, because the Install Windows wizard can detect many LAN and Internet settings and configure your computer automatically.

Starting the Installation

Before starting the installation process, you need to take a few steps, depending on whether you are installing on a blank hard disk, upgrading an existing Windows installation, or creating a dual-boot system.

Installing Windows on a Blank Hard Disk

You must be able to start the computer to start the Windows installation. If you don't have an operating system installed on your hard disk, you need to be able to boot from the Windows Vista DVD.

CAUTION *Formatting your hard disk (or a partition) deletes everything on it. You can't use the Recycle Bin or other unerase programs to get files back. Be sure to make and verify a backup copy of all the files you want to save (see Chapter 10).*

The Windows Vista DVD is bootable; that is, it contains startup operating system files so that you can use it to start your computer. However, your computer must be configured to boot from the CD-ROM/DVD drive. Your computer may look first in the floppy drive and then on the hard drive for operating system files at startup. Try putting the Windows Vista DVD in the DVD drive and starting your computer to see if the computer loads the Install Windows wizard from the DVD. If not, follow the instructions in the rest of this section.

To tell your computer to look on the DVD during startup, you need to change your computer's BIOS setup. The method to do this varies from computer to computer, and you should check your computer's documentation. Generally, you press a key (usually F2, F6, F10, or DELETE) during startup, while the computer manufacturer's logo is on the screen, before you see the Windows logo. Some computers display a prompt to tell what to press (for example, "Press <DEL> key if you want to run setup").

Once you press the correct key, you see your computer's BIOS configuration screen. Follow the instructions on the screen (or in your computer's documentation) to change the boot sequence (or boot order) to start with the CD-ROM (or DVD if that is listed). Then follow the instructions to save your changes and reboot with the Windows Vista DVD in the drive. The Setup program should run. Follow its instructions to install Windows Vista.

Upgrading to Windows Vista

When you upgrade to Windows Vista, the Install Windows wizard can save your old operating system's files and settings, so that you don't need to reinstall all of your programs. You can upgrade to Windows Vista if your computer has Windows XP installed on it.

If your hard disk has become full of junk, or your Windows installation is unreliable, you may want to start from scratch anyway, rather than installing Windows on top of what you already have on the hard disk. Installing from scratch is called a *clean install*, and it reduces problems with older, incompatible program files and with unneeded files that waste disk space. You can save the data files you want to keep, reformat the hard disk, install Windows, install the programs you want to use, and restore your data files. The Install Windows wizard can even do the reformatting for you. A clean install usually saves time in the long run, even though you need to reinstall your programs.

TIP *We prefer to make a separate partition for data (usually D:), move our data files there, and use the C: partition for only Windows and programs (see "Partitions, File Systems, and Drive Letters" in Chapter 34). This allows us to reinstall Windows any time we like without disturbing our data.*

To upgrade from a previous version of Windows, follow these steps:

1. Start your current version of Windows.

2. Put the Windows Vista DVD in the DVD drive. You see the Install Windows window (see Figure A-1). If you don't see this window, use Windows Explorer to look at the contents of the DVD and run the Setup.exe program. Another way to run the program is to choose Start | Run, type **d:\dvd**, and press ENTER (if your DVD drive is drive D:).

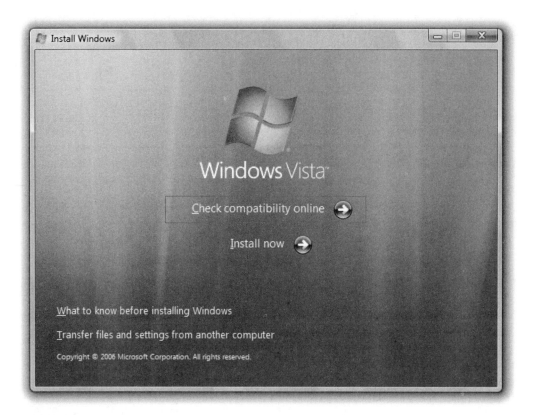

Figure A-1   The Install Windows window.

3. Click Check Compatibility Online to run the compatibility check for your computer hardware and software. The compatibility test creates a report that lists hardware and software issues that may cause problems. If there are problems and Windows Vista can still install, the compatibility test tells you that. You can proceed. Any known issues can be looked at after Windows Vista installs. For issues that cannot be resolved, Windows Vista will not allow you to continue with the installation process. You must fix the problems (such as add more memory if you have less than 512 MB installed) before continuing.

4. After the Check Compatibility tool runs and you get a clean bill of health (or at least your computer does), click Install Now.

5. Follow the instructions that the Install Windows wizard displays (see the next section).

Answering the Install Windows Wizard's Questions

Follow the steps outlined in this section to install Windows once you have started the Install Windows wizard and you see the Welcome To Microsoft Windows Vista window, shown in Figure A-1. (The second option, Install Optional Windows Components, appears only when you run the program on a system that is already running Windows Vista.) You can press ESC at any time to cancel your installation. Click Next to move from one screen of the Install Windows wizard to the next.

1. To start the installation, click Install Windows Vista.

2. In the first Install Windows screen, you're prompted whether you want to check the Windows Vista Update site to download any updates (see Figure A-2). You also can bypass this procedure by clicking Do Not Get The Latest Updates For Installation.

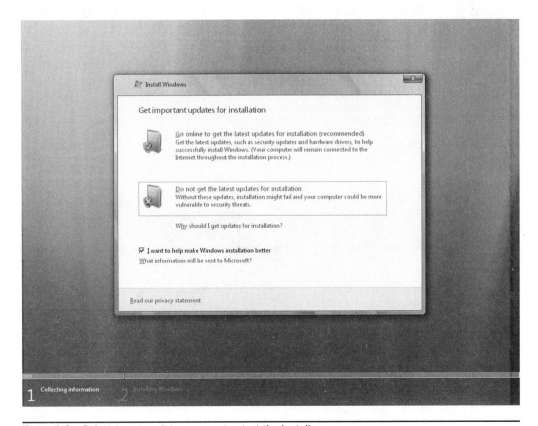

FIGURE A-2   Select to get updates now or to start the install process.

3. In the next Install Windows dialog box, enter your product key number (see Figure A-3). Click Next.

4. If you do not enter a product key in Step 2, an Install Windows dialog box appears asking you to select the Windows Vista edition you purchased. Select the version, click I Have Selected The Edition Of Windows That I Purchased, and click Next.

5. Click I Accept The License Terms and click Next.

FIGURE A-3 Enter your 15-digit product key.

6. In the Install Windows dialog box, set the installation type to either Upgrade or Custom (as shown in Figure A-4).

Choose Custom if you want to specify on which partition you want to install Windows Vista. The Upgrade choice sets up Windows Vista on the partition on which Windows XP was installed.

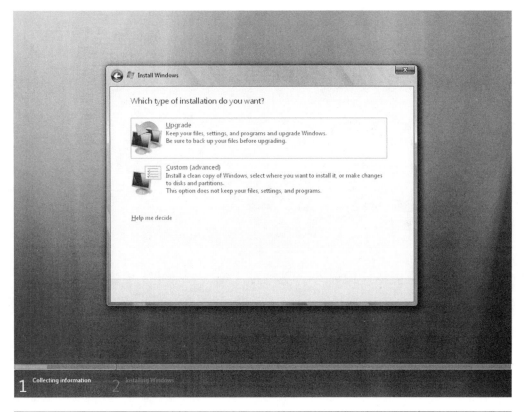

FIGURE A-4   Specify the installation type.

7. If you chose Upgrade, the Install Windows wizard displays the Compatibility Report screen, which shows a report of any compatibility problems Window discovered on your computer. Figure A-5, for example, shows that the device drivers for the sound card in my system need to be upgraded for sound to work correctly.

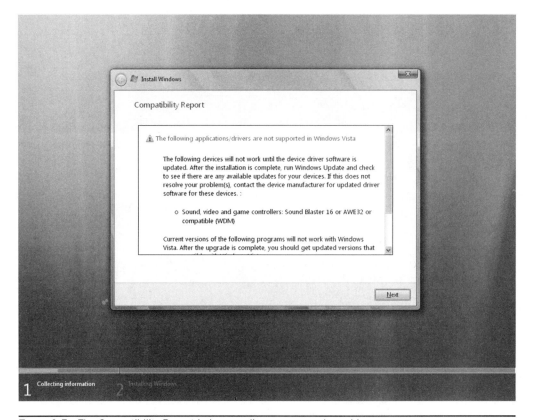

FIGURE A-5   The Compatibility Report helps you diagnose upgrade problems.

8. If you chose the Custom installation option, you can choose the drive on which Windows Vista installs, as well as other options (see Figure A-6).

9. The Install Windows wizard begins the lengthy install process. The Installing Windows screen (see Figure A-7) appears to show you the progress of the installation. Do not shut down your computer or try to remove the DVD during this stage. It takes several hours for Windows Vista to install. During the installation process, Windows

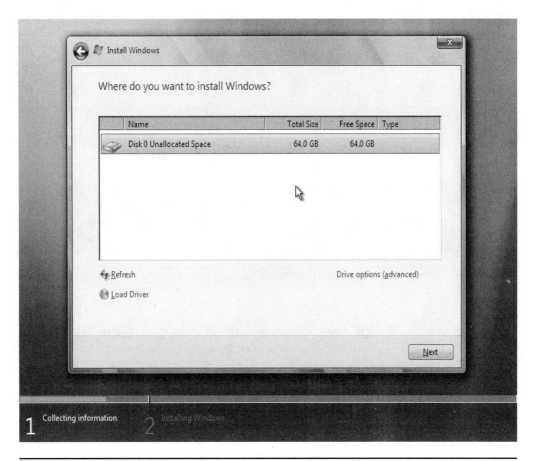

FIGURE A-6   To change partition setup parameters, click Drive Options (Advanced).

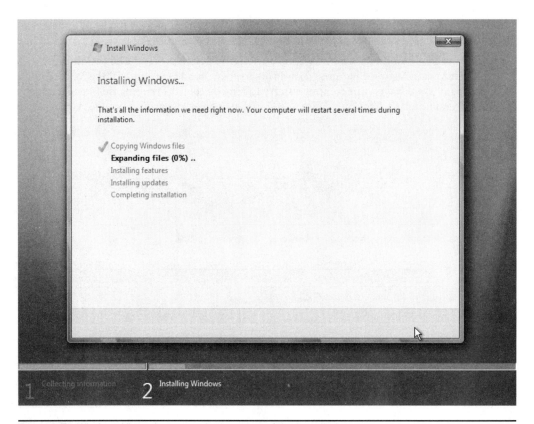

FIGURE A-7 Windows Vista shows you the progress of the installation process.

Vista will shut down and reboot your computer automatically. When it does, just leave it alone. Windows Vista will take care of everything. When it reboots the first time, Windows displays a text-mode (nongraphical) screen (see Figure A-8).

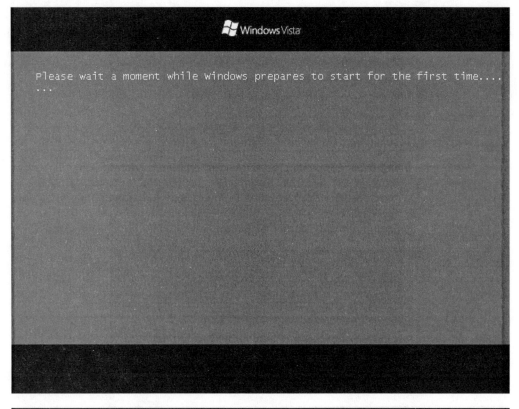

Figure A-8   Windows Vista displays this text-mode screen after it reboots your computer.

10. After some time (usually a couple of hours), you will need to interact with the Install Windows wizard. If you chose the Upgrade installation option, you are asked to confirm the regional settings for your area (see Figure A-9). Click Next. If you chose to perform a new installation, Windows displays the Choose A User Name And Picture dialog box. Here you can enter a username, password, password hint to help you remember your password, and a user account picture. Click Next to continue.

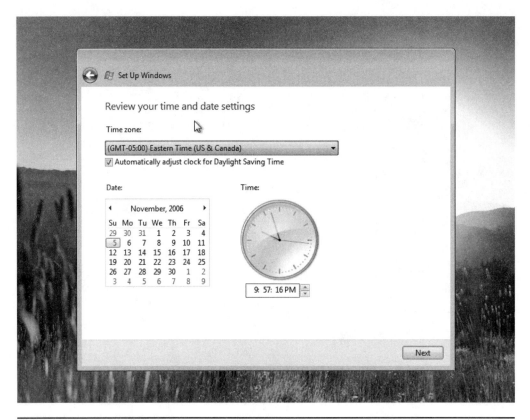

FIGURE A-9 Confirm or change the regional settings.

11. If you chose the new installation option, the Type A Computer Name And Choose A Desktop Background screen appears (see Figure A-10). Type the name you want to use for your computer. If your computer is connected to a LAN, the LAN administrator might want to issue a name for your computer.

12. Click Next. The Help Protect Windows Automatically screen appears (this is for either installation). The best option here is Use Recommended Settings. This way your computer is protected from potentially harmful programs that can be downloaded from the Internet as you navigate the Web. (Note: You may want to

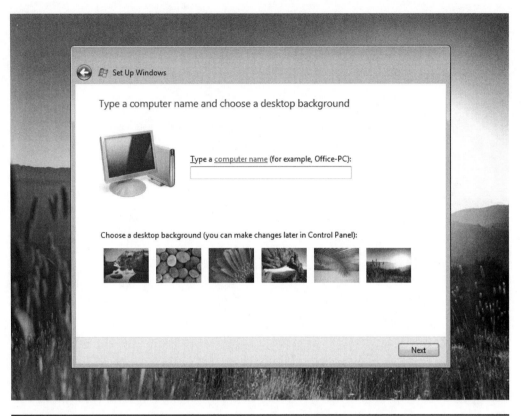

FIGURE A-10   Specify a computer name and background image.

augment Windows Vista's security tools with other ones after you get Vista set up.) Click an option.

13. For new installs, the Review Your Time And Date Settings screen appears (see Figure A-9). Confirm or change the settings here. Click Next.

14. The Select Your Computer's Current Location screen appears (see Figure A-11) to help you choose the type of network your computer uses. The choices are self-explanatory, but if you are not sure which one to choose, click Public Location.

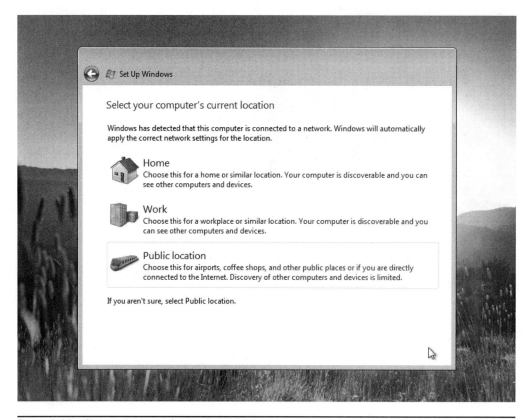

Figure A-11   Choose the type of network you use.

15. Windows displays the Thank You screen. Click Start. Windows may take some more time to install more features and perform additional setup procedures.

16. Eventually the user account screen appears. Enter your password and click the right-arrow button onscreen or press ENTER on your keyboard.

17. After several minutes again, you are shown the Windows Vista desktop and the Welcome Center window (see Figure A-12).

FIGURE A-12   Finally, after several hours of installation, Windows Vista is ready for you!

Checking Your System after Installing Windows

Here are things to do after Windows is installed:

- **Configure your hardware**   Check that all of your hardware was correctly detected by Windows, including your modem, network cards, scanners, video cameras, digital cameras, and printer. Choose Start, right-click Computer, and choose Properties. Then click the Device Manager link on the Tasks pane on the left side of the window (see "What Is the Device Manager?" in Chapter 14). If any of the computer components listed in the Device Manager window have exclamation marks on their icons, something is wrong. Refer to Chapter 14 for information about how to reinstall hardware.

TIP   *You can print a summary of your Windows configuration. Choose Start | All Programs | Accessories | System Tools | System Information. Then choose File | Print.*

- **Check your network connection** If your computer is connected to a LAN, check that the network communication is functioning normally. If it's not, see "Troubleshooting Your Network" in Chapter 30, or talk to your LAN administrator.

- **Reinstall programs** If you didn't reformat your hard disk to install Windows from scratch, and if you installed Windows Vista in the same folder as your previous version of Windows, you shouldn't need to reinstall the application programs that were installed on your hard disk. The Install Windows wizard looks for installed programs and installs them in Windows Vista, too. Otherwise, get out your installation CDs or DVDs and start installing programs.

- **Test your Internet connection** The Install Windows wizard can usually locate and set up your Internet connection during the installation process. This is especially true if you have a working broadband or LAN Internet connection. To test your connection, choose Start | Internet to launch Internet Explorer 7. If you see the MSN web site, you're on!

- **Update your antivirus program** If you have antivirus software (and you should if your computer connects to the Internet), check whether it is compatible with Windows Vista. Go to the program's web site and check whether you need to upgrade the antivirus program. Also make sure that you have an up-to-date virus database.

Index